The New Zealand
Bed & Breakfast
Book 2003

HOMESTAYS · FARMSTAYS · B&B INNS

Published by Moonshine Press
PO Box 6843, Wellington, New Zealand
Telephone: (04) 385-2615
Fax: (04) 385-2694
Website: www.bnb.co.nz
Email: info@bnb.co.nz

© Moonshine Press, 2002

ISBN 0-9582149-7-2

Typeset and design by Moonshine Press, Wellington
Printed by PrintLink, Wellington

Every effort has been made to ensure that the information in this
book is as up to date as possible at the time of going to press. All
listing information has been supplied by the hosts. The publishers
do not accept responsibility arising from reliance on any contents
in the book.

Introduction

Welcome to the 15th edition of *The New Zealand Bed & Breakfast Book.*

The popularity of bed and breakfast in New Zealand has increased each year since we first published *The New Zealand Bed & Breakfast Book* in 1987. The amazing growth is not only a reflection of changing holiday trends but a response by New Zealanders to open their homes and share their experiences with travellers. Bed & breakfast in New Zealand means a warm welcome and a unique holiday experience. Most B&B accommodation is in private homes with a sprinkling of guesthouses and small hotels. Each listing in the guide has been written by the host themselves and you will discover their warmth and personality through their writing. *The New Zealand Bed & Breakfast Book* is not simply an accommodation guide but an introduction to a uniquely New Zealand holiday experience.

The best holidays are often remembered by the friends one makes. How many of us have loved a country because of one or two memorable individuals we have encountered there? For the traveller who wants to experience the real New Zealand and get to know its people, bed and breakfast offers an opportunity to do just that. If you have time, we recommend you don't try to travel too far in one day. Take time to enjoy the company of your hosts and other locals. You will find New Zealand hosts friendly and generous, and eager to share their local knowledge with you.

All properties inspected
All B&Bs which are newly listed are inspected to ensure that they meet our required standard. We expect that all B&Bs in *The New Zealand Bed and Breakfast Book* will offer excellent hospitality.

Finding your way around - using *The New Zealand Bed & Breakfast Book*
We travel from north to south listing the towns as we come to them. In addition, we've divided New Zealand into geographical regions, a map of which is included at the start of each chapter. In some regions, such as Southland, our listings take a detour off the north-to-south route, and follow their nose - it will soon become obvious.

Your comments
We welcome your views on the *Bed & Breakfast Book* and the hosts you meet. Please visit our website www.bnb.co.nz or write to us at PO Box 6843, Wellington, New Zealand.

Happy travelling

Moonshine Press

About B&B

Our B&Bs range from homely to luxurious, but you can always be assured of superior hospitality.

Types of accommodation

Traditional B&B: generally small owner-occupied home accommodation usually with private guest living and dining areas.

Homestay: a homestay is a B&B where you share the family's living area.

Farmstay: country accommodation, usually on a working farm.

Self-contained: separate self-contained accommodation, with kitchen and living/dining room. Breakfast provisions usually provided at least for the first night.

Separate/suite: similar to self-contained but without kitchen facilities. Living/dining facilities may be limited.

Bathrooms

Ensuite and private bathrooms are for your use exclusively.
Guests share bathroom means you will be sharing with other guests.
Family share means you will be sharing with the family.

Tariff

The prices listed are in New Zealand dollars and include GST. Prices listed are subject to change, and any change to listed prices will be stated at time of booking. Some hosts offer a discount for children - this applies to age 12 or under unless otherwise stated. Most of our B&Bs will accept credit cards.

Reservations

We recommend you contact your hosts well in advance to be sure of confirming your accommodation. Most hosts require a deposit so make sure you understand their cancellation policy. Please let your hosts know if you have to cancel, they will have spent time preparing for you. You may also book accommodation through some travel agents or via specialised B&B reservation services.

Breakfast & Dinner

Breakfast is included in the tariff, with each host offering their own menu. You'll be surprised at the range of delicious breakfasts available, many using local produce. If you would like dinner most hosts require 24 hours notice.

Smoking

Most of our B&Bs are non-smoking, but smoking is permitted outside. Listings displaying the no smoking logo do not permit smoking anywhere on the property. B&Bs which have a smoking area inside mention this in their text.

The New Zealand Bed & Breakfast Book is online at www.bnb.co.nz

Have you heard about *The Australian Bed & Breakfast Book?* Contact Moonshine Press, PO Box 1, Brooklyn, NSW 2083, Australia. Or visit our website www.bbbook.com.au

The difference between a hotel and a B&B is that you don't hug the hotel staff when you leave.

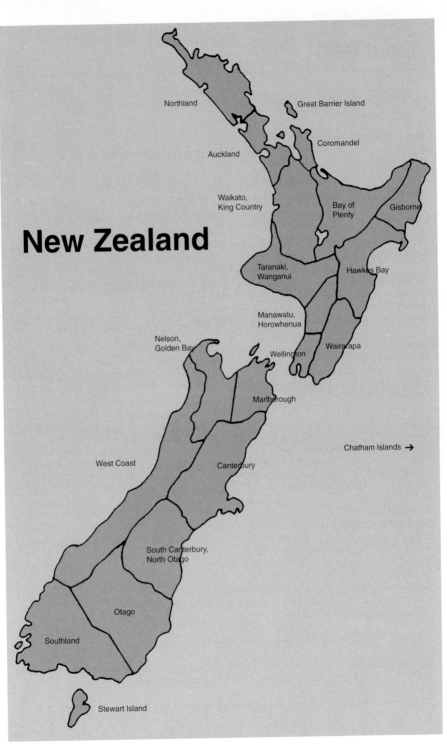

New Zealand

Northland

Great Barrier Island

Coromandel

Auckland

Waikato,
King Country

Bay of
Plenty

Gisborne

Taranaki,
Wanganui

Hawkes Bay

Manawatu,
Horowhenua

Nelson,
Golden Bay

Wairarapa

Wellington

Marlborough

Chatham Islands →

West Coast

Canterbury

South Canterbury,
North Otago

Otago

Southland

Stewart Island

Contents

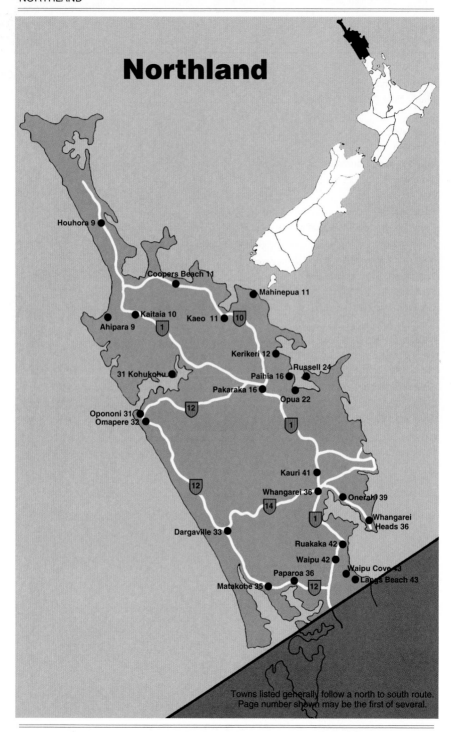

Northland

Houhora 9

Coopers Beach 11

Mahinepua 11

Kaitaia 10   Kaeo 11   10

Ahipara 9   1

Kerikeri 12

31 Kohukohu

Russell 24

Paihia 16

Pakaraka 16   Opua 22

Opononi 31
Omapere 32   12

1

Kauri 41

Whangarei 36   Onerahi 39

14

Dargaville 33   1

Whangarei
Heads 36

Ruakaka 42

Waipu 42

Paparoa 36   Waipu Cove 43

Matakohe 35   12   Langs Beach 43

Towns listed generally follow a north to south route.
Page number shown may be the first of several.

Houhora *Homestay   44km N of Kaitaia*

Houhora Lodge & Homestay
Jacqui & Bruce Malcolm
3994 Far North Rd, Houhora, RD 4, Kaitaia
Tel: (09) 409 7884 Fax: (09) 409 7884
Mob: 025 926 992   houhora.homestay@xtra.co.nz
www.topstay.co.nz

Double $125 Single $80 (Continental & Full Breakfast)
Dinner $30 by arrangement Credit cards accepted
Pet on property Children welcome
3 King/Twin (3 bdrm) 2 Ensuite 1 Private

We have fled our largest city to live on the shores of Houhora Harbour, and look forward to sharing this special part of New Zealand with you. Come and enjoy the remote coastal walks, shell-collecting, Cape Reinga, 90 mile beach and other attractions. We can arrange 4x4 trips, sport or game fishing and provide relaxed and quality accommodation on your return. Homemade bread, homegrown fruit, home-pressed olive oil, vegetables and eggs. Fresh or smoked fish a speciality. Email, internet and fax facilities available.

Ahipara - Ninety Mile Beach *Self-contained B&B Guesthouse*
16km W of Kaitaia

Siesta Lodge
Carole & Alan Harding
PO Box 30, Ahipara, Northland
Tel: (09) 409 2011 Fax: (09) 409 2011 Mob: 025 293 9665
ninetymile@xtra.co.nz www.ahipara.co.nz/siesta

Double $140-$160 (Continental & Full Breakfast)
Dinner by arrangement apartments $180-$250
Credit cards accepted
4 Queen 1 Twin (5 bdrm) 4 Ensuite 4 Private

The Siesta is a Mediterranean style house set in private grounds with panoramic views overlooking the sheltered Ahipara Bay, sand-dune wilderness and the magnificent Ninety Mile Beach. Each room has private balcony, queen-size bed and ensuites. Sleep to the sound of the sea with sea-views from your bed, enjoy spectacular sunsets from your balcony. The adjacent villa has 2 luxury self-contained, spacious apartments with spectacular views, and are an ideal base for longer stays. We have a very friendly cat and dog. Phone for directions.

Ahipara - Ninety Mile Beach *Self-contained B&B*   *17km W of Kaitaia*

Foreshore Lodge
Maire & Selwyn Parker
269 Foreshore Road, RD 1,
Kaitaia
Tel: (09) 409 4860 Fax: (09) 409 4860
www.ahipara.co.nz/foreshore

Double $70-$90 Single $70 (Continental Breakfast)
Child $5 under 12yrs Breakfast $7.50pp extra
Credit cards accepted
1 Super King 1 King 2 Double 2 Single (3 bdrm)
1 Ensuite 1 Private

2 Self-contained units with fully equipped kitchens, situated on the water's edge at Ahipara Bay, the southernmost sheltered end of 90 mile beach. BBQ on your covered terrace. Relax and enjoy lovely seaviews from your comfortable unit. Safe swimming, fishing, surfing, walking just across the road. All tours can be arranged. Golf course - 5 minutes away. Restaurants, takeaways and dairies nearby. Enquire tariff for long stays, extra guests. Children very welcome. Sorry no pets.

Kaitaia - Ahipara   *Homestay B&B   15km W of Kaitaia*

Beachside
Maire & Brian Veza
72 Foreshore Road, RD 1, Kaitaia
Tel: (09) 409 4819 Fax: (09) 409 4819
www.bnb.co.nz/beachside.html

Double $70-$80 Single $50-$55 (Full Breakfast)
Child $20 Dinner $20 Credit cards accepted
1 Twin 2 Single (2 bdrm)
1 Ensuite 1 Family share

Welcome to our comfortable house. Relax and enjoy views from the deck of Ninety Mile Beach stretching to the Cape. A private walkway 50 metres leads to the beach. Activities Ahipara offers are surfing, swimming, horse riding, quad bike hire, fishing. Golf course 2km drive. For those interested in farming, visit our beef farm at Herikino. Dinner available on request. Directions: Take road to Ahipara from Kaitaia. Turn left at Ahipara School, follow road around corner, 3rd house on beach side.

Kaitaia - Lake Ngatu   *B&B Countrystay   14km N of Kaitaia*

Lake Ngatu Lodge
Diane & Graeme Jay
Sweetwater Road, RD 1, Awanui, Northland
Tel: (09) 406 7300 Fax: (09) 406 7300
lakengatulodge@hotmail.com
www.bnb.co.nz/lakengatulodge.html

Double $100 Single $80 (Continental Breakfast)
Dinner by arrangement Credit cards accepted
Pet on property
2 King/Twin (2 bdrm) 1 Private

Our lakeside home, set on 10 acres of mature garden, orchard and paddocks, is the ideal centralised Northern retreat. Relax in your upstairs room or private lounge, swim, walk or kayak the Lake, 3 minutes to 90 mile Beach - the choice is yours! 100kms to Cape Reinga, bus tours pass our gate daily, three golf-courses and Okahu Estate winery within a half hour drive, or fishing/diving trips can be arranged. Special continental breakfast with homegrown organic produce, meals on request, undercover parking and saltwater pool top off the experience - Diane, Graeme and Jif the dog welcome you!

Kaitaia - Pamapuria   *Self-contained Homestay B&B   7min S of Kaitaia*

Plane Tree Lodge
Rosemary & Mike Wright
State Highway 1
Tel: (09) 408 0995 Fax: (09) 408 0959 Mob: 025 338 859
reservationsplanetreelodge@xtra.co.nz
www.plane-tree-lodge.net.nz

Double $100-$120 Single $70-$90 (Special Breakfast)
self-contained cottage $150 - $180
Credit cards accepted Pet on property
3 Queen 3 Single (5 bdrm) 3 Ensuite 1 Private

Our native timber home is idyllically situated on one and a half acres of English style garden, with a touch of the South Pacific. We offer guests a real get away from it all, stress-free, country stay, within easy reach of all popular attractions. Experience game fishing, dolphins, Cape Reinga, and visit the nocturnal park. Wake up each morning to a delicious, bountiful breakfast, which could include such delights as fresh picked strawberries and raspberries (in season), home made muesli, yoghurt and conserves, followed by a cooked course to boast about. Our 5 cats ensure a mouse-free environment.

Coopers Beach   *Homestay Separate/Suite*   *3km N of Mangonui*

Mac'n'Mo's
Maureen & Malcolm MacMillan
PO Box 177, Mangonui
Tel: (09) 406 0538 Fax: (09) 406 0538
Mob: 025 286 5180
MacNMo@xtra.co.nz
www.bnb.co.nz/macnmos.html
Double $65-$80 Single $40-$60
(Continental Breakfast) Dinner $25
1 Queen 2 Double 2 Single (4 bdrm)
2 Ensuite 2 Guests share

Enjoy a "million dollar" view of Doubtless Bay while you enjoy Mac's smoked fish on your toast. The bus to Cape Reinga stops at our gate, you may visit glowworms, kiwi house, go on a craft or wine trail, swim with dolphins, go fishing, diving or just relax on our unpolluted uncrowded beaches, there's one across the road. There are several fine restaurants and the "world famous" fish and chip shop nearby. Have a memorable stay with Mac'n'Mo, they will take good care of you.

Coopers Beach   *B&B*   *3km N of Mangonui*

Doubtless Bay Lodge
Harry & Berwyn Porten
33 Cable Bayblock Road, Coopers Beach,
Mangonui 0557
Tel: (09) 406 1661 Fax: (09) 406 1662
Mob: 025 275 2144 hporten@xtra.co.nz
www.bnb.co.nz/doubtlessbaylodge.html
Double $90 Single $65 (Full Breakfast) Child $20
Dinner $25 by arrangement   Credit cards accepted
3 Queen 2 Single (4 bdrm)   4 Ensuite

Our B/B is 800 mtrs north of the Coopers Beach shops. We are 1 hour north of Paihia. Each room has ensuite bathroom, Sky-Cable TV, fridge, tea and coffee making facilities. We have a guest laundry and barbecue and two pussy cats. We arrange scenic bus tours to Cape Reinga, fishing trips and dolphin watching. Enjoy the sea and rural views of this lovely place where you can visit the many isolated beaches in the area, knowing you are 150 kms from the nearest traffic lights.

Mahinepua - Kaeo   *Homestay*   *22km E of Kaeo*

Waiwurrie
Vickie & Rodger Corbin
Mahinepua, RD 1, Kaeo/Whangaroa, Northland
Tel: (09) 405 0840 Fax: (09) 405 0854
Mob: 021 186 7900
wai.wurrie@xtra.co.nz
www.bnb.co.nz/waiwurrie.html
Double $150-$175 Single $125 (Full Breakfast)
Dinner $35pp Credit cards accepted Pet on property
1 King 1 Queen (2 bdrm)
1 Ensuite 1 Private

Would you like a chance to see some of Northland's spectacular scenery? Have we the place for you! Situated on the East coast with views of the Pacific Ocean, Cavailli Islands and home of one of the famous Marlin deep sea fishing grounds. Golf at Kauri Cliffs, sightsee to Cape Reinga, visit the Bay of Islands, Kerikeri, Whangaroa or just relax. We have a dog called Benson and Moppet the cat and we love to entertain and would enjoy meeting you. For more information please phone us.

Kerikeri   *Homestay B&B*   *3km E of Kerikeri*

Matariki Orchard
Alison & David Bridgman
Pa Road, Kerikeri, Bay of Islands
Tel: (09) 407 7577 Fax: (09) 407 7593
Mob: 025 278 2423
matarikihomestay@xtra.co.nz
www.bnb.co.nz/matarikiorchard.html
Double $100 Single $50 (Full Breakfast) Child $20
Dinner $40pp Credit cards accepted
1 Queen 2 Single (2 bdrm)
1 Guests share

We welcome guests to our home, large garden, swimming pool and citrus orchard. Its a pleasant walk to the historic area and 4 mins by car to township, clubs and craft outlets. David has a vintage car which is used for personalised historic scenic and craft tours. We are 5th generation New Zealanders love to help with "where to go and what to do", can make tour bookings. We enjoy providing a 3 course dinner with wine. Can meet coach or plane, no cost. Directions please phone.

Kerikeri - Okaihau   *Farmstay B&B*   *12km W of Kerikeri*

Clotworthy Farmstay
Neville & Shennett Clotworthy
Wiroa Road, RD1, Okaihau,
Bay of Islands
Tel: (09) 401 9371 Fax: (09) 401 9371
www.bnb.co.nz/clotworthyfarmstay.html
Double $80 Single $40 (Full Breakfast)
Dinner $25 by arrangement Credit cards accepted
1 Queen 4 Single (3 bdrm)
1 Guests share

We farm cattle, sheep, and horses on our 310 acres. There are panoramic views of the Bay of Islands area from our home 1,000 ft above sea level. Of 1840's pioneering descent, our interests are travel, farming, genealogy and equestrian activities. We have an extensive library on Northland history and families. Directions: SH10 take Wiroa/Airport Road at the Kerikeri intersection. 9kms on the right OR SH1, take Kerikeri Road just south of Okaihau. We are 4th house on the left, past the golf course (8kms).

Kerikeri   *Homestay*   *5km N of Kerikeri*

Kilernan Homestay
Heather & Bruce Manson
Silkwood Lane, RD 2, Kerikeri
Tel: (09) 407 8582 Fax: (09) 407 8317
Mob: 027 4790 216
brucemanson@xtra.co.nz
www.truenz.co.nz/kilernan
Double $120 Single $80 (Full Breakfast) Child n/a
Dinner $35 Credit cards accepted Pet on property
1 Queen 2 Single (2 bdrm)
2 Ensuite

"Simply superior" wrote one of our guests and at "Kilernan" we strive to maintain that standard. Close to the Kerikeri Village but with magnificent rural views our home offers quality accommodation, your own ensuite; full breakfast; and dinner with all the trimmings. We can also assist with a full range of local tours and sightseeing activities. Together with 'Monty' our pedigree boxer we look forward to extending a welcome and superior hospitality to our guests.

Kerikeri *Farmstay Homestay B&B   10km Kerikeri Central*

Kerikeri Inlet View
Trish & Nolan Daniells
Inlet Road, RD 3, Kerikeri
Tel: (09) 407 7477 Fax: (09) 407 7478 Mob: 025 612 0021
www.bnb.co.nz/kerikeriinletview.html
Double $70 Single $45 (Full Breakfast) Child $15
Dinner $18 by arrangement Children welcome
Backpackers (not on hill) $25 - no breakfast
Child at home Pet on property
1 Queen 2 Double 2 Single (3 bdrm)
2 Ensuite 1 Guests share

We welcome you to our 7 bedroom home on top of our 1100 acre beef and sheep farm. Enjoy the superb views of the inlet and the Bay of Islands while you relax in our spa pool. Join us for breakfast consisting of seasonal fruit and juice, homemade bread and butter, free-range chook eggs, our own sausages, before exploring the many attractions around Kerikeri. Backpackers has 6 lockable bedrooms, large lounge, kitchen and laundry. Note: please phone first for bookings, detailed directions or pick-up. We speak Japanese.

Kerikeri *Self-contained B&B Orchardstay   8km S of Kerikeri*

Puriri Park
Paul & Charmian Treadwell
Puriri Park Orchard, State Highway 10, Box 572, Kerikeri
Tel: (09) 407 9818 Fax: (09) 407 9498
puriri@xtra.co.nz
www.bnb.co.nz/puriripark.html
Double $85 Single $65 (Full Breakfast) Child $10
Dinner $30 Credit cards accepted
3 Double 2 Twin 1 Single (4 bdrm)
1 Private 2 Guests share

Puriri Park has long been known for its hospitality in the Far North. Guests are welcome to wander around our large garden, explore the orange and kiwifruit orchards, sit by the lilypond or feed our flock of fantail pigeons. We have five acres of bird-filled native bush, mostly totara and puriri. We are in an excellent situation for trips to Cape Reinga and sailing or cruising on the beautiful Bay of Islands. We can arrange tours for you or pick you up from the airport.

Kerikeri *Homestay B&B   7km N of Kerikeri*

Sunrise Homestay B&B
Judy & Les Remnant
140 Skudders Road, Skudders Beach, RD 1, Kerkeri
Tel: (09) 407 5447 Fax: (09) 407 8448
Mob: 021 774 941 sunrisehomestay@xtra.co.nz
www.bnb.co.nz/sunrisehomestaybb.html
Double $90 Single $60 (Full Breakfast)
Dinner $30pp by prior arrangement
Credit cards accepted
1 Double 4 Single (3 bdrm) 1 Ensuite 1 Guests share

A warm welcome awaits you at our restful homestay ovelooking Kerikeri inlet, magnificent water views and often spectacular sunrises and sunsets. Occasional visits from dolphins. Plenty to see and do in Bay of Islands. We are only too happy to help arrange your trips. Tea and coffee available at all times. Laundry facilities available. Courtesy pick up from bus or airport. Phone, fax or leave phone number on answer phone, we will call you back. One of the best locations in Kerikeri. Do come and share it with us. Non smokers. We have no pets.

Kerikeri *Homestay*   *2.6km N of Kerikeri*

Glenfalloch
Rick & Evalyn Pitelen
Landing Road, Kerikeri
Tel: (09) 407 5471 Fax: (09) 407 5473
Mob: 025 280 0661 glenfall@ihug.co.nz
www.bnb.co.nz/glenfalloch.html

Double $80-$90 Single $60 (Full Breakfast) Child $20
Dinner $25pp Credit cards accepted Children welcome
1 King 1 Queen 1 Double 1 Single (3 bdrm)
2 Ensuite 1 Private

Venture down Glenfalloch's tree lined driveway to a peaceful garden paradise. Evalyn and Rick welcome guests with refreshments to be enjoyed in the lounges or outdoors on the decks. You are welcome to wander about the garden, use the swimming pool and tennis court, or just relax in our private retreat. Breakfast can be enjoyed at your leisure outdoors, weather permitting. Laundry facilities available. Directions: travel 0.6km from the Stone Store to second driveway on left after Department of Conservation sign.

Kerikeri *B&B*   *3km S of Kerikeri*

Graleen
Graeme & Colleen Wattam
578a Kerikeri Road, RD 3, Kerikeri,
Bay of Islands
Tel: (09) 407 9047 Fax: (09) 407 9047
Mob: 025 940 845 graleen@xtra.co.nz
www.kerikeri.co.nz/graleen

Double $70 Single $40 (Full Breakfast)
Credit cards accepted
1 Queen 1 Double 2 Single (3 bdrm) 3 Ensuite

After extensive travel we have designed and built a new home with guest accommodation and comfort in mind. All bedrooms have ensuites and TV with direct access to our lovely sheltered veranda. Breakfast in our large guest lounge. Historic Kerikeri is surrounded by orchards, farms, and is centrally situated to Bay of Islands and Northland's many tourist attractions. "Graleen" is 200 metres from SH10, only 20 minutes from historic Waitangi and Paihia beaches, 3 minutes from the township, restaurants, golf course and many craft galleries.

Kerikeri *Homestay B&B*   *3km E of Kerikeri*

Holmes Homestay
Jane & Tony Holmes
30b Blacks Road, Kerikeri
Tel: (09) 407 7500 Fax: (09) 407 7500
Mob: 025 241 9448 tony_holmes@xtra.co.nz
www.bnb.co.nz/holmeshomestay.html

Double $75-$90 Single $50 (Full Breakfast)
Dinner $25 Credit cards accepted
1 Queen 1 Twin (2 bdrm)
1 Ensuite 1 Private 1 Family share

If you want tranquillity, relaxing on the deck watching boats come up the Inlet, a warm welcome awaits you, in our large, comfortable bungalow. The adventurous can paddle canoes up to the Stone Store. Our yacht is close by. Bush walks, night kiwi walks, fishing, horse trekking can be arranged. Bird life is abundant, sheep munch next door and we have two pet calves. At Kerikeri roundabout turn right into Hobson, left into Inlet - at 2.3km turn left into Blacks. We're half way down the hill. See you.

Kerikeri *Homestay Coastal 12km E of Kerikeri*

Oversley
Maire & Tone Coyte
Doves Bay Road, RD 1, Kerikeri
Tel: (09) 407 8744 Fax: (09) 407 4487
Mob: 025 959 207 oversley@xtra.co.nz
www.bnb.co.nz/oversley.html
Double $110-$140 Single $90-$120 (Full Breakfast)
Dinner $35 Credit cards accepted
1 King 1 Queen 2 Single (3 bdrm)
2 Ensuite 1 Private

Welcome to 'Oversley' and enjoy magnificent panoramic water views, sweeping lawns and private native bush walks to the water. Our spacious, comfortable home, set in 18 acres, offers a friendly relaxed atmosphere with quality accommodation and laundry facilities. We are an easy going, well travelled, retired couple, enjoy all sports, sailing and fishing on our 13 metre yacht, golfing on Kerikeri's first class course 15 minutes away (Kauri Cliff's course only 35 minutes away) and are animal lovers. Your company at dinner, to share good food and wine with us, is most welcome.

Kerikeri *Homestay B&B 2km S of Kerikeri*

Gannaway House
Jill & Roger Gardner
Kerikeri Road, RD 3, Kerikeri
Tel: (09) 407 1432 Fax: (09) 407 1431
Mob: 025 798 115 gannaway@xtra.co.nz
www.bnb.co.nz/gannawayhouse.html
Double $85-$105 Single $55-$75 (Full Breakfast)
Child $30 Dinner $30 by arrangement
Credit cards accepted Pet on property
2 Queen 1 Twin (3 bdrm) 1 Ensuite 1 Guests share

Jill and Roger welcome you to Gannaway House. Our comfortable home, set in 2 acres of garden and orchard is situated down a tree-lined driveway, close to town but in the quiet of the country. We offer one large ground floor room with ensuite and private entrance. Upstairs, two rooms (1 Queen and 1 Twin) with shared facilities. Enjoy our beautiful tranquil garden - also the sheep and lambs in the orchard. We are also breeders of pedigree cats. Directions: From S.H. 10 - first driveway on left past Makana Chocolate Factory.

Kerikeri *Self-contained 14km N of Kerikeri*

Cavalli View Cottage
Sharon Burgess & Richard Harris
Te Ra Road, Takou Bay, RD2, Kerikeri
Tel: (09) 407 9019
Fax: (09) 407 9018
Mob: 021 118 5047
cavallicottage@hotmail.com
www.bnb.co.nz/cavalliviewcottage.html
Double $150 Child $7.50 extra adult $15
also Futon in lounge
1 Queen (1 bdrm) 1 Private

Cavalli view cottage overlooks Takou Bay, a beautiful unspoiled surf beach, and the magnificent Cavalli Islands. The characteristic cottage was purpose-built in 2002 on a 10 acre rural property & features extensive use of natural timber. It is completely self-contained and private from hosts home with a full kitchen allowing self-catering, queensize bedroom and extra futon couch double bed. Private sundecks with barbecue allow alfresco dining. We have two cats, 'Kimo' a friendly border collie and chooks in the orchard.

Kerikeri   *Homestay*

Pukanui Lodge B&B
Dale Simkin & Dale Hutchinson
322 Kerikeri Road, Kerikeri,

Tel: (09) 407 7003 Fax: (09) 407 7068
Mob: 0274 444 955 pukanui@igrin.co.nz
www.bnb.co.nz/pukanui2.html

Double $110-$140 Single $55-$70
(Continental Breakfast) Credit cards accepted
2 Queen 1 Twin (3 bdrm)
3 Ensuite

Tranquility 400m from Kerikeri township. Subtropical gardens and citrus orchard have influenced both decor and cuisine of Pukanui. Generous breakfast can be served on private decks off your ensuite bedroom in garden setting or overlooking pool in summer. Cosy lounge in winter. Local produce features significantly in our culinary delights with dinner by prior arrangement. Friendly hosts will help olan youru visit to make it memorable. Fax and email facilities available. Complimentary airport/bus transfers.

Pakaraka - Paihia   *Farmstay B&B*   *10km N of Kawakawa*

Bay of Islands Farmstay - B&B Highland Farm
Glenis & Ken Mackintosh
Pakaraka, 6627 State Highway 1, RD 2, Kaikohe 0400

Tel: (09) 404 0430 Fax: (09) 404 0430
Mob: 027 249 8296 Ken@soft.net.nz
www.bnb.co.nz/bayofislandfarmstaybb.html

Double $85 Single $60 (Full Breakfast) Child $10
Dinner $20 - $30 (byo & comp.) twin room $80
Credit cards accepted Pet on property Children welcome
1 Double 1 Twin 3 Single (2 bdrm) 2 Ensuite

Beautiful 51 acres, stone walls, barberry hedges. Sheep, cattle. Ken trains dogs and pups daily! Enjoy watching help shift animals. Meet and photograph with "Mr Angus" our lovable steer. "Monkey" our cat will enjoy your visit. Swimming pool or cosy warm home in winter. Good Central Base! Five golf courses, bowls, beaches, hot pools, shopping! Situated 15 minutes Paihia, Kerikeri, Kaikohe. Welcome to Bay of Islands. Book early or take pot luck! (10 minutes North Kawakawa or 2 south Pakaraka Junction). "Highland Farm" on entrance.

Paihia   *Countrystay*   *8km N of Paihia*

Puketona Lodge
Heather and Maurice Pickup
769 Puketona Road, RD 1, Paihia 0252

Tel: (09) 402 8152 Fax: (09) 402 8152
Mob: 025 260 7058 puketonalodge@xtra.co.nz
www.bnb.co.nz/puketonalodge.html

Double $115 King $120 Single $90
(Full Breakfast) Dinner $35
Credit cards accepted Pet on property
1 King/Twin 1 Double (2 bdrm) 1 Ensuite 1 Private

Our home, on 10 acres, is large and modern, built by Maurice of native timbers. Of English/NZ origins, we have American connections too. Our bedrooms are spacious and private and open onto our large garden. We are close to Haruru Falls, Waitangi, beaches, walks, golf and historic places. Our breakfasts feature homemade breads, preserves, fresh fruit, and more. We can book tours and cruises. Complimentary refreshments on arrival. Heather teaches ceramics and enjoys showing guests over the studio. We have two dogs and one cat.

Paihia   *B&B   Paihia Central*

The Totaras - Hilltop B&B
C & F Habicht
6 School Rd, Paihia
Tel: (09) 402 8238 Fax: (09) 402 8238
thetotaras@ihug.co.nz
www.bnb.co.nz/thetotarashilltopbb.html
Double $130-$175 (Special Breakfast) Dinner $40pp
Rate applies to B&B Book holders only
Credit cards accepted
1 King/Twin 1 Queen 1 Single (2 bdrm) 2 Ensuite

...For the sophisticated traveller...luxury with charm. Two scenic ensuite apartments uniquely located on a hilltop reveal breathtaking panoramic views over historic Waitangi, the harbour, Russell the islands and the endless horizon. Start your day with delicious Austrian pancakes, stroll along the beach to Waitangi, ride the ferry to Russell, cruise the islands.... Christine has a degree in Hotel Management, Frank is an international photographer. His latest book depicts the beauty of the Bay. Honeymooners paradise, pleasant ambience. Wir sprechen Deutsch. Minimum stay two nights.

Paihia   *Countrystay   7km N of Paihia*

Lily Pond Estate B&B (Est 1989)
Allwyn & Graeme Sutherland
Puketona Road, RD 1,
Paihia
Lily Pond Orchard sign at gate
Tel: (09) 402 7041
www.bnb.co.nz/lilypondorchardbb.html
Double $85 Single $45 (Full Breakfast)
1 Double 1 Twin 1 Single (3 bdrm)
1 Guests share with seperate toilet

Drive in through an avenue of mature Liquid Amber trees to our comfortable timber home on our 5 acre Country Estate growing citrus and pip fruit. The guest wing has views of the fountain, bird aviary, small lake and black swan with the double and twin rooms having private verandah access. Fresh orange juice, fruit and homemade jams are served at breakfast. We are born NZ'ers, sailed thousands of miles living aboard our 50ft yacht in the Pacific and will gladly share our Bay of Island knowledge to make your visit most memorable.

Central Paihia   *Self-contained B&B*

The Cedar Suite Spas
Jo & Peter Nisbet
5 Sullivans Road, Paihia
Tel: (09) 402 8516 Fax: (09) 402 8555
Mob: 025 969 281 Cdr.Swt@xtra.co.nz
www.bnb.co.nz/thecedarsuite.html
Double $89-$150 Single $89-$150
(Continental Breakfast) Breakfast extra, $10.50 pp
Credit cards accepted
3 Queen 1 Single (3 bdrm) 3 Ensuite

The Cedar Suite Spas offers first class accommodation in our modern cedar home amidst beautiful native trees. Suites are separate, 3 with PRIVATE SPAS, and their own superior ensuites. Both of us enjoy music, Peter managing the New Zealand Symphony Orchestra for over twenty years, and Jo enjoys photography and interior design. Breakfast we call Kiwi: - continental plus - and local fruit plays a big part in that. There is private parking, comfortable beds, fine linen, a French style room, filtered water and TV.

Paihia   *Homestay B&B   1.5km S of Paihia*

Te Haumi House
Enid & Ernie Walker
12 Seaview Road,
Paihia
Tel: (09) 402 8046 Fax: (09) 402 8046
www.bnb.co.nz/tehaumihouse.html

Double $80 Single $45 (Continental Breakfast)
Credit cards accepted
2 Queen 1 Single (2 bdrm)
1 Guests share 1 Family share

Millennium Sunrise. Welcome to our modern waterfront home, set amongst subtropical gardens with expansive harbour views, just minutes from tourist activities and town centre. Guests enjoy privacy through a clever split-level design. Buffet breakfast with a choice of dining room, garden deck or courtyard. Laundry facilities, ample off-street parking and courtesy pickup from bus available. Descendants of early settlers, we have a good knowledge of local history. Ernie is a Masonic Lodge member.

Paihia   *Self-contained   Central Paihia*

Craicor Accommodation
Garth Craig & Anne Corbett
PO Box 15, 49 Kings Road,
Paihia, Bay of Islands
Tel: (09) 402 7882 Fax: (09) 402 7883
craicor@actrix.gen.nz
www.bnb.co.nz/craicoraccommodation.html

Double $120 Single $90 (Continental Breakfast)
Breakfast optional $7.50 each   Credit cards accepted
2 King 2 Single (2 bdrm) 2 Ensuite

The perfect spot for those seeking a quiet, sunny and central location. Discover the Garden Suite and Tree House. Self contained modern units nestled in a garden setting with trees that almost hug you, native birds and sea views. Each unit has ensuite bathroom, fully equipped kitchen for self catering, super king bed, T.V, insect screens and is tastefully decorated to reflect the natural colours of the surroundings. Safe off street parking, all within a five minute stroll to the waterfront, restaurants and town centre.

Paihia   *Self-contained   Paihia Central*

Iona Lodge
Mary & Malcolm Sinclair
29 Bayview Road, Paihia, Bay of Islands
Tel: (09) 402 8072 Fax: (09) 402 8072
ionas@xtra.co.nz
www.bnb.co.nz/ionalodge.html

Double $85-$115 Single $70 (Continental Breakfast)
Credit cards accepted
2 Double 1 Single (2 bdrm)
2 Ensuite

Share with us the best views in the Bay, from the comfort of your quiet sunny units, situated in Bayview Road, overlooking Central Paihia. Conveniently situated to shops, wharf and restaurants. One unit has a double and single bed. Upstairs are the bathroom, lounge, and kitchen. The studio has a double bed, kitchen and ensuite. Both are fully equipped with TV, BBQ and decks for you to relax on and enjoy the panoramic views. We supply generous breakfast provisions each day for you to enjoy at your leisure.

Paihia   *Homestay B&B   1km N of Paihia*

Bay of Islands Bed & Breakfast
Laraine & Sid Dyer
48 Tahuna Road, Paihia, Bay of Islands
Tel: (09) 402 8551 Fax: (09) 402 8551
Mob: 025 657 6815
larained@ihug.co.nz
www.bnb.co.nz/bayofislandsbedbreakfast.html
Double $70 Single $40 (Continental Breakfast)
Pet on property
1 Queen 2 Single (3 bdrm)
1 Family share

We invite you to stay and relax in our home, only minutes from the beach, with bush walks and golf course nearby. On arrival a warm welcome awaits you, with tea or coffee and a chance to unwind. Assistance with your itinerary is offered should you need help. We look forward to the pleasure of your company and ensuring your stay is as comfortable and memorable as possible. Our courtesy car will meet you if travelling by bus. We have a friendly dog named Tessa.

Paihia   *Self-contained B&B   Paihia Central*

Marlin House
Christopher & Angela Houry
15 Bayview Road, Paihia, Bay of Islands
Tel: (09) 402 8550 Fax: (09) 402 6770
Mob: 025 487 937 or 021 487 937
chris.houry@xtra.co.nz
www.bnb.co.nz/marlinhouse.html
Double $95-$160 Single $90-$100 (Special Breakfast)
Dinner B/A Credit cards accepted Pet on property
1 King/Twin 1 King 1 Queen 1 Twin (4 bdrm)
4 Ensuite

Marlin House is a beautiful neo-colonial building with spacious accommodation for eight persons in four (One Super Luxury) self-contained suites with fridge, TV and off-road parking. Situated in a quiet tree-clad spot above Paihia with million dollar views of the Bay. It is only three minutes walk to the beach shops and restaurants. We serve special continental breakfasts in your suite or on the deck, or order a full cooked breakfast. Ask us for 10% discounts on local excursions.

Paihia   *Self-contained B&B   0.5km NW of Paihia*

Windermere
Richard & Jill Burrows
168 Marsden Road, Paihia, Bay of Islands
Tel: (09) 402 8696 Fax: (09) 402 5095
windermere@igrin.co.nz
www.windermere.co.nz
Double $80-$150 Single $80-$100
(Continental Breakfast) Child $25
Credit cards accepted Pet on property
2 Queen 4 Single (2 bdrm) 2 Ensuite

'Windermere' is a large modern family home set in a bush setting and yet located right on one of the best beaches in the Bay of Islands. Superior accommodation is provided with suites having their own ensuite and kitchen facilities. For longer stays one suite has its own laundry, dryer and fully equipped kitchen. The other suite has microwave and fridge only. Each suite has its own decks where you can sit and enjoy the view enhanced by spectacular sunsets. Jill and Richard would welcome your company to enjoy our own little part of paradise.

Paihia   *Self-contained B&B   Paihia Central*

Admiral's View Lodge
Robyn & Peter Rhodes, 2 McMurray Road, Paihia, Bay of Islands

Tel: (09) 402 6236 Fax: (09) 402 6237
Mob: 025 779 997 Reservations: 0800 247 234
admiralsview@actrix.gen.nz
www.bnb.co.nz/admiralsviewlodge.html

Double $75-$175 (Continental Breakfast)
Credit cards accepted Pet on property
4 King 6 Queen 3 Double 9 Twin 11 Single (13 bdrm)
9 Ensuite 2 Private

OPENING OCTOBER 2002 Admiral's View Lodge has been purposely built for your comfort and enjoyment. Set in a peaceful location off the busy main road with views across to historic Russell and beyond.

Our new units are large and well equipped, fully self-contained, and air-conditioned. Executive studios, luxury suites with two-person spa baths. One and two-bedroom apartments plus our popular B&B suites. Italian-style bathrooms with extra large showers, and double vanities. Sunny terraces and patios. Units sleep 2-6.

We offer a secure environment, ideal for business, pleasure, or that ROMANTIC time out. Tours can be arranged for you - swim with the dolphins, sail the bay, visit the 'hole in the rock' and golf at Waitangi only minutes away. Group bookings, multi-night and off-season rates. Tarrif includes generous buffet breakfast. Restaurant adjacent and cafes and town centre all within walking distance.

If you are looking for something SPECIAL, Robyn and Peter would love to welcome you to Admiral's View Lodge.

Features and attractions:
• LOCATION LOCATION
• Sea views
• rooms serviced daily
• guests laundry
• free tennis and bikes
• business & Internet facilities
• Sky TV in rooms
• Bush and coastal walks

Paihia *B&B and Self-contained*   *3km N of Paihia*

Villa Casablanca
Barbara & Derek Robertson,
18 Goffe Drive,
Haruru Falls,
Paihia

Tel: (09) 402 6980 Fax: (09) 402 6980 Mob: 021 666 567
derek@bestprice.co.nz
www.bestprice.co.nz

Double $110-$200 Single $90-$160
(Special Breakfast) Child n/a Dinner $45
Holiday Apartments $90 -$170   Credit cards accepted
2 King/Twin 4 Queen 4 Single (5 bdrm)
4 Ensuite 2 Private

Our romantic hacienda is surrounded by private gardens
where the only sound you hear is the murmuring of the
waterfall at night and bird songs at daybreak. Located on
a ridge at historic Haruru Falls, it enjoys breathtaking
views over Russell and The Bay of Islands.

Choose traditional bed and breakfast in our guest wings
or the privacy of self-catering accommodation in our
holiday apartments.

The villa is your home away from home. The spacious
sunny bedrooms, each have tea and coffee facilities, a
bar fridge and a private or en-suite bathroom. There is a
tv lounge and library, a guest laundry, barbeque and sun
decks.

Villa Casablanca makes an ideal base for your stay in
Northland. It is within easy driving distance from all the
main sites and less than five minutes to Paihia's beach
and shops. Your hosts: Barbara and Derek.

Paihia - Bay of Islands   *Homestay Self contained*   *6km W of Paihia*

Appledore Lodge
Janet & Jim Pugh
Puketona Road, Paihia, Bay of Islands
Tel: (09) 402 8007 Fax: (09) 402 8007
Mob: 021-1795839 appledorelodge@xtra.co.nz
www.bnb.co.nz/appledore.html
Double $80-$150 Single $60-$75 (Special Breakfast)
Child Negotiable s/c riverside lodge $150 - $200
Credit cards accepted Pet on property
1 King 1 Double (2 bdrm) 2 Ensuite

Welcome and relax in our home. Waitangi River gently tumbles over miniature waterfalls and rapids just 25 mars away. Spellbinding river views from your King or Double Four Poster with ensuite facilities, harmonising gracefully with the out door Spa Pool bringing you ever closer with nature. Special breakfast all home made served on our antique Kauri table or grand deck. We enjoy classic cars, golf, travel and meeting new guests, Janet, Jim & our Golden Retriever look forward to making your stay memorable "Yours to enjoy"

Paihia   *B&B*   *3km Paihia*

Fallsview
Shirley & Clive Welch
4 Fallsview Road, RD 1, Haruru, Paihia
Tel: (09) 402 7871 Fax: (09) 402 7861
Mob: 025 627 1652 www.bnb.co.nz/fallsview.html
Double $75-$90 Single $40-$50 (Full Breakfast)
Child $40 Credit cards accepted
Pet on property Children welcome
1 Queen 1 Twin 1 Single (3 bdrm)
1 Guests share

Our studio apartment has all the comforts of home, a beautiful sunny lounge with fridge, microwave, stereo, TV, tea/coffee facilities, laundry, barbecue and undercover parking. All surrounded by a semi tropical garden. With breakfast upstairs you will enjoy the beautiful panoramic view of the surrounding countryside. Extra twin beds are available upstairs if in a group. We share our home with a small gregarious poodle and 3 reclusive cats. Situated only 3km from main tourist attractions. We offer you a warm welcome.

Paihia - Opua   *Homestay B&B*   *5km S of Paihia*

Pt. Veronica Lodge
Audrey & John McKiernan
Pt. Veronica Drive, Opua, Bay of Islands
Tel: (09) 402 5579 Fax: (09) 402 5579
Mob: 021 1820697   pt.veronicalodge@xtra.co.nz
www.bnb.co.nz/ptveronicalodge.html
Double $100-$160 Single $70-$120
(Continental & Full Breakfast) Dinner by arrangement
Credit cards accepted Pet on property
2 Queen 1 Double (3 bdrm)
2 Ensuite 1 Private

We are between Paihia & Opua just above the coastal track with views of the bay towards Russell; this is our special place that nestles in a reserve. 40 minutes walk to Opua wharf or 50 to Paihia. Enjoy a soak in our Spa or rest on the decks. T.V. in your room and Sky channels in the lounge. Golf, sailing, fishing & historic buildings within 10 minutes drive. Audrey & John welcome you to our home. Our two friendly dogs live on the lower deck.

Paihia - Bay of Islands *Homestay B&B   6km W of Paihia*

Blue Heron Country Lodge
Beverly and George Barke
621B Puketona Road, R.D.1 Paihia, Bay of Islands
Tel: (09) 402 8195 Fax: (09) 402 8194
george.barke@xtra.co.nz
www.bnb.co.nz/blueheron.html
Double $120 Single $90
(Continental Breakfast)
Child $40 Children welcome
1 Queen 1 Twin (2 bdrm)
1 Ensuite 1 Guests share

We invite guests to share peace and tranquillity in our home. We are situated 3.5 hours north of Auckland, and 6kms from Paihia beaches, restaurants and entertainment. You can stroll around our large garden, watch bird life, view skydivers descending, and a few minutes away experience golfing, fishing, boating, scuba diving, or coastal walks. We enjoy gardening, nature, woodturning, boating, fishing, country living, travelling and meeting new people. A warm welcome awaits you with complementary refreshments on your arrival.

Paihia - Opua *Self-contained Separate/Suite B&B 5km S of Paihia*

Waterview Lodge
Antionette & Jess Cherrington
14 Franklin Street, Opua, Bay of Islands 0290
Tel: (09) 402 7595 Fax: (09) 402 7596
Mob: 021 102 3950 waterviewlodge@hotmail.com
www.bnb.co.nz/waterview.html
Double $140-$220 Single $90-$120
(Continental Breakfast) Child $20 Dinner $30 - $40
Credit cards accepted Child at home Children welcome
3 Queen 2 Single (3 bdrm) 3 Ensuite

Overlooking the picturesque Port of Opua, Waterview Lodge is a quality accomodation establishment. The Harbour and River suites, with private balcony's, have expansive sea views of Opua and the upper harbour. Our 3 bedroom cottage also has beautiful sea views.Our 2 bedroom Garden unit is located downstairs, next to the Garden suite, with their own private garden and native bush backdrop. Both my husband & I are originally from the area. Waterview Lodge has been my family home for over 40 years. My husband and I live here with our 2 sons, Ben 15 and Oliver 8, and our little dog Amy.

Paihia - Opua *B&B   5km S of Paihia*

Rose Cottage
Pat & Don Jansen
37a Oromahoe Road, Opua 0290, Bay of Islands
Tel: (09) 402 8099 Fax: (09) 402 8096
Mob: 025 605 9560
www.bnb.co.nz/rosecottageopua.html
Double $80-$100 (Continental Breakfast)
1 King/Twin 1 Double (2 bdrm)
1 Guests share

Welcome to our home set in a lovely bush garden and enjoying picturesque upper harbour and rural views. Our guest wing offers a private entrance and deck area, fridge and microwave, TV, and tea/coffee facilities. Both guest rooms have extensive sea views. Private bathroom by arrangement. Don is a retired carpenter ant Pat, a retired nurse. We have been hosting guests for many years and look forward to helping you enjoy your stay. Inspection welcome.

Paihia - Opua   *Self-contained Homestay B&B   300m E of Opua*

Margaret Sinclair
7 Franklin St, Opua
Tel: (09) 402 8285 Fax: (09) 402 8285
bbopua@xtra.co.nz
www.bnb.co.nz/sinclair.html

Double $70 Single $40 (Continental Breakfast)
S/C Flat 1 double 2 single
$70 - $90 Double $10 Single
1 Double 2 Single (2 bdrm)
1 Family share

Welcome to my lovely home above Opua harbour. Enjoy panoramic views of water and boat activities - always something happening. Tourist activities are nearby. Relax in the spa after your day's outing. You may like to wander in my garden - my big interest. Downstairs is a 2 roomed unit, separate shower, toilet and private deck with stunning views. Take the Whangarei - Paihia road. Turn right for Opua - Russel ferry. This is Franklin St. My house is clearly visible on the seaward side.

Paihia - Opua   *Self-contained B&B   5km S of Paihia*

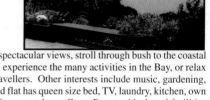

Seascape
Vanessa & Frank Leadley
17 English Bay Road, Opua
Tel: (09) 402 7650 Fax: (09) 402 7650
Mob: 027 4756 793 frankleadley@xtra.co.nz
www.bnb.co.nz/leadley.html

Double $80 Single $60 (Special Breakfast)
S/C flat $90 - $100 Credit cards accepted
1 Queen 2 Single (2 bdrm)
1 Ensuite 1 Family share

"Seascape" is on a tranquil bush-clad ridge. Enjoy spectacular views, stroll through bush to the coastal walk-way, enjoy our beautifully landscaped garden, experience the many activities in the Bay, or relax on your deck. We are keen NZ and international travellers. Other interests include music, gardening, fishing, boating, and Rotary. Our fully self-contained flat has queen size bed, TV, laundry, kitchen, own entrance and deck. Join us for breakfast, or look after yourselves. Guest Room with shared facilities also available.

Russell   *Homestay B&B   4mins N of Russell*

Kays Place
Kay Bosanquet
67 Wellington Street, Russell
Tel: (09) 403 7843 Fax: (09) 403 7853
Mob: 025 2723 672
kaysplace@xtra.co.nz>
www.bnb.co.nz/kaysplace.html

Double $120-$150 Single $65 (Continental Breakfast)
1 Queen 1 Double 1 Twin 1 Single (4 bdrm)
1 Ensuite 2 Private

My home overlooks Russell Bay with breathtaking water and bush views. Born and bred in Northland I take great pride in showing my guests NZ finest capital. I love every kind of fishing and frequently escort my guests out game fishing. Meals are usually served on the terrace and I find my guests like to explore and sample the different fish restaurants that abound in Russell. Lots of lovely walks handy. All I ask of my guests is to completely relax and use my home as theirs.

Russell *Self-contained B&B   Russell Central*

Te Manaaki
Sharyn & Dudley Smith
2 Robertson Road, Russell
Tel: (09) 403 7200 Fax: (09) 403 7537
Mob: 027 497 2177 triple.b@xtra.co.nz
www.bay-of-islands.co.nz/accomm/tmanaaki.html
Double $150-$250 Single $150-$250 (Full Breakfast)
Child $20 Credit cards accepted
2 Superking (2 bdrm)
2 Ensuite

"Te Manaaki" overlooks the picturesque harbour and village of historic Russell with its delightful seaside restaurants, shops and wharf a gentle stroll away. Magnificent harbour, bush and village views are a feature of guests private accommodation. The Villa is an attractively appointed sunny spacious de-luxe unit set in its own grounds (with garden spa) adjacent to the main house. The Studio is a self contained suite-styled apartment on the ground floor of our new modern home. Both units have mini-kitchen facilities and off-street parking.

Russell *B&B   19km E of Russell*

Gasthaus Waipiro Bay
Beate & Thomas Lauterbach
Waipiro Bay - Manawaora Road 392,
PO Box 224, Russell
Tel: (09) 403 7095 Fax: (09) 403 7095
gasthaus@ihug.co.nz www.lauterbach.co.nz
Double $165-$185 Single $135-$150 (Full Breakfast)
Child $45pp Dinner $48 pp by arrangement
Credit cards accepted Children welcome
2 Queen 1 Single (2 bdrm) 1 Ensuite 1 Private

Dream of a place, an artist's home above a bay, the Pacific Ocean on the horizon, islands, beaches, forests - nature at your doorstep. This world of space and light inspires artist Thomas Lauterbach to paint strong images of land, sea and the Maori people. A warm, imaginative home, comfortable bedrooms with spectacular views. Enjoy your private living-room with open fire place and works of art. We love to cook gourmet meals with flavours from Italy to the South Pacific. For a taste of heaven on earth - come and let us spoil you a little.

Russell *Self-contained Homestay B&B   5km S of Russell*

Treetops
Vivienne & Andy Nathan
6 Pinetree Lane, Te Wahapu, Russell
Tel: (09) 403 7475 Fax: (09) 403 7459
Mob: 025 272 8881 vnathan@xtra.co.nz
www.bnb.co.nz/treetopsrussell.html
Double $95 Single $85 (Full Breakfast) Dinner $35
S/C Cottage $105 Credit cards accepted
1 King 1 Double (2 bdrm)
1 Guests share

Our home is situated at the end of Te Wahapu Peninsula. We are surrounded by native bush and tuis & fantails are our constant companions. Kiwis are sometimes heard during the night. Both upstairs bedrooms have beautiful sea views from your bed. Guests are welcome to sit in the spa pool and watch the sun set over Paihia across the Bay. A track through the bush leads down to the beach and the self-contained historic cottage, where you are welcome to use the dinghy and barbecue.

Russell   *Self-contained Homestay B&B*

Inn-The-Pink B&B
Mary & Kent Maclachlan
1 Oneroa Road, Russell

Tel: (09) 403 7347 Fax: (09) 403 7347
Mob: 025 289 3562 mary&kent@xtra.co.nz
www.bay-of-islands.co.nz/inthepnk

Double $110 Single $70 (Full Breakfast)
Child $35 (under 12) S/C $150 Credit cards accepted
1 King/Twin 1 Queen 2 Single (2 bdrm)
1 Ensuite 1 Private

Welcome to our magical house on the hill with magnificent harbour views, colourful gardens and spectacular Russell sunsets. We're super friendly Kiwi Canadian sailors who have been welcoming guests to our slice of paradise for 12 years. Relax on your own deck in the self-contained unit with queen bed, ensuite bathroom, fridge, microwave, TV. Our home has a comfortable guestroom with king/twin beds and private bathroom. Experience our delicious cooked breakfasts, a highlight of your stay. We're a five minute stroll from Russell village.

Russell   *Homestay   1km E of Russell*

Lesleys
Lesley Coleman
1 Pomare Road, Russell, Northland

Tel: (09) 403 7099 Mob: 021 108 0369
three.gs@xtra.co.nz
www.bnb.co.nz/bay-of-islands.co.nz/accomm/lesley.html

Double $105 Single $75 (Special Breakfast)
Child $30 Dinner $20 Credit cards accepted
Pet on property Children welcome
1 Double 1 Single (1 bdrm) 1 Private

Our home is 10 minutes walk to historic Russell and the design inspired by having lived in Greece. In warm weather breakfast on the verandah looking out to Matauwhi Bay and Russell Boat Club otherwise relax in the glassed-in breeze way with fresh waffles and maple syrup. Or you may like a traditional English breakfast using fresh eggs from our chickens. We have only one guestroom with its own entrance, large bathroom and antique bath. Our combined interests include travelling, art, sport and our cat and dog. Welcome!

Russell - Okiato   *Self-contained Separate/Suite B&B   9km S of Russell*

Aimeo Cottage
Annie & Helmuth Hormann
Okiato Point Road, RD 1, Russell

Tel: (09) 403 7494 Fax: (09) 403 7494
Mob: 025 272 2393 aimeo-cottage.nz@xtra.co.nz
www.bnb.co.nz/aimeocottage.html

Double $120 Single $110 (Special Breakfast)
Three bedroom holiday home tariff on request
Child $25 Credit cards accepted Children welcome
4 King/Twin 1 Single (2 bdrm)
1 Ensuite 1 Private

"A quiet place to relax." We have sailed half way around the world to find this beautiful quiet place in the heart of the Bay of Islands and would be happy to share this with you for a while. Aimeo Cottage is built on the hill of Okiato Point, a secluded peninsula overlooking the Bay. In 10 minutes you are in New Zealand's first capital, Russell, the site of many historic buildings, an interesting museum and art galleries. Children are welcome. For golfers a complete set of clubs (men) complementary available.

Russell - Matauwhi Bay *Historic Guesthouse & Self-contained Cottage*

1km E of Russell

Ounuwhao B&B
Marilyn & Allan Nicklin
Matauwhi Bay, Russell
Tel: (09) 403 7310 Fax: (09) 403 8310
thenicklins@xtra.co.nz
www.bnb.co.nz/ounuwhaobb.html

Double $160-$200 Single $120-$150 (Full Breakfast) Child $35 under 12 yrs Dinner n/a
Detached garden-suite $185 Credit cards accepted
1 King/Twin 4 Queen 2 Twin 2 Single (6 bdrm)
4 Ensuite 1 Private

Welcome to historic Russell; take a step-back into a bygone era and spend some time with us in our delightful, nostalgic, immaculately restored Victorian Villa (Circa 1894).

Enjoy your own large guest lounge; tea/coffee and biscuits always available, with open fire in the cooler months, and wrap-around verandahs for you to relax and take-in the warm sea breezes.

Each of our four queen rooms have traditional wallpapers and paintwork, with handmade patchwork quilts and fresh flowers to create a lovingly detailed, traditional romantic interior.

Breakfast is served in our farmhouse kitchen around the large kauri dining table or al-fresco on the verandah if you wish. It is an all homemade affair; from the freshly baked fruit and nut bread, to the yummy daily special and the jam conserves.

Our self-contained cottage is set in park-like grounds for your privacy and enjoyment: with two double bedrooms, it is ideal for a family or two couples travelling together. It has a large lounge overlooking the reserve and out into the bay, a sun-room and fully self-contained kitchen. Wonderful for people looking for that special place for peace and time-out. Max 4 persons. Breakfast is available if required.

Complimentary afternoon tea on arrival. Laundry service available. We look forward to meeting you soon. Our homes are SMOKE-FREE.

We are closed June and July.

We are a member of NZ Heritage Inns Group.

EXPERIENCE OUR HISTORIC B&B.

ENJOY A WORLD OF DIFFERENCE.

Russell   *Self-contained Homestay B&B Studio Unit   0.25km E of Russell*

Brown Lodge
Joan & Roly Brown,
6 Ashby Street, Russell

Tel: (09) 403 7693 Fax: (09) 403 7683 brown.lodge@xtra.co.nz
http://webnz.co.nz/bbnz/brown1.htm
Double $160-$180 Single $160 Extra person in room $60 (Full Breakfast) Credit cards accepted
3 Queen 2 Single (3 bdrm)
3 Ensuite

Quite central position with fine sea views over Russell and the Bay. One of the interesting new homes architecturally designed in keeping with the historic nature of Russell. An all timber construction featuring New Zealand Kauri, Rimu, Douglas Fir and Pine.   A look at craftsmanship of today with old world atmosphere combined with modern private facilities and true home comforts.

Friendly and personal attention is assured. Breakfast at our antique Kauri table amongst Rimu wood panelling, old bricks and over 100 years old re-sited arched windows. Furnished with antiques, Persian carpets throughout and examples of Roly's Kauri furniture and cabinetry. Air conditioning and heating for all year round comfort.

Two private spacious suites, each with their own entrance from the main foyer, both have sea views, queen size beds, ensuites, TV, fridge and tea/coffee making facilities.

Studio unit with private entrance and own verandah to enjoy the view over Russel and the Bay. Air conditioning, queen bed and one large single, fridge, TV, large ensuite.

Russell township is easy 3 minute walk to restaurants, shops, wharf. We can advise and book restaurants, boat cruises around the Bay and bus trips to Cape Reinga etc. Smoke free home, safe off street parking, no wheel chair access.

Russell - Te Wahapu   *Self-contained B&B   7km S of Russell*

Brisa
Jenny & Peter Sharpe
Te Wahapu Road, RD 1, Russell
Tel: (09) 403 7757 Fax: (09) 403 7758 Mob: 025 58 22 31
brisa@xtra.co.nz
www.bay-of-islands.co.nz/accomm/brisa.html
Double $160 Single $140 (Full Breakfast) (Special Breakfast)
Dinner by arrangement $30pp Credit cards accepted
1 King/Twin 2 Queen (3 bdrm)
3 Ensuite

Our home and garden are hidden among the trees at the water's edge. In the morning wake to the sound of the birds and the sunrise over Orongo Bay.

We offer warm hospitality and quiet, clean, high quality accommodation with safe off street parking.

Our guests can enjoy total privacy within their self contained cottage or studio which has a kitchenette with fridge and cooking facilities, a spacious bedroom/lounge area and ensuite bathroom.

Each cottage has its own area of flowers shrubs and trees, a separate entrance and large deck that overlooks the bay.

The emphasis is on tasteful, comfortable surroundings with all the essential extras such as fresh flowers, home baking, toiletries and bathrobes. Top quality beds and bedding, cotton sheets and soft absorbent towels ensure a feeling of luxury. In each suite a television, books and magazines are provided for your enjoyment.

Our breakfast table is set with white linen, silver and fine china and features fresh baking, home grown fruit, our own preserves and eggs from our free range hens.

The menu changes daily. Picnic hampers and dinners are also available by arrangement

A dinghy is at hand for a leisurely paddle from our beach and historic Russell's museum, restaurants and galleries are just seven minutes away by car.

Come and enjoy this private and tranquil place with us.

Russell - Te Wahapu   *Separate/Suite B&B Lodge   7km S of Russell*

Mako Lodge & Fishing Charters
Jean & Graeme McIntosh
92a Te Wahapu Rd, Russell
Tel: (09) 403 7770 Fax: (09) 403 7713
Mob: 025 739 787 Tollfree: 0800 625 669
makolodge.charters@xtra.co.nz www.makolodge.co.nz
Double $110 Single $110 (Full Breakfast) Dinner b/a
Lodge From $170 Credit cards accepted Pets welcome
1 King/Twin 2 Queen 1 Double 6 Single (4 bdrm)
4 Ensuite

Secluded waterfront location just 7 mins from Russell village. Choose from the luxury of our lodge - sleeps up to 8 persons - (Qualmark **** rated 2002/3 Homestay suite (double) and Studio - sleeps 1 double, 2 singles, all fully self-contained with own e nsuites. Services include telephone, TV & video library and BBQ's. Pets by arrangement. Complimentary dinghy and kayak for use on our sheltered estuary. Resident Golden Labrador (Tessa). Optional light tackle, saltfly, gamefishing or sightseeing trips on our modern fully equipped charter vessel "MAKO 1".

Russell   *Homestay   0.5km N of Russell*

La Veduta
Danielle & Dino Fossi
11 Gould Street, Russell, Bay of Islands
Tel: (09) 403 8299 Fax: (09) 403 8299
laveduta@xtra.co.nz www.laveduta.co.nz
Double $130-$150 Single $95-$110   Child $45
(Continental & Full Breakfast) Dinner by arrangement
Credit cards accepted Pet on property
4 Double 1 Twin 1 Single (5 bdrm)
2 Ensuite 2 Private 1 Guests share

LA VEDUTA (the view). Enjoy our mix of traditional European culture in the midst of the beautiful Bay of Islands. Historic heartland of New Zealand. La Veduta is the perfect pied a terre for your Northland holiday. We offer our guests a warm welcome and personalised service. A delicious breakfast is served on the balcony. Enjoy refreshments watching the sunset over the Bay. Relax or we can arrange tours and activities. Restaurants, beach and ferries handy, transport available. French & Italian spoken. TV room, billiard room, laundry.

Russell   *Self-contained   7km S of Russell*

Whare Tainui
Eleanor & William Stegall
PO Box 54, Te Wahapu, Russell
Tel: (09) 403 8339 Fax: (09) 403 8339
Mob: 025 244 3178
www.bnb.co.nz/wharetainui.html
Double $125-$145 (Continental Breakfast)
Credit cards accepted
2 Queen (2 bdrm)
1 Ensuite 1 Private

On Te Wahapu Peninsula stay in secluded modern hilltop villa - fully equipped kitchen, liv/din room and bath, to plan day trips by car or bus tour - Cape Reinga; air or boat tours - Bay of Islands or local ferry boat trips - Russell to Paihia w/shopping, museums return to your 'treehouse' plan picnic track to Tore Tore Island at the end of Peninsula just beyond boat ramp at low tide or stay on your private patio and decks enjoy NZ's natural habitat with ever-changing bay views.

Russell   *Self-contained Separate/Suite B&B studio*   *Russell Central*

A Place in the Sun
Pip & Oliver Campbell
57 Upper Wellington Street,
Russell, Bay of Islands
Tel: (09) 403 7615 Fax: (09) 403 7610
Mob: 025 777 942   sailing@paradise.net.nz
www.bay-of-islands.co.nz/accomm/sunny.html
Double $100-$150 Single $90 (Continental Breakfast)
Credit cards accepted
1 Queen 1 Double 1 Single (3 bdrm) 2 Ensuite

'Romantic Russell, where the present means the past', is this retired sailing couple's perfect anchorage. Our home (and your separate accommodation) overlooks the village, with great views across the Bay. Close to uncrowded beaches, heritage trails, restaurants, and convenient departure for all cruises and activities. Two new apartments and studio (for longer stay), open through ranchsliders on to a covered terrace at lawn level (no stairs). You will find a peaceful setting, bordering a bush reserve, comfortable beds, bathrobes, toiletries. We serve a substantial coontinental breakfast.

Kohukohu   *Homestay B&B Guesthouse*   *80km S of Kaitaia*

Harbour Views Guest House
Jacky Kelly & Bill Thomson
Rakautapu Road,
Kohukohu, Northland
Tel: (09) 405 5815 Fax: (09) 405 5865
www.bnb.co.nz/harbourviewsguesthouse.html
Double $80 Single $40 (Full Breakfast)
Dinner $20 Pet on property
1 Queen 2 Single (2 bdrm)
1 Private

Historic Kohukohu, now a friendly and charming village,is situated on the north side of the Hokianga Harbour. Our beautifully restored Kauri home is set in two acres of gardens and trees and commands a spectacular view of the harbour. The guest rooms, opening on to a sunny verandah, are in a private wing of the house. Meals are prepared using home-grown produce in season. We are interested in and knowledgeable about the history and geography of the area. We have two cats.

Opononi   *Homestay B&B*   *50km W of Kaikohe*

Koutu Lodge
Tony and Sylvia Stockman
Koutu Loop Road, Opononi, RD 3, Kaikohe
Tel: (09) 405 8882 Fax: (09) 405 8893
koutulodgebnb@xtra.co.nz
www.bnb.co.nz/koutulodge.html
Double $90 Single $55 (Full Breakfast)
Dinner $30 by arrangement Credit cards accepted
1 King 1 Queen 1 Double 1 Single (3 bdrm)
2 Ensuite 1 Private

Situated on Koutu Point overlooking the beautiful Hokianga Harbour, our home has views both rural and sea. Two rooms have private decks, ensuites, and all rooms are tastefully decorated and very comfortable.We are a friendly Kiwi couple, and our aim is to provide a memorable stay, peaceful, or as active as you wish. Our friendly dog lives outside. Koutu Loop Rd is 4.3 kms north of Opononi then left 2.3 kms on tar seal to Lodge on right.

Opononi *Homestay B&B   57km W of Kaikohe*

Opononi Dolphin Lodge
Rob & Pam Jensen
Cnr SH12 & Fairlie Cres, PO Box 28, Opononi
Tel: (09) 405 8451 Fax: (09) 405 8451
<shirley@xtra.co.nz
www.bnb.co.nz/dolphinlodge.html
Double $65-$85 Single $50 (Continental Breakfast)
Credit cards accepted
1 Queen 1 Double 1 Twin 1 Single (3 bdrm)
2 Ensuite 1 Private 1 Guests share

Situated on the corner of SH12 and Fairlie Cres, opposite a beach reserve on the edge of the pristine Hokianga Harbour, only 20 minutes from 'Tane-Mahuta' the largest Kauri tree in the world. From our decks there are picture postcard views up and down and across the harbour to the huge golden sand dunes. Machine embroidery, patchwork, quilting, fishing, boating, service clubs activities and indoor bowls are our main interests. Come to the Hokianga - the West Coast diamond.

Omapere *B&B   60km W of Kaikohe*

Harbourside Bed & Breakfast
Joy & Garth Coulter
PO Box 10, Omapere
Tel: (09) 405 8246
harboursidebnb@xtra.co.nz
www.bnb.co.nz/harboursidebedbreakfast.html
Double $85 Single $55 (Continental Breakfast)
Credit cards accepted Pet on property
1 Queen 2 Single (2 bdrm)
2 Ensuite

Our beachfront home on State Highway 12 overlooking the Hokianga Harbour is within walking distance of restaurants and bars. The beach is 50 metres away. Both rooms have ensuites, tea making facilities, refrigerators and TV with separate entrances onto private decks to relax and enjoy superb views. We're close to the Waipoua Forest, West Coast beaches and sand hills. We have an interest in farming, forestry and education. Stay and share our home and cat. Extra to above a self-contained flat is available.

Omapere *B&B   60km W of Kaikohe*

Hokianga Haven Omapere Beachfront
Heather Randerson
226 State Highway 12, Omapere, Hokianga
Tel: (09) 405 8285 Fax: (09) 405 8215
Mob: 021 393 973
tikanga2000@xtra.co.nz
www.bnb.co.nz/omaperebeachfront.html
Double $130 (Full Breakfast)
1 Queen (1 bdrm)
1 Private

Snuggled into this peaceful private, beachfront location, our new home embraces the continuously inspiring sea scape of the dramatic harbour entrance and magnificent dune. Simply relaxing in this harbourside haven is reviltalizing. Bush and forest walks, horse riding, harbour cruising, fishing, river and coastal swimming are some of the natural delights to be enjoyed in this historic area. Our dog will be a willing walking companion. Star gazing in the warmth of the hot tub is a wonderful way to finish the day. Range of healing therapies available.

Dargaville   *Self contained suites*   *2km Dargaville*

Awakino Point Boutique Motel
June & Mick
PO Box 168, Dargaville
Tel: (09) 439 7870 Fax: (09) 439 7870
awakinopoint@xtra.co.nz
www.awakinopoint.co.nz
Double $75-$95 (Continental Breakfast)
Dinner by arrangement 2/brm, 4 persons $135 - $155
Rates Seasonal Credit cards accepted
3 Queen 4 Twin (5 bdrm) 3 Ensuite

This unique property set on its own acreage surrounded by attractive gardens is just 2kms from Dargaville on SH14 (The Whangarei Road). The best features of a motel scheme and a New Zealand bed and breakfast have been amalgamated to produce something a little different. You will enjoy your own self contained suite with private bathroom, friendly personal service and a good breakfast. Three well appointed one and two bedroom self contained ground floor units. One of them has a kitchen, bath and log fire.   Smoking outdoors please.

Dargaville - Bayly's Beach   *Self contained*

Ocean View
Paula & John Powell
7 Ocean View Terrace, Bayly's Beach, RD7, Dargaville
Tel: (09) 439 6256 Mob: 025 623 3821
baylys@win.co.nz
www.bnb.co.nz/oceanview.html
Double $75 Single $45 (Continental Breakfast)
Child $10 under 12yrs Credit cards accepted
Child at home Pet on property Children welcome
1 Double 1 Single (1 bdrm) 1 Ensuite

Just off the trail, this sometimes wild, always wonderful, expansive west coast beach is a great place to relax. With a glimpse of the sea, your cottage is two minutes walk to the beach and clifftop walkways. We have two great cafes and 18-hole golf locally, with Kai Iwi Lakes and forests an easy day trip. Enjoy your sunny, comfortable cottage (great shower!) and breakfast at your leisure - provided in cottage for you. With our two children and Ruby the cat we look forward to welcoming you. Directions: Drive through the village, you will see our sign at the foot of the big hill.

All our B&Bs are non-smoking
unless stated otherwise in the text.

Dargaville   *Farmstay B&B luxury accomodation*   *1.5km S of Dargaville*

Kauri House Lodge
Doug Blaxall
PO Box 382, Bowen Street,
Dargaville

Tel: (09) 439 8082 Fax: (09) 439 8082
Mob: 025 547 769
kaurihouse@infomace.co.nz
www.bnb.co.nz/kaurihouselodge.html

Double $175-$225 Single $150-$160 (Full Breakfast)
Credit cards accepted
1 King/Twin 2 King (3 bdrm)
3 Ensuite

Kauri House Lodge sits high above Dargaville amongst mature trees. The 1880's villa retains all it's charm, style and grace with original Kauri panelling and period antiques in all rooms.

Start your day woken by native birds, walk through extensive landscaped grounds or read in our library. In summer enjoy a dip in the large swimming pool. In winter our billiard room log fire is a cozy spot to relax for the evening.

Join us to explore beautiful mature native bush on our nearby farm overlooking the Wairoa River and Kaipara Harbour.

The area offers many activities including deserted beaches, lakes, river tours, horse treks, walks and restaurants.

THE MOST COMMON COMMENT IN VISITOR BOOK: "SAVE THE BEST TO LAST".
WE HAVE BEEN HOSTING BED AND BREAKFAST FOR 30 YEARS.

Dargaville *B&B 2km S of Dargaville*

Turiwiri B&B
Bruce & Jennifer Crawford
Turiwiri RAPID 6775,
State Highway 12, Dargaville
Tel: (09) 439 6003 Fax: (09) 439 6003
www.bnb.co.nz/turiwiribb.html

Double $70 Single $35 (Continental Breakfast)
Pet on property
2 Queen (2 bdrm)
1 Guests share

We enjoy sharing our local knowledge with guests in our modern, one level home 2ks from Dargaville on SH 12, minutes from quality restaurants. Excellent parking for vehicles, and an expansive garden. We thank our guests for not smoking and offer the use of our enclosed Spa Pool. Our family of three grown children, all live away from home, and interests include Family, Farming, Rotary International, Gardening and Big Game Fishing. Our pets include two cats and a friendly deaf corgi.

Dargaville *B&B Dargaville central*

Birch's B&B
Wally Birch
18 Kauri Street, Dargaville,
Tel: (09) 439 7565 Fax: (09) 439 7520
Mob: 025 586 554
birch@kauricoast.co.nz
www.bnb.co.nz/birchsbb.html

Double $70 Single $45 (Continental Breakfast)
Child negotiable Credit cards accepted
2 Queen 2 Twin (4 bdrm)
2 Guests share

If you enjoy a good night's sleep, love a nice hot shower and insist on cleanliness then look no further. My Kauri bungalow was built in 1912 has 4 queen and twin bedrooms well decorated for your comfort. A large family lounge with log fire and a lovely modern kitchen, dining room with coal range. I'm close to the town centre which has excellent eating out houses. If it's a friendly homely stay you require call in, your inspection is welcome.

Matakohe *Farmstay 4km S of Matakohe*

Maramarie
Elinor & Tom Beazley
Tinopai Road, RD 1, Matakohe
Tel: (09) 431 6911 maramarie@xtra.co.nz
www.bnb.co.nz/maramarie.html

Double $80 Single $50 (Continental Breakfast)
Child 1/2 price Dinner $20 B/A Credit cards accepted
Child at home Pet on property Children welcome
1 Double (1 bdrm)
1 Private

"Maramarie" is a secluded Kauri homestead set in a mature garden. Located 4km from Matakohe and the unique Kauri museum where Kauri history is beautifully displayed and is a must see on your visit to Northland. We are beef farmers and our farm overlooks the Kaipara Harbour. I am Swedish and Tom is a Kiwi with three school age children. We have working dogs and a lazy cat. Come and visit our family and relax on our farm. Please phone for reservations and directions.

Matakohe   *Homestay B&B   9km S of Matakohe*

Petite Provence
Linda & Guy Bucchi
Tinopai Road, RD1, Matakohe
Tel: (09) 431 7552 Fax: (09) 431 7552
www.bnb.co.nz/petiteprovince.html
Double $100 Single $80 (Continental Breakfast)
Dinner by arrangement Credit cards accepted
Pet on property
2 Queen (2 bdrm) 2 Ensuite

Bienvenue to Petite Provence, our new colonial style home (French provencal interior) set amongst rolling farmland with neighbouring native bush and views of Kaipara Harbour. Guy is French, I am a New Zealander, our South of France family home was also a homestay. Mediterranean/vegetarian/local produce meals. Smoking outdoors. Pets: one outside dog. Directions: from Matakohe Kauri Museum travel 9kms south towards Tinopai. Drive to end of private road (500m) in front of St. Michael on the hill church. Bookings preferred.

Pahi - Paparoa   *Self-contained B&B   7km W of Paparoa*

Palm House
Len & Pam Byles
Pahi Road, RD 1, Paparoa, Northland
Tel: (09) 431 6689 Fax: (09) 431 6689
Mob: 021 178 9789
palmhouse@paradise.net.nz
www.bnb.co.nz/palmhouse.html
Double $100 Single $70 (Full Breakfast)
Dinner $35 by arrangement S/C Garden Cottage $80
Credit cards accepted Pet on property
2 Queen 1 Twin (3 bdrm) 1 Ensuite 1 Guests share

Get off the beaten track for a night or two and enjoy staying in this quiet backwater on the Kaipara Harbour.Just relax, amble along the tideline, visit the largest Morton Bay Fig Tree, stroll to the wharf, watch the fish jump in the water. Enjoy tasty home cooked meals, NZ wines in peaceful surroundings. Just 13kms from Matakohe Kauri Museum on S/H12. Turn south at Paparoa,travel 7kms to Pahi. Palm House is on the left. Two signs above the gate. Two smoochy cats

Whangarei   *Self-contained Homestay B&B   10km E of Whangarei*

Waikaraka Harbourview
Marrion & John Beck
477 Whangarei Heads Road, Waikaraka,
RD 4, Whangarei
Tel: (09) 436 2549 Fax: (09) 436 2549
becksbb@xtra.co.nz
www.bnb.co.nz/waikarakaharbourview.html
Double $55-$75 Single $40-$50
(Continental Breakfast) Credit cards accepted
1 Double 2 Single (2 bdrm) 1 Ensuite 1 Family share

Happily retired, we enjoy outdoors, travel, sport, gardening, fishing and guests. We have a twin, self-contained studio with en-suite and double room with conservatory and family share bathroom. Spectacular sea and landscape views - tea/coffee facilities, refrigerator, table and chairs, TV, radio, adjoining covered decks. Enjoy gardens, beaches, forest and mountain walks, golf, fishing, boating, swimming. DIRECTIONS: From Whangarei city centre, head east to Onerahi (5km) - at BP station, turn left on Whangarei Heads Road, 5km to B&B (sign on left). Phone answered 24 hours.

Whangarei Heads *Self-contained B&B* *31km SE of Whangarei*

Manaia Gardens
Audrey & Colin Arnold
RD 4, Whangarei
Tel: (09) 434 0797 arnoldac@igrin.co.nz
www.bnb.co.nz/manaiagardens.html

Double $65 Single $50 (Continental Breakfast)
Child under 5 free Extra person $15
Self-catering $50 - $60
Credit cards accepted Children welcome
Smoking area inside
2 Queen 1 Single (3 bdrm) 2 Private

We have a small farm and a large garden, with two quaint old self-contained cabins in the garden. They have comfortable beds and basic cooking facilities. We have a rowboat you are welcome to borrow, nearby shops and galleries. Laundry available. This is a beautiful area with rocky bush clad hills, harbour and ocean beaches, lots of Conservation land for walks. Or just relax in private. We are the only buildings in the bay. Red mailbox 2487 on the Whangarei Heads Road.

Whangarei Heads *Homestay* *28km SE of Whangarei*

Bantry
Karel & Robin Lieffering
Little Munro Bay, RD 4, Whangarei
Tel: (09) 434 0751 Fax: (09) 434 0754
lieffrng@igrin.co.nz
www.bnb.co.nz/bantry.html

Double $100 Single $55 (Full Breakfast)
Child 1/2 price under 12yrs Dinner $30
1 Queen 2 Single (2 bdrm)
1 Guests share

We are a semi-retired couple with dog. We speak Dutch, French, German, and Japanese and we like to laugh. Our unusual home with some natural rock interior walls is on the edge of a safe swimming beach, and bush reserve with walking tracks and several good fishing spots. A photographically fascinating area with wonderful views of coastal "mountains" bay and sea. Guests have own entrance and sitting room, all sea views. Enjoyable food and NZ wine. Directions: Phone, fax, email for reservations and directions.

Whangarei *Self-contained Homestay B&B* *10km E of Whangarei*

Waikaraka Harbourview
Marrion & John Beck
477 Whangarei Heads Road, Waikaraka,
RD 4, Whangarei
Tel: (09) 436 2549 Fax: (09) 436 2549
becksbb@xtra.co.nz
www.bnb.co.nz/waikarakaharbourview.html

Double $55-$75 Single $40-$50
(Continental Breakfast) Credit cards accepted
1 Double 2 Single (2 bdrm) 1 Ensuite 1 Family share

Happily retired, we enjoy outdoors, travel, sport, gardening, fishing and guests. We have a twin, self-contained studio with en-suite and double room with conservatory and family share bathroom. Spectacular sea and landscape views - tea/coffee facilities, refrigerator, table and chairs, TV, radio, adjoining covered decks. Enjoy gardens, beaches, forest and mountain walks, golf, fishing, boating, swimming. DIRECTIONS: From Whangarei city centre, head east to Onerahi (5km) - at BP station, turn left on Whangarei Heads Road, 5km to B&B (sign on left). Phone answered 24 hours.

Whangarei   *Farmstay Homestay   17km E of Whangarei*

Parua House
Pat & Peter Heaslip, Parua Bay, RD 4, Whangarei

Tel: (09) 436 5855 Fax: (09) 436 5105
paruahomestay@clear.net.nz
www.paruahomestay.homestead.com

Double $125 Single $75 (Full Breakfast) Child 1/2 price Dinner $35
Credit cards accepted
Pet on property
2 Queen 3 Single (4 bdrm)
2 Ensuite 1 Private

Parua House is a classical colonial house, built in 1883, comfortably restored and occupying an elevated site with panoramic views of Parua Bay and the Whangarei Harbour. The property covers 29 hectares of farmland including two protected reserves which are rich in native trees (including kauri) and birds.

Guests are welcome to explore the farm and bush, milk the Jersey cow, explore the olive grove and subtropical orchard or just relax in the spa-pool or on the verandah. A safe swimming beach adjoins the farm, with a short walk to the fishing jetty, two marinas and a golf course are nearby.

Our wide interests include photography, patchwork quilting and horticulture. The house is attractively appointed with antique furniture and a rare collection of spinning wheels.

Awake to home-baked bread and freshly squeezed orange juice. Dine in elegant surroundings with generous helpings of home produce with our own meat, milk, eggs, home-grown vegetables, olive and subtropical fruit (home-made icecream a speciality). Pre meal drinks and wine are provided to add to the bonhomie of an evening around a large French oak refectory table. As featured on TV's "Ansett NZ Time of Your Life" and "Corban's Taste NZ".

Whangarei - Onerahi *Self-contained B&B Luxury*   *9km Whangarei*

Channel Vista
Jenny & Murray Tancred
254 Beach Road, Onerahi, Whangarei
Tel: (09) 436 5529 Fax: (09) 436 5529
Mob: 025 973 083 tancred@igrin.co.nz
www.bnb.co.nz/channelvista.html

Double $90-$150 (Full Breakfast)
Credit cards accepted Pet on property
2 Queen (2 bdrm) 2 Ensuite

'Channel Vista' is situated on the shores of Whangarei Harbour. We have 2 luxury self contained units each with their own private decks where you can relax and watch the boats go by. We offer a smoke free environment and have laundry, fax and email facilities available. Salty (dog) and Pepe (cat) are our friendly pets. Local shopping centre is only 3 minutes away. All sports facilities (eg golf, diving, walks, game fishing, bowls etc) nearby. We are only 1 hour from the Bay of Islands, so it is a good place to base yourself for your Northland holiday.

Whangarei *B&B*   *4.5km NE of Whangarei*

Graelyn Villa
Joanie Guy
166 Kiripaka Road, Whangarei
Tel: (09) 437 7532 Fax: (09) 437 7533
graelyn@xtra.co.nz
www.bnb.co.nz/graelynvillla.html

Double $80 Single $65 (Continental Breakfast)
Child by arrangement Credit cards accepted
Pet on property Children welcome Pets welcome
2 Queen 2 Single (3 bdrm) 3 Ensuite

Welcome to my turn-of-the-century villa, which has been lovingly restored to offer comfort and luxury. My rooms offer superbly comfortable beds, TV, tea/coffee, heaters and electric blankets. FOR YOUR PRIVACY, ALL ROOMS ARE SEPARATE TO OWNERS ACCOMMODATION AND ALL HAVE ENSUITES. Five minutes to city centre with a wide variety of top class restaurants, 25 minute drive to Tutukaka Coast, handy to spectacular Whangarei Falls. I have two quiet dogs and a cat named Koko. Your pets welcome. Laundry facilities available.

Whangarei *Homestay B&B*   *16km W of Whangarei*

Taraire Grove
Jan & Brian Newman
Tatton Rd, RD 9, Whangarei
Tel: (09) 434 7279 Fax: (09) 434 7279
cooper@igrin.co.nz
www.bnb.co.nz/tarairegrove.html

Double $80 Single $50 (Full Breakfast)
Child 1/2 price Dinner $12 - $20 pp Children welcome
Credit cards accepted Pet on property
1 Queen 2 Single (2 bdrm) 1 Guests share

We welcome you to our charming country residence at Maungatapere, within easy driving distances to East and West Coast beaches. We are a semi-retired couple, and welcome the opportunity to return hospitality experienced overseas. Our home overlooks a stream and we are gradually developing the 3 1/2 acres into lawns, gardens and ponds. The guest wing is private - TV room - tea\coffee making facilities - smoke free area. Whangarei, 15 minutes away, has excellent restaurants or you can choose to dine with us and enjoy hospitality.

Whangarei   *Homestay B&B*

City Lights
Kevin McMahon & Doug Simpson
40A Vale Road Riverside, Whangarei
Tel: (09) 438 2390 Fax: (09) 438 2480
Mob: 027 479 1266
dougkevin@xtra.co.nz
www.bnb.co.nz/citylights.html

Double $80 Single $50 (Continental & Full Breakfast)
Credit cards accepted Pet on property
1 Queen 2 Single (2 bdrm)
1 Guests share

Our comfortable elevated home is 1.2 km from the Mall and Post Office. We overlook the Hatea River, Western Hills with views over city. The Town Basin is at the bottom of the street with restaurants, cafes and the Aquatic Centre. Forum North, Whangarei area hospital is close by. Unfortunately our place is not suitable for children. Meet Cara our lovable Boxer. Smokers outside. Pick up from Airport. We look forward to meeting you. Please phone ahead.

Whangarei   *Self-contained   10km NE of Whangarei CBD*

Country Garden Tearooms
John & Margaret Pool
526 Ngunguru Road,
RD 3, Whangarei
Tel: (09) 437 5127
Mob: 025 519 476
www.bnb.co.nz/countrygarden.html

Double $70 Single $50 (Full Breakfast)
Dinner $20 by arrangement
2 Queen (2 bdrm)
2 Ensuite

Enjoy a warm friendly welcome. We have over three acres of beautiful trees, shrubs, bulbs, perennials, succulents and a large variety of bird life. Feel at home in a spacious self-contained unit with fridge, microwave and tea making facilities. Enjoy cooked or continental breakfast in our dining room overlooking the garden. We are 10km from central Whangarei on Ngunguru-Tutukaka highway. 5km from Whangarei Falls. Beautiful beaches, restaurants, diving, fishing and golfing within 10km.

Whangarei   *Homestay B&B   12km SW of Whangarei*

Owaitokamotu
M & G Whitehead
PO Box 6067, Otaika, Whangarei
Tel: (09) 434 7554 Fax: (09) 4347554
minniegeorge@xtra.co.nz
www.bnb.co.nz/owaitokamotu.html

Double $75 Single $45 (Full Breakfast) Dinner $20
Children welcome Pets welcome
2 King/Twin 2 Queen (3 bdrm)
2 Guests share

Come and enjoy the absolute tranquillity of "Owaitokamotu" which is a place of water, magnificent rocks of all shapes and sizes, and pristine native bush awaiting your rambling walks, all set on 10 1/2 acres of easy contour and newly created gardens. Our home is newly built and is wheelchair friendly. Bedrooms have private access form exterior. TV, tea, coffee and cookies. A wide verandah offers pleasant relaxation. Smoking outside only please. Laundry facilities available.

Whangarei   *Self-contained Homestay B&B   In House   6km W of Whangarei*

The Stranded Mariner
Errol & Sharon Grace
State Highway 14, RD 9, Whangarei
Tel: (09) 438 9967 Fax: (09) 438 7967
Mob: 027 414 2006 info@strandedmariner.co.nz
www.strandedmariner.co.nz

Double $90-$120 Single $65-$85 (Full Breakfast)
Dinner by arrangement Credit cards accepted
1 Queen 1 Double 1 Twin 1 Single (4 bdrm)
1 Ensuite 2 Private

"Stranded Mariner", 6km from central Whangarei. In a very peaceful country, native bush surrounding. Walkways lead from boundaries to Museum, 18th century Clarke homestead, Bird Recovery Centre, Kiwi house. Sherwood Golf Course, 3km. Errol handcrafted our home from native timbers (floors, ceilings), featuring leadlight windows, bricked fireplaces. Cottage garden waterwheel, organic vegetables. Breakfast, and evening meals prepared in our kitchen emphasizing freshness-top quality. Whangarei's a great base to explore Northland, Bay of Islands, Kauri forest, Kauri Museum, Poor Knights Islands all easy day trips.

Whangarei - Kauri   *Homestay B&B   4km N of Whangarei*

Karamea House
Eliza and Denis Snelgar
184 Apotu Road, Kauri, Whangarei
Tel: 09 435 3401 Fax: 09 435 3495 Mob: 025 451 961
karamea@xtra.co.nz   www.karamea.co.nz

Double $180 Single $140
(Continental & Full Breakfast) Child $50 Dinner $50
Credit cards accepted Pet on property
Children welcome
3 Queen 1 Single (3 bdrm) 3 Ensuite

'Magical & enchanting'. Retreat and indulge yourself in peace and tranquillity, or use as a base to explore magnificent Northland. Your stay will be memorable with luscious food, generous hospitality and ultimate comfort in a spacious, two storey Georgian Manor. Breakfast alfresco, overlooking fragrant gardens or in the large country kitchen. Facilities include outdoor swimming and spa pools, astroturf tennis court, email & fax, central heating, air conditioning and large log fires. Your hosts will delight in ensuring your stay is an exceptional one.

All our B&Bs are non-smoking
unless stated otherwise in the text.

Whangarei- Glenbervie   *Homestay B&B*   *12km NE of Whangarei*

Lupton House Homestay B&B
Marie & John Dennistoun - Wood
555 Ngunguru Road, Glenbervie, RD 3, Whangarei
Tel: (09) 437 2989 Fax: (09) 437 2989
Mob: 025 203 9805 dennistoun-wood@xtra.co.nz
www.truenz.co.nz/luptonhouse
Double $95-$140 Single $70-$90 (Full Breakfast)
Dinner By arrangement Credit cards accepted
Child at home Pet on property Smoking area inside
2 Queen 2 Single (3 bdrm)3 Ensuite

Welcome to our home which is located in the dry-stone walled farmland of Glenbervie, between Whangarei and the beautiful beaches of Tutukaka coast. Lovingly restored and furnished and with extensive gardens, swimming pool and games room, our colonial villa offers guests comfort and relaxation in a friendly old-world country atmosphere which we share with our grandson, golden retriever dogs and two donkeys. We offer a full breakfast and by arrangement, dinner. Diving, fishing, golf, watersports and country walks within a 15km radius.

Ruakaka   *Self-contained Farmstay B&B*   *30km S of Whangarei*

Bream Bay Farmstay
Joyce & Vince Roberts
Doctor's Hill Road, RD 2, Waipu
Tel: (09) 432 7842 Fax: (09) 432 7842
Mob: 025 419 585
robertsb.b@xtra.co.nz
www.bnb.co.nz/breambayfarmstay.html
Double $80 Single $50 (Full Breakfast) Child $20
Dinner $25 Credit cards accepted
Children welcome Pets welcome
2 Queen 2 Single (3 bdrm) 1 Private 1 Family share

We offer awesome sea views from your own private terrace plus a free tour by arrangement, over our 160 acre dry stock farm & bush. Cooking facilities available. Our wetland area is home to the rare brown bitten. Beautiful beaches, golf course, racetrack where Vince trains our racehorses and good restaurants are a short drive from our home. As ex dairy farmers with a grown up family of four children, other interests include B&B for the past 12 years, travel, golf gardening.

Waipu   *Self-contained Farmstay*   *10km S of Waipu*

Andre & Robin La Bonte
PO Box 60, Waipu,
Northland
Tel: (09) 432 0645 Fax: (09) 432 0645
labonte@xtra.co.nz
www.bnb.co.nz/labonte.html
Double $80 Single $50 (Continental Breakfast)
Dinner $20 Credit cards accepted
1 King 2 Double 2 Single (3 bdrm)
2 Private

Sleep to the sound of the ocean in a separate efficiency apartment or in guest bedrooms on our 36 acre seaside farm. Explore our limestone rock formations or just sit and relax under the mature trees that grace our shoreline. The beach at Waipu Cove is a ten minute walk along the sea. We are a licensed fish farm, graze cattle and have flea free cats. Glow worm caves, deep-sea fishing, scuba diving and golf available locally. No smoking please. American spoken. Bookings recommended.

Waipu *Self-contained Farmstay B&B* *6km SE of Waipu*

The Stone House
Gillian & John Devine
Cove Road, Waipu
Tel: (09) 432 0432 Fax: (09) 432 0432
Tollfree: 0800 007 358 stonehousewaipu@xtra.co.nz
www.bnb.co.nz/thestonehouse.html

Double $80-$100 Single $60 (Full Breakfast)
Child $20 Dinner $20 Credit cards accepted
Pet on property Children welcome Pets welcome
1 King/Twin 2 Queen 1 Double 3 Single (4 bdrm)
1 Ensuite 3 Private

Relax in a charming seaside cottage or with your hosts Gillian and John in their unique solid Stonehouse.
Either way you will enjoy the green pastures of our farm, fringed with mature pohutakawa trees and the
sound of surf on a magnificent ocean beach. Picturesque rock gardens, croquet lawn and sheltered
patios complete the setting. Canoes and dinghys are available for exploring the adjacent lagoon and
bird sanctuary. Lots to do, lots to discover and to end each day, warm company around a log fire.

Waipu Cove *Self-contained B&B Downstairs Flat* *8km SE of Waipu*

Flower Haven
53 St Anne Road, Waipu Cove,
RD 2, Waipu 0254
Tel: (09) 432 0421 Mob: 025 287 2418
flowerhaven@xtra.co.nz
www.bnb.co.nz/flowerhaven.html

Double $95-$115 (Continental Breakfast)
Credit cards accepted
2 Double (2 bdrm)
1 Private

Flower Haven is elevated with panoramic coastal views, being developed as a garden retreat. The
accommodation is a self-contained downstairs flat with separate access; kitchen includes stove,
microwave, fridge/freezer. Washing machine, radio, TV, linen, duvets, blankets and bath towels provided.
Reduced tariff if continental breakfast not required. Our interests are gardening, genealogy and meeting
people. Near to restaurants, bird sanctuary, museums, golf, horse treks, fishing, caving, walking tracks,
oil refinery. 5 minutes to shop, sandy surf beach, rocks. Whangarei 35 minutes, Auckland 1 1/2 hours.

Langs Beach *B&B* *12km SE of Waipu*

Lochalsh Bed & Breakfast
Graham & Billie Long
Cove Road, Langs Beach, Waipu
Tel: (09) 432 0053 Fax: (09) 432 0053
Mob: 025 203 1660 lochalsh@clear.net.nz
www.lochalsh.co.nz

Double $80-$110 Single $60 (Full Breakfast)
Child POA Dinner $25 by arrangement
Credit cards accepted Pet on property
Children welcome
1 King 1 Twin (2 bdrm) 2 Ensuite

Our great grandfather settled this area in 1853. Our home is the original Lang home, right beside this
most beautiful of white surf beaches, lined by Pohutukawa trees. Our sunny guest lounge/kitchen/
dining area runs right along the front of the house, looking over the beach, bay and Hen and Chicken
Islands. Comfortable rooms with ensuites make this a delightful place for rest and relaxation. Billie &
Graham look forward to your company. From our visitors book: 'Our best stay in New Zealand!'

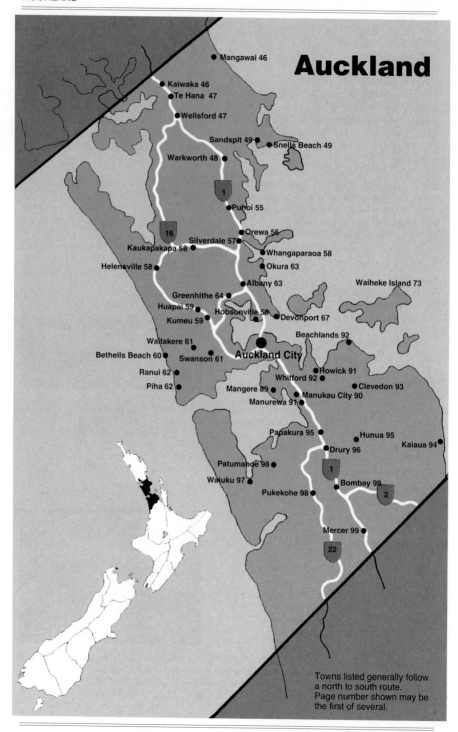

Auckland

Mangawai 46

Kaiwaka 46
Te Hana 47

Wellsford 47

Sandspit 49
Snells Beach 49

Warkworth 48

1

Puhoi 55

16
Orewa 56

Silverdale 57
Kaukapakapa 58
Whangaparaoa 58

Helensville 58
Okura 63

Albany 63
Waiheke Island 73

Greenhithe 64
Huapai 59
Hobsonville 59
Devonport 67
Kumeu 59

Beachlands 92

Waitakere 61
Auckland City
Bethells Beach 60
Swanson 61
Howick 91
Ranui 62
Whitford 92
Piha 62
Clevedon 93
Mangere 89
Manukau City 90
Manurewa 91

Papakura 95
Hunua 95

Drury 96
Kaiaua 94

Patumahoe 98
1
Waiuku 97
Bombay 99
Pukekohe 98
2

Mercer 99

22

Towns listed generally follow
a north to south route.
Page number shown may be
the first of several.

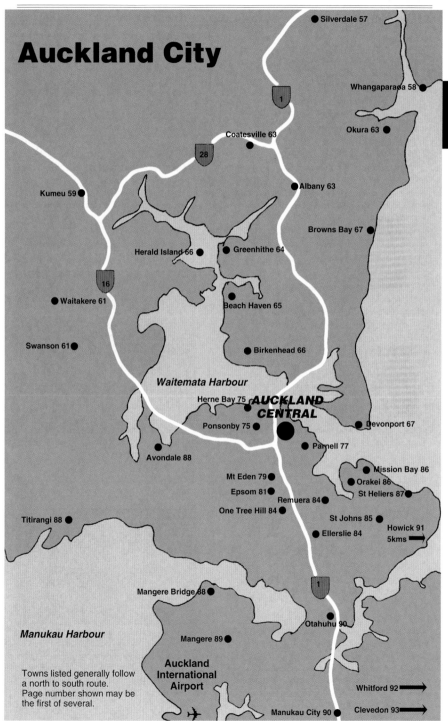

Auckland City

Silverdale 57

Whangaparaoa 58

Okura 63

1

Coatesville 63

28

Albany 63

Kumeu 59

Browns Bay 67

Herald Island 66
Greenhithe 64

16

Waitakere 61

Beach Haven 65

Swanson 61

Birkenhead 66

Waitemata Harbour

Herne Bay 75
AUCKLAND CENTRAL

Ponsonby 75

Devonport 67

Parnell 77

Avondale 88

Mission Bay 86

Mt Eden 79
Orakei 86

Epsom 81
St Heliers 87

Remuera 84

One Tree Hill 84

Titirangi 88

St Johns 85

Howick 91
5kms

Ellerslie 84

1

Mangere Bridge 88

Manukau Harbour

Otahuhu 90

Mangere 89

Auckland International Airport

Whitford 92

Towns listed generally follow
a north to south route.
Page number shown may be
the first of several.

Clevedon 93

Manukau City 90

Mangawhai *Homestay* *7km S of Mangawhai*

Fallowfield
Jean & Don Goldschmidt
Staniforth Road, RD 5, Wellsford
Tel: (09) 431 5096 Fax: (09) 431 5063
Mob: 0274 829 736
goldschmidt@xtra.co.nz
www.webnz.co.nz/bbnz/fallowfd.htm
Double $95-$105 (Full Breakfast) Dinner $30
Credit cards accepted
1 Queen 1 Twin (2 bdrm)
1 Private 1 Guests share

'A little out of the way, quite out of the ordinary'. Breathtaking views over rolling pasture to a Pacific ocean dotted with islands can be seen from our eyrie tucked into the hills above the seaside haven of Mangawhai. After a game of croquet or a beach visit for swimming or fishing, we can share the evening meal. Within our home built with architectural flair the guestroom is private, has tea and coffee facilities, a bed with a firm mattress, good heating and good lighting.

Mangawhai Heads *boutique bed and breakfast Inn* *1km SE of Mangawhai Heads*

Mangawhai Lodge -
a room with a view Boutique B&B Inn
Jeannette Forde
4 Heather Street, Mangawhai Heads
Tel: (09) 431 5311 Fax: (09) 431 5312
mlodge@xtra.co.nz   www.seaviewlodge.co.nz
Double $120-$150 Single $95-$130
(Special Breakfast) Credit cards accepted
3 King/Twin 2 Queen 8 Single (5 bdrm)
3 Ensuite 2 Private

Indulge yourself - escape to the tranquillity and magic that's Mangawhai Lodge. Five stylish guest rooms open onto wrap-around verandas of this colonial Inn. Spectacular sea and island views of the Hauraki Gulf, and white sandy beaches ensure Mangawhai Lodge is the ultimate "room with a view". Spend your days on the championship golf course, exploring the beaches and walkways or curled up reading or watching the boats sail by. Ideal for social golfing groups. Adjacent to award winning cafe, bowls/golf. Water access 3 minutes.

Kaiwaka *Self-contained Separate/Suite B&B* *19km N of Wellsford*

Serenity Gardens
Graham Mansfield
59 Gibbons Road, RD 2, Kaiwaka
Tel: (09) 431 2310 Mob: 025 209 3847
www.bnb.co.nz/serenitygardens.html
Double $90 Single $50 (Continental Breakfast)
Child Negotiable Children welcome
1 Queen 1 Single (1 bdrm)
1 Ensuite

Very warm welcome to new self-contained B&B accommodation bounded by tall totara bush, river and extensive gardens. Modern facilities include large double bedroom with river views (TV, radio); kitchenette (breakfast bar, microwave, fridge, all usual electrical appliances); shower; gamesroom (table tennis, snooker, laundry/ironing facilities). Privacy, comfort, quietness assured with friendly unobtrusive service. Ample secure parking, advice concerning sightseeing and free pamphlets. Leave main highway (Kaiwaka, famed "town of little lights"), at superstore, signposted Mangawhai Heads, 16 km. Located 1/2 km along Gibbons Road.

Wellsford - Te Hana   *Historic Farmhouse*   *6km N of Wellsford*

The Retreat
Colleen & Tony Moore
Te Hana, RD 5, Wellsford
Tel: (09) 423 8547
booking@sheepfarmstay.com
www.sheepfarmstay.com
Double $95 (Full Breakfast) Dinner $25pp self-contained cottage $85
Credit cards accepted Pet on property
2 Queen 1 Single (2 bdrm)
1 Private

Tony and Colleen welcome you to The Retreat, a spacious 1860's farmhouse built for a family with 12 children. Set well back from the road, the house is surrounded by an extensive landscaped garden, including a productive vegetable garden and orchard.

Fresh produce from the garden is a feature in our home cooking. Colleen is a spinner and weaver and our flock of sheep provides the raw material for the woollen goods that are hand made and for sale from the studio. If you haven't got close up to a sheep this is your chance, as we always have friendly sheep to hand feed.

We have hosted guests at The Retreat since 1988 and appreciate what you require. We know New Zealand well, our families have lived in NZ for several generations and we have visited most places in

our beautiful country, so if you have any questions on what to see or do, we are well equipped to provide the answers. We host only one group at a time, so you won't have to share a bathroom with someone you don't know.

The Retreat is very easy to find. Travelling North on SH 1, we are 6km North of Wellsford, look for the Weaving Studio sign on your left. You will pass through Te Hana before arriving at The Retreat. Kaiwaka is 13km north of The Retreat.

Now available a self contained cottage in the garden, sleeps 3.

Wellsford *Farmstay B&B*   *7km N of Wellsford*

Rosandra Homestay
Ross & Sandra Williams
557 SH1, RD5, Wellsford,

Tel: (09) 423 9343 Fax: (09) 423 9343
Mob: 021 179 9311   rosandra@xtra.co.nz
www.bnb.co.nz/rosandrahomestay.html

Double $150 Single $120 (Full Breakfast)
Credit cards accepted
3 Queen 1 Twin (4 bdrm)
1 Ensuite 1 Guests share

Welcome to our 90 acre lifestyle farm. Beautifully covered with mature trees, where our sheep and beef cattle graze. Privately set in landscaped gardens our modern home offers you warm spacious guest rooms with ensuite, private lounge, opening on to a sunny outdoor deck area. Swim all year round in the indoor 15m heated pool or watch the big screen TV while relaxing in the spa pool. Situated close to golf courses and East Coast beaches, find us easily on SH1, 7km north of Wellsford and opposite Mangawhai turn off. Two cats.

Warkworth *Farmstay*   *13km E of Warkworth*

Blue Hayes Farmstay
Rosalie & Rod Miller
44 Martins Bay Road, RD 2, Warkworth

Tel: (09) 425 5612 Fax: (09) 425 5612
Mob: 025 776 873
www.bnb.co.nz/bluehayesfarmstay.html

Double $75-$85 Single $50 (Full Breakfast)
Child $20 under 12yrs Dinner $25
Credit cards accepted
4 Single (2 bdrm) 1 Ensuite 1 Family share

We live on a 214 acre farm overlooking Kawau Bay and Mahurangi Heads 80km north of Auckland, farming sheep, cattle. Private setting, open space, farm walks, bush reserves and restored old school. Close to safe beaches. Participation in farming activities welcome. Family home is 50 years old, comfortable and relaxed with open fireplace. Rod, commercial pilot, flying instructor, scenic flights available. Near Goat Island Marine reserve and historic Kawau Island. We welcome you to share our hospitality and three course dinner. One cat.

Warkworth *Bed and Breakfast*   *Self-contained*   *0.5km N of Warkworth*

Homewood Cottage
Ina & Trevor Shaw
17 View Rd, Warkworth

Tel: (09) 425 8667 Fax: (09) 425 9610
Mob: 025 235 7469
www.bnb.co.nz/homewoodcottage.html

Double $80 (Continental Breakfast)
Credit cards accepted
1 Queen 2 Twin (2 bdrm)
2 Ensuite

Our home is in a peaceful, quiet garden with views of Warkworth and the hills. The bed-sitter style rooms are a good size. Each has own entrance, tea making, TV and patio with car parking. No cooking. The rooms are private but feel free to come in and chat. Breakfast is substantial continental with choice. We enjoy walking and golf. Ina is an artist. Close to town and a selection of restaurants. Our home is smoke free. Please phone. View Road is off Hill Street..

Warkworth - Snells Beach *Farmstay Homestay B&B   9km E of Warkworth*

Mahurangi Lodge
Alison & Rodney Woodcock
416 Mahurangi East Road, Snells Beach, Warkworth
Tel: (09) 425 5465 Fax: (09) 425 5465
mahulodge@ihug.co.nz www.pacificviewlodge.co.nz
Double $50-$85 Single $25-$50 (Special Breakfast)
Child $10 - $15 Dinner by arrangement
Credit cards accepted Pet on property
3 Double 2 Twin 3 Single (4 bdrm)
2 Ensuite 1 Guests share 1 Family share

Mahurangi Lodge, a 30 acre farmlet 1 hour Nth of Auckland (1 1/2 hour International Airport) is set on a hilltop. Enjoy magnificent views of Kawau, Little & Great Barrier Islands, & Coromandel from large rooms. A welcome "cuppa"on arrival, meet our manx cat relax, dine in or at good restaurants nearby. 20 min from Goat Island Marine Reserve (some snorkel gear available) only minutes to Kawau Island Ferry with our special guest discounts. Many good walks, kayaking, wineries, craft shops around. Free email access. Turn East Warkworth lights, 9km to Snells Beach.

Warkworth - Sandspit *Homestay   7km E of Warkworth*

Belvedere Homestay
M & R Everett
38 Kanuka Road,
RD 2, Warkworth

Tel: (09) 425 7201 Fax: (09) 425 7201
Mob: 025 284 4771 belvederehomestay@xtra.co.nz
www.belvederehomestay.co.nz
Double $105-$125 Single $70 (Special Breakfast)
Dinner $40 Pet on property
2 Queen 1 Twin (3 bdrm) 1 Ensuite 2 Private

"Sandspit" the perfect stop to and from The Bay of Islands. "Belvedere" has 360 degree views, sea to countryside and is 'awesome' plus relaxing decks, barbecue, garden, orchards, native birds and bush, peace and tranquillity with good parking. Airconditioned, spa, games room, comfortable beds are all here for your comfort. Many attractions are within 7 kms and Margaret's flair with cooking is a great way to relax after an adventurous day with pre-drinks, 3 course meal and wine. Come and stay with Margaret, Ron and our friendly dog "Nicky".

Warkworth *Self-contained Homestay B&B   4.5km W of Warkworth*

Willow Lodge
Paddy & John Evans
541 Woodcocks Road, Warkworth
Tel: (09) 425 7676 Fax: (09) 425 7676
Mob: 025 940 885 paddywarkworth@xtra.co.nz
www.bnb.co.nz/willowlodgewarkworth.html
Double $100-$120 Single $60-$80 (Full Breakfast)
Child $20 Dinner $30
1 Queen 2 Double 4 Single (4 bdrm)
2 Ensuite 1 Private

Your hosts, John & Paddy have more than 30 years experience in the hospitality field and have lived in Warkworth for the past 27 years. Our wealth of local knowledge will ensure your stay is both memorable and enjoyable. Willow Lodge boasts tranquil rural views over rolling farmland and is set in two acres of landscaped gardens. We offer superior self-contained accommodation complete with own ensuite , kitchen facilities, TV, BBQ all of which opens onto your own private courtyard. We are well know for our fabulous breakfasts.

Warkworth *Self-contained Homestay* *13km E of Warkworth*

Barbara & John Maltby
Omaha Orchards, 282 Point Wells Road,
RD 6, Warkworth

Tel: (09) 422 7415 Fax: (09) 422 7419
www.bnb.co.nz/maltby.html

Double $50-$75 (Seasonal) Single $40-$65
(Continental Breakfast) Extra persons $12
Dinner $15 - $20 by arrangement
In-house accommodation available if preferred
1 Queen 1 Double (1 bdrm)
1 Ensuite

Our home and self-contained unit (built 1999) is set on 11 acres nestled beside the Whangateau Harbour. Relax in the extensive gardens and swim in the beautifully appointed pool. Nearby is Omaha Beach, golf course, tennis courts, restaurants, art and craft studios, pottery works, museum, Sheep World, Honey Centre and Kawau Island. This is some of the prettiest coastline in New Zealand. John and Barbara look forward to sharing their little slice of paradise with you.

Warkworth *B&B Country Homestay* *3km W of Warkworth*

Bellgrove
Julie & John Bell
346 Woodcocks Road, RD 1, Warkworth

Tel: (09) 425 9770 Fax: (09) 425 9770
bellgrove@xtra.co.nz
www.bnb.co.nz/bellgrove.html

Double $100 Single $60 (Full Breakfast)
Dinner $25 Credit cards accepted
1 Queen 1 Twin 1 Single (3 bdrm)
1 Ensuite 1 Private

Nestled in a valley beside the Mahurangi Stream with a bush backdrop, Bellgrove is a tasteful country home and farmlet only 3km on a sealed road from Highway 1. Enjoy our large inground swimming pool, hot spa pool, friendly farm animals, manicured gardens and extensive decks. Guest's private upstairs accommodation is separate from the family with rural views. John has been involved in tourism for 10 years and has travelled extensively. Julie's interests include cooking and entertaining. Bellgrove is recommended by Lonely Planet travel guide.

Warkworth *Self-contained studio loft apartment* *9km E of Warkworth*

Island Bay Retreat
Joyce & Bill Malofy
105 Ridge Rd, Scotts landing,
RD 2, Warkworth

Tel: (09) 425 4269 Fax: (09) 425 4265
Mob: 025 262 8358
www.bnb.co.nz/islandbayretreat.html

Double $115
1 Queen 1 Single (1 bdrm)
1 Ensuite

Secluded intimate retreat on the beautiful Mahurangi Peninsula. Set amongst 2 acres of lovely gardens right on Mahurangi Harbour's foreshore. Idyllic magical place to relax in total privacy, captivating panoramic sea & rural views from our cosy open plan accommodation. Facilities for weekend or longer stays (self-catering). Sundecks, reclining chairs, bbq, kitchen, TV, ensuite (own entrance). Stroll along the bays to historic Scott's Landing, bush trails, swimming, boating, fishing (rods provided). Friendly village atmosphere, licensed restaurants, shopping and attractions. (Auckland 1 hour)

Warkworth   *Farmstay   6km S of Warkworth*

Ryme Intrinseca
Elizabeth & Cam Mitchell
121 Perry Road, RD 3, Warkworth
Tel: (09) 425 9448 Fax: (09) 425 9458
rymeintrinseca@xtra.co.nz
www.bnb.co.nz/rymeintrinseca.html

Double $100 Single $60 (Full Breakfast)
Child 1/2 price Dinner $30 by arrangement
Credit cards accepted Pet on property
2 Queen 2 Single (3 bdrm) 1 Private

Our sheep and cattle farm is 50 minutes from Auckland just 1km off SH1, and our spacious home is set in a quiet, secluded valley overlooking native bush and surrounded by gardens. Join in farm activities or just relax. The upstairs guest bedrooms, with extensive farm views, open into a large guest sitting room with TV and tea/coffee making facilities. Local sightseeing attractions include historic Kawau Island, vineyards, Sheep World, horse riding, and many lovely beaches. We are widely travelled and warmly welcome visitors to our home. We only take one party at a time.

Warkworth - Sandspit   *Self-contained B&B   6km E of Warkworth*

Jacaranda Cottage Rhondda & Les Sweetman
1186 Sandspit Rd, RD 2, Warkworth
Tel: (09) 425 9441 Fax: (09) 425 9451
Mob: 025 912 281   Tollfree: 0800 80 0 537
rhondda@xtra.co.nz
www.bnb.co.nz/jacarandacottagesandspit.html

Double $100-$120 (Full Breakfast)
Child $40 Dinner $30 Self-contained $80-$100
Credit cards accepted
1 King 1 Queen (2 bdrm)   2 Ensuite

Welcome to Jacaranda Cottage, our new house. The views of the Sandspit harbour are magnificent and so close you will feel part of the panorama. We are one hour from Auckland. Warkworth is a picturesque area which provides many opportunities for sightseeing and relaxation, including restaurants, vineyards, art galleries etc. We are a few minutes walk form Sandspit wharf, from where ferries leave for Kawau Island. We have a 10m catamaran and will take you sailing or fishing, by arrangement. Our dog is a border collie.

Warkworth - Sandspit   *Self-contained B&B   10km E of Warkworth*

Sea Breeze
Di & Robin Grant
14 Puriri Place, RD 2, Sandspit Heights, Warkworth
Tel: (09) 425 7220 Fax: (09) 425 7220
Mob: 021 657 220 robindi.grant@xtra.co.nz
www.bnb.co.nz/seabreeze.html

Double $110 Single $80 (Continental Breakfast)
Credit cards accepted Pet on property
1 Queen (1 bdrm)
1 Ensuite

SEA BREEZE is a self-contained luxury apartment with magnificent sea views and surrounding bush. Breakfast is provided in the kitchenette to be enjoyed at your leisure and a bedsettee in the lounge doubles for extra guests. There are lovely bush walks to the beaches immediately below the property. Take a cruise to Kawau Island or visit the many vineyards, galleries and cafes. Your hosts have travelled extensively and now enjoy gardening and boating in their spare time. Phone/fax for directions.

Warkworth - Sandspit   *B&B*   *7km E of Warkworth*

The Saltings
Maureen & Terry Baines
1210 Sandspit Road, RD 2, Warkworth
Tel: (09) 425 9670 Fax: (09) 425 9674
Mob: 021 625 948 relax@saltings.co.nz
www.saltings.co.nz

Double $140-$165 Single $125-$150 (Full Breakfast)
Child Unsuitable Credit cards accepted
1 King/Twin 1 King 1 Queen 4 Single (3 bdrm)
3 Ensuite

An enchanting hideaway up a tree lined driveway. This tranquil home on 6 acres has magical views of Sandspit Estuary. The Mediterranean ambience, white linen, tiles, candles and flowers give a sense of romance. All rooms have French doors opening onto private courtyards. Refreshments served on arrival or available in separate guest lounge. Maureen's special three-course breakfast is surpassed only by the view. Boutique vineyards, restaurants, cafes, potteries and beaches nearby. A short walk to Kawau ferry. Golden retriever on site. Smoke free home.

Warkworth - Matakana   *Self-contained Beauty Farm   7km Warkworth*

Casa Alegria
Claudia & Alex Schenz
180 Monarch Downs Way, Warkworth
Tel: (09) 422 7211 Fax: (09) 422 7833
casaalegria@xtra.co.nz
www.bnb.co.nz/casaalegria.html

Double $120-$140 Single $85-$100
(Special Breakfast) Dinner $30 - $50
Credit cards accepted Child at home
2 King/Twin 1 King (2 bdrm) 1 Ensuite 1 Private

As a happy family, Claudia, Alex and Julia(10), we welcome you in our brand new home. We have a peaceful setting close to Warkworth, Sandspit and Matakana with an awesome view of Kawau Bay, deerfarm, vineyards. Tastefully decorated, well appointed rooms (TV, Tea/Coffee), one with own patio, make your stay enjoyable. Luxurious bathrooms offer underfloorheating & hairdryer.As wine and food connaisseurs we offer on request 3-course dinners. Visit top-wineries, Kawau, Goat Island, go horseriding, fishing, golfing or just enjoy being pampered in Claudia's beauty studio ... German, French, Japanese spoken.

Warkworth - Snells Beach   *B&B*   *9km E of Warkworth*

Wings and Waves B & B
Sue Bunce
25 Fidelis Ave., Snells Beach,
Warkworth
Tel: 09 425 6399 Mob: 025 403 299
pinkperil@xtra.co.nz
www.bnb.co.nz/bunce.html

Double $80-$90 Single $50 (Continental Breakfast)
1 Queen 1 Double (2 bdrm)
1 Guests share

Awake to beautiful sea views from your room and sounds of birdsong. Walk uphill in the adjoining nature reserve for panoramic views of Kawau Island and beyond. Attractions include: Kawau Island, Wineries, Snorkelling at Goat Island, beautiful beaches and scenic walks. Rooms have TV and coffee facilities. I'm a Commercial Pilot and keen sailor, walker and kayaker. I live the outdoor Kiwi life to the full. I've travelled extensively in NZ and worldwide. Bill & Ben are my tame chooks. Sorry, no children or smoking.

Warkworth Central   *B&B*   *Warkworth Village*

Emerald House
Angie & Barrie Mullins
Cnr Falls & Bank St, Warkworth,
Tel: (09) 425 7279 Mob: 025 276 5160
emeraldhouse@clear.net.nz
www.bnb.co.nz/emeraldhouse.html
Double $110-$150 Single $85 (Full Breakfast)
Credit cards accepted Child at home Pet on property
2 King 1 Twin (2 bdrm)
1 Ensuite 1 Private

Situated in the heart of Warkworth Village, Emerald House was once home to the local police constabulary. This historic house built in 1920 has been lovingly restored to ensure comfort and privacy. Enjoy king size posturepedic beds, luxurious linen, individual dining tables, huge separate guest lounge, saltwater pool plus much more. We are a well travelled Irish couple and promise you the best of Irish hospitality in New Zealand. Jack Russell kept separate. Children under 12 not catered for. Ample off street parking.

Warkworth Rural   *Homestay B&B*   *9km SE of Warkworth*

Te Kauri Birding Lodge
Karen Baird and Chris Gaskin
346 Cowan Bay Road,, RD 3, Warkworth
Tel: (09) 422 2115 Fax: (09) 422 2358 Mob: 021 366 744
info@kiwi-wildlife.co.nz   www.bnb.co.nz/tekauri.html
Double $140 (Oct - Mar) $85 (Apr - Sept)
(Continental & Full Breakfast) Child $100
Suite $190 (Oct - Mar) $110 (Apr - Sept)
Dinner $40 Packed lunch avail. on request
Credit cards accepted Children welcome
1 Queen 1 Double (2 bdrm) 1 Ensuite 1 Private

The hosts run Kiwi Wildlife Tours a company offering specialised birdwatching holidays. Te Kauri birding Lodge is an ideal place for nature enthusiasts to start their holiday. Karen and Chris can help guests plan their itinerary to take in the best nature places in NZ. Guided excursions $150 per day pp, plus expenses. Self drive itinerary planning, including making reservations, $70. Te Kauri Birding Lodge is set on poles over a regenerating kauri forest which they are helping to protect.

Warkworth   *Self-contained*   *20km E of Warkworth*

Tui Haven
Lynn McNabb
7 George Street,
RD2, Warkworth
Tel: (09) 425 6922 Mob: 025 426 926
mcnabblynn@hotmail.com
www.bnb.co.nz/tuihaven.html
Double $120 Pet on property
1 Double 1 Single (1 bdrm)
1 Private

Tui Haven is situated at the end of the Mahurangi Peninsula. We are surrounded by native bush and the Tui, Fantails and pigeons are our constant companions. The apartment is completely private, fully self-contained with own entrance, patio, and barbeque. Superb views of the harbour and beyond, and a short bush track to a private beach where you can swim, fish or just sunbathe. You are welcome to use the dinghy. No Pets or children under 5yrs please.

Warkworth - Matakana   *B&B   12km E of Warkworth*

Olive Hill
Jacky & Tony Whincop
671 Matakana Valley Road, Matakana, Warkworth
Tel: (09) 422 9593 Fax: (09) 422 9593
Mob: 025 685 2702
olivehill.matakana@xtra.co.nz
www.bnb.co.nz/olivehill.html

Double $140 Single $120 (Special Breakfast)
Credit cards accepted Pet on property
2 Queen (2 bdrm) 2 Ensuite

Your search is over! Olive Hill, a Tuscan-inspired property nestled comfortably amongst olive trees and atop a secluded and private hill, promises privacy and hospitality but offers so much more. Only 10 minutes from the golf course, stunning beaches, vineyards, and restaurants - you're close enough to sample the delights of the region, but can hideaway and relax if you prefer. Enjoy breakfast Alfresco on your own private deck, relax in the spacious guest lounge, or just enjoy the country air - welcome to your paradise!!

Warkworth   *B&B Private entrance/patio   2.5km S of Warkworth*

Warkworth Country House
Alan & Pauline Waddington
18, Wilson Road, RD1, Warkworth

Tel: (09) 422 2485 Fax: (09) 422 2485
Mob: 021 680 6016   paulalan@xtra.co.nz
www.bnb.co.nz/warkworthco untry.html

Double $110-$130 Single $80-$100 (Full Breakfast)
Child 12 + years Credit cards accepted
1 Queen 1 Twin (2 bdrm)
2 Ensuite

Set in 2 peaceful acres,1 hour north of Auckland. Each tasteful room has en-suite, private entrance and patio with tea/coffee making facilities, hairdryer, radio alarm, T.V. and toiletries. E-mail and laundry facilities available. Enjoy delicious cooked or continental breakfasts in the dining room or alfresco,weather permitting. Visit historic Warkworth Museum, Kawau Island, antique and craft shops, vineyards and pottery. Enjoy horse riding, golf, fishing, or just strolling on the nearby sandy beaches. We look forward to welcoming you to our country home.

Warkworth - Matakana   *3km NE of Warkworth*
Homestay B&B Luxury Country accommodation

Stargate Lodge
Jane & Neil Peterken
139 Clayden Road, PO Box 275, Warkworth 1241
Tel: (09) 425 9995 Fax: (09) 425 9778
Mob: 025 991 115 stargate@surfer.co.nz
www.bnb.co.nz/stargate.html

Double $185-$265 Single $150-$225
(Full Breakfast) Credit cards accepted
1 King/Twin 2 King (2 bdrm) 2 Ensuite

New,purpose built, designed as a peaceful, retreat, Lodge is set on 10 acres, including 8 acres of mature, native bush, overlooking panoramic farmlands. Designer decor suites are warm, sunny,including TV, tea and coffee, fridge, phone facitlities, with own balcony. Comfortable guest lounge with log fire, adjoining elegant dining. Small conference facility. Not suitable for children. Surrounded by golf courses, wineries, restaurants, fishing. Your caring,well travelled hosts will assist wherever possible. A portrait artist, Jane has Diplomas in Natural Therapies, appoinments welcomed.

Warkworth   *B&B   Studio room   7km E of Warkworth*

Shoalwater
Don & Jocelyn Adolph
1 Kanuka Road (entrance between 7 & 9 Kanuka Rd),
Sandspit, RD2, Warkworth
Tel: (09) 425 0566 Fax: (09) 425 0566
Mob: 021 126 0081   Tollfree: 0800 110 925
shoalwater@xtra.co.nz   www.shoalwater.co.nz
Double $100-$150 Single $90-$120
(Continental Breakfast) Credit cards accepted
2 Queen (2 bdrm) 2 Ensuite

Our brand new home on the waterfront has two large studio rooms with breathtaking views over tidal Sandspit. In luxury and comfort you each have your own entrance, ensuite with Egyptian cotton towels, queen bed with imported linen, comfortable lounge chairs, dining suite, TV, alarm clock, heater, electric blanket, hairdryer, ironing facilities, tea/coffee facilities and heating facilities for light meals. Visit local vineyards, cafes, potters, galleries, walkways and beaches. Kayaks available. A short walk to the wharf to fish, or catch the ferry to Kawau Island. Small dog on site.

Puhoi   *Farmstay   20km N of Orewa*

Nichola(s) & Peter Rodgers
Krippner Rd, Puhoi, Auckland
Tel: (09) 422 0626 Fax: (09) 422 0626
Mob: 021 215 5165   ofp@friends.co.nz
www.farmstaynz.com
Double $105-$190 Single $90-$150 (Full Breakfast)
Child under 16 free Dinner included Guest Wing
Credit cards accepted Children welcome
1 Queen 2 Twin (2 bdrm) 1 Private

Farmstay, the gentle, organic way. Tariff includes taste-filled organic meals; fruit & vegetables; fresh baking ... very comfortable beds. Children welcomed (babysitting?) Come relax (no children if not yours), sleep off 'jet-lag'. Share panoramic views, fresh air, clean water; share expreiences, ideas and knowledge over dinner. Walk in the hills through trees streams, bird life & native flora & fauna, secluded private places. Use our library and business facilities ... We farm with kindness sheep, Belted Galloway cows, horses, ducks, poultry running free, providing milk, butter, yoghurt, ice-cream, cheeses ... more information at www.farmstaynz.com.

Puhoi   *Homestay   9km N of Orewa*

Westwell Ho
Fae & David England
34 Saleyards Road, Puhoi
Tel: (09) 422 0064 Fax: (09) 422 0064
Mob: 025 280 5795   dhengland@xtra.co.nz
www.bnb.co.nz/westwellho.html
Double $90 Single $70 (Full Breakfast)
Child $30 Credit cards accepted
Pet on property Children welcome
1 Queen 1 Double 1 Single (2 bdrm)
1 Ensuite 1 Private

We welcome you to our sunny colonial style home in the lovely Puhoi Valley. We are only 2 minutes by car west of Main North Highway up a small road behind the old pub in this historic Puhoi Village. The homestead has wide verandahs around 3 sides where you can relax as you view the gardens, winding paths and beautiful trees. Nearby are the fantastic Waiwera Thermal Pools, or you could hire a canoe and paddle down the Puhoi River to Wenderholm Beach and Park. Sky T.V. available.

Orewa   *Lodge*   *2km N of Orewa*

Moontide Lodge
Jurgen & Monika Resch
19 Ocean View Road,
Orewa - Hatfields Beach

Tel: (09) 426 2374 Fax: (09) 426 2398
Mob: 025 263 0102   moontde@nznet.gen.nz
www.bnb.co.nz/moontidelodge.html

Double $150-$200 (Special Breakfast)
Credit cards accepted Pet on property
4 Queen (4 bdrm) 3 Ensuite 1 Private

Overlooking the native bush and the sheltered bay of beautiful Hatfields Beach Moontide Lodge offers a high standard of "boutique" accommodation. We are situated on a cliff with beach access. Each of our four luxuriously appointed bedrooms features ensuite or private bathroom and breathtaking seaviews. Enjoy your complimentary tea/coffee and sherry/port in our elegant guest lounge with open fireplace. Breakfast and dinner (by appointment) is served in our formal dining room or on the verandah. German and French spoken. Timmy, our dog, is a friendly extra.

Orewa - Auckland   *Self-contained Homestay B&B*   *20min N of Auckland Central*

Villa Orewa
Sandra & Ian Burrow
264 Hibiscus Coast Highway,
Orewa, Auckland

Tel: (09) 426 3073 Fax: (09) 426 3053
Mob: 021 626 760 rooms@villaorewa.co.nz
www.villaorewa.co.nz

Double $150 Single $100 (Full Breakfast)
Dinner by arrangement Credit cards accepted
1 King/Twin 2 Queen (3 bdrm) 3 Ensuite

Welcome to our beautifully appointed unique new Mediterranean style home, with white-washed walls and blue vaulted roofs, purpose built as aboutique Bed and Breakfast for the discerning traveller - a taste of the Greek Isles here in New Zealand on beautiful Orewa Beach, just 20 minutes drive north of downtown Auckland. Stay in one of our self-contained rooms, each with private balcony, and enjoy the panoramic beach and sea views, or socialise with us in ourspacious living areas as you wish. We will do everything we can to make sure that your stay is an enjoyable and memorable one.

Orewa Beach   *B&B*   *Orewa*

Orewa Bach
Lesley & Grahame Gilbertson
309A Hibiscus Coast Highway,
Orewa Beach, Auckland 1461

Tel: (09) 426 3510 Fax: (09) 426 3509
Mob: 025 237 9567 grahame.g@xtra.co.nz
www.bnb.co.nz/orewabach.html

Double $150-$200 Single $130-$180 (Full Breakfast)
Credit cards accepted
2 Queen (2 bdrm) 2 Ensuite

Welcome to Orewa Bach, situated on the picturesque Hibiscus Coast, with absolute beach frontage to popular Orewa Beach. The central shopping area with a variety of cafes, restaurants and bars is immediately adjacent. Our luxurious bedrooms feature ensuites, heated towel rail, hairdryer, toiletries and quality bed linen. The guest lounge has modern furniture, Sky TV, complimentary refreshments are provided. Enjoy delicious breakfasts served in the dining alcove or outdoors on the patio. Local attractions include golf courses, hot pools, factory and craft shops and wineries.

Orewa *B&B* *1.5km E of Orewa*

Orewa Heights
Gail & Bill Cotton
114 Westhoe Heights, Orewa
Tel: (09) 426 8299
Fax: (09) 426 8299
jammmed@xtra.co.nz
www.bnb.co.nz/orewaheights.html
Double $110 Single $55 (Full Breakfast)
Child $25 Dinner $25 Children welcome
1 Queen 1 Double 1 Twin (3 bdrm)
1 Ensuite 1 Private

Gail and Bill invite you to enjoy the friendly hospitality in their modern open plan home overlooking Orewa Beach and surrounding islands. Enjoy a home cooked meal or sample the many restaurants in our area. We are located 1.5km from the beach and shops. Our interests are golf, fishing and travel.

Orewa *Homestay* *3.5km SE of Orewa*

Red Beach Homestay
Loretta Austin
13a William Bayes Place,
Red Beach, Orewa
Tel: (09) 426 7204 Fax: (09) 426 7204
Mob: 025 619 5659 l.austin@xtra.co.nz
www.bnb.co.nz/redbeachhomestay.html
Double $65 Single $35 (Continental Breakfast)
1 Double 1 Single (2 bdrm)
1 Ensuite 1 Guests share

Escape the city. Relax by the park! Walk to our safe surf beach (body boards available). Red Beach is 30 mins north of the harbour bridge, one hour from Auckland and has easy access to highways north. It is a casual, relaxed seaside suburb, with 3 golf courses, yacht marine, hot pools, and beach and bush walks. My house is light and sunny, the beds have electric blankets and the double ensuite room has tea and coffee facilities and TV. Some German spoken.

Silverdale *B&B* *1km S of Silverdale*

The Ambers
Gerard & Diane Zwier
146 Pine Valley Road,
Silverdale, Auckland
Tel: (09) 426 0015 Fax: (09) 426 0015
gzwier@xtra.co.nz www.the-ambers.co.nz
Double $150 Single $110 (Special Breakfast)
Child $75 Credit cards accepted Pet on property
1 King/Twin 2 Double 1 Twin (4 bdrm)
3 Ensuite 1 Family share

Looking for a romantic weekend away or just wanting to relax in elegant surroundings during your travels around New Zealand, then come and stay at The Ambers. Share our tranquil country atmosphere and warm hospitality - unwind with complimentary pre-dinner drinks. We have travelled extensively and enjoy meeting people. Three friendly German Shepherd dogs are part of our family. We are 30 minutes north of Auckland and are minutes from beaches, restaurants and shops. Please phone for reservations and directions. Warm regards, Di and Gerard.

Whangaparaoa   *Self-contained*   *40km N of Auckland*

Jan & Ernest's Place
Jan Collins & Ernest Davenport
18A Brixton Road, Manly, Whangaparaoa
Tel: (09) 424 7281 Mob: 025 264 2962
codav@xtra.co.nz
www.bnb.co.nz/janandernests.html
Double $65-$95 Single $45-$65
(Continental Breakfast)
$5 pp optional breakfast Pet on property
2 Single (1 bdrm) 1 Private

We offer a comfortable twin studio unit with private bathroom and mini-kitchen with fridge, microwave and top-cook stove. Separate guest entrance and private patio surrounded by trees and garden. TV, linen and towels are provided. Beds have electric blankets and duvets. We are within walking distance to beaches, shops, bowling club and restaurants. Within 5km is Shakespeare Park, Gulf Harbour Marina and golf course. Our home is smoke-free and we have two Balinese cats 'Chino' and 'Phoebe'. Directions - please phone

Kaukapakapa   *Homestay*   *14km N of Kaukapakapa*

Kereru Lodge
Mrs B Headford
Arone Farm, RD 3, Kaukapakapa
Tel: (09) 420 5223 Fax: (09) 420 5223
Mob: 021 420 522   Bheadford@xtra.co.nz
www.bnb.co.nz/kererulodgekaukapakapa.html
Double $70 Single $45 (Full Breakfast) Dinner $20
Credit cards accepted
1 Queen 1 Double 2 Single (3 bdrm)
1 Ensuite 1 Guests share

Relax in comfort and enjoy the warm hospitality of our large Kiwi country home. Set in a large much loved garden, in a quiet rural valley our home has lots of indoor/outdoor living. You may wish to play petanque or darts or pool, or just relax with a drink in the Summerhouse. Locally there are bushwalks, golf and tennis. We have many interests from shell collecting to geology and fossils. We enjoy sharing the delights of country living and meeting people from around the world.

Helensville   *Self-contained B&B*   *4km SW of Helensville*

Rose Cottage
Dianne & Richard Kidd
2191 State Highway 16,
RD 2, Helensville
Tel: (09) 420 8007 Fax: (09) 420 7966
Tollfree: 0800 755 433   kidds@xtra.co.nz
www.bnb.co.nz/rosecottagehelensville.html
Double $110 Single $80 (Full Breakfast)
Credit cards accepted
1 Queen (1 bdrm) 1 Ensuite

"Rose Cottage" offers comfort and privacy set within peaceful gardens. Whenuanui is a 350 ha Helensville sheep and beef farm providing magnificent farm walks. The family homestead and gardens have panoramic views over Helensville and the Kaipara Valley. Tasteful accommodation includes ensuite, TV and kitchenette. All-weather tennis court available for guests to use. Just 35 minutes from downtown Auckland on State Highway 16. A base to explore the Kaipara region or a great start or end to your Northland tour. Smoking outdoors appreciated.

Huapai - Kumeu *Farmstay Homestay B&B   15km W of Auckland*

Foremost Fruits
Andrea & Jim Hawkless
45 Trigg Road, Huapai, Auckland
Tel: (09) 412 8862 Fax: (09) 412 8869
jrhawkless@xtra.co.nz
www.bnb.co.nz/foremostfruits.html
Double $80 Single $60 (Full Breakfast) Child $25
Dinner $20 Credit cards accepted
2 Queen 3 Single (3 bdrm) 1 Guests share

Foremost Fruits is surrounded by several top NZ wineries and is on a small orchard with a greenhouse growing export table grapes. We provide comfort and relaxation plus use of a swimming pool. Guests have an upstairs to themselves - 2 bedrooms have TV. Breakfast is of choice and we offer selection of homemade breads and jams. There are several top restaurants in the area plus casual dining and take-away. Local attractions: beaches, gannet colony, horse riding, golf. Directions from Auckland: take Northwestern motorway to end. Turn left to Kumeu (8km) past garden centre, over railway line to Trigg Road (left before 100km sign), no. 45 on left.

Kumeu *Homestay B&B Countrystay   26km NW of Auckland*

Nor-West Greenlands
Kay & Kerry Hamilton
303 Riverhead Rd, RD 2, Kumeu
Tel: (09) 412 8167 Fax: (09) 412 8167
Mob: 025 286 6064 Tollfree: 0800 501 850
bed@farm-stay.co.nz www.farm-stay.co.nz
Double $110 Single $80 (Full Breakfast)
Dinner $30 by arrangement Credit cards accepted
Pet on property
1 Queen 1 Double 2 Single (3 bdrm)
1 Private 1 Guests share

Nor-West Greenlands is 15 acres nestled in a tranquil valley of native bush setting with a large garden, and a flock of tame coloured sheep. A swimming pool and guest lounge, with tea and coffee facilities, compliment the two storied house, home to Kerry and Kay, three cats, a hug of teddy bears and various crafts (lessons available). Kumeu has numerous wineries and restaurants, and Muriwai is home to the Gannet Colony. If you want peace and quiet 30 mins from Auckland city we have it.

Hobsonville *Homestay B&B   15mins NW of Auckland*

Eastview
Don & Joane Clarke
2 Parkside Road, Hobsonville, Auckland
Tel: (09) 416 9254 Fax: (09) 416 9254
eastview@xtra.co.nz www.bnb.co.nz/eastview.html
Double $95-$110 Single $80-$90 (Special Breakfast)
Child $30 Dinner by arrangement exta adult discount
Credit cards accepted Pet on property
1 Queen 1 Double 2 Single (3 bdrm)
2 Private 1 Guests share

EASTVIEW: 15 minutes nor/west of Auckland. Make the most of our EASY-TO-FIND location, and easy access to explore Auckland. Relax in comfort, with panoramic water/city views, over a delightful garden. Warm spacious guest bedrooms and lounge soak up all day sun where you can enjoy tea/coffee with home-baked cookies anytime, or watch sky/TV. Stroll to the nearby marina, discover superb beaches, wineries, great restaurants, thermal pools, native bush clad hills, gannet colony, golf courses, harbour cruises.

Bethells Beach *Self-contained Self-contained Cottages & 100 Seater Summer Pavilion*

15km W of Swanson

Bethell's Beach Cottage

Trude & John Bethell-Paice, PO Box 95057, Swanson, Auckland

Tel: (09) 810 9581 Fax: (09) 810 8677 info@bethellsbeach.com www.bethellsbeach.com

Double $175-$275 Child uner 12yrs 1/2 price Dinner $35pp + GST by arr.

Breakfast extra $20pp + GST   Credit cards accepted Pet on property Children welcome

2 Queen 2 Double 3 Single (3 bdrm)

2 Private

Drive 30 minutes from Auckland city to one of the most unique parts of the West coast. The Bethell's settled this area 6 generations ago and Trude and John continue the long family tradition of hospitality. They have created two magic cottages and venue in this spectacular place where the best sunsets and seaviews are to be experienced - as seen in magazines: Grace, & Elle Aus, Feb 2000, Elle Singapore, March 2000. Both cottages have a sunny north facing aspect and are surrounded by 200-year-old pohutukawa's (NZ Christmas tree). Each one is totally separate, private and has a large brick barbecue. The vast front lawn is ideal for games and the gardens are thoughtfully designed for relaxation. The cottages are made up with your holiday in mind - not only are beds made and towels/linen put out, but Trude and John have attended to too many details to mention and laundry facilities are available. Even the cats will welcome you. As seen in Vogue Australia 1998. Life/The Observer (Great Britain 1998) - 'one of twenty great world wide destinations'. British TV Travel Show 1998. She magazine (February 1999) - 'one of the 10 most romantic places to stay in NZ'. North and South magazine (January 1999) - 'one of the 14 best Bed and Breakfasts in NZ' and many more.

'TUREHU' COTTAGE has a studio atmosphere with double bi-folding doors from the conservatory. For outdoor dining sit under a pohutukawa tree at your own bench and table on the hillside with views over the beach and Bethell's valley. Cork floor in the kitchen, TV and bedroom area, gentle cream walls and white trim. Warm slate floors in the conservatory with lounge, dining table and bathroom (shower and toilet). Kitchen has microwave, large fridge/freezer, stove and coffee plunger, with all kitchen and dining amenities. Suitable for a couple and one child or two friends.

'TE KOINGA' COTTAGE, this superb home away from home is 80sqm and has two bi-folding doors onto a 35sqm wooden deck for outdoor dining and relaxation in this sun trap. Set under the shade of a magnificent spralling pohutukawa tree and surrounded by garden. A fireplace for winter warmth and sixteen seater dining

table. The two bedrooms have carpet and terracotta tiles expand to the dining, kitchen, bathroom and toilet. Wood panelled and cream/tan rag rolled walls for a relaxing atmosphere. The bathroom offers a bath and shower. Open planned kitchen has microwave, large fridge/freezer, stove, dishwasher and coffee maker. Suitable for a family, 2 couples or a small function. Trude is a marriage celebrant and Trude and John specialise in weddings, private functions and company workshops. A local professional chef is available for these occasions.

LOCAL ADVENTURES - Bethell's beach is a short drive or walk. Pack a picnic lunch and discover Lake Wainamu for fresh water swimming and expansive sand dunes or go on a bush walk with excellent examples of New Zealand native flora. If you head in the direction of the beach you may enjoy exploring the caves (at night the magic of glow worms and phosphorescence in the shallows), or go surfing or fishing. You are close to many world class Vineyards and restaurants/cafes. You may fancy a game of golf - two courses within 10-20 minutes drive from your cottage. Many more activities in a short driving distance. No pets please. Children under 12 half price.

Bethells Valley - West Auckland
Self-contained Farmstay   15km W of Henderson

Greenmead Farm
Averil & Jon Bateman
115 Bethells Road, RD 1, Henderson
Tel: (09) 810 9363 Fax: (09) 810 8363
jabat@greenmead.co.nz
www.greenmead.co.nz

Double $90 breakfast additional charge
Extra guests $20 Pet on property Children welcome
4 Single (2 bdrm)
1 Private

Guests have sole use of comfortable holiday home - two bedrooms, bathroom, lounge (TV) and large kitchen/dining room with excellent cooking facilities. Additional guests $20 each. Breakfast extra. Foldout double bed available. The main house and guest cottage are surrounded by a large country garden - swings for children. Cattle, two Border collie working dogs, bees and chooks. Located in rural valley in the Waitakere Ranges. Good walking tracks in the area - forest, beach and lake. 30 minutes drive west of central Auckland. Beach 5 minutes.

Waitakere - Swanson
Homestay B&B   10km W of Henderson

Abode de Fleur
Janice & John Reece
1194 Scenic Drive North, Swanson, Auckland
Tel: (09) 833 4288 Fax: (09) 833 4288
Mob: 025 786 788 fleursb&b@xtra.co.nz
stay@fleurs.co.nz www.fleurs.co.nz

Double $95-$120 Single $65-$75 (Special Breakfast)
Dinner by arrangement Credit cards accepted
Pet on property   2 Queen 1 Twin (3 bdrm)
1 Ensuite 1 Private 2 Family share

Our romantic home is set in a peaceful valley amongst 17 acres of pasture and native bush. We are on the 'Twin Coast Discovery Route'. Easy access to walking tracks through native rainforests, wonderful unspoilt west coast beaches (Piha, Bethells, Kare Kare, Muriwai). Zena, Hercules and The Piano were filmed in this area. Local attractions: wineries, golf courses, cafes, excellent restaurants and shopping centres. We offer a selection of beautifully appointed rooms with tea and coffee-making facilities. A very warm welcome awaits you in this unique part of New Zealand.

Waitakere Ranges - Swanson
Self-contained B&B   4km W of Swanson

Panorama Heights
Paul & Allison Ingram
42 Kitewaho Road, Swanson,
Waitakere City, Auckland
Tel: (09) 832 4777 Fax: (09) 833 7773
Mob: 025 272 8811 Tollfree: 0800 692 624
nzbnb4u@clear.net.nz www.panoramaheights.co.nz

Double $115-$125 Single $80-$90 (Full Breakfast)
Dinner by request Credit cards accepted
2 Queen 1 Twin 1 Single (4 bdrm) 3 Ensuite 1 Private

Private and peaceful with breathtaking panoramic views located high in the Waitakere Ranges on the "Twin Coast Discovery Route". Watch the sun rise across native kauri trees, bush and Auckland City beyond. We are within easy access to over 200 km of walking tracks through 17,000 hectares of native rainforest. 10-15 minutes from West Coast beaches (Piha, Bethells, Karekare, Muriwai) wineries and two scenic golf courses, art trails, shopping centers. Indoors non-smoking. A warm welcome awaits you. Please phone for bookings and directions. Airport pick up available.

Ranui   *Homestay B&B   Detached B&B*   *15mins W of Auckland*

The Garrett
Alma & Rod Mackay
295 Swanson Road, Waitakere City, Auckland 8
Tel: (09) 833 6018 Fax: (09) 833 6018
www.bnb.co.nz/mackay.html
Double $75 Single $45
(Continental Breakfast) Child $22
2 King/Twin 1 King 2 Single (2 bdrm)
1 Ensuite

Just 15 minutes form Auckland City and five minutes from historical Henderson, The Garrett offers villa style accommodation with ensuite and private terrace. Twin beds or king size if you prefer. We can accommodate extra guests with folding beds on request. High ceilings and period furniture and decor create an atmosphere of old in this delightful Homestay, just minutes away from Waitakere City. Leading attractions include wine trails, Art Out West Trail - including Lopdell House Gallery. Waitake Ranges, bush walks, Aratiki Heritage and Environment Centre, golf courses. West City Shopping Centre, Lynn Mall and St Lukes. No pets; no campervans.

Piha   *Self-contained Separate/Suite*   *20km W of Henderson*

Piha Cottage
Tracey & Steve Skidmore
PO Box 48, Piha, Waitakere City, Auckland
Tel: (09) 812 8514 Fax: (09) 812 8514
Mob: 025 657 8669
piha_cottage@yahoo.co.nz
www.bnb.co.nz/pihacottage.html
Double $95 Single $95 (Continental Breakfast)
Child $20 Child at home Pet on property
Children welcome
1 Double 1 Single (1 bdrm) 1 Private

Piha Cottage is secluded in quiet bush surrounds within easy walking distance of beach and tracks. Its studio style includes a kitchen, dining and living area. Piha is on the rugged West Coast nestled into native rainforest. The beach is renown for surfing and is patrolled for swimmers in summer. There is a network of outstanding tracks to choose from - spectacular cliffs and wild beaches, streams and waterfalls. We can provide maps and advice on the tracks which we know intimately.

Piha   *Self-contained*   *40mins W of Auckland*

Piha Lodge
Shirley Bond
117 Piha Road, Piha
Tel: (09) 812 8595 Fax: (09) 812 8583
Mob: 021 639 529 pihalodge@xtra.co.nz
www.pihalodge.co.nz
Double $130 (Continental Breakfast) Child $20
Additional adults $30 Credit cards accepted
Pet on property Children welcome
3 Queen 1 Double 1 Single (4 bdrm) 2 Private

Winner of the 2001 Bank of New Zealand Waitakere Eco City "BEST ACCOMMODATION" Award. Situated in the sub-tropical rainforest of the Waitakere Ranges and on the wild West Coast, Piha has one of New Zealand's top surfing beaches and magnificent sunsets that are legendary. Relax in the swimming pool, hot spa or games room. Our quality self-contained units give you all the comforts of home plus privacy, homemade bread each morning and stunning panoramic sea and bush views. Our two very friendly little Bichon dogs are kept separately.

Piha   *Self-contained Separate/Suite   25km W of Henderson*

Westwood Cottage
Dianne & Don Sparrow
95 Glenesk Road, Piha, Auckland
Tel: (09) 812 8205 Fax: (09) 812 8203
Mob: 025 278 8110
westwoodcottage.piha@clear.net.nz
www.bnb.co.nz/westwoodcottage.html
Double $100 Single $80 (Continental Breakfast)
Child $20 Credit cards accepted Children welcome
1 Queen 1 Single (2 bdrm)
1 Private

Westwood Cottage offers a unique experience. Nestled in a secluded corner of our property, amongst beautiful bush overlooking Piha Valley. The Cottage is self-contained, open plan design, flowing on to a private deck. Full kitchen facilities with continental breakfast supplied. A cozy log fire for your enjoyment on cooler evenings. Off road parking provided. Children 5 and over welcome. A short walk leads to Piha Surf Beach and bush walks include Kitekite Waterfall and Black Rock Dam.

Okura   *Self-contained B&B   20km N of Auckland Central*

Okura B&B
Judie & Ian Greig
20 Valerie Crescent, Okura,
RD 2, Albany, Auckland
Tel: (09) 473 0792 Fax: (09) 473 1072
ibgreig@clear.net.nz
www.bnb.co.nz/okurabb.html
Double $85 Single $65 (Continental & Full Breakfast)
Credit cards accepted
1 Queen 1 Single (2 bdrm) 1 Private

Situated on Auckland's North Shore, Okura is a small settlement bounded by farmland and the Okura River, an estuary edged with native rain-forest. If you like peace, quiet, with only bird song nearby, estuary and forest views, then this is for you.   Accommodation includes your own, not shared, TV lounge, tea-making facilities, fridge, shower and toilet. Nearby are a wide variety of cafes, shops, beaches, walks, North Shore Stadium, Massey University and golf courses. Okura - one of Auckland's best kept secrets.

Coatesville - Albany   *Farmstay   7km N of Albany*

Camperdown
Chris & David Hempleman
455 Coatesville/Riverhead Highway,
RD 3, Albany, Auckland
Tel: (09) 415 9009 Fax: (09) 415 9023
Tollfree: 0800 921 479 chris@camperdown.co.nz
www.camperdown.co.nz
Double $110 Single $80 (Full Breakfast)
Child $40 Dinner $40 Children welcome
1 King/Twin 2 Queen 1 Double 2 Single (4 bdrm)
2 Private 1 Guests share

We are only 25 minutes from Auckland City. Relax in secluded tranquillity, our home opens into beautiful gardens, native bush and stream offering the best of hospitality in a friendly atmosphere. On the farm we have sheep, cattle and pet lambs. Guest areas consist of the entire upstairs. Guests may use our games room, play tennis on our court, row a boat on the lake, or just stroll by the stream. Directions. travel North to Albany, onto Highway 17, turn left at 'BP' into Coatesville/Riverhead Highway (28).

Albany - Coatesville *B&B Country Homestay   3km N of Albany*

Te Harinui Country Homestay
Mike & Sue Blanchard
102 Coatesville Highway,
RD 3, Albany, Auckland
Tel: (09) 415 9295
sue@teharinui.co.nz   www.teharinui.co.nz

Double $85 Single $65 (Full Breakfast)
Child by arrangement Dinner $25 by arrangement
Pet on property
1 Queen 2 Single (2 bdrm)
1 Guests share

A home from home in the country only 20 minutes from the city. Stroll in the bush and paddocks; meet our old horse, goat, pet coloured sheep, two dogs and cat all very friendly. Learn to spin and browse our craft shop. We can arrange outings to local attractions including beaches. Close to stadium and Massey University. Generous breakfasts; coffee and teas are always available. Sue speaks French and is learning Mandarin.

Greenhithe *B&B Rural Homestay   15km N of Auckland*

Waiata Tui Lodge (The Song of the Tui)
Therese & Ned Jujnovich
177 Upper Harbour Drive, Greenhithe, Auckland
Tel: (09) 413 9270 Fax: (09) 413 9217
theresewa@xtra.co.nz
www.bnb.co.nz/waiatatuilodge.html

Double $75-$90 Single $60 (Special Breakfast)
Dinner $25 Credit cards accepted
2 Queen 1 Twin 2 Single (3 bdrm) 2 Private

You will be warmly welcomed to Waiata-Tui Lodge. Our haven of 9 acres is only 15 mins to Auckland City and 6 mins to Albany University. A handy starting off place for travelling North. You can relax here. Waken to bird song. Look out over Kauris to the tranquil water below and the more distant Waitakere Ranges. Walk in our lush rainforest with massive trees a few centuries old. Swim in our pool. Meet Harry our friendly goat and his mates. Therese is a keen wine-maker. We have both travelled extensively in New Zealand and overseas. A Lockwood Home. Homestay since 1986.   Please phone for directions.

Ensuite and private bathrooms
are for your use exclusively.
Guest share bathroom means you
will be sharing with other guests.
Family share means you
will be sharing with the family.

Coastal Beach Haven   *Homestay B&B   15 min N of Auckland Central*

Port O' Call
Jill & Bernie Cleal
12 Amelia Place, Coastal Beach Haven, Auckland
Tel: (09) 483 4439 Fax: (09) 483 4439 Mob: 025 227 2639
portocall.b&b@xtra.co.nz
www.bnb.co.nz/portocall.html
Double $150-$160 Single $100-$120 (Full Breakfast) Credit cards accepted Pet on property
1 King 1 Queen (2 bdrm)
2 Ensuite

Welcome to "Port O'Call", a secret hideaway overlooking the tranquil sparkling waters of the glorious Upper Waitemata Harbour. Enjoy watching the many water activities or partake in them yourselves. We can take you sailing on our 28' Catamaran "Akarana Express" or enjoy a leisurely paddle in a kayak around these calm waters viewing the bird life that abounds ...

Come and enjoy our warm and relaxed hospitality in one of two spacious private, tastefully decorated bedrooms with a nautical theme with TV & CD player, ensuites featuring hair drier, toiletries, bath-robes, heated towel rail; all leading out to a large salt water pool and spa pool for your enjoyment, whilst still enjoying the relaxing views over the water and soak up the sunshine from the wide verandahs. Tea and coffee making facilities, fridge, laundry and ironing facilities, fresh flowers ...

To get away for a peaceful read or just to ponder, dis-cover the "Secret Garden" amongst the tropical palms and native plants, or cuddle up in front of the log fire during winter with a complimentary glass of fine New Zealand wine. 15 mins from America's Cup Village, Wine/Craft and Sightseeing Tours, Charter Fishing Trips arranged.

THE ULTIMATE PLACE TO UNWIND.

P.S. There are three resident cats. Jill and Bernie look forward to making your stay totally enjoyable.

Birkenhead Point   *Luxury B&B*   *3km N of Auckland City*

Stafford Villa
Chris and Mark Windram
2 Awanui Street,
Birkenhead Point, Auckland
Tel: 64 9 418 3022 Fax: 64 9 419 8197
Mob: 021 61 3022   rest@staffordvilla.co.nz
www.staffordvilla.co.nz
Double $245-$275 Single $245 (Full Breakfast)
Credit cards accepted
1 King/Twin 1 King (2 bdrm) 2 Ensuite

An historic Colonial Villa; romantic, elegant, tranquil and private. Located in a quiet street of native and tropical trees, nine minutes to Auckland city by car or ferry, walking distance to cafes, restaurants, boutique shopping, galleries, beaches, coastal and bush walks. Two guests rooms - China Blue with antique carved four poster bed, large ensuite dressing room and balcony overlooking the garden, Tuscany Summer with ensuite, in soft cream and terracotta tonings reminiscent of the Tuscan countryside. Exquisite linens, complimentary tea/coffee, sherry/port fresh flowers, fruit and chocolates.

Birkenhead   *Self-contained*   *2km N of Auckland Central*

Aorangi Gardens
Bruce & Raihi Taylor
29b Aorangi Place, Birkenhead, Auckland
Tel: (09) 480 1973 Mob: 025 284 1704
aorangi-gardens@xtra.co.nz
www.aorangi-gardens.co.nz
Double $150 Single $110 (Special Breakfast)
Child $40 Credit cards accepted Child at home
Pet on property Children welcome
1 King (1 bdrm) 1 Ensuite

Can you imagine being in a tranquil garden setting so close to the excitement of the America's Cup Village and all the attractions that vibrant Auckland city has to offer? Aorangi Gardens is 10 minutes from the city and our spacious self-contained bedroom and living area has a studio kitchen. Our special breakfasts include fresh homemade bread/muffins daily. Cafes, restaurants, shops are close by as is an amazing walk through established bush to a beach close to the Harbour Bridge. Private entrance. Off-street parking.

Herald Island   *Homestay Separate/Suite B&B*   *6km NW of Henderson*

Harbour View Homestay
Les Pratt, 84 The Terrace, Herald Island
Tel: +64 (9) 416 7553 Fax: +64 (9) 416 7553
harbourviewhomestay@nznet.gen.nz
www.bnb.co.nz/harbourview.html
Double $80-$110 Single $45-$65 (Full Breakfast)
Child half price Dinner $20 Credit cards accepted
Pet on property Pets welcome Smoking area inside
1 Queen 4 Single (3 bdrm)
1 Ensuite 1 Private 1 Guests share

Your host has a two storey home with superb accommodation, right on waters edge. Upstairs has 2 bedrooms, 1 Queen, 1 Twin, each with its own sundeck, with views of harbour. Own lounge, bathroom, and tea & coffee making facilities. Downstairs has 1 Twin (large) with own ensuite. Very homely. Easy access. Within 20 mins radius, wine tasting, horse riding, golf course, bush walks, vintage car museum & model world. Close to various restaurants and reception lounges at vineyards. A hearty home cooked meal can be provided.

Browns Bay   *B&B*   *1.5km W of Browns Bay*

Amoritz House
Carol & Gary Moffatt
730 East Coast Road, Browns Bay, Auckland
Tel: (09) 479 6338 Fax: (09) 479 6338
Mob: 025 806958 Tollfree: 0800 936 338
amoritz@ihug.co.nz   www.aucklandaccommodation.co.nz
Double $90-$120 Single $70-$90 (Full Breakfast)
Dinner $10 - $30pp Credit cards accepted
2 King/Twin 1 Double 1 Single (3 bdrm)
2 Ensuite 1 Private

Spend some peaceful nights in our quiet guest bedrooms with Sky TV, garden and rural outlooks. Separate guest entrance leads into kitchenette with fridge, microwave, washing machine, dryer etc. Adjoining dining room. Internet, e-mail, fax etc available. Minutes from North Harbour Stadium, Millennium Stadium, Massey University, a variety of cafes, restaurants, beaches, shopping and Auckland City Centre with all its attractions. Bus stop at door. Large garden, barbeque. Off street parking, 2 minutes to Motorway. Non smoking. Dinners $10, $20, $30 pp with prior notice.

Devonport   *Homestay*   *8km N of Auckland*

Cheltenham-By-The-Sea
Gayle and Mark Mossman
2 Grove Road, Devonport, Auckland
Tel: (09) 445 9437 Fax: (09) 445 9432
Mob: 021 251 6920 mgmossman@clear.net.nz
www.cheltenhambythesea.co.nz
Double $100-$130 Single $75-$100
(Continental Breakfast) Child $50
1 Queen 1 Double 1 Twin 1 Single (4 bdrm)
1 Ensuite 1 Private 1 Guests share

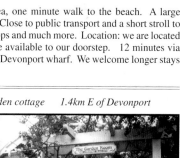

Mark & Gayle welcome you to Cheltenham By The Sea, one minute walk to the beach. A large contemporary home set amongst native trees and garden. Close to public transport and a short stroll to the village with cafes, restaurants, art galleries, antique shops and much more. Location: we are located 45 minutes from the International Airport. Airport shuttle available to our doorstep. 12 minutes via ferry to downtown Auckland City. Courtesy pick-up from Devonport wharf. We welcome longer stays and can arrange favourable rates accordingly.

Devonport   *Homestay B&B Self-contained Garden cottage*   *1.4km E of Devonport*

The Garden Room
Perrine & Bryan Hall
23 Cheltenham Rd, Devonport
Tel: (09) 445 2472 Fax: (09) 445 2472
Mob: 025 989 643   perrinehall@xtra.co.nz
www.devonportgardenroom.co.nz
Double $150-$170 Single $120-$130
(Special Breakfast) Child $50 Credit cards accepted
longstay & Winter rates avail. neg.
1 King 1 Queen 1 Single (2 bdrm) 1 Ensuite 1 Private

Private sunny garden cottage with ensuite, own entrance and parking. A few steps from Cheltenham Beach, short stroll to Devonport village where a ferry ride takes 10 mins to city. French doors open onto tranquil villa garden. Guests are served delicious breakfast in sunny courtyard or in privacy of room - fresh juices, tropical or local fruits, muesli, yoghurt, warm homemade breads, croissants, muffins, choice of cooked. Crisp cotton sheets, bathrobes, flowers, fruit,selection of teas, coffee bodum, refrigerator, TV, in room - fax/email, laundry in villa, where one king bedroom offered.

Devonport *B&B Self-contained cottage 4km N of Auckland Central*

Karin's Garden Villa
Karin Loesch & Family
14 Sinclair Street, Devonport, Auckland 1309

Tel: (09) 445 8689 Fax: (09) 445 8689 stay@karinsvilla.com
www.karinsvilla.com

Double $145-$175 Single $90-$135 (Continental Breakfast) Child $25 Dinner By arrangement
S/C cottage $185 Credit cards accepted Pet on property Children welcome, cot available
1 King/Twin 2 Double 3 Single (4 bdrm)
1 Ensuite 1 Private 1 Guests share

Tucked away at the end of a quiet cul-de-sac, Karin's Garden Villa - a DEVONPORT DREAM - offers real home comfort with its light cosy rooms, easy relaxed atmosphere and the warmest of welcome from Karin and her family. A beautifully restored spacious Victorian villa surrounded by large lawns and old fruit trees.

Karin's Garden Villa has also been featured on NZ and Australian television advertising for its relaxed, peaceful setting. Just 5 minutes stroll from tree-lined Cheltenham Beach, sailing, golf, tennis, shops and restaurants and only a short drive or pleasant 10 minute walk past extinct volcanoes to the picturesque Devonport centre with its many attractions.

Your comfortable room offers separate private access through French doors, opening onto a wide verandah and cottage garden. And for those visitors wanting ultimate comfort and privacy, there is even a self-contained studio cottage with balcony and full kitchen facilities to rent (min. 3 days). Sit down to a nutritious breakfast in the sunny dining room with its large bay windows overlooking everflowering purple lavender and native gardens. Guests are welcome to join the family barbecue and relax on our large lawn. We welcome longer stays and can arrange favourable discounts accordingly.

Help yourself to tea and German-style coffee and biscuits anytime, check your e-mail and feel free to use the kitchen and laundry.

Karin comes from Germany and she and her family have lived in Indonesia for a number of years. We have seen a lot of the world and enjoy meeting other travellers. Always happy to help you arrange island cruises, rental cars, bikes and tours.

From the airport take a Shuttle Bus to our doorstep or to Downtown Ferry Terminal. Courtesy pick-up from Devonport Wharf. By Car: After crossing Harbour Bridge, take Takapuna-Devonport turnoff. Right at T-junction, follow Lake Road to end, left into Albert, Vauxhall Road and then first left into Sinclair Street.

Devonport *B&B* *8km N of Auckland*

Devonport Villa B&B Inn
Keith & Lesley Wilkinson

46 Tainui Road, Devonport, Auckland
Tel: (09) 445 8397 Fax: (09) 445 9766
dvilla@ihug.co.nz
www.bnb.co.nz/devonportvillabbinn.html

Double $175-$245 (Full Breakfast) Credit cards accepted Pet on property Children welcome
2 King 4 Queen 2 Twin 1 Single (7 bdrm)
7 Ensuite

Devonport Villa Inn, winner of the NZ Tourism Awards for hosted accommodation, is in the heart of Devonport, 2 minutes walk from Auckland's best kept secret, sandy and safe Cheltenham Beach.

There is something special about every aspect of this exquisite historic home built in 1903 by a wealthy retired English doctor. Edwardian elegance, spacious individual rooms with king and queen beds, extensive guest library, rich woollen carpets, restored colonial furniture, outstanding stained glass windows and the guest lounge with its amazing vaulted ceiling and polished native timber floor.

Choose from the unique upstairs Turret Room, the romantic and sunny Rangitoto Suite with its private balcony, the colonial style Beaconsfield Suite with antique clawfoot bath and four-poster king bed or the Oxford and Gold rooms.

Each cosy room is individually decorated with firm beds, soft woollen blankets, flowers from the garden, plump pillows and crisp white linen. And in the morning you will be cooked a delicious full breakfast, including freshly squeezed juice, natural yoghurt, nutritious muesli, muffins baked daily, pancakes, double smoked bacon with eggs and preserves.....join other guests in the dining room overlooking the garden, or if you like we can serve breakfast in some rooms at a time to suit.

Please ask when booking. Sit in the sunny shell courtyard overlooking the Edwardian style garden with lavender hedges, old roses and spacious lawns. Enjoy a moonlit stroll along the beach to North Head and dinner at a nearby restaurant.

Devonport Villa is within easy walking distance of the major wedding reception venues and the historic sights of Devonport. Let us help you to make your stay in Devonport relaxing, pleasant and unique. Fax and E-mail available. Smoking is not permitted in the house.

Devonport   *B&B*   *2km N of Auckland Central*

Villa Cambria
Kate & Clive Sinclair, 71 Vauxhall Road, Devonport, Auckland
Tel: (09) 445 7899 Fax: (09) 446 0508 Mob: 025 843 826
info@villacambria.co.nz   www.villacambria.co.nz
Double $150-$230 Single $130-$150 (Full Breakfast) Credit cards accepted
3 Queen 1 Double 1 Twin (5 bdrm)   5 Ensuite

Villa Cambria is among one of the finest Bed & Breakfast Inns in Devonport. The elegant, historic Villa is a typical Devonport Victorian home. Built in 1904 of native kauri timber, it has been lovingly restored to its former glory and tastefully furnished with an eclectic mix of antique, asian, interesting and homely items. The Villa is situated in an unbeatable location, just a few minutes walk to beautiful Cheltenham Beach and the picturesque Waitemata Golf Course (18 holes).

Each of the guest rooms is decorated individually. Choose from the romantic Garden Loft with its own balcony, or one of our four beautifully appointed guest bedrooms. From the hand-selected sprigs of lavender in the bathrooms to the complimentary tea, coffee, port and toiletries, you'll be pampered during your stay. All our rooms have phone connections, irons and hairdryers. Breakfast is wholesome, enjoy hand selected fresh fruit, yoghurt, a choice of cooked breakfasts and a selection of continental favourites.

Breakfast is made with fresh produce from the market and is accompanied by home made bread, followed by freshly brewed coffee and a choice of teas. The finishing touch though, is without a doubt the warm, friendly spontaneity of owners Clive and Kate, who live in a completely separate part of the house.

After breakfast you can enjoy the many nearby attractions, take a 12 minute ferry ride into the centre of the city (ferries cross every 30 minutes), or explore the many islands in the Hauraki Gulf. Devonport boasts more than 30 restaurants and offers excellent shopping, a cinema, many lovely walks and one of 49 extinct volcanic cones dotted around Auckland. Indeed Devonport has the enviable reputation of being the 'Jewel in Auckland's Crown' and one of the safest places to live within the city.

Visit our web site at www.villacambria.co.nz for full details and room descriptions.

DIRECTIONS: From the airport take a shuttle bus door to door service. By car: Travelling north, cross Auckland Harbour bridge. Travel 1.5kms and take the Esmonde Road exit Highway 26 to Takapuna-Devonport. Follow signs to Devonport along Lake Road. At the roundabout turn left into Albert Road, then at the T junction turn left into Vauxhall Road, Inn on left.

Devonport *Homestay*

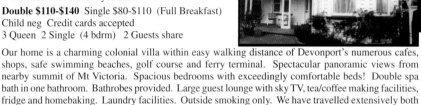

Amberley B & B
Mary & Michael Burnett
3 Ewen Alison Avenue, Devonport, Auckland 1309
Tel: (09) 446 0506 Fax: (09) 446 0506
Mob: 025 288 0161
amberley@xtra.co.nz
www.bnb.co.nz/amberleybb.html

Double $110-$140 Single $80-$110 (Full Breakfast)
Child neg Credit cards accepted
3 Queen 2 Single (4 bdrm) 2 Guests share

Our home is a charming colonial villa within easy walking distance of Devonport's numerous cafes, shops, safe swimming beaches, golf course and ferry terminal. Spectacular panoramic views from nearby summit of Mt Victoria. Spacious bedrooms with exceedingly comfortable beds! Double spa bath in one bathroom. Bathrobes provided. Large guest lounge with sky TV, tea/coffee making facilities, fridge and homebaking. Laundry facilities. Outside smoking only. We have travelled extensively both here and overseas and look forward to making your stay in our beautiful country an enjoyable experience.

Devonport *Homestay B&B   1.5km N of Devonport*

Ducks Crossing Cottage
Gwenda & Peter Mark-Woods
58 Seabreeze Road, Devonport, Auckland
Tel: (09) 445 8102 Fax: (09) 445 8102
duckxing@splurge.net.nz
www.bnb.co.nz/duckscrossingcottage.html

Double $90-$120 Single $65-$85
(Full Breakfast) Child $30
1 Queen 1 Double 2 Single (3 bdrm)
1 Ensuite 2 Private

Welcome to our charming modern home, built in 1994, surrounded by trees and gardens. Peaceful, spacious and sunny bedrooms with attractive country decor. All rooms have TV and clock radios. Tea and coffee facilities available with delicious home cooking. we are adjacent Waitemata Golf course and 5 minutes from Narrow Neck Beach. Swim, sail and explore. Devonport village is 2 minutes by car and has a variety of restaurants, cafes and antique shops. Hosts are well travelled, informative and enjoy hospitality.

Devonport *B&B*

Rainbow Villa
Judy McGrath
17 Rattray Street, Devonport, Auckland
Tel: (09) 445 3597 Fax: (09) 445 4597
rainbowvilla@xtra.co.nz
www.rainbowvilla.co.nz

Double $130-$160 Single $100-$130
(Full Breakfast) Credit cards accepted
1 King 1 Queen 2 Single (3 bdrm)
3 Ensuite

Welcome to our pretty Victorian Villa (1885) nestled in a quiet cul-de-sac on the lower slopes of Mt Victoria. there are three elegant spacious rooms with ensuites and Sky TV. A hot Spa Pool is available in the garden. We serve a delicious full breakfast and coffee and tea are available at all times. Situated just 100 metres from the Historic Devonport Village, 5 minute walk to the ferry which is a 10 minute ride to downtown Auckland. Directions: Rattray street is the first on the left past the Picture theatre. Not suitable for children or pets. www.rainbowvilla.co.nz, e-mail rainbowvilla@xtra.co.nz.

Devonport   *Self-contained B&B Quality Accommodation*

Badgers of Devonport
Heather & Badger Miller
30 Summer Street, Devonport, Auckland
Tel: (09) 445 2099 Fax: (09) 445 0231
Mob: 025 720 336 badgers@clear.net.nz
www.badger.co.nz

Double $119-$149 Single $89-$119 (Full Breakfast)
Dinner $35pp Credit cards accepted
4 Double 4 Twin 2 Single (4 bdrm)
3 Ensuite 1 Private

Welcome to our home. Let us pamper you in our quiet, sunny Victorian Villa furnished with antiques, oriental carpets and memorabilia from our extensive travels. Laze on your Victorian brass bed, soak in your Victorian claw footed bath. Complimentary drinks, chocolates. All bedrooms have ensuite, private bathrooms, bathrobes, toiletries, flowers, teddy bears to cuddle. Self-contained guest wing complete with kitchen facilities. Laundry, airport transfers available. Off-street parking. Sumptuous breakfast for vegetarians and meat lovers. Stroll to the beach, restaurants, cafes, art galleries, shops, museums.

Devonport   *Self-contained B&B Apartment*   *3km NE of Devonport*

Ivanhoe Apartments
Coralie & Philip Luffman
82 Wairoa Road, Devonport, Auckland 9
Tel: (09) 445 1900 Fax: (09) 446 0039
ivho@xtra.co.nz   www.bnb.co.nz/ivanhoe.html

Double $120-$140 Single $85-$100
(Continental Breakfast) Child $5 over 5 yrs
rates seasonal $ monthly negotiable
Credit cards accepted
1 Queen 1 Twin 1 Single (2 bdrm)   2 Ensuite

Ivanhoe has 2 fully furnished one bedroom apartments situated on the ground floor of our home at Narrow Neck beach Devonport. These apartments have private entrances, cozy lounge, spacious bedrooms and bathrooms. Kitchens have full cooking facilities. Each has its own private patio. Bed & breakfast available 3 nights minimum stay. Beach, park, golf course adjacent with walking trails only a minutes walk away. Historic Devonport only minutes by bus or car enables you to enjoy restaurants and shopping. A ferry sails regularly to down-town Auckland in minutes.

Devonport   *Self-contained B&B Cottage*   *1km NE of Devonport*

Devonport Sea Cottage
John Lethaby & Michele van Zon
3A Cambridge Terrace, Devonport, Auckland
Tel: (09) 445 7117 Fax: (09) 445 7117
lethabys@ihug.co.nz
www.homestaysnz.co.nz/listings/46

Double $120 Single $100 (Continental Breakfast)
Child $10 Weekly & Winter rates avail.
Pet on property
1 Queen 1 Single (1 bdrm) 1 Ensuite

A charming and private, beautifully appointed cottage only meters from the sea and park. The ideal location. A short 10 minute stroll along the waterfront in different directions takes you to lovely Cheltenham Beach, reception lounges and Devonport Village. Our cottage is light, serene and airy with full facilities including lounge/bedroom, bathroom, kitchen/dining and private verandah. Full breakfast available on request. We welcome either short term or longer stays. John, Michele and family, including small dog and cat, warmly invite you to stay.

Devonport   *Self-contained B&B Cottage*   *4km N of Auckland Central*

The Jasmine Room
Joan & John Lewis
20 Buchanan Street,
Devonport, Auckland
Tel: (09) 445 8825 Fax: (09) 445 8605
Mob: 021 120 9532
joanjohnlewis@xtra.co.nz
www.bnb.co.nz/thejasmineroom.html
Double $100 (Full Breakfast)
1 Queen (1 bdrm)
1 Ensuite

Welcome to our cosy smoke-free quiet and private guest cottage. We are right in the heart of historic Devonport Village with all its attractions, cafes, beaches, golf course, scenic walks. The ferry to Auckland City and the Hauraki Gulf is 3 minutes walk away. A breakfast basket is delivered to your door and provides fruit juice, cereals, home made muesli and yoghurt, a platter of seasonal fruits, breads, English muffins, jams, spreads, cheeses, free range eggs, breakfast teas and freshly brewed coffee. TV, fax.

Devonport   *Self-contained B&B*   *2km W of Devonport*

Devonport Clifftop Apartment
Sandra & Bruce McLachlan
31 Stanley Point Road, Devonport, Auckland
Tel: (09) 446 1130 Mob: 021 550 814
clifftop@ihug.co.nz
www.bnb.co.nz/clifftop.html
Double $200-$230 Single $165 (Continental Breakfast)
Child $10 Dinner by arrangement each extra adult $30
Credit cards accepted Child at home
1 Queen 1 Double (1 bdrm) 1 Ensuite

Devonport Clifftop is a self contained apartment on the ground floor of our large modern home overlooking Stanley Bay and Auckland harbour. Luxuriously furnished with lounge/dining opening out to private courtyard, kitchen with all modern appliances, spacious bedroom and large bathroom which includes washing machine, dryer and ironing facilities. Separate entrance and off street parking. The garden leads down to the cliff edge with superb water views and steps down to shoreline. The apartment kitchen is stocked with provisions for a light breakfast, tea/coffee and home baking.

Waiheke Island   *B&B*

Blue Horizon
David & Marion Aim
41 Coromandel Road,
Sandy Bay, Waiheke Island
Tel: (09) 372 5632
www.bnb.co.nz/bluehorizon.html
Double $80-$95 Single $55-$70
(Continental Breakfast)
2 Queen (2 bdrm)
1 Ensuite 1 Family share

We live above Sandy Bay which is 2-3 mins walk away with spectacular sea views. All the rooms of our modest home face due north catching the sun all day. Waiheke caters for adventuring, dining out, sandy beaches, rock pools, which we enjoy after farming and owning a garden centre which our 4 children helped with. We really enjoy our B & B and look forward to sharing our beautiful island with you. Directions: Ferry from Auckland. Car ferry Howick. Complimentary ferry transfers.

Devonport   *B&B Boutique   10 min N of Auckland Central*

Buchanan's of Devonport B&B Inn
Eric & Cecille Charnley
22 Buchanan Street,
Devonport, Auckland

Tel: (09) 445 3333 Fax: (09) 445 3333 Mob: 025 207 6738
info@buchanansofdevonport.co.nz
www.buchanansofdevonport.co.nz

Double $140-$230 Single $120-$180 (Full Breakfast) Credit cards accepted Child at home
1 King/Twin 1 Queen 2 Double (4 bdrm)
4 Ensuite

Welcome to the luxury and "olde-worlde" elegance of Buchanan's of Devonport, our gracious 2 storey home in the heart of Devonport - a historical, picturesque, seaside village on Auckland's North Shore. Built in 1933 in the Edwardian architecture and immaculately restored in 1998 to its original era, our home is tastefully furnished throughout with genuine NZ and colonial antiques and artworks.

A private lounge with a gas-log fireplace, tea and coffee-making facilities, filtered water & complimentary biscuits is available for guests' use. Upstairs, we offer 4 luxuriously appointed, colour themed guestrooms, all with balconies and ensuites with complimentary toiletries, hairdryers & demist mirrors.

Each room has its own unique charm (which sometimes give our guests some difficulty as to which room they want to stay!) and are individually furnished with an antique wooden bed & furnishings, imported fine beddings, plush Egyptian cotton towels , a comfortable couch, fresh flowers, TV, CD player, alarm clock, heater & electric blankets, ironing facilities, tea and coffee-making facilities and complimentary biscuits & sherry. The Honeymoon Suite has an added VCR and matching his-and-hers bathrobes!

Allow us to pamper your taste buds in the morning with a choice of delicious, hearty continental or cooked breakfast, which is served between 7.30am-9.30am in the formal dining room, or outside in the sunny courtyard with Kauri & other native trees and a 3-tier fountain.

After your day's outing, relax in the warm waters of our new therapeutic spa-in-gazebo to soothe your body and mind. Only a 5-min stroll to the Devonport ferry wharf and a stone's throw away from all the village's international restaurants & cafes, special attractions and amenities, including major wedding reception venues, an 18 hole golf course (advanced bookings required) and lovely white-sand beaches! A complimentary tour of Devonport by your hosts is also on offer.

We can be a venue for small conferences too, with or without catering. 24-Hr. Security/Safety deposit box available. Ample off street parking. Unsuitable for children. A warm welcome awaits you at Buchanan's of Devonport from Eric, Cecille & Helena (our lovely 7 year old daughter who is our pride & joy!)

Please check out our website for a "virtual reality tour" of our B&B Inn.

Herne Bay - Auckland Central

Homestay B&B   2.5km W of Auckland central

Moana Vista
Tim Kennedy & Matthew Moran
60 Hamilton Road, Herne Bay, Auckland
Tel: (09) 376 5028 Mob: 021 376 150
Tollfree: 0800 213 761
info@moanavista.co.nz
www.moanavista.co.nz
Double $140-$160 Single $120 (Full Breakfast)
Credit cards accepted
1 King 1 Queen (2 bdrm)
1 Guests share

Relax and enjoy the hospitality of one of Auckland's grand old homes. Recently refurbished to include all modern amenities but retaining its early colonial charm. Lovely water views, stroll to the Ponsonby cafes and restaurants and beaches. Kayak available. Continental or cooked breakfast supplied. The entire upstairs is available for guests with high water pressure/heated towel rail, drier and toiletries. Gas and electric heating and TV in both bedrooms with free Internet in the adjoining library.

Herne Bay - Auckland   *B&B*

Sunderland House Bed & Breakfast
Donald & Kathy Sunderland
1a Cox Street, Herne Bay, Auckland
Tel: 025 249 9025 Mob: 025 249 9025
sunderlandhouse@ihug.co.nz
www.bnb.co.nz/sunderlandhousebb.html
Double $130-$150 Single $115 (Continental Breakfast)
traditional NZ roast by req. Pet on property
2 King/Twin 1 Queen (3 bdrm)
3 Ensuite

Television personality & interior designer Donald Grant Sunderland, wife Kathy, and springer spaniel Ben, invite you to share their elegant and sumptuous replica Victorian villa. Your privacy and comfort is paramount in 3 beautiful, spacious ensuite rooms. Especially for romantics, the principle suite features a claw foot bath set luxuriously in the bedroom. Indulge yourself with leisurely breakfasts, home baking, and complimentary sherry in the library, conservatory or on the patio. Just 3km to the city, and a short stroll to local cafes, restaurants, and great shopping.

Ponsonby - Auckland Central   *B&B   Small Hotel   Auckland Central*

The Great Ponsonby B&B
Sally James & Gerry Hill
30 Ponsonby Terrace, Ponsonby, Auckland
Tel: (09) 376 5989 Fax: (09) 376 5527
great.ponsonby@xtra.co.nz
www.ponsonbybnb.co.nz
Double $160-$275 Single $140-$200 (Full Breakfast)
Double Suites Credit cards accepted Pet on property
6 King/Twin 5 Queen (11 bdrm)
11 Ensuite

Chic B&B hotel close to all the razzmatazz of Ponsonby Road's bars, cafes and shopping, yet in a quiet cul-de-sac. Close to everything in the ciy by bus which passes every ten minutes. An 1898 villa restored with bold use of colour and NZ and Pacific art works. Leisurely breakfasts served from our extensive menu in the dining room or alfresco on the veranda overlooking the large garden. Eight double rooms and three suites. Each is beautiful and comfortable with ensuite, sky tv, DDI phones, hairdryer, tea making facilities. A gentle dog and cat on site.

Ponsonby - Auckland Central *Self-contained* *3 k W of Auckland Central*

Ponsonby Potager
Marsha & Ray Lawford
43 Douglas Street,
Ponsonby, Auckland 2
Tel: (09) 378 7237 Fax: (09) 378 7267
raywarby@xtra.co.nz
ponsonbypotager.co.nz
Double $120 Single $90
(Full Breakfast) Pet on property
2 Double (2 bdrm)
1 Private

Prepare to be pampered at the "Ponsonby Potager". Enjoy a self-help breakfast in the garden room or on one of the two private decks. You have your own entrances, bathroom, lounge (with video and book library), fully equipped kitchen, fresh fruit and flowers, off-street parking and Sky TV. It is peaceful here but only a 3 minutes stroll to the shops, cafes and restaurants of Ponsonby. Marsha, Ray and Danny (4 legged son) respect your privacy but are here if you need advice.

Ponsonby - Auckland Central *Homestay B&B* *2km E of Auckland Central*

Summer Street
Selwyn Houry
6 Summer Street, Ponsonby, Auckland
Tel: (09) 361 3715 Fax: (09) 361 3715
Mob: 021 535 635 selwyn_houry@hotmail.com
www.bnb.co.nz/summerstreet.html
Double $100-$130 Single $80-$100
(Continental Breakfast) Child by arrangement
Pet on property
2 King/Twin 1 King 3 Queen (4 bdrm)
4 Ensuite 1 Family share

Summer Street is very quiet but less than one minute's walk from Auckland's busy and vibrant Ponsonby Road with all its fantastic shops cafes and restaurants. Public transport is very close (Auckland centre 10 minutes) Importantly we provide off-street parking, large quality beds, linen and towels. A continental buffet breakfast is laid out either in our dining area or in the garden. Alternatively you've got a great choice of reasonably priced quality cafes and bistros a minute away on Ponsonby Road.

Ponsonby - Auckland *B&B* *1km W of Inner City*

Amitee's on Ponsonby
237 Ponsonby Road, Ponsonby, Auckland
Tel: (09) 378 6325 Fax: (09) 378 6329
Mob: 025 721 344
relax@amitees.com
www.amitees.com
Double $135 Single $135 (Continental Breakfast)
queen $150 penthouse $200 Credit cards accepted
Pet on property
1 King/Twin 5 Queen 2 Double (8 bdrm)
8 Ensuite

Cool and contemporary - your choice for accommodation on vibrant Ponsonby Road. Eight attractive comfortable bedrooms with ensuites designed with flair. Two suites with awesome city views. Private garden, wine cellar with guest selection, free internet, DD phones, guest kitchen, cosy fireplace in winter. Small friendly family-owned in great neighbourhood. Restaurants, cafes, bars, boutiques a step away. "Link" bus at gate every 10 mins around city and all the sights.Credit Cards Visa/MC.

Parnell - Auckland *B&B Small Hotel*   *1.5km E of Auckland Central*

Ascot Parnell
Bart & Therese Blommaert, 32 St Stephens Avenue, Parnell, Auckland 1
Tel: (09) 309 9012 Fax: (09) 309 3729
AscotParnell@compuserve.com
www.ascotparnell.com

Double $165-$250 Single $165 (Full Breakfast) $50 extra person ask about Winter rates
Credit cards accepted
7 King/Twin 2 Queen 2 Single (11 bdrm)
10 Ensuite 1 Private

Ascot Parnell is a convenient, central and quiet location to visit all Auckland city attractions. The airport shuttle bus will bring you to the door. Built in 1910, this large mansion has been carefully restored to its former elegance, maintaining its old-fashioned charm. As a small B&B hotel it offers spacious guest-rooms with European character. Also ideal for the business traveller who requires everything nearby.

The Downtown ferry terminal is 1 mile (1.5km) away, and there is a Link-bus every 8 minutes on the corner of the street. It is an easy walk to the Rose Gardens, Auckland Museum, Parnell Village and Newmarket with its many boutiques, craft-shops, art galleries, cafes and restaurants.

There is a choice from spacious superior queen-rooms to modestly priced but comfortable single rooms. All are non-smoking, immaculate and tastefully decorated, they have their own bathroom, hair-drier, telephone and Internet access.

A sumptuous breakfast is served in the morning room overlooking the subtropical garden. Refreshments are offered throughout the day.

Although it is not necessary to rent a car, there is parking in the courtyard. Visit http://www.ascotparnell.com/ and use the reservations form.

The friendly hosts Bart and Therese also speak Flemish/ Dutch, French and German and look forward to welcoming you. We recommend to book well in advance! Ask for our reduced winter rates (May-September).

Parnell - Auckland *B&B*   *2km S of Auckland Central*

Redwood Bed & Breakfast
Dawn Feickert, 11 Judges Bay Road, Parnell, Auckland
Tel: (09) 373 4903 Fax: (09) 373 4903 Tollfree: 0800 349 742
kotuku@wave.co.nz   www.redwood-bed-breakfast.ws
Double $120-$165 Single $85-$120 (Special Breakfast) Child $25 Credit cards accepted
2 Queen 1 Double 2 Single (3 bdrm)   2 Ensuite 1 Family share

THE REDWOOD offers you a very warm welcome. Stroll through our peaceful inner-city native garden and you will find a stand of tree ferns, Nikau palms and cabbage trees. Native birds frequent the garden and as we do, you shall enjoy their evensong. We are adjacent to the famous Parnell Rose Gardens and Dove-Myer Robinson Park. You are invited to use the lounge and deck from where you will experience our ever-changing view of pleasure craft and shipping over the Waitemata harbour to Devonport and Mt Victoria.

You will have the same views while enjoying our gourmet breakfast having choices of fresh fruit, yoghurt, cereals, daily baked muffins, breads and pastries, and choice of cooked breakfast. We are located close to many popular attractions, including Parnell Village and its restaurants, the Auckland Domain and museum, Kelly Tarlton's Underwater World, the salt water Parnell pools and the waterfront as well as many golf courses. If you are enjoying a day of sightseeing picnic hampers can be supplied on request. We are just a one-stop bus ride or a twenty-minute walk from the city centre and waterfront, including the yacht basin.

You will enjoy the shopping, galleries, cinemas, theatre and many more restaurants in the down town area. Door to door shuttle buses are available to and from the Airport. We are happy to advise and assist you with onward travel.

Our rooms are comfortable and have queen, double or single beds with all the conveniences you would expect, including colour TV and tea and coffee making facilities. You will find us well travelled and conversant on many topics of interest, including wine. We aim to provide you with a home away from home and every effort has been made to ensure that your stay - be it business or pleasure - is a pleasant and enjoyable one.

In house pre or post jet-lag therapeutic massage and other beauty therapy treatments are available. Email. fax and office facilities available.

Parnell - Auckland   *B&B   B&B Hotel   1.5km E of Downtown Auckland*

Chalet Chevron
Brett & Jennie Boyce
14 Brighton Road, Parnell, Auckland
Tel: (09) 309 0290 Fax: (09) 373 5754
chaletchevron@xtra.co.nz   www.chaletchevron.co.nz
Double $110-$130 Single $80-$90 (Full Breakfast)
Child $25 Family room - sleeps 4 $140 - $170
Credit cards accepted Pet on property Children welcome
2 King/Twin 1 Queen 5 Double 2 Twin
11 Single (12 bdrm)   12 Ensuite

Ideally positioned near Parnell Village with its restaurants, boutiques and art galleries, we are a small hotel offering quiet, well-appointed, charming guestrooms, all with own bathrooms and many boasting stunning harbour and bay views. Our typically 'kiwi' breakfast has an individually cooked course. We are conveniently close to public transport, making Downtown Auckland, harbour ferries and other city locations readily accessible. Starship Children's Hospital, University, Museum, the Domain, Wintergardens, Rose Gardens, cinemas and shopping areas are all situated within easy walking distance.

Parnell - Auckland   *B&B   Guesthouse   1.5km Auckland City*

St Georges Bay Lodge
Bonnie Jensen and Kit and Nicola Wong
43 St Georges Bay Road, Parnell, Auckland
Tel: (09) 303 1050 Fax: (09) 303 1055
Mob: 025 896 959
enquiry@stgeorge.co.nz
www.stgeorge.co.nz
Double $195-$245 Single $165-$205
(Full Breakfast) Credit cards accepted
2 King 1 Queen 1 Twin (4 bdrm)
3 Ensuite 1 Private

St Georges Bay Lodge is an elegant Victorian Villa which has the charm of a by-gone era, with the comfort of modern amenities. There is no better location for your stay in Auckland City. We are minutes from: picturesque Parnell Village, designer boutiques and speciality stores, great cafes, restaurants, and night club life, health centres, swimming pools, gardens, parks, and the Museum in Auckland Domain and Holy Trinity Cathedral.

Mt Eden - Auckland   *B&B   Auckland Central*

811 Bed & Breakfast
Bryan Condon & David Fitchew
811 Dominion Road, Mt Eden, Auckland 1003
Tel: (09) 620 4284 Fax: (09) 620 4286
Mob: 025 289 8863   www.bnb.co.nz/bedbreakfast.html
Double $75 Single $50 (Full Breakfast)
Pet on property
2 Double 1 Twin (3 bdrm)
2 Guests share

All are welcome at 811 Bed and Breakfast. Your hosts Bryan and David, Pfeni and their Irish Water Spaniels welcome you to their turn of the century home. Our home reflects years of collecting and living overseas. Centrally located on Dominion Road (which is an extension of Queen Street city centre). The bus stop at the door, only 10 minutes to city and 20 minutes to airport, shuttle bus from airport. Easy walking to Balmoral shopping area (banks, excellent restaurants). We have operated a bed and breakfast on a farm in Digby County, Nova Scotia, Canada. The nicest compliment we can receive is when Guests tell us, it's like visiting friends when they stay with us.

Mt Eden - Auckland
B&B Small Hotel   *2km S of Auckland Central*

Bavaria B&B Hotel
Ulrike Stephan & Rudolf Schmidt
83 Valley Road, Mt Eden, Auckland 3
Tel: (09) 638 9641 Fax: (09) 638 9665 bavaria@xtra.co.nz
www.bavariabandbhotel.co.nz
Double $99-$135 Single $70-$95 (Full Breakfast) Child $12 over 2 yrs
Credit cards accepted Children welcome
1 King/Twin 4 Queen 2 Double 2 Twin 4 Single (11 bdrm)
11 Ensuite

We invite you to stay at our charming small hotel offering quality B&B with all modern facilities yet combined with a homely and welcoming atmosphere.

Our picturesque, colonial villa with its 11 guestrooms is tastefully decorated with contemporary native timber furniture. It is designed generously and maintained immaculately.

All rooms have ensuites, quality commercial beds (extra length), telephones, suitcase racks, desks, electric blankets and internet access for your laptop computer.

Relax in our large sunny guest lounge which looks on to a private sun deck and small exotic garden.

Our breakfast buffet is a house speciality offering a wide selection of freshly prepared healthy foods with a touch of German cuisine. Refreshments are offered during the day.

There is plenty of off-street parking available in the court yard. The city is only 2km away and can be easily reached by bus or car. Within walking distance you will find excellent restaurants, cafes, banks, a modern supermarket, an internet cafe and many other shops.

Despite the proximity to the city, you will enjoy the quiet atmosphere of Mount Eden with its colonial villas, pretty gardens and Mt. Eden summit lending panoramic views over the city and harbour.

Your hosts are always happy to give advice on rental cars, tours or on any other topic about New Zealand.

Mt Eden - Auckland   *B&B   B&B Hotel   3km S of Auckland Waterfront*

Pentlands B&B Hotel
Brian Hopkins
22 Pentland Avenue, Mt Eden, Auckland
Tel: (09) 638 7031 Fax: (09) 638 7031
hoppy.pentland@xtra.co.nz
www.pentlands.co.nz
Double $79-$89 Single $49-$59
(Continental Breakfast) Extra people $20-$25
Credit cards accepted Children welcome
7 Double 3 Twin 5 Single (15 bdrm)
4 Guests share

Peace and quiet in the heart of Auckland. Ideal for travellers, families and groups. Top-rated villa style in sunny garden setting with tennis court. Guest lounge with open fire, Sky TV, internet facilities. Off street parking, laundry and cooking facilities. Close to Eden Park and to shops, restaurants etc. Rated "best by guests" and great value for money.

Epsom - Auckland   *Homestay B&B   6km S of Auckland Central*

Hey's Homestay
Kathy & Roger Hey
2/7 Tahuri Road, Epsom 3, Auckland
Tel: (09) 520 0154 Fax: (09) 520 0184
Mob: 021 642 652
R.K.Hey@xtra.Co.NZ
www.bnb.co.nz/hey.html
Double $85 Single $55 (Continental Breakfast)
Child neg Dinner $25 Children welcome
1 King 1 Twin (2 bdrm)
1 Guests share

We offer home comforts. Two minutes from the motorway, in a central quiet garden suburb, with many facilities. Airport 20 minutes , on a door to door shuttle bus service. Excellent city bus service nearby. Juice, tea, coffee provided. Laundry facilities. Off street parking. Family group welcome. We are experienced travellers and enjoy our guests. Directions: Leave Motorway at Market Road, travel West, cross over Great South Road, first left into Dunkerron Ave, Tahuri Road 2nd left.

Epsom - Auckland   *Homestay B&B   5km S of Auckland Central*

Auckland Homestay
Isobel & Ian Thompson
37 Torrance Street, Epsom, Auckland
Tel: (09) 624 3714 aucklandhomestay@xtra.co.nz
www.aucklandhomestay.co.nz
Double $115-$135 Single $75-$100
(Continental & Full Breakfast) Child Neg
Dinner $25. by arrangement Credit cards accepted
2 Queen 1 Single (3 bdrm)
1 Ensuite 1 Guests share

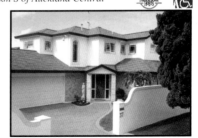

Experience warm, friendly hospitality in our large modern home in a quiet tree lined street. Just 5 minutes from motorway and 15 minutes from Airport and City CBD. Our central location is ideally positioned to explore the many attractions, whether by car or one of the nearby bus routes. Use of full laundry facilities. Telephone, email by request. Evening meals by prior arrangement. Off Street Parking. We look forward to sharing our non-smoking home with you.

Epsom - Auckland *Homestay* *5km S of Auckland City Centre*

Millars Epsom Homestay
Janet & Jim Millar, 10 Ngaroma Road, Epsom, Auckland 1003
Tel: (09) 625 7336 Fax: (09) 625 7336 Mob: 025 659 2817
jmillar@xtra.co.nz
www.bnb.co.nz/millarsepsomhomestay.html

Double $80-$90 Single $60-$70 (Full Breakfast) Child $10 Dinner $30 Credit cards accepted
1 King 1 Queen 2 Single (3 bdrm)
1 Ensuite 2 Private

Our home, a spacious 1919 wooden bungalow, is surprisingly quiet and restful, set in a garden suburb in a tree-lined street, 200 metres from Greenwoods Corner Village with its bank, post office, reasonably priced non-tourist restaurants, and bus stop on direct route (15 minutes each way) between the airport and CBD.

There is a short walk to One Tree Hill, one of Auckland's loveliest parks with a playground, farm animals, groves of trees, the Observatory, and a magnificent pano-rama of Auckland from the summit. A 15 minute walk through the park leads to the Expo centre and Greenlane Hospital.

There are two accommodation areas - either the 'Garden Suite' with its Queen-sized double bedroom, large lounge with 3 single beds, patio, desk and TV, own bathroom, and which is the area we find really suitable for families; or the 'Upstairs' bedroom (king-size, can be converted to twin beds) with own ensuite, desk and TV.

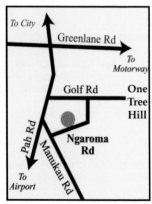

We have travelled widely both in NZ and overseas (our son lives in Finland) and very much like conversing with guests and assist-ing in making their stay as pleasant as possible in our country and especially in this attractive suburb of Auckland. We are a smoke-free family. Jim and I were both born in NZ, and we belong to NZ Association Farm and Home Hosts, and also to Home and Farmstay Auckland.

Epsom - Auckland   *Homestay B&B   5km S of Auckland*

Epsom House
Kathy & Rick
18 Crescent Road, Epsom, Auckland
Tel: (09) 630 0900 Fax: (09) 630 0900
Mob: 025 834 779   Tollfree: 0800 118 448
kathyvb@xtra.co.nz www.epsombb.com
Double $200 Single $160 (Special Breakfast)
Dinner $40 Credit cards accepted Pet on property
2 King 1 Twin (2 bdrm)
2 Ensuite

Nestled on the slopes of One Tree Hill in a tree-lined street, Epsom House is within 4 minutes flat walk of the local Greenlane and National Women's Hospitals, Expo and Conference Centre, Showgrounds and Collectors Markets. Luxurious suites, superior bed and bedding and quality furnishings, ensuite bathrooms with spa bath. Relax in the private sunny courtyard garden or private comfortable guest lounge. All suites have fast internet and e-mail facilities. Tariff includes complimentary continental or gourmet breakfasts, airport transfers, coffee, special teas and juices. We offer you warm hospitality.

Epsom - Auckland   *B&B   5KM SE of Auckland CBD*

Hillier House Luxury Bed and Breakfast
Christine and Chris Hillier
144 Mountain Road, Epsom, Auckland 1003
Tel: +64 9 6230777 Fax: +64 9 6230778
Mob: 025 289 1075   hillierhouse@xtra.co.nz
www.hillierhouse.co.nz
Double $195-$245 Single $150-$200
(Full Breakfast) Child $35 Credit cards accepted
Pet on property
1 King/Twin 1 King 1 Queen (3 bdrm)   3 Ensuite

As you will know from previous travelling experiences, location is one of the most important factors. Hillier House is a beautiful home in a beautiful and very central suburb, not only 5 minutes by car from the city, harbour and America's Cup Village but also within strolling distance of numerous cafes and boutiques. A bus to the city stops outside the front door. Inside, the rooms are spacious and newly decorated. They all have TV and direct dial phone. Two have stereos, desk, modem connection and a view to the harbour. Guest lounge with gas fire. Swimming pool on site. One outside cat.

Epsom - Auckland   *Self-contained B&B   5km SE of Auckland CBD*

Laurel Cottage
Pene & Steve Ryan
83 Ranfurly Road, Epsom, Auckland
Tel: (09) 630 4384 Fax: (09) 630 4384
Mob: 025 986 909
enquiry@laurelcottage.co.nz
www.bnb.co.nz/laurelcottage.html
Double $170-$195 Single $150-$170 (Full Breakfast)
Credit cards accepted Child at home Pet on property
1 Queen (1 bdrm) 1 Ensuite

Laurel Cottage is a newly renovated 1910 cottage situated in Epsom, a gracious and very central suburb. Only five minutes by car from Auckland City and America's Cup Village and within strolling distance of numerous cafes and shops. 20 minutes from airport. The cottage has superior bedlinen and furnishings, fully-equipped kitchen for self-catering, plus a barbeque. Full breakfast provisions included. Laundry available. There is a television, stereo, modem connection and direct dial phone. We look forward to welcoming you and are nearby for advice and assistance. Two outside cats.

One Tree Hill - Auckland   *Self-contained Homestay   5km S of Newmarket*

Ron & Doreen Curreen
39B Konini Road,
One Tree Hill, Auckland 5
Tel: (09) 579 9531 Fax: (09) 579 9531
www.bnb.co.nz/curreen.html
Double $65-$75 Single $45
(Continental Breakfast)
Child $12 Dinner $25
1 King 1 Queen 1 Double (3 bdrm)
1 Private 1 Guests share

A warm friendly welcome awaits you at 39B. Situated 15 minutes from the airport and city centre our large contemporary home in a secluded garden setting on private right of way offers pleasant views and peaceful surroundings. We are close to Ellerslie Racecourse, One Tree Hill Domain, Alexandra Park, Epsom Showgrounds and Ericsson Stadium, Restaurants, Antique shops, Supermarket, and bus service are a short distance away. Our spacious self-contained unit has a large bedroom with king sized bed. Private bathroom lounge with TV, kitchenette, microwave, washing machine and extras.

Ellerslie - Auckland   *Homestay   8km SE of Auckland Central*

Taimihinga
Marjorie Love
16 Malabar Drive, Ellerslie, Auckland 5
Tel: (09) 579 7796 Fax: (09) 579 7796
mlovebnb@ihug.co.nz
www.bnb.co.nz/taimihinga.html
Double $80 Single $50 (Full Breakfast)
Dinner by arrangement Credit cards accepted
1 Double 1 Twin 1 Single (3 bdrm) 1 Guests share

Taimihinga - softly calling o'er the ocean. Answer the call - enjoy the welcome at this comfortable home in quiet garden with pleasant northerly outlook. Ellerslie offers convenient access to Auckland's Business and Entertainment Centres, Scenic and Recreational Attractions. It is close to motorway (1km), transport, racing, parks, hospitals, shops, restaurants. Interests: people, family (now in faraway places), arts, music, travel, church (Anglican), Probus, gardening. Refreshment trolley, hairdrier and bathrobes in rooms. Laundry and fax facilities (small charge). Smoking outside only, please. Directions: Please phone, fax or write.

Remuera - Auckland   *Homestay B&B   7km N of Auckland Central*

Woodlands
Judi & Roger Harwood
18 Waiatarua Road, Remuera, Auckland 1005
Tel: (09) 524 6990 Fax: (09) 524 6993
Mob: 025 602 5592 Woodlands@ake.quik.co.nz
www.bnb.co.nz/woodlands.html
Double $130-$145 Single $100 (Special Breakfast)
Child not suitable Dinner $45 pp Credit cards accepted
1 King 1 Double 1 Single (2 bdrm)
1 Ensuite 1 Private

Guest book comments "Absolutely purr-fect". "A superb stay". "Very comfortable with stunning food". "A lovely oasis of calm with wonderful breakfasts". "Peaceful retreat with excellent breakfasts". Our breakfasts ARE special using seasonal fruit and produce. Join us for a Cordon Bleu candlelit evening dinner - booking essential. "Woodlands" is very quiet, surrounded by native trees and palms and central to many places of interest. The two guest bedrooms have tea/coffee facilities, heated towel rails, and coloured TV's. Safe off street carparking. Arrive a guest - leave a friend.

St Johns Park - Remuera - Auckland *Homestay*

8km SE of Auckland Central

Amity Homestay
Jean & Neville Taylor
47 Norman Lesser Drive,
St Johns Park, Remuera, Auckland
Tel: (09) 521 1827 Fax: (09) 521 1863
jean@amity.co.nz   www.amity.co.nz
Double $90 Single $45 (Full Breakfast)
3 Single (2 bdrm) 1 Guests share

Relax in our lounge, conservatory, or garden . Our warm comfortable smoke free home has off street parking in quiet residential area surrounding the Remuera Golf Course. All bedrooms have smoke alarms, electric blankets, cosy duvets, fans, and for cooler nights, heaters. Laundry and ironing facilities are available. There is a range of restaurants nearby. Bus stop to and from Downtown Auckland at gate. We are handy to Tamaki University Campus and Ascot Hospital. Members of New Zealand Association of Farm and Home Hosts.

Remuera - Auckland *Homestay B&B* *1km N of Newmarket*

The Brooks, Longwood
54 Seaview Road, Remuera, Auckland 1105
Tel: (09) 523 3746 Fax: (09) 523 3756
Mob: 025 744 035
longwood@ihug.co.nz
www.brooksnz.co.nz

Single $95-$140 (Continental Breakfast)
Credit cards accepted
1 Queen 3 Single (2 bdrm)
2 Ensuite

We invite you to stay in our beautiful old home. Longwood is a fully restored farmhouse, built in the 1880s. We have two guest rooms, each with ensuite and our spacious home features sunny verandahs overlooking the gardens and pool. Breakfast to suit - healthy or indulgent or a little of both. We are superbly located close to the shops, galleries, theatres and parks of Auckland City, Parnell, Newmarket and Remuera. We ask no smoking please indoors. We have a friendly cat. The airport shuttle will bring you to our door, or phone for easy directions.

Remuera - Auckland *Self-contained B&B*

Lillington Villa
Carol and Peter Dossor
2/24 Lillington Road, Remuera, Auckland
Tel: (09) 523 2035 Fax: (09) 523 2036
Mob: 025 927 063   caropet@xtra.co.nz
www.bnb.co.nz/lillingtonvilla.html

Double $120 Single $100 (Continental Breakfast)
Child $20 Dinner $40 full week $520
Credit cards accepted
2 Single (1 bdrm) 1 Ensuite

A home away from home. Large, sunny, welcoming one bedroom flat in well-restored villa 10 minutes from central Auckland. Own entrance and courtyard. Lock-up garage available. Security and fire alarm system. Gas heating. Telephone and Sky TV. Full modern open-plan kitchen and new bathroom. Dishwasher, microwave, fridge/freezer, stove, washing machine, dryer. Full sets of crockery, cutlery, etc. Comfortable twin Sealy posturepedic beds, can be made up as queen. Also double bed-settee in living room so can sleep four.

Remuera - Auckland   *Self-contained Homestay B&B   1.5km E of Newmarket*

Green Oasis
James & Joy Foote
25a Portland Rd, Remuera, Auckland 5
Tel: (09) 520 1921 Fax: (09) 522 9004
Mob: 021 175 8291   footes1@xtra.co.nz
www.bnb.co.nz/greenoasis.pl.net.html
Double $110 Single $75 (Full Breakfast) Child $65
Children welcome
1 Queen 1 Single (2 bdrm)   1 Private 1 Family share

Green Oasis offers a secluded and tranquil location in a much-loved garden of native trees and ferns - 10 mins to city centre. We are close to the Museum, antique and specialty shops, restaurants and cafes of Remuera, Newmarket and Parnell. Ours is an informal home of natural timbers and sunny decks where you will find us relaxed and welcoming, sensitive to your needs, be it to withdraw and rest, or to engage with us. Your accommodation, entered from a private garden, is self-contained with fully equipped kitchen, tea and coffee-making facilities, washing machine and TV. A special breakfast of seasonal and homemade taste sensations!

Orakei - Okahu Bay   *Homestay   5km E of Auckland Central*

Nautical Nook/Free Sailing
Trish & Keith Janes & Irish Setter
23b Watene Crescent, Orakei, Auckland
Tel: (09) 521 2544 Fax: (64-9) 521 2542
Mob: 025 397 116   Tollfree: 0800 360 544
nauticalnook@bigfoot.com   www.nauticalnook.com
Double $110-$120 Single $80-$85 (Full Breakfast)
Credit cards accepted
2 Queen 1 Single (3 bdrm)
1 Ensuite 1 Private 1 Family share

Friendly, relaxed beachside hospitality, 5km from Downtown. 100 metres from Okahu Bay, fringed by Pohutukawa trees. Gourmet breakfast. Stroll to Kelly Tarlton's Underwater World and Mission Bay Beach and cafes along picturesque promenade. Bus to city, Americas Cup Village, ferry terminal. Unwind for 2-3 day stopver. COMPLIMENTARY SAILING on our sparkling harbour on 34' yacht. We have travelled extensively internationally and within NZ and can assist with local sightseeing, travel planning and rental car. Take taxi or shuttle from airport. WELCOME!

Mission Bay - Auckland   *Homestay   6km E of Auckland Central*

Bryan & Jean Cockell
41 Nihill Cresent,
Mission Bay,
Auckland
Tel: (09) 528 3809 www.bnb.co.nz/cockell.html
Double $85 Single $60
(Full Breakfast) Dinner $25
Credit cards accepted
1 Double (1 bdrm)
1 Private

We warmly welcome you to our modern split level home. The upper level is for your exclusive use including a private lounge. 5 minutes walk to Mission Bay beach, cafes and restaurants and 10 minutes scenic car or bus ride to down town Auckland and ferry terminal for harbour and islands in the Gulf. We are retired and look forward to sharing our special part of Auckland with you. Please phone for directions or airport shuttle bus to our door. Please no smoking.

St Heliers - Auckland *B&B* *10km E of Auckland*

Jill & Ron McPherson
102 Maskell Street,
St Heliers, Auckland
Tel: (09) 575 9738 Fax: (09) 575 0051
Mob: 0274 752 034
ron&jill_mcpherson@xtra.co.nz
www.bnb.co.nz/mcpherson.html
Double $110 Single $75 (Continental Breakfast)
1 Queen 1 Twin (2 bdrm)
1 Private

Welcome to our modern home with off street parking in a smoke free environment. One group of guests is accommodated at a time. Having travelled extensively ourselves we are fully aware of tourists' needs. Eight minutes walk to St Heliers Bay beach, shops, restaurants, cafes, banks and post office. Picturesque 12 minutes drive along the Auckland waterfront past Kelly Tarlton's Antarctic and Underwater Encounter to Downtown Auckland. Interests including all sports, gardening and Jill is a keen cross-stitch embroiderer. Not suitable for children/pets.

St Heliers - Auckland *Homestay B&B* *10km E of Auckland Central*

Pippi's Bed and Breakfast
Pippi & Philip Wells
15 Tuhimata Street,
St Heliers, Auckland
Tel: (09) 575 6057 Fax: (09) 575 6055
Mob: 021 989 643 pswells@xtra.co.nz
go.to/pippis
Double $140-$170 Single $120-$140 (Full Breakfast)
Credit cards accepted Pet on property
1 Queen 1 Double (2 bdrm) 1 Ensuite 1 Private

Our character home with pretty cottage garden offers guests a sunny retreat only a short walk to lovely beach, village and restaurants. Spacious bedroom with easy access, ensuite bathroom, electric blankets, feather duvets, Sky TV, tea/coffee etc. Delicious breakfast of fruit, home-made bread/muesli, and/or full breakfast, espresso coffee/tea. Telephone, fax, email, hairdryer, laundry, off street parking available. With Bess (golden retriever) and Bertie (toy poodle) we look forward to offering you a warm welcome to our smoke-free home.

St Heliers *B&B* *10km E of Auckland City*

Burnt Fig
Dianne & Alister Benvie
2/1 Walmsley Road, St. Heliers, Auckland
Tel: (09) 575 4150 Mob: 025 281 6893
benvie@xtra.co.nz
www.bnb.co.nz/burntfig.html
Double $130 Single $110 (Full Breakfast)
Credit cards accepted
2 Queen 1 Twin 2 Single (3 bdrm)
1 Ensuite 1 Private

Welcome to Burnt Fig, a modern architect-designed house located in beautiful St. Heliers Bay. Only minutes walk to local beaches and great cafes. A stunning waterfront drive takes you to downtown Auckland and the Americas Cup Village. Among the facilities available are tea and coffee in a separate guest lounge, off-street parking and use of laundry. Tia, the Belgian Shepherd will also welcome you. We both play golf at Titirangi, one of New Zealand's finest Championship courses where tee times can be arranged.

Titirangi - Auckland   *B&B*   *20min W of Auckland City*

Kaurigrove
Gaby & Peter Wunderlich
120 Konini Road,
Titirangi, Auckland 7
Tel: (09) 817 5608 Fax: (09) 817 5608
Mob: 025 275 0574
www.bnb.co.nz/kaurigrove.html
Double $85-$90 Single $45-$50 (Special Breakfast)
Credit cards accepted
1 Queen 1 Single (2 bdrm)
1 Guests share

Welcome to our home! Situated at Titirangi, the gateway of the Waitakere Ranges and Auckland's historic West Coast with its magnificent beaches and vast native bush areas! Nearby are other attractions such as the Titirangi Golf course, cafes, restaurants and walking tracks. Gaby and Peter, your hosts of German descent, are keen trampers themselves and are happy to introduce you to the highlights of Auckland and its surrounding areas. PS: We have a shy cat called Coco. Non smoking inside residence.

Avondale - Auckland   *Self-contained B&B*   *10km W of Auckland Central*

Kodesh Community
Kodesh Trust
31B Cradock Street, Avondale, Auckland
Tel: (09) 828 5672 Fax: (09) 828 5684
Kodesh_Trust@free.net.nz
www.bnb.co.nz/kodeshcommunity.html
Double $55 Single $35 (Continental Breakfast)
Child $20 Dinner $8 Flat $60 - $80
2 Queen 1 Double 1 Twin 3 Single (2 bdrm)
2 Private 2 Family share

Kodesh is an ecumenical, cross cultural Christian community of around 25 residents, about 8 minutes by car from downtown Auckland. Guest rooms in a large modern home have full cooking facilities available, a self contained flat sleeps four. An evening meal is available in the community dining room Monday - Friday. Bookings essential. The atmosphere is relaxed and guests can amalgamate into the life of the community as much or little as desired. No smoking, no pets, children under 12 welcome in self contained unit.

Mangere Bridge - Auckland Airport   *Homestay*   *14km S of Auckland Central*

Mangere Bridge Homestay
Carol & Brian
146 Coronation Road,
Mangere Bridge, Auckland
Tel: (09) 636 6346 Fax: (09) 636 6345
www.bnb.co.nz/mangerebridgehomestay.html
Double $70 Single $45-$50 (Full Breakfast)
Child $20, 12 & under
Dinner $20 by prior arrangement Pet on property
2 Double 2 Single (3 bdrm)
1 Guests share 1 Family share

We invite you to share our home which is within 10 minutes of Auckland Airport, an ideal location for your arrival or departure of New Zealand. We enjoy meeting people and look forward to making your stay an enjoyable one. We welcome you to join us for dinner by prior arrangement. Courtesy car to or from airport, bus and rail. Off street parking available. Handy to public transport. Please no smoking indoors. Although we have a cat we request no pets. Inspection welcomed.

Mangere - Auckland *B&B* *4km from Airport*

Airport Pensione B&B
Gleny Phillips
1 Westney Rd,
Mangere, Auckland
Tel: (09) 275 0533 Fax: (09) 275 0533
Mob: 025 296 9329 airportbnb@paradise.net.nz
www.bnb.co.nz/airportpensionebb.html
Double $65-$80 Single $50 (Continental Breakfast)
Child $10 shared pp $25 Credit cards accepted
10 Double 8 Twin 8 Single (10 bdrm)
2 Ensuite 2 Private 3 Guests share 1 Family share

Friendly, comfortable, courtesy van from Airport. 24 hr free tea/coffee, large lounge/dining, fridge, TV, microwave, toilet/showers. Car storage and free luggage storage. Rental cars/vans and tours can be arranged. Handy to restaurants/take-aways/supermarkets. City bus 100 metres outside lodge. Double room with ensuite/TV with two adjoining rooms ideal for group or family, can sleep up to 11 people. Direct free phone at Airport Information No. 28 and we will transport you to our lodge in five minutes.

Mangere - Auckland Airport *Homestay B&B* *2km from Mangere*

Airport Homestay/B&B
May Pepperell
288 Kirkbride Road, Mangere, Auckland
Tel: (09) 275 6777 Fax: (09) 275 6728
Mob: 025 289 8200
www.bnb.co.nz/airporthomestay.html
Double $60 Single $40 (Continental Breakfast)
Child $15 Pet on property
3 Single (2 bdrm)
1 Guests share

Clean comfortable home five minutes from airport but not on flight path. Easy walk to shops and restaurants. Ten minutes from shopping centres and Rainbows End amusement park. Aviation golf course near airport, winery and Lakeside Convention Centre nearby. My interests are golf, travel, Ladies' Probus and voluntary work. Beds have woollen underlays and electric blankets. There is a sunny terrace and fenced swimming pool. Courtesy car to/from airport at reasonable hour. Vehicles minded while you're away from $1 day. One timid outdoors cat.

Mangere Bridge - Auckland Airport *16km S of Auckland Central*

B&B

Tudor House
Gill Whitehead
1 Banbury Place, Mangere Bridge, Auckland
Tel: (09) 634 3413 Fax: (09) 622 3238
Mob: 025 605 7257 gill.w@xtra.co.nz
www.bnb.co.nz/tudorhouse.html
Double $80 Single $50 (Full Breakfast) Child $30
Dinner $20 B/A King/Twin with ensuite $90
Credit cards accepted Pet on property
1 King/Twin 1 Queen 1 Single (3 bdrm) 1 Ensuite 1 Guests share

Enjoy breakfast overlooking the harbour/bird reserve from our comfy, peaceful, waterfront home just 10 mins drive from Auckland airport, shops, restaurants, and Villa Maria winery, but not on the flight path. Stroll along Kiwi Esplanade to local shops and takeaways. Amble up Mangere Mountain for a spectacular view. Visit Ambury park/farm. City bus stop across the road, take advantage of the $8 Auckland pass for buses and ferries. A cat and small dog are in residence. Airport courtesy car at a reasonable hour.

Mangere Bridge - Auckland Airport   *7.5km N of Auckland Airport*

Homestay B&B

Mountain View B&B
Ian & Jenny, and cat Oscar Davis
85A Wallace Road, Mangere Bridge, Auckland
Tel: (09) 636 6535 mtviewbb@xtra.co.nz
Fax: (09) 636 6126 www.bnb.co.nz/mountainviewbb.html
Double $75-$120 Single $55-$80 (Full Breakfast)
Child $20 Dinner b/a Credit cards accepted
1 King/Twin 4 Queen 1 Twin 2 Single (6 bdrm)
4 Ensuite 1 Guests share

8 minutes Auckland Airport, travel north on George Bolt Drive, left into Kirkbride Road, follow Kirkbride through to Wallace Road. Downtown Auckland and other attractions including Eden Park/Ericsson Stadium within 25 minutes drive. Restored Kauri Villa, quiet locality, off street parking, public transport at gate. Enjoy quality décor, expansive harbour views and delicious breakfasts. Friendly, hospitable NZ Hosts. Ian is building a Q2 aircraft. L&M Klima,USA recorded "Thanks for your generous hospitality, sound suggestions and lively conversations. Great B&B - Great Location - Great Hosts!

Otahuhu - Auckland   *B&B   17km S of Auckland*

Jerrine & Gerard Fecteau
70 Mangere Road,
Otahuhu, Auckland
Tel: (09) 276 9335 Fax: (09) 276 9235
oasisbb@xtra.co.nz
www.bnb.co.nz/fecteau.html
Double $60 Single $40 (Full Breakfast) Child neg
Dinner $20 Credit cards accepted Pet on property
Children welcome Pets welcome
1 Queen 1 Double 1 Twin (3 bdrm)
2 Guests share

We welcome you to the oasis in Otahuhu. We can help you plan your holiday route and rent a car. The motorways, train, bus and airport are minutes away. 70 is a rest stop before your long flights "home". We are collectors of amazing things, cactus, coins of the world, depression glassware, brass birds, Canadian art and a cat called Alice. Washing facilities available. Dinner by arrangement. Phone, fax or email to reserve. Our courtesy van will pick you up at the airport, train or bus.

Manukau - Auckland   *Homestay   6.5km NE of Manukau City*

Tanglewood
Roseanne & Ian Devereux
5 Inchinnam Road, Flat Bush, Auckland
Tel: (09) 274 8280 Fax: (09) 634 6896
tanglewood@clear.net.nz
www.bnb.co.nz/tanglewoodmanukau.html
Double $80-$90 Single $60 (Full Breakfast)
Child $10 Credit cards accepted Pet on property
1 Queen 1 Double 2 Single (3 bdrm)
1 Ensuite 1 Guests share

Our homely country cottage, set in two acres is close to the international airport. The garden loft is separate from the house with ensuite, TV, fridge, deck overlooking large peaceful gardens and ponds. Accommodation inside the house has its own bathroom. We are 30 minutes from downtown Auckland, close to bush walks, Regional Botanic gardens and restaurants. Delicious home cooked breakfast includes eggs from our free range hens. We have a swimming pool and a friendly dog 'Daisy'. We are non-smoking. Booking is essential.

Manurewa - Auckland   *Homestay*   *2km S of Manukau City*

Hillpark Homestay
Katrine & Graham Paton
16 Collie Street, Manurewa, Auckland 1702
Tel: (09) 267 6847 Fax: (09) 267 8718
Mob: 021 215 7974   hillpark.homestay@xtra.co.nz
www.bnb.co.nz/hillparkhomestay.html
Double $70 Single $50 (Full Breakfast) Child $20
Dinner $15 by arrangement Credit cards accepted
Pet on property Children welcome
1 Double 3 Single (3 bdrm) 1 Ensuite 1 Guests share

Welcome to our sunny, spacious home and meet our friendly Tonkinese cat. We are 15 minutes from Auckland Airport, 20 minutes from Auckland City Centre, by motorway, gateway to the route south and Pacific Coast Highway. Nearby are Manukau City Shopping Centre, Rainbow's End Adventure Park, restaurants, cinemas, souvenir shops, Community Arts Centre, Regional Botanic Gardens (Ellerslie Flowershow), and bush walks. Our interests include Red Cross, teaching, classical music, painting, gardening, photography, Christian interests, reading and travel. We're a smoke-free home.

Howick - Auckland   *Homestay B&B*   *1km NE of Howick*

Above the Beach
Max & Marjorie Fisher
141 Mellons Bay Road, Howick, Auckland
Tel: (09) 534 2245 Fax: (09) 534 2245
kea.nz@attglobal.net
www.bnb.co.nz/abovethebeach.html
Double $90-$110 Single $60 (Continental Breakfast)
Credit cards accepted
1 Queen 1 Double 2 Single (4 bdrm)
1 Ensuite 1 Private 1 Guests share

Relax with us 50 metres 'Above The Beach', Kauri trees and views across the gulf. Auckland: 16km by road, or 35 minute stressfree ferry ride. Airport: 25 minutes. Howick is a delightful village with 16 cafes and restaurants and historic church. Six beaches, two golf courses and ferry within 2 km radius. Feather duvets, electric blankets, heaters, easy chairs, fridge and TV for your convenience. Home away from home and super breakfasts. Directions: shuttle from airport. Please phone for directions. Easy walk to village.

Howick - Auckland   *Homestay B&B*   *1/2 k E of Howick*

Mellons Bay Lodge
June & Owen Williams
64 Mellons Bay Road, Howick, Auckland
Tel: (09) 535 0535 Fax: (09) 535 2713
Mob: 025 504 352   ojw@takeiteasy.co.nz
www.takeiteasy.co.nz
Double $105-$115 Single $80-$90
(Continental & Full Breakfast) Credit cards accepted
1 Queen 1 Double 1 Single (3 bdrm)
1 Private 1 Guests share

We offer warm relaxed hospitality in a charming setting with excellent facilities - your own sunny lounge, private bathroom, bathrobes, hairdryer, great breakfasts with homemade foods. Offstreet parking, laundry and office facilities. Only 30 min from CBD by local ferry or motorway (offpeak) and 20 min from airport. Short stroll to beach, lookout views, and Howick village with many restaurants, cafes, pubs, interesting shops. 10 min drive to 5 safe beaches, historic village, golf courses. We look forward to sharing our home and our company with you.

Beachlands   *Homestay B&B*   *25km E of Howick*

Enid & Terry Cripps
51 Wakelin Road,
Beachlands 1705
Tel: (09) 536 5546 Fax: (09) 536 5546
etcripps@slingshot.co.nz
www.bnb.co.nz/cripps.html
Double $90 Single $50 (Full Breakfast)
Dinner $25 by arrangement
1 Queen (1 bdrm)
1 Private

Enid and Terry offer you a warm welcome to the Marine Garden suburb of Beachlands which is situated on the East Coast, 40 km South East of Auckland City. Our converted cottage is only 3 minutes walk from the beach at Sunkist Bay, local shops and licensed restaurant. The Formosa Auckland Golf Course and Pine Harbour marina are 5 minutes drive away. We are both in our 60's, have travelled widely. Guest accommodation is a large upstairs bedroom with sitting area, TV and a shaded balcony facing the sea.   Shuttle bus from the Airport or phone for directions.

Beachlands - Pohutukawa Coast   *40 km SE of Auckland*

Self-contained Separate/Suite B&B
Beachlands Waterfront B&B
Barry & Suzi Keon
3 Pohutukawa Rd, Auckland
Tel: 09 536 5195 Fax: 09 536 5198
Mob: 025 508 091   barry.keon@clear.net.nz
www.beachlandsbungalow.com
Double $120 Single $100
(Continental & Full Breakfast) Credit cards accepted
2 Queen 1 Twin (3 bdrm)
1 Private 1 Guests share 1 Family share

Sensational north facing sea views, pool, fishing & ski boats, kayaks, sailing dinghy, rings & skis. Fabulous bush & coast walks, handy to international golf course, marina, restaurants. 15 min to largest & newest shopping centre, Botany Town centre, theatres & fun park. Only 40 minutes to the c.b.d, 25 mins by new fast ferry. 25 mins from international airport, 20 mins to polo & vineyards. Five star with exquisite furnishings. Sky t.v.secluded sandy beach & 5 others to choose from. Two free of charge award winning regional parks only minutes away .

Whitford   *Farmstay*   *25km SE of Auckland*

Springhill Country Homestay
Judy & Derek Stubbs
Polo Lane, Whitford, RD, Manurewa, Auckland
Tel: (09) 530 8674 Fax: (09) 530 8274
Mob: 021 251 2518   djstubbs@ihug.co.nz
www.bnb.co.nz/springhillfarmstay.html
Double $95 Single $70 (Full Breakfast)
Child $35 Dinner $30pp by arrangement
1 Queen 2 Single (2 bdrm)
1 Ensuite 1 Family share

Springhill is an 8 hectare farm in Whitford, an attractive rural area approximately 25km SE of Auckland. We are close to a beautiful golf course, beaches and Auckland Airport. We breed Angora goats and pets include a cat and a dog. We have a large comfortable home and spacious garden. Guest accommodation is one detached double room with ensuite, and 1 room with twin single beds. TV, tea & coffee making facilities,and a private spa pool are available. Directions: Left off Whitford Park Road. 1km past Golf Course.

Whitford   *Homestay   12km Howick*

Albertine
Averill & Bart Allsopp - Smith
298 Clifton Road, Whitford,
RD 1, Howick, Auckland
Tel: (09) 530 9441 Fax: (09) 530 9441
Mob: 021 974 119
albertinestay@xtra.co.nz
www.bnb.co.nz/albertine.html
Double $90 Single $65 (Full Breakfast)
Credit cards accepted
1 Double (1 bdrm) 1 Ensuite 1 Private

Enjoy a game of tennis on our peaceful rural five acre block. Wake up in your separate self-contained loft to the sound of the birds. We are 30 minutes from Auckland City and within 15 minutes. of cinemas, shopping, restaurants, cafes and craft shops. Nearby is a Marina where sailing/boating and fishing are available by arrangement. We are close to beaches, golf courses and polo ground, or you may prefer a quiet country walk. Unsuitable for children or animals.

Clevedon   *Homestay B&B   40km SE of Auckland*

Willowgrove
Sallie McDonald and David Hooper
764 Clevedon - Kawakawa Bay Road,
RD5 Clevedon, Papakura
Tel: (09) 292 8456 Fax: (09) 534 8465
Mob: 021 991 499
mcdonaldsm@paradise.net.nz
www.bnb.co.nz/willowgrove.html
Room Rate $90-$120 (Full Breakfast) Child 1/2 price
Dinner $25 Credit cards accepted Pet on property
2 Queen (2 bdrm) 2 Ensuite

Willowgrove is located near the rural village of Clevedon on the Pacific Coast Highway - just 40 mins from Central Auckland and the Airport (we are happy to pick-up at a small charge. The house is set in 2 acres of mature gardens, and a further 9 acres is established as an Olive Grove. We are close to beaches, golf and polo and enroute to the Coromandel. A warm hospitable welcome awaits you. Directions please phone.

Clevedon   *Homestay   7km E of Clevedon*

Fairfield Country Homestay
Christopher & Paddy Carl
Clevedon, RD 5, Papakura
Tel: (09) 292 8852 Fax: (09) 292 8631
carl.fairfield@xtra.co.nz
www.bnb.co.nz/fairfieldcountryhomestay.html
Double $135 Single $100 (Full Breakfast)
Dinner $40pp Credit cards accepted
1 Queen (1 bdrm)
1 Ensuite

Fairfield
COUNTRY HOME STAY

Our home is set in 14 acres with extensive rural views. Mangere Airport and Auckland City are 40 mins away. We offer a self contained bed/sitting room ensuite with TV, tea and coffee making facilities and private courtyard. There are beaches nearby along the Scenic Route to Coromandel. Locally polo, winery, horse riding, golf available. Paddy is involved in the fashion industry, Christopher is a retired naval officer. Kennel facilities available on site.

Clevedon   *Self-contained B&B*   *3km S of Clevedon Village*

The Gables
Phil & Cathy Foulkes
122 Tourist Road, Clevedon, RD 2 Papakura
Tel: (09) 292 8373 Fax: (09) 292 8629
Mob: 025 941 249 foulkes@xtra.co.nz
www.the-gables.co.nz

Double $120 ,Single $90 Child $20
(Continental & Full Breakfast) Dinner By arrangement
Additional person $20   Credit cards accepted
2 Queen 2 Double (2 bdrm)   2 Ensuite

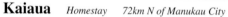

In 1988 Phil and Cathy Foulkes set out to create a dream country home and garden for themselves and their family. Tucked away in their garden are two self contained spacious cottage units where they invite guests to share their hospitality. Set on 10 acres, handy to Clevedon Village each cottage unit offers a queensize bedroom with ensuite, lounge/dining room with double bed settee, laundry and cooking facilities. Clevedon features green pastures, friendly people and old fashioned hospitality within 30 minutes drive from Auckland CBD and International Airport.

Kaiaua   *Homestay*   *72km N of Manukau City*

Corovista
Julia & Bob Bissett
1841B East Coast Road, Kaiaua, RD 3, Pokeno
Tel: (09) 232 2842 Fax: (09) 232 2862
Mob: 025 245 5269
www.bnb.co.nz/corovista.html

Double $65-$90 Single $40-$50 (Full Breakfast)
Child 1/2 price Dinner $30pp Credit cards accepted
1 King/Twin 1 Double (2 bdrm)
1 Guests share 1 Family share

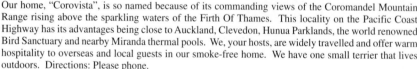

Our home, "Corovista", is so named because of its commanding views of the Coromandel Mountain Range rising above the sparkling waters of the Firth Of Thames. This locality on the Pacific Coast Highway has its advantages being close to Auckland, Clevedon, Hunua Parklands, the world renowned Bird Sanctuary and nearby Miranda thermal pools. We, your hosts, are widely travelled and offer warm hospitality to overseas and local guests in our smoke-free home. We have one small terrier that lives outdoors. Directions: Please phone.

Kaiaua   *B&B Lodge*   *85km SE of Auckland*

Kaiaua Seaside Lodge
Fran Joseph & Denis Martinovich
1336 Pacific Coast Highway, Kaiaua
Tel: (09) 232 2696 Fax: (09) 232 2699
Mob: 025 274 0534
kaiaua_lodge@xtra.co.nz
www.bnb.co.nz/kaiauaseasidelodge.html

Double $95-$110 Single $75 (Special Breakfast)
2 Queen 1 Double 2 Single (5 bdrm)
2 Ensuite 1 Guests share

Situated on the water's edge, 4km north of Kaiaua township, the Lodge has panoramic views of the Coromandel across the Firth of Thames. It is ideally positioned for leisurely seashore strolls or more active tramps in the Hunua Ranges. Boating and fishing facilities are available and breakfast includes flounder or snapper, in season. Ensuite rooms are spacious and the separate guest lounge has a refrigerator and television. The Seabird Coast is renowned for its birdlife, thermal hot pools, nearby Regional Parks and "fish 'n chips".

Papakura   *Homestay B&B Country stay   5km E of Papakura*

Hunua Gorge Country House
Joy, Ben & Amy Calway
482 Hunua Road, Papakura, South Auckland
Tel: (09) 299 9922 Fax: (09) 299 6932
Mob: 021 669 922   hunua-lodge@xtra.co.nz
www.friars.co.nz/hosts/hunua.html
Double $90-$120 (Full Breakfast)
Child depending on age Credit cards accepted
1 King 1 Queen 1 Double 2 Twin 5 Single (5 bdrm)
1 Ensuite 1 Private 1 Family share

Welcome to our wilderness on the doorstep of Auckland City. A great place to start or end your NZ holiday. Peace, tranquility, great food, magic sunsets, wild scenery, leafy greenery views, from all rooms. Large comfortable newly decorated home, verandas, lawns, garden, bush and rural setting on 50 acres with sheep, ponies, cattle, birdlife Stay a few days and discover the wonders of Auckland. Fresh food, fresh air, comfortable beds guaranteed. Please phone. Dinner from $25 or $35, 3 courses by prior arrangement. Pets and children welcome.

Papakura   *Homestay   1.5km W of Papakura*

Campbell Clan House
Colin & Anna Mieke Campbell
57 Rushgreen Ave, Papakura
Tel: (09) 298 8231 Fax: (09) 298 7792
Mob: 025 967 754   colam@pl.net
www.campbellclan.co.nz
Double $100-$110 Single $55-$65 (Full Breakfast)
Child Neg Dinner $25/$35 by arrangement
Credit cards accepted Children welcome
1 Queen 2 Single (2 bdrm)   1 Private 1 Family share

If you are looking for a peaceful location close enough to Auckland to visit city attractions (20 minutes) yet also handy to the airport (15 minutes) or motorway system (2 minutes) our family home will meet your requirements. Our upstairs guest bedrooms and lounge (with TV, library, fridge, tea/coffee facilities) open onto a private balcony overlooking Pahurehure Estuary Reserve. We are happy to assist with any holiday arrangements and offer fax, internet and laundry facilities. We offer a discounted rate for 3+ night bookings.

Hunua - Paparimu   *Self-contained Homestay   20mins S of Papakura*

Erathcrih Country Cottage
Rob & Gillian Wakelin
10 Wilson Road, Paparimu, RD 3, Papakura, Auckland
Tel: (09) 292 5062 Fax: (09) 292 5062
Mob: 021 128 1547   gillrob@xtra.co.nz
www.bnb.co.nz/erathcrihcountrycottage.html
Double $110 Single $80 (Continental Breakfast)
Child reduced rate Dinner $35 pp by arrangement
Additional person $30 (bed settee in lounge)
Credit cards accepted Pet on property
1 Queen 1 Double (2 bdrm)   1 Private

On clear summer nights, dine under incredibly bright stars - no city lights here - within easy reach of Auckland Airport and City, beaches, hotpools, walks in the bushclad Hunuas, and State Highway 2 for travel South. The self-contained cottage nestles peacefully under mature trees, a garden stroll from the main house. Guineafowl wander freely, eels cruise the stream, cattle graze the paddocks. We guarantee a warm, friendly welcome in our home, whether you eat a home-cooked meal with us or decide to self-cater.

Drury   *Homestay B&B   5km S of Drury*

Tuhimata Park
Susan & Pat Baker
697B Runciman Road, Runciman, RD 2, Drury
Tel: (09) 294 8748 Fax: (09) 294 8749
tuhimata@iprolink.co.nz
www.bnb.co.nz/tuhimatapark.html
Double $100-$110 Single $55-$70 (Full Breakfast)
Child neg Dinner $30 - $35 Credit cards accepted
Pet on property Children welcome
2 Double 2 Single (3 bdrm)
1 Ensuite 1 Private

Our spacious, comfortable, and relaxing home is an ideal place to start or finish a NZ holiday. Only 20 minutes from Auckland Airport and 30 minutes from the city centre. Set in expansive lawns and giant oak trees, with wide verandahs, overlooking rolling green farmland, indoor garden and BBQ in a large conservatory, tennis court, swimming pool, spa pool, and games room. 2 or 3 course dinners, including pre dinner drinks and nibbles, wine, and liqueurs with coffee. Laundry facilities. Pets - a family cat.

Drury   *Farmstay B&B   6km S of Drury*

Briardale
Archie & Sue McPherson
23 Maxted Road, Ramarama,
RD 3 Drury, Auckland
Tel: (09) 294 7417 Fax: (09) 238 7592
Mob: 025 736 313   sue.mcpherson@icn.co.nz
www.farmstay.net.nz
Double $100 Single $50 (Special Breakfast)
Child neg Dinner by arrangement
1 Queen 2 Twin 1 Single (3 bdrm)   2 Guests share

Warm country hospitality in a delightful country setting - the perfect start or end to your holiday. Stroll through the large garden,mingle with the hobby farm menagerie, soak in the hot spa or enjoy a candlelit supper and good company. A restful and private visit is guaranteed. Archie and Sue are seasoned travellers and have worked in the food and media industries for more than 30 years. Directions: Take Ramarama exit on southern motorway (airport 20 minutes), Maxted Road is third right on Ararimu side of motorway. Visit us at www.farmstay.net.nz

Drury   *Homestay B&B*   *3km E of Drury*

The Homestead
Carolyn & Ron Booker
349 Drury Hills Road,
RD 1, Drury 1750
Tel: (09) 294 9030 Fax: (09) 294 9035
www.bnb.co.nz/user90.html
Double $90 Single $60 (Full Breakfast)
Child negotiable Dinner $25 Pet on property
Children welcome
2 Queen (2 bdrm)
2 Ensuite

The Homestead is an early colonial home (1879) with an interesting history. Lovingly restored by Ron and Carolyn this character filled family home nestles on 15 acres with mature native bush and a tumbling stream creating a wonderful peaceful haven, only 30 mins from the centre of Auckland. Close to excellent restaurants or let us cook for you using the best of fresh local produce. Guest lounge and TV, laundry facilities. Family cat and dog. Please phone for directions. 20 mins to airport.

Drury   *Homestay*   *3km S of Papakura*

Southawk
Lynn Lockhart & Rod Campbell
249 Sutton Road, PO Box 203, Drury, Auckland
Tel: (09) 298 0670 Fax: (09) 298 0673
Mob: 021 354 024   southawk@xtra.co.nz
www.bnb.co.nz/southawk.html
Double $110 Single $70 (Full Breakfast)
Child neg Dinner $25 Credit cards accepted
2 Queen 1 Single (3 bdrm) 2 Private 1 Family share

Southawk is a secluded country home set in 10 acres with beautiful gardens, swimming pool an petanque. Only 25 mins from Auckland City; 20 mins from Auckland International Airport; 3 kilometres from the Southern Motorway. Close to all Auckland's most famous attractions. Join us for an evening meal or NZ style BBQ. Large modern guest bedrooms, own bathrooms and lounge with TV/music and tea/coffee facilities. Relax around the open fire in the winter and the pool in the summer. A warm welcome awaits you. We will be pleased to assist and advise on further travel arrangemants. Internet, fax & laundry facilities available.

Waiuku   *Homestay*   *5km E of Waiuku*

Totara Downs
Janet & Christopher de Tracy-Gould
Baldhill Road, RD 1,
Waiuku, South Auckland
Tel: (09) 235 8505 Fax: (09) 235 8504
Mob: 021 154 8713   totaradw@ihug.co.nz
www.totaradowns.co.nz
Double $120 Single $80 (Full Breakfast)
Credit cards accepted Pet on property
1 King/Twin 1 Queen (2 bdrm)
1 Ensuite 1 Private

Just 50 minutes drive from Auckland's International Airport and city, "Totara Downs" is found on a quiet country road. Set in large country house gardens with breath taking rural views. We offer feather and downs pillows and duvets, sitting room with open fire, swimming pool, lawn croquet. Historic Waiuku boasts wonderful peninsula beaches and country garden tours. With Flora our westie and two cats we look forward to meeting you. Not suitable for children under 12. Smoke free home.

Pukekohe - Waiuku   *Homestay plus self-contained*   *10km W of Pukekohe*

Deveron   Sally & Tony McWilliams
77 Sommerville Road, Patumahoe
Tel: (09) 236 3673 devmark@eudoramail.com
Tollfree: Aust. tel/fax 1800 126 077
Fax: (09) 236 3631   www.bnb.co.nz/deveron.html

Double $105 Single $85 (Full Breakfast)
Child $15 under 15 Dinner $30 by arrangement
Guest House $140, $25 extra adult Credit cards accepted
2 King/Twin 2 Queen 2 Single (4 bdrm)
1 Private 2 Guests share

We extend to you a warm invitation to relax with us at Deveron, our comfortable country home, set in 11 acres of beautiful native bush and extensive gardens. Guests' wing ensures peace and privacy. In addition we can offer our spacious, comfortable 2 bedroom guest apartment with large lounge and wood burning stove, fully equipped kitchen and laundry and deck with gas BBQ. Breakfast provisions are included. Weekly rates apply. Nearby are several golf courses, excellent restaurants, surf beaches, vintage railway and water gardens.

Pukekohe   *Homestay*

Nirvana B&B
Kevin & Maxine Sleyer
47 Calcutta Road, Pukekohe
Tel: (09) 238 8462 Fax: (09) 238 8462
Mob: 025 585 844   kev.max@ihug.co.nz
www.bnb.co.nz/nirvanabb.html

Double $95-$100 Single $65 (Special Breakfast)
Child neg. Dinner $25 pp by arrangement
Credit cards accepted Pets welcome
2 Queen 2 Single (3 bdrm)   2 Private

Where town meets country. A modern expansive family homestay in a picturesque, rural setting with magnificent views of Greater Auckland. Nirvana's friendly service complemented by its close proximity to the region's top facilities will ensure a memorable stay. Just 49km from the airport, your breakaway begins with our pick-up service. Soak in the spa, cool off in the pool, and enjoy a drink in the bar/ lounge before a delicious home-cooked meal. Nirvana is close to beaches, golf courses, shops, restaurants, Grand Prix/horse racing tracks.

Patumahoe - Pukekohe   *Farmstay*   *15km W of Pukekohe*

Willowbrook
Phillip Cassrels
63 Speedy Road, Patumahoe
Tel: (09) 236 4344 Fax: (09) 236 4343
Mob: 021 877 383   charityevents@xtra.co.nz
www.bnb.co.nz/willowbrookbb.html

Double $100-$120 Single $90 (Full Breakfast)
Dinner $30 Credit cards accepted Pet on property
Children welcome
1 Queen 1 Single (2 bdrm)   1 Private

Willowbrook commands sensational views through to Auckland, 50km away. Our two black labradors, Nelson and Tiki, will introduce you to the beef cattle on our 10-acre farmlet. We have a golf practice range, a practice bunker and pre-dinner drinks are served whilst playing Petanque! Access to lovely beaches, golf courses and tennis courts are only a few minutes away. The 'accomodation wing' continues the rural views and has its own private bathroom with bath and shower. Phillip and Clare have travelled extensively both in NZ and overseas and enjoy meeting new people.

Bombay - Auckland *B&B   Country Homestay   25min S of Airport*

Brookfield Lodge
Noreen & Ray Lee
State Highway 1, RD, Bombay
Tel: (09) 236 0775 Mob: 025 292 1422
Tollfree: 0800 37 75 80
mcvicarr@xtra.co.nz
www.bnb.co.nz/brookfieldlodge.html
Double $110 Single $80 (Full Breakfast)
Dinner $30 by arrangement
1 Queen 2 Single (2 bdrm)   1 Private

Easily accessed on the Southern Motorway 'Brookfield Lodge' is the perfect place to begin and end your holiday or for a weekend retreat. Relax and savour country cuisine and warm hospitality. The large gracious home is set in an extensive beautiful garden on a 5 acre property. Attractive bedrooms are adjacent to a Jacuzzi (spa) room. Enjoy wonderful breakfasts. Three course meals by arrangement. Restaurants nearby. Resident Labrador. From North: Pukekohe-Bombay exit. 50 metres into BP Centre. Brookfield access Rd beside McDonalds. 1 minute. From South: 1km past Beaver Rd.

Mercer *Farmstay Homestay Separate/Suite B&B   24km SE of Pukekohe*

Dorothy & Alan McIntyre
233 Koheroa Road,
Mercer
Tel: (09) 232 6837 Fax: (09) 232 6837
www.bnb.co.nz/mcintyre.html
Double $85 Single $50
(Full Breakfast) Child Neg
Dinner $20
1 Queen 1 Double (2 bdrm)
1 Private

We live on a cattle farm with a modern brick home. We have a large swimming pool surrounded by one acre of interesting garden. We are 3km off the main Auckland-Hamilton highway. Our views are panoramic. Very happy to provide dinner - alternative restaurants available. 30-40 minutes from Auckland Airport. Directions: Travel SH1 to Mercer. At Mercer do not enter Mobil Service Centre. Travelling from north turn left across railway line. Travelling from south turn right across railway line 3km up Koheroa Rd - meet Kellyville Rd - House visible on left.

The difference between a B&B and a hotel
is that you don't hug the hotel staff when you leave.

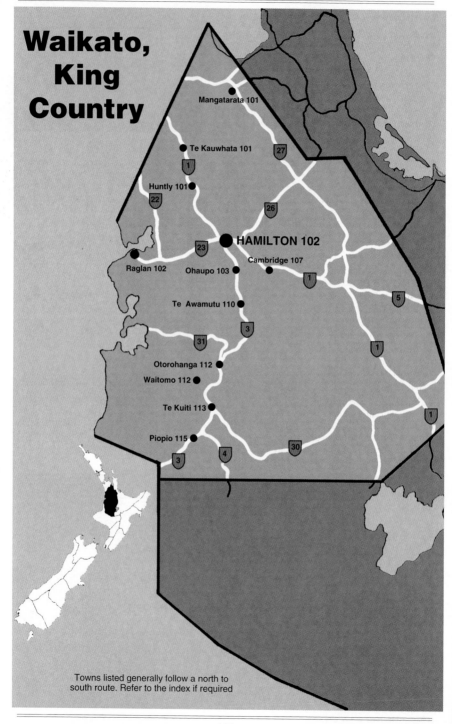

Waikato, King Country

Mangatarata 101

Te Kauwhata 101 — 27

1

Huntly 101
22

26

23 ● HAMILTON 102

Cambridge 107

Raglan 102   Ohaupo 103   1

Te Awamutu 110   5

3

31

Otorohanga 112
Waitomo 112

Te Kuiti 113   1

Piopio 115
30

3   4

Towns listed generally follow a north to
south route. Refer to the index if required

Mangatarata   *Farmstay   13km W of Ngatea*

Clark's Country Touch
Betty & Murray Clark
209 Highway 27, Mangatarata, RD 6, Thames
Tel: (07) 867 3070 Fax: (07) 867 3070
Mob: 021 808 992   bmclark@xtra.co.nz
www.bnb.co.nz/clarkscountrytouch.html
Double $65 Single $45 (Continental Breakfast)
Child Discount Dinner $15 Credit cards accepted
Pet on property Children welcome
1 King/Twin (1 bdrm) 1 Family share

Welcome to our beef farm with views of rolling pasture, bush and Coromandel ranges. Our sunny guestroom with TV, tea, coffee, cookies is opposite the bathroom. We are handy to the Hauraki Golf Course, Bowling Club, Seabird Coast, Miranda Hot Pools, Ngatea Gemstone Factory and Thames Coromandel coast. Our friendly dog Becky lives outside and our cat Watson shares our home. We are aged 50ish and enjoy handcrafts, gardening, four wheel driving and vintage machinery. Warm country hospitality awaits you. Non-smoking indoors.

Te Kauwhata   *Self-contained Farmstay   7km E of Te Kauwhata*

Herons Ridge
David Sharland
1131 Waikare Road, RD 1, Te Kauwhata
Tel: (07) 826 4646 Fax: (07) 826 4646
herons_ridge@xtra.co.nz
www.webnz.co.nz/bbnz/heron.htm
Double $80 Single $50 (Full Breakfast)
Child discount Dinner By arrangement
S/C studio $120 Pet on property Pets welcome
1 King 2 Queen 1 Double 1 Single (4 bdrm)
2 Ensuite 1 Private

Welcome to your home in the Waikato. Our farm and Horse Stud is the perfect setting for your first nights stay. Horses. Livestock, Pets, Ponds and Pinewoods enhance our rural location on Lake Waikare Scenic Drive. Our quality air conditioned Garden Studio gives the opportunity for self catering. Breakfast and Dinner are served in our dining room. For peace and quiet, country walks, honeymoon suite, golfing, horse riding, natural hot springs near by or our pool; the choice is yours.

Huntly   *Self-contained Farmstay   4km NW of Huntly*

Parnassus Farm & Garden
David & Sharon Payne
Te Ohaki Road, RD 1, Huntly
Tel: (07) 828 8781 Fax: (07) 828 8781
Mob: 021 458 525   parnassus@xtra.co.nz
www.bnb.co.nz/parnassus.html
Double $90 Single $45 (Full Breakfast)
Child According to age Dinner by arrangement
Credit cards accepted Pet on property
2 Double 4 Single (3 bdrm)
1 Private 1 Guests share 1 Family share

Parnassus offers you all the calm and beauty of the New Zealand countryside yet is only minutes off SH1. We are a working farm combining dairying, forestry, sheep and beef and have an extensive garden incorporating formal rose beds, woodland area, orchard, berry fruit courtyard and kitchen gardens. Children enjoy our delightful range of birds and small animals. We're easy to find, from SH1 cross Waikato River just south of Huntly township, right into Harris St 2km, right into Te Ohaki Road, 1.9 kms on LHS.

Raglan *Self-contained Farmstay   20km S of Raglan*

Matawha
Jenny & Peter Thomson
61 Matawha Road, RD 2, Raglan
Tel: (07) 825 6709 Fax: (07) 825 6715
Mob: 025 162 6405 jennyt@wave.co.nz
www.bnb.co.nz/matawha.html
Double $60-$80 Single $30-$40 (Full Breakfast)
Dinner $20
1 Double 4 Single (2 bdrm)
1 Private 1 Family share

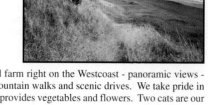

We are fortunate to have our own private beach and farm right on the Westcoast - panoramic views - providing surfing, fishing, hanggliding, bush and mountain walks and scenic drives. We take pride in farming this land for over 100 years. A large garden provides vegetables and flowers. Two cats are our resident pets. Seperate studio and spa. Directions: Take Hamilton/Raglan Rd route 23. Turn off at Kauroa/Bridal Veil Falls - turn R) at Te Mata into Ruapuke Rd, Turn L) into Tutu Rimu Rd follow to junction and our entrance 61 on cattlestop and name on letterbox.

Hamilton *Homestay   3km N of Hamilton*

Kantara
Mrs Esther Kelly
7 Delamare Road,
Bryant Park, Hamilton
Tel: (07) 849 2070 Mob: 025 263 9442
esther@enlighten.co.nz
www.bnb.co.nz/kelly.html
Double $80 Single $55 (Continental Breakfast)
Dinner $20 Credit cards accepted
2 Single (1 bdrm)   1 Private

I have travelled extensively throughout New Zealand and overseas and welcome tourists to my comfortable home. I live close to the Waikato River with its tranquil river walks and St Andrews Golf Course. My interests are travel, golf, tramping, Mah Jong and gardening. A member of NZ Association Farm & Home Hosts and Probus. I look forward to offering you friendly hospitality. Directions: From Auckland - leave main Highway north of Hamilton at 2nd round intersection into Bryant Road. Turn left into Sandwich Road and 2nd street on right.

Hamilton *Homestay B&B   1.5km E of Hamilton Central*

Matthews B&B
Maureen & Graeme Matthews
24 Pearson Avenue, Claudelands, Hamilton
Tel: (07) 855 4269 Fax: (07) 855 4269
Mob: 025 747 758
mgm@xtra.co.nz
www.bnb.co.nz/matthews.html
Double $65 Single $45 (Full Breakfast)
Child 1/2 price Dinner $20 Credit cards accepted
Pet on property
3 Single (2 bdrm)   1 Guests share 1 Family share

Welcome to our home two seconds off the city bypass on Routes 7 and 9 at Five Crossroads. We are adjacent to the showgrounds, Ruakura Research Station and handy to the university and only three minutes from central city. Our home is a 'lived-in' comfortable home, warm in winter and cool in summer, with a pool available. We enjoy spending time with visitors from NZ and overseas . We have travelled extensively and enjoy helping to plan your holiday. Dinner by arrangement.

Hamilton *Homestay B&B*

Glenys & John Ebbett
162 Beerescourt Rd,
Hamilton
Tel: (07) 849 2005 Fax: (07) 849 8405
johnebbett@xtra.co.nz
www.bnb.co.nz/ebbett.html
Double $80 Single $55
(Full Breakfast) Dinner $20
2 Single (1 bdrm)
1 Private

Only minutes from town centre, our ten year old home has a spectacular view of the Waikato River - New Zealand's longest. We travel extensively and love sharing travel anecdotes, but also respect our guests privacy. Your room has its own tea/coffee facility and private bathroom. Eighty-five minutes from Auckland International Airport appeals to tourists arriving or departing New Zealand. Our interests include gardening, music, sport, travel and people. We don't have young children or pets, and are smoke free. Full breakfast available.

WAIKATO

Hamilton *Homestay* *Hamilton Central*

Judy & Brian Dixon
50A Queenwood Avenue,
Chartwell, Hamilton
Tel: (07) 855 7324
jdixon@voyager.co.nz
www.opotiki2.co.nz/waiotahi
Double $65 Single $45
(Continental Breakfast)
2 Single (1 bdrm)
1 Private

Haere mai - Welcome to our comfortable smoke free, homely Lockwood nestled within a quiet garden. Guests have sole access to their bathroom and bedroom. Our aim is to provide a warm environment where guests relax and enjoy themselves. Within walking distance are popular "Cafe en Q", "The Platter Place". Chartwell Square and Waikato River walks. We also have a beach home with magnificent sea views near Opotiki if requested. We share our home with a friendly cat named Zapper. Directions: please phone.

Hamilton - Ohaupo *Homestay B&B* *4km SW of Hamilton*

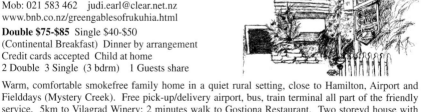

Green Gables of Rukuhia
Earl & Judi McWhirter
35 Rukuhia Road, RD 2, Ohaupo
Tel: (07) 843 8511 Fax: (07) 843 8514
Mob: 021 583 462   judi.earl@clear.net.nz
www.bnb.co.nz/greengablesofrukuhia.html
Double $75-$85 Single $40-$50
(Continental Breakfast) Dinner by arrangement
Credit cards accepted Child at home
2 Double 3 Single (3 bdrm)   1 Guests share

Warm, comfortable smokefree family home in a quiet rural setting, close to Hamilton, Airport and Fielddays (Mystery Creek). Free pick-up/delivery airport, bus, train terminal all part of the friendly service. 5km to Vilagrad Winery; 2 minutes walk to Gostiona Restaurant. Two storeyd house with guest rooms, lounge downstairs; dining, hosts upstairs. Fresh home baked bread and selection of coffees to suit. Judi lectures statistics, University of Waikato. Earl is a "retired" school teacher. One daughter still lives at home. Non-smokers preferred.

Hamilton *Homestay Home & Garden* *4km S of Hamilton*

The Poplars
Lesley & Peter Ramsay
402 Matangi Road, RD 4, Hamilton
Tel: (07) 829 5551 Mob: 025 668 0985
ramsay@waikato.ac.nz
www.bnb.co.nz/thepoplars.html
Double $90 Single $65 (Full Breakfast)
Dinner $25pp by arrangement
Credit cards accepted Pet on property
1 King 2 Single (2 bdrm) 1 Private

Just minutes from Hamilton, Mystery Creek and Cambridge, The Poplars offers a haven of peace and quiet. Set in a majestic three acre garden with internationally acclaimed daffodils, 800 roses and many water features. Each guest room has tea and coffee making facilities, electric blankets and TV. Solar heated swimming pool and spa are adjacent to guest rooms. Hosts Peter and Lesley, themselves seasoned travellers, offer you the charms of country living. A warm welcome shared with family pets awaits you. A unique and special place to stay. Directions: Please phone.

Hamilton *Farmstay Homestay B&B Farmlet* *6km S of Hamilton*

PORT Williams
Roger & Pat Williams
Pencarrow Road, Tamahere, RD 3, Hamilton
Tel: (07) 856 2499 Fax: (07) 856 2499
Mob: 025 261 1959 port.williams@clear.net.nz
www.bnb.co.nz/portwilliams.html
Double $115 Single $75 (Continental Breakfast)
Dinner by arrangement Queen (ensuite) $110
Credit cards accepted
1 Queen 1 Double 1 Twin 1 Single (2 bdrm) 2 Ensuite

Come and join us in our Mediterranean-style Villa, placed for maximum sunshine in a landscaped garden with goats and sheep grazing the gully below. We are a friendly couple and now our family have left home, we wish to share our new surroundings. Having travelled extensively, we understand the importance of hospitality. See our many art and craft interests on display. Our 5 acre farmlet is conveniently 3kms from Hamilton Airport, Mystery Creek and just off SH1. Enjoy tranquillity and glorious sunsets. Please ring for directions.

Hamilton - Lake Rotokauri *4km NW of Hamilton*

Self-contained Country Gardenstay
Cathy & David Dewes
Exelby Rd, Hamilton
Tel: (07) 849 9020 Fax: (07) 849 9020
Mob: 025 202 1978
dcdewes@xtra.co.nz
www.bnb.co.nz/dewes.html
Double $120 Single $90 (Special Breakfast)
Credit cards accepted
1 Queen (1 bdrm) 1 Ensuite

Our home is nestled in 3 acres of garden, offering privacy and relaxation. Enjoy magnificent views of Lake Rotokauri and Mt. Pirongia from our upstairs guest rooms where there is a kitchen, lounge and dining area. Our special self-serve breakfast is full of homemade treats. Soak in the hydrotherapy spa or relax having a professional therapeutic massage (available by appointment). We, with our children are keen outdoors people and can direct you to local attractions ... the Hamilton zoo with its famous 'free flight' sanctuary is just 2 minutes away. Please phone for reservations and directions.

Hamilton   *Homestay B&B   Hamilton Central*

Hillcrest Heights Homestay B&B
Barbara & Tony
54 Hillcrest Road, Hillcrest, Hamilton
Tel: (07) 856 4818 Fax: (07) 856 4831
Mob: 025 226 7386   hillcrest.bb@clear.net.nz
home.clear.net.nz/pages/hillcrest.bb/index.html.

Double $75-$85 Single $55-$65
(Continental Breakfast) Child $15
Dinner $20 by arrangement Pet on property
4 Queen 4 Single (4 bdrm) 2 Ensuite 1 Guests share

We extend a warm welcome to all visitors. Our home is spacious, clean and comfortable with views over Hamilton City. Quality accommodation in a friendly, relaxed environment. Off street parking, complimentary tea and coffee, laundry facilities, gym equipment and swimming pool. Great breakfast guaranteed. Dinner provided by arrangement. On city bus route. Free transport to and from local airport, bus and train stations. Waikato University, Hamilton gardens, river walks, cafes, restaurants and bars minutes away. Our children have flown the nest but Turbo the cat remains.

Hamilton - Tamahere   *B&B   10km S of Hamilton*

Lenvor B&B
Lenora & Trevor Shelley
540E Oaklea Lane, RD 3, Tamahere, Hamilton
Tel: (07) 856 2027 Fax: (07) 856 4173
lenvor@clear.net.nz
www.bnb.co.nz/lenvorbb.html

Double $100 Single $50 (Full Breakfast) Child $25
Dinner by arrangement Children welcome
2 Queen 1 Twin 1 Single (4 bdrm)
1 Ensuite 1 Guests share 1 Family share

Lenora and Trevor warmly invite you to relax and to share the comfort of our smoke free home "Lenvor", which is set in a rural area, down a country lane. Our two storeyed home has guest rooms, small lounge upstairs; dining, lounge, hosts, downstairs. 10 minutes to Hamilton or Cambridge; 5 minutes to Mystery Creek or airport. Lenora's interests are floral art and cake icing. Trevor enjoys vintage cars. Breakfast includes cereals, home made jams, preserved fruits, bacon and eggs.

Hamilton   *Homestay B&B   28km S of Hamilton*

Country Quarters Homestay
Ngaere & Jack Waite
No 11 Corcoran Road,
Te Pahu, Hamilton
Tel: (07) 825 9727 graeme.waite@xtra.co.nz
www.bnb.co.nz/countryquartershomestay.html

Double $80 Single $40 (Full Breakfast) Child $10
Dinner $20 Caravan $15 Pet on property
Children welcome Pets welcome
1 Queen 1 Twin 3 Single (5 bdrm)
1 Guests share

We welcome you to the peace and tranquillity of country life. Our place is central from Te Awamutu and Hamilton and are located in the little farming community of Te Pahu, right under Mount Pirongia. We are in the middle of a block of Chestnut trees and are quite secluded. We have our small dog and two fat cats. Our home is very large and roomy and we have special facilities for the elderly person. Comfort and nice meals is what we offer you.

Hamilton *B&B 0.5 E of Hamilton Central*

Sefton
Jan Short
213B River Road, Hamilton
Tel: (07) 855 9046 Fax: (07) 855 9041
Mob: 025 221 4681 jshort@xtra.co.nz
www.bnb.co.nz/sefton.html
Double $100 Single $50 (Continental Breakfast)
Pet on property
1 Queen 1 Single (2 bdrm) 1 Guests share

Stay and enjoy Sefton where you can expect a warm and friendly welcome, a comfortable room, a tasty breakfast, easy off-street parking and more. From Sefton, you can enjoy views of the river or the lights as you stroll across the Claudelands Bridge direct to Hamilton's centre for great coffee and food at a wide variety of cafes and restaurants. Or, choose to explore the peaceful river walks through nearby park ans gardens. Sefton is close to so much of Hamilton. Come and enjoy.

Hamilton *Self-contained Country Cottage* *10km E of Hamilton*

A&A Country Stay
Ann & Alan Marsh
275 Vaile Road, RD 4, Hamilton
Tel: (07) 824 1908 Fax: (07) 824 1908
Mob: 025 763 014
aacountrystay@xtra.co.nz
www.bnb.co.nz/aacountrystay.html
Double $90 Single $60 (Continental & Full Breakfast)
Child neg. Dinner $20pp $15 Extra Person
Credit cards accepted
1 Queen 1 Double 2 Single (2 bdrm) 1 Private

Welcome to "THE COTTAGE". We offer a self-contained cottage with cooking facilities, laundry, sky digital and phone. Set in 2 acres of garden just a few metres away from our home giving you peace and privacy. Overlooking our 47 acres with herefords and suffolk sheep. We are close to all amenities,just 10 minutes from Hamilton Central, 5 minutes from shopping centre. We welcome long term stayers, so come and enjoy your stay in our relaxed and informal surroundings. Please phone for directions.

Hamilton - Ohaupo *B&B* *15km S of Hamilton*

Ridge House
Joy and Patrick Trail
15 Main Rd, Ohaupo
Tel: 07 823 6555 Fax: 07 823 6550
Mob: 025 206 5154 joyandpatrick@xtra.co.nz
www.bnb.co.nz/ridgehousebnb.html
Double $70-$80 Single $60-$70
(Continental Breakfast) Child $15 Dinner $20
Credit cards accepted Pet on property Pets welcome
1 Queen 2 Double 1 Twin 1 Single (4 bdrm)
2 Guests share

Relax and enjoy the warm atmosphere of our home with lake and pastoral views as far as the eye can see. An ideal base for days trips to Hamilton, Cambridge, Waitomo Caves, Rotorua and Tauranga. 6 mins to Hamilton International Airport and Mystery Creek (home of the Fieldays). We share our home with a small dog named Blake and a cat named Blaze. We look forward to meeting you and sharing our home with you. A home away from home. Safe and happy travelling.

Hamilton   *Homestay B&B*

Kinnear Cottage
Heather & Graham Campbell
467 River Road, Hamilton
Tel: (07) 855 1832 Fax: (07) 855 1824
Mob: 021 781 429   pineapplelump@xtra.co.nz
www.bnb.co.nz/kinnearcottage.html
Double $110 Single $80 (Continental & Full Breakfast)
Dinner by arrangement Pet on property
1 Queen 2 Single (2 bdrm) 1 Ensuite 1 Guests share

WAIKATO

Kinnear Cottage overlooking the Waikato River offers character, colour, art, warmth, good food and good company. Upstairs spacious double suite with private balcony, views of flowing water, willows, reflections, ducks, and rowers. Only minutes from town centre, walk riverbank paths, canoes and bicycles available. Hosts - Graham (ex-boarding house master, teacher of history and English, now in school management) and Heather (ex-physiotherapist now artist exhibiting watercolours in Venice) have travelled widely, love history, art, books, sport, meeting fellow travellers and sometimes gardening. Oliver Twist is resident cat.

Hamilton   *Self-contained B&B   3km City Centre*

Las Palmas
Caroline & Malcolm Baigent
16a Acacia Cres, Hamilton,
Tel: (07) 843 3769 Fax: (07) 843 3242
Mob: 025 275 5200   las_palmas2002@hotmail.com
www.bnb.co.nz/laspalmas.html
Double $135 Single $115 (Special Breakfast)
Child $20 Dinner $30 Queen rooms $80
Credit cards accepted Pet on property
Children welcome Pets welcome
1 King/Twin 2 Queen (3 bdrm)
1 Ensuite 1 Guests share

We extend a warm welcome to our home set in a beautiful quiet country setting right on the city boundary. We have 3.5 acres of parklike grounds to walk around, hit a golf ball or have a game of petanque. Enjoy the heated swimming pool in the summer and the spa in the winter. Also our 'library' or listen to music. Transfers available to or from the airport (10 mins) and dinner by arrangement.

Cambridge   *B&B   Cambridge Central*

Park House
Pat & Bill Hargreaves
70 Queen Street, Cambridge
Tel: (07) 827 6368 Fax: (07) 827 4094
Park.House@xtra.co.nz
www.parkhouse.co.nz
Double $160 Single $120 (Full Breakfast)
Credit cards accepted
1 King/Twin 1 Queen (2 bdrm)
1 Ensuite 1 Private

Park House, circa 1920, is for guests of discernment who appreciate quality and comfort. For 15 years we have offered this superb setting for guests. Throughout this large home are antiques, traditional furniture, patchworks and stained glass windows creating an elegant and restful ambience. The guest lounge features an elaborately carved fireplace, fine art, library, TV and complimentary sherry. Bedrooms in separate wing upstairs ensues privacy. Unbeatable quiet location overlooking village green, 2 minute walk to restaurants, antique and craft shops. Member of Heritage Inns.

Cambridge *Farmstay Separate/Suite B&B* *5km SW of Cambridge*

Birches
Sheri Mitchell & Hugh Jellie
263 Maungatautari Road, PO Box 194, Cambridge
Tel: (07) 827 6556 Fax: (07) 827 3552
Mob: 021 882 216 birches@ihug.co.nz
birches.cambridge.net.nz

Double $95 Single $60 (Special Breakfast)
Child by arrangement Dinner by arrangement
Credit cards accepted Child at home Pet on property
1 Queen 1 Double 1 Single (2 bdrm) 1 Ensuite 1 Private

Our 1930's character farmhouse offers open fires in guests' sitting room, tennis and swimming pool set in country garden amongst picturesque horse studs. Proximity to Cambridge and Lake Karapiro makes Birches an ideal base for lake users. Hugh, a veterinarian, and I are widely travelled. Olivia, 10, is happy to show her farm pets and cat. Little Cherry Tree cottage (queen/ensuite) is ideal for couples wanting privacy. The twin room in farmhouse has private bathroom with spabath. We serve delicious farmhouse breakfasts alfresco or in dining room.

Cambridge *Homestay B&B* *Cambridge Central*

White's Homestay
Diane & Paul White
7 Marlowe Drive, Cambridge
Tel: (07) 823 2142 Fax: (07) 823 2143
Mob: 025 963 224
www.bnb.co.nz/whiteshomestay.html

Double $85 Single $55 (Full Breakfast) Child n/a
Dinner by arrangement Credit cards accepted
2 Queen (2 bdrm)
2 Ensuite

We look forward to welcoming you to our centrally located spacious comfortable home near the Waikato River. Guestrooms have TVs, tea/coffee making facilities and ensuite bathrooms. A guest lounge/library/music room is available for guests wanting privacy or join us in our lounge for coffee, a glass of wine or a chat. Easy to find, peaceful and tranquil location. Directions: cross bridge at south end of Victoria Street (main street) turn right off bridge, Marlowe Drive is first on right.

Cambridge *B&B* *5min walk Cambridge*

Hansel & Gretels B&B
Debbie Worth
58 Hamilton Road, Cambridge
On the corner of Hamilton Road and Bryce Street
Tel: (07) 827 8476 Fax: (07) 827 8476
Mob: 027 453 7928 HanselGretel@hotmail.com
www.bnb.co.nz/hanselgretelsbb.html

Double $90 Single $75 (Continental Breakfast)
Credit cards accepted Pet on property
Children welcome Pets welcome Smoking area inside
1 Queen 1 Double 2 Single (3 bdrm) 2 Private

Wanting home comfort and privacy or want to chat you will find it here. Located 5 minutes from the town centre, restaurants, antique and gift shops, harness racing and golf club.This is the centre of the thoroughbred horse industry (horse studs 5 min drive). Daily leisurely drives to Waitomo Caves 40 mins, Rotorua 55 mins, Hamilton Field Days 10 mins, Lake Karapiro 10 mins and a host of other interesting drives and walks. We're happy to pick you up from the bus stop or Hamilton Airport.

Cambridge   *Homestay B&B   2km N of Cambridge*

Glenelg
Ken & Shirley Geary
6 Curnow Place, Leamington, Cambridge
Tel: (07) 823 0084 Fax: (07) 823 4279
glenelgbedbreakfastnz@hotmail.com
www.bnb.co.nz/glenelg.html
Double $100 Single $65
(Continental & Full Breakfast) Child $20
Dinner $20 by arrangement Credit cards accepted
3 Queen 1 Twin (4 bdrm) 3 Ensuite 1 Private

Glenelg welcomes you to Cambridge to a new home with quality spacious accommodation - warm quiet and private overlooking Waikato Farmland, with plenty of off street parking. Beds have electric blankets and woolrests. 200 Rose bushes in the garden. 5 Mins to Lake Karapiro. Mystery Creek where NZ National Field Days and many other functions are held is only 15 mins away. Sky TV, laundry facilities available. No smoking indoors please. "Home away from Home". For a brochure and directions please phone. Evening dinner by arrangement.

Cambridge   *B&B Countrystay   10km S of Cambridge*

Dunfarmin
Jackie & Bob Clarke
55 Gorton Road, RD 2, Cambridge
Tel: (07) 827 7727 Fax: (07) 823 3357
Mob: 025 611 5247   dunfarmin@wave.co.nz
www.bnb.co.nz/dunfarmin.html
Double $90 Single $50 (Full Breakfast) Child $25
Dinner $25 by arrangement Credit cards accepted
1 Queen 1 Double 3 Single (3 bdrm)
1 Ensuite 1 Guests share

Welcome to our country home, situated just off State Highway One. Positioned on a commanding knoll, 20 acres sheltered by mature trees offering the weary traveller peace and tranquillity. The outlook from the spacious home provide panoramic views of the surrounding Waikato countryside. We have an inground swimming pool and floodlit tennis court. Five minutes to Lake Karapiro, twenty minutes to Mystery Creek. Within one hours drive to Tauranga, Rotorua , Waitomo Caves. Please feel at home with us, farm animals and Possum the cat.

Cambridge   *Self-contained B&B   2km S of Cambridge*

Pamade B&B
Paul & Marion Derikx
229 Shakespeare Street, Leamington
Tel: (07) 827 4916 Fax: (07) 827 4988
Mob: 021 261 7122   pamades@hotmail.com
www.bnb.co.nz/pamade.html
Double $70-$90 Single $50-$60 (Special Breakfast)
Dinner By Arrangement
1 King/Twin 1 King 1 Queen
1 Double 2 Single (3 bdrm) 2 Ensuite 1 Private

Pamade is a character home, very comfortable with beautiful gardens. We are situated 2 minutes from central Cambridge with its wonderful selection of fascinating Art, Craft, Boutique and Antique Shops, Restaurants, Stud Farms and Golf Course. Just around the corner from Lake Karapiro (5 minutes drive), with its water-skiing, rowing and other aquatic sports. Mystery Creek (Fieldays) is only 10 minutes drive away. Self contained unit plus large double room (ensuite and coffee and tea arrangements) with private exit. Ideal for longer stays. Great breakfast guaranteed.

Cambridge   *Self-contained B&B*   *1km Cambridge central*

Clanfield House
Wayne Good & Raymond Parker
155 Victoria Street, Cambridge,
Tel: (07) 823 2018 Fax: (07) 823 1412
Mob: 027 485 6016
wayne.good@xtra.co.nz
www.findus.co.nz/clanfieldhouse
Double $100-$125 Single $100
(Continental Breakfast) Credit cards accepted
Pet on property
1 Double (1 bdrm) 1 Ensuite

Clanfield House, circa 1900, is a beautifully restored Victorian Villa in the heart of Cambridge. We offer delightfully decorated, separate accommodation with ensuite facilities, and a courtyard with private Spa Pool, in peaceful surroundings. All your breakfast provisions are left in your room, to enjoy at your leisure. Our home makes an ideal base for visiting the surrounding countryside. We look forward to making you welcome.

Cambridge   *Homestay*   *5 NE of Cambridge*

Gainsborough House
Julie and Michael Thorpe
1-103 Maungakawa Road, RD 4, Cambridge
Tel: +64 7 823 2473 Fax: +64 7 823 1678
GainsboroughHouse@xtra.co.nz
www.gainsboroughhouse.co.nz
Double $120-$150 Single $90
(Continental & Full Breakfast) Dinner By arrangement
Credit cards accepted Pet on property
1 King 1 Double 1 Twin (3 bdrm) 3 Ensuite

Country House Living with Style: elegant, superior accommodation in a peaceful rural setting near Cambridge, in stunning gardens and furnished with quality artwork and antiques (many available for sale in our adjacent interior design studio). Stroll through our gardens and neighbouring farmland, or relax with a book in our library. With Thomas Gainsborough Esq the cat we offer a haven for jet-lagged travelers: we are only 90 min from Auckland Airport, and are within easy reach of many of NZ's major tourist attractions.

Te Awamutu   *Farmstay Guesthouse*   *4.5km N of Te Awamutu*

Mrs R Bleskie & C Bleskie
Storey Road, Te Awamutu
Tel: (07) 871 3301
www.bnb.co.nz/bleskie.html
Double $115 Single $60 (Full Breakfast)
Child $25 Dinner $25
Children welcome Pets welcome
1 Double 8 Single (5 bdrm)
1 Ensuite 1 Guests share 1 Family share

The 85 acre farm, situated in beautiful country side with cattle, horses, pigs, poultry, sheep, goats and pets. A spacious home welcomes you with swimming pool and tennis court. Large guest rooms with doors to garden. Specials: Horseback riding and gig rides for children and adults for $10 a ride. Raspberry picking in season and access to the milking of 500 dairy cows.

Te Awamutu   *Farmstay B&B*   *2km S of Te Awamutu*

Leger Farm
Beverley & Peter Bryant
114 St Leger Rd,
Te Awamutu

Tel: (07) 871 6676 Fax: (07) 871 6679
www.bnb.co.nz/legerfarm.html

Double $125 Single $85
(Full Breakfast) Dinner $30
1 Queen 1 Double 1 Twin 3 Single (4 bdrm)
1 Ensuite 1 Private 1 Guests share

'Leger Farm' is a private residence with country living at its finest. The discerning leisure traveller seeking quality accommodation, in peaceful, relaxing surroundings, will find warm hospitality and every comfort here. Spacious bedrooms share stunning panoramic views of surrounding countryside. Each bedroom has its own balcony with beautiful garden vistas. We farm cattle and sheep, and are centrally based for visiting Waitomo Caves and black water rafting, Rotorua with its thermal activity and NZ's dramatic West Coast and ironstone sands. Golf course nearby. Smoke free home.

WAIKATO

Te Awamutu   *Homestay B&B*   *4km S of Te Awamutu*

Morton Homestay
Marg and Dick Morton
10 Brill Road,
RD 5, Te Awamutu

Tel: (07) 871 8814 Fax: (07) 871 8865
www.bnb.co.nz/mortonhomestay.html

Double $75 Single $45 (Full Breakfast)
Dinner $20 Credit cards accepted
1 Double 2 Single (2 bdrm)
1 Private

We welcome visitors to enjoy our hospitality and the peacefulness of our home 5 minutes from the centre of New Zealand's "Rosetown". Waitomo, Rotorua and Lake Taupo are within easy driving distance from us. Hamilton airport and Mystery creek are 20 minutes away. Te Awamutu is an excellent base for bushwalking, golfing, fishing and garden visits. Gardening, philately and woodturning are among our interests. Prior notice for dinner, would be appreciated. Direction. Please phone or fax for reservations and directions.

Te Awamutu   *Farmstay*   *19km SE of Te Awamutu*

Poplar Ridge Farm
Ross & Valda Sutton
1614 Arapuni Road, Parawera,
RD 2, Te Awamutu

Tel: (07) 872 7958 Mob: 025 677 4032
poplar.ridge@xtra.co.nz
www.fairfieldintermediate.school.nz/poplar.ridge/index.html

Double $95 Single $60 (Full Breakfast)
Child 1/2 price Dinner $25
1 Twin 1 Single (2 bdrm)
1 Guests share

Poplar Ridge Farm is a 24 hectare block in the middle of the lush Waikato. It is a maize and beef farm. There are panoramic views and spectacular sunsets. We have traditional gardens with colour all year and in winter lots of native birdlife. Our home has recently been totally refurbished and reflects our passion for NZ art, Persian rugs and English china. See our own toy museum or trout fish twelve minutes away. Rotorua and Waitomo Caves are just sixty minutes. We have two cats and one dog.

Te Awamutu   *Homestay*   *2.5km N of Te Awamutu Post Office*

Tregamere
Bev & Chris Johnson
2025 Ohaupo Road, Te Awamutu 2400
Tel: (07) 870 1950 Fax: (07) 870 1952
Mob: 025 291 3162
c.b.john@xtra.co.nz
www.bnb.co.nz/tregamere.html

Double $100 Single $80 (Full Breakfast) Child $30
Dinner $35 Campervans $30 Credit cards accepted
1 Queen 3 Single (2 bdrm)
1 Ensuite 1 Guests share

A warm welcome awaits you at Tregamere, where you'll share our large, well-appointed home, and slumber in comfort. Enjoy fabulous sunsets over Mt Pirongia, savour our lush garden, explore the impressive Kahikatea stand, or amuse yourself in the games room. Set in tranquil surroundings on Te Awamutu's northern boundary, our central location is great for exploring - west coast beaches, the renowned Waitomo Caves, Hamilton and Rotorua are all within an easy drive.

Otorohanga - Waitomo District   *8km NW of Otorohanga*

Self-contained Farmstay B&B
Meadowland
Jill & Tony Webber
746 State Highway 31, RD 3, Otorohanga
Tel: (07) 873 7729 Fax: (07) 873 7719
Tollfree: 0800 687 262   meadowland@xtra.co.nz
www.bnb.co.nz/meadowland.html

Double $75 Single $50 (Full Breakfast) Child $20
Credit cards accepted Children welcome
2 Queen 1 Double 1 Twin 2 Single (5 bdrm)
1 Private 1 Guests share

Welcome to Meadowland, on State Highway 31, on the right hand side at the top of the second hill. Our accommodation is: a self-contained unit which can sleep up to six. One twin and two double bedrooms in homestead with guest shared bathroom and separate toilet. All beds have woolrests and electric blankets. We have a tennis court, swimming pool and spa pool on site. We are five minutes from the Otorohanga Kiwi House and Aviary, twenty minutes from Waitomo Caves area. We have three outside cats.

Please let your hosts know if you have to cancel
they will have spent time preparing for you.

Waitomo Village - Waitomo District *Self-contained B&B*

Dalziel Waitomo Caves Guest Lodge
Andree & Peter Dalziel
PO Box 16,
Waitomo Caves

Tel: (07) 878 7641 Fax: (07) 878 7466
www.bnb.co.nz/dalzielwaitomocaves.html

Double $70 Single $50 (Continental Breakfast)
Credit cards accepted
3 Queen 1 Double 2 Single (5 bdrm)
5 Ensuite

Our home is only 100 metres from the Museum of Caves information office in the centre of the village and a few hundred metres from the Glow Worm Caves. Our detached rooms with their individual ensuite facilities are of the highest standard. With a variety of cave adventure trips, excellent bush walks and a top golf course we recommend at least two days to spend with us. We will arrange your meals. You will find a place with warm and friendly hospitality.

WAIKATO

Waitomo Caves *Self-contained B&B* *9.7km W of Waitomo Village*

Te Tiro
Rachel & Angus Stubbs
970 Caves Te Anga Road, Waitomo Village,

Tel: (07) 878 6328 Fax: (07) 878 6328
Mob: 027 226 7681 stubbs.a_r@xtra.co.nz
www.bnb.co.nz/tetiro.html

Double $80-$95 Single $60 (Continental Breakfast)
Child $15 Credit cards accepted Child at home
Pet on property Children welcome Pets welcome
2 Queen 5 Single (2 bdrm) 2 Private 1 Guests share

Te Tiro (The View) 'welcomes you'. Enjoy fantastic panoramic views of the central North Island and mountains. At night enjoy glowworms nestled in lush NZ bush only metres from your cottage. Situated on an established sheep farm with 350 acres of reserve bush. Our new self-contained pioneer style cottages can accommodate up to five people in a cosy open plan room. Hosts Rachel and Angus have thirty years of tourism experience between them and would be happy to advise you on the wonders of Waitomo.

Te Kuiti - Waitomo District *Homestay B&B* *1km S of Te Kuiti*

Te Kuiti B&B
Pauline Blackmore
5 Grey St, Te Kuiti

Tel: (07) 878 6686
pauline.blackmore@xtra.co.nz
www.bnb.co.nz/tekuitibb.html

Double $70-$80 Single $50 (Full Breakfast)
Credit cards accepted
2 Queen 2 Single (3 bdrm)
2 Ensuite 1 Private

We live only 50 metres off Highway 3. Expect a warm welcome, peace and relaxation in our 1920's bungalow. The bedrooms have tea and coffee-making facilities, quality beds and bedding and heaters. Breakfast can be timed to suit you and includes cereals, fruit, juice and toast followed by cooked English breakfast and brewed coffee or tea. Feel free to use the TV in one of the lounges. We can help you with advice about local attractions including great places to walk or tramp.

Te Kuiti - Waitomo District   *Farmstay   20km NW of Te Kuiti*

Tapanui Country Home
Sue & Mark Perry
1714 Oparure Rd,
RD 5, Te Kuiti 2500

Tel: (07) 877 8549 Fax: (07) 877 8541
Mob: 025 949 873   info@tapanui.co.nz
www.tapanui.co.nz

Double $155-$170 Single $145-$160 (Full Breakfast)
Dinner By Arrangement Credit cards accepted
3 King/Twin (3 bdrm) 1 Ensuite 1 Private

Luxury accommodation located 25 mins from the world famous Waitomo Caves. Large, magnificently appointed homestead providing warm hospitality that ensures every comfort. Set High in the quiet rolling hills, with spectacular formations of limestone, the views from the spacious bedrooms induce a feeling of tranquillity. 770 hectare sheep and cattle farm. Pet sheep an added attraction. Complete relaxation is the keynote. Children not catered for. Dinner served by prior arrangement only. Check in: after 4 pm. Check out: 10am.   NEW ZEALAND AT ITS VERY BEST.

Te Kuiti - Waitomo District   *Farmstay B&B   6km E of Te Kuiti*

Panorama Farm
Michael & Raema Warriner
65 Carter Road, RD 2, Te Kuiti

Tel: (07) 878 5104 Fax: (07) 878 8104
panoramab.b@xtra.co.nz
www.bnb.co.nz/panoramafarm.html

Double $72 Single $36 (Full Breakfast)
Child $18 Dinner $20 Credit cards accepted
1 Double 3 Single (2 bdrm)
1 Guests share

Raema, Michael and the cat welcome you to our hill top home, overlooking bush clad hills, fertile valleys and distant peaks with golden dawns and spectacular sunsets. We offer comfortable beds and the quiet surroundings of a 30 hectare farm plus 40 years experience of the district and its attractions. Waitomo is 25 mins away, Rotorua, Taupo 2 hours so come and enjoy the company, the scenery and a good night's rest. Arriving or departing from Auckland - we are 2 1/2 hours to the Airport.

Te Kuiti - Waitomo District   *Farmstay B&B   2km N of Te Kuiti*

Margaret & Graeme Churstain
137 Gadsby Road,
RD 5, Te Kuiti

Tel: (07) 878 8191 Fax: (07) 878 5949
Mob: 021 735 853
www.bnb.co.nz/churstain.html

Double $70 Single $40 (Continental Breakfast)
Pet on property Children welcome
1 Queen 1 Double 1 Twin 2 Single (3 bdrm)
1 Private 1 Guests share

Welcome to the 'peace and tranquility' of our hilltop farmlet, signposted on SH3, northern end of Te Kuiti. We have welcomed travellers for many years so come and enjoy our wonderful rural views and kiwi hospitality. Being the sheep shearing capital of the world, Te Kuiti and surrounding areas offer many leisure activities, with Waitomo Caves 10 mins away. Rooms with guest-share bathroom upstairs, or if you prefer, a unit downstairs ideal for families with private bathroom. By the way . . . the cat and dog are harmless.

Te Kuiti - Waitomo District

Homestay B&B   1 km S of Te Kuiti PO

Sanaig House
Mike & Sue Wagstaff
35 Awakino Rd,
Te Kuiti
Tel: 0064 7 878 7128 Fax: 0064 7 878 7128
sanaig@xtra.co.nz
www.bnb.co.nz/sanaighouse.html
Double $90 Single $70 (Continental Breakfast)
1 Queen 1 Double (3 bdrm)
1 Ensuite 1 Private

Welcome to Sanaig House one of Te Kuiti's gracious homes built in 1903. The guest bedrooms in our spacious home are attractive, sunny & open onto or overlook the lovely garden & its mature trees. Attractions Waitomo Caves, rafting, caving, fishing, golf, bird-watching, gardens, scenicwalks. With prior notice we are able to arrange visits to prestigious private King Country gardens & also to observe the endangered native Kokako.

WAIKATO

Piopio - Waitomo District   *24km SW of Te Kuiti*
Homestay B&B   Country Homestay

Bracken Ridge
Susan & Rob Hallam
Aria Road, Piopio 2555
Tel: (07) 877 8384 Mob: 025 610 4001
www.bnb.co.nz/hallam.html
Double $80 Single $50 (Full Breakfast)
Dinner $20 by arrangement
1 Queen 3 Single (2 bdrm)
1 Private

Enjoy a peaceful, relaxing time at our large, modern home set in landscaped gardens on a small sheep and cattle farmlet. Our elevated site provides panoramic views of green pastures, trees and limestone rocks. All rooms have a garden or rural outlook. Spacious heated bedrooms have comfortable beds and electric blankets. Our interests encompass gardening, music, sailing and meeting people from all over the world. Piopio 1km and Waitomo Caves just 35 minutes away. Please phone ahead for reservations and directions.

Our B&Bs range from homely to luxurious,
but you can always be assured of superior hospitality.

Pio Pio - Waitomo District *Farmstay Homestay B&B   19km S of Te Kuiti*

Carmel Farm
Barbara & Leo Anselmi
Main Road, PO Box 93, Pio Pio
Tel: (07) 877 8130 Fax: (07) 877 8130
Carmelfarms@xtra.co.nz
www.bnb.co.nz/carmelfarm.html

Double $100 Single $50 (Continental Breakfast) Dinner $25pp (with complementary wine)
Children welcome Pets welcome
2 King/Twin 4 Single (4 bdrm)
1 Ensuite 1 Family share

Barbara and Leo Anselmi own and operate a 1200 acre sheep, beef and dairy farm. You will be welcomed into a 3000 square feet modern home set in picturesque gardens, in a lovely limestone valley.

You will be treated to delicious home cooked meals and the warmth of our friendship. Whether enjoying the excitement of mustering mobs of cattle and sheep, viewing the milking of 550 cows, driving around the rolling hills on the four-wheeled farm-bike, relaxing as you bask in the sun by the pool or wandering through the gardens, you will experience unforgettable memories of breathtaking scenery, a clean green environment.

We have farm pets who love the attention of our guests. The donkeys are waiting to be fed. We look over a beautiful 18 hole golf course which welcomes visitors.

The property is a short distance from Black Water Rafting and canoeing activities, The Lost World Cavern, and the famous Waitomo Caves. Nearby are bush walks and the home of the rare Kokako bird. We can help to arrange activities for people of all ages and interests including garden visits and horse riding. Please let us know your preference.

We are 140 kms from Rotorua/Taupo.

Directions: Travel 19 kms south of Te Kuiti on SH3 towards Piopio. Carmel Farm is on the right. We can arrange to pick up from Otorohanga, Te Kuiti or Waitomo, if required.

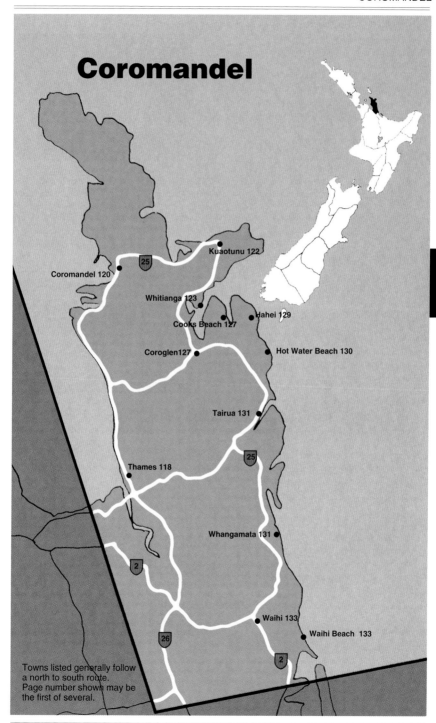

Coromandel

Kuaotunu 122

Coromandel 120

Whitianga 123

Cooks Beach 127

Hahei 129

Coroglen127

Hot Water Beach 130

Tairua 131

Thames 118

Whangamata 131

Waihi 133

Waihi Beach 133

Towns listed generally follow
a north to south route.
Page number shown may be
the first of several.

Thames   *Self-contained Farmstay   8km SE of Thames*

Wharfedale Farmstay
Rosemary Burks
RD 1, Kopu,
Thames

Tel: (07) 868 8929 Fax: (07) 868 8926
www.bnb.co.nz/wharfedalefarmstay.html

Double $100-$120 Single $80 (Full Breakfast)
Credit cards accepted
1 Double 2 Single (2 bdrm)
2 Private

For 11 years our guests have enjoyed the beauty of Wharfedale which has featured in Air NZ airwaves and Japans my country magazines. We invite you to share our idyllic lifestyle set in 9 acres of park like paddocks and gardens surrounded by native bush. Delight in private river swimming, abundant bird life, our dairy goats. We enjoy wholefood and organically grown produce. There are cooking facilities in the studio apartment. We have no children or indoor animals. Cool shade in summer and cozy log fires and electric blankets in winter. We look forward to meeting you.

Thames   *Self-contained   3km SE of Thames*

Grafton Cottage
Ferne & David Tee
304 Grafton Road, Thames

Tel: (07) 868 9971 Fax: (07) 868 3075
Mob: 021 139 4012
graftcot@ihug.co.nz
www.bnb.co.nz/graftoncottage.html

Double $110-$150 Single $95 (Continental Breakfast)
Credit cards accepted
1 Queen 4 Double 2 Single (6 bdrm)
6 Ensuite

A small elegant lodge nestled in the foothills of the Coromandel Peninsula overlooking the historic gold and timber town of Thames. We are 1 hours drive from Auckland International Airport. The tree lined property offers 4 luxury chalets set apart which have generous decks with magnificent views. Thames is the ideal base to explore the rest of the Peninsula and is away for the hustle and bustle of the city. Included are 2 studios and 2 two bedroom chalets all with tea/coffee, fridge, sinks, and microwave.

Thames   *B&B   1.5km SE of Thames*

Brunton House
Albert & Yvonne Sturgess
210 Parawai Road, Thames

Tel: (07) 868 5160 Fax: (07) 868 5160
Mob: 025 627 4272 www.bnb.co.nz/bruntonhouse.html
bruntonhouse@xtra.co.nz   asturgess@paradise.net.nz

Double $95 Single $60 (Full Breakfast)
Dinner $25by arrangement Credit cards accepted
2 Queen 1 Double 2 Single (3 bdrm)
1 Guests share 1 Family share

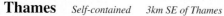

Share in Thames' early history, stay in our Lovely Victorian House which is comfortable, homely and smokefree. Our large grounds include mature trees, swimming pool (summer) and grass tennis court. The house features large comfortable bedrooms, guest lounge with TV, stereo and extensive library, billiard room, S/S tea and coffee. Our interests include travel, steam trains, embroidery, dancing, reading, gardening and our lovable cat and dog. Directions: Opposite Toyota Plant turn into Banks Street. Right into Parawai Rd and find us 200m further on left.

Thames   *Homestay   8km E of Thames*

Huia Lodge
Val & Steve Barnes
589 Kauaeranga Valley Road, Thames
Tel: (07) 868 6557 Fax: (07) 868 6557
huia.lodge@xtra.co.nz
www.thames-info.co.nz/HuiaLodge

Double $75 Single $40 (Full Breakfast)
Child $20 Dinner $20 by arrangement
Credit cards accepted Pet on property
2 Queen 2 Single (3 bdrm)
2 Ensuite

Each guest has an ensuite and tea/coffee facilities. Relax and enjoy the tranquility of the Valley, hike in the nearby Forest Park or circle the Peninsula to view the famous Coromandel scenery. We're in our mid 50's, enjoy meeting travellers, love the rural lifestyle, grow fruit/vegetables and pamper Bart the cat on our 4 acre property. Turn at BP corner (south end of township) into Banks Street then follow Parawai Road into the Valley. We're 8km from BP. Just 1 1/2 hours from Auckland.

Thames   *Homestay   6.4km E of Thames*

Mountain Top B&B
Allan Berry & Elizabeth McCracken
452 Kauaeranga Valley Road, RD 2, Thames
Tel: (07) 868 9662 Fax: (07) 868 9662
nzh_mountain.top@xtra.co.nz
www.bnb.co.nz/mountaintopbb.html

Double $90-$95 Single $50 (Full Breakfast)
Child 1/2 price Dinner $20 - $30
Credit cards accepted Pet on property Pets welcome
1 Queen 1 Double 1 Single (2 bdrm) 1 Guests share

Allan and I grow mandarins, olives, native trees & raise coloured sheep on a small organic farm. Our guest wing with lounge, fridge, TV and extensive library has bedrooms with decks overlooking river and mountains. Coromandel forest park has superb walking tracks or nearby you can amble over neighbouring farmland or swim in forest pools. We have a relaxed garden, Jack Russell Roly and cat Priscilla. We love meeting people often cooking for guests mostly from farm produce. Come and let us look after you.

Thames   *B&B   4km E of Thames*

Acorn Lodge
Dennis & Pat
161 Kauaeranga Valley,
RD 2, Thames
Tel: (07) 868 8723 Fax: (07) 868 8713
AcornLodge@xtra.co.nz
www.bnb.co.nz/acornlodge.html

Double $100 Single $65 (Full Breakfast)
Child Neg Dinner $30 by arrangement
Credit cards accepted Pet on property
1 Queen 1 Double 1 Single (3 bdrm) 2 Private

Relax and enjoy the tranquil views from our spacious home set in 2 acres of park-like grounds. Enjoy a pot of tea or coffee and home baking on your sunny patio or relax in your comfortable lounge featuring an atrium and waterfall. At night marvel at the glow worms - only 2 mins walk. Our interests include tramping in the nearby "Forest Park", fishing and gardening. We, Dennis and Pat, along with Penny our cat and Coco our friendly German Shepherd, assure you of a warm welcome.

Coromandel   *Homestay   11km S of Coromandel*

Coromandel Homestay   Hilary & Vic Matthews
74 Kowhai Drive, Te Kouma Bay, Coromandel
Tel: (07) 866 8046 Fax: (07) 866 8046
vc.hm.matthews@xtra.co.nz
www.bnb.co.nz/coromandelhomestay.html

Double $90-$105 Single $60-$70
(Continental Breakfast) Dinner $40 by arrangement
Credit cards accepted Pet on property
1 Queen 1 Double 1 Single (2 bdrm)
1 Ensuite 1 Private

Our homestay is near an attractive safe beach. We have a bush setting and beautiful views of Coromandel Harbour. The area is very quiet and peaceful. Vic is a professional furniture/designer maker. Hilary enjoys gardening, spinning and woodturning. We have a cat. The house is unsuitable for young children. Take SH25 for 50kms travelling north from Thames. Turn sharp left into Te Kouma Road. After 3kms turn left into Kowhai Drive. We are 15 minutes drive south of Coromandel town. Dinner by prior arrangement.

Coromandel   *Farmstay B&B   3km S of Coromandel*

Jacaranda Lodge
Gayle & Gary Bowler
3195 Tiki Road, RD 1, Coromandel
Tel: (07) 866 8002 Fax: (07) 866 8002   also.as/bowler
jacarandaCOROMANDEL@xtra.co.nz

Double $90-$125 Single $50-$100 (Special Breakfast)
Dinner $30 - $40 Beach House $80 - $130
Credit cards accepted Pet on property
3 Queen 1 Double 1 Twin 1 Single (6 bdrm)
2 Ensuite 1 Private 1 Guests share

Welcome to Jacaranda, a warm relaxing home set on 6 acres of peaceful farmland and beautiful gardens with rural and mountain views. We offer spacious bedrooms, guest lounges and kitchen and ample verandahs. Our meals are delicious, featuring fresh home grown foods plus local seafood, served overlooking the rose garden whenever possible. Jacaranda is an excellent base close to all the peninisula's attractions. Gayle loves tramping the amazing local trails. Gary loves fishing, golf and tennis and we will happily organise these or any other activities. Website: http://also.as/bowler

Coromandel   *Self-contained B&B   0.5 E of Coromandel*

Country Touch
Colleen & Geoff Innis
39 Whangapoua Road, Coromandel
Tel: (07) 866 8310 Fax: (07) 866 8310
Mob: 025 971 196
countrytouch@xtra.co.nz
www.bnb.co.nz/countrytouch.html

Double $90 Single $65 (Continental Breakfast)
Child $10 Credit cards accepted Children welcome
2 Queen 4 Single (4 bdrm)
4 Ensuite

Geoff and I are a retired couple who enjoy meeting people, and invite you to a restful holiday in a country setting. With newly established trees and gardens, roses a speciality. You have the independence of 4 units situated apart from our home, all with fold out sofas, TV, fridge, tea and coffee making facilities. You have a country touch feeling with only a 10 minute stroll to Coromandel township, where you can enjoy our local arts, crafts and restaurants. Come and enjoy.

Coromandel   *Homestay   10km S of Coromandel*

AJ's Homestay
Annette & Ray Hintz
24 Kowhai Drive, Te Kouma, RD, Coromandel
Tel: (07) 866 7057 Fax: (07) 866 7057
Mob: 025 581 624   rm.aj.hintz@actrix.gen.nz
www.bnb.co.nz/ajshomestay.html
Double $85-$120 Single $70 (Continental Breakfast)
Dinner $25 - $35 Credit cards accepted
Children welcome
1 Queen 1 Double 1 Single (2 bdrm)
1 Ensuite 1 Family share

AJ's HOMESTAY with panoramic sea views overlooking the Coromandel Harbour, spectacular sunsets. Five-minute walk to a safe swimming beach. Most mornings breakfast is served on the terrace. Our games room has a billiard and table tennis table. Dinner can be arranged. Directions, Thames coast main road (SH25) Approx. 50 mins. At the bottom of the last hill overlooking Coromandel Harbour. Turn sharp left, at the Te Kouma Rd sign. Travel past the boat ramp, next turn left. Kowhai Drive, we are No 24.

Coromandel   *B&B   0.5km S of Coromandel*

The Green House
Gwen Whitmore
505 Tiki road, Coromandel
Tel: (07) 866 7303
whitemore@wave.co.nz
www.bnb.co.nz/thegreenhouse.html
Double $100 Single $50 (Continental Breakfast)
Credit cards accepted
2 Queen 2 Single (3 bdrm)
1 Ensuite 1 Guests share

Be our guests in beautiful Coromandel. We have three guest bedrooms and guest lounge with TV, tea/coffee making facilities. Views to the East are bush clad hills and to the West sea views and spectacular sunsets. Enjoy breakfast served in the garden. Take a leisurely 5-10 minutes stroll into Coromandel Town with lovely craft shops and restaurants. Experience a walk in indigenous forest, ride a unique miniature railway and visit beautiful gardens. Golf course, bowls and beaches nearby. Internet/web access.

A homestay is a B&B where you
share the family's living area.

Kuaotunu   *B&B   Country Stay   17km N of Whitianga*

The Kaeppeli's
Jill & Robert Kaeppeli
Grays Avenue, Kuaotunu, RD 2, Whitianga
Tel: (07) 866 2445 Mob: 025 656 3442
kaeppeli.kuaotunu@paradise.net.nz.
www.whitianga.co.nz/kaeppeli

Double $70-$120 Single $50-$80 (Full Breakfast)
Child negotiable Dinner $28 Credit cards accepted
Child at home Pet on property Pets welcome
2 King 4 Single (4 bdrm)   2 Ensuite 1 Guests share

"Country Living in Style and Comfort", with Swiss/Kiwi family on small farm above the Pacific. Exquisite Meals - Swiss Chef using top quality produce and woodfired oven served in guests dining room or Panoramic Gazebo. Walk to clean, safe, white sandy beaches, enjoy the peace and tranquility of Kuaotunu. Bushwalks, tennis, fishing, kayaking, swimming, Eco-Adventure feeding Kiwi. Matarangi Golf Course and horse trekking nearby. Ideal starting point for exploring glorious Coromandel Peninsula or relaxing. Paradise found. AND OUR VIEW? JUST THE BEST!

Kuaotunu   *Self-contained B&B   17km N of Whitianga*

Blue Penguin Glenda Mawhinney & Barbara Meredith
11 Cuvier Crescent, Kuaotunu, RD 2, Whitianga
Tel: (07) 866 2222   holidayhomes@bluepenguin.co.nz
Fax: (07) 866 0228   www.bluepenguin.co.nz

Double $95-$110 Single $65 (Continental Breakfast)
Child $30 Dinner $20 by arrangement
Credit cards accepted Pet on property
Children welcome Pets welcome Smoking area inside
1 King/Twin 1 Double 4 Single (2 bdrm)
1 Guests share

We offer you the upper level of our architecturally designed home with spectacular views over the beach and pohutukawa trees to the Mercury Islands and Great Barrier. The master (or mistress) guestroom has queen bed, window seats and small private balcony. Children love the family guestroom, double bed, two singles, bunks, cot, TV/video, plenty of toys, games, kids' videos. Our lifestlye is enhanced by our Retriever, Poodle and little Foxy. We are two professional women whom also manage 250 Private Beach Houses available for holiday rental - see our web site.

Kuaotunu   *Self-contained Homestay B&B   18km N of Whitianga*

Kuaotunu Bay Lodge
Lorraine and Bill Muir
State Highway 25, Kuaotunu, RD 2, Whitianga
Tel: (07) 866 4396 Fax: (07) 866 4396
Mob: 025 601 3665
muir@kuaotunubay.co.nz
www.kuaotunubay.co.nz

Double $150-$170 Single $100
(Continental Breakfast) Dinner $45pp
Credit cards accepted Pet on property
2 Queen 2 Single (3 bdrm)   2 Ensuite 1 Private

Situated on the coast our home has been purpose built for guests with ensuites and underfloor heating. Enjoy breakfast in the sunny conservatory or on the deck listening to the waves. The safe beach is just a short walk through the garden. Ideal for all sea activities, fishing, kayaking or explore the local art and craft. Whitianga with its restaurants and tourist activities is a 20 minute drive. Our 10 acre property has a small bush reserve, sheep and a friendly dog. Welcome.

Kuaotunu   *Homestay B&B   17km N of Whitianga*

Drift In B&B
Yvonne & Peppe Thompson
16 Grays Avenue, Kuaotunu, RD 2, Whitianga
Tel: (07) 866 4321 Fax: (07) 866 4321
Mob: 025 245 3632
www.bnb.co.nz/driftinbb.html
Double $85-$95 Single $50 (Full Breakfast)
Child $30 (5-12yrs) Dinner by arrangement
Visa/MC accepted Children welcome
1 Queen 2 Single (2 bdrm) 1 Guests share

Welcome is assured at Drift In. This tranquil comfortable modern cedar home is designed to take full advantage of the sun and breathtaking views of the Great Barrier and Mercury Islands, by day and moonlit night. An unique beach theme pervades our house and garden. Breakfast is a memorable occasion with sight and sounds of birds and sea complimenting an excellent range of home cooking. Only a minute walk to safe white-sand beaches and rock pools. Drift in, relax and enjoy this special part of New Zealand.

Kuaotunu   *14km N of Whitianga*
Self-contained Farmstay B&B Self-contained Chalet

Pitoone
Annegrit, Michael & Jessica (10yrs) Brueck
1120 State Highway 25, Kuaotunu, RD 2, Whitianga
Tel: (07) 866 2690 info@pitoone.com
annegrit.brueck@pitoone.com
www.bnb.co.nz/pitoone.html

Double $130-$150 (Full Breakfast)
Dinner by arrangement Child at home
Pet on property Children welcome
1 Queen 2 Single (open mezzanine floor) 1 Private

"PITOONE" B&B is a 30 ha hilly Farm, with 7ha of wonderful native bush.Short drive away from some of NZ's most beautifull white sandy beaches,Matarangi Golf Course, Restaurants.The very charming and comfortable Chalet, setting privat, overlooking the native bush to the Pacific Ocean has fully cooking facilities, open fire place, barbeque on the terrace. Have your wine to the sound of bush and sea. Feel the tranquillity. The perfect "Get Away".

Whitianga   *Self-contained B&B   1km S of Whitianga*

Cosy Cat Cottage
Gordon Pearce
41 South Highway, Whitianga
Tel: (07) 866 4488 Fax: (07) 866 4488
Mob: 025 798 745   cosycat@whitianga.co.nz
www.bnb.co.nz/cosycatcottage.html
Double $80-$105 Single $50-$75 (Full Breakfast)
Cottage $80 - $160 Credit cards accepted
Pet on property
2 Queen 1 Double 1 Single (3 bdrm)
2 Ensuite 1 Private

Welcome to our picturesque two storied cottage filled with feline memorabilia! Relax with complimentary tea or coffee served on the veranda or in the guest lounge. Enjoy a good nights rest in comfortable beds & choose a variety of treats from our breakfast blackboard menu. You will probably like to meet Sylvie the cat or perhaps visit the cat hotel in the garden. A separate cottage is available with Queen beds, bathrooms and kitchen. Friendly helpful service is assured - hope to see you soon!

Whitianga   *Homestay*

Anne's Haven
Anne & Bob
119 Albert St, Whitianga
Tel: (07) 866 5550
anneshaven@paradise.net.nz
www.bnb.co.nz/anneshaven.html
Double $65 Single $40 (Full Breakfast)
Child $20 Dinner $20
1 Double 2 Single (2 bdrm)
1 Family share

Welcome to our comfortable modern home and the tranquility of the garden. Guests share the lounge/ TV room. The shower, toilet and bathroom are each separate rooms for easy access. We are 400 metres from shops and restaurants and walking distance to six lovely beaches. Bob enjoys building and flying radio controlled model planes. Anne makes pottery, dabbles with watercolours, and gardens. Let us make your stay a memorable one. Our moggie 'Gordon Bennett' is friendly also.

Whitianga   *Homestay B&B   3.5km S of Whitianga*

Camellia Lodge
Pat & John Lilley
South Highway, RD 1, Whitianga
Tel: (07) 866 2253 Fax: (07) 866 2253
Mob: 021 217 6612
camellia@wave.co.nz
www.whitianga.co.nz/camellia-lodge
Double $90-$110 Single $65 (Full Breakfast)
Child 1/2 price Dinner $25 Credit cards accepted
1 Queen 2 Double 2 Twin (4 bdrm)
2 Ensuite 2 Guests share

Welcome to our friendly home, which is nestled in a secluded park-like garden, which includes native, and many mature trees. We also offer you a spa and swimming pool and lots of lovely gardens to relax in. You would normally be woken up to the tune of bellbirds, then you settle into a hearty breakfast which will set you up for the whole day. We have a guest lounge and tea and coffee making facilities. We can assure you of a warm friendly welcome and a comfortable stay.

Whitianga   *Homestay B&B Bedsit   3.2km S of Whitianga*

A Hi-Way Haven
Joan & Nevin Paton
1 Golf Road, Whitianga
Tel: (07) 866 2427 Fax: (07) 866 2424
Mob: 025 627 2044   a-haven@paradise.net.nz
www.bnb.co.nz/ahiwayhaven.html
Double $70-$90 Single $40-$50
(Continental & Full Breakfast) Pet on property
1 King/Twin 1 Queen 1 Double 2 Single (4 bdrm)
1 Ensuite 1 Guests share

Looking for comfortable affordable accommodation 3.2km from Whitianga. Hearty cooked breakfast will keep you going all day. 18 hole golf course is adjacent and central to all amenities on the Coromandel Peninsula.   Short drive to Whitianga township with many restaurants and your hosts will be happy to arrange all holiday wishes.   Guest lounge, TV, Tea/Coffee and laundry facilities. Ensuite bedsit also available for disabled people. Friendly dog and cat. We at A Hi-way Haven know that you will come as a visitor and depart as a friend.

Whitianga *Homestay B&B*   *16km N of Whitianga*

The Peachey's
Yvonne & Dale Peachey
15 Kawhero Drive,
Kuaotunu RD 2, Whitianga
Tel: (07) 866 5290 Fax: (07) 866 5290
DYPeachey@xtra.co.nz
www.bnb.co.nz/thepeacheys.html

Double $100-$120 Single $80 (Special Breakfast)
Dinner $25pp Credit cards accepted Pet on property
1 King 1 Double 2 Single (2 bdrm)   2 Ensuite

Welcome. Our new home and B&B at Kuaotunu, is on SH25 between Whitianga and Coromandel. A short stroll through the reserve opposite your accommodation is Kuaotunu Beach. The place for the "travel weary" to unwind. We are a semi retired couple (and Barley the cat) who have lived in the area for many years and enjoy meeting people. Swimming, tennis, golf, fishing, cycling, bush walks and relaxation at your doorstep. Cafes and restaurants at Whitianga and Matarangi are only a 15 minute drive away.

Whitianga *B&B Hotel style*   *4km N of Whitianga*

At Parkland Place
Maria & Guy Clark
14 Parkland Place, Brophys Beach, Whitianga
Tel: (07) 866 4987 Fax: (07) 866 4946
Mob: 025 291 7495   parklandplace@wave.co.nz
www.atparklandplace.co.nz

Double $135-$200 Single $100-$150
(Special Breakfast) Child Neg Dinner by arrangement
Credit cards accepted Children welcome
2 King 3 Queen 3 Single (5 bdrm) 4 Ensuite 1 Private

Enjoy European hospitality in Whitianga's most luxurious Boutique Accommodation. Maria, a ships chef from Poland and New Zealand husband Guy, a master mariner, will make your stay a memorable experience. Large luxuriously appointed rooms. Magnificent breakfasts. Superb candle-lit dinners or BBQ by arrangement. Sunny picturesque outdoor area with spa pool. Large guest lounge with TV, library, music and refreshments. Situated near the beach and next to reserves and farmland ensures absolute peace and quiet. Privacy and discretion assured. You will not regret coming.

Whitianga *Self-contained B&B*   *6km S of Whitianga*

Riverside Retreat
Maree & Richard Prestage
309 Road, RD 1,
Whitianga
Tel: (07) 866 5155 Fax: (07) 866 5155
retreat@xtra.co.nz
www.riversideretreat.co.nz

Double $120 Single $120 (Continental Breakfast)
1 Queen (1 bdrm)
1 Private

You are invited to share our Riverside Retreat beside the waters which run through the beautiful Mahakirau Valley. Your cottage, nestled amongst native trees in 3 acres of landscaped gardens, has fully equipped kitchen, sunny lounge, and queen bedroom upstairs in loft, with views over the garden and river. You can fly-fish for trout, bush walk, or just relax by the river with a book. The perfect place to unwind, soothe the spirit and leave the world behind. Your hosts and moggy "Woz" assure you a relaxing and memorable stay.

Whitianga   *B&B*   *1km N of Whitianga*

The Beach House
Helen & Allan Watson
38 Buffalo Beach Road, P O Box 162, Whitianga
Tel: (07) 866 5647 Fax: (07) 866 5647 Mob: 025 668 2781
ahwatson@paradise.net.nz
www.bnb.co.nz/thebeachhousewhitianga.html

Double $110-$150 Single $100-$140 (Continental Breakfast) Child n/a Credit cards accepted
1 King/Twin 1 Queen 1 Single (2 bdrm)
2 Ensuite

UNBEATABLE BEACHFRONT LOCATION   180 degree sea views from both spacious first floor rooms, opening onto a balcony. Safe swimming at any tide 30 meters across the grass reserve. High quality accommodation with individual tea/coffee making facilities, refrigerators, TV's, electric blankets, reading lights and ensuites with heated towel rails.

Watch the fishing, sailing and pleasure craft plying our sparkling clean bay, beach lovers can swim, (we provide the towels) walk the 3 km sandy beach, gather shells, or just breathe the clean fresh air.

A five minute level walk to waterfront cafe's, restaurants, ferry and shopping centre, the Intercity Bus stops at our entrance on request. 30 minutes to Hot Water Beach, Cathedral Cove and Cooks Beach.

We are fortunate to have lived in Whitianga for over 40 years and enjoy sharing our home and our love of the Peninsula with our guests. Allan is a classic Motorcycle enthusiast and Helen is a Licenced Marriage Celebrant.

Our generous special continental breakfast is served on our deck facing the beach.   Rooms have secure doors giving total privacy when required, guests own entrance and off street parking.

Our tariff is seasonally priced and we offer a discount for a three night stay. High season mid December to end February. Courtesy transport to local bus/airfield.

Closed June & July

Whitianga - Cooks Beach   *Homestay Rural   17km N of Tairua*

Mercury Orchard
Heather and Barry Scott
141 Purangi Road, RD1, Whitianga
Tel: (07) 866 3119 Fax: (07) 866 3115
Mob: 025 283 0176   mercorchard@xtra.co.nz
www.mercuryorchard.co.nz

Double $105 Single $75 (Full Breakfast)
Dinner $25 S/C Cottage $120
Credit cards accepted Pet on property
3 Queen 2 Single (4 bdrm)
2 Ensuite 1 Family share

Mercury Orchard is 5 acres of country garden and organic orchard close to Cooks, Hahei and Hot Water Beaches. Our large guest room opens to private garden and swimming pool, has tea & coffee facilities, ensuite bathroom and adjoining queen bedroom. Also available - Fig Tree Cottage, self contained country style comfort, opening through French doors into orchard, crisp cotton bed linen, fresh fruit and flowers, breakfast hamper and use of BBQ. We share our smoke-free home with 2 small dogs and a cat.

Whitianga - Coroglen   *14km S of Whitianga*

Self-contained Farmstay B&B

Coroglen Lodge
Wendy & Nigel Davidson
2221 State Highway 25, RD 1, Whitianga 2856
Tel: (07) 866 3225 Fax: (07) 866 3235
clover@wave.co.nz
www.mercurybay.co.nz/coroglen.html

Double $75-$85 Single $50-$60 Child $35
(Continental Breakfast) Credit cards accepted
2 Queen 2 Single (3 bdrm) 2 Guests share

Coroglen Lodge is situated on 17 acres of farmland with cattle, sheep and friendly chickens. Surrounded by hills and nestled in a valley with views of Coromandel Ranges and Whitianga Estuary, this is rural tranquillity. Halfway between Whitianga Township and Hot Water Beach there is easy access to both areas and all attractions. We have a garden to roam in, barbecue area with fuel, and full cooking facilities. Two showers, two toilets and laundry facilities are available. Guest area is separate and spacious with a large sunny lounge area for your comfort.

Whitianga   *B&B   500m Whitianga*

Cottage by the Sea
Gayle & Max Murray
11 The Esplanade, Whitianga
Tel: (07) 866 0605 Fax: (07) 866 0675
Mob: 025 237 6163
staying@acottagebythesea.com
www.bnb.co.nz/cottagebytheseawhitianga.html

Double $80-$150 Single $90 (Full Breakfast)
Credit cards accepted
1 King 2 Queen (3 bdrm)
1 Ensuite 1 Guests share

Our charming cottage is located opposite the wharf offering peaceful harbour views. A 1 minute stroll takes you to Buffalo Beach. The township, a 2 minute easy walk has excellent restaurants, cafes and shopping. A 4km drive takes you to the 18 hole golf course and busy airfield. Guest share the family lounge with open fire during the cooler months. Breakfast served on sunny deck or room service. Guests own entrance with safe private off street parking. Our lovely home is shared with two quiet cats.

Hahei Beach   *Homestay*   *36km N of Tairua*

Spellbound Homestay - B&B
Barbara & Alan Lucas
Grange Road, Hahei Beach, RD 1, Whitianga
Tel: (07) 866 3543 Fax: (07) 866 3003 Mob: 025 720 407
spellbound@whitianga.co.nz
www.bnb.co.nz/spellboundhomestaybb.html
Double $125-$150 Single $85-$110 (Special Breakfast) Credit cards accepted
2 King/Twin 2 Queen (4 bdrm)
3 Ensuite 1 Private

Barbara and I live overlooking the sea with panoramic views from the Alderman Islands to the Mercury Islands. We are five minutes from Hahei Beach and are on the road to Cathedral Cove and its beaches, a must when visiting this area. Hot Water Beach is just a short distance away where you can enjoy a warm soak at any time of the year.

The area offers bush walks, surf beaches, fishing and spectacular views for photography. "The Paradise Coast". Most rooms have sea views with ensuites/private bathrooms, all beds have electric blankets and insect screens are fitted to most windows.

We have tea/coffee making facilities and a refrigerator for the use of all guests. Weather permitting, our generous continental breakfast is served on our front deck. Hahei has three good restaurants, for lunches and evening meals.

We thank you for not smoking in the house. We have no animals.

Please give us a telephone call when you wish to come and we can promise you a most enjoyable stay. Reservations essential.

Directions: Turn off at Whenuakite (Highway 25). Grange Road is on left by Hahei Store. We are on left near top of hill. Look for 'Spellbound' signs, follow Service Road. Street numbers not consecutive.

Hahei Beach   *B&B   200m NE of Hahei shops and cafe's*

Hawleys Bed and Breakfast Hahei
Peter and Rhonda Hawley
19 Hahei Beach Road, RD 1, Whitianga
Tel: 07 8663272 Fax: 07 8663273 Mob: 025 971090
Tollfree: 0800 2 SURVEY
hawleysb&b@haheibeach.co.nz
www.haheibeach.co.nz
Double $120 Single $110
(Continental & Full Breakfast) Credit cards accepted
Children welcome
1 Queen 2 Single (2 bdrm) 1 Private

Situated on the flat, half-way (200m) between the beach and the shops and cafes. Ideal for those who enjoy extra space and comfort. The purpose built two double bedrooms (house completed mid 2000) share a spacious bathroom and take up all of the second storey at the rear of the house. The larger room has a balcony and a queen size bed and the smaller room two single beds. A cot is available. There is secure garaging. No children at home and no pets.

Hahei   *Self-contained B&B   38km S of Whitianga*

The Church
Richard Agnew & Karen Blair
87 Beach Road, Hahei, RD 1, Whitianga
Tel: (07) 866 3533 Fax: (07) 866 3055
Mob: 025 596 877   hahei4ch@xtra.co.nz
www.thechurchhahei.co.nz
Double $90-$140 Single $80-$100
(Continental Breakfast) Child $15 Dinner Menu
Credit cards accepted Pet on property
11 Queen (11 bdrm) 11 Ensuite

The Church is Hahei's newest and most unique accommodation and dining experience. The Church building provides a character dining room/licensed restaurant for wholesome breakfasts and delicious evening meals. Eleven cosy wooden cottages scattered through delightful bush and gardens offer a range of accommodation and tariffs, with ensuites, fridges and tea and coffee facilities (some fully self-contained). Enjoy our warm hospitality, the wonders of Cathedral Cove, Hot Water Beach, and the Coromandel Peninsula. We live on site with our 12yr old daughter, dog and cat. Seasonal rates.

Hahei Beach   *Homestay   36km N of Tairua*

Cedar Lodge
Jenny & John Graham
36 Beach Road, Hahei, RD 1, Whitianga
Tel: (07) 866 3789 Fax: (07) 866 3978
cedarlodge@wave.co.nz
www.bnb.co.nz/cedarlodge.html
Double $90 Single $60 (Full Breakfast)
Credit cards accepted
1 Queen 1 Single (1 bdrm)
1 Private

Come and unwind in our comfortable private upstairs studio apartment with its own entrance. Enjoy the sea views and relaxing atmosphere. Take a 200m stroll to the beautiful beach and experience the magic of Hahei. Cathedral Cove walkway and Hot Water beach are nearby. Scenic boat/dive trips are easily arranged with local operators. We have an adult family scattered around the world and two friendly cats. We thank you for not smoking indoors. We enjoy an active retired lifestyle, so please phone ahead for bookings and directions.

Hahei Beach   *Homestay B&B Cottage*   *36km N of Tairua*

Bon Appetit Hahei
Andy & Monika Schuerch
Orchard Road, Hahei, RD 1, Whitianga
Tel: (07) 866 3116 Fax: (07) 866 3117
Mob: 027 24 591 42   schuerch@wave.co.nz
www.bonappetit.co.nz
Double $85-$95 (Full Breakfast)
Child at home Pet on property
Children welcome
1 Queen (1 bdrm) 1 Private

Relax and enjoy the breathtaking views and the absolute privacy of our Bed and Breakfast. Having Cathedral Cove and Hot Water Beach just 5 minutes away, we are perfectly situated for your stay in Hahei. We offer you a warm, homely stay with excellent breakfast. Our cottage, surrounded by native bush, contains ensuite, tea and coffee making facilities and fridge. Feel free to use our laundry and barbecue terrace. Portacot available. We have two children and a friendly cat. Directions: Please telephone for directions.

Hot Water Beach   *Self-contained*   *24km N of Tairua*

Auntie Dawns Place
Dawn & Joe Nelmes
Radar Road, Hot Water Beach, RD 1, Whitianga
Tel: (07) 866 3707 Fax: (07) 866 3701
AuntieDawn@MercuryBay.co.nz
www.bnb.co.nz/auntiedawnsplace.html
Double $75-$90 Single $40 (Continental Breakfast)
Child $15 Credit cards accepted
2 Queen 1 Double (2 bdrm)
2 Private

Hot Water Beach is a beautiful surf beach. At low tide hot water bubbles up at a particular place in the sand and you dig yourself a "hot pool". Our house is surrounded by huge Pohutukawa trees, 150 metres from the sea. We have a terrier and Joe makes home-brew beer. Apartments are comfortably furnished and we provide tea, coffee, bread, butter, jam, milk and cereals. Guests prepare breakfast at preferred time. Nearest restaurant 10 minutes away at Hahei. Directions: Turn right into Radar Road 200 metres before shop.

Hot Water Beach   *Homestay B&B*   *32km S of Whitianga*

Hot Water Beach B&B
Gail & Trevor Knight
48 Pye Place, Hot Water Beach, RD 1, Whitianga
Tel: (07) 866 3991 Fax: (07) 866 3291
Mob: 025 799 620   Tollfree: 0800 146 889
TKnight@xtra.co.nz
www.hotwaterbedandbreakfast.co.nz
Double $140-$160 Single $120-$140 (Full Breakfast)
Dinner by arrangement Credit cards accepted
Pet on property
3 Queen (3 bdrm)   2 Ensuite 1 Private

We have a spacious elevated home with extensive decks, on which you can have fresh coffee or juice, while enjoying sweeping panoramic sea/beach views. Sit under the brilliant southern stars in our spa pool or play on our full sized billiard table. You can swim, surf, dive, fish, kayak, play golf, bushwalk, horse trek or visit spectacular Cathedral Cove or alternatively just dig a hole and soak in the natural hot springs on our beach. We have two cats and a sociable boxer.

Tairua *Homestay* *30km E of Thames*

On the Edge - Tairua
Andrea Patten
219 Paku Drive, Tairua,
Coromandel Peninsula
Tel: (07) 864 8285 Fax: (07) 864 8232
Mob: 025 736 176 ontheedge@hotmail.com
www.bnb.co.nz/ontheedgetairua.html
Double $140-$180 Single $100-$130 (Full Breakfast)
Child $50 Dinner $30 Credit cards accepted
Pet on property Children welcome
2 Queen 2 Double (2 bdrm) 2 Ensuite

'On The Edge' of Paku Hill, panoramic views of the Pacific Ocean and islands. Ideally situated for walks to Paku Hill with spectacular views of Pauanui and Tairua. 20mins north - Hot Water Beach and Cathedral Cove. Close to 18 hole golf course and good restaurants. Andrea and James have travelled extensively, spending their leisure time diving, fishing and skiing. With their intimate knowledge of the Coromandel Peninsula they can provide a tour of the Coromandel in their green coach.

Tairua *B&B* *45km E of Thames*

Harbour View Lodge
Sheryl Allan & John Goldstone
179 Main Road, Tairua
Tel: (07) 864 7040 Fax: (07) 864 7042
info@harbourviewlodge.co.nz
www.harbourviewlodge.co.nz
Double $120-$150 Single $110-$120
(Special Breakfast) Credit cards accepted
1 King 1 Queen 1 Double 1 Twin 3 Single (4 bdrm)
3 Ensuite 1 Guests share

Situated on the foothills of Tairua. Our boutique accommodation offers Rest and Tranquillity for that perfect break. Our bedrooms have own ensuite with fridge, tea & coffee making facilities. The Guest TV lounge opens onto BBQ area, swimming pool and garden. Breakfast is a house specialty, delicious continental choices served in the dining room with its ever-changing views of Tairua Harbour and Paku Mountain. Enjoy our beaches, bush walks, fishing, diving, and golfing. Close to Cathedral Cove & Hot Water Beach.

Whangamata *Guest Lodge* *2km W of Whangamata*

Brenton Lodge
Jan & Paul Campbell
1 Brenton Place, Whangamata
Tel: (07) 865 8400 Fax: (07) 865 8400
Mob: 025 780 134
brentonlodge@xtra.co.nz
www.brentonlodge.co.nz
Double $295 Single $275 (Full Breakfast)
Extra person $80 Credit cards accepted
3 Queen (3 bdrm)
3 Ensuite

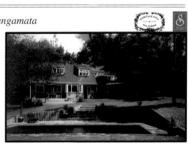

Brenton Lodge provides superior boutique accommodation with style. A superb country retreat for the discerning visitor ..... intimate and personal. Escape & Enjoy, Peace, Privacy & Pampering. Glorious sea views, beautiful gardens & swimming pool, situated just 2 km's from the surf beach and village. Charming Guest Cottages are tastefully decorated, cotton sheets, fresh flowers. Gourmet Breakfasts served in the privacy of your room or alfresco on your balcony.

Whangamata *Homestay   1km N of Whangamata*

Waireka Homestay
Gail & Dick Wilson
108 Waireka Place, Whangamata
Tel: (07) 865 8859 Fax: (07) 865 8859
waireka@whangamata.co.nz
www.thepeninsula.co.nz/waireka

Double $95-$120 Single $75-$85 (Full Breakfast)
Child $25 Dinner $25 Credit cards accepted
Pet on property
1 Queen 2 Single (2 bdrm) 1 Ensuite 1 Guests share

Extra touches, something special. Free Whangamata tour. Two hours from Rotorua or Auckland. Use our delightful modern homestay in riverside setting as a base to explore the superb beaches and bushwalks of Whangamata and the Coromandel Peninsula. Enjoy quality cuisine with produce from our garden. Your party will be our only guests. Children welcome. We will help you share our interests - golf, fishing, boating, snorkelling, travel, petanque, floral art, gardening, kite flying. Free guest double kayak. Help with your itinerary. Individualised tours with licensed operator - luxury car. Cat.

Whangamata (Rural) *B&B   8km N of Whangamata*

Copsefield B&B
Richard and Trish Davison
1055 SH25, RD 1, Whangamata
Tel: (07) 865 9555 Fax: (07) 865 9555
Mob: 025 289 0131 copsefield@xtra.co.nz
www.copsefield.co.nz

Double $140 Single $100
(Full Breakfast) Child under 5 free
Credit cards accepted Children welcome
2 Queen 2 Single (3 bdrm) 3 Ensuite

Character country home situated on 3 acres, at the Southern end of the stunning Coromandel Peninsula. Copsefield is purpose built for your comfort, with 3 ensuite rooms. All rooms are non-smoking. Two beaches close by . Canoes, bikes, walks, spa pool. Peace and tranquility beside native bush and river. Guest lounge with TV, tea and coffee . Complimentary wine. Full breakfast including home grown eggs and fresh fruit. Your hosts Trish & Richard offer you a warm and friendly welcome, and personal attention.

Whangamata *Homestay B&B   200m N of town centre*

Sandy Rose Bed & Breakfast
Shirley & Murray Calman
Corner Hetherington & Rutherford Roads,
Whangamata
Tel: (07) 865 6911 Fax: (07) 865 6911
Mob: 025 711 220 sandyrose@whangamata.co.nz
www.sandyrose.whangamata.co.nz

Double $110 Single $85 (Special Breakfast)
Credit cards accepted Pet on property
1 Queen 2 Twin (3 bdrm) 3 Ensuite

A charming B&B in the Coromandel Peninsula's popular holiday destination, we have three tastefully decorated guest bedrooms, all with ensuite bathrooms, comfortable beds and in-room TVs. Complimentary tea and coffee is available in the guest lounge. We are ideally located, close to Whangamata's shops, cafes and restaurants, and an easy stroll to the surf beach, harbour and wharf. Enjoy our extensive continental breakfast and use our home as a base to relax and enjoy the natural attractions that Whangamata and area has to offer.

Waihi *Homestay B&B 1km N of Waihi*

West Wind Gardens
Josie & Bob French
22 Roycroft Street, Waihi
Tel: (07) 863 7208 westwindgarden@xtra.co.nz
www.bnb.co.nz/westwind.html
Double $65 Single $35 (Continental Breakfast)
Child $15 Dinner $20 Credit cards accepted
Children welcome
4 Single (2 bdrm)
1 Guests share

We offer a friendly restful smoke-free stay in our modern home and garden. Waihi is the gate way to both the Coromandel with its beautiful beaches and the Bay of Plenty. Waihi is a historic town with vintage railway running to Waikino, a working gold mine discovered 1878 closed 1952. Reopened in 1989 as a open-cast mine. Free mine tours available. Beach 10 min away, beautiful bush walks, golf courses, trout fishing. Enjoy a home cooked meal or sample our restaurants. Our interests are gardening, dancing and travel.

Waihi Beach *B&B Self catering 13km E of Waihi*

Waves
Margaret & George Collins
169 Seaforth Road, Waihi Beach
Tel: (07) 863 4771 Fax: (07) 863 4772
Mob: 025 487 603
wavesatwaihibeach@yahoo.co.nz
www.bnb.co.nz/waves.html
Double $100 Single $80 (Full Breakfast)
Up to 4 people self catering $120 Children welcome
2 Queen 1 Twin 1 Single (3 bdrm) 2 Private

"Waves" is just a few sandy steps to the Pacific surf. Swimming, fishing, golfing, flying, boating, bowling, tennis, adventure activities are all close by. A great year round holiday place. Waihi is the gateway to the beautiful Coromandel Peninsula and The Bay Of Plenty fruit bowl. "Waves" offers comfortable, friendly Bed & Breakfast or fully equipped self - catering accommodation. Discuss your options with Margaret & George. They are a much travelled, hospitable couple who will help make your stay memorable. "Waves" is smoke free. Children welcome.

Waihi Beach *Self-contained 11km E of Waihi*

Waterfront Homestay
Kay & John Morgan
17 The Esplanade (off Hinemoa Street), Waihi Beach
Tel: (07) 863 4342 Fax: (07) 863 4342
Mob: 025 287 1104
k.morgan@xtra.co.nz
www.bnb.co.nz/waterfronthomestay.html
Double $90 (Continental Breakfast)
Credit cards accepted Children welcome
1 King 1 Double 1 Single (2 bdrm) 1 Private

Waterfront Homestay Fully self contained two double bedrooms plus single bed. Very suitable for two couples or small family group. Unit on lower floor of family home. Situated on waterfront of beautiful uncrowded ocean beach. Walk from front door directly onto sandy beach. Safe ocean swimming, surfcasting, surfing and coastal walks. 9 hole golf course with club hire in township, 18 hole golf course 11km away. Restaurant within walking distance of accommodation or use facilities provided with accommodation. Tariff $90 per couple bed & breakfast, $10 per extra persons.

Waihi   *Homestay B&B Studio*   *2km W of Waihi*

Trout & Chicken at Drift House
Michael & Adrienne Muir
9137 State Highway 2, RD 2, Waihi
Tel: (07) 863 6964 Fax: (07) 863 6966
Mob: 025 206 4080   troutandchicken@paradise.net.nz
www.troutandchicken.co.nz

Double $110 Single $90 (Special Breakfast)
Dinner $30 by arrangement Studio $80
Credit cards accepted Pet on property
1 Queen 2 Twin (2 bdrm) 2 Ensuite

Welcome to our nearly new home 300m's off the main highway, quiet, peaceful and situated on an organic blueberry orchard. Look for trout and eels in the bordering stream, sit on your own deck with coffee and blueberry muffins or visit the local organic cafe, restaurants, shops, local historic sites and walk in the beautiful countryside. Enjoy a relaxing breakfast on the deck or in our comfortable dining room. Have a walk in the orchard accompanied our friendly Labrador, or just relax with your favourite book.

Waihi   *Homestay Separate/Suite*   *2km S of Waihi*

Ashtree House
Anne & Bill Ashdown
20 Riflerange Road, Waihi
Tel: (07) 863 6448 Fax: (07) 863 6443
www.bnb.co.nz/waihi.html

Double $80 Single $50 (Full Breakfast)
Dinner $20pp Garden unit $35 pp
Pet on property
1 King 1 Double 2 Single (3 bdrm)
2 Private 1 Guests share

Modern brick home set on the side of a hill with extensive views and access to trout river. Private guest wing comprising 2 double bedrooms, large private bathroom with shower and bath. Guest lounge with TV, stereo and large selection of New Zealand books. Laundry and separate toilet. Eight acres, large attractive garden and pond area. I breed kakarikis, New Zealand's endangered parrots. One house dog. Situated 2 minutes to centre of Waihi, complete privacy and quiet guaranteed. Self-contained unit with wheelchair facilities.

Waihi   *Homestay B&B*   *.5km W of Waihi*

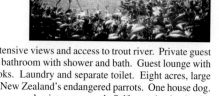

Chez Nous
Sara Parish
41 Seddon Avenue, Waihi
Tel: 07 863 7538 Sara.P@xtra.co.nz
www.bnb.co.nz/cheznous.html

Double $65 Single $45 (Continental Breakfast)
Child $20 Dinner $20pp by arrangement
Credit cards accepted Pet on property
1 Queen 1 Twin (2 bdrm)
1 Guests share

Enjoy a relaxed and friendly atmosphere in a spacious, modern home in an attractive garden setting. Shops and restaurants are within easy walking distance. Discover past and present gold mining activities (tours available), sandy surf beaches, bush walks, 9 and 18 hole golf courses, art, craft and wine trails. Waihi is an ideal stopover for the traveller who wants to explore the Coromandel Peninsula, Bay of Plenty and Waikato.

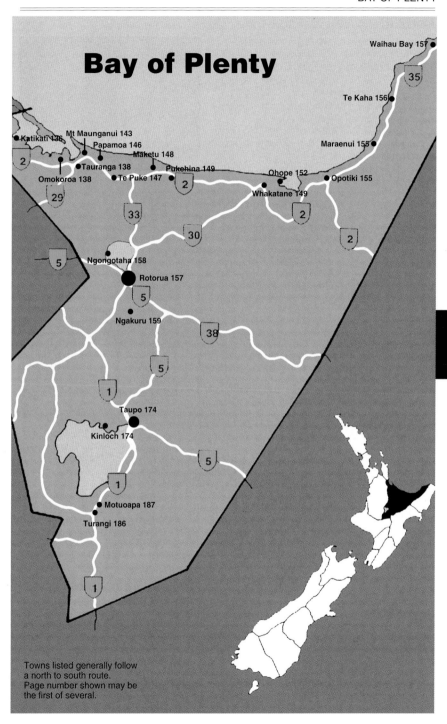

Bay of Plenty

Waihau Bay 157

35

Te Kaha 156

Katikati 136
Mt Maunganui 143
Papamoa 146
Maraenui 155
Maketu 148
2
Tauranga 138
Pukehina 149
Ohope 152
Opotiki 155
Omokoroa 138
Te Puke 147
2
Whakatane 149
29
33
2
30
5
Ngongotaha 158
Rotorua 157
5
Ngakuru 159
38
5
1
Taupo 174
Kinloch 174
5
1
Motuoapa 187
Turangi 186
1

Towns listed generally follow
a north to south route.
Page number shown may be
the first of several.

Katikati *Farmstay B&B Self-contained Cottage* *30km N of Tauranga*

Jacaranda Cottage Lynlie & Rick Watson
230 Thompson's Track, RD 2, Katikati
Tel: (07) 549 0616 Fax: (07) 549 0616
Mob: 025 272 8710   jacaranda.cottage@clear.net.nz
www.jacaranda-cottage.co.nz

Double $80 Single $50 (Full Breakfast)
S/C Cottage (2 night min.stay) $85 Dble
$25per extra adult Child discount Credit cards accepted
House:1 Queen 2 Single (2 bdrm) 1 Guests share
SC: 1 Double 1 Single (1 bdrm) 1 Ensuite

Spectacular 360 degree views, from forests and farmlands to mountains and the sea - your introduction to the true spirit of rural New Zealand with its unsurpassed hospitality and warm generosity. Our modest, clean and comfortable family home is on a five acre farmlet, 8km south of Katikati Mural Town. Or you may prefer instead our fully equipped, self-catering hillside cottage. We enjoy children 'helping' us with our friendly small-farm animals. Swimming pool, horses, glowworms at night. Near beaches, tramping, golf, hot pools, bird gardens, winery, restaurants, arts/crafts.

Katikati *Self-contained* *20km S of Katikati*

Jones Lifestyle
Thora & Trevor Jones
Pahoia Road, RD 2, Tauranga
Tel: (07) 548 0661 Fax: (07) 548 0661
joneslifestyle@clear.net.nz
www.bnb.co.nz/joneslifestyle.html

Double $85 Single $60 (Continental Breakfast)
Child $20 Credit cards accepted
1 Queen (1 bdrm)
1 Private

This modern self-contained apartment has all amenities including lounge (with convertible divan), fully equipped kitchen and laundry. For a larger family extra bedrooms and a private bathroom are available in the main house. A deluxe continental breakfast is provided for self-service. Other amenities are BBQ, dinghy, games rooms for billiards, table tennis etc. We share our peaceful horticultural lifestyle property on Pahoia peninsula with many birds. There are spectacular views of Tauranga harbour (water's edge 200m away) and sunset over the Kaimai Ranges.

Katikati *Farmstay B&B* *3km N of Katikati*

Aberfeldy
Mary Anne and Rod Calver
164 Lindemann Road, RD 1, Katikati
Tel: (07) 549 0363 Fax: (07) 549 0363
Mob: 025 909 710   Tollfree: 0800 309 064
aberfeldy@xtra.co.nz   www.bnb.co.nz/aberfeldy.html

Double $100 Single $55 (Full Breakfast) Child $30
Dinner By arrangement Credit cards accepted
Pet on property Children welcome Pets welcome
1 Double 1 Twin 1 Single (2 bdrm) 1 Private

Large attractive home set in extensive gardens with private sunny guest accommodation. The private lounge opens onto a patio, and has TV and coffee making facilities. One party at a time in guest accommodation. We farm sheep and cattle. Rod's long been associated with Kiwifruit and is a Rotarian. Panoramic views of bush-clad hills, farmland and harbour. Activities include bush and farm walks, meeting tame animals especially Sue the Kune Kune pig. Golf course, horse riding, music, cooking. Jax, our Australian terrier will welcome you.

Katikati *B&B 1km N of Katikati*

Waterford House (katikati.8k.com)
Alan & Helen Cook
15 Crossley Street, Katikati
Tel: (07) 549 0757
www.katikati.8k.com

Double $65 Single $40 (Full Breakfast)
Child discounted Dinner $20 by arrangement
Credit cards accepted Pet on property
1 Queen 1 Double 2 Twin 1 Single (5 bdrm)
3 Guests share

Waterford House, situated in a quiet semi-rural area, provides spacious accommodation with wheelchair access throughout. A large comfortable lounge with television, stereo-radio, fridge-freezer, microwave and tea/coffee making facilities. Cot and highchair are available. Local attractions include Twickenham Homestead Cafe, Morton Estate Winery, Bird Gardens, Ballantyne Golf Course, Sapphire Springs Hot Pools, Kaimai bush walks, Uretara River Walkway and craft workshops. 32 murals and sculptures depict the history of Katikati "Mural Town", located on Pacific Coast Highway. Our cat is called Matilda.

Katikati *B&B Countrystay 7km N of Katikati*

Cotswold Lodge
Alison & Des Belsham
183 Ongare Point Road, RD 1, Katikati
Tel: (07) 549 2110 Fax: (07) 549 2109
cotswold@ihug.co.nz
www.cotswold.co.nz

Double $115-$125 Single $90 (Full Breakfast)
Dinner By arrangement Credit cards accepted
2 Double 2 Single (3 bdrm)
3 Ensuite

We offer warm Kiwi hospitality, a little luxury and a relaxed environment in our rural 'home away from home', Cotswold Lodge. Gourmet breakfasts included. Evening meals by prior arrangement. Wander through the gardens, a Kiwifruit orchard or down to the Harbour. Enjoy the views to the Kaimai Ranges or relax in the hot spa and listen to the birds. Rotorua and Coromandel only 1.5 hours away. Nearby: restaurants, murals, bird gardens, heritage museum, hot pools, beaches, coastal and bush walks, wineries, galleries, and several golf courses.

Katikati *B&B Private suite 9km N of Katikati*

Peaceful Panorama Lodge
Phil & Barbara McKernon
901 Main Road North, SH2, RD1, Katikati 3063
Tel: (07) 549 1882 Fax: (07) 549 1882
Mob: 021 165 5875   mckernon@xtra.co.nz
www.beds-n-leisure.com/peacefulpanorama

Double $95 Single $85 (Special Breakfast) Child $30
  Dinner $25 by arrangement $120 suite dble
Group discounts Credit cards accepted Pet on property
2 Double 3 Single (3 bdrm) 1 Ensuite 1 Private

Conveniently located only minutes from beautiful Waihi beach and nestling in the foothills of the Kaimais. We offer stylish accommodation with all rooms having spectacular ocean views. The private suite with own lounge and TV opens out to the swimming pool area. Tea and coffee facilities and a generous home-cooked breakfast served on the terrace. Feel free to roam the 10 acres of gardens and fruit orchards which are home to an abundance of flora and fauna. Nearby: thermal hot pools, bush walks, golf courses, wineries, harbour, dolphin 'sea faris' ... we love it here, so will you!

Tauranga - Omokoroa   *15km N of Tauranga*
Self-contained Homestay B&B Cottage

Walnut Cottage
Ken & Betty Curreen
309 Plummers Point Road, Omokoroa, RD 2, Tauranga
Tel: (07) 548 0692 Fax: (07) 548 1764
walnuthomestay@actrix.co.nz
www.cybersurf.co.nz/curreen
Double $75-$95 Single $50-$80
(Continental Breakfast) Dinner $15
1 Queen 1 Double (2 bdrm) 2 Ensuite

Walnut Cottage is situated on scenic Plummers Point Peninsula overlooking Tauranga Harbour. We invite our guests to enjoy the tranquility our "little-corner-of-the-world" has to offer. Stroll along the Peninsula with its superb views, amble to boat jetty and reserve or relax in mineral hot pools. Golf courses(spare clubs available),wineries,tramping tracks, quarry "gardens" and eating houses are in the vicinity. Fishing trips can be arranged. Both accomodations have own private entrances, T.V.and tea/ coffee. Directions: Plummers Point Rd.is opposite Caltex Service Station on SH2.

Tauranga - Omokoroa   *Homestay B&B*   *20K N of Tauranga*
SERENDIPITY
Sarath and Linda Vidanage
77 Harbour View Road, Omokoroa, Tauranga
Tel: (07) 548 2033 Mob: 027 499 9815
sarathv@yahoo.com
www.bnb.co.nz/vidanage.html
Double $100 Single $75 (Full Breakfast)
Child $30.00 Dinner $30.00 Children welcome
4 Double (2 bdrm)
2 Private

Welcome to our home and garden nestled above spectacular Omokoroa Beach. The beach is a short walk down the steps. Leisurely walking treks take you through the groves and gardens of the peninsula. A beautiful golf course and local hot pools are minutes away. We are a well-traveled couple who have found our paradise. We love to cook and offer a varied cuisine from traditional to exotic. In one stop you will experience the best of the Bay of Plenty.

Omokoroa   *B&B*   *17km N of Tauranga*
Seascape
Geoff & Sue Gripton
5 Waterview Terrace, Omokoroa
Tel: (07) 548 1027
grippos@xtra.co.nz
www.bnb.co.nz/seascape.html
Double $65-$75 Single $45 (Continental Breakfast)
Credit cards accepted Pet on property
1 Double 2 Single (2 bdrm)
1 Ensuite 1 Guests share

Come share our stunning views of Tauranga Harbour and Kaimais. On our doorstep are beaches, walkways, golf, hot pools, boat ramps etc. Just halfway (15 mins) between Tauranga and Katikati, we offer a double room with ensuite and TV, twin room with shared bathroom, both with tea/coffee. Breakfast on cereals, juice, homemade bread and jams while gazing at the everchanging view. Only 3.5km from SH2, left at roundabout, first right, first left into Waterview Terrace. Geoff, Sue and our cat will welcome you.

Tauranga   *Homestay B&B   2km W of Tauranga*

Christine Ross
8A Vale Street,
Bureta, Tauranga
Tel: (07) 576 8895
rossvale@xtra.co.nz
www.bnb.co.nz/ross.html
Double $70 Single $40
(Continental & Full Breakfast)
1 Twin 1 Single (2 bdrm)
2 Private

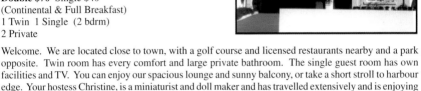

Welcome. We are located close to town, with a golf course and licensed restaurants nearby and a park opposite. Twin room has every comfort and large private bathroom. The single guest room has own facilities and TV. You can enjoy our spacious lounge and sunny balcony, or take a short stroll to harbour edge. Your hostess Christine, is a miniaturist and doll maker and has travelled extensively and is enjoying retirement. Breakfast of your choice. Off street parking plus a garage. Will meet public transport.

Tauranga   *Homestay B&B   5km E of Tauranga*

Bolney Gate
Joyce & Jack Ingram
20 Esmerelda St, Welcome Bay, Tauranga
Tel: (07) 544 0107 or (07) 544 3228
Fax: (07) 544 3228   www.bnb.co.nz/bolneygate.html
Double $60 Single $35 (Full Breakfast)
Child $20, under 10yrs $15, nuder 3 ni
Credit cards accepted
1 King/Twin 2 Queen 2 Twin 2 Single (3 bdrm)
1 Family share

Bolney Gate is a comfortable 4 level home overlooking a mature park. We have a secluded pool, Sky TV and an interesting cuisine. Tauranga has world renowned surf beaches - salt and fresh water fishing - scenic walks - rafting and jet water facilities. Rotorua is within easy reach - the thermal areas - Coromandel near at hand with a wealth to offer. Interests - history - current affairs - art - creative writing. Jack and I have travelled widely both in NZ and overseas. Off street parking and pick up facilities available.

Tauranga - Matua   *B&B   6km N of Tauranga*

Christiansen's B&B
Heather & John Christiansen
210 Levers Road, Matua, Tauranga
Tel: (07) 576 6835 Fax: (07) 576 6464
christiansensbandb@clear.net.nz
www.bnb.co.nz/christiansensbb.html
Double $90 Single $60 (Full Breakfast)
Credit cards accepted
1 Queen 2 Single (2 bdrm)
1 Guests share

Our home in the pleasant suburb of Matua is set in a garden of NZ native trees, shrubs and ferns. The guest wing is quiet and comfortable. Please use our lounge and enjoy the garden. Our home is smoke-free. Breakfast - see our menu of special choices. Can cater for food allergies. Close to harbour beaches and parks; seven minutes drive to Tauranga city centre and fifteen minutes to Mount Maunganui's Ocean Beach. Our interests include growing native plants, the performing arts and motorcycling.

Tauranga - Oropi   *Farmstay Homestay*   *9km S of Tauranga*

Grenofen
Jennie & Norm Reeve
85 Castles Road, Oropi,
RD 3, Tauranga
Tel: (07) 543 3953 Fax: (07) 543 3951
n.reeve@wave.co.nz
www.bnb.co.nz/grenofen.html

Double $100 Single $70 (Full Breakfast)
Child by age Dinner $35
1 King 2 Single (2 bdrm)
2 Ensuite

We invite you to stay with us in our spacious home overlooking the countryside, sea, Tauranga city and Mt Maunganui. Our property is a sheltered 3 1/2 acres with trees, gardens and lawns. You may relax in quiet and privacy, enjoy the spa, or swim in our pool. both rooms have ensuite, electric blankets, TV, and comfortable chairs. Tea facility in guest area, laundry done overnight if required. We love to share our home and travel experiences with guests. Be sure of a warm welcome.

Tauranga - Bethlehem   *6km NW of Tauranga*

The Hollies
Shirley & Michael Creak
Westridge Drive, Bethlehem, Tauranga 3001
Tel: (07) 577 9678 Fax: (07) 579 1678
stay@hollies.co.nz   www.hollies.co.nz

Double $120-$250 Single $95-$165 (Full Breakfast)
Dinner $40 pp Credit cards accepted
2 King/Twin 1 Queen 2 Single (3 bdrm)
1 Ensuite 2 Private

Hollies, an elegant sophisticated modern country house, acre of gardens. Large luxuriously appointed rooms, panoramic views of gardens and rolling hills. The spacious suite has super king (or twin) bed, ensuite, lounge & TV, kitchenette, alternative private entrance and balcony. Hairdryers, bathrobes and toiletries. Fresh flowers, chocolates and crisp linen and every attention to detail combine to ensure your stay is truly memorable. Complimentary tea/coffee. Landscaped gardens, swimming pool. Breakfast: home made bread, muffins, fresh fruit and tempting cooked dishes. Muffee our cat. Children by arrangement.

Tauranga   *Homestay*   *6km N of Tauranga*

Matua Homestay
Peter & Anne Seaton
34 Tainui Street, Matua, Tauranga
Tel: (07) 576 8083 Mob: 025 915 566
pa_seaton@clear.net.nz
www.bnb.co.nz/matuahomestay.html

Double $70 Single $40 (Continental Breakfast)
Child $20 Children welcome
1 Double 1 Twin (2 bdrm)
1 Guests share

Welcome to quality accommodation in our spacious well appointed home in a peaceful garden setting. Stroll 200 metres to the harbour beach to see spectacular estuary views. Enjoy a good nights sleep in tastefully furnished guest rooms. Tea,coffee and milo are available at any time. We have travelled extensively and are happy to help you plan visits to local places of interest. We look forward to meeting you, offering Kiwi hospitality and making your stay with us very special. Phone now for reservation and directions.

Tauranga *Homestay B&B* *3km N of Tauranga Central*

Harbinger House
Helen & Doug Fisher
209 Fraser Street, Tauranga
Tel: (07) 578 8801 Fax: (07) 579 4101
Mob: 025 583 049   d-h.fisher@xtra.co.nz
www.harbinger.co.nz
Double $75-$90 Single $55-$70 (Special Breakfast)
Child 1/2 price Dinner $25 Credit cards accepted
2 Queen 2 Single (3 bdrm) 1 Guests share

Harbinger House is centrally located to hospital, conference centres, beaches and downtown shopping. Our upstairs has been renovated with your comfort a top priority, using quality furnishings and linen. The queen rooms have vanity units and private balconies. A guest phone and laundry facilities are available. Breakfast is a gourmet event, using local produce where possible. We offer complimentary pick up from public transport depots and have off street parking. Our house is smoke free inside and we have a cat called Bronson.

Tauranga *Homestay B&B* *10km E of Tauranga*

Birch Haven
Judy & George McConnell
R403 Welcome Bay Road, RD 5, Tauranga
Tel: (07) 544 2499 Mob: 025 414 289
george.mcconnell@paradise.net.nz
www.bnb.co.nz/birchhaven.html
Double $80 Single $50 (Full Breakfast) Child $25
Dinner $25 Pet on property
1 King/Twin 1 Queen (2 bdrm)
1 Private 1 Family share

Luxurious, comfortable one-level 'home away from home' on 3 1/2 acres growing tamarillos and avocados. We enjoy meeting people, have travelled extensively and our interests include Blackie our cat, sport, reading, gardening, good food and wine. We offer a 3 course dinner option, swimming and spa pools, tour information and local courtesy pickup. Tauranga, Mt Maunganui, cafes and restaurants are a ten minute drive. Make us your base for day trips to Lake Taupo, Rotorua, Waitomo Caves or Coromandel Peninsula. Go sightseeing - have fun - return and relax!

Tauranga *B&B* *10km SW of Tauranga*

Redwood Villa
Mike & Dee Forsman
17 Redwood Lane, Tauriko RD 1, Tauranga
Tel: (07) 543 4303 Fax: (07) 543 4303
Mob: 025 296 5565   redwoodvilla@ihug.co.nz
www.bnb.co.nz/redwoodvilla.co.nz.html
Double $100 Single $75 (Continental Breakfast)
Dinner $30 Full breakfast by arrangement
Pet on property
1 Queen (1 bdrm) 1 Ensuite 1 Private

Relax in a completely refurbished 100 year old villa. This historic dwelling was originally the Tauriko Post Office and serviced river traders during the saw-milling era early last century. Rural property comprising 3 acres with house situated amongst giant redwood and oak trees. Your own lounge, bathroom (claw foot bath), verandahs and outdoor areas. Only 12 minutes to downtown Tauranga and over Harbour bridge to Mt Maunganui. Attractions: stroll to river, tramping, parks, wineries, beaches, restaurants. We have two cats and a dog. Smoking outside only.

Tauranga *Homestay B&B*   *12km S of Downtown Tauranga*

Floribunda
John & Sue Speirs
70 Gargan Road, RD 1, Tauranga
Tel: (07) 543 0454 Fax: (07) 543 0454
Mob: 021 778 414
s.phillips@clear.net.nz
www.bnb.co.nz/floribunda.html

Double $95 Single $75 (Full Breakfast)
Dinner $30pp
1 Queen (1 bdrm)
1 Private

A warm welcome awaits you at our elegant country home, just 15 minutes from downtown Tauranga. Relax amongst the Bays' finest gardens, set on 5 acres with magnificent rural views. Enjoy tennis, swimming in Summer, the putting green, walking or cycling. Your room offers every facility to ensure your utmost in comfort. Restaurants, golf courses, beaches, wineries, shopping etc. all very close by.

Tauranga *B&B*   *3km S of Tauranga*

Fieldview 15th Avenue
Tui and Brian Henry
143c Fifteenth Ave,
Tauranga
Tel: 07 579 0919
www.bnb.co.nz/bandbtauranga.html

Double $70 Single $50
(Continental Breakfast)
Credit cards accepted
1 Double (1 bdrm)
1 Ensuite

Welcome to our modern, open plan townhouse, with off street parking, conveniently located close to CBD, restaurants, hospital, main highways. Our guest room, with ensuite, is on the ground floor. Join us for tea, coffee and home baking in our spacious lounge, or relax in the sunny open aspect of our courtyard. Cut lunches for travellers can be arranged. We look forward to welcoming you to our home, where your every comfort is our concern.

Tauranga - Pahoia *Homestay B&B*   *20km N of Tauranga*

Bayview Homestead
Verna & Bill Morris
567 Esdaile Rd, Pahoia, RD 6 Tauranga
Tel: (07) 548 1551 Fax: (07) 548 1551
Mob: 025 464 488
bayviewhomestead@xtra.co.nz
www.bnb.co.nz/bayviewhomestead.html

Double $125-$150 Single $95-$110 (Special Breakfast)
Dinner $20 - 35 BYO Credit cards accepted
1 King/Twin 1 Queen (2 bdrm) 1 Private

If you like friendly hospitality, delicious food and stunning views you'll love staying at Bayview Homestead. Our home sits amid 3 acres of lawns and gardens, and all rooms are spacious with views of farmland, mountain and the sea. Our extensive breakfast menu offers everything from the traditional bacon and eggs to American pancakes and our own house specials. With plenty of indoor and outdoor living areas, guests can choose either to socialize or have privacy. French, German and Spanish spoken. Children by arrangement.

Tauranga   *Self-contained Farmstay B&B*   *11km SW of Tauranga*

Totara Vale Lodge
Fran & Brian Smith
48 Redwood Lane, RD 1, Tauriko

Tel: (07) 543 0883 Fax: (07) 543 0883
fran&brian@xtra.co.nz
www.bnb.co.nz/totaravalelodge.html

Double $80 Single $50 (Continental Breakfast)
Dinner $25 full breakfast by arrangement
Credit cards accepted Pet on property
2 Twin (2 bdrm)
1 Private 1 Guests share

Our peaceful, secluded 35 acre farm is on the banks of the Wairoa River, just off the Hamilton-Tauranga highway. We offer a detached self-contained unit, or a twin room upstairs in our home, sharing facilities. Character farmhouse surrounded by large cottage garden with rhododendroms, and many beautiful trees. Swim, canoe, fish or relax and enjoy views of river and countryside. We have travelled widely overseas and in New Zealand, and enjoy our two classic cars. Phone for directions.

Tauranga   *Self-contained B&B self-catering*   *Central Tauranga*

Avenue Eleven
Paul & Daria Lowe
26 Eleventh Avenue, Memorial Park, Tauranga

Tel: (07) 577 1881 Fax: (07) 577 1881
Mob: 025 204 8290
avenue11tauranga@yahoo.co.nz
www.bnb.co.nz/avenueeleven.html

Double $80-$125 Single $80 (Continental Breakfast)
Children welcome
2 King/Twin 2 Queen (4 bdrm)
4 Ensuite

Avenue Eleven is centrally located with pleasant views over Tauranga Harbour and Memorial Park. All suites are self-contained, have ensuite bathrooms and water views . Two suites also have self-catering facilities. The rooms are newly renovated with many stylish interior design features. There are excellent restaurants, cafés and shops only a short walking distance away and a stroll across the road will take you through the park to the open air pool and harbour's edge. One of the best locations in Tauranga.

Mt Maunganui   *Self-contained Homestay*   *4km N of Mt Maunganui*

Homestay on the Beach
Bernie & Lolly Cotter
85C Oceanbeach Road, Mt Maunganui

Tel: (07) 575 4879 Fax: (07) 575 4828
Mob: 025 766 799   bernie.cotter@xtra.co.nz
www.bnb.co.nz/homestayonthebeachcotter.html

Double $130 Single $80 (Continental Breakfast)
Child negotiable $25pp extra guests Suite Double $160
Credit cards accepted Children welcome
2 Queen 1 Single (2 bdrm) 1 Ensuite 1 Private

Welcome to our magnificent home by the sea. Choose from our self-contained suite, sleeping 5 guests (suitable for children) with private deck. 1 min to beach for those casual walks. Upstairs is our Queen ensuite with TV. Your continental breakfast includes eggs any style. International golf course 500 metres. The famous "Mount Walk" up or around with 360 degree views is breathtaking. 4kms are shops, hot salt water pools, and restaurants for your enjoyment. Sorry no pets. Off street parking. Look forward to having you stay.

Mt Maunganui   *Self-contained Homestay*   *8km E of Tauranga*

Beachfront Homestay
Barbara Marsh
28A Sunbrae Grove, Mount Maunganui
Tel: (07) 575 5592 Fax: (07) 575 5592
Mob: 021 707 243
www.bnb.co.nz/beachfronthomestaymtmaunganui.html

Double $100 Single $70 (Continental Breakfast)
Credit cards accepted Pet on property
1 Queen 2 Single (2 bdrm)
1 Guests share

Welcome to our absolute oceanfront Paradise, where you can relax in beautiful surroundings at one of the country's finest beaches. We are close to great restaurants, excellent shopping, bowls, golf and hot salt pools. We have one twin and one queen-sized bedroom, guest bathroom, lounge with kitchen facilities, TV etc. This unit is available to rent, also, at a separate rate. Undercover, off-street parking, laundry facilities offered, smoke-free home. Your well travelled hostess and resident cat (Bella) look forward to meeting you.

Mt Maunganui   *Self-contained Homestay*   *3km S of Mt Maunganui*

Fairways
Philippa & John Davies
170 Ocean Beach Road, Mt. Maunganui
Tel: (07) 575 5325 Fax: (07) 578 2362
pipjohn@clear.net.nz
www.bnb.co.nz/fairways.html

Double $95 Single $75 (Full Breakfast)
Dinner incl. wine $35pp B/A Credit cards accepted
1 Queen 1 Double (2 bdrm)
1 Ensuite 1 Family share

A Golfer's paradise. Our comfortable, timbered, character home adjoins the 8th fairway of the Mount golf course, and is across the road from the wonderful ocean beach. Enjoy with us interesting food, wine, art, music, conversation, and a bonus golf lesson. John is a retired solicitor, teacher and former scratch golfer, and Pippa a registered nurse involved in natural health. Our leisurely dinners are fun occasions, and John's desserts legendary. We are well travelled both in New Zealand and abroad, and look forward to meeting you.

Mt Maunganui   *B&B*   *9km S of Mt Maunganui*

Pembroke House
Graham & Cathy Burgess
12 Santa Fe Key, Royal Palm Beach Estate,
Papamoa/Mt Maunganui
Tel: (07) 572 1000 PembrokeHouse@xtra.co.nz
www.bnb.co.nz/pembrokehouse.html

Double $90-$95 Single $70-$75 (Full Breakfast)
Child $35 Credit cards accepted Pet on property
2 Queen 2 Single (3 bdrm)
2 Ensuite 1 Private

Welcome to our modern home. Cross the road to the Ocean Beach, where you can enjoy swimming, surfing and beach walks. Enjoy stunning sea-views while dining at breakfast. Near Palm Beach Shopping Plaza and restaurants. Separate guest lounge with TV and tea-making facilities. Cathy is a primary school teacher and Graham semi-retired - your host. We are widely travelled and both enjoy meeting people. We share our home with two precious cats - Twinkle and Crystal. (Not suitable for children under five years.) No smoking.

Mt Maunganui   *B&B*   *10km E of Mt Maunganui - Tauranga*

Royal Palm Beach Waters
Val & Dick Waters
36 Palm Beach Boulevard, Royal Palm Beach,
Papamoa/Mt Maunganui
Tel: (07) 575 8395 Fax: (07) 575 8395
Mob: 021 510 900   waters.royalpalms@xtra.co.nz
www.bnb.co.nz/royalpalmbeachwaters.html
Double $95-$125 Single $75 (Full Breakfast)
Credit cards accepted
2 Queen 2 Single (3 bdrm)   1 Ensuite 1 Guests share

Award winning home on the lakeside, with beautiful sunset views to the Papamoa hills and only 300 metres from safe surf beach and close to all amenities. Our spacious executive suite is fully self contained with spa bath, TV and complimentary tea making facilities. A separate guest lounge also has complimentary tea making facilities, TV and large deck for sunbathing. Courtesy pick up from airport, buses, information centres. Coffee and cake served on arrival. We offer luxury at an affordable price. Not suitable for small children.

Mt Maunganui   *Self-contained B&B*   *3km S of Mt Maunganui*

Oceanbeach B&B
Marilou & Gerard Meyers
14 Oceanbeach Road, Mt Maunganui
Tel: (07) 574 5568 Mob: 025 218 5682
www.bnb.co.nz/oceanbeachbb.html
Double $80 Single $50
(Continental Breakfast) Child $15
1 Queen 1 Double 2 Single (3 bdrm)
2 Private

Marilou and Gerard welcome you to our home at Mount Maunganui, with the best beach in the Bay of Plenty, just across the road for swimming, surfing, sunbathing and beach walks. Hot water pools, golf course, shops and restaurants are all close at hand. The fully self-contained apartment has two bedrooms, a bathroom, kitchen, lounge with TV and laundry facilities. A double bedroom upstairs with own bathroom is available. No smoking. Off street parking and garaging is provided. There are two friendly resident cats.

Mt Maunganui   *Homestay*   *5km S of Mt Maunganui*

Beachfront Homestays
Christine Mora
3/323 Oceanbeach Road, Mt Maunganui 3002
Tel: (07) 575 6501 Fax: (07) 574 6501
Mob: 025 604 2135   beachfront@clear.net.nz
www.bnb.co.nz/beachfronthomestays.html
Double $120 Single $80 (Full Breakfast)
Dinner by arrangement Credit cards accepted
1 Queen 2 Single (2 bdrm)
1 Guests share

We invite you to share the relaxing atmosphere of our beachfront home. Enjoy walking the beach, restful seaviews and ultimate "at home" comforts - fine linens - fresh flowers - robes - toiletries. Breakfast to suit, healthy or indulgent, al fresco on the deck if you wish. Dinner by prior arrangement. Off street parking and laundry facilities for guests. non-smokers preferred. Two minutes to Bayfair shopping centre and ten to Downtown Mount Maunganui, with hot saltwater pools and many tempting restaurants, cafes and shops. looking forward to welcoming you.

Mt Maunganui *B&B Detached villa*   *4km S of Mt Maunganui*

Fairvue Villas
Winston & Kathy Spence
164 Ocean Beach Road, Mount Maunganui,
Tel: (07) 575 7457 Fax: (07) 575 6457
Mob: 0274 943 714   Tollfree: 0800 302 342
fairvilla@xtra.co.nz
www.bnb.co.nz/fairvuevillas.html
Double $120-$160 Single $80-$110
(Special Breakfast) Dinner by arrangement
detached villa extra $25 pp Credit cards accepted
2 Queen 1 Double 2 Twin (5 bdrm) 3 Ensuite 3 Private 1 Guests share

Welcome to Fairvue Villas. Our French flair villa is situated on the Mount golf course and across the road is the Ocean Beach. Choose from two luxurious bedrooms with private ensuites, TV, coffee facilities, and quality linen, or our self-contained detached villa with laundry, and cooking facilities. Sleeps up to six guests. You can stroll along the beach, play a round of golf, or relax in private surroundings in our elegant lounge overlooking the golf course. Off street parking. A warm greeting awaits you.

Mt Maunganui *B&B holiday flats*   *1km E of Mount Manganui*

Mt Maunganui Bed & Breakfast
Nellie McQueen & Daphne William
463 Maunganui Road, Mt Maunganui,
Tel: (07) 575 4013 Fax: (07) 575 3014
Mob: 025 272 6342   bednbrekkie@ihug.co.nz
www.bnb.co.nz/themountbnb.html
Double $80-$90 Single $50-$60 (Full Breakfast)
Credit cards accepted
3 Double 2 Twin 1 Single (5 bdrm)
2 Guests share

Are you looking for a relaxed friendly atmosphere? Mt Maunganui B&B offers real hospitality at affordable prices, comfortable rooms, electric blankets, TVs, pool table/games room, tea & coffee on tap. Breakfast is great: cereal, fruit, bacon & eggs. We are close to downtown Mt Maunganui featuring excellent restaurants, cafes, clubs, Blake Park sporting complex, golf courses. Minutes away from the best beach in New Zealand and wonderful hot water salt pools. We are warm and caring hosts, ensuring that our guests enjoy their stay with us.

Papamoa *Self-contained Homestay*   *12km E of Mt Maunganui*

Markbeech Homestay
Joan & Jim Francis
6 Beachwater Drive, Papamoa
Tel: (07) 572 3588 Fax: (07) 572 3588
Mob: 025 318 132   2jaysfrancis@free.net.nz
www.bnb.co.nz/markbeechhomestay.html
Double $90 Single $45 (Continental & Full Breakfast)
Child 1/2 price Dinner $20 by arrangement
Credit cards accepted
1 Queen (s/c with kitchenette and ensuite)
1 Single (2 bdrm) 1 Ensuite 1 Private

We welcome you to our new home in Beachwater. We are in our 60's, and now into our 13th year of hosting. Our hobbies are gardening, travel, and entertaining guests. Our high level of personal service will, we hope, make you feel comfortable and relaxed. We are a five minute walk to the local shops and restaurants. Ten minutes walk to the beach, to swim or stroll. 'Arrive to us as guests, and leave as friends.' Please phone for directions.

Papamoa   *Homestay B&B*   *7km S of Bay Fair*

Tara Homestay B&B
Rose & Graeme Wilson
118 Tara Road, Papamoa, RD 7, Te Puke
Tel: (07) 542 3785 Fax: (07) 542 3787
Mob: 027 450 1254   grwilson.tarabb@clear.net.nz
www.bnb.co.nz/tarahomestaybb.html

Double $90 Single $60 (Full Breakfast)
Child $15 under 12yrs Dinner $20 - $25
Credit cards accepted Pets welcome
2 Queen 2 Single (3 bdrm) 1 Ensuite 1 Guests share

Rose and Graeme welcome you to their home on three acres, with extensive gardens highlighted with objects of old plus ceramics and mosaics created by Rose. We are retired farmers who have travelled and enjoy meeting and entertaining in our relaxed country atmosphere. Only 2km to beach, Palm Beach Mall. Handy to golf, walks, hot pools and 12kms to Mt Maunganui or Tauranga. Come and relax with us. Directions: From SH2 (Rotorua-Tauranga) turn at Domain Rd, Papamoa signpost. Proceed 150m. Turn right onto Tara Road. 1km down.

Papamoa Hills   *Homestay B&B Golf Course*   *13km W of Te Puke*

Summerhill
Brent & Rachel
Reid Road, R.D. 7 Te Puke, Bay of Plenty
Tel: (07) 542 1442 Fax: (07) 542 1445
Mob: 025 286 3613   res@summerhill.co.nz
www.bnb.co.nz/summerhill.html

Double $120-$150 Single $80-$100
(Continental & Full Breakfast) Dinner By Arrangement
Credit cards accepted Pet on property
3 Queen (3 bdrm) 3 Ensuite

Splendid golf house using natural timbers, stone and a turf roof. Overlooking a forested sheep and beef farm plus panoramic views of the Bay of Plenty sea and Islands. A challenging 9 hole golf course - par 36, runs through a chestnut orchard. Clubs for hire. Farm walks and mountain bike trails through established native and exotic forests. Adjacent to a famous Maori pa site/close to Kaiate water falls/Te Puke the kiwi-fruit capital/golden sand beaches of Papamoa with shops and restaurants/hot salt water pools of Mt Maunganui, and airport.

Te Puke   *Homestay*   *2km NW of Te Puke*

Lindenhof
Sandra & Henry Sutter
58 Dunlop Road,
Te Puke
Tel: (07) 573 4592 Fax: (07) 573 9392
henryandsandra@xtra.co.nz
www.bnb.co.nz/lindenhof.html

Double $100-$120 Single $70 (Full Breakfast)
Dinner $20 Credit cards accepted Pet on property
1 Queen 4 Single (3 bdrm)
1 Ensuite 2 Private

Lindenhof is an imposing building in the style of a Georgian country home. You are able to indulge in affordable luxury. Te Puke is the heart of Kiwifruit country. Close to town, semi rural. Tennis court, swimming pool. Languages spoken, English, Swiss German, German and French. Hobbies: vintage cars and spinning. No smoking in house. Not suitable for children. SH2 from Tauranga, Dunlop Rd turns right by Gas Centre (international B/B sign) 1 km. Up Dunlop Rd on left.

Te Puke   *Homestay Separate/Suite B&B*   *4.5km E of Te Puke*

Aotea Villa
Leigh & Jerry Basinger
246 Te Matai Road, Te Puke
Tel: (07) 573 9433 Fax: (07) 573 9463
Mob: 025 821 842   Tollfree: 0800 821 842
Leigh.Pool@xtra.co.nz   www.aoteavilla.co.nz

Double $100 Single $80 (Continental & Full Breakfast)
Child $30 Dinner by arrangement Credit cards accepted
1 Queen 2 Double 2 Twin 1 Single (4 bdrm)
1 Ensuite 1 Guests share

Welcome to AOTEA VILLA Te Puke, built in 1910 and recently renovated. Quiet location. Enjoy our spa, swimming pool, or relax on our wide verandas, viewing the gardens or sunsets. Close to Baypark Speedway, golf, beaches, tourists attractions, and only 40 minutes from Rotorua, Whakatane, 20 minutes from Mt. Maunganui, Tauranga. Gourmet meals by arrangement. Personality pet dog and cat. Well travelled hosts that will assist you with your interests in this area, to maximise an enjoyable stay. Visit our website www.aoteavilla.co.nz

Te Puke   *Self-contained Farmstay B&B*   *14km W of Te Puke*

Tui Heights Cottage
Theo & Lynlie Mills
1384 No 3 Road, RD 3, Te Puke 3071
Tel: (07) 573 5185 Fax: (07) 573 5185
millse@xtra.co.nz
www.bnb.co.nz/tuiheights.html

Double $90 Single $50 (Full Breakfast)
Child $20 Dinner $25 Credit cards accepted
Children welcome Pets welcome
1 King (1 bdrm) 1 Private

Theo and Lynlie welcome you to our rural farmstay. Enjoy the tranquility, awake to the sounds of Tuis, Bellbirds and possible to sight feral fallow deer wondering the farm. Most welcome to farm walks, native bush on our boundary. We are unique, living in Te Puke's Kiwifruit Country, enjoying natures paradise but being only 25mins to Mt Maunganui beaches, downtown Tauranga. We are keen outdoor people interested in tramping, travel, cooking & crafts. Kitchen, bar-b-que facilities available in our separate accommodation. Full breakfast available. Children welcome.

Maketu Beach   *Self-contained Homestay B&B*   *8km E of Te Puke*

Blue Tides Beachfront B&B/Homestay
Patricia Haine
7 Te Awhe Road, Maketu Beach, Bay of Plenty
Tel: (07) 533 2023 Fax: (07) 533 2023
Mob: 025 261 3077   Tollfree: 0800 359 191
info@bluetides.co.nz   www.bluetides.co.nz

Double $90-$120 Single $75 (Full Breakfast)
Dinner $25 - $35 S/C Unit $100 - $120
Credit cards accepted Pets welcome
2 King/Twin 2 Queen (4 bdrm)
3 Ensuite 1 Private 1 Guests share

So central to exciting tourist activities, shops and a choice of beaches. So much to see and do. Located on the water's edge in a multicultural village full of ancient history. Cafes and restaurants near by, amazing sunsets and night skies. Safe swimming and walks, boat ramp and hunting, warm and cozy year round. Kiwi home cooking, easy to find. Very relaxed with caring extras and genuine hospitality. We searched the world and settled here - come and see why! Great for all seasons!

Pukehina Beach   *Homestay*   *21km N of Te Puke*

Homestay on the Beach
Alison & Paul Carter
217 Pukehina Parade, Pukehina Beach, RD 9, Te Puke
Tel: (07) 533 3988 Fax: (07) 533 3988
Mob: 025 276 7305   p.a.carter@pukehina-beach.co.nz
www.homestays.net.nz/pukehina.htm
Double $100 Single $65
(Continental & Full Breakfast) Child 1/2 price
Unit $120 Dinner $30 Credit cards accepted
2 Double (2 bdrm)   1 Guests share

Welcome to our Absolute Beachfront Home situated on the Pacific Ocean. Your accommodation situated downstairs, allowing you complete privacy, if you so wish, includes, T.V. lounge with coffee/tea, fridge and laundry facilities, also available at separate rate. Enjoy magnificent views from your own private sundeck, including White Island volcano and occasional visits from the friendly dolphins. Golf course 13km. 30-40 minute drive from Tauranga, Mount Maunganui, Whakatane and Rotorua. Two licensed restaurants within 4km, surf casting, swimming walks or relax and enjoy our unique paradise.

Whakatane   *Homestay*   *7km W of Whakatane*

Leaburn Homestay
Kathleen and Jim Law
237 Thornton Road, RD 4, Whakatane
Tel: (07) 3087487/308 Fax: (07) 308 7487
kath.law@theredbarn.co.nz
www.bnb.co.nz/leaburnhomestay.html
Double $70 Single $40 (Full Breakfast)
Dinner $25 Credit cards accepted
1 Queen 2 Single (2 bdrm)
1 Guests share

Whakatane is off the beaten tourist track, yet it is the centre for a wide range of activities. We can arrange sightseeing trips, including White Island. Relax in peaceful surroundings - watch the activities in our Red Barn Country Kitchen and Craftshop, which promotes 270 Bay of Plenty artisans. Two 50/50 sharemilkers manage our properties and milk over 400 cows. We grow citrus and breed black and coloured sheep. As "young oldies" we enjoy bowls, Lions Club, genealogy, and organic gardening. Currently no domestic pets.

Whakatane   *Farmstay*   *18km S of Whakatane*

Omataroa Deer Farm
Jill & John Needham
Paul Road, RD 2, Whakatane
Tel: (07) 322 8399 Fax: (07) 322 8399
Mob: 025 449 250
jill-needham@xtra.co.nz
www.bnb.co.nz/needham.html
Double $90 Single $60 (Continental & Full Breakfast)
Child $40 Dinner $25 Pet on property
1 King 1 Queen (2 bdrm)
1 Ensuite 1 Private

We invite you to stay with us in our contemporary home which sits high on a hill commanding panoramic views. We farm deer organically and grow Hydrangeas for export. You will be the only guest so you have sole use of a quiet private wing. Your evening meal will be 'special', venison - lamb or fresh seafood with home-grown vegetables. We dive, fish, tramp, ski, golf and love to travel. We have a friendly chocolate Labrador and a Burmese cat. Laundry available.

Whakatane   *Farmstay   14km W of Whakatane*

Rakaunui
Lois & Tony Ranson
Western Drain Road, RD 3, Whakatane
Tel: (07) 304 9292 Fax: (07) 304 9292
Mob: 025 246 6077   ranson@wave.co.nz
www.bnb.co.nz/rakaunui.html

Double $80 Single $50 (Continental & Full Breakfast)
Child $25 Dinner $25 Credit cards accepted
1 Queen 1 Double 2 Single (3 bdrm)
1 Ensuite 1 Private 1 Family share

Enjoy warm and friendly hospitality in our comfortable home set in extensive gardens where the peace and tranquillity of rural life can be truly appreciated. Check out our kiwifruit orchard, feed the guinea fowl, doves and hens, who supply the breakfast eggs. Lois is the gardener (camellias and roses are her favourites) also collector of antiques, quiltmaker, and embroiderer and examples of her handiwork abound. Tony is the "background support force" and provides essential services such as cork pulling. Tea making in bedrooms. Children welcome.

Whakatane   *Homestay   Whakatane Central*

Travellers Rest
Karen & Jeff Winterson
28 Henderson Street, Whakatane
Tel: (07) 307 1015 Mob: 025 276 6449
travrest@wave.co.nz
www.bnb.co.nz/travellersrest.html

Double $70 Single $35 (Continental Breakfast)
Credit cards accepted Pet on property
Children welcome Pets welcome
1 King/Twin 2 Single (2 bdrm) 1 Guests share

Needing Time Out? Join Jeff and Karen in their quiet home and garden beside the Whakatane River. Enjoy scenic river walks, rest in their garden, or visit the vibrant, local, art, craft, or garden trail. Take a short drive to Ohope beach, Hot Pools, River or Sea activities. Our Interests are: family, roses, gardening, photography, walking our dog, model cars, pen and stamp collecting. We look forward to sharing time with our guests, as does our friendly cat. Internet facility available. Unavailable May-Nov. 2003.

Whakatane   *Homestay B&B Private Cottage   10km S of Whakatane*

Baker's
Lynne & Bruce Baker
40 Butler Road, RD 2, Whakatane
Tel: (07) 307 0368 Fax: (07) 307 0368
Mob: 025 284 6996   bakers@world-net.co.nz
www.bnb.co.nz/bakers.html

Double $100-$110 Single $75
(Continental & Full Breakfast) s/c private cottage
Credit cards accepted Dinner $25 by arrangement
1 King/Twin 2 Queen 2 Single (4 bdrm)
2 Ensuite 1 Private

Welcome. Enjoy country charm in our modern attractively appointed Homestay. Share the peace and tranquillity of our park like property with quail, tui, wild pigeon and doves. Practice, or learn croquet on our full size lawn. Relax in a spa and if you prefer privacy, your own lounge. Fishing! There is parking for your boat. Day trip and enjoy our fantastic deep water, or land base fishing. Your fish will be kept chilled, or by negotiation smoked. Sea, coast, bush river or mountain - it is all here. Please phone for directions. We will pick up if needed. See you soon.

Whakatane   *Self-contained Homestay B&B Private Cottage*

Briar Rose
Annette & David Pamment
54 Waiewe Street, Whakatane
Tel: (07) 308 0314 Fax: (07) 308 0317 Mob: 0274 942 589
Briarrosewhk@hotmail.com
www.bnb.co.nz/briarrose.html

Double $80-$100 Single $60 (Continental Breakfast) (Special Breakfast) Child neg Dinner $25
1 Queen 1 Double 1 Single (2 bdrm)
1 Ensuite 1 Family share

On the hilltop above the town, Briar Rose and Rose Cottage are nestled in a peaceful cove of native bush where you can relax on the wagon wheel seat and watch and listen to the birdlife. You can also enjoy our beautiful cottage garden specialising in old fashioned roses.

Annette and David have a vast knowledge of the region which boasts many attractions, Ohope beach, sun and surf. Many walking tracks nearby. There is a good selection of cafes, bars brasseries and restaurants. But alternatively you can dine with us and enjoy fresh wild game meals or something to your taste.

* Our Guests say *

"Close your eyes, you could be in heaven."

"Very cosy, romantic and welcoming".

"So friendly, peaceful, relaxed and warm, I recommend it to all."

"Ledgendary Kiwi hospitality, thats what all the guide books say, I believe WE have experienced it here at BRIARROSE". *

Whakatane   *Homestay B&B*   *1.5km S of Whakatane Post Office*

Crestwood Homestay
Jan & Peter McKechnie
2 Crestwood Rise, Whakatane, Bay of Plenty

Tel: (07) 308 7554 Fax: (07) 308 7551
Mob: 025 624 6248   pandjmckechnie@xtra.co.nz
www.bnb.co.nz/crestwoodhomestay.html

Double $80 Single $60 (Continental Breakfast)
Dinner $25 $100 Private Bathroom
Credit cards accepted
1 Queen 2 Single (2 bdrm) 1 Private 1 Guests share

Scenic surroundings with beautiful sea, bush and rural views. A friendly relaxing atmosphere, quiet and peaceful and rooms tastefully furnished. Cosy lounge with writing desk, comfy sofas, and TV. Also fridge, crockery and utensils for making light snacks tea and coffee. Accommodation is upstairs and private and does not intrude into main host area. Peter and Janet enjoy coastguard interests, fishing from our boat, travelling and gardening. You are welcome to join us for evening drinks or an evening meal with notice.

Whakatane   *Farmstay B&B*   *13 W of Whakatane*

Kanuka Cottage
Carol & Ian Boyd
880 Thornton Road, RD 4, Whakatane

Tel: (07) 304 6001 Fax: (07) 304 6001
Mob: 021 883 684
kanuka1@xtra.co.nz
www.bnb.co.nz/kanukacottage.html

Double $70-$90 (Full Breakfast) Child neg
Dinner $25 by arr. Credit cards accepted
1 King/Twin 1 Queen 3 Single (2 bdrm) 2 Ensuite

Enjoy expansive sea and active volcano views from our B & B and Self Contained units. Set in 23 secluded acres of coastal kanuka with private access to sandy surf beach. Good surf casting/kontiki fishing. White Island tours, deep sea fishing, and other recreational activities arranged. Handy to golf courses. Large and interesting succulent, cacti and bromeliad gardens with plants for sale. Feed our friendly alpaca, goats and chickens. Sample our fresh vegetables, fruit and eggs organically produced on our property. Kanuka Forest Organic vineyard and winery next door.

Ohope Beach   *Self-contained Homestay B&B*   *6km E of Whakatane*   ♿

Shiloah
Pat & Brian Tolley
27 Westend, Ohope Beach

Tel: (07) 312 4401 Fax: (07) 312 4401
www.bnb.co.nz/shiloah.html

Double $66-$80 Single $35-$45
(Full Breakfast) Child 1/2 price
Dinner $18 - $25 by arrangement S/C unit
1 Queen 1 Twin 4 Single (3 bdrm)
2 Private 1 Guests share

Homestay: Paradise on the beach - view White Island and enjoy our hospitality. Facilities available for disabled guests. Classic car enthusiasts - well travelled. Self contained unit 1 twin bedroom, 1 single bed with bed settee (2) if required. Tariff $30-$35 own bedding, $40-$45 supplied. Access to beach across road. Fishing, swimming, surfing, and bush walks.

Ohope Beach *Self-contained*   *8km Whakatane*

The Rafters
Pat Rafter
261A Pohutukawa Ave, Ohope Beach
Tel: (07) 312 4856 Fax: (07) 312 4856
www.bnb.co.nz/therafters.html

Double $80-$90 Single $75-$80 (Continental Breakfast) Child $10 Dinner $30 - $45 Pet on property
Children welcome Pets welcome Smoking area inside
1 King 1 Single (2 bdrm)
1 Ensuite

Panoramic sea views: White, Whale islands, East Coast. Safe swimming. Many interesting walks. Golf, tennis, bowls, all within minutes. Licensed Chartered Club Restaurant opposite. Trips to volcanic White Island, fishing, jet boating, diving, swimming with dolphins arranged. Full cooking facilities; private entrance, sunken garden, BBQ. Complimentary: tea, coffee, biscuits, fruit, newspaper, personal laundry service. By special arrangement, dinner with Host and his Weimaraner dog, Gazelle, in Library - dining room, $30 - $45, includes pre dinner drinks and wines. Pat's interests are: philosophy, theology, history, English literature, the making of grape wines and all spirits, golf, bowls, music and tramping.

I have a friendly Weimaraner dog. Courtesy car available. House trained animals welcomed. Two restaurants and Oyster farm within 5 minutes drive.

I look forward to your company and assure you unique hospitality.

Directions: On reaching Ohope Beach turn right, proceed 2 km to 261a (beach-side) name "Rafters" on a brick letterbox with illuminated B&B sign.

For further information goto - www.wave.co.nz/pages/macaulay/The_Rafters.htm

Ohope Beach   *B&B*   *5km SE of Whakatane*

Turneys Bed & Breakfast
Marilyn & Em Turney
28 Pohutukawa Ave, Ohope Beach
Tel: (07) 312 5040 Fax: (07) 312 5040
Mob: 025 960 894   Tollfree: 0800 266 269
turneys@xtra.co.nz
www.businessonline.co.nz/turneys/
Double $150 Single $100 (Continental Breakfast)
Dinner by arrangement Credit cards accepted
1 King 1 Queen (2 bdrm)
2 Ensuite

Base yourselves with us and 'day trip', erupting White Island or Rotorua, fishing or golfing, to mention a few activites available. We offer luxury, multi-level accommodation, opposite a safe beach, cafe and shops. Treat yourself to the special 'Blue' room with its private deck overlooking the ocean, or the 'Garden' room. Both are spacious and tasteful with all amenities, and with little extras which make it so special. Come and share all we have to offer - you won't be disappointed.

Ohope Beach   *Homestay B&B Self-contained cottage*   *8km SE of Whakatane*

Oceanspray Homestay
Frances & John Galbraith
283A Pohutukawa Avenue, Ohope, Bay of Plenty
Tel: (07) 312 4112 Mob: 025 286 6824
frances@oceanspray.co.nz
www.bnb.co.nz/oceansprayhomestay.html
Double $90-$110 Single $55-$75 (Special Breakfast)
accepted Pet on property Children welcome
3 Queen 4 Twin (5 bdrm)
2 Private

Panoramic views and a warm welcome greet you at Oceanspray Homestay - a beachfront property with views to White Island, also East Cape. Our downstairs separate unit within our home has three attractively furnished bedrooms, lounge/kitchen/bathroom. Adjacent to our house, a two bedroom furnished self-contained cosy cottage. Home comforts of cookies, TV, books, toys for children. Special breakfasts - homemade bread, preserved fruits. We enjoy providing fish dinners for our guests upstairs overlooking the sea - John catching the fish kayaking with longline, Frances - her speciality: cooking and entertaining.

Ohope Beach   *Homestay B&B*   *6km E of Whakatane*

Noel & Jenny Davis
123 Pohutukawa Ave, Ohope
Tel: (07) 312 6090 Mob: 025 287 0532
jenny.noel@xtra.co.nz
www.bnb.co.nz/davis.html
Double $85-$100 Single $65-$80
(Continental Breakfast) Child neg.
Dinner by arrangement full breakfast optional $10
1 King 1 Twin (2 bdrm)
2 Ensuite

Welcome to our new home right on the beach. Relax in our modern surroundings. Enjoy breakfast in our dining room or on the large patio overlooking our stunning view. Have a warm outside shower after your swim in our safe beach. Before we moved to London 20 years ago, we enjoyed entertaining homestay guests; now that we are back in New Zealand, we are keen to make new friends. Our interests include opera, 60s and 70s music, theatre, travel, art, sport and our worldwide friends.

Opotiki *Self-contained Farmstay B&B* *18km E of Opotiki*

Coral's B&B
Coral Parkinson
Morice's Bay, Highway 35, RD 1, Opotiki
Tel: (07) 315 8052 Fax: (07) 315 8052
Mob: 021 299 9757 coralsb.b@wxc.net.nz
www.bnb.co.nz/coralsbb.html
Double $80-$125 Single $40-$62.5
(Continental Breakfast) Child $15 Dinner $25
Child at home Pet on property Pets welcome
2 Queen 1 Double 2 Single (3 bdrm) 2 Private

We provide two self contained accommodation options located on our hobby farm. As well as pets and farm animals we collect English classic cars and varied memorabilia. Enjoy the beach and bird life, swim at nearby sandy beach. Fish, ramble over the rocks, explore caves. The two storied cottage features lead-light windows, native timbers, large decks look out across the bay and native bush. The mews has separate bedroom, large lounge, all on one level. Looks out into our garden. Covered parking, home made bread, preserves.

Opotiki - Maraenui *Self-contained Farmstay B&B* *40km E of Opotiki*

Oariki Farm House Chris Stone
Maraenui Beach/Houpoto, Box 486, Opotiki
Tel: (07) 325 2678 Fax: (07) 325 2678 Mob: 025 531 678
oariki@clear.net.nz
www.bnb.co.nz/oarikifarmhouse.html
Double $100 Single $50 (Full Breakfast) Child $25
Dinner $30 S/C Cottage $90 - $130 Credit cards accepted
Pet on property Children welcome Pets welcome
1 King 2 Queen 1 Double 1 Single (3 bdrm)
1 Ensuite 1 Private 1 Guests share

Nestled in bush on a secluded coastal farmlet near the mouth of the Motu River, OARIKI FARMHOUSE offers farmhouse accommodation, bed and breakfast, or a two bedroom self contained cottage with kitchen. Our farmlet grows organic produce ,often we have fresh fish or mussels. Our dog will take you on beach walks, and our cat escorts you fishing! The perfect place to relax for a few days in peaceful surroundings. Sleep to the sound of the ocean , wake to the sound of the birds. Some maps show Maraenui as Houpoto. Directions are essential.

Opotiki - Tirohanga *Self-contained* *7km E of Opotiki*

Tirohanga Beach Holiday Home
Natalie & Jeff Jaffarian
#787 State Highway 35E, Opotiki
Tel: (07) 315 8899 Fax: (07) 315 8896
Mob: 027 412 6411 jaffarian@xtra.co.nz
www.beachholidayhomenewzealand.com/
Double $90 Single $45 (Continental Breakfast)
Child $30 up to 10yrs Dinner $25 by arrangement
Weekly/monthly rates Credit cards accepted
1 Queen 1 Double 1 Twin 3 Single (4 bdrm) 2 Private

Tirohanga Beach Holiday Home is an ideal get-away for all seasons. Magnificent ocean view right from your bed! Beautiful beach extends for miles in each direction. Swimming, surfing, fishing, beach walking at your doorsteps. Enjoy breathtaking sun-rises and sun-sets from the large deck overlooking White and Whale Islands. We offer 2 self-contained units, each with everything you need to relax and enjoy your holiday, complete with cooking facilities, barbecue and washing machine. Dinners by arrangement. Try our authentic Russian cuisine - borsch soup with hot cutlets!

Opotiki   *Homestay*   *11km W of Opotiki*

Fantail Cottage
Meg & Mike Collins
318 Ohiwa Harbour Road, RD 2, Opotiki
Tel: (07) 315 4981 Fax: (07) 315 4981
Tollfree: 0800 153 553
wendylyn@wave.co.nz
www.bnb.co.nz/fantailcottage.html

Double $85 Single $50 (Full Breakfast)
Dinner $25
1 Twin (1 bdrm)
1 Ensuite

Welcome to Fantail Cottage. Set on a sunny, bush-clad spur, your room and hot spa have breathtaking views overlooking Ohiwa Spit and the open sea our to Whale Island. Meg and Mike have travelled widely overseas and enjoy cooking with homegrown organic produce. 34km from Whakatane and 11km from Opotiki, this is a great place to relax, bird-watch, fish, walk and swim. From Whakatane turn left on SH2 at Waiotahi Bridge. Follow signs to Ohiwa Holiday Camp and Fantail Cottage.

Opotiki - Wairata   *Farmstay*   *40km S of Opotiki*

Wairata Station Farmstay
M & B Redpath
Private Bag 1070, Wairata, Opotiki
Tel: (07) 315 7761 Fax: (07) 315 7761
rl.redpath@xtra.co.nz
www.bnb.co.nz/wairatastation.html

Double $80 Single $50 (Full Breakfast)
Child $25 Dinner $20
1 Queen 4 Single (2 bdrm)
1 Private

Join us on our 1900 hectare hill country sheep, cattle, deer and goat farm in the heart of the scenic Waioeka Gorge. Numerous tracks to walk, glowworms and crystal clear Waioeka River at doorstep for trout fishing, eeling, swimming, kayaking. We can take guests on 4WD excursion or guided deer or pig hunting. Guest self-contained accommodation adjoins house we serve hearty home baked meals. We have 4 children, two of whom still live at home. We always welcome guests and look forward to meeting you. Please phone for directions.

Opotiki - Te Kaha   *B&B Inn*   *66 E of Opotiki*

Tui Lodge Garden Resort
Joyce, Rex & Peter Carpenter
201 Copenhagen Road, Te Kaha, BOP 3093
Tel: (07) 325 2922 Fax: (07) 325 2922
jorex@xtra.co.nz
www.bnb.co.nz/tuilodgegardenresort.html

Double $95-$125 Single $65-$95 (Full Breakfast)
Child $25 Dinner $30pp self-contained cabin $65
Credit cards accepted Pet on property
3 Queen 1 Twin 4 Single (6 bdrm) 3 Ensuite 1 Private

Set in 3 acres of gardens "our lodge" features ambience, comfort and tranquility without equal on "the coast". Purpose built in 1998, our guests tell us that we have something that is very special. From our visitor book; "the lodge is a dream. I could stay for life" Horst Kersten, Germany. "Our first homestay, wonderful experience, wonderful location" B&D Morrison, Gisborne. "So gracious and what wonderful food" J&C Daley, North Carolina USA. "on a par with paradise, great hosts and a magnificent location" A&S Goss, Napier.

Opotiki - Te Kaha   *Self-contained B&B*   *1hr N of Opotiki*

Waikawa B&B
Bev & Kev Hamlin
7541 State Highway 35, RD 3, Opotiki
Tel: (07) 325 2070 Fax: (07) 325 2070
WAIKAWA.BnB@xtra.co.nz
www.bnb.co.nz/waikawabb.html

Double $80-$85 Single $50 (Continental Breakfast)
Child 1/2 price under 12 Dinner $25
Self-contained $80 Credit cards accepted
Pet on property Pets welcome
1 King/Twin 2 Queen (3 bdrm) 3 Ensuite

Welcome to Waikawa Bed & Breakfast. 200 metres down driveway off State Highway 35. Our dwelling is on the water's edge facing north in tranquil surroundings. The west views, spectacular seascapes and stunning sunsets with White Island guarding on the horizon. Our detached guest rooms have ensuites, TV, fridge, tea and coffee facilities. Stroll the 2 acre property and enjoy the farm yard animals. We also have a cat and small dog. We have fresh organic fruit and vegetables in season.

Opotiki - Waihau Bay   *Self-contained Homestay B&B*   *112km N of Opotiki*

Waihau Bay Homestay   Noelene & Merv Topia
RD 3, Opotiki
Tel: (07) 325 3674 Fax: (07) 325 3679
Mob: 025 674 2157   Tollfree: 0800 240 170
n.topia@clear.net.nz
www.nzhomestay.co.nz/topia.html

Double $80-$100 Single $55-$75
(Continental & Full Breakfast) Child 1/2 price
Dinner $25 Credit cards accepted Pets welcome
1 King 1 Queen 1 Double 2 Twin (4 bdrm)
2 Ensuite 2 Private 1 Guests share

Surrounded by unspoiled beauty we invite you to come and enjoy magnificent views, stunning sunsets, swim, go diving, kayaking (we have kayaks) or just walk along the sandy beach. You are most welcome to join Merv when he checks his craypots each morning and his catches are our cuisine specialty. Fishing trips, horse treks and guided cultural walks are also available.We have two self-contained units with disabled facilities, and a double room with ensuite. Our cat Whiskey, and dog Meg enjoy making new friends.

Rotorua   *Self-contained B&B*   *10km W of Rotorua*

Rhodohill
Ailsa & Dave Stewart
569 Paradise Valley Road, Rotorua
Tel: (07) 348 9010 Fax: (07) 348 9041
Mob: 025 672 4009
www.bnb.co.nz/rhodohill

Double $80 Single $60 (Continental Breakfast)
Child $20 Credit cards accepted Children welcome
1 Queen (1 bdrm)
1 Ensuite

"Rhodohill" is set in a mature 4 acre garden in picturesque Paradise Valley, 10km west of Rotorua. Its hillside setting, large trees and hundreds of rhododendrons, camellias etc and many native birds offer a relaxing retreat within easy distance of major tourist attractions, golf courses and cafes and restaurants. The renowned Ngongotaha trout stream flows through the valley. Modern, self-contained accommodation with own entrance, fully equipped kitchen, dining room-lounge. Smoke free indoors. We operate a specialist plant nursery. Our retired sheep dog "Max" enjoys escorting guests around the garden.

Rotorua - Ngongotaha   *Self-contained Farmstay*   *17km N of Rotorua*

Deer Pine Lodge
John Insch, PO Box 22, Ngongotaha, Rotorua
Tel: (07) 332 3458 Fax: (07) 332 3458 Mob: 025 261 9965
deerpine@xtra.co.nz
www.bnb.co.nz/deerpinelodge.html
Double $85-$100 Single $70-$85 (Continental Breakfast) Child $20 - $25
Dinner $30 by arrangement Credit cards accepted
3 King 1 Queen 4 Single (5 bdrm)
5 Ensuite

Welcome to Deer Pine Lodge. Enjoy the panoramic views of Lake Rotorua and Mt Tarawera. We farm deer, our property surrounded with trees planted by the New Zealand Forest Research as experimental shelter belts on our accredited deer farm.

The nearby city of Rotorua is fast becoming New Zealand's most popular tourist destination offering all sorts of entertainment. We have a cat and a Boxer (Jake), very gentle. Our four children have grown up and left the nest. Our bed/breakfast units are private, own bathroom, TV, radio, fridge, microwave, electric blankets all beds, coffee/tea making facilities, heaters. Heaters and hair dryers also in all bathrooms.

Our two bedroom fully self contained units, designed by prominent Rotorua architect Gerald Stock, each having private balcony, carport, sundeck, ensuite, spacious lounge, kitchen, also laundry facilities, TV, radio, heater etc. Cot and highchair available. Security arms fitted on all windows, smoke detectors installed in all bedrooms and lounges, fire extinguisher installed in all kitchens.

Holding NZ certificate in food hygiene ensuring high standards of food preparation and serving. Guests are free to do the conducted tour and observe the different species of deer and get first hand knowledge of all aspects of deer farming after breakfast. If interested please inform host on arrival. Three course meal of beef, lamb, or venison by prior arrangement, pre dinner drinks.

Hosts John and Betty, originally from Scotland have travelled extensively overseas and have many years experience in hosting look forward to your stay with us. Prefer guests to smoke outside. Budget accommodation available.

Rotorua *Farmstay   4km SW of Rotorua*

Hunts Farm
Maureen and John Hunt
363 Pukehangi Road,
Rotorua
Tel: (07) 348 1352
www.bnb.co.nz/hunt.html
Double $95 Single $60
(Full Breakfast) Child $20
1 King/Twin 1 Queen 2 Single (2 bdrm)
2 Ensuite

Come rest awhile with us in our new home as we help you plan your itinerary and book your local tours. Explore our farm of 150 acres, running beef and deer, by foot or farm vehicle. Now our children have flown, Tigger, our trusty farm dog who lives in the garden is our chief helper. The views are magical. 360 degrees of lake, island, forest, city and farm land. Guest area has private entrance; lounge with tea, coffee making facilities, TV, fridge and laundry available. Two triple rooms, each with ensuite lead out to sunny private terraces.

Rotorua *Homestay   2km Rotorua centre*

Rotorua Lakeside Homestay
Ursula and Lindsay Prince
3 Raukura Place, Rotorua
Tel: (07) 347 0140 Fax: (07) 347 0107
Tollfree: 0800 223 624
the-princes@xtra.co.nz
www.bnb.co.nz/rotorualakesidehomestay.html
Double $85-$95 Single $65-$75 (Special Breakfast)
1 King/Twin 1 Queen (2 bdrm)
1 Ensuite 1 Private

We invite you to make our spacious, modern home in it's tranquil lake setting your base to explore Rotorua's many attractions. Home-hosts since 1988, we are interested in world and local affairs and care about environmental issues. Now retired, we have lived overseas and still travel extensively. We enjoy outdoor activities and offer you free use of our Canadian canoe. While sharing with you a generous, healthy breakfast with many home-made goodies, we'll help you plan activities and happily arrange local bookings. Minimum stay, 2 nights.

Rotorua - Ngakuru *Farmstay Cottage Homestead   32km S of Rotorua*

Te Ana Farmstay
Heather & Brian Oberer
Poutakataka Road, Ngakuru, RD 1, Rotorua
Tel: (07) 333 2720 Fax: (07) 333 2720
Mob: 025 828 151   teanafarmstay@xtra.co.nz
babs.co.nz/teana
Double $95-$150 Single $75 (Special Breakfast)
Child $35 Dinner by arrangement Pet on property
2 Queen 4 Single (4 bdrm) 2 Ensuite 1 Family share

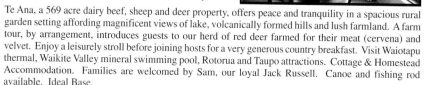

Te Ana, a 569 acre dairy beef, sheep and deer property, offers peace and tranquility in a spacious rural garden setting affording magnificent views of lake, volcanically formed hills and lush farmland. A farm tour, by arrangement, introduces guests to our herd of red deer farmed for their meat (cervena) and velvet. Enjoy a leisurely stroll before joining hosts for a very generous country breakfast. Visit Waiotapu thermal, Waikite Valley mineral swimming pool, Rotorua and Taupo attractions. Cottage & Homestead Accommodation. Families are welcomed by Sam, our loyal Jack Russell. Canoe and fishing rod available. Ideal Base.

Rotorua   *Homestay B&B   4km S of Rotorua*

Serendipity Homestay
Kate & Brian Gore
3 Kerswell Terrace, Tihi-o-tonga, Rotorua
Tel: (07) 347 9385 Mob: 025 609 3268
b.gore@clear.net.nz
www.bnb.co.nz/serendipityrotorua.html
Double $95 Single $60 (Full Breakfast) Child $30
Dinner $25 by arrangement Credit cards accepted
1 Double 2 Twin (2 bdrm)
1 Private

MARVEL - at unsurpassed views of geysers, city, lakes and beyond. RELAX - in all day sun, on the deck, in the conservatory or in the privacy of our garden. INDULGE - in comfort, home cooked cuisine and the friendly folk who have been enjoying hosting for many years. Our interests are, golf, tramping, gardening, antiques and sharing our extensive local and national knowledge with you. Let us advise you on the "must see" list while in Rotorua and other highlights of our beautiful country. WELCOME!!

Rotorua   *Self-contained Homestay B&B   1.5km S of Rotorua*

Heather's Homestay
Heather Radford
5A Marguerita Street, Rotorua
Tel: (07) 349 4303 heathermr@xtra.co.nz
www.bnb.co.nz/heathershomestay.html
Double $75 Single $45 (Full Breakfast)
self-contained, sleeps 6 from $110 dbl
Credit cards accepted Children welcome
1 Queen 1 Twin (2 bdrm)
2 Private

Haeremai - Welcome to my comfortable home in the heart of the thermal area, minutes from the city centre yet quiet and private. An adjoining property at 5b Marguerita St is available as a self-contained unit. Rotorua born and bred I am proud of my city and enjoy sharing what knowledge I have with my guests. For 10 years I have enjoyed being a B & B host and I look forward to many more visitors to my home and unique city. Directions - off Fenton Street.

Rotorua   *Farmstay Homestay B&B   10km E of Rotorua*

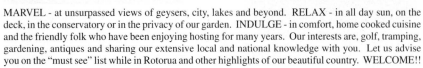

Peppertree Farm
Elma & Deane Balme
25 Cookson Road, RD 4, Rotorua
Tel: (07) 345 3718 Fax: (07) 345 3718
Mob: 025 776 468
peppertree.farm@xtra.co.nz
www.bnb.co.nz/peppertreefarm.html
Double $90 Single $60 (Full Breakfast)
Child 1/2 price Credit cards accepted Pet on property
1 Queen 2 Twin (3 bdrm)
1 Ensuite 1 Private

Handy to airport our quiet rural retreat overlooking Lake Rotorua will provide a welcome homely atmosphere. Farm animals are horses, cows, sheep, working dogs, chickens and goats. Horse riding and trout fishing can be arranged. Our interests include horse racing, fishing, gardening and travel. We can arrange for a visit to a Maori Hangi and Concert. For the latter you can be collected and returned home. Two house pets: "Lucy" Fox Terrier, "Edie" the cat. Pet lambs in spring. Children welcome.

Rotorua - Ngongotaha   *Homestay Lakestay   10km N of Rotorua*

Waiteti Lakeside Lodge
Val & Brian Blewett, 2 Arnold Street, Ngongotaha, Rotorua
Tel: (07) 357 2311 Fax: (07) 357 2311 Mob: 025 615 6923
waitetilodge@xtra.co.nz
www.waitetilodge.co.nz

Double $145-$210 Single $135-$200 (Full Breakfast) Child $35 12 & over
multiple-night rates available   Credit cards accepted
4 Queen 2 Single (5 bdrm)
3 Ensuite 1 Private 2 Guests share

Waiteti Lakeside Lodge is situated on the shores of Lake Rotorua at the mouth of the picturesque Waiteti Trout Stream, away from the sulphur fumes and traffic noise of Rotorua City but close to all of Rotorua's attractions, fine restaurants, and Maori culture.

The timber and natural stone lodge offers luxury private accommodation in traditional style and an extremely quiet and tranquil setting. There are five supremely comfortable bedrooms, three with ensuites and other two sharing a bathroom. The ensuite rooms have TVs and open on to balconies overlooking the lake, and in addition there is a private guests' lounge with satellite TV, video, library, pool table, and tea and coffee facilities.

All rooms enjoy spectacular views of the lake and stream mouth, and the lodge's gardens extend to the water's edge, home to numerous native birds and waterfowl.

Enjoy trout fishing (with or without professional guide) from the lodge's grounds, on the lake in the lodge's own charter boat, or on one of the many productive local trout streams - your catch can be fresh smoked for a superb breakfast or lunch treat.

Alternatively you may prefer to take a guided boat trip to historic Mokola Island, a sacred Maori site and wildlife sanctuary, where native flora and birdlife, including several rare and endangered species, abound.

Your experienced hosts Brian and Val Blewett are available to advise and/or guide you at all times to ensure that your stay is highly enjoyable. Brian is a professional fishing guide with more than 30 years experience, so success is virtually guaranteed.

Brian and Val will arrange bookings for all local attractions and activities including:
* Rotorua's best cafes and restaurants
* maori culture and entertainment
* six golf courses
* back country/wilderness trout fishing
* white water rafting
* canoeing
* forest walks
* mountain biking
* float plane trips from the lodge

Rotorua   *Self-contained Homestay B&B*   *5km SE of Rotorua*

Walker Homestay
Colleen & Isaac Walker
13 Glenfield Road, Owhata, Rotorua
Tel: (07) 345 3882 Mob: 025 289 5003
colleen.walker@clear.net.nz
www.bnb.co.nz/walkerhomestay.html

Double $65-$70 Single $40-$45
(Continental Breakfast) Child 1/2 price
Dinner by arrangement Extra adult $15
Credit cards accepted Pet on property
2 Double 1 Twin 1 Single (3 bdrm) 1 Ensuite 1 Private

The cottage, situated in its own garden area has one double and one twin bedroom, lounge, kitchen, bathroom and laundry. Room in the house has one double; one single bed; ensuite; tea/coffee facilities; microwave; separate entrance as well as access to hosts living area. Have complete privacy or be one of the family. Colleen is a Technical Institute tutor and Ike is a tour guide. Two friendly little dogs will welcome you. OFF ROAD PARKING. 24 hours notice if evening meal required.

Rotorua   *Homestay B&B*   *3km W of Rotorua*

West Brook
Judy & Brian Bain
378 Malfroy Road, Rotorua
Tel: (07) 347 8073 Fax: (07) 347 8073
www.bnb.co.nz/westbrook.html

Double $70 Single $45 (Continental Breakfast)
Child under 12 half price Dinner $25
Credit cards accepted
4 Single (2 bdrm)
1 Family share

Retired farmers with years of hospitality involvement, live 3km from city on Western outskirts. Interests include meeting people, farming, international current affairs. Brian a Rotorua Host Lions member, Judy's interest extend to all aspects of homemaking and gardening. Both well appointed comfy guest rooms are equipped with electric blankets. The friendly front door welcome and chatter over the meal table add up to our motto "Home away from Home". Assistance with sightseeing planning and transport to and from tourist centre available.

Rotorua - Hamurana   *Farmstay*   *20km NE of Rotorua*

Daniel Farmstay
Rod & Dianne Daniel
Te Waerenga Road,
RD 2, Rotorua
Tel: (07) 332 3560 Fax: (07) 332 3560
www.bnb.co.nz/danielfarmstay.html

Double $90 (Full Breakfast)
Dinner $25pp by arrangement
1 Queen 1 Double 3 Single (3 bdrm)
1 Private 1 Guests share

Come and enjoy our deer farm situated close to Rotorua's renowned tourist attractions. Rod is happy to take guests over the farm, with opportunity to feed a tame hind and pet Tan our friendly outdoor dog. Our modern home has panoramic views over Rotorua lake and city. Upstairs accommodation which is for guests exclusive use has two bedrooms, bathroom, and games area. Downstairs has a twin guest room with private toilet and vanity. Rod is a keen trout fisherman, Dianne a teacher. We enjoy meeting people.

Rotorua - Ngongotaha *Homestay B&B 10km N of Rotorua*

Alrae's Lake View B&B
Raema & Alf Owen, 124 Leonard Road, PO Box 14, Ngongotaha
Tel: (07) 357 4913 Fax: (07) 357 4513 Mob: 025 275 0113
Tollfree: 0800 RAEMAS
alraes@xtra.co.nz
www.beds-n-leisure.com/alraes.htm

Double $95-$140 (Full Breakfast) Dinner $40 Credit cards accepted
1 King/Twin 1 Queen 1 Double (3 bdrm)
1 Ensuite 1 Private 1 Guests share

Welcome to our HOMESTAY/BED & BREAKFAST WITH THE MILLION DOLLAR VIEW and our two acre lifestyle block with the black sheep and friendly atmosphere where your comfort is our priority. Just 10 mins from Rotorua City, handy to major tourist attractions, and walking distance to Lake Rotorua and Waiteti Stream where you can fly fish and then smoke your catch in our smoker. We can arrange any other sightseeing you wish to do ... be it Bungy Jumping or White Water Rafting or just taking a ramble through some of our beautiful bush and Redwood groves in the surrounding lake district.

Breakfast on scrumptious food in the conservatory while you enjoy the stunning 200 degree plus views of Lake Rotorua, Tarawera and Ngongotaha Mountains. You will have the choice of three bedrooms, king/twin, Queen or double, guaranteed to give you a restful nights sleep, all with comfortable innersprung mattresses, electric blankets, reading lights, shaver points & hairdryer ... Bathrooms have full facilities and the ensuite has a jacuzzi. All bedrooms have a pleasant outlook over the garden.

Enjoy our company or the privacy of the guest lounge with it's peaceful lake and garden views. There are no sulphur fumes and traffic noises. The guest lounge has CTV with teletext, stereo/radio, books and magazines. In the conservatory there is tea/coffee making facilities, available 24 hours for your convenience. If you wish you can enjoy a drink on the sunny garden patio and listen to the bird life. Laundry is available Dinner is an option but prior notice please. We have secure off street parking. Our accommodation is smoke free. We have no pets.

Your hosts have been hosting for many years and enjoy the wonderful experience of meeting people from all over the world. Our interest includes, Lions, Music, Masonry, gardening, walking, yachting, trout fishing, surfcasting and boating. Alf is a retired commercial builder and we have travelled extensively to many places in the world.

Directions: to find the BED & BREAKFAST WITH THE MILLION DOLLAR VIEW, take highway 5 to Ngongotaha, thru the township, over railway line, turn second right into Waiteti Road, then 1st left into Leonard Road. We are 200 metres on left. Please phone/fax/ email write for reservations. Relax in a HOME AWAY FROM HOME. We hope to meet you soon.

Rotorua   *Homestay*   *6km E of Rotorua*

Kairuri Home Hosts
Anne & Don Speedy
24 Mark Pl, Lynmore 3201, Rotorua
Tel: (07) 345 5385 Fax: (07) 345 7119
Mob: 025 929 254   dspeedy@clear.net.nz
www.babs.com.au/nz/kairuri.htm.

Double $140 Single $90 (Special Breakfast)
Dinner $35 - $45 Credit cards accepted
Pet on property Children welcome
1 King/Twin 1 Queen (2 bdrm)
1 Ensuite 1 Private

Anne and Don invite you to share their private rural retreat, six minutes from city centre. Enjoy friendly hospitality, share an entertaining evening meal, or relax in your private suite, featuring panoramic views of the lake, forest and city. Don can assist with personalised tours and will take pride in showing you the splendour of local forest walks and the glow worms. Anne's garden is her passion, and with Foxy the resident supervising cat, encourages guests to share their love of Rotorua's best kept secret.

Rotorua City   *Homestay B&B*   *100m N of Tourism Centre*

Inner City Homestay
Susan & Irvine Munro
1126 Whakaue Street, Rotorua
Tel: (07) 348 8594 Fax: (07) 348 8594
Mob: 025 359 923
innercityhomestay@yahoo.com
www.bnb.co.nz/innercityhomestay.html
Double $85 Single $50 (Full Breakfast) Child $30
Pet on property Children welcome
1 Double 2 Single (2 bdrm)   1 Guests share

"Innercity Homestay", 1126 Whakaue Street, the most central bed and breakfast/homestay in Rotorua. In the central city close to major tourist attractions and Lake Rotorua. Comfortable home with two guest bedrooms, thermally heated (pool also available). Cooked or continental breakfasts with special diets catered for. Most restaurants, cafes and tourism centre are within a short walking distance. Buses met at tourism centre. We are happy to make reservations for tours, Maori hangi, and concerts. Laundry service available. We welcome your enquiries.

Rotorua   *Self-contained Homestay*   *14km E of Rotorua*

Lake Edge Homestay & Trout Fishing Charters
Glenda & Paul Norman
8 Parkcliff Road, RD 4, Rotorua
Tel: (07) 345 9328 Fax: (07) 345 9328
Mob: 025 758 750   lake.charters@xtra.co.nz
www.lured.co.nz

Double $85-$100 Single $65-$85
(Continental Breakfast)
Dinner $25pp Credit cards accepted Pet on property
1 King 2 Single (2 bdrm)   1 Ensuite

Lake edge home of professional fishing guide with the most productive rainbow trout fishing at the front doorstep. You can go fishing, charter a cruise with special hot pool charter for guests or simply enjoy the tranquillity of the lakeside lifestyle and be only 10 minutes from all the attractions of Rotorua. Your accommodation has a separate entrance, cooking facilities, Sky TV, electric blankets, tea and coffee, own private ensuite and can be as self-contained or catered for as you request. We can help you arrange sight seeing, golf, rafting and of course trout fishing, or simply relax.

Rotorua - Ngongotaha   *Homestay B&B   10km N of Rotorua*

Ngongotaha Lakeside Lodge
Ann & Gordon Thompson
41 Operiana Street, Ngongotaha, Rotorua
Tel: (07) 357 4020 Fax: (07) 357 4020 Mob: 025 200 7539
Tollfree: 0800 144020
lake.edge@xtra.co.nz
www.bnb.co.nz/ngongotahalakesidelodge.html

Double $115-$150 Single $105-$135 (Full Breakfast) Child Children over 10 welcome $25. Dinner $45 by arrangement Credit cards accepted
1 King 1 Queen 1 Twin 4 Single (3 bdrm)
3 Ensuite

Welcome to our friendly and comfortable lodge on the shore of **Lake Rotorua**, where we have panoramic views of the lake and surrounding mountains. Our lodge is central to all major tourist attractions in the Rotorua area but far enough away to be **sulphur free**. The upper level of our two-storey home is exclusively for guests with three **ensuite bedrooms** equipped with everything you need for a comfortable stay including TV. The **guest lounge** opens onto a **conservatory** which overlooks the lake. It has Sky TV, video, library. We offer **complimentary** tea and coffee facilities and a fridge. A laundry service is available on request.

A full breakfast is served every morning while we help you plan your day using our **complimentary** map and knowledge of the region. Gordon is an experienced fisherman and will happily share his knowledge with you so you can try your luck for the **fighting trout** just metres from the lodge. We'll also cook your catch for you. Ample off street parking. Canoes, fishing rods, golf clubs free to guests.

Directions: Take state highway 5 to Ngongotaha Drive through the village. After the railway line turn right into Wikaraka Street, left into Okana crescent then left into Operiana Street and the lodge is on the right.

"A UNIQUE PLACE TO STAY"

Rotorua - Ngongotaha *Farmstay Homestay B&B Countrystay*   *17km N of Rotorua*

Clover Downs Estate
Lyn & Lloyd Ferris
175 Jackson Road, RD 2, Ngongotaha
Tel: (07) 332 2366 Fax: (07) 332 2367 Mob: 027 471 2866
Tollfree: 0800 3687 5323
Reservations@cloverdowns.co.nz
www.cloverdowns.co.nz

Double $175-$250 Single $160-$235 (Special Breakfast) Child neg Credit cards accepted
Pet on property Children welcome
3 King/Twin 1 King (4 bdrm)
4 Ensuite

For the discerning, a place to unwind and rediscover the simple pleasures in life. Magnificent Deer & Ostrich farm retreat set amidst 35 acres of green pasture, only 15 minutes drive north from Rotorua city centre.

We can offer you the Governor's Suite, or one of our three beautifully appointed spacious guestrooms, complete with ensuite bathrooms. Each room is equipped with tea & coffee facilities, refrigerator, TV, video. Rooms are serviced daily and there are laundry facilities available

After a sumptuous breakfast, join Lloyd and our friendly dogs on our farm tour, try a game of pentanque, or just relax on your individual outdoor deck and enjoy the peace and tranquility of Clover Downs Estate.

There are many things to do and see in Rotorua. Visit our many cultural and scenic tourist attractions, go horse riding, play a round of golf , or try trout fishing with an experienced guide at one of the many lakes and rivers in the area.

Rotorua has some wonderful restaurants and cafes or maybe enjoy a Maori hangi & concert. We have extensive overseas and New Zealand travel experience so let us help make your stay in our country relaxing, pleasant and memorable.

We are proud members of Superior Inns of NZ, Boutique Lodgings of NZ, Heritage & Character Inns of NZ & Kiwi Host.

Rotorua *Homestay B&B*   *3km S of Rotorua*

Thermal Stay
Wendy & Rod Davenhill
367 Old Taupo Road, Rotorua
Tel: (07) 349 1605 Fax: (07) 349 1641
Mob: 025 377 122   davenhill@clear.net.nz
www.thermalstay.co.nz
Double $95-$120 Single $65 (Full Breakfast)
Child 1/2 price Dinner $30pp by arrangement
Credit cards accepted   Pet on property
1 King 2 Queen 2 Single (3 bdrm)
1 Private 1 Guests share 1 Family share

"An Oasis In the City" (Scene Lifestyle magazine) Quiet, central, private. Thermally heated home and swimming pool, spa in winter. Tranquil gardens featuring waterfall, fish and native birdlife. Walking distance to city centre, thermal activities, forests and golf courses. Well travelled hosts who enjoy good food, wine and conversation. Our company, or time in the guest lounge with private patio. Dine with us or sample one of our many restaurants or Maori hangi/concerts. Off road parking, table tennis. Laundry, e-mail and fax available.

Rotorua *Farmstay Homestay B&B*   *15km N of Rotorua*

Panorama Country Homestay
Dave Perry & Chris King
144 Fryer Road, Hamurana, Rotorua
Tel: (07) 332 2618 Fax: (07) 332 2618
Mob: 021 610 949 Tollfree: 0800 303 703
panorama@wave.co.nz
www.bnb.co.nz/panoramacountryhomestay.html
Double $135-$170 Single $100-$110 (Continental & Full Breakfast)
Child $50 Dinner $50 Credit cards accepted Pet on property
1 King/Twin 1 King 1 Queen 1 Double 1 Twin 1 Single (3 bdrm)
2 Ensuite 1 Private

This is an ideal base to stay whilst visiting Rotorua. The architecturally designed cedar and brick home takes full advantage of the panoramic views of Lake Rotorua and surrounding countryside, away from the sulphur smells of Rotorua. All bedrooms have ensuites or private bathroom with heaters, toiletries, hair dryers and heated towel rails. Play tennis or relax in the heated jaccuzi, or go for walks to Hamurana Springs, or Redwood Forest. Five golf courses and fishing close by. There are friendly sheep and working dogs.

Rotorua *B&B Guesthouse*   *Rotorua Central*

Dudley House
Bobbie & Philip Seaman
1024 Rangiuru Street, Rotorua
Tel: (07) 347 9894
www.bnb.co.nz/dudleyhouse.html
Double $65-$70 Single $45 (Full Breakfast)
1 Queen 1 Double 1 Twin 1 Single (4 bdrm)
2 Guests share

"Dudley House" is a typical English Tudor style house built in the 1930's, with rimu doors and trims and matai polished floors. The house is tastefully and warmly decorated, with thermal heating. The dining room is adorned with military and police memorabilia. Non-smoking. Your hosts are happy to sit and chat about the numerous attractions around Rotorua, some within walking distance. Restaurants, cafes or bars, shops and banks are 5 minutes walk, also a 2 minute walk to lake front and village green. We welcome your inquiry.

BAY OF PLENTY

Rotorua   *Homestay B&B Country Homestay*   *12km NE of Rotorua*

Eucalyptus Tree Country Homestay
Manfred & Is Fischer
66 State Highway 33, RD 4, Rotorua
Tel: (07) 345 5325 Fax: (07) 345 5325
Mob: 025 261 6142
euc.countryhome@actrix.co.nz
www.bnb.co.nz/actrix.co.nz/users/euc.countryhome.html
Double $80 Single $55 (Full Breakfast) Dinner $25
1 King/Twin 2 Queen 1 Double (3 bdrm)
1 Guests share 1 Family share

Welcome to our quiet, smokefree, high quality country home. On our small farm near Lake Rotorua, close to Lake Rotoiti and Okataina, we have a donkey, calves, sheep, chickens, rabbits, bees, organic vegetables and fruit trees. Native bush drive to clear trophy trout fishing lakes and bush walks, thermal area, Maori culture, Hotpools, horseriding, skydiving, whitewater rafting. Our hobbies are troutfishing from boat, and fly fishing in lakes and rivers, hunting and shooting. We lived in the USA, Canada, Indonesia, Mexico and Germany and speak their languages.

Lake Rotorua   *Homestay B&B   7km NE of Rotorua*

The Lake House
Susan & Warwick Kay
6 Cooper Avenue, Holdens Bay, Rotorua
Tel: (07) 345 3313 Fax: (07) 345 3310
Tollfree: 0800 002 863
SusanK@xtra.co.nz
www.babs.co.nz/lakehouse/index.htm
Double $110-$130 Single $80-$100
(Special Breakfast) Child $35
Dinner $40 by arrangement Credit cards accepted
2 Queen 2 Single (3 bdrm) 1 Ensuite 1 Private

The Lake House was chosen to give guests the best beach front location on Lake Rotorua. Enjoy good food and great coffee, the beauty and peace. Wonderful lake views from all rooms, comfortable beds and friendly attentive hosts will make your stay memorable. 4 course dinner with NZ wines by arrangement. Free use of kayaks, email and laundry. Directions: Holdens Bay is down Robinson Avenue off Te Ngae Road (SH30). Turn right into Cooper Avenue, The Lake House is 200m along on the left.

Rotorua   *Homestay B&B   4km W of Rotorua City Centre*

The Towers Homestay
Doreen & Des Towers
373 Malfroy Road, Rotorua
Tel: (07) 347 6254 Tollfree: 0800 261 040
ddtowers@xtra.co.nz
www.mist.co.uk/homestaynz/
Double $80 Single $45 (Continental Breakfast)
Child $25, 12 & under Dinner $25 by arrangement
Credit cards accepted
1 Double 1 Twin (2 bdrm) 1 Private

Welcome to our elevated smoke free home with views over Rotorua. We really enjoy home hosting, and our lifestyle enables us to spend time (as required) with our guests. Guest bedrooms/bathroom downstairs. Breakfast is served upstairs in our spacious lounge. We offer free pickup from bus, train or plane. Off street parking is available. Des has many years experience with a national organisation providing both local and NZ touring information. Doreen, originally from South Wales, likes gardening and reading, and enjoys meeting people. We host only one party at a time.

Rotorua   *Homestay B&B*   *20km E of Rotorua*

Lakeside B & B
Laurice & Bill Unwin
155G Okere Road, RD 4, Rotorua
Tel: (07) 362 4288 Fax: (07) 362 4288
Mob: 0274 521 483   tengae.physio@xtra.co.nz
www.bnb.co.nz/unwin.html

Double $100 Single $80 (Full Breakfast)
Dinner $25pp Credit cards accepted Pet on property
1 King/Twin 2 Queen (3 bdrm)
2 Ensuite 1 Private

We have a new home in a beautiful setting beside Lake Rotoiti (Okere Arm). Within a short walking distance there are bushwalks, glowworms, waterfalls, river and lake fishing. Each B&B is centrally heated with ensuite, comfortable new beds, TV, refrigerator, tea/coffee making facilities. Smokefree inside, Boat mooring, BBQ and laundry facilities available. We share convivial meals with many guests. Our outdoor dog is small and friendly. We are easy to find just one minute from Highway 33. Please ring for directions.

Rotorua   *Countrystay*   *10km N of Rotorua*

Country - Villa
Anneke & John Van Der Maat
351 Dalbeth Road, RD 2, Rotorua
Tel: (07) 357 5893 Fax: (07) 357 5890
Mob: 025 272 6807
countryvilla@xtra.co.nz
www.countryvilla.biz

Double $175-$195 Single $155-$175
(Full Breakfast) Child Neg. Credit cards accepted
4 Queen 3 Single (5 bdrm)
3 Ensuite 1 Private

A peaceful country retreat, 10 minutes from Rotorua and its many attractions. Your stay in this magnificently restored Victorian style villa, which was originally built in 1906 in Auckland and 90 years later moved to this splendid site, will be a memorable one. The views over rolling pasture to the lake and in the distance Mount Tarawera are unforgettable. Country Villa is an ideal base to stay for several days, with Taupo and Tauranga only an hour away. Country Villa is smoke free inside.

Rotorua   *Homestay B&B*   *4km E of Rotorua*

Honfleur
Bryan & Erica Jew
31 Walford Drive, Lynmore, Rotorua
Tel: (07) 345 6170 Fax: (07) 345 6170
Mob: 025 233 9741
www.bnb.co.nz/honfleur.html

Double $100 Single $50-$75 (Full Breakfast)
Dinner $35 Credit cards accepted Pet on property
1 Double 2 Twin (2 bdrm)
1 Ensuite 1 Family share

"Honfleur" is a French country-style home in quiet, semi-rural surroundings close to lakes and forest. We offer generous hospitality amid antique furnishings and a beautiful garden featuring roses and perennials. Downstairs double bedroom with ensuite bathroom has a private entrance. Upstairs a twin bedroom has lake views and shares family bathroom (separate toilet). We are long-term Rotorua residents with sound local knowledge - retired medical professionals with friendly Labrador dog. We offer a three course dinner (with wine) by arrangement. Not suitable for young children.

Rotorua   *Homestay B&B   4km E of Rotorua*

Lynmore B&B Homestay
Leonie & Paul Kibblewhite
2 Hilton Road, Lynmore, Rotorua
Tel: (07) 345 6303 Fax: (07) 345 6353
kibble@xtra.co.nz
www.bnb.co.nz/lynmorebbhomestay.html

Double $100 Single $70 (Special Breakfast)
Credit cards accepted Pet on property
1 Queen 1 Double (2 bdrm) 1 Ensuite 1 Private

Welcome ... bienvenue, willkommen! Discover real character nestled beside forest walks, yet just 5 minutes drive from the centre. Leonie, ex-teacher, and Paul, scientist, delight in being New Zealanders - share our love of this remarkable area over refreshments, or a wine on the patio (or before a cosy fire ...) Meet the charming Officer, Paul's guide dog. Enjoy well-appointed rooms (great showers); relax in the lounge, sunroom, patio, or beautiful garden - nature ; relax in the guest lounge, patio, or beautiful garden - native trees a feature. Delicious breakfast - this couple enjoys food! Leonie parle francais (und ein bisschen Deutsch).

Rotorua - Lake Tarawera   *Self-contained Homestay B&B   15 SE of Rotorua*

Boatshed Bay Lodge
Lorraine van Praagh
95 Spencer Road, Lake Tarawera, RD 5, Rotorua
Tel: (07) 362 8441 Fax: (07) 362 8441
Mob: 025 279 9269
boatshedbay@xtra.co.nz
www.bnb.co.nz/boatshedbaylodge.html

Double $105 Single $85 (Full Breakfast) Child $25
Dinner $30 S/C $85 Credit cards accepted
2 Queen 1 Double 2 Single (2 bdrm) 2 Ensuite

Boatshed Bay is located on the shore of scenic Lake Tarawera with its sparking waters fringed by native bush at the foot of majestic Mount Tarawera. We offer boat charter, world renowned trout fishing, tramping (Mountain trek), bushwalks or just relax in peace and tranquillity only 15km from Rotorua. All facilities are available, including laundry, kitchen and nearby licensed restaurant "The Landing Cafe". We provide home style breakfast and meals on request. Your host Lorraine is well travelled and enjoys meeting people. My place is your place.

Rotorua   *Farmstay B&B Luxury Farmstay   15km NW of Rotorua*

Kahilani B&B/Farmstay
Yvonne & David Medlicott
691 Dansey Road, RD 2, Rotorua
Tel: (07) 332 5662 Fax: (07) 332 5552
Mob: 025 990 690   kahilani@wave.co.nz
www.bnb.co.nz/kahilanifarm.html

Double $160-$175 Single $120-$135
(Special Breakfast) Child 1/2 price Dinner $35 - $75
Credit cards accepted Pet on property
1 King/Twin 2 Queen 1 Single (4 bdrm)
1 Ensuite 1 Private

Warm hospitality, great food and country comforts await you at Kahilani. Easily located, just minutes from Rotorua's attractions, but a feeling of world's away with the homestead beautifully sited in the midst of a 100 hectare (250 acre) Deer/Sheep farm, offering panoramic rural, forest and lake views. Upstairs guest suites, cool in summer, centrally heated in winter, provide all the facilities discerning travellers may expect. Classy comfort food is the House Specialty! Extensive gardens, Labradors (in compound) and two Tonkinese cats complete the picture.

Rotorua - Lake Tarawera   *Homestay B&B   20km SE of Rotorua*

Lake Tarawera Rheinland Lodge
Gunter & Maria
484 Spencer Road, RD 5, Rotorua
Tel: (07) 362 8838 Fax: (07) 362 8838
Mob: 025 234 3024
tarawera@ihug.co.nz
www.bnb.co.nz/rheinlandlodge.html
Double $100-$120 Single $75-$85 (Special Breakfast)
1 King/Twin 1 Queen (2 bdrm)
1 Private 1 Family share

Located at the magic Lake Tarawera renowned for its scenery and history we offer warm hospitality with a personal touch. Expect total privacy, magnificent lake views, luxurious and relaxing outdoor whirlpool, spacious bathroom with shower and bath, fitness area, stereo, TV, internet connection, lake beach 5 minutes on foot, sea 45 minutes by car, bush walks, fishing and hunting trips by arrangement, home-made bread, German cuisine on request, organic garden, German/English spoken, free pick-up from airport or city.

Rotorua - Lake Tarawera   *23km SE of Rotorua*
Self-contained Homestay B&B Tourist flat

Bush Haven
Rob & Marie Dollimore
588 Spencer Road, Lake Tarawera, Rotorua
Tel: (07) 362 8447 Fax: (07) 362 8447
www.bnb.co.nz/bushhaven.html
Double $95-$125 Single $75-$95
(Continental Breakfast) Pet on property
1 Queen 1 Double 2 Single (3 bdrm)
1 Private 1 Guests share

"Bush Haven" is nestled in 5 acres of attractive gardens and bush reserve with views across Otumutu Island and bay to the south western section of Lake Tarawera. The tourist flat is the ground floor. Hosts Rob and Marie and friendly pet Spaniels live in the upper level. There is a delightful 300 metre bush walk from the garden down to a secluded bay. Native flora and fauna in abundance. "Bush Haven" is quiet and peaceful away from the main settlement. Dinghy available for hire.

Rotorua - Central   *B&B   Rotorua Central*

Tresco
Gwyn & John Hanson
3 Toko Street, Rotorua
Tel: (07) 348 9611 Fax: (07) 348 9611
Tollfree: 0800 TRESCO (0800 873 726)
trescorotorua@xtra.co.nz   www.bnb.co.nz/tresco.html
Double $85 Single $50 (Full Breakfast)
Credit cards accepted Pet on property Children welcome
2 King/Twin 2 Queen 2 Single (6 bdrm)
3 Ensuite 1 Private 2 Guests share

CENTRAL LOCATION - A warm welcome awaits you at our comfortable friendly home, situated on a tree-lined street only 150 metres from Central Rotorua with its many attractions and excellent restaurants. Established over 30 years and recently renovated, Tresco offers all the comforts of home. You will enjoy a substantial cooked and/or continental breakfast. 24-hour complimentary refreshments. Genuine hot mineral pool. FREE pick-up from airport or bus terminal.   Off-street parking. Laundry facility with drying room.

Rotorua - Ngongotaha   *Self-contained Farmstay   12km N of Rotorua*

Emerald Fields
John & Maree Bellerby
304 Central Rd, RD2, Rotorua
Tel: (07) 332 2351 Fax: (07) 332 2351
Mob: 025 260 9893   emeraldfields@xtra.co.nz
www.bnb.co.nz/emeraldfields.html
Double $150-$170 Single $120-$150
(Continental Breakfast) Child $15
Credit cards accepted Children welcome
1 King/Twin 1 Double (1 bdrm) 1 Ensuite 1 Private

Share with John, Maree and family our enviable farming lifestyle and enjoy good old-fashioned kiwi hospitality. At Emerald Fields the only thing not 'kiwi' is our Aussie cattle dog, Tammy, who loves visitors. Hand feed the pet deer we are now farming, after years of John catching them from helicopters. Home away from home. Your cottage is sumptuously appointed, with every convenience to ensure a luxurious stay. Clean, fresh air with magnificent rural and lake views, only minutes from major tourist attractions and Rotorua city. Double bed is a fold out.

Rotorua   *5km NW of Rotorua City Centre*
Self-contained B&B Boutique Hotel / Lodge

Swiss Lodge Rotorua   Heiko & Christina Kaiser
207 - 209 Kawaha Point Road, Rotorua
Tel: (07) 348 5868 Fax: (07) 348 5869
Mob: 021 119 1000   stay@swisslodge.co.nz
www.swisslodge.co.nz
Double $189-$279 Single $179 (Special Breakfast)
Child $35 Dinner $45 - $65
penthouse & lakeside chalet $319 - $479
Credit cards accepted Pet on property
6 King 3 Queen 3 Twin (12 bdrm) 9 Ensuite 1 Private

Swiss Lodge is a unique lake front retreat, offering panoramic views, near the tip of Kawaha Point. It is just 5 minutes drive from the city centre, but away from traffic noise and sulphur fumes.   Guests have a choice of either an ensuite bedroom, a penthouse apartment or lakeside chalet.   Our private beach and jetty provide a convenient starting point for boating and floatplane excursions. Relax in our lakeside spa and sauna or make use of the comlimentary green fee for a round of golf.

Rotorua   *Homestay B&B   15km N of Rotorua*

Montrose Deer Farm
Alan & Mary Mandeno
453 Tauranga Direct Road, Rotorua
Tel: (07) 332 2322 Fax: (07) 332 2323
Mob: 025 598 775   mandeno.family@xtra.co.nz
www.montrose-farmstay.co.nz
Double $125-$145 Single $90 ((Special Breakfast)
Child by arrangement Dinner by arrangement
 Credit cards accepted Pet on property
1 King/Twin 1 Queen 1 Double (3 bdrm)
1 Ensuite 1 Private 1 Guests share

Montrose Deer Farm is the perfect tranquil base for your stay in Rotorua whether you are here to see the wonderful thermal attractions, play golf, to trout fish or on business. Our large house is elevated on 180 acres of beautiful native bush and lush rolling farmlands just 15 mins from city centre. Enjoy breakfast then stroll around our extensive gardens or take a farm tour with Alan to feed deer and Scottish Highland Cattle and hear native birds in the bush.

Rotorua - Lake - Central
Boutique lodge & s/c waterfront apartment

Jack & Di's Lake Road Lodge
Diana Bradshaw
21 Lake Road, Rotorua,
Tel: (07) 346 8482 Fax: (07) 346 8486
Mob: 021 1385 369
Tollfree: 0800 522 526
jdbedbreakfast@wave.co.nz
www.bnb.co.nz/lakeroadlodge.html

Double $99-$175 for Single $75-$120 (Continental Breakfast)
Child neg. 2 bedroom apartment $250, 3 bedroom apartment $350
Credit cards accepted Children welcome over 10 years
3 Queen 1 Twin 3 Single (5 bdrms)
3 Ensuite 1 Private

Hosts reside at Fenton Street - see below.
Visitors never cease to be amazed and delighted at what Lake

Road Lodge offers. The setting by the lake is unique - panoramic views of Lake Rotorua, Mokoia Island, the steaming historic Maori village of Ohinemutu, St Faith's Church and yet is only a five minute walk to the city centre, cafes and shopping. The Lodge offers luxury, comfort, fresh breakfast supplies and relaxing deck living with hot pool and barbecue, off-street parking, laundry, courtesy local pick- up, plus penthouse apartment. Jack and Diana have anticipated all visitor needs.

Rotorua - Central *B&B*

Jack & Di's Fenton St Lodge
Diana Bradshaw,
313 Fenton Street, Rotorua,
Tel: (07) 346 8482 Fax: (07) 346 8486
Mob: 021 138 5369
Tollfree: 0800 522 526
jdbedbreakfast@wave.co.nz
www.jdbedbreakfast.co.nz

Double $99-$175 Single $75-$120
(Continental Breakfast) Child neg.
Credit cards accepted Children welcome
1 Superking 1 Queen 3 Double 1 Twin 3 Single (6 bdrm)
2 Ensuite 1 Private 1 Guests share

Opened April 2002, Jack and Diana's exclusive Lodge offers spacious, luxurious guest only accommodation, including new fully tiled bathroom and en-suite facilities, sunny balcony and views

of Mt Ngongotaha. In the heart of Rotorua's Golden Mile and within walking distance to the city, Whakarewarewa Thermal Reserve, racecourse and transport to tourist attractions where weary travellers can enjoy relaxing sleep, nourishing continental breakfast and charming décor, with Jack and Diana's local knowledge for itineraries. There is a Honeymoon suite, wheelchair access, laundry, off-street parking and is non-smoking.

Kinloch   *Self-contained Homestay*   *20km W of Taupo*

Tom Sawyer's B&B
Trish & Tom Sawyer
34 Angela Place, Kinloch, Taupo
Tel: (07) 377 2551 Fax: (07) 377 2551
Mob: 025 764 739
sawyer@reap.org.nz
www.bnb.co.nz/tomsawyers.html

Double $95 Single $50 (Full Breakfast)
Child under 5 free Dinner $25 Pet on property
1 King/Twin 1 Queen 1 Single (2 bdrm)
2 Ensuite

A warm welcome waits you at Trish & Tom's B&B. Our lovely lakeside village 15 minutes from Taupo. We have a choice of golf courses, superb fishing and bush walks. Offstreet parking is right at your door. Hearty breakfasts and our home-smoked trout are our specialities. Accommodation is a self-contained unit plus a double room with ensuite in-home. Trish and Tom are keen golfers and fishers and love to share these activities with guests. You can join us for a kiwi BBQ at days end.

Taupo   *Homestay B&B*   *2km E of Taupo*

Yeoman's Lakeview Homestay
Colleen & Bob Yeoman
23 Rokino Road,
Taupo 2730
Tel: (07) 377 0283 Fax: (07) 377 4683
www.bnb.co.nz/yeomans.html

Double $100 Single $50 (Full Breakfast)
Child $25 Dinner $30 by arrangement
1 Queen 3 Single (3 bdrm)
1 Ensuite 1 Guests share

Bob and I have enjoyed hosting for over fifteen years, our Lakeview Homestay with beautiful mountains backdrop makes our guests' stay in Taupo very special. Our home is spacious, comfortable and relaxing. All Taupo's attractions are nearby, golf courses, thermal pools, Huka Falls and fishing. We are retired sheep and cattle farmers, Bob excels at golf and is in charge of cooked breakfasts. Home made jams and marmalade are my specialty. It is a pleasure to provide dinner by arrangement. Laundry facilities are always available. Off street parking.

Taupo   *Self-contained Homestay*   *3km S of Taupo*

Hawai Homestay
Jeanette & Bryce Jones
18 Hawai Street, 2 Mile Bay, Taupo
Tel: (07) 377 3242 Mob: 025 234 0558
jeanettej@xtra.co.nz
www.beds-n-leisure.com/hawai.htm

Double $80 Single $50 (Full Breakfast) Child $20
Dinner $20 Marmite Cottage $55 double
Credit cards accepted Pet on property
1 Queen 1 Twin (2 bdrm) 1 Guests share

Taupo is great for holidays any season, swimming, fishing, tramping, skiing. Our modern warm house has wonderful lake views from lounge and deck. Quiet and comfortable guest bedrooms are downstairs with shared bathroom. Home made muesli, preserves, fresh cooked bread and muffins our breakfast specialty. Two minutes walk to lake and excellent restaurants. Self-contained cottage, 3 bedrooms, sleeps seven, open plan lounge, potbelly stove, linen and firewood supplied. Great for families. Interests include church, Probus, roses, WW2 memorabilia and adorable shitzu dog.

Taupo - Acacia Bay   *Homestay*   *6km W of Taupo*

Leece's Homestay
Marlene and Bob Leece
98 Wakeman Road, Acacia Bay,
Taupo 2736
Tel: (07) 378 6099
www.bnb.co.nz/leeceshomestay.html

Double $80 Single $50
(Continental Breakfast) Child neg
1 King 1 Double 2 Single (2 bdrm)
1 Guests share

Your hosts Bob and Marlene extend a warm welcome to our large Lockwood home with woodfire for winter and north facing sunny deck from guest bedroom. Also magnificent view of Lake Taupo from lounge and front deck. There are bush walks and steps down to lake to swim in summer. We are awaiting your arrival with anticipation of making friends. You are welcome to smoke but not inside. Please phone for directions.

Taupo - Acacia Bay   *Homestay*   *5km W of Taupo*

Pariroa Homestay
Joan & Eric Leersnijder
77A Wakeman Road, Acacia Bay, Taupo
Tel: (07) 378 3861 Fax: (07) 378 3866
Mob: 025 530 370
pariroa@xtra.co.nz
www.bnb.co.nz/.html

Double $75 Single $50 (Full Breakfast)
Credit cards accepted
1 Queen 2 Single (2 bdrm)
1 Guests share

VIEWS VIEWS. Our home is Scandinavian style with wooden interior. Situated in a very quiet area and minutes form the beach, we have magnificent, uninterrupted views of Lake Taupo and The Ranges from bedrooms and living room. We have travelled extensively and Eric was previously a tea planter in Indonesia, having lived in The Netherlands, Spain and Italy. Directions: Turn down between 95 and 99 Wakeman Road. We are the last house on this short road (200 metres).

Taupo   *Homestay*   *2km S of Taupo*

Nolan's Homestay
Betty & Ned Nolan
30 Rokino Road, Taupo
Tel: (07) 377 0828 Fax: (07) 377 0828
Mob: 027 144 9035   nolans@beds-n-leisure.com
www.beds-n-leisure.com/nolans-homestay

Double $90 Single $50 (Full Breakfast)
Child 1/2 price Dinner $25 Pet on property
2 Twin 4 Single (2 bdrm)
1 Ensuite 1 Private 1 Family share

Our one level home is located up a tree lined drive with ample parking, nestled among trees. Superb views of town, lake mountains and ranges. Retired sheep and cattle farmers we have travelled widely with many tangible reminders furnishing our home. Relax or enjoy trout fishing, tramping, sightseeing or golf. Betty loves to cook but Taupo abounds in good restaurants. This is not just a Bed and Breakfast but a HOMESTAY! Directions: Lakefront Take Taharepa Road to Hilltop shops turn left into Rokino road. No 30 is on right after Waihora Street. (One loved cat)

Taupo   *Self-contained Homestay   1km S of Taupo*

Pataka House
Raewyn & Neil Alexander
8 Pataka Road, Taupo
Tel: (07) 378 5481 Fax: (07) 378 5461
Mob: 025 473 881
www.beds-n-leisure.com/pataka/htm

Double $100 Single $70
(Full Breakfast) Child $30 S/C $110
Pet on property Children welcome
2 Queen 4 Single (4 bdrm)
1 Ensuite 1 Private 1 Guests share

'Pataka House' is highly recommended for its hospitality. We assure guests that their stay lives up to New Zealand's reputation as being a home away from home. We are easily located just one turn off the lake front and up a tree-lined driveway. Our garden room is privately situated, has an appealing decor and extremely popular to young and old alike. Stay for one night or stay for more as Lake Taupo will truly be the highlight of your holiday.

Taupo   *Lakestay   6km W of Taupo*

Kooringa
Robin & John Mosley
32 Ewing Grove, Acacia Bay, Taupo
Tel: (07) 378 8025 Fax: (07) 378 6085
Mob: 025 272 6343   kooringa@xtra.co.nz
www.kooringa.co.nz

Double $110 Single $100 (Full Breakfast)
Credit cards accepted
1 Queen 1 Double 2 Single (2 bdrm)
1 Ensuite

"Kooringa" is situated in sheltered Acacia Bay (2 mins walk to Lake), surrounded by native bush and gardens with magnificent views of Lake Taupo and Mt Tauhara. We are a retired professional couple, lived overseas and travelled extensively with our two sons. We are within easy distance of all major attractions. Your private guest suite includes lounge, Sky TV and deck. A generous breakfast with plenty of variety is served in the conservatory overlooking the Lake. Please phone, fax or email for bookings. Directions: www. kooringa.co.nz

Taupo   *Self-contained Homestay   Taupo Central*

Lakeland Homestay
Lesley, Chris & Pussycats
11 Williams Street, Taupo
Tel: (07) 378 1952 Fax: (07) 378 1912
Mob: 025 877 971   lakeland.bb@xtra.co.nz
www.bnb.co.nz/lakelandhomestay.html

Double $100 Single $60 (Continental Breakfast)
$120 dble + $20 pp Self-contained flat
Credit cards accepted Pet on property
1 Queen 2 Double 2 Twin (4 bdrm)
1 Ensuite 1 Private 1 Family share

Nestled in a restful tree-lined street, a mere five minutes stroll form the Lake's edge and shopping centre "Lakeland Homestay" is a cheerful and cosy home that enjoys views of the lake and mountains. Keen gardeners, anglers and golfers Chris and Lesley work and play in an adventure oasis. For extra warmth on winter nights all beds have electric blankets, and laundry facilities are available. A courtesy car is available for coach travellers and there is off-street parking. Please phone for directions.

Taupo - Acacia Bay   *Homestay B&B*   *5km W of Taupo*

Paeroa Lakeside Homestay
Barbara & John Bibby
21 Te Kopua Street, Acacia Bay, Taupo
Tel: (07) 378 8449 Fax: (07) 378 8446 Mob: 025 818 829
bibby@reap.org.nz
www.taupohomestay.com

Double $175-$225 Single $175-$225 (Full Breakfast) (Special Breakfast) Child $75 Dinner $40
Triple (2 Rooms) $225 - $250 Credit cards accepted
1 Queen 2 Single (3 bdrm)
3 Ensuite

UNIQUE GENUINE LAKEFRONT LOCATION PAEROA'S hosts Barbara and John welcome you to their spacious modern quality Homestay at sheltered ACACIA BAY, developed on three levels to capture the MAGNIFICENT UNINTERRUPTED, PANORAMIC VIEWS of world famous LAKE TAUPO and beyond.

The flower filled garden gently descends to the private beach, jetty where you can swim, relax. Use the rowboat or catch a FISHING CHARTER with John in his 30-ft cruiser. John has fished Lake Taupo and its rivers successfully for 35 years. We can cook your large RAINBOW TROUT for breakfast or smoke it for your lunch.

The house is large, comfortable and well appointed for your comfort and privacy with spacious lounge areas, sundecks, patios and outdoor seats in the garden to enjoy the abundant birdlife, flowers and Lake Views. The rooms have comfortable beds, TV, electric blankets and heaters, great views, ensuite bathrooms with heated towelrails and hairdriers - serviced daily. Laundry service is available. A large guest lounge for your use with tea and coffee facilities, TV, piano, books and comfort. Private decks off the rooms. Breakfasts are a specialty.

We are retired sheep and beef farmers enjoying living in our quiet peaceful and private home beside the beach, just minutes from the town centre, 3 golf courses, bush walks, restaurants, shops, boating, thermal hot springs, and all the many major attractions the area provides.

Plan to STAY SEVERAL DAYS and base your CENTRAL NORTH ISLAND visits to Napier, Rotorua, Tongariro National Park and ski-fields from here. There is so much to do in Taupo. Amongst your hosts' interests are travel, golf, gardening, fishing, entertaining and family. We have a detailed knowledge of the region and members of the NZ Assn Farm & Home Hosts.

Taupo *Homestay* *1km S of Taupo*

Tui Glen
Robbie & Stan Shearer
10 Pataka Road, Taupo
Tel: (07) 378 7007 Fax: (07) 378 2412
Mob: 025 239 2931
stanrob@ezysurf.co.nz
www.bnb.co.nz/tuiglen.html
Double $110 Single $75 (Full Breakfast)
Dinner B/A Credit cards accepted
1 King 2 Single (2 bdrm)
1 Ensuite 1 Private

A few metres from the lakefront beach and a short stroll to town we are close to all local facilities and attractions. Hospitality is our priority. We enjoy sharing the ambience of our much admired home and garden with our guests. Bedrooms are comfortable and attractive with facilities to match - one party at a time. A widely travelled retired couple with numerous interests we are the recipients of the coveted National Travel Courtesy Award. Telephone for directions. Courtesy car available if required.

Taupo *Self-contained Homestay* *15km W of Taupo*

Ben Lomond
Mary & Jack Weston
1434 Poihipi Road, RD 1, Taupo
Tel: (07) 377 6033 Fax: (07) 377 6033
Mob: 025 774 080   benlomond@xtra.co.nz
www.bnb.co.nz/benlomond.html
Double $90 Single $45 (Full Breakfast) Child $22
Dinner $25 by arrangement S/C price on inquiry
Credit cards accepted Pet on property
1 Queen 1 Twin (2 bdrm)
1 Guests share

Welcome to Ben Lomond. Jack and I have farmed here for 40 years and our comfortable family home is set in a mature garden. There is a self contained cottage in the garden or 2 bedrooms available in the house. We have interests in fishing, golf and the Equestrian world and are familiar with the attractions on the Central Plateau. Our pets include dogs and cats who wander in and out. Taupo restaurants are 15 minutes away or dine with us by arrangement.

Taupo *Homestay* *3km SE of Taupo*

Ann & Dan Hennebry
28 Greenwich Street,
Taupo
Tel: (07) 378 9483 Mob: 025 297 4283
brie@xtra.co.nz
www.bnb.co.nz/hennebry.html
Double $90 Single $60
(Full Breakfast) Dinner $30
1 King 1 Single (2 bdrm)
1 Guests share

We enjoy having guests in our spacious home overlooking farmland and bordering Taupo's Botanical gardens. We hope you will join us for dinner (maybe a barbecue in the summer) and complimentary wine in our pleasant dining room. There are many good restaurants in Taupo should you prefer that. Our launch "Bonita" is available for fishing or sight seeing on the beautiful lake - Dan is an excellent skipper. We (and our elderly cat Ginny) look forward to welcoming you to our warm, comfortable, home.

Taupo - Countryside   *Self-contained Homestay B&B   35km NW of Taupo*

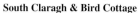

South Claragh & Bird Cottage
Lesley & Paul Hill
South Claragh, Poihipi Road,
RD 1, Mangakino, Taupo
Tel: (07) 372 8848 Fax: (07) 372 8047
lhill@reap.org.nz   www.countryaccommodation.co.nz
Double $90-$120 Single $80-$90 (Full Breakfast)
Child $10-$45 Dinner $40pp Bird Cottage $90-$100 dbl
$25/$10 extras Credit cards accepted Pet on property
1 Queen 1 Double 1 Single (3 bdrm)   2 Private

Turn into our leafy driveway and relax in tranquil, rambling gardens. Meet our gentle donkeys, coloured sheep, outdoor dog. Accommodation options: 1. Enjoy bed & breakfast in our comfortable, centrally heated farmhouse. Delicious farm breakfasts. Homegrown produce and excellent cooking make dining recommended.   2. Settle into Bird Cottage which is self-contained and cosy, with delightful views. Perfect for two, will sleep 4/5. Firewood and linen provided. No meals included, but breakfast/dinner happily prepared by arrangement. More details and pictures on our web site.

Taupo   *Homestay B&B   2km S of Taupo*

Bramham
Julia & John Bates
7 Waipahihi Avenue, Taupo
Tel: (07) 378 0064 Fax: (07) 378 0065
Mob: 025 240 9643   info@bramham.co.nz
www.bramham.co.nz
Double $100-$110 Single $60-$70
(Full Breakfast) Pet on property
1 Double 2 Twin 1 Single (3 bdrm)
2 Ensuite 1 Private

Bramham is situated just two minutes walk form the Hot Beach of Lake Taupo and offers tremendous views of the lake and mountains to the south.   John and Julia, having spent 24 years in the RNZAF, including service with the USAF in Tucson Arizona, welcome you to our quiet, homely and peaceful atmosphere. Hearty breakfasts are our specialty. Local knowledge is our business. Bus terminal and airport service complimentary. Being non smokers our dogs, Bob and Daisy, ask you not to smoke in our home.

Taupo   *Homestay   3km S of Taupo*

Catley's Homestay
Beverley & Tom Catley
55 Grace Crescent, Taupo
Tel: (07) 378 1403 Fax: (07) 378 1402
taupo@actrix.gen.nz
www.bnb.co.nz/catleyshomestay.html
Double $100 Single $70 (Full Breakfast) Child $30
Credit cards accepted Children welcome
1 Queen 1 Double 2 Single (3 bdrm)
1 Private 1 Family share

If you want a quiet Homestay with panoramic views of lake and mountains, generous breakfasts and warm hospitality, this is the place for you. Upstairs guest rooms open onto a sheltered sundeck with extensive views of the lake and snow capped volcanoes. We also have a comfortable self-contained unit with its own garden entrance. All Taupo's famous attractions are nearby including Huka Falls and thermal pools. Laundry facilities are available. You will enjoy your stay in this lovely area. To avoid disappointment booking is recommended.

Taupo   *Homestay   Rural Homestay   14km NW of Taupo*

Minarapa
Barbara & Dermot Grainger
620 Oruanui Road, RD 1, Taupo
Tel: (07) 378 1931 Mob: 025 272 2367
info@minarapa.co.nz   www.minarapa.co.nz

Double $90-$120 Single $70-$90 (Full Breakfast)
Child $30 Dinner by arrangement
Credit cards accepted Pet on property
1 King/Twin 2 Queen 2 Single (4 bdrm)
2 Ensuite 1 Private

Wend your way along a tree-lined drive to enter the tranquillity of our 11 acre rural retreat, just 12 minutes from Taupo, 45 minutes from Rotorua and central to tourist attractions. Our large home has billiard room with fridge for guest use, lounge with feature fireplace and covered verandah. The spacious, well appointed guest rooms, two with ensuite and balcony, overlook park-like grounds with colourful gardens, mature trees, grass tennis court and beyond pond and stream, friendly farm animals. Barbara speaks fluent German.

Taupo   *B&B*

Gillies Lodge
Kay & Gerry English
77 Gillies Ave, Taupo
Tel: (07) 377 2377 Fax: (07) 377 2377
genglish@reap.org.nz
www.bnb.co.nz/gillieslodge.html

Double $85 Single $65 (Full Breakfast)
Child under 12 free Credit cards accepted
Children welcome
4 Double 12 Single (9 bdrm)
9 Ensuite

With a view across Lake Taupo to Acacia Bay we are flanked by rhododendrons and a small park, enjoying peace and privacy in a residential area, 2km from the city centre. From our upstairs (lounge, bar dining area) we have enjoyed brilliant sunsets with our guests from all parts of the planet. We specialise in arranging your activities (boating to bungy) prior to or on arrival. We will meet you at local transport terminals if required. Please phone.

Taupo   *Homestay   2km S of Taupo*

Mountain Views Homestay
Jack & Bridget Grice
17B Puriri Street, Taupo
Tel: (07) 378 6136 Fax: (07) 378 6134
Mob: 025 200 5437
mtviews@reap.org.nz
www.bnb.co.nz/mountainviewshomestay.html

Double $70 Single $40 (Continental Breakfast)
Child negotiable Dinner by arrangement
Credit cards accepted
1 Queen 1 Twin (2 bdrm)   1 Guests share

You will get a warm welcome in our home. Stay two nights or more, and Jack will take you for a FREE cruise on Lake Taupo's replica steamboat "Ernest Kemp" (conditions apply). Breakfast is served in the main living room, and includes Bridget's home baked bread and home-made jams. (Cooked breakfast optional extra.) We are able to recommend and book local attractions. Off street parking available. We appreciate guests not smoking in the house. Please phone for directions.

Taupo *Self-contained Homestay B&B* *3km S of Taupo*

Above the Lake
Judi & Barry Thomson
32 Harvey Street, Taupo
Tel: (07) 378 4558 Fax: (07) 378 4071
Mob: 025 817 443   relax@canapecruises.co.nz
www.abovethelake.co.nz

Double $110 Single $85 (Special Breakfast)
Child POA Credit cards accepted Pet on property
1 Queen (1 bdrm)
1 Private

Welcome to our completely private guest area which includes queen size bed, separate sitting room with fridge, log fire, TV and two single beds. Plus private bathroom, ktchenette, laundry facility, easy access to indoor thermal spa and outdoor salt pool. We invite you to join us for breakfast and enjoy the lake and mountain views. Georgia, our social Labrador, looks forward to your company. Armchair cricketers and active golfers especially welcome. We are happy to suggest 'what's hot and what's not' with local activities and eateries.

Taupo *Homestay Country Homestay* *8km E of Taupo*

Richlyn Homestay
Lyn & Richard James
1 Mark Wynd, Bonshaw Park, Taupo
Tel: (07) 378 8023 Fax: (07) 378 8023
Mob: 025 908 647   richlyn.james.taupo@xtra.co.nz
www.richlyn.co.nz

Double $140-$150 Single $100-$110 (Full Breakfast)
Child neg Credit cards accepted Pet on property
1 King 2 Queen 2 Single (4 bdrm)
1 Ensuite 1 Private

Welcome to our dream: "Richlyn" warm, spacious, comfortable, smokefree. Eight park-like peaceful acres, views of mountain, and countryside. Outdoor spa pool, gardens, places to walk and relax, two cats, two poodles. Richard and Lyn enjoy travelling, and provide what they expect, comfortable beds, great breakfasts and genuine friendship guests say "Richlyn", is a haven of peace and tranquility from the rush of life. Directions: From Taupo, up Napier Road 6 km, right into Caroline Drive, 2 km to Mark Wynd turn left, first driveway left.

Taupo *Homestay B&B* *2km S of Taupo*

Ambleside Homestay and Bed & Breakfast
Patricia & Russell Jensen
5 Te Hepera Street, Taupo
Tel: (07) 378 1888 Fax: (07) 378 1888
Mob: 025 836 888   scandic@xtra.co.nz
www.ambleside.co.nz

Double $125-$145 Single $110 (Special Breakfast)
Credit cards accepted Pet on property
2 Queen (2 bdrm)
1 Ensuite 1 Private

Enjoy the warm hospitality and relaxed atmosphere in our sunny home, situated in a quiet cul-de-sac, just a stroll to the lake and restaurants. Upstairs is exclusive to you; two double bedrooms offer panoramic views; both equipped with cable TV, refrigerators and tea/coffee facilities. One bedroom and guest lounge open onto a sunny balcony overlooking lake. Soak in our hot mineral pool in the garden - totally private except for our friendly cat. Home baking and delicious continental/countrystyle cooked breakfasts a speciality. Free E mail facilities. Telephone anytime. **1849**

Taupo   *Homestay   2km S of Taupo*

Pavlova House
Terri McCallum
45 Arrowsmith Avenue, Taupo
Tel: (07) 378 1171 Mob: 021 120 4961
terri.max@xtra.co.nz
www.bnb.co.nz/pavlova.html

Double $90 Single $60-$85 (Full Breakfast)
Child $15 Pet on property Children welcome
1 Queen 1 Double (2 bdrm)
1 Guests share

Expansive views of the lake to Mt Ruapehu. Close to town and a menagerie of activities. Botanical Gardens, hot thermal pools, 'around the corner'. Friendly helpful hosts in comfortable pleasant and interesting surroundings. Small well-behaved dog. Children welcome. We appreciate you not smoking in our home. We are members of NZAFHH and look forward to hearing from you. Please phone for directions. Inspections by appointment.

Taupo   *Farmstay   12km NW of Taupo*

Whitiora Farm
Judith & Jim McGrath
1281 Mapara Road, RD 1, Taupo
Tel: (07) 378 6491 Fax: (07) 378 6491
mcg.whitiora@xtra.co.nz
www.bnb.co.nz/whitiorafarm.html

Double $100 Single $60 (Full Breakfast)
Child $25 Dinner $30, lunch $15, by arrangement
1 Queen 4 Single (3 bdrm)
2 Family share

Three course dinner by arrangement. Breakfast: your choice of cereal, homegrown fruit, eggs, bacon, sausages, home-made bread, conserves, coffee, English/herb tea. Our 461 acre farm grazes sheep, cattle, deer, goats thoroughbred horses, which we breed and Jim trains and races. Judith, NZAFHH member enjoys gardening, especially organic vegetables. We enjoy sharing our large comfortable home, garden, farm, welcome children (5-12 half price, under 5 negotiable). We appreciate you not smoking in our home. Booking advisable to avoid disappointment.

Taupo   *Self-contained Farmstay B&B   13KM N of Taupo*

Bellbird Ridge Alpaca Farm
Mike & Lorraine Harrison
68 Tangye Road, RD 1, Taupo
Tel: +64 7 377 1996 Fax: +64 7 377 1992
Mob: 025 668 7754   lharrison@xtra.co.nz
www.bnb.co.nz/bellbirdridge.html

Double $130 Single $90 (Full Breakfast)
Dinner $40 pp by arrangement Credit cards accepted
Pet on property Pets welcome
1 Queen (1 bdrm) 1 Ensuite

Our new one bedroom self-contained cottage is warm and welcoming with quality fittings throughout. The cottage is private and nestled into extensive park like gardens with a deck overlooking the pond where you can enjoy the serenity of rural life and listen to the Bellbirds and Tuis. Our 10 acre farm has sweeping rural views and is 15 minutes easy drive from Taupo, 45 minutes from Rotorua and only 1.5 hours from the snowfields. Breakfast provisions are included and there is parking for your boat.

Taupo - Acacia Bay   *B&B*   *5km W of Taupo*

The Loft
Todd & Linda Gilchrist, 3 Wakeman Road, Acacia Bay, Taupo
Tel: (07) 377 1040 Fax: (07) 377 1049 Mob: 025 851 347
book@theloftnz.com
www.theloftnz.com

Double $120-$170 Single $90 (Continental Breakfast) (Full Breakfast) (Special Breakfast)
Child $75 Dinner Gourmet dinners $55pp Credit cards accepted
3 Queen 1 Single (3 bdrm)
3 Ensuite

Situated 5 minutes from Taupo township, The Loft is nestled on a hillside overlooking LAKE TAUPO. Your hosts LINDA AND TODD welcome you into their world of luxury, fine food and romance. Their years of experience in the hospitality industry, make them a couple who excel in the art of entertainment.

Todd is an internationally travelled CHEF and he and Linda are both culinary masters. Their enthusiasm for good food and wine is something that spills over into everything that they do. Sumptuous breakfasts of homemade preserves, freshly squeezed orange juice, fresh baked muffins and croissants, smoked salmon scrambled egg and piping hot waffles are an experience not to be missed.

Arrange an evening meal at The Loft and you will be treated to a four course CANDLELIT BANQUET that will leave you with a lasting memory of New Zealand hospitality. The Loft boasts three very private Queen sized rooms with ensuite bathrooms. Their style is RUSTIC, ROMANTIC AND WARM where the attention to detail shows that your comfort takes top priority. The guest lounge with a large open fire welcomes you to relax, enjoy afternoon tea, or complimentary pre-dinner drinks and port while you chat about the Taupo region and your sight-seeing plans.

TROUT FISHING TRIPS & ADVENTURE TREKS can be arranged by your hosts along with a myriad of other more relaxing activities. Linda & Todd look forward to sharing their home and their company with you, assuring you of a warm welcome and a luxurious stay. Directions: www.theloftnz.com

Taupo   *Homestay B&B*   *5km S of Taupo centre*

Beside the Lake
Irene & Roger Foote
8 Chad Street, Taupo

Tel: (07) 378 5847 Fax: (07) 378 5847
Mob: 025 804 683
foote.tpo@xtra.co.nz
www.bnb.co.nz/besidethelake.html

Double $180 (Continental & Full Breakfast)
Credit cards accepted
2 King/Twin (2 bdrm)
1 Ensuite 1 Private

We invite you to enjoy the tranquillity of our beautiful property beside Lake Taupo. Our luxury accommodation is smokefree, offers breakfast of your choice and has air conditioning and central heating. All rooms have lake views and a balcony or terrace. Totally relax beside the lake, in the lake (swimming), on the lake (boating, fishing) or around the lake, fishing in world famous trout rivers; walking trails; ski slopes; golf courses, thermal pools and unique volcanic countryside. Enjoy your break beside the lake.

Taupo   *Homestay Boutique Accommodation*   *2.5km S of Taupo*

Fairviews
Brenda Watson
8 Fairview Terrace, Taupo

Tel: (07) 377 0773
fairviews@reap.org.nz
www.reap.org.nz/~fairviews

Double $110-$135 Single $95-$110 (Full Breakfast)
Credit cards accepted
1 Queen 2 Single (2 bdrm)
1 Ensuite 1 Private

You are invited to stay at my modern smoke-free homestay situated in a tranquil neighbourhood within walking distance of Hot Pools and Lake. Relax and enjoy Fairviews gardens. Be as private as you wish or socialise with hosts. Rooms are tastefully decorated and comfortable. Double room is large with private entrance, TV, fridge, tea/coffee facilities, robe and hairdryer. Generous breakfasts provided. Email facilities and laundry are available at small charge. My knowledge of region is extensive. Interests include theatre, antiques/collectables, travel, tramping.

Taupo   *Homestay B&B*   *KM 2 SE of TAUPO*

Finial House
Jan & Neil Fleming
51 Ngauruhoe St, Taupo

Tel: 07 377 4347 Fax: 07 377 4348
Mob: 025 685 8255
n.j.fleming@xtra.co.nz
www.finial-homestay.co.nz

Double $100-$135 Single $70-$95 (Full Breakfast)
Dinner $20-25 Pet on property
2 King/Twin 2 Queen (3 bdrm)
2 Ensuite 1 Family share

Finial House is a spacious home in a peaceful setting, with magnificent views of the lake and volcanic mountains. Close to town and lake with its many attractions. We are widely travelled and enjoy chatting with guests from other places. Having recently moved from our dairy farm at Matamata our interests are: travel, sports, music, walking, running and gardening. Our three children have families of their own and we are left with our two timid cats.

Taupo - Acacia Bay   *Homestay B&B*   *7km W of Taupo*

Hazeldene Lodge
Judy & Tony Pratt
119 Acacia Heights Drive,
Acacia Bay, Taupo

Tel: (07) 377 0560 Fax: (07) 377 0560 Mob: 025 609 2647
hazeldene@xtra.co.nz
www.hazeldenelodge.co.nz

Double $175-$215 Single $150-$215 Child POA Credit cards accepted Pet on property
Children welcome
1 Queen 3 Double 1 Twin (5 bdrm)
5 Ensuite

Hazeldene Lodge is a stunning newly created up-market home planned specifically for the comfort of guests. Set on two acres of land on the brow of a hill in a picturesque rural setting, yet only 7 kilometres drive from town.

After operating a very successful bed & breakfast in England for three years, your hosts Judy & Tony decided to immigrate to New Zealand and offer the same high standard of 'Home from Home' accommodation.

All our bedrooms have been very tastefully furnished and fitted out with all the luxuries in life, such as TVs, electric blankets, hair dryers, iron and ironing board, coffee and tea-making facilities, also from your rooms you have spectacular views during the day, and by night twinkling lights of Taupo township are gorgeous.

We are within easy distance of the famous Huka Falls, and also international golf courses, geothermal activity, and also some excellent restaurants.

We assure you a warm welcome and a comfortable stay.

Please phone, fax, or email for bookings, or visit our website.

Taupo   *Self-contained Homestay Separate/Suite B&B   16km N of Taupo*

Brackenhurst
Ray & Barbara Graham
801 Oruanui Road, RD1, Taupo
Tel: (07) 377 6451 Fax: (07) 377 6451
Mob: 0274 456 217   rgbg@xtra.co.nz
www.bnb.co.nz/brackenhurst2.html

Double $100 Single $60
(Continental & Full Breakfast) Child $30
Dinner $35 Credit cards accepted
1 Queen 1 Double 4 Single (3 bdrm)
2 Ensuite 2 Private

Brackenhurst is a warm modern lockwood design home on 14 acres of peaceful countryside with fantails, tuis, bellbirds flitting from tree to tree. We offer a warm welcome with peace and tranquility. You can also practise your chipping and putting, work out in the gym, or enjoy a peaceful game of petanque or croquet. A private guest wing in the house or a separate annex offer the ultimate in away from home comforts. Breakfast to suit, either continental style or full english. Dinner is available by arrangement.

Taupo - Acacia Bay   *Homestay   6km W of Taupo*

Bay View Homestay
Marion & Guy Whitehouse
50/1 Wakeman Road, Acacia Bay, Taupo
Tel: (07) 378 7873 Fax: (07) 378 7893
Mob: 021 211 2904
www.bnb.co.nz/bayviewhomestay.html

Double $90 Single $50 (Continental Breakfast)
Dinner by arrangement Credit cards accepted
1 Queen 1 Twin (2 bdrm)
1 Guests share

Enjoy the warm hospitality with your hosts Marion and Guy, retired deer farmers and friendly cat 'Kita'. Our modern contemporary home of native timbers offers open-plan living, air conditioning, double glazing, off-road parking. Spectacular panoramic views of Lake Taupo and mountains. Taupo's shimmering lights by night. Minutes from lake, fishing, tennis, native walks, restaurant. 6km to Taupo township and local attracions, thermal pools, Huka Falls, Huka jet, chartered fishing, bungy, golf. Bookings can be arranged. Please phone for directions.

Turangi   *Homestay B&B + Self-contained cottage   1.5km E of Turangi Central*

The Andersons'
Betty & Jack Anderson
3 Poto Street, Turangi
Tel: (07) 386 8272 Fax: (07) 386 8272
Mob: 025 628 0810   jbanderson@xtra.co.nz
www.bnb.co.nz/anderson.html

Double $90 Single $55 (Full Breakfast)
Child in cottage only Dinner $30pp by arrangement
S/C Cottage $70 - $140 Credit cards accepted
2 Queen 1 Twin (3 bdrm)   3 Ensuite

Welcome to our smoke-free home, with ENSUITE bathrooms for your comfort, in QUIET street, beside Tongariro RIVER walkway and fishing, handy to restaurants and town, with arranged transport to TONGARIRO NATIONAL PARK at your door. LAKE TAUPO and THERMAL baths 5 minutes drive. Upstairs QUEEN rooms with balconies, separated for PRIVACY by tea, coffee making area. Downstairs is twin suite, laundry and lounge where we'll share interests in flying, skiing, fishing, tramping, and maps, of our VOLCANIC area. Guest-shy cat. Cottage suitable for families.

Turangi *Self-contained B&B*   *53km S of Taupo*

Akepiro Cottage
Jenny & John Wilcox
PO Box 256, Turangi
Tel: (07) 386 7384
Fax: (07) 386 6838
jennywilcox@xtra.co.nz
www.bnb.co.nz/akepirocottage.html

Double $90 Single $50 (Continental Breakfast)
Breakfast on req. $10 Credit cards accepted
2 Queen 2 Single (2 bdrm)
1 Private

Set in half-acre woodland garden, featuring rhododendrons and native plants, which attracts many species of birds. Access through the garden gate to the Tongariro River and major fishing pools. Perfect retreat for a restful break. 4 mins from excellent golf course, 1/2 hour to the mountains. Our home and garden are adjacent, but allows utmost privacy to cottage. Full modern kitchen and laundry, all linen supplied. Full breakfast can be provisioned prior to arrival. Come, share this corner of nature's paradise with us.

Turangi *Self-contained Homestay B&B*   *1km E of Turangi*

Ika Fishing Lodge
Suzanne & Kerry Simpson
155 Taupahi Road,
PO Box 259, Turangi
Tel: (07) 386 5538 Fax: (07) 386 5538
ikalodge@xtra.co.nz
www.ika.co.nz

Double $120-$160 Single $90-$120 (Full Breakfast)
Dinner $40pp Credit cards accepted
2 King/Twin 3 Queen (4 bdrm)
3 Ensuite

You open the back gate and there is the Island Pool. We can now offer 1 self contained unit with 2 bedrooms, kitchen, lounge and sun deck. 2 double rooms inside the lodge with ensuites. A spacious lounge with open fire is available along with Sky TV. Kerry, your guide has fished the area for 50 years and has been a guide for some 30 years. Suzanne, the other Simpson partner is your resident chef and is renowned for her trout sashimi. Please come and "enjoy".

Turangi - Motuoapa *B&B*   *10km N of Turangi*

Meredith House
Frances & Ian Meredith
45 Kahotea Place, Motuoapa, RD 2, Turangi
Tel: (07) 386 5266 Fax: (07) 386 5270
meredith.house@xtra.co.nz
www.bnb.co.nz/meredithhouse.html

Double $90 Single $60 (Continental & Full Breakfast)
Self-cont. (breakfast extra) $100 - $120
Credit cards accepted Children welcome
1 Queen 3 Single (2 bdrm)   1 Private

Stop and enjoy this outdoor Paradise. Just off SH1 (B & B Sign). Overlooking Lake Taupo, our two-storey home offers ground-floor self-contained accommodation with own entrance. Fully equipped Kitchen, Dining room, Lounge. Two cosy bedrooms (each with TV). Vehicle/Boat off-street parking. Minutes to Marina and World-renowned Lake/river fishing. Beautiful bush walks. 45 minutes to ski fields and Tongariro National Park. Our association with Tongariro/Taupo area spans over 30 years, through work and outdoor pursuits. Welcome to our Retreat.

Turangi   *Self-contained*   *52km S of Taupo*

River Birches
Gill & Peter Osborne
21A Koura Street, Turangi
Tel: (07) 386 5348 Fax: (07) 386 5948
gillo@xtra.co.nz
www.bnb.co.nz/riverbirches.html

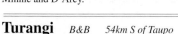

Double $150 Single $95 (Full Breakfast)
Credit cards accepted
1 King/Twin 2 Single (2 bdrm)
1 Private

On the banks of the Tongariro River in tranquil gardens this perfect hideaway cottage has a fully equipped kitchen, TV, potbelly and a host of other above average details to ensure your comfort. Enjoy breakfast at your leisure. Fish in world famous pools adjacent to our boundary, participate in the myriad of outdoor activities offered in the area or relax with a book in our beautiful garden. We have travelled extensively and enjoy meeting people. We are enthusiastic gardeners, 'helped' by our dachshunds, Minnie and D'Arcy.

Turangi   *B&B*   *54km S of Taupo*

Founders Guest Lodge
Peter & Chris Stewart
253 Taupahi Road, Turangi
Tel: (07) 386 8539 Fax: (07) 386 8534
Mob: 025 854 000   founders@ihug.co.nz
www.founders.co.nz

Double $150 Single $80 (Full Breakfast)
Whole lodge, 12-13 persons negotiable
Credit cards accepted
1 King/Twin 3 Queen (4 bdrm)
4 Ensuite

Welcome to Turangi and to our New Zealand colonial-style home. Relax and enjoy the unique beauty of the "trout fishing capital of the world". Many outdoor activities are available at his "place for all seasons" - with rivers, mountains and magnificent Lake Taupo on our doorstep. Four ensuite bedrooms open on to the veranda. Enjoy breakfast outside in the summer or pre-dinner drinks by the fire apres ski in the winter! Our friendly dog has her own kennel. Whole Lodge available - sleeps 13 self-catered.

Turangi   *B&B*   *52km S of Taupo*

The Birches
Tineke & Peter Baldwin
13 Koura Street, Turangi
Tel: (07) 386 5140 Fax: (07) 386 5149
Mob: 021 149 6594
tineke.peter@xtra.co.nz
www.bnb.co.nz/thebirches.html

Double $120 Single $90 (Special Breakfast)
Dinner by arrangement Credit cards accepted
1 Queen (1 bdrm)
1 Ensuite

Close to the world renowned Tongariro River we offer a charming and gracious residence in a quiet street. This unique setting has exceptional access to tramping, fly fishing, skiing, rafting or purely a retreat from life's hustle and bustle. Enjoy superior and spacious ensuite accommodation with TV and coffee/tea making facilities in a separate part of the house. Your Dutch/Canadian hosts have considerable international experience and can speak Dutch and French. Dinner by arrangement.

Turangi   *B&B   16km NW of Turangi*

Wills' Place
Jill & Brian Wills
145 Omori Road, Omori
Tel: (07) 386 7339 Fax: (07) 386 7339
Mob: 027 228 8960   willsplace@wave.co.nz
Double $100 Single $75 (Special Breakfast)
Child neg Dinner by arrangement
Credit cards accepted Pet on property
1 Queen 2 Single (1 bdrm)   1 Ensuite

Our home is lakeside in the beautiful southwest corner of Lake Taupo with wonderful views, excellent fishing, boating, swimming, bush walks. We are off the beaten track, yet only 10-15 minutes to shops, restaurants, thermal pools, Tongariro River, rafting, kayaking, eco-tours etc. 40 minutes to Tongariro National Park and mountains. We offer a comfortable suite with separate entry and complete privacy. Ensuite bathroom with bath and shower. Tea-making facilities, fridge, microwave, television, laundry. A special place we'd love to share it with you.

www.laketaupo.co.nz/turangi/motels/willsplace/index.htm

Turangi   *Farmstay B&B   2km N of Turangi centre*

Skighaugh
Robert & Patrika Salmon
114 Grace Road, Turangi
Tel: (07) 386 6739 www.bnb.co.nz/skighaugh.html
Double $70-$100 Single $70-$90
(Special Breakfast)
Child $20 Dinner by arrangement
Credit cards accepted
Dogs on property
7 King/Twin (7 bdrm)
3 Guests share

Situated between Tongariro River and Lake Taupo's Stump Bay our home is perfect for people who want to fish, ski or explore the National Park. We live in an historic villa on 8 acres, the house is eco-friendly, using solar water heating, recycled timber and wool insulation. The land is farmed bio-dynamically; we specialize in tree crops. The accommodation is suitable for family groups as well as individuals and the guest wing has its own central heating, kitchen and social room.

If you would like dinner
most hosts require 24 hours' notice.

Gisborne and District

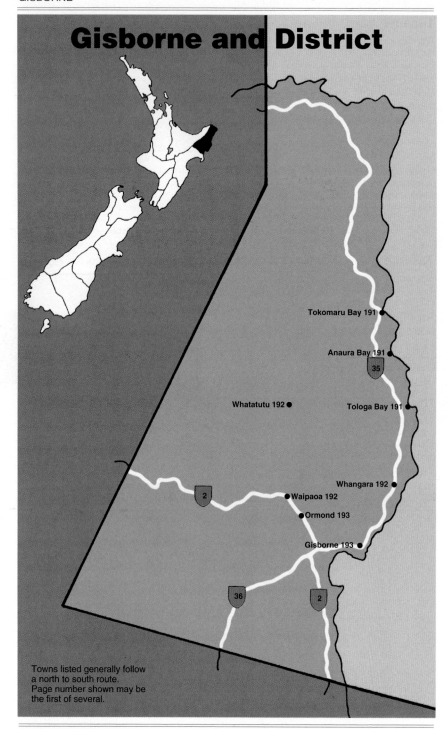

Tokomaru Bay 191

Anaura Bay 191

35

Whatatutu 192

Tologa Bay 191

Whangara 192

Waipaoa 192

2

Ormond 193

Gisborne 193

36

2

Towns listed generally follow
a north to south route.
Page number shown may be
the first of several.

Tokomaru Bay   *Farmstay Homestay*   *7km W of Tokomaru Bay*

Rahiri
Meg & Bill Busby
263 Mata Road, Tokomaru Bay, East Coast
Tel: (06) 864 5615 Fax: (06) 864 5817
Mob: 027 246 2619 Tollfree: 0800 347 411
Info@Rahiri.com www.rahiri.com

Double $350 Single $250 (Full Breakfast)
Price INCLUDES wine & dinner Credit cards accepted
1 King 1 Double 1 Twin (3 bdrm)
2 Ensuite 1 Guests share

Welcome to 'Rahiri' a gracious 100 year old homestead situated on 7500 acre Pauariki Station, 7km inland from Tokomaru Bay. We offer spacious relaxing accommodation for those wanting a break away from a busy stressful life. Situated amongst mature trees and gardens, with swimming pool, tennis court and wonderful views of Mt Hikurangi. Open fire places in 5 rooms. Flowers, antique furniture, Alfresco dining in summer. Price includes dinner with top quality local wines & cheeses & breakfast. Laundry facilities available. (Single party booking prefered)

Anaura Bay   *Self-contained Farmstay Homestay B&B Beachstay*   *12km N of Tolaga Bay*

Anaura Beachstay or Willowflat Farmstay B&B
June & Allan Hall
Tolaga Bay, Gisborne
Tel: (06) 862 6341 Fax: (06) 862 6371
Mob: 021 267 4909 willowflat@xtra.co.nz
www.bnb.co.nz/anaurabeachstay.html

Double $80 Single $50 (Full Breakfast) Child Half price
Dinner $25 S/C Beachfront Cottage with 2 Double,
$150-$200p.n. min 2 nights Child at home Pet on property
1 Queen 1 Double (2 bdrm) 1 Guests share 2 Family share

Paradise - the best of both worlds - Breakfast with us at our beachfront cottage in picturesque Anaura Bay, glorious sunrises, white sand and backdrop of beautiful native bush, fishing, walkways, or at Willowflat, our sheep, cattle and cropping farm, 12km, spacious home and grounds, an hour north of Gisborne. Village, Cashmere Company, fishing charters, hunting, golf, reserves within 12 km of Willowflat or 23 km of Beachstay. Self-contained option available at both venues $150-$200 per night. Beachstay 2 doubles plus, Farmstay 3 doubles plus.

Tolaga Bay   *Self-contained Homestay*   *3km N of Tolaga Bay, Gisborne 55km*

Papatahi
Nicki & Bruce Jefferd
427 Main Road North, Tolaga Bay,
Tel: (06) 862 6623 Fax: (06) 862 6623
Mob: 025 283 7178   b.n.jefferd@xtra.co.nz
www.bnb.co.nz/papatahi.html

Double $95 Single $60 (Full Breakfast)
Child 1/2 price Dinner $25 Child at home
1 Queen 1 Double (2 bdrm)
1 Ensuite 1 Guests share

Papatahi Homestay is very easy to find being just 3km north of the Tolaga Bay township, on the Pacific Coast Highway. We have a comfortable, modern, sunny home set in a wonderful garden. Papatahi offers separate accommodation with ensuite. A golf course, fishing charters, the Tolaga Bay Cashmere Co and several magnificent beaches are all just minutes away. Daily farm activities are often of interest to our guests. Friendly farm pets and three children add to the experience! Great country meals and good wine are a speciality. Inspection will impress!

Whangara   *Self-contained Farmstay*   *50km E of Gisborne*

The Roost
Nick Reed
Mataurangi Station, RD 3, Gisborne
Tel: (06) 862 2858 Fax: (06) 862 2857
Mob: 025 242 2449   Tollfree: 0800 398 411
mataurangi@xtra.co.nz
www.bnb.co.nz/theroost.html

Double $80 Single $50
(Continental Breakfast) Child $25
1 Double 1 Single (1 bdrm)
1 Private

Mataurangi is a 607 Ha Hill Country sheep and cattle station situated 14km up Panikau Rd, off SH35 between Tolaga Bay and Gisborne. You will stay in "The Roost"; a secluded, fully refurbished, self contained shepherds cottage. (Full kitchen facilities, BBQ, sundeck and small garden). While we may be slightly off the beaten track, we know you will enjoy the experience, and look forward to meeting you and sharing our corner of New Zealand. Please phone for detailed direction.

Whatatutu   *Farmstay*   *50km NE of Gisborne*

Te Hau Station
Chris and Jenny Meban
332 Te Hau Road, Whatatutu, Eastland 3871
Tel: (06) 862 1822 Fax: (06) 862 1997
Mob: 025 844 574   Tollfree: 0800 686218
tehaustn@xtra.co.nz   www.bnb.co.nz/tehaustation.html

Double $95 Single $60 (Full Breakfast)
Child 1/2 price Dinner $30 Credit cards accepted
Child at home Pet on property Pets welcome
1 Queen 2 Double 2 Single (3 bdrm)
1 Ensuite 1 Guests share 1 Family share

Our Colonial Farmhouse, on a 6000 acre hill country station, is an easy 40 minute drive from Gisborne, off SH2 North. Enjoy hands-on farm experiences, learning about life on a sheep and cattle station; watch the shepherds riding horses, expertly handling stock with their sheepdogs. Walking, clay-bird shooting and hunting are all options, or choose to relax and enjoy the many facilities we have to offer including our pool and hot spa. Our two young sons take pleasure in showing guests their many pets.

Waipaoa   *Farmstay*   *20km N of Gisborne*

The Willows
Rosemary & Graham Johnson
& Montgomerie the Labrador
Waipaoa, RD 1, Gisborne
Tel: (06) 862 5605 Fax: (06) 862 5601
Mob: 025 837 365
www.bnb.co.nz/thewillows.html

Double $80 Single $50 (Full Breakfast)
Child 10% discount Dinner $30 by arrangement
2 Queen 2 Single (3 bdrm)
1 Private 1 Guests share

Our home is situated on a hill amid a park like garden with some wonderful trees planted by our forefathers. We enjoy the amenities available in the city and also the country life on our 440 acre property involving deer, cattle, sheep, grapes and cropping. This year we can now offer a double bedroom with a private bathroom. The bedroom has its own access so you can enjoy privacy if you so desire. We are situated 20km north of Gisborne on SH2 through the scenic Waioeka Gorge.

Ormond   *Self-contained*   *18km N of Gisborne*

Hide-a-way Cottage
Paul and Pauline Manning
1354 Matawai Rd, Ormond RD 1, Gisborne
Tel: (06) 862 5456 Fax: (06) 862 5802
Mob (Paul): 021 151 1873   Tollfree: 0800 100 430
paulandpauline@xtra.co.nz
www.bnb.co.nz/user98.html

Double $90 Single $70 (Continental Breakfast)
Child $10 Dinner $20 Children welcome
1 Double 3 Single (2 bdrm)   1 Private

Your hosts, Paul and Pauline welcome you to Hide-a-way Cottage. We have two friendly cats and four chooks. Hide-a-way cottage is situated on our mandarin orchard with a rural outlook overlooking the mandarin trees and surrounding vineyards to the hills. The cottage captures the sun from early morning to late evening. The cottage is very clean and tidy, private and peaceful, fully self-contained with ramps and bathroom set up for the disabled. By arrangement and for a small cost guests can share dinner with us.

Ormond   *Self-contained B&B Orchard Stay B&B, self-contained*   *18km N of Gisborne*

Kiwifruit Orchard Stay
Jenny & Greig Foster
37 Bond Road, RD1, Ormond, Gisborne
Tel: (06) 862 5688 Fax: (06) 862 5688
Mob: 027 441 2876   jdfoster@ihug.co.nz
www.bnb.co.nz/kiwifruitorchardstay.html

Double $85-$95 Single $65 (Special Breakfast)
Child $25 Dinner $30 Pet on property Pets welcome
2 Queen 1 Double 1 Single (2 bdrm)
2 Private

Country Living with style and comfort. Stay in our Villa Moderna, self-contained or our home with private lounge and bathroom. Spend lazy afternoons in the sun sampling wine from our local wineries. During the chillier winter nights take a long soak in our indoor spa and watch the stars set amongst the chardonnay capital of NZ. Come relax with us and our cats and dogs on our kiwifruit orchard and sample the fruit. Five minutes to restaurant bar/grill. Sky, fax, internet, email, spa, swimming pool available. Pets welcome.

Gisborne   *Self-contained Homestay B&B*   *Gisborne Central*

Thomson Homestay
Barbara & Alec Thomson
16 Rawiri Street, Gisborne
Tel: (06) 868 9675 Fax: (06) 868 9675
Mob: 025 265 5350
Tollfree: 0800 370 505
www.bnb.co.nz/thomsonhomestay.html

Double $70 Single $50
(Continental & Full Breakfast) S/C $85
1 Queen 1 Double 2 Twin 2 Single (3 bdrm)
1 Guests share

From our spacious home it is only a five minute stroll to the city centre, wharf complex, museum, rose gardens etc. Secure off-street parking available. We are happy to meet bus or plane. Guests have own TV lounge with tea and coffee making facilities etc. Sight seeing can be arranged at an agreed price. We also have a self-contained unit at $85 per night. Alec and I enjoy a game of bridge, and are also keen bowlers.

Gisborne *Farmstay   25km S of Gisborne*

Wairakaia Farmstay
Sarah & Rodney Faulkner
1894 State Highway 2, Muriwai, Gisborne
Tel: (06) 862 8607 Fax: (06) 862 8607
Mob: 025 611 5778   Tollfree: 0800 329 060
wairakaia@xtra.co.nz
www.bnb.co.nz/wairakaiafarmstay.html

Double $120-$150 Single $80 (Special Breakfast)
Child $30 Dinner $25 - $40 Credit cards accepted
Pet on property Children welcome
1 King/Twin 1 Queen (2 bdrm)   1 Ensuite 1 Private

Welcome to our home - the centre of farm and family life for 3 generations. We are surrounded by a large garden and 1,600 acres of sheep, beef and forestry. Our interests include travelling, cooking, reading and gardening. Breakfast is special and is served in the sunporch overlooking the bay. Join us for an evening meal and enjoy excellent homegrown produce, local wines and award winning cheese. Meet our two cats and Lewis the corgi. Laundry facilities available as is our tennis court.

Gisborne *Farmstay   40km W of Gisborne*

Sally & Andrew Jefferd
RD 2, Ngatapa, Gisborne
Tel: (06) 867 1313 Fax: (06) 867 6311
Tollfree: 0800 469 4401313
jefferd@xtra.co.nz
www.bnb.co.nz/jefferd.html

Double $95 Single $60 (Full Breakfast)
Child 1/2 price Dinner $25 Pets welcome
1 Double 1 Twin (2 bdrm)
1 Ensuite 1 Private 1 Family share

We live 5 minutes drive from the famous Eastwood Hill arboretum. Eastwood Hill is internationally recognized comprising 65 hectares of numerous varieties of trees and shrubs. We have a 1400 acre hill country property, farming sheep, cattle and deer. Farm tours and walks easily arranged. In a tranquil setting we offer our guests separate accommodation with ensuite just a few metres from the main house, giving them the privacy they may desire. Guests are welcome to use the swimming pool and tennis court.

Please let your hosts know if you have to cancel
they will have spent time preparing for you.

Gisborne   *Homestay B&B   Gisborne Central*

Sea View
Raewyn & Gary Robinson
68 Salisbury Road, Gisborne
Tel: (06) 867 3879 Fax: (06) 867 5879
Tollfree: 0800 268 068   raewyn@regaleggs.co.nz
www.bnb.co.nz/seaviewgisborne.html
Double $95 Single $70 (Continental Breakfast)
Children welcome
2 Double 1 Twin 1 Single (3 bdrm)
2 Private

Absolute luxury and comfort. Beachfront bed and breakfast. Seaview is situated on the foreshore of Waikanae beach with unsurpassed panoramic views of Young Nicks head and beautiful Poverty Bay. Just 50 metres from front door to golden sand, and warm blue waters of Poverty Bay. Only two minutes drive to the city (easy walking distance) and visitor information centre. Relax and enjoy safe swimming and great surfing. Five minutes to international golf course and Olympic pool complex. We offer 2 double bedrooms and twin room. 2 private bathrooms. Internet facilities available.

Gisborne   *B&B Beachstay   5km NE of Gisborne*

Beach Stay
Peter & Dorothy Rouse
111 Wairere Road, Wainui Beach, Gisborne
Tel: (06) 868 8111 Fax: (06) 868 8162
Mob: 025 794 929   pete.dot@xtra.co.nz
www.bnb.co.nz/beachstaygisborne.html
Double $85 Single $50 (Continental & Full Breakfast)
Child $10 Dinner $25 Credit cards accepted
Smoking area inside
1 Queen 2 Double 2 Single (2 bdrm)
1 Ensuite 1 Private

GISBORNE

We welcome you to our home which is situated right on the beach front at Wainui. The steps from the lawn lead down to the beach, which is renowned for its lovely clean sand, surf, pleasant walking and good swimming. Gisborne can also offer a host of entertainment, including golf on one of the finest golf courses, charter fishing trips, wine trails, Eastwood Hill Arboretum, horse trekking etc, or you may wish to relax on the beach for the day with a light luncheon provided.

Gisborne   *Homestay   24km W of Gisborne*

Manurere
Joanne & John Sherratt
RD 2, Ngatapa, Gisborne
Tel: (06) 863 9852 Fax: (06) 863 9842
john.sherratt@xtra.co.nz
www.bnb.co.nz/manurere.html
Double $100 Single $60 (Full Breakfast)
Dinner $20 Credit cards accepted
1 Queen 1 Single (1 bdrm)
1 Ensuite

We have a lovely old villa in a peaceful setting in an old established country garden, only 20 minutes from the city centre and beaches. We have a tennis court and swimming pool available in season. We enjoy meeting people and regard homestaying as a wonderful way of achieving this by sharing our home and hospitality with others. Come and enjoy the Ngatapa Valley with our famous 'Eastwoodhill Arboretum' 5 minutes away and also local crafts and furniture makers. Reservations by appointment only.

Gisborne   *Homestay Gallery   Gisborne Central*

Studio 4
Judy & Gavin Smith
4 Heta Road, Gisborne
Tel: (06) 868 1571 Fax: (06) 868 1457
Mob: 0274 386 502   Tollfree: 0800 370 398
Studioart@clear.net.nz
www.bnb.co.nz/studiogisborne.html

Double $90 Single $60 (Continental Breakfast)
Dinner $25pp Credit cards accepted
1 Queen 3 Single (2 bdrm)
1 Ensuite 1 Family share

Welcome to our American-style character home, set amongst old English trees. We offer peaceful surroundings with off-street parking. An 8 min. walk along the riverbank will take you to the city centre, the "wharf" area, the museum and a variety of restaurants. Gavin is a well-known watercolour artist and we have an art gallery on site. We have travelled overseas ourselves and enjoy meeting people in our comfortable user-friendly home.

Gisborne   *Homestay   8km N of Gisborne*

Makorori Heights
Roger & Morag Shanks
36 Sirrah St, Wainui Beach, Gisborne
Tel: (06) 867 0806
Fax: (06) 868 7706
Mob: 021 250 4918
www.bnb.co.nz/makororiheights.html

Double $80 Single $45 (Full Breakfast)
Dinner $25 Credit cards accepted
1 Double 2 Single (2 bdrm)
1 Guests share 1 Family share

Our home is 1/2 km off Highway 35 at the northern end of Wainui Beach. With beautiful sea and sunrise views, surrounded by farmland and our own young olive grove. Handy to bush and coastal walkways. We have travelled overseas and enjoy the company of others. Roger is a water colour artist with examples of his overseas and local works available for viewing or purchase. Horse trekking, fishing trips, country excursions by arrangements. We have one friendly small dog not allowed indoors.

Gisborne   *Homestay B&B   1km E of Gisborne*

Fox Street Retreat
Jan & Alan Saunders
103 Fox Street, Gisborne
Tel: (06) 868 8702 Fax: (06) 868 8702
Mob: 025 907 777   Tollfree: 0800 868 8702
jan.saunders@clear.net.nz
www.bnb.co.nz/geocities.com/fox_street_retreat.html
Double $70 Single $50
(Continental Breakfast) Child $25
1 Queen 1 Twin (2 bdrm)
1 Family share

Welcome to our tasteful retreat situated in our delightful gardens in a quiet location within easy walking distance of city. Relax around our pool and enjoy use of our BBQ. Sky TV in bedrooms. We play bowls and bridge and will gladly arrange for guests with free use of clubs and trolleys. We are Tuberous Begonia enthusiasts with lovely display in gardens, pots and baskets in season. We will gladly arrange tours. Cut lunches on request. Off street parking available.

Gisborne   *B&B*   *Gisborne*

Riverbank Homestay
Judy, David and Marney Newell
100 Oak Street, Gisborne

Tel: 021 633 372 Fax: (06) 868 9940
Mob: 021 633 372   anaurastay@xtra.co.nz
www.bnb.co.nz/riverbankhomestay.html

Double $75-$85 Single $50 (Full Breakfast)
Child $20 Dinner $25 Credit cards accepted
Pet on property Children welcome
1 Queen 1 Double 1 Twin (3 bdrm)
1 Ensuite 1 Private 1 Guests share

We are a retired couple used to travel during working lives-our guests now keep us (and daughter Marney) in touch with the outside world and are a welcome source of new friendships. Our home is on a quiet riverbank section 5 minutes by car from city centre. We offer a large, airy, private studio with ensuite, TV, and deck or rooms, with private bathroom, in the family living area. We also have a beachfront homestay "Rangimarie" at beautiful Anaura Bay on SH 35.

Gisborne - Wairoa   *Self-contained Farmstay*   *60km SW of Gisborne*

Rongoio Farm Stay
Matt & Jude Stock
Ruakaka Rd, Tiniroto, Gisborne

Tel: (06) 867 4065 Fax: (06) 863 7018
rongoio@paradise.net.nz
www.bnb.co.nz/rongoiostation.html

Double $100 Single $80 (Full Breakfast) Child $20
Dinner $30 Surcharge for 1 night only $10
1 King 1 Queen 2 Single (3 bdrm)
1 Private

Join us on our 440 hectare hill country sheep and cattle farm and enjoy all that rural NZ life offers. Very close to the homestead but secluded by established trees is a three bedroom totally self contained cottage. From this cosy home feel the remote peace and tranquillity along with the magnificent views of the trout filled Hangaroa River and waterfall. We encourage guests to participate in rural activities including fishing, wild game shooting, horse and motor bike riding, possum shooting and eeling. Warm friendly back country hospitality is our specialty. Children most welcome but no pets.

Please let us know how you enjoyed your B&B experience.
Ask your host for a comment form.

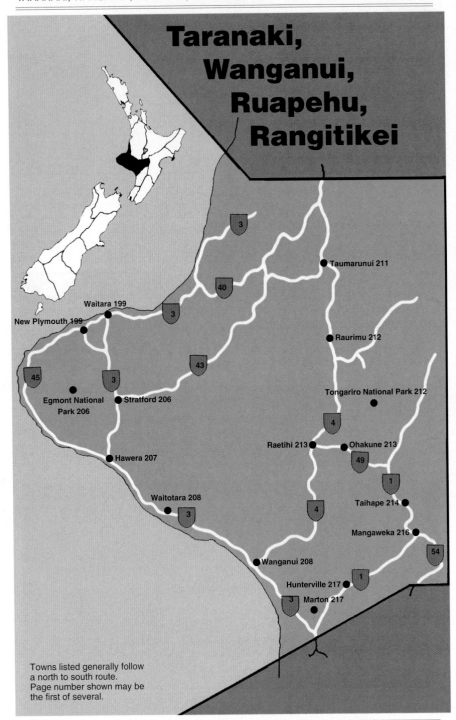

Taranaki, Wanganui, Ruapehu, Rangitikei

Taumarunui 211

Waitara 199

New Plymouth 199

Raurimu 212

Tongariro National Park 212

Egmont National Park 206

Stratford 206

Raetihi 213

Ohakune 213

Hawera 207

Taihape 214

Waitotara 208

Mangaweka 216

Wanganui 208

Hunterville 217

Marton 217

Towns listed generally follow
a north to south route.
Page number shown may be
the first of several.

Waitara   *Self-contained Homestay B&B*   *15kms No of New Plymouth*

Trenowth Gardens
Sherril and Ken George
2 Armstrong Avenue, Waitara, Taranaki
Tel: (06) 754 7674 Fax: (06) 754 8884
Mob: 025 736 055   sherril@trenowth.co.nz
www.trenowth.com

Double $80 Single $65 (Continental & Full Breakfast)
Child $15 Dinner $25pp Credit cards accepted
2 Double 1 Single (2 bdrm)
1 Ensuite 1 Private

Garden Homestay plus self-contained B&B cottage situated right on the main north-south Auckland/New Plymouth/Wellington highway at historic Waitara. Large family house with guest homestay(ensuite) plus additional B&B cottage with separate bedroom,lounge/dining/kitchen area with separate bathroom/laundry/toilet. Fully equipped with TV/music/library; all set in 18 acres of landscaped gardens, private lake and orchards. Close to 4 golf courses, local fishing, bush and mountain walks. Ten minutes from New Plymouth restaurants, twenty minutes from the mountain.

New Plymouth   *Homestay*   *6km SE of New Plymouth*

Blacksmiths Rest
Evelyn & Laurie Cockerill
481 Mangorei Road, New Plymouth
Tel: (06) 758 6090 Fax: (06) 758 6078
Mob: 025 678 8641
www.bnb.co.nz/blacksmithsrest.html

Double $70-$80 Single $45 (Full Breakfast)
Dinner $20 by arrangement Credit cards accepted
2 Queen 2 Single (2 bdrm)
1 Ensuite 1 Private

Relax and enjoy our rural views although we are only five minutes drive from city centre while the well known "Tupare Gardens" are just next door.   Each guest room has a queen and a single bed with an ensuite in the upstairs bedroom. We have a large garden, some sheep and a friendly dog called Bill who lives outside. Interests, equestrian, sport, gardening. There is plenty of off street parking. Mangorei Road can be easily found when approaching New Plymouth from either north or south.

New Plymouth   *Homestay B&B*   *2km N of New Plymouth*

Brooklands B&B
Neal Spragg
39 Plympton Street, Brooklands,
New Plymouth
Tel: (06) 753 2265 Mob: 025 285 7602
brooklandsbb@freenet.co.nz
www.bnb.co.nz/brooklandsbb.html

Double $65 Single $35 (Continental Breakfast)
1 Queen 2 Single (2 bdrm)
1 Private

My home is located in a peaceful and tranquil setting overlooking a bush clad walkway leading to the renowned Pukekura and Brooklands Parks and city centre. The guest wing consists of bathroom and toilet facilities, two bedrooms, one queen size and the other a twin room. I enjoy sharing my comfortable home with visitors from abroad and New Zealand travellers. I offer you a warm and friendly welcome and a relaxed stay in New Plymouth. I request please no smoking in the house.

New Plymouth   *B&B   4.5km NE of New Plymouth*

Merrilands Homestay
A & E Howan
11 Tamati Place, Merrilands, New Plymouth
Tel: (06) 758 8932 Fax: (06) 758 8932
ahowan@xtra.co.nz
www.bnb.co.nz/howan.html

Double $60 Single $40 (Continental Breakfast)
twin $60 Credit cards accepted
1 Double 3 Single (3 bdrm)
1 Guests share

We live in a comfortable modern home, looking out on beautiful Mt Egmont/Taranaki. We are easily found from both north and south approaches to New Plymouth, located in a quiet cul-de-sac just off Mangorei Road. As an active retired couple our interests are varied, including walking, travel, gardening and needlework. We enjoy meeting new friends, and provide hospitality in a relaxed atmosphere for your pleasure. Light refreshments, laundry facilities and off-street parking are available. Guests are requested not to smoke in the house.

New Plymouth - Omata   *B&B   5km S of New Plymouth*

Rangitui
Therese & Tony Waghorn
Waireka Road, RD 4, New Plymouth
Tel: (06) 751 2979 Fax: (06) 751 2985
twaghorn@clear.net.nz
www.accommodationtaranaki.co.nz

Double $70-$90 Single $60-$80 (Full Breakfast)
Dinner $40 Credit cards accepted Pet on property
1 Queen 2 Single (2 bdrm)
1 Ensuite 1 Private

10 minutes from New Plymouth. Separate chalet with ensuite, queen bed, TV, and balcony overlooking bush and sea. Twin room with guest facilities in house. Your choice of breakfast (except kippers!) Dinner with wine, $40 per head, by arrangement. Enjoy bush or orchard walks, relax by our pool, or visit some of the nearby attractions: beautiful Mt Taranaki, some of the best surf in the world, famous gardens, art gallery, museum, historic sites and golf courses. Bookings: Please phone for reservations/directions.

New Plymouth   *Homestay B&B Farmlet   5km W of New Plymouth Central*

Birdhaven
Ann & John Butler
26 Pararewa Drive, New Plymouth
Tel: (06) 751 0432 Fax: (06) 751 3475
Tollfree: 0800 306 449   info@birdhaven.co.nz
www.bnb.co.nz/birdhaven.html

Double $77-$100 Single $54-$80 (Special Breakfast)
Child by arrangement Dinner by arrangement
Credit cards accepted Pet on property
1 King/Twin 1 Queen 2 Single (2 bdrm) 1 Private

Ensuring your comfort and pleasure is important to us. We have lived in three continents and enjoy travelling. We love welcoming guests to Birdhaven and endeavouring to exceed your expectations. Share our tranquil, spacious, tastefully furnished home, secluded gardens and spectacular mountain view. Relax on the patios overlooking our beautiful native bush, woodlands and birdlife. Indulge in the complimentary refreshments and the special breakfast of seasonal and homemade temptations. A peaceful haven only five minutes from city. Cedric, our cat, is gregarious and well behaved.

New Plymouth *Self-contained Farmstay* *3km S of New Plymouth*

Oak Valley Manor
Pat & Paul Ekdahl
248 Junction Road, RD 1, New Plymouth
Tel: (06) 758 1501 Fax: (06) 758 1052
Mob: 025 420 325   kauri.holdings@xtra.co.nz
www.bnb.co.nz/oakvalleymanor.html

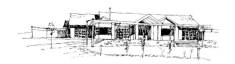

Double $105 Single $75 (Full Breakfast)
Child $1 per year up to 12yrs Dinner $30
Pets welcome   Credit cards accepted
2 Queen 1 Single (2 bdrm)   2 Ensuite

Your hosts, Pat and Paul, two friendly people with a wealth of experience in the hospitality industry, invite you to a unique bed and breakfast in their beautifully appointed home with views from each room to Mount Egmont. These beautiful views make an impression which we will everlasting. Guests can choose their own privacy or socialise with us. We have a variety of animals, donkey, peacocks, pigs, aand dogs. Ducks and geese enjoy the lake. Golf course 10 minute drive. Laundry available.

New Plymouth *Homestay* *New Plymouth Central*

Kirkstall House
Ian Hay & Lindy MacDiarmid
8 Baring Terrace, New Plymouth
Tel: (06) 758 3222 Fax: (06) 758 3224
Mob: 025 973 908   kirkstall@xtra.co.nz
www.bnb.co.nz/kirkstallhouse.html

Double $80 Single $60 Ensuite room $75/95
Credit cards accepted Pet on property
(3 bdrm)
2 Private

"Kirkstall House" invites you to experience its old world beauty and comfort, in an atmosphere of easy hospitality and relaxed surroundings. "Kirkstall House" is one of surprise. Enjoy our superb mountain views, cosy open fire, and delightful garden leading down to the river. The sea, beaches, and walkways, restaurants and shops are all within easy walking distance. Lindy, a practising physiotherapist, and Ian, involved with tourism, are here to help you enjoy Taranakai to the utmost. We are smoke free and have four great cats.

New Plymouth *Self-contained* *25km N of New Plymouth*

Cottage by the Sea
Nancy & Hugh Mills
66 Lower Turangi Road,
RD 43, Waitara
Tel: (06) 754 7915 Fax: (06) 754 7915
nancy.mills@clear.net.nz
www.bnb.co.nz/cottagebytheseanewplymouth.html

Double $95 Single $75 (Continental Breakfast)
Child neg extra person $25 Pet on property
1 Queen 1 Double (1 bdrm)
1 Ensuite

Go to sleep with the sound of the waves...wake with the birds. This modern, peaceful cottage, nestled amongst landscaped gardens and lawns, offers complete privacy. You may take a short bushwalk down 100 steps to the beach, relax on the veranda watching ever-changing sea views, or request a tour of our small commercial flower business. There is a comfortable sofabed in the lounge. The kitchen is fully equipped. Subtract $7.50 pp if providing your own breakfast. Our family dog may greet you.

T'NAKI, W'NUI,
R'PEHU, R'TIKEI

New Plymouth   *Homestay*

The Grange
Cathy Thurston & John Smith
The Grange, 44B Victoria Road,
New Plymouth Central

Tel: (06) 758 1540 Fax: (06) 758 1539
Mob: 027 4333 497   cathyt@clear.net.nz
www.bnb.co.nz/thegrange.html

Double $110 Single $85 (Full Breakfast)
Credit cards accepted Pet on property
1 King/Twin 1 Queen 2 Single (2 bdrm)
2 Ensuite

Come and stay in our modern architecturally designed award-winning home built with the privacy and comfort of our guests in mind. With unique bush views and a house designed to take full advantage of the sun our guests can enjoy relaxing in the lounge or the extensive tiled courtyards. The Grange is centrally heated, security controlled and located adjacent to the renowned Pukekura Park and Bowl of Brooklands. The city is within a short 5 minute walk.

New Plymouth   *B&B separate suite*   *New Plymouth Central*

93 By the Sea
Patricia & Bruce Robinson
93 Buller Street, New Plymouth

Tel: (06) 758 6555 Mob: 025 230 3887
pat@93bythesea.co.nz
www.pat@93bythesea.co.nz

Double $100 Single $80 (Special Breakfast)
Dinner by arrangement Children welcome
1 King/Twin 1 Double (2 bdrm)
1 Private

Exclusive use of downstairs facility with off-street parking, lounge, bedrooms, bathroom (spa bath, super shower, laundry), ONE PARTY ONLY. Share breakfast with us while enjoying sights, sounds, and feel of garden, surf, ocean. Centrally situated on the N.P.Coastal walkway, means access to parks, beaches, city centre, is simple and enjoyable. Guests' Comments, 2002: 'Beautiful home, beautiful people, great breakfast! Thankyou!', G&P, Canada; 'A delightful experience', M.C. England; 'A beautiful spot, so many options', H&M, USA.

New Plymouth   *B&B*   *1km S of Civic Centre*

The Treehouse
Herbert & Lorraine Abel
75 Morley Street,
New Plymouth

Tel: (06) 757 4288 herbabel@xtra.co.nz
www.bnb.co.nz/thetreehouse.html

Double $80 Single $50 (Full Breakfast)
Dinner $25 by arrangement Credit cards accepted
1 King 1 Queen 2 Twin (3 bdrm)
1 Guests share

Lorraine and Herb invite you to our stunning Treehouse. Our guest accommodation is situated downstairs with all rooms opening on to our attractive garden, but please feel free to join us upstairs or lounge on our sunny deck anytime. We are just minutes from all amenities and beautiful Pukekura Park. Our home is smoke free but not suitable for children or pets. Ample off street parking available. Lorraine, Herb and our friendly house cat, Sam, look forward to meeting you.

New Plymouth   *Guest House*   *New Plymouth central*

Issey Manor
Carol & Lewis
32 Carrington Street, New Plymouth
Tel: (06) 758 2375 Fax: (06) 758 2375
Mob: 025 248 6686   issey.manor@actrix.co.nz
www.isseymanor.co.nz
Double $100-$150 (Full Breakfast)
Child by arrangement corporate rates available
Credit cards accepted Pet on property
1 King/Twin 3 Queen (4 bdrm)   4 Ensuite

Issey Manor offers 4 luxury contemporary suites, all with designer bathrooms, 2 having spa baths. All rooms have beautiful bedding, refreshments, phones, work desks, data points comfortable seating, email, fax available. Separate guest dining/lounge, Sky TV. An inner city location just minutes stroll to many cafes, seaside promenade, art galleries, Information Centre, Pukekura Park and Brooklands Bowl. Enjoy our many books, artwork, collectables and relax on the enormous decking overlooking a tranquil bush and stream vista. For business or pleasure your comfort and privacy assured.

New Plymouth   *Self-contained B&B*   *500m W of New Plymouth Central*

Airlie House
Lisa McCready & Trevor Masters
161 Powderham Street, New Plymouth
Tel: (06) 757 8866 Fax: (06) 757 8866
Mob: (021) 499697   email@airliehouse.co.nz
www.airliehouse.co.nz
Double $95 Single $75 (Special Breakfast)
Child neg Credit cards accepted
1 King/Twin 2 Queen 2 Single (3 bdrm)
3 Ensuite

Airlie House (formerly 'Balconies') is nestled amongst lovely gardens in the heart of the city, just 5 min walk to New Plymouth's city centre and seafront. Our warm, comfortable 110 year old character home offers two downstairs guest rooms with ensuites plus a studio flat. High-speed internet access in all rooms as well as a computer for shared use in the library. Off-street parking available. Guests are requested not to smoke inside. We are within walking distance to many attractions, restaurants and parks.

T'NAKI, W'NUI,
R'PEHU, R'TIKEI

New Plymouth   *B&B*   *500m Central New Plymouth*

Alice Jane Bed and Breakfast
Bill & Vicki Lovell-Smith
60 Pendarves Street,
New Plymouth 4601
Tel: (06) 758 1440 Fax: (06) 758 1440
Mob: 021 259 5772
alice_jane@wave.co.nz
www.bnb.co.nz/alicejanebb.html
Double $80 Single $60
1 King/Twin 2 Queen 1 Single (4 bdrm)
1 Guests share

Encounter the mountain to surf experience that is the city of New Plymouth, whether it be for business or pleasure. Stay at Bill and Vicki's spacious and tastefully restored 1915 villa. Guests will be pampered and refreshed by the successful blend of the old and new. Your comfort is our immediate goal in your home away from home. Secure off-street parking and a courtesy car are available. Touring motorcyclist friendly ammenities. (There are pets on the premises).

New Plymouth   *B&B*   *New Plymouth Central*

Summerfield House
Wendy & Murray Boulter
1 Victoria Rd, New Plymouth,
Tel: 06 758 8962 Fax: 06 758 8962 Mob: 025 609 4813
boulters@xtra.co.nz
www.bnb.co.nz/user161.html
Double $125 Single $90 (Full Breakfast)
Child B/A Dinner by arrangement
Credit cards accepted Children welcome
2 Queen (2 bdrm)   1 Private 1 Guests share

Sited amidst an old orchard and private gardens, Summerfield House is conveniently located just across the road from Pukekura Park and Brooklands Bowl. Downtown shops, cafes, restaurants, art galleries, heritage walkways and foreshore promenade are a 5 minute walk. We offer luxury accommodation with beautiful large bedrooms decorated in English Country or French Provincial style with everything for your comfort. The guest lounge is furnished with English antiques, original NZ art and Sky TV. Be assured of fine accommodation and a warm welcome.

Ensuite and private bathrooms
are for your use exclusively.
Guest share bathroom means you
will be sharing with other guests.
Family share means you
will be sharing with the family.

New Plymouth   *Homestay B&B   8km New Plymouth*

Churchwood Manor
Jo-Anne & Warren
1148 Devon Road, R.D.3, New Plymouth
Tel: (06) 7551947 Fax: (06) 7588520
Mob: 025 718 660
churchwoodmanor@xtra.co.nz
www.bnb.co.nz/churchwoodmanor.html

Double $95 Single $75 (Special Breakfast)
Child $25 - under 5 free Dinner by arrangement
Credit cards accepted Pets welcome
2 Queen 1 Twin 1 Single (3 bdrm)   2 Ensuite

Churchwood is a 1920's bungalow set on 3 arces of mature grounds, mins from New Plymouth city &
Airport. Swim indoors or soak in the spa. Curl up with a book by the fire, Stroll though the garden with
major (the cat). Dine inside or out with Dinners and small functions tailored to suit by arrangement.
Bookings for sightseeing within the Taranaki region and New Zealand avaliable. Jo-Anne & Warren
welcome guests with warm hospitality and are only too happy to help.

New Plymouth   *B&B   5km W of City Centre*

Bradford Way B&B
Robbie & Joy Peel
186 South Road, New Plymouth,
Tel: (06) 751 0551 bradfordway@ihug.co.nz
www.bnb.co.nz/bradfordwaybb.html

Double $60-$85 Single $40-$65 (Full Breakfast)
Child half price Dinner $20 by arrangement
Credit cards accepted
2 Queen 1 Twin (3 bdrm)
2 Ensuite 1 Private

We are the closest city B&B to surf highway and fabulous beaches. Also nearby to bush walks on Mt
Taranaki or Pukekura and Brooklands. Visit the art galleries or enjoy a game of golf at one of our
excellent golf courses. Our spacious guest wing has its own TV lounge/sporting library and a separate
entrance off a large courtyard where breakfast can be served on a lovely morning. We have travelled
extensively overseas giving us a great appreciation of true hospitality.

New Plymouth   *Homestay B&B   6km N of New Plymouth*

Rockvale Lodge
Neil and Jeannette Cowley
97 Manutahi Road, R.D. 2, New Plymouth
Tel: (06) 755 0750 Fax: (06) 755 0750
Mob: 025 682 1236   jeannette.neil@xtra.co.nz
www.bnb.co.nz/user200.html

Double $80 Single $60 (Full Breakfast) Child $30
Dinner $25 By Arrangement Credit cards accepted
1 Queen 2 Single (2 bdrm)
1 Guests share

We welcome you to our large, country-style home, recently renovated, surrounded by deer farm, with
beautiful Mt. Egmont/Taranaki as a backdrop. Guests' double room and adjoining lounge open onto a
balcony, with rural views. Relax in your private spabath, and join us for dinner, on the deck in summer,
or by the fire in winter. We are close to airport, city, beaches, parks and the mountain. Six 18-hole golf
courses are within 15 minutes drive. You will receive a warm welcome from Mallory, our Labrador,
who lives outdoors. We look forward to sharing our home with you. Families welcome.

New Plymouth *Homestay B&B   4km E of New Plymouth*

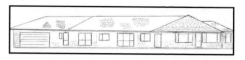

Struan Lodge
Mary and Andrew Sylvester
399A Mangorei Road, New Plymouth,
Tel: To be sent Fax: To be sent
Mob: 021 317 8100
struan.lodge@xtra.co.nz
www.bnb.co.nz/struanlodge.html

Double $120 Single $100 (Full Breakfast)
Dinner $30 Credit cards accepted
2 Queen 1 Twin (3 bdrm)
3 Ensuite

Struan Lodge is set in a perfectly, private and peaceful semi rural environment. With your own en suite, bathrobe, guest lounge, tea coffee making facilities and much more, Struan Lodge has been purposely built to offer you a fine Scottish welcome. Ideally situated, we are very close to a secluded water hole and only a few minutes drive from many Taranaki attractions. Come and sample the wonderful hospitality Taranaki has to offer. Mary, Andrew and Meg (our little bichon frese) await your arrival.

Stratford *Farmstay Homestay B&B   1/2km N of Stratford*

Stallard B&B
Billieanne & Corb Stallard
3514 State Highway 3, Stratford Northern Boundry
Tel: (06) 765 8324 Fax: (06) 765 8324
stallardbb@infogen.net.nz
www.bnb.co.nz/stallardbb.html

Double $70 Single $40 (Special Breakfast)
Child $20 Family room sleeps 4 $95
Credit cards accepted Smoking area inside
2 Double 2 Twin 2 Single (4 bdrm)   4 Ensuite

1900 "Upstairs Downstairs" comfort. Cooked or continental breakfast included. Free self catering kitchen, tea, coffee, biscuits. Homely or private. Own key. Optional separate lounge. Restaurants, taverns, shops nearby. Rooms are antique, romantic with TV, heaters, electric blankets, serviced daily. Gardens, BBQ, row boat, bush bath, river walks. 15 mins Mt Egmont skifields, climbing, tramping. Centrally located on edge of Stratford, easy distance to New Plymouth, museums, famous gardens, tourist attractions. We are semi retired farmers. Interests include gemstones travel, art. Welcome.

Egmont National Park *Farmstay Homestay   9km W of Stratford*

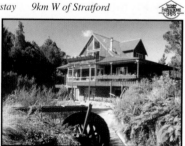

Anderson's Alpine Lodge   Keith & Berta Anderson
PO Box 303, Stratford, Taranaki
Tel: (06) 765 6620 Fax: (06) 765 6100
Mob: 025 412 372   Tollfree: 0800 668 682
mountainhouse@xtra.co.nz   www.mountainhouse.co.nz

Double $125-$155 Single $125 (Full Breakfast)
Dinner $35 - $40 Mountain House Motor Lodge $105
Credit cards accepted Pets welcome
1 King/Twin 1 Queen 1 Double 2 Single (3 bdrm)
3 Ensuite

Swiss style chalet surrounded with native gardens and bush. Spectacular views of Mount Egmont/Taranaki and Egmont National Park opposite our front gate. Five kilometers to Mountain House and its famed restaurant, further 3km to Stratford Plateau and skifields. Tramps, summit climbs, trout stream, gardens & museums nearby. Private helicopter summit flights. Pet sheep, pig, ducks etc. Kiwi Keith and Swiss Berta Anderson owned mountain lodges since 1973, winning many awards. Keith is noted Taranaki artist specializing in mountain scenes.

Stratford   *Country Retreat*   *15km NE of Stratford*

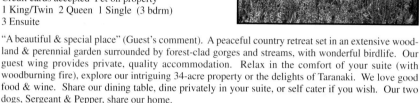

Sarsen House
Bruce & Lorri Ellis
Te Popo Gardens, 636 Stanley Road, RD 24, Stratford
Tel: (06) 762 8775 Fax: (06) 762 8776
tepopo@clear.net.nz   www.tepopo.co.nz
Double $120-$140 Single $100-$120
(Special Breakfast) Dinner $25 - $35
Credit cards accepted Pet on property
1 King/Twin 2 Queen 1 Single (3 bdrm)
3 Ensuite

"A beautiful & special place" (Guest's comment). A peaceful country retreat set in an extensive woodland & perennial garden surrounded by forest-clad gorges and streams, with wonderful birdlife. Our guest wing provides private, quality accommodation. Relax in the comfort of your suite (with woodburning fire), explore our intriguing 34-acre property or the delights of Taranaki. We love good food & wine. Share our dining table, dine privately in your suite, or self cater if you wish. Our two dogs, Sergeant & Pepper, share our home.

Hawera   *B&B Inn*   *1.5km S of Hawera Central*

Tairoa Lodge
Linda & Steve Morrison
3 Puawai Street, PO Box 117, Hawera
Tel: (06) 278 8603 Fax: (06) 278 8603
Mob: 027 2435782   tairoa.lodge@xtra.co.nz
www.tairoa-lodge.co.nz
Double $120-$130 Single $100 (Full Breakfast)
Dinner by arrangement Credit cards accepted
Child at home Pet on property
2 Queen 1 Single (2 bdrm) 2 Ensuite

TAIROA LODGE
◎ BED & BREAKFAST ◎

Originally built in 1875 our Kauri villa has been renovated to its former Victorian glory and is nestled amongst established grounds. Polished Kauri floors add a golden glow to the tastefully decorated rooms. Each bedroom is spacious and has views over the woodland garden and swimming pool. Breakfasts are served in the dining room, verandah or privately on the balcony of the master suite. Romance package available for that special occasion or weekend retreat. Linda and Steve assure you a memorable stay at Tairoa Lodge.

Hawera   *B&B*

Linden Park
Douglas & Merilyn Tippett
69 Waihi Road, Hawera,
Tel: (06) 278 5421 Fax: (06) 278 5421
Mob: 025 281 6216
www.bnb.co.nz/lindenpark.html
Double $80 Single $60 (Full Breakfast)
Dinner $15, on request Credit cards accepted
2 Queen 1 Double (3 bdrm)
1 Guests share

Welcome to our home, named after the old English Linden trees growing at the entranceway. We are situated on SH3, directly opposite King Edward Park and Hawera's aquatic centre, and are in close proximity to Hawera's amenities, restaurants and local attractions. The mountain, intensive dairy farming, trout streams, parks, gardens, beaches, golf courses, museums and local industry offer a variety of activities. We trust ours will be a home away from home as you enjoy the loveliness of South Taranaki.

Waitotara - Wanganui   *Self-contained Farmstay   29km W of Wanganui*

Ashley Park
Barry Pearce & Wendy Bowman
State Highway 3, Box 36, Waitotara, Wanganui
Tel: (06) 346 5917 Fax: (06) 346 5861
ashley_park@xtra.co.nz
www.bnb.co.nz/ashleypark.html

Double $70-$90 Single $40 (Full Breakfast)
Dinner $25 Credit cards accepted
1 Queen 4 Single (3 bdrm)
1 Ensuite 1 Guests share

We have a 500 acre sheep and cattle farm and live in a comfortable home, set in an attractive garden
with a swimming pool and tennis court. Also in the garden is an antique shop selling Devonshire teas.
100 metres from the house is a 4 acre park and lake, aviaries and a collection hand fed pet farm animals.
We welcome guests to have dinner with us. Self-contained accommodation is available in the park.

Wanganui   *Homestay   3km W of Wanganui*

Janet Dick
156 Great North Road,
Wanganui
Tel: (06) 345 8951 Mob: 025 235 2733
janetdick@infogen.net.nz
www.bnb.co.nz/dick.html
Double $75 Single $50
(Continental Breakfast)
2 Single (1 bdrm)
1 Private

My home is a modern Lockwood set amongst mature trees, three kilometres from the centre of Wanganui
on the main Wanganui./New Plymouth Highway. I have travelled extensively overseas and enjoy meeting
and conversing with people from all countries. My many interests include sport, tramping, gardening,
bridge, travel and fishing. Wanganui has many attractions including excellent sporting facilities, museums
an art gallery and the scenic Wanganui river which offers everything from paddle steam cruises to
kayaking to jetboating to the famous Bridge to Nowhere.

Wanganui   *Farmstay   45km N of Wanganui*

Operiki Farmstay
Trissa & Peter McIntyre
3302 River Rd, Operiki, RD 6, Wanganui
Tel: (06) 342 8159
www.bnb.co.nz/operikifarmstay.html
Single $35 (Full Breakfast) Child $15 Dinner $20
Credit cards accepted
1 Double 2 Single (2 bdrm)
1 Family share

Farmstay overlooking the Whanganui River - en route to the Bridge to Nowhere - sheep, cattle and deer
farming. Pottery and macadamia nuts and cat. Enjoy a country picnic and/or walk. Other activities
along the river can be arranged: canoeing, jet boat rides, horse riding, mountain bike riding, Marae visit
and farm activities according to season.

Wanganui   *Homestay B&B   5min walk Wanganui Centre*

Bradgate
Frances
7 Somme Parade,
Wanganui
Tel: (06) 345 3634 Fax: (06) 345 3634
www.bnb.co.nz/bradgate.html

Double $70-$75 Single $40-$50 (Full Breakfast)
Dinner $25 Pet on property
2 Queen 1 Double 2 Single (3 bdrm)
1 Guests share

Welcome to Bradgate, a gracious 2 storey home. With its beautiful entrance hall and carved rimu staircase which reflects the original character and gracefulness of the house. 28 years ago my husband and I came to New Zealand. We owned Shangri-La Restaurant by Virginia Lake. 20 years later the family have flown the nest. We decided to welcome guests into our home. My Mum and I share an energetic young labrador named Crunchy. I enjoy playing golf, gardening and meeting people. Non-smoking house, Dinner by arrangement.

Wanganui   *Homestay B&B   2km NW of Wanganui*

Kembali
Wes & Marylyn Palmer
26 Taranaki Street, St Johns Hill, Wanganui
Tel: (06) 347 1727 Mob: 025 270 1879
wespalmer@xtra.co.nz
www.bnb.co.nz/kembali.html

Double $80 Single $50 (Full Breakfast)
Credit cards accepted
1 Queen 1 Twin (2 bdrm)
1 Private

In a quiet cul-de-sac, 'Kembali' is a modern, centrally heated, sunny home. Upstairs are the guest bedrooms and lounge with TV, fridge, tea/coffee facilities. The house overlooks trees and 'wetlands' where native birds roam. Semi-retired, no pets, our children married, we offer a restful stay for one party/group at a time. Off-street parking and laundry available. Five minutes drive to restaurants and walks - historic Wanganui is 'well worth the journey'. We look forward to welcoming you.

Wanganui   *Farmstay   30km NE of Wanganui*

Omaka Homestay
Ann & John Handley
1622 River Road,
RD 6, Whanganui
Tel: (06) 342 5597 omakaholiday@xtra.co.nz
www.bnb.co.nz/omakahomestay.html

Single $40 (Full Breakfast) Child half price
Dinner $20 campervans $10
1 Twin (1 bdrm)
1 Family share

Come as strangers, leave as friends when you stay at Omaka, a 1000 hectare mixed farm beside the historic and scenic Whanganui River bounding the Whanganui National Park. Stay in our comfortable home with spectacular bush views, join in farm activities, enjoy three hour canoe trips, horseride, swim, walk our bush and farm tracks. John's hobbies include running and trout fishing; Ann's books, herbs, gardening and cooking. We enjoy people and have travelled extensively. We have two cats and a sheep dog.

Wanganui *Farmstay* *20km NE of Wanganui*

Misty Valley Farmstay
Linda & Garry Wadsworth
RD 5, 97 Parihauhau Road, Wanganui
Tel: (06) 342 5767
linda.garry.wadsworth@xtra.co.nz
www.bnb.co.nz/mistyvalley.html

Double $70 Single $45 (Full Breakfast) Child $20
Dinner $30 Credit cards accepted Children welcome
2 Double 2 Twin (2 bdrm)
1 Guests share

Misty Valley is a small organic farm at 3.7 hectares. We prefer to use our own produce whenever possible. There are farm animals for you to meet including our Brittany George and cats Alice and Calico, who all live outside. Our two grandchildren visit us regularly and children will be made very welcome. We are non-smoking, but have pleasant deck areas for those who do. Our famous river and historical city offer plenty of activities for the whole family to enjoy.

Wanganui *Homestay* *20km N of Wanganui*

Chestnut Farm
Brenda Wilson
1690 State Highway 3 North, RD4, Maxwell
Tel: (06) 342 9998 Fax: (06) 342 9998
Mob: 025 856 036
chestnutfarm@paradise.net.nz
www.bnb.co.nz/chestnutfarm.html

Double $60 Single $40 (Full Breakfast) Child $20
Dinner $20 Pet on property Smoking area inside
1 Queen 1 Twin (2 bdrm) 1 Guests share

Come and experience tranquil rural environments. Your hosts, a border collie and two nurses, Brenda & Judi, establishing a lifestyle farm. Enjoy bush, farmlands, get close to nature and our farmyard animals. Soak up the sun, enjoying sea views from extensive gardens. Canoe the duckpond. Enjoy homegrown vegetables, free range eggs. Children welcome. The perfect base to explore the Whanganui River City, two National Parks, local beaches, botanical gardens. Picnics on request. Each room contains TV, tea & coffee making facilities. Discount for two or more nights.

Wanganui *B&B* *2km E of Wanganui*

The Pepper Tree
Jenny & David Pitt
19 Young Street, Wanganui
Tel: (06) 343 9933 Mob: (025) 264 7603
pittman@xtra.co.nz
www.bnb.co.nz/thepeppertree.html

Double $90 Single $65 (Continental & Full Breakfast)
Dinner by arrangement Pet on property
1 Double 1 Twin (2 bdrm)
1 Guests share

Enjoy warm and friendly hospitality when you visit our lovingly restored 1920's Californian Bungalow. Relax in our guest lounge, or take a stroll by the Wanganui River at the end of the street, and watch the Waimarie paddle steamer pass by. Situated just a few metres off State Highway 4, we are a short drive from the city centre. Dave's interests include making and repairing musical instruments, Karate and cooking. Jenny enjoys home decor, gardening and folk art. We look forward to sharing your company.

Wanganui   *2 min Wanganui centre*

Braemar House
Gail and Mike Helleur
2 Plymouth Street,
Wanganui
Tel: (06) 347 2529 Fax: (06) 347 2529
www.bnb.co.nz/user186.html
Double $70 Single $45
Pet on property Children welcome
4 Double 8 Single (8 bdrm)

Welcome to 'Old World Charm'. This restored character home was built in 1895 and has a homely atmosphere that makes your stay restful and enjoyable. The graceful entrance leads to character bedrooms, lounge and dining room, which are all centrally heated. Laundry facilities and fully equipped kitchen are available. Off-street parking is surrounded by lovely gardens. The location is close to town and many tourist attractions. We look forward to you staying here. Gail, Mike, family, and Pippin, the resident cat, will welcome you.

Taumarunui   *Farmstay   10km E of Taumarunui*

Orangi Farmstay
Gayle & Dave Richardson
Orangi Road, RD 4, Taumarunui
Tel: (07) 896 6035 Fax: (07) 896 6035
daveandgayle@xtra.co.nz
www.bnb.co.nz/orangifarmstay.html
Double $70 Single $40 (Full Breakfast)
Child 1/2 price Dinner $15 Campervans $20
Child at home Pet on property Smoking area inside
1 Queen 3 Single (2 bdrm)
1 Family share

Welcome to Orangi, it's your home away from home, spacious, quiet and private. Comfortable rooms with electric blankets and duvets. Toby 14 and Jana 13 and our friendly cats enjoy the company of other children. Our friendly little dog will greet you on arrival. Go trout fishing, or walk along the river bank. We look forward to enjoying your company in our friendly and casual home. Join us for a good country meal, and the kettle is always on. Laundry available.

Taumarunui   *Farmstay   5km NE of Taumarunui*

Shirley & Allan Jones
213 Taringamotu Road, Taumarunui,
Tel: (07) 896 7722 costleyj@xtra.co.nz
www.bnb.co.nz/user194.html
Double $90 Single $60
(Continental & Full Breakfast) Child half price
Dinner by arrangement Pet on property
1 Double 1 Twin (2 bdrm)
1 Private

Our spacious home is situated 5km from the centre of Taumarunui surrounded by a peaceful one-acre garden with a native bush backdrop filled with NZ native birds. The bedrooms open on to a large veranda. Laundry available. A stream runs along one boundary of the property suitable for walks and summertime swimming. A well renowned golf course is located within 2km, along with guided mountain walks, canoeing, hot pools, scenic flights, skiing, trout fishing and white-water rafting are all within an hours drive.

Raurimu *Homestay B&B Self-contained cabin* *7km N of National Park*

Spiral Gardens
Phil & Margaret Hawthorne
Raurimu Road, Raurimu
Tel: (07) 892 2997 Fax: (07) 892 2997
Mob: 025 753 482 spiralgardens@xtra.co.nz
www.bnb.co.nz/spiralgardens.html

Double $130 Single $110 (Full Breakfast)
Child $40 Dinner by arrangement
Self-contained cabin $130 double Credit cards accepted
2 Queen 3 Double 3 Single (3 bdrm)
3 Ensuite 1 Private

Our new home overlooks the Piopiotea Stream and a magnificent stand of native bush. We are 5 mins from National Park Village, gateway to Tongario and Wanganui National Parks. The Whakapapa ski area is a 25 min drive. We can organise any of the many adventure activities offered in the Ruapehu and Taupo Districts. Our luxury suits feature a queen bed, a bed settee, casual chairs, dresser and writing bureau. The bunk room sleeps 5, ideal for larger families. Our cosy cabin is self-catering.

Tongariro National Park *Self-contained B&B Lodge* *2km S of National Park*

Mountain Heights Lodge
Wendy and Chris Howard
PO Box 43, National Park
Tel: (07) 892 2833 Fax: (07) 892 2850
mountainheights@xtra.co.nz
www.mountainheights.co.nz

Double $90-$140 Single $60 (Full Breakfast) Child $30
Dinner B/A S/C $70 - $120 Credit cards accepted
1 Queen 2 Double 2 Twin (5 bdrm)
4 Ensuite 1 Guests share

Welcome to Mountain Heights, situated at the edge of Tongariro National Park. We offer bed and breakfast in comfortable ensuite rooms in the lodge. Viewa across farmland to bush and mountains. Hot spa, central heating. Large lounge with log fire. Ideal for tramping, fishing, canoeing, skiing, mountain biking or just relaxing. We will help you organise activities including transport to the Tongariro Crossing. Our self-catering units are adjacent to the lodge and have their own bathroom, kitchen with cooking utensils and TV. Sleep 2-6.

Just as we have a variety of B&Bs
you will also be offered a variety of breakfasts,
and they will always be generous.

Raetihi *Self-contained Homestay B&B*   *0.5km N of Raetihi*

Log Lodge
Jan & Bob Lamb
5 Ranfurly Terrace, Raetihi
Tel: (06) 385 4135 Fax: (06) 385 4835
Lamb.Log-Lodge@Xtra.co.nz
www.bnb.co.nz/loglodge.html
Double $95 Single $50 (Full Breakfast)
Child $40
Credit cards accepted
2 Double 4 Single (2 bdrm)
2 Private

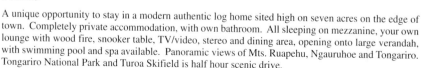

A unique opportunity to stay in a modern authentic log home sited high on seven acres on the edge of town. Completely private accommodation, with own bathroom. All sleeping on mezzanine, your own lounge with wood fire, snooker table, TV/video, stereo and dining area, opening onto large verandah, with swimming pool and spa available. Panoramic views of Mts. Ruapehu, Ngauruhoe and Tongariro. Tongariro National Park and Turoa Skifield is half hour scenic drive.

Ohakune *Farmstay Homestay*   *6km W of Ohakune*

Mitredale
Audrey & Diane Pritt
Smiths Road, RD, Ohakune
Tel: (06) 385 8016 Fax: (06) 385 8016
Mob: 025 531 916   www.bnb.co.nz/mitredale.html
Double $80 Single $50 (Continental Breakfast)
Dinner $25pp Credit cards accepted
Pet on property Pets welcome
1 Double 2 Single (2 bdrm)
1 Family share

We farm sheep, Bull Beef and run a Boarding Kennel in a beautiful peaceful valley with magnificent views of Mt Ruapehu. Tongariro National Park for skiing, walking, photography. Excellent 18 hole golf course, great fishing locally. We are members of Ducks Unlimited a conservation group and our local wine club. Have 2 Labradors and 1 large cat. We offer dinner traditional farm house (Diane, a cook book author), or breakfast with excellent home made jams. Take Raetihi Road, at Hotel/BP Service Station Corner. 4kms to Smiths Road. Last house 2kms.

Ohakune *Homestay*   *1km SW of Ohakune*

Kohinoor
Nita & Bruce Wilde
1011 Raetihi Road, Ohakune
Tel: (06) 385 8026 Mob: 025 620 5326
kohinoor@xtra.co.nz
www.bnb.co.nz/kohinoor.html
Double $80-$120 Single $50 (Full Breakfast)
Child $35 Dinner $25
2 Double 2 Single (3 bdrm)
1 Ensuite 1 Private 1 Family share

Enjoy spectacular views of volcanic Mt Ruapehu while relaxing in our tranquil 3 acre garden. Kohinoor (a gem of rare beauty) is an ideal base from where you can ski Turoa or Whakapapa skifields. Tramp in the world famous Tongariro World Heritage Park and enjoy golf, trout fishing and kiwi encounters. We are just 1 km from Ohakune with its cafes, restaurants and apres ski activities. Our interests include gardening, photography, trout fishing, skiing and giving genuine kiwi hospitality. Midweek ski deals available.

T'NAKI, W'NUI, R'PEHU, R'TIKEI

Taihape   *Homestay B&B*   *1km on hill above Taihape*

Korirata Homestay
Pat & Noel Gilbert
25 Pukeko Street, Taihape
Tel: (06) 388 0315 Fax: (06) 388 0315
korirata@xtra.co.nz
www.bnb.co.nz/koriratahomestay.html
Double $70 Single $50 (Special Breakfast)
Child 1/2 price under 10yrs Dinner by arrangement
Credit cards accepted
4 Single (2 bdrm)   1 Guests share

A warm welcome awaits you at the top of the hill in Taihape, where panoramic views of the mountains, ranges and surrounding countryside, add to the tranquil surroundings. 3/4 acre has been landscaped with shrubs. Hydroponics and orchid houses are found along with chrysanthemums in season. Meals, if desired, are with hosts, using produce from the garden where possible. Comfortable beds with electric blankets. Rafting, Bungy Jumping and farm visits can be arranged. 1 hour to Ruapehu, Lake Taupo and 2 1/2-3 hours to Wellington and Rotorua.

Taihape   *Homestay B&B*   *10km N of Taihape*

Harmony
Christine & John Tarrant
RD 5, Taihape
Tel: (06) 388 1117 Fax: (06) 388 1117
Mob: 025 297 5957   harmonybandb@xtra.co.nz
www.bnb.co.nz/harmony.html
Double $75 Single $40 (Continental Breakfast)
Child half price under 12 Dinner by arrangement
Full breakfast $2.50 extra pp Credit cards accepted
Pet on property Children welcome
1 Double 2 Single (2 bdrm)   1 Guests share

Situated on State Highway One, 10 km north of Taihape and 20 km south of Waiouru, we offer comfortable accommodation in our spacious farm homestead. A separate guest lounge is available with tea and coffee making facilities. The farm is home for stud Romney sheep, Angus cattle, deer, farmdogs and two cats. 'Harmony' is an ideal stop over - halfway between Rotorua and Wellington. Turoa Skifield is an hour away. Taihape offers good shops and restaurants and is central to a host of outdoor adventures.

The difference between a B&B and a hotel
is that you don't hug the hotel staff when you leave.

Taihape/Rangitikei *Self-contained Farmstay Homestay Fishingstay/Retreat*

26km Taihape

Tarata Fishaway

Stephen & Trudi Mattock, Mokai Road, RD 3, Taihape

Tel: (06) 388 0354 Fax: (06) 388 0954 Mob: 025 227 4986

fishaway@xtra.co.nz

www.tarata.co.nz

Double $80-$140 Single $40-$75 (Continental Breakfast) Child half price Dinner $25pp
Credit cards accepted
1 King/Twin 3 Queen 2 Double 4 Single (6 bdrm)
1 Ensuite 1 Private 1 Guests share

We are very lucky to have a piece of New Zealand's natural beauty. Tarata is nestled in bush in the remote Mokai Valley where the picturesque Rangitikei River meets the rugged Ruahine Ranges. With the Ruahines towering above us, stunning views, farm pets and unique trout fishing right at our doorstep, it is the perfect environment to bring up our three children.

Stephen offers guided fishing and rafting trips for all ages. Raft through the gentle crystal clear waters of the magnificent Rangitikei River, vertical papa gorges and stunning scenery you will never forget.

Our spacious home and garden allow guests private space to unwind. Whether it is by the pool on a hot summers day with a book or spending a cosy winters night in front of our open fire with a good wine. There is something special for the whole family and our spotlight safari and farm tour are free for all our guests.   Location, Location, Location. Our new "River Retreat" has a fully self-contained kitchen, lounge, bathroom and two bedrooms (wheelchair friendly). Soak in the spa-bath with "million dollar views" of the river or relax on the large decking amidst native birds and trees. Peace, privacy and tranquillity at its best! We will even deliver a candle light dinner to your door if you prefer.

We think Tarata is truly a magic place and we would love sharing it with you. Approved pets welcome.

Directions: Tarata Fishaway is 26 scenic kms from Taihape. Turn off state highway one, 6km south of Taihape at the Bungy sign. Follow the Bungy and Tarata Fishaway signs (14km) to the Bungy bridge. We are 6kms past here on Mokai Road.

Features and Attractions

- Homestead Accommodation
- River Retreat
- Fisherman's Cottage
- Honeymoon Suite
- Spotlight Safaris
- Clay bird Shooting
- Bush Walks/4WD Treks
- Farm Tours

T'NAKI, W'NUI,
R'PEHU, R'TIKEI

Mangaweka *Farmstay B&B* *12km E of Mangaweka*

Mairenui Rural Retreat
Sue, David & Matt Sweet, Ruahine Road, Mangaweka 5456
Tel: (06) 382 5564 Fax: (06) 382 5885 Mob: 025 517 545
mairenui@xtra.co.nz
www.mairenui.co.nz

Mairenui Rural Retreat offers three accommodation options and meals are available at the Homestead for guests in the self contained houses. On the farm there is a concrete tennis court, a full size petanque court, a croquet lawn and river swimming. There is also a trout stream for catch and release fishing only. Locally there are the renowned Rangitikei gardens, river adventure, historic home tours and four scenic golf courses. Sue, David and Matt, Bess the terrierX dog, and cats Norman & Nicky welcome guests of all nationalities. French and German are spoken here (except by the animals!)

The Homestead

The Homestead offers quality in house accommodation for up to four people. One heritage-style double room with a small sitting area and a slate floored ensuite bathroom with sunken bath, toiletries, hairdryer and its own verandah. The twin room is larger with shower /toilet and also its own verandah.

Double $120-$190 Single $85-$100
(Special Breakfast)
Dinner $35 Credit cards accepted Pet on property

1 Queen 1 Twin (2 bdrm)
2 Ensuite

The Retreat

A 1977 Comeskey designed open plan, three and a half storey building set in a stand of 700 year old native trees. A semi circular living room leads up to a brick paved kitchen which is fully equipped with electric oven, microwave and a wood burning stove. Double-hung doors lead through to a tiled breakfast conservatory. The bricked central circular stair tower leads to the first storey double bedrooms and the twin room which is up a vertical ladder. A "seventies" experience! Meals available at Homestead

Double $100 Single $50 (Special Breakfast)
Dinner $35 min.$100, max. $200 Breakfast $10-$15
Credit cards accepted Children welcome Pets welcome

1 Queen 1 Double 1 Twin (3 bdrm)
1 Guests share

The Colonial Villa

A restored hundred year old dwelling with polished wooden floors, a wind up gramophone, a small pool table, two open fires and a wood stove. There's a refrigerator, stove, some electric blankets and heaters. The beds have duvets and blankets, there is a separate shower and the bath is an original claw foot beauty! Verandahs on two sides of the house provide plenty of room for relaxing on the comfortable seats in the sun. Meals available at Homestead

Double $60 Single $30 (Special Breakfast) Dinner $35
min $60.00, max $200.00 breakfast $10-$15 Credit cards accepted Children welcome Pets welcome

3 Double 2 Twin (5 bdrm)
2 Guests share

Hunterville *Farmstay* *10km NE of Hunterville*

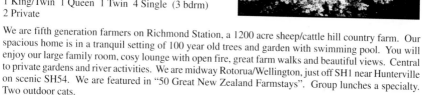

Vennell's Farmstay
Oriel & Phil Vennell
Mangapipi Road, Rewa, RD 10
Tel: (06) 328 6780 Fax: (06) 328 6780
Mob: 025 407 164   Tollfree: 0800 220 172 Pin
www.bnb.co.nz/vennellsfarmstay.html
Double $100 Single $50 (Full Breakfast)
Child neg Dinner $30
1 King/Twin 1 Queen 1 Twin 4 Single (3 bdrm)
2 Private

We are fifth generation farmers on Richmond Station, a 1200 acre sheep/cattle hill country farm. Our spacious home is in a tranquil setting of 100 year old trees and garden with swimming pool. You will enjoy our large family room, cosy lounge with open fire, great farm walks and beautiful views. Central to private gardens and river activities. We are midway Rotorua/Wellington, just off SH1 near Hunterville on scenic SH54. We are featured in "50 Great New Zealand Farmstays". Group lunches a specialty. Two outdoor cats.

Marton *Farmstay Separate/Suite B&B private guest wing* *5km N of Marton*

Ridgewood Farm
Gay & Jarrah Greenough
Rural #5990, Snellgrove Road, RD 2, Marton 5460
Tel: (06) 327 8887 Fax: (06) 327 8767
Mob: 025 467 057   gay@ridgewood-farm.co.nz
www.ridgewood-farm.co.nz
Double $120-$140 Single $70-$90 (Special Breakfast)
Child 1/2 price under 12yrs Dinner by arrangement
Credit cards accepted Pet on property
2 Double 2 Twin (4 bdrm)   1 Private 1 Guests share

Ridgewood is a lovingly restored and furnished historic homestead with old world charm and commands one of the best vistas in the Rangitikei. Private native bush at the back door teams with birdlife. Mature rhododendrons and camellias fringe the large garden and tennis court. We are home to Cape Baron Geese, free ranging pure bred land and water fowl, 3 shy cats and 1 friendly dog. For a relaxing weekend away , an adventure holiday or a peaceful retreat. Let our warm hospitality welcome you. Bookings recommended.

Marton *Homestay B&B* *45km N of Palmerston North*

Rea's Inn
Keith and Lorraine Rea
12 Dunallen Avenue, Marton,
Tel: (06) 327 4442 Fax: (06) 327 4442
Mob: 025 799589
keithandlorraine@xtra.co.nz
www.bnb.co.nz/reasinn.html
Double $80 Single $45 (Continental Breakfast)
Child Half price Dinner $20 Credit cards accepted
Pet on property Children welcome
1 Queen 1 Twin (2 bdrm)   1 Private

We have a warm comfortable home where we offer hospitality, peace and tranquility. Situated in quiet cul-de-sac with a private garden setting. Wide range of local attractions. Close to Nga Tawa and Huntley Schools. Ideal for weekend retreat or stopover.(Only 2hrs from Wellington Ferry.) Tour around Organic Farm available by arrangement. Your comfort and pleasure are important to us. Our 2 cats like people too, and we all welcome you to come, relax and enjoy the friendly atmosphere at Rea's Inn.

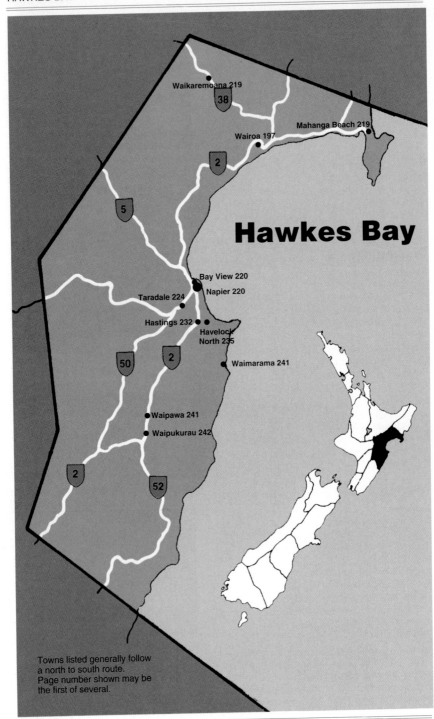

Waikaremoana 219
38
Mahanga Beach 219
Wairoa 197
2
5

Hawkes Bay

Bay View 220
Napier 220
Taradale 224
Hastings 232
Havelock
North 235
50 **2**
Waimarama 241

Waipawa 241
Waipukurau 242

2 **52**

Towns listed generally follow
a north to south route.
Page number shown may be
the first of several.

Mahanga Beach *Self-contained Farmstay* *50km N of Wairoa*

Reomoana
Louise Schick
RD 8, Nuhaka, Hawkes Bay
Tel: (06) 837 5898 Fax: (06) 837 5990
louiseschick@hotmail.com
www.bnb.co.nz/reomoana.html

Double $100 Single $60 (Continental Breakfast)
Dinner $30 Cottage $100 Credit cards accepted
Pet on property
2 Queen 1 Single (3 bdrm) 1 Ensuite 1 Private

"Reomoana" - The voice of the sea. Pacific Ocean front farm at beautiful Mahia Peninsula. The spacious, rustic home with cathedral ceilings, hand-crafted furniture overlooks the Pacific with breathtaking views. Enjoy the miles of white sandy beaches, go swimming, surfing or fishing. A painter's paradise. Attractions in the area include: Morere Hot Springs, Mahia Reserve and Golf Course. Horse riding and fishing charters by arrangement. 6km to 'Sunset Point Restaurant'. Outside pets: Golden Labrador and cat. Also self-contained cottage in avocado orchard, ideal for families.

Waikaremoana *Homestay B&B* *50km W of Wairoa*

Waikaremoana Homestay
Bev Macharper
Tuai Village, RD5, Wairoa
Tel: (06) 837 3701 Fax: (06) 837 3709
ykarestay@xtra.co.nz
www.bnb.co.nz/waikaremoana.html

Double $85 Single $50 (Special Breakfast)
Dinner $25 Pet on property
Children welcome Pets welcome
1 King/Twin 1 Double (2 bdrm) 1 Guests share

Lake Waikaremoana is a unique native forest wilderness bordering eastern Te Urewera National Park. The homestay, set in the picturesque village of Tuai, is an ideal base for hiking, flyfishing or boating. Tuai Village is nestled around Lake Whakamarino, 1km from Highway 38. The house, 70 years old, is cosy and comfortable and from the verandah you view the lake and may see native birds. Homecooking uses garden and local produce. A fishing dinghy is available. Relax in outdoor spa. Flexible hours - laundry service.

Bay View - Napier   *Homestay Beach   12km N of Napier*

Kilbirnie

Jill & John Grant, 84 Le Quesne Road, Bay View, Napier

Tel: (06) 836 6929 Mob: 025 234 7363

jill.johng@xtra.co.nz

www.bnb.co.nz/kilbirnie.html

Double $70-$90 (Full Breakfast) (Special Breakfast) Child not suitable
Dinner $20 - $30pp by arrangement Credit cards accepted Pet on property
1 Queen 1 Double (2 bdrm)
1 Ensuite 1 Private

We moved in 1996 to the quiet end of an unspoiled fishing beach by the Esk river, attracted by the beauty and position away from the traffic noise, while only 15 minutes from the main attractions. Nearby are vineyards, gardens, walks and a full range of harbourside restaurants north of Napier. Kilbirnie is near the Taupo Road intersection with the Pacific Highway to Gisborne, with off road parking. Upstairs, guest rooms have restful views of the Pacific Ocean one side, vineyards on the other, private bathrooms, excellent showers, abundant hot water, comfortable firm beds and guest lounge. Special breakfast overlooking the ocean is an experience which makes lunch superfluous. We are retired farmers with time to share good company, fresh imaginative food and juice, real coffee, an eclectic range of books, who invite you to enjoy our hospitality in modern surroundings. We have 12 years home hosting experience and are non-smokers.

Directions: From Taupo first left after intersection Highway 2 & 5 Franklin Road to Le Quesne, proceed to far end beachfront. From Napier first right after "Mobil" Station.

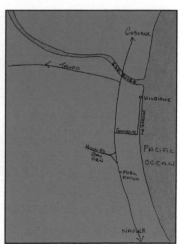

The View

Bay View - Napier   *Farmstay B&B and self-contained lodge*   *12km N of Napier*

The Grange
Roslyn & Don Bird, 263 Hill Road, Eskdale, Hawkes Bay
Tel: (06) 836 6666 Fax: (06) 836 6456 Mob: 025 281 5738
stay_at_the_grange@xtra.co.nz
www.thegrangelodge.com

Farmstay B&B: Double $75-$85 Single $60-70 (full or special breakfast)
S/C Lodge: $75-$85 dbl, $60-70 sgl, $20 extra pp, breakfast provisions optional
Dinner $30 Credit cards accepted Child at home Pet on property Children welcome
Beds: 2 King/Twin 1 Double 2 Single (3 bdrm)
Bathrooms: 2 Private

In the heart of a thriving <u>WINE REGION</u> overlooking the picturesque Esk Valley nestles "<u>THE GRANGE</u>" our delightfully modern "<u>FARMSTAY</u>" and superior <u>SELF-CONTAINED</u> "<u>LODGE</u>". Private, spacious accommodation in relaxing peaceful surrounds with spectacular rural, coastal and city views. Feel the comforts of home as we tempt you with our farm produce, baking, and preserves.

We're an outgoing family who really enjoy the company of guests. Hospitality is guaranteed! Experience our <u>FARM</u> life with Roslyn and Sparkie (the cat). Feed the Sheep, Cows, Pigs, Chickens and Dairy Goats. Try milking Nancy the Goat or bottle-feeding a Lamb - seasonal. Don a passionate 3rd generation <u>WINEMAKER</u> combines 26 years knowledge with tasting over dinner or at our Wishart Estate <u>WINERY</u>. You might like to try hand plunging the reds at Vintage or a Barrel sample of future releases.

Explore the world's <u>ART DECO</u> Capital <u>NAPIER 12 MINUTES</u> drive away and Hawke's Bay's many regional attractions within 30 minutes. Unwind on the Deck to the soothing chorus of native birds in the surrounding gardens and trees and at day's end spend time romancing over our wonderful night sky. Taupo (Kinloch) holiday home and email access available.

Share our home or retreat in the Lodge. "Our Place Is Your Place." 1 km off SH5 at Eskdale or 3km off SH2 at Bay View.

Bay View   *Self-contained Homestay B&B*   *12km N of Napier*

Beachfront Homestay
Christine & Jim Howard
20a Le Quesne Rd, Bay View, Napier

Tel: (06) 836 6530 Fax: (06) 836 6531
Mob: 021 159 0162   j-howard@clear.net.nz
www.beachfronthb.co.nz

Double $80 Single $50 (Special Breakfast)
Child $10 Dinner $25 Credit cards accepted
1 Queen 2 Single (2 bdrm)
1 Private

Jim, Christine and Sarcha (Jack Russell) will welcome you to their new beachfront home with breathtaking views of Hawkes Bay and walking distance to local wineries. Guests are offered self contained accommodation and own entrance on ground floor. Jim a local stock agent and Christine works at a local winery both enjoy meeting people and their interests are fishing and the outdoor life. Surfcasting and Kontiki fishing available. Beachfront homestay is just 5 mins from the Napier Taupo turn off and 12 minutes from Napiers Marine Parade & Cafes.

Bay View - Martha's Vineyard   *B&B*   *10km N of Napier*

Bay View Estate
Jeff Franklin
Kaimata Heights,
Bay View, Napier

Tel: (06) 836 7516 Fax: (06) 836 7517
www.bayviewnz@xtra.co.nz

Double $155-$175 Single $125 (Special Breakfast)
Credit cards accepted
1 King/Twin 1 King 1 Queen 1 Twin (0 bdrm)
1 Ensuite 1 Private

Picture the glistening sun flickering across the expansive Pacific Ocean as you enjoy alfresco breakfast. Our architect's brief was to exploit the natural beauty and tranquility of the area. He succeeded in creating a stunning ultramodern, stylish hilltop country retreat, with first class facilities. Take your time to meander through the magical 'Esk Valley' and enjoy the world class wineries and restaurants. For your 'urban cravings' Art Deco Napier is only minutes away.

Napier   *Homestay*   *1km N of Napier*

Spence Homestay
Kay & Stewart Spence
17 Cobden Road, Napier

Tel: (06) 835 9454 Fax: (06) 835 9454
Mob: 025 235 9828   Tollfree: 0800 117 890
ksspence@actrix.gen.nz
www.bnb.co.nz/spence.html

Double $120 Single $85 (Full Breakfast)
Credit cards accepted
1 Queen 1 Single (1 bdrm)   1 Ensuite

Welcome to our comfortable new home, next door to where we have home hosted for 10 years. Quiet area 10-15 minutes walk from art deco city centre. Guest suite opens out side to guest patio, lounge includes double bed - settee, TV, teamaking, fridge, microwave. Bedroom with Queen and Single beds, ensuite bathroom. Walled garden being established with petanque court. Able to meet public transport. Directions: Port end Marine Parade, Coote Road, right into Thompson Road, and left into Cobden Road opposite water tower.

Napier   *Homestay*   *1.3km NW of Napier*

A ROOM WITH A VIEW
Helen & Robert McGregor
9 Milton Terrace, Napier
Tel: (06) 835 7434 Fax: (06) 835 1912
roomwithview@xtra.co.nz.
www.bnb.co.nz/mcgregor.html

Double $90 Single $60 (Continental Breakfast)
Credit cards accepted Smoking area inside
1 Double (1 bdrm)
1 Private

We welcome you to our modern home with a spectacular sea view, large garden and sunny hill location. We're a fifteen minute walk to shops and restaurants at historic Port Ahuriri or our Art Deco City Centre. Private bath and shower. Laundry facilities at nominal charge. No smoking inside please. Pick-up service at no charge. Our interests are travel, gardening, the arts and local history (Helen's an Art Deco Walk Guide and Robert is Executive Director of the Art Deco Trust). We enjoy hosting, conversation and laughter. Please phone or write first.

Napier   *Homestay B&B*   *Napier Central*

Hillcrest
Nancy & Noel Lyons
4 George St,
Hospital Hill, Napier
Tel: (06) 835 1812 lyons@inhb.co.nz
www.hillcrestnapier.co.nz

Double $85 Single $60 (Continental Breakfast)
Credit cards accepted
1 Double 2 Single (2 bdrm)
1 Guests share

If you require quiet accommodation just minutes from the city centre, our comfortable home provides peace in restful surroundings. Relax on wide decks overlooking our garden, or enjoy the spectacular sea views. Explore nearby historic places and the Botanical Gardens. Your own lounge with tea/coffee making; laundry and off street parking available. We have travelled extensively and welcome the opportunity of meeting visitors. Our interests are travel, music, bowls and embroidery. We will happily meet you at the travel depots. Holiday home at Mahia Beach available.

Napier City   *Homestay*

Madeira Bed & Breakfast
Julie & Eric Ball
6 Madeira Road,
Napier
Tel: (06) 835 5185
julieball@clear.net.nz
www.bnb.co.nz/madeirabedbreakfast.html

Double $85 Single $50 (Full Breakfast)
1 Queen (1 bdrm)
1 Family share

We welcome you to our beautiful old home situated above Napier city, with outstanding views over Hawke Bay. A three minute walk takes you to the Art Deco buildings, cafes and shops. Parking on site. Laundry facilities available. Your double room has a queen size bed and adjoining toilet and hand basin. Also tea making facilities. Weather permitting, breakfast may be served on the veranda or in the garden, in the morning sun. We have a cat.

Taradale - Napier   *B&B   8km W of Napier*

Kerry Lodge
Jenny & Bill Hoffman
7 Forward Street, Greenmeadows, Napier
Tel: (06) 844 9630 Fax: (06) 844 1450
Mob: 025 932 874 kerrylodge@xtra.co.nz
www.kerrylodge.co.nz

Double $85-$90 Single $60 (Full Breakfast)
Child $40 Credit cards accepted Pet on property
1 King 1 Queen 2 Twin (3 bdrm)
1 Ensuite 1 Guests share

Set in tranquil gardens, we invite guests to share the warmth and comfort of our home. Our large rooms offer heating, refreshment facilities and colour television. A mobility ensuite and wheelchair access is available for guests convenience. Also a laundry. Your day with us begins with a scrumptious breakfast and a chat to help plan your day's activities. Relax in our sparkling pool or indoor spa. Situated near Church Road and Mission wineries. Our dogs Tess and Hogan and cat Tabitha wait to welcome you.

Napier   *Homestay   City Location*

Treeways Homestay
Cheryl & Maurie Keeling
1 Lighthouse Road, Bluff Hill, Napier
Tel: (06) 835 6567 Fax: (06) 835 6567
mckeeling@xtra.co.nz
www.bnb.co.nz/treeways.html

Double $105 Single $75 (Full Breakfast)
Dinner $30 by arrangement
1 King/Twin 1 Queen (2 bdrm)
2 Ensuite

Peaceful, private, 15 minutes walk to Bluff Hill lookout or city. A large sunny terrace with spa pool, flower garden and lily pond with pleasant views over the sea and northern coastline. Our home with spacious living areas, rimu timber floors and comfortable furnishings is warm and friendly. Bedrooms have electric blankets,TV, heating and writing desk. Home grown vegetables and fruits, complimentary local wine with dinner. We have travelled extensively, enjoy theatre, the outdoors and Digby our Jack Russell dog. Email& laundry service available.Good off street parking.

Napier   *Self-contained Homestay   5km S of Napier*

Snug Harbour
Ruth & Don McLeod
147 Harold Holt Avenue,
Napier
Tel: (06) 843 2521 Fax: (06) 843 2520
donmcld@clear.net.nz
www.bnb.co.nz/snugharbour.html

Double $80-$90 Single $55 (Full Breakfast)
Dinner $25 by arrangement Credit cards accepted
1 Queen 1 Twin 1 Single (3 bdrm)
1 Ensuite 1 Family share

Ruth & Don welcome you to our modern smoke free home with its rural outlook and sunny attractive patio. The garden studio with ensuite and tea making facilities has its own entrance. We are situated on the outskirts of Napier City, the Art Deco City of the World, and in close proximity to wineries and many other tourist attractions. We both have a background in teaching, with interests in travel, gardening and photography.

Napier *B&B* *1km N of Napier*

Ourhome
N & N Hamlin
4 Hospital Terrace,
Hospital Hill, Napier
Tel: (06) 835 7358 Fax: (06) 835 7355
Mob: 025 852 304
ourhomeb&b@xtra.co.nz
www.bnb.co.nz/ourhome.html
Double $90 Single $60 (Continental Breakfast)
1 King/Twin 1 Double (1 bdrm)
1 Private

Kick off your shoes, put up your feet, and drink in the magical view with your cuppa and G&T while relaxing on your own patio or private lounge. Our superking/twin beds have been described by guests as "pamper" beds. Double bed-settee in lounge (4 in one party). Our aim is to make your stay as comfortable as possible; to this end tea/coffee/cookies, TV, fridge, iron, laundry facilities, parking, and total privacy are all offered. All attractions within easy driving distance. Pick up from public transport.

Napier *Self-contained* *1km N of Napier*

The Coach House
Jan Chalmers
9 Gladstone Road,
Napier
Tel: (06) 835 6126 Mob: 025 657 3263
www.bnb.co.nz/thecoachhouse.html
Double $100 Single $80 (Full Breakfast)
Child $25 - babies free 4 people $160 Pets welcome
1 Queen 2 Single (2 bdrm)
1 Private

On the hill over-looking a gorgeous Mediterranean garden and sea views, the historic Coach-house is tastefully renovated and totally self-contained. It contains 2 bedrooms , open plan kitchen, dining, living rooms, bathroom and separate loo. The fridge will be full of a variety of breakfast supplies. TV and radio included and fresh flowers in all rooms. The sunny deck has a table and chairs and gas barbecue. Off-street parking and easy access plus peace and privacy complete the picture.

Napier *Homestay B&B* *0.5 E of Napier Central*

No 11
Phyllida & Bryan Isles
11 Sealy Road, Napier Hill,
Napier
Tel: (06) 834 4372 Mob: 025 246 3968
phyllbry@xtra.co.nz
www.bnb.co.nz/nonapier.html
Double $100 Single $75 (Special Breakfast)
1 King/Twin 2 Queen (3 bdrm)
2 Guests share

The name says it all! You will score our home more than 10 for Comfort, Convenience, Conviviality. Comfort: Spacious, sunny, warm, bedrooms with TV, tea making facilities, electric blankets, sun lounge. Convenience: Quality new home with wonderful views. Easy stroll to city, cafes, and tourist attractions. Off-street parking. Conviviality: Our aim is to assist you to make your stay enjoyable. A selection of specialty breakfast choices is offered. We have a dog and a cat. Please no smoking indoors. We look forward to meeting you.

Napier   *Self-contained B&B*   *Napier Central*

Inglenook
Phyl Olsen
3 Cameron Terrace,
Napier
Tel: (06) 834 2922 Mob: 025 414 992
www.bnb.co.nz/inglenook.html
Double $95 Single $60
(Special Breakfast) Child $20
1 Queen 2 Double 1 Twin (4 bdrm)
4 Ensuite

Inglenook is situated on the hill in a garden setting overlooking city and sea and only five minutes stroll to shops and restaurants. Inglenook offers privacy and a quiet restful atmosphere. It is immaculately presented and serviced. Guest suites are self contained with their own separate entrances and keys. A special breakfast including fruit is served to guests at a pre-arranged time outdoors or in guests rooms as required. Tea/coffee making facilities available in each suite. You are welcome to make further enquiries.

Napier   *B&B Guesthouse*

Blue Water Lodge Ltd
471 Marine Parade,
Napier
Tel: (06) 835 8929 Fax: (06) 835 8929
bobbrown2@xtra.co.nz
www.bnb.co.nz/bluewaterlodgeltd.html
Double $70-$80 Single $40 (Continental Breakfast)
Child $10 under 14 yrs Credit cards accepted
6 Double 9 Single (9 bdrm)
1 Ensuite 2 Guests share

Blue Water Lodge is on the beach front opposite the Aquarium on Napier's popular Marine Parade. Close to all local tourist attractions and within walking distance to the city centre, information centre, family restaurants, RSA and Cosmopolitan Club. Owner operated.

Taradale - Napier   *B&B*   *8km SW of Napier*

Greenwood Bed and Breakfast
Ann & Peter Green
62 Avondale Road, Taradale, Napier
Tel: (06) 845 1246 Fax: (06) 845 1247
Mob: 025 795 403   greenwood@clear.net.nz
www.greenwoodbnb.co.nz
Double $90-$105 Single $60-$70 (Full Breakfast)
Dinner $30 Credit cards accepted
2 Queen 2 Single (3 bdrm)
3 Ensuite

Relax in our guest lounge or on the deck as trees filter the afternoon sun. Savour Ann's homemade preserves and eggs benedict. Put the world to rights as we discuss the follies of presidents and kings. Laugh as Peter tries to converse in German and French. Our loves are family and entertaining. Our interests are history, language, art, computers and golf. A short walk takes you to Taradale shops, restaurants and wineries. Tourist attractions and golf courses within easy driving distance. Dinner by arrangement.

Taradale - Napier   *Self-contained B&B*   *10km W of Napier*

Otatara Heights
Roy & Sandra Holderness
57 Churchill Drive, Taradale, Napier
Tel: (06) 844 8855 Fax: (06) 844 8855
sandroy@xtra.co.nz
www.bnb.co.nz/otataraheights.html

Double $85 (Continental Breakfast)
Credit cards accepted
1 Queen 1 Double (1 bdrm)
1 Private

Comfortable, quiet apartment in the heart of our foremost wine producing area. Superb day and night views over Napier and local rural scenes. 10 minutes drive to the Art Deco capital of the world. 2km to Taradale village. Safe off-street parking. Top quality restaurants and wineries nearby. We are a friendly couple who have enjoyed B&B overseas and like meeting people. Our interests are travel, theatre, good food and wine. Bella, our cat, keeps to herself. Handy to E.I.T and golf course.

Taradale - Napier   *Homestay B&B*   *7.5km SW of Napier*

'279' Church Road
Sandy Edginton
279 Church Road, Taradale, Napier
Tel: (06) 844 7814 Fax: (06) 844 7814
Mob: 025 265 6706
sandy.279@homestaynapier.co.nz
www.homestaynapier.co.nz

Double $100 Single $70 (Full Breakfast)
Dinner by arrangement Credit cards accepted
Smoking area inside
1 Queen 1 Twin (2 bdrm) 1 Guests share

"279", an elegant and spacious home set amongst mature trees and gardens, offers excellent hospitality in a relaxed, friendly atmosphere to Domestic and International visitors. Located adjacent to Mission Estate and Church Road wineries,restaurants and craft galleries, "279" is within a short drive of 'Art Deco' Napier, Hastings, golf courses, and tourist activities. I welcome you to "279" and will help make your visit the highlight of your travels.

A homestay is a B&B where you
share the family's living area.

Napier   *Homestay   Napier Central*

Cameron Close
Joy & Graeme Thomas
33 Cameron Road, Napier
Tel: (06) 835 5180 Fax: (06) 835 4115
Mob: 021 683 551
BESCO@xtra.co.nz
www.bnb.co.nz/cameronclose.html
Double $90 Single $60
(Special Breakfast) Pet on property
2 Double 1 Single (3 bdrm)
1 Guests share

Come and share our 1920's home, garden and pool situated above the lovely Art Deco city of Napier. A five minute stroll will have you amongst the Art Deco buildings and town, or relax poolside and enjoy our garden. We offer home cooked goodies using fresh produce from Hawkes Bay. Our interests include food, wine, classic cars, art deco and good company. Let us share our knowldge of NZ with you. We offer laundry facilities and have bikes available. Phone for easy directions.

Napier   *Homestay B&B   1 N of Napier*

Cobden Garden Homestay
Rayma and Phillip Jenkins
1 Cobden Crescent, Bluff Hill, Napier
Tel: 06 834 2090 Fax: 06 834 2090
Mob: 025 540062   Tollfree: 0800 426 233
info@cobden.co.nz   www.cobden.co.nz
Double $110-$160 Single $90-$140
(Special Breakfast) Credit cards accepted
Pet on property
1 King/Twin 1 King (2 bdrm)
2 Ensuite

We invite you to stay in our quiet, warm and sunny colonial villa on Bluff Hill. We have two double rooms, each with its own ensuite. There is a beautiful garden for your enjoyment. We invite you to join us each evening for complimentary tastings of local wine and produce. Each morning choose your gourmet breakfast from the menu of local foods and homemade delights. We make sure your stay will be extra special and memorable. There are two unobtrusive cats in residence.

Napier Hill   *B&B   1km N of Napier*

Maison Bearnaise
Christine Grouden
25 France Road, Bluff Hill, Napier 4001
Tel: (06) 835 4693 Fax: (06) 835 4694
chrisgraham@xtra.co.nz
www.bnb.co.nz/user180.html
Double $100-$120 Single $75-$85
(Continental & Full Breakfast) Pet on property
2 Queen (2 bdrm)
2 Ensuite

Christine, Graham and Brewster (our short-haired cat who keeps to himself), welcome you to our attractive and peaceful home. Walking distance to city centre, restaurants, tourist attractions and Bluff Hill lookout. Off street parking available. Comfortable beds/electric blankets. Each bedroom has an en suite for total privacy. Relax with tea or coffee in your room or curl up in the guest lounge. Delicious breakfasts alfresco (weather permitting) or indoors. Helpful travel tips and warm friendly atmosphere - our visitor's book reflects it all.

Napier   *Luxury B&B   1KM Napier City Centre*

Cobden Villa Bed & Breakfast
Amy and Cornel Walewski, 11 Cobden Road, Bluff Hill, Napier
Tel: (06) 835 9065 Fax: (06) 833 6979 Mob: 025 286 1789
stay@cobdenvilla.com   www.cobdenvilla.com

Double $185-$365 Single $185 (Full Breakfast) (Special Breakfast)
Credit cards accepted Child at home
1 King 2 Queen 2 King Single (4 bdrm)   3 Ensuite 1 Private

A Picturesque 1870 Villa has been completely restored and fully furnished in the Art Deco Style. To which your hosts, Amy and Cornel, brought their enthusiastic interest together with artistic talent from America, to live in   Napier - "The Art Deco City".

Situated on top of Bluff Hill... you may start your day enjoying a full gourmet breakfast in the spacious conservatory while watching the Ocean Sunrise. Then relax after day's end with a glass of local wine and watch the Harbour sunset from the surrounding Veranda or elegant Dining Room.

We offer four creatively designed bedrooms with ensuites or private bath, custom-comfort beds, fine quality linens and European down duvets. The Honeymoon Suite offers a 'romantic' King bedroom with an ensuite that includes a deluxe Jacuzzi spa with a double shower steam-room and adjoining private garden veranda.

All rooms have central heating and air conditioning with accessible porches for outdoor smoking. Off street parking, email and fax are available. German is well understood.   10 minute walk into 'Down Town'.

Directions: Marine Parade toward the port, make a left onto Coote Rd (at Centennial gardens) - Right turn onto Thompson Road - follow up around and remain left- Left turn onto Cobden Road (#11)

Napier - Marine Parade   *Boutique hotel B&B*   *Napier*

Mon Logis
Gerard Averous, 415 Marine parade, PO Box 871, Napier
Tel: (06) 835 2125 Fax: (06) 835 8811 Mob: 025 725 332
monlogis@xtra.co.nz www.bnb.co.nz/monlogis.html

Double $140-$160 Single $120 (Continental Breakfast) (Full Breakfast) Credit cards accepted
2 King/Twin (4 bdrm) 3 Ensuite 1 Private

A little piece of France nestled in the heart of the beautiful wine growing region of Hawke's Bay.

Built as private Hotel in 1915 this grand colonial building overlooking the pacific's breakers is only a few minutes walk from the city centre.

Now lovingly renovated Mon Logis will cater to a maximun of eight guests and is modelled on the small privately owned french hotel. Charm, personnal service and french cuisine are the specialities. Of the upstairs individualy furnished rooms, two have twin beds and all have their own private facilities.

Owner frenchman Gerard Averous has decorated each guest room differently but in a style in keeping with the original charm of the building. Iron bedsteads, feather duvets, lace covers and fine cotton linen all create a special elegance and one room is totally furnished with pieces bought from France.

Downstairs, an informal guest lounge invites relaxation, television viewing, a quiet time reading or perhaps a game of chess or bridge. Guests can help themselves to coffee or tea and home made biscuits any time of the day.

Breakfast, served in the privacy of your own rooom or downstairs Dining Room, could be a basket of freshly baked breads, croissants, or brioche, with a compote of locally grown fruits or a wonderful herb omlettee.

Should you want to dine out, Gerard is happy to give recommendations and as a trained guide with the Art Deco Society, can help with insight into Napier's unique architecture.

All perfectly designed for comfort and relaxation, Mon Logis is a non-smoking establishment and does not cater for children. French and Spanish spoken; exclusive customised vineyard tours with host by arrangement. Casual elegance at a price you can afford.

Napier *B&B* *centr Napier*

The Green House
Ruth Buss and Jeremy Hutt
18b Milton Oaks, Milton Rd, Napier
Tel: (06) 835 4475 Fax: (06) 835 4475
Mob: 021 187 3827
ruthzmail@clear.net.nz
www.bnb.co.nz/thegreenhousebb.html

Double $80 Single $50 (Special Breakfast)
Dinner $20 Credit cards accepted
1 Queen 1 Twin (2 bdrm) 1 Guests share

The Green House is a Vegetarian Bed and Breakfast, 5 minutes walk from the heart of 'Art Deco Napier', yet surrounded by woodland, with plenty of native birds ... and sea views! We aim to provide a peaceful, smokefree environment for our guests.Homemade breads and preserves for breakfast! Our hillside home is built on several levels and unsuitable for wheelchairs or small children, although babies or older chidren would be very welcome. We have ample parking, or can pick up from Airport, buses etc. Internet access available.

Napier *B&B*

Mornington Private Lodge
Diana Swayn and Matt Sinden
20a Sealy Road, Napier,
Tel: (06) 835 4450 Fax: (06) 835 4452
Mob: 025 538 820   stay@mornington.co.nz
www.mornington.co.nz

Double $230 Single $195 (Full Breakfast)
Child $50 Credit cards accepted Pet on property
1 Queen 1 Twin (2 bdrm)
1 Private

Renowned architect Louis Hay designed Mornington in 1921 on Napier Hill. The bungalow-style house, overlooking the city with views to the Pacific Ocean and Cape Kidnappers features arts and crafts interiors, period furniture and William Morris fabrics and wallpapers. Accommodation comprises the red queen room, green twin room, each with fine linens, fresh flowers and quality confectionary. Both rooms open to a sunny verandah providing panoramic sunrises. Single party bookings ensure the privacy to make your stay in Napier relaxing and memorable.

Napier *Homestay* *1km N of Napier*

Gladstone Homestay
Joan and Bill Richardson
4 Gladstone Road, Napier,
Tel: (06) 835 7870 Fax: (06) 835 7870
Mob: 025 265 1463
billoany@clear.net.nz
www.bnb.co.nz/gladstonehomestay.html

Double $85 Single $65 (Full Breakfast) Child neg.
Dinner $25pp by arrangement
1 Queen 1 Twin (2 bdrm)
1 Private

Enjoy the old world charm of our comfortable home situated in an idyllic spot on the hill above Napier. Relax in the picturesque gardens with sea views. Walk to the city and restaurants or enjoy a New Zealand cuisine meal at Gladstone Homestay. The independent guest accommodation upstairs with its own entrance provides for up to four in a group and also includes a private sitting room with tea/coffee making facilities and complimentary extras. A warm welcome awaits you with safe off-street parking.

Napier   *B&B*   *Napier*

Freemans On Clyde
Anthony & Sue Freeman
17 Clyde Road, Napier,
Tel: (06) 835 9124 or (06) 835 3922 (cafe)
Mob: 021 171 0209
freemo@iprohome.co.nz
www.bnb.co.nz/freemansonllyde.html

Double $180 (Special Breakfast) Winter rates avail.
Credit cards accepted Child at home Pet on property
2 Queen 1 Double (3 bdrm)
3 Ensuite

Originally built in 1854, Freemans on Clyde is one of Napier's earliest farmhouses that survived the devastating 1931 earthquake. Located on Napier Hill, this colonial farmhouse features cape cod style architecture and now offers three ensuite guestrooms. Guests enjoy relaxing on the large verandah and garden in summer, or beside the open fire in the guest lounge in winter. For breakfast guests wander five minutes down the hill to the city to Sue and Anthony's 'Caffe Aroma' for a full cafe menu included in the room rate.

Napier - Hastings   *Self-contained B&B*   *btw Napier/ Hastings*

Copperfields
Pam & Richard Marshall
Copperfields, Pakowhai Road, Napier
Tel: (06) 876 9710 Fax: (06) 876 9710
Mob: 021 256 7590   rich.pam@clear.net.nz
www.bnb.co.nz/copperfields.html

Double $95-$110 Single $80 (Full Breakfast)
Child neg Dinner $30pp Credit cards accepted
Pet on property Children welcome
1 Double 3 Single (2 bdrm) 1 Private 1 Family share

Copperfields: A lifestyle orchard between the Art Deco cities of Napier/Hastings. Wineries, craft trails, golf courses and tourist attractions are readily accessible. Pam and Richard are involved in weaving, crafts , furniture restoration and antiques. Non-smokers. We have a labrador dog and a pet pig. Guests stay in "Glen Cottage" large self contained cottage attached to our house (own private entrance). Includes fully equipped kitchen. Guests are welcome to join us for breakfast or dinner (three courses). Family rates negotiable. Dogs welcome (conditions apply)

Napier - Hastings   *Farmstay Homestay*   *15km E of Napier/Hastings*

Bill and Heather Shaw
Charlton Road,
RD 2, Hastings
Tel: (06) 875 0177 Fax: (06) 875 0525
www.bnb.co.nz/shaw.html

Double $150 Single $100
(Full Breakfast)
Dinner by arrangement
4 Single (2 bdrm)
1 Ensuite 1 Family share

Our home is situated in Charlton Road Te Awanga which is approximately twenty minutes form both Napier and Hastings and right next door to the gannets at Cape Kidnappers and one of Hawkes Bay leading winery restaurants. With us you can enjoy space, tranquillity, and fine hospitality while receiving every assistance to make your stay in our area as interesting and enjoyable as possible. We have two Jack Russel dogs. Directions: Charlton Road is the first road on your right after passing through Te Awanga village.

Napier - Hastings   *Farmstay Homestay*   *50km W of Hastings - Napier*

Waiwhenua Farmstay
Kirsty Hill & Family
808 River Road, RD 9, Hastings

Tel: (06) 874 2435 Fax: (06) 874 2465
Mob: 027 479 4094   kirsty.hill@xtra.co.nz
www.bnb.co.nz/waiwhenuafarmstay.html

Double $100 Single $50 (Continental Breakfast)
Child $40 Dinner $25 Campervan/Backpacker Lodge
Child at home Pet on property Children welcome
2 Queen 3 Single (2 bdrm)   1 Private

Experience a genuine farmstay, delicious home produce and food, trout fishing and friendly rural hospitality at our historic homestead and farm. Our family and pet Foxy Becky enjoy meeting people and catering for individuals or families interested in the outdoor life (two nights recommended) on our large sheep, beef and deer farm, and organic apple and pear orchard. Enrich your stay by experiencing outdoor activities at our backdoor including, guided farm tours, trout fishing, hunting, bush and farm walks, jet boating and extensive mountain hikes.

Napier - Hastings   *Self-contained B&B Self-contained cottage*   *2.5km N of Clive*

Kerry & Jan McKinnie
PO Box 38, Clive, Napier

Tel: (06) 870 0759 Fax: (06) 870 0528
Mob: 025 211 0464   ker.jan@xtra.co.nz
www.bnb.co.nz/mckinnie.html

Double $75 Single $50 (Full Breakfast)
Dinner by arrangement Credit cards accepted
Child at home Pet on property
Children welcome Pets welcome
1 Queen 1 Double 4 Single (3 bdrm)
3 Ensuite

Riverbank house is set amongst the trees on 1.5 acres of land. Our two well appointed cottages include tea/coffee facilities, fridge, microwave etc and suit all types of travellers. We are a well-travelled family who enjoy looking after our guests. We have three cats, one dog and a mini horse. At 2.5km north of Clive we are central to everything. See you soon!

Napier - Hastings   *Self-contained Homestay*   *12km E of Napier/Hastimgs*

Merriwee Boutique Homestay
Jeanne Richards
29 Gordon Road, Te Awanga, Hawkes Bay

Tel: (06) 875 0111 Fax: (06) 875 0111
Mob: 021 214 5023   merriwee@xtra.co.nz
www.merriwee.co.nz

Double $100-$180 Single $100-$130 (Full Breakfast)
Dinner B/A Credit cards accepted Pet on property
1 King 1 Queen 1 Double 1 Twin (4 bdrm)
2 Ensuite 1 Private

Merriwee was built in 1908 and is set in an apricot orchard just a stroll from Te Awanga beach. It is close to Napier/Hastings and Havelock North, with Cape Kidnappers and wineries nearby. The home is spacious, with quality furnishings, open fires and sea views across to Napier. French doors access bedrooms to verandahs and garden. The main guest area is self contained with sitting room, open fire and kitchen. There is a swimming pool and pentanque court. Terrier 'Mags' and cat Floyd will greet you. Gorden Road is the first on the right as you enter Te Awanga Village.

Napier - Hastings *Homestay*   *18km W of Napier*

Silverford
Chris & William Orme-Wright
Puketapu, Hawkes Bay
Tel: (06) 844 5600 Fax: (06) 844 4423
homestay@paradise.net.nz
www.silverford.co.nz

Double $145-$165 Single $115 (Full Breakfast) Credit cards accepted
1 King 1 Queen 1 Double (3 bdrm)
1 Ensuite 1 Guests share

Situated on the Wine Trail, 'Silverford' - one of Hawkes Bay's most gracious Homesteads - is spaciously set in 17 acres of farmland, established trees and gardens. Drive through our half a kilometre long gorgeous Oak lined avenue to the sweeping lawns, bright flower gardens and ponds surrounding our elegant home designed by Natusch at the turn of the century.

We are relaxed and friendly and offer a warm ambience in private, comfortable and tranquil surroundings - a romantic haven with tastefully furnished bedrooms, charming guest sitting room and a courtyard to dream in.

Silverford is an idyllic welcoming haven for a private, peaceful and cosy stay whilst at the same time being close to all the amenities and attractions that Hawkes Bay has to offer. Friendly deer, cow, pigeons, ducks and dogs. Central Heating. Swimming Pool. Good restaurants close by.

We are smokefree and regret the property is unsuitable for children. Some French and German spoken.

Hastings - Havelock North *2.5km SE of Havelock North*

Self-contained Homestay B&B

Jill & Jock Taylor
134 Kopanga Road, Havelock North
Tel: (06) 877 8797
Fax: (06) 877 2335
jilljock@paradise.net.nz
www.bnb.co.nz/taylor.html

Double $90 Single $50 (Continental Breakfast)
Credit cards accepted Pet on property
1 Queen 2 Single (2 bdrm)
2 Private

Welcome to our home and garden. In rural surroundings only five minutes to Havelock North. Hastings and Napier approximately fifteen minutes. We are gardeners and golfers and what better place to be than Hawkes Bay with four excellent golf courses, superb gardens and many wineries. Our four children

Hastings - Havelock North *16km S of Havelock North*

Farmstay Homestay

Ros Phillips
Wharehau, RD 11,
Hastings
Tel: (06) 877 4111
Fax: (06) 877 4111
www.bnb.co.nz/phillips.html

Single $40 (Full Breakfast)
Child 1/2 price Dinner $25 Beach Bach
1 Queen 2 Twin 1 Single (4 bdrm)
1 Guests share 1 Family share

20 minutes from Hastings, Havelock North or Waipawa, enjoy the beautiful Hawkes Bay. We are handy to the many attractions Hawkes Bay has to offer. Gannets - wineries - art deco - golf courses - Splash Planet - a local trout river (guide available) or just relax in peace and space. Dinner (featuring local produce) available on request. If interesetd and weather permits a farm tour in 4WD.

Hastings City *Homestay   Hastings Central*

McConchie Homestay
Barbara & Keta McConchie
115A Frederick Street, Hastings
Tel: (06) 878 4576 Mob: 025 610 2902
barbaramcconchie@xtra.co.nz
www.bnb.co.nz/mcconchie.html

Double $80 Single $45 (Full Breakfast)
Child $15 Dinner $20 by arrangement
Credit cards accepted Pet on property
1 Queen 2 Single (2 bdrm)   1 Guests share

Enjoy our peaceful garden back section, away from all traffic noises, yet central to Hastings City. Our Siamese cat says 'Hi'. Nearby are parks, golf courses, wineries, orchards and the best icecream ever. Short trips take you to spectacular views, Cape Kidnapper's Gannet colony, or Napier's Art Deco. Activities include ballooning, Clydesdale wagon ride, hot pools, wine trails, or relaxing having coffee on our deck. Directions: From Wellington, take the Napier/Stortford Lodge route, left off main highway at Paki Paki. From Taupo ring. No smoking please.

Hastings   *Self-contained B&B   9km W of Hastings*

A Cottage
Anne & Peter Wilkinson
Box 2116, 79 Carrick Road,
Twyford (residential), Hastings
Tel: (06) 879 9357 Fax: (06) 879 9357
Mob: 021 1835144   ph-aawilkinson@clear.net.nz
www.bnb.co.nz/wilkinson.html
Double $90 Single $75 (Full Breakfast)
Credit cards accepted Pet on property
1 King/Twin (1 bdrm)   1 Private

We look forward to giving you a warm welcome to the Hawkes Bay which offers a wide variety of attractions, in particular wineries and the Art Deco buildings of Napier. We are close to the Ngaruroro River for good trout fishing during the season and within easy reach of a variety of other rivers and lakes. Guided fishing is offered by Peter. Our accommodation has a small kitchen and living room. Non smoking and not suitable for children. Owners have two dogs. Ring for directions.

Hastings   *Homestay   2.5km Hastings*

Woodbine Cottage
Ngaire & Jim Shand
1279 Louie Street, Hastings
Tel: (06) 876 9388 Fax: (06) 876 9666
Mob: 025 529 522
nshand@xtra.co.nz
www.bnb.co.nz/woodbinecottage.html
Double $100 Single $55 (Continental Breakfast)
Dinner $25pp by arrangement Credit cards accepted
1 Double 1 Twin (2 bdrm)
1 Guests share

Our home is set in half acre of cottage garden on the Hastings boundary close to Havelock North. Swimming pool and tennis court for the energetic and a spa bath to relax in at night Hastings city centre is five minutes by car and Havelock North 2 minutes. 'Splash Planet', with its many water features and hot pools is only two minutes away. We look forward to your company and can assure you of a comfortable and relaxing stay. Non smoking and not suitable for small children or pets.

Hastings   *Self-contained B&B   3km S of Hastings*

Raureka
Tim & Rosemary Ormond
26 Wellwood Road, RD 5, Hastings
Tel: (06) 878 9715 Fax: (06) 878 9715
Mob: 025 627 5887
r.t.ormond@xtra.co.nz
www.bnb.co.nz/raureka.html
Double $90 Single $70
(Continental & Full Breakfast) Pet on property
1 Queen (1 bdrm)
1 Ensuite

We welcome you to our home situated in a quiet rural setting. 'Raureka' is an apple orchard 3 km from town, close to restaurants, golf courses and wineries. We have an attractive detached room with a queen size bed, ensuite, TV and tea & coffee making facilities. Guests are welcome to use our pool and tennis court set in an attractive garden with a view out to 100 year old oak trees. We offer you a relaxed, quiet, friendly stay. Smoking outside only.

Hastings   *Homestay B&B   12km W of Hastings, 12km S of Taradale*

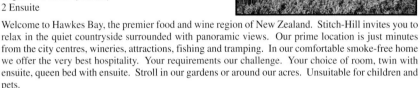

Stitch-Hill Farm
Charles Trask
170 Taihape Road, RD 9, Hastings
Tel: (06) 879 9456 Fax: (06) 879 9806
cjtrask@xtra.co.nz
www.bnb.co.nz/stitchhill.html

Double $85 Single $50 (Continental Breakfast)
Dinner by arrangement
1 Queen 1 Twin (2 bdrm)
2 Ensuite

Welcome to Hawkes Bay, the premier food and wine region of New Zealand. Stitch-Hill invites you to relax in the quiet countryside surrounded with panoramic views. Our prime location is just minutes from the city centres, wineries, attractions, fishing and tramping. In our comfortable smoke-free home we offer the very best hospitality. Your requirements our challenge. Your choice of room, twin with ensuite, queen bed with ensuite. Stroll in our gardens or around our acres. Unsuitable for children and pets.

Hastings   *Self-contained Homestay   9km W of Hastings*

Wharenikau   John & Anne Porter
172 Taihape Road, RD 9, Okawa, Hastings
Tel: (06) 879 5899 Fax: (06) 879 5896
Mob: 025 381 477   john.porter@leather.co.nz
www.bnb.co.nz/wharenikau.html

Double $100-$120 (Full Breakfast)
Dinner $130 per couple(Gourmet)
Credit cards accepted Pet on property Pets welcome
1 King 1 Queen 1 Twin (3 bdrm)
1 Private 1 Guests share

Set high on 15 acres, planted with 2000 trees, Wharenikau overlooks Hawkes Bay's world-renowned vineyards and the picturesque Ngaruroro river. Newly built, Wharenikau represents John and Anne's desire to offer guests exceptional accommodation, food and wine. We serve a gourmet three course dinner with premium Hawkes Bay wines. Architecturally designed to enjoy the magnificent views, peace and tranquillity, Wharenikau is ideally suited for relaxing in style and therefore not suitable for children. Privacy is afforded by way of a separate cottage. Pets by arrangement.

Hastings   *Self-contained B&B   3km S of Hastings*

Primefruit Orchard
Dick & Elly Spiekerman
74 Longlands Road East, Hastings,
Tel: (06) 876 4163 Fax: (06) 876 4163
Mob: 027 444 8798
info@holidaynewzealand.co.nz
www.holidaynewzealand.co.nz

Double $90 Single $70 (Continental Breakfast)
cottage $110 Pet on property
1 Queen 1 Double 1 Single (3 bdrm)
2 Private

We like to be your host on our orchard where we have an abundance of fruit and guided tour and season. We offer a double bedroom with continental breakfast, explore our indoor games room or gazebo. If you like privacy then we have a self-contained cottage with two bedrooms, barbecue on deck or enjoy swimming pool, spa, table tennis, petanque and lawn croquet. Dutch spoken. All welcome.

Havelock North - Hastings *Farmstay Homestay 1km S of Havelock North*

Peak View Farm
Dianne & Keith Taylor
92 Middle Road, Havelock North
Tel: (06) 877 7408 Fax: (06) 877 7410
www.bnb.co.nz/peakviewfarm.html

Double $70 Single $45 (Full Breakfast) Child neg. Dinner $25
Credit cards accepted
Children welcome
1 Double 2 Single (2 bdrm)
1 Family share

We invite you to relax in our century old home admidst large trees, gardens and lawns on 25 acres of horticulture land. Enjoy our friendly, personal and caring hospitality, or a separate lounge is available with TV and books if you want a quiet time. Comfortable beds with firm mattresses and electric blankets make for a good night's sleep. Sit and chat, when time allows, over a generous breakfast - cooked or continental with homemade preserves and goodies. Wholesome dinners on request.

Interests include tramping, bushwalks, gardening and genealogy. We have travelled extensively and enjoy meeting local and overseas visitors. Can also advise on travel throughout New Zealand. Afer nearly 15 years of "Happy Hosting", we have an ever-increasing circle of friends - with many returning.

Dianne is one of few in New Zealand who has a Certificate in Homestay Management.

Panoramic views from Te Mata Peak - 10 minutes to the top. Visit the many wineries, safari trip to the gannets, trout fishing and orchard tours are just a few of the wonderful activities to enjoy. A short walk to lovely boutique shops, cafes and restaurants. Hastings and Splash Planet are only 4kms away, and Napier, the Art Deco City of the World is 20 kms.

We look forward to meeting you and our aim is to make your stay a memorable one. Be welcomed with juice, real coffee or tea. Laundry facilities available. No smoking inside please.

Havelock North   *Farmstay Homestay*   *4km E of Havelock North*

Overcliff
Joan & Nigel Sutton
Waimarama Rd, RD 12, Havelock North
Tel: (06) 877 6852 Fax: (06) 877 6852
jn.partners@clear.net.nz
www.bnb.co.nz/overcliff.html

Double $90 Single $65 (Full Breakfast)
Dinner $25 Credit cards accepted Pet on property
Children welcome Pets welcome
1 Double 1 Twin 1 Single (3 bdrm)
1 Private

Our comfortable family home is set in ten acres next to the Tukituki River near Te Mata Peak, five minutes from Havelock North. We have a number of friendly animals: dogs, cats, birds, coloured sheep, kunekune pigs and horses. Come for a walk to the river with the dogs, meeting and feeding the other animals enroute or you can relax by the pool or play tennis on the grass court. We are close to local restaurants and wineries and fifteen minutes from Ocean Beach.

Havelock North   *Homestay B&B Boutique*   *1km N of Havelock North*

Weldon Boutique Bed & Breakfast   Pracilla Hay
98 Te Mata Road, Havelock North, Hawkes Bay
Tel: (06) 877 7551 Fax: (06) 877 7051
Tollfree: 0800 206 499   pracilla@weldon.co.nz
www.weldon.co.nz

Double $120-$140 Single $80-$110
(Special Breakfast) Dinner $35 Queen $130-$150
Twin $120 Credit cards accepted Pet on property
1 Queen 2 Double 1 Twin 1 Single (5 bdrm)
2 Private 1 Guests share

In a quiet picturesque garden at the end of a lavender lined lane, WELDON offers comfort and quality with romantic olde worlde charm. Accommodation is offered in spacious elegantly appointed bedrooms, furnished with period and antique furniture. TV & tea/coffee are provided in each room. Fresh flowers, fine linen and fluffy towels reflect the luxury of fine accommodation. Breakfast of fresh local fruits & gourmet cooked options is served outdoors among the roses in summer or in the dining room during winter. Two toy poodles (James and Thomas) will greet you enthusiastically!

Havelock North   *Homestay*   *5km E of Hastings*

Belvedere
Shirley & Mervyn Pethybridge
51 Lucknow Road, Havelock North
Tel: (06) 877 4551 Fax: (06) 877 4550
pethybridge@actrix.gen.nz
www.bnb.co.nz/belvedere.html

Double $80 Single $45 (Continental & Full Breakfast)
Dinner $25 by arrangement Smoking area inside
1 Queen 1 Double 1 Twin (3 bdrm)
1 Ensuite 1 Private

Belvedere is a large 2 storeyed home set in half an acre of well kept lawns and gardens. The elegant rooms have balconies with great views. It is a short walk to Havelock North village where there are a great variety of shops and restaurants. Hawkes Bay is a well known tourist resort with something for everyone. Having travelled extensively within New Zealand and Overseas we have enjoyed the hospitality of many Homestays and are pleased to be able to offer the same in return. Not suitable for children under 12yrs.

Havelock North   *Homestay B&B*   *5 km N of Havelock North*

Totara Stables
John W. Hayes & Sharon A. Bellaart
324 Te Mata - Mangateretere Road,
Havelock North, RD 2, Hastings

Tel: (06) 877 8882 Fax: (06) 877 8891
Mob: 025 863 910   totarastables@xtra.co.nz
www.geocities.com/totarastables

Double $90-$105 Single $75 Credit cards accepted
1 King/Twin 1 Queen 1 Twin (3 bdrm)
1 Ensuite 1 Private

Offering a unique Bed & Breakfast experience in a lovingly restored 1910 villa. Take a peek into the museum of early pioneer farming displayed in the century old stables or marvel at the simplicity of early stationary motors. Feed the hand reared deer or arrange a ride in a classic 1951 Sunbeam Talbot motor car. We are located in the heart of the Te Mata wine region only minutes from the pictureque village of Havelock North. Non smoking and not suitable for children under 12 years.

Havelock North   *Homestay B&B*   *1km E of Havelock North*

Poona
Joan & David Donaldson
29 Simla Avenue, Havelock North, Hawkes Bay

Tel: (06) 877 1706 Fax: (06) 877 1709
Mob: 021 181 2506
www.bnb.co.nz/poona.html

Double $90 Single $70 (Continental Breakfast)
Credit cards accepted Pet on property
1 Queen (1 bdrm)
1 Private

Poona is a picturesque arts and crafts style house in the heart of the wine country on the slopes of Te Mata Peak. Only minutes from restaurants, village markets and art deco architecture. Suite comprises Queen bedroom, private bathroom and sitting room with TV, tea making facilities and fridge. Complimentary delicacies. Comfortably furnished with antiques. Breakfast of seasonal local produce served on our terrace overlooking pretty gardens with old brick paving or in the dining room with open fire, fresh flowers and one cat, Cleo. Non smoking.

Take it easy
Don't try to travel too far in one day.

Waimarama Beach *Homestay* *34km SE of Hastings*

Rita & Murray Webb
68 Harper Road,
Waimarama, Hawkes Bay
Tel: (06) 874 6795 rwebb@xtra.co.nz
www.bnb.co.nz/webb.html

Double $80 Single $45
(Full Breakfast) Dinner $25
Credit cards accepted Pet on property
2 Double (2 bdrm)
1 Guests share

Lovely beach for surfing, swimming, diving, boating, fishing etc. Bushwalks and golf course nearby. Situated only 5 minutes walk from beach with lovely views of sea, local park and farmland. Nearest town is Havelock North - 20 minutes drive, with Napier 40 minutes. We have 2 double rooms available, a spa pool and separate toilet and bathroom for guests. Cooked breakfast is offered and dinner is available if required. Please phone for reservations 06-874 6795. No smoking inside please. Pets: 2 cats, 1 dog.

Waipawa *Farmstay Country Home* *2km E of Waipawa*

Haowhenua
Caroline & David Jefferd
77 Pourerere Road, RD 1, Waipawa 4170
Tel: (06) 857 8241 Fax: (06) 857 8261
Mob: 025 2684 854
d.jefferd@xtra.co.nz
www.bnb.co.nz/haowhenua.html

Double $100 Single $75 (Full Breakfast)
Child 1/2 price Dinner $25pp Credit cards accepted
Pet on property Children welcome
1 Queen (1 bdrm)   1 Ensuite

Come and enjoy an evening or two at "Haowhenua" with a farming family in a spacious and comfortable old country home set in park like surrounds with lovely gardens and swimming pool, and share your adventures with us. We have two cats and a labrador and only 2km off State Highway 2 and in close proximity to all of Hawkes Bay's attractions. No smoking inside. Please phone for directions.

Waipawa *Homestay* *2km N of Waipawa*

Corgarff Homestay
Judy & Neil McHardy
104 Great North Road, Waipawa, Hawkes Bay
Tel: (06) 857 7828 Fax: (06) 857 7055
corgarff@xtra.co.nz
www.bnb.co.nz/corgarffhomestay.html

Double $100 Single $50
(Continental & Full Breakfast) Child $25
Dinner $20 Credit cards accepted Pet on property
2 King/Twin 2 Twin 1 Single (3 bdrm)
1 Ensuite 1 Guests share 1 Family share

A warm welcome awaits you at Corgarff, our very sunny and comfortable home, set in 13 acres amongst lovely old trees. We have a flock of Texel sheep and a Birman Cat 'Mollie'. Our guest wing has a separate entrance and also a small private sitting room with TV. Our facilities are very suitable for wheelchair or disabled persons. Children under 12 half price. Three hours easy run to ferry in Wellington. Four challenging golf courses within easy reach. Five safe sandy beaches.

Waipukurau   *Self-contained Farmstay*   *20km S of Waipukurau*

Hinerangi Station
Caroline & Dan von Dadelszen
615 Hinerangi Road, RD 1, Waipukurau
Tel: (06) 855 8273 Fax: (06) 855 8273
carovond@amcom.co.nz
hinerangi_farmstay.homestead.com/Farmstay.html

Double $100-$120 Single $80 (Full Breakfast)
Child $30 Dinner $30pp $110 Double
$40 each extra person S/C cottage Pet on property
Children welcome Pets welcome
2 Queen 1 Double 5 Single (4 bdrm)   2 Private

Hinerangi Station is an 1800 acre sheep, cattle and deer farm set in the rolling hills of Central Hawkes Bay. Our spacious 1920 homestead was designed by Louis Hay of Napier Art Deco fame. It has a full size billiard table and there is a tennis court and swimming pool in the garden. Guests have their own private entrance. "The Cookhouse",a recently renovated 100 yr old cottage offers self contained accomodation for couples and families. We have one terrier and a cat.

Waipukurau   *Farmstay*   *9km W of Waipukurau*

Mynthurst
Annabelle & David Hamilton
912 Lindsay Road, RD 3, Waipukurau
Tel: (06) 857 8093 Fax: (06) 857 8093
Mob: 025 232 2458   mynthurst@xtra.co.nz
www.chapelwick.co.nz

Double $150 Single $85 (Full Breakfast)
Child $25 Dinner $35pp Extra space avail for families
Pet on property Children welcome
1 King/Twin 1 Double 1 Single (3 bdrm) 1 Ensuite 1 Private

Mynthurst, genuine working sheep and cattle farm 560 hectares. Guests from NZ and overseas welcomed for 18 years. The homestead is large, warm and comfortable. Observe farm activities, enjoy swimming, trout fishing, golf, tennis, wineries. Dinner available on request, using finest local produce. Whether travelling North or South, visiting beautiful Hawkes Bay, you'll find Mynthurst the perfect retreat. 1/2 hour from Hastings SH2. Booking avoids disappointment. Phone for directions. No smoking. Children welcome. Two Cats. Expect Excellence. Farm tour included. Superb Environment.

Waipukurau   *Homestay*   *Waipukurau Central*

Airlie Mount
Aart & Rashida van Saarloos
South Service Lane, off Porangahau Road,
PO Box 368, Waipukurau
Tel: (06) 858 7601 Fax: (06) 858 7609
Mob: 025 249 9726   salos@xtra.co.nz
www.bnb.co.nz/airliemount.html

Double $90 Single $60 (Full Breakfast)
Child $30, 12 & under Pet on property
1 King/Twin 1 Queen 1 Single (2 bdrm)   2 Ensuite

Historic fully restored "Airlie Mount", built in 1870, is situated in the exact centre of Waipukurau, a few steps away from shops and restaurants - yet it's an island of tranquillity, surrounded by cottage gardens and native bush. The comfortable (non-smoking) homestead offers verandahs, billiard room and swimming pool. The guest rooms are very private, have their own bathrooms, TV and outside courtyards. Your hosts have travelled extensively and have two children and a Labrador who all enjoy meeting new guests.   Historic Homestead walks arranged.

Waipukurau *Farmstay* *7km E of Waipukurau*

Mangatarata Country Estate
Judy & Donald Macdonald
415 Mangatarata Road, RD 5, Waipukurau
Tel: (06) 858 8275 Fax: (06) 858 8270 Mob: 021 480 769
Tollfree: 0800 858 857
mangatarata@xtra.co.nz
www.hawkesbaynz.com/pages/mangatarata
Double $150-$160 Single $85 (Full Breakfast)
Dinner $35pp
2 Queen 1 Double 3 Single (3 bdrm)
1 Private 1 Guests share

Retreat to a beautiful historic homestead nestled in the heart of Hawkes Bay, Wine Country. Unwind with uninterrupted farm views from the gracious Victorian verandah.

Experience beef and sheep farming first hand or wander through the extensive gardens with swimming pool, pathways and a pond where birdlife prevails.

Enjoy a generous breakfast and good coffee in the private dining room or on the verandah, weather providing. Other sumptuous meals may be arranged by request. Gourmet lamb is Judy's speciality, complimented with fresh produce from the kitchen garden or grown locally.

Meet Mac the Scottish terrier and the two cats who arrived and stayed.

Mangatarata is one of Hawkes Bay's most historic sheep stations and is still a working farm of 2,500 acres. The perfect location for a memorable getaway with truly New Zealand uniqueness.

Waipukurau   *B&B   44km SE of Waipukurau*

Chapelwick
Lorna and Rodger Dix
482 Hunter Road, RD4, Porangahau, Waipukurau

Tel: (06) 855 5119 Fax: (06) 855 5119
Mob: 025 520 843   chapelwick@flatnet.co.nz
www.porangahau.co.nz

Double $135 Single $80 (Full Breakfast) Child $25
Dinner $30 Children welcome
1 Queen 1 Double 1 Twin (3 bdrm)
1 Ensuite 1 Private

Established in 1854 this imposing country home and chapel are set in 18 acres of NZ countryside. The large bedrooms provide a magnificent view of the estate, right out to sea and the formal dining room, lounge and billiard room recall the ambience of yesteryear. From the starched linen nappery, homemade preserves and fresh flowers in your room, Chapelwick will leave you with a wonderful impression of throughtful care and detail. Hosts Lorna and Rodger make every endeavour to ensure your stay is a memorable one.

Waipukurau   *Self-contained   4.5km S of Waipukurau*

Pukeora Vineyard Cottage   Kate Norman
Pukeora Scenic Road, RD1, Waipukurau
(off SH2 south of Waikpukurau)

Tel: (06) 858 9339 Fax: (06) 858 6070
Mob: 021 701 606   enquiries@pukeora.com
www.pukeora.com

Double $80 Single $60 (Continental Breakfast)
Child $25   Child at home
1 Queen 1 Double 2 Twin 1 Single (3 bdrm)
1 Guests share

The charming 3-bedroom cottage is located alongside our house at the edge of a gum forest with stunning views over the vineyard and beyond. The cottage built c1920, has character wooden floors throughout, open plan lounge/kitchen with TV and log fire. The verandah is perfect for a leisurely sunny breakfast or enjoying a wine at sundown.   Pukeora Estate is a working 4Ha vineyard, boutique winery and a conventions venue. Your hosts Kate, Max, baby Jessica, dog Harlem and 5 cats welcome you to our unique experience.   For further details, please see our website.

Please let us know how you enjoyed your B&B experience. Ask your host for a comment form,

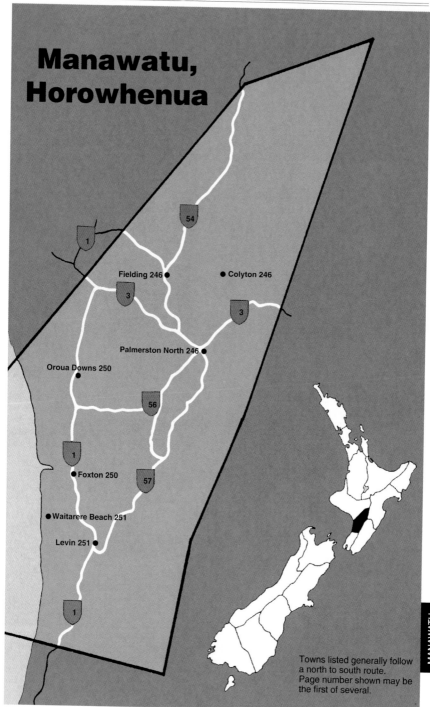

Manawatu, Horowhenua

54

1

Fielding 246 ●

● Colyton 246

3

3

Palmerston North 246 ●

Oroua Downs 250 ●

56

1

● Foxton 250

57

● Waitarere Beach 251

Levin 251 ●

1

Towns listed generally follow
a north to south route.
Page number shown may be
the first of several.

Colyton - Feilding   *Farmstay*   *16km E of Feilding*

Hiamoe
Toos and John Cousins
Waiata, Colyton, Feilding
Tel: **(06) 328 7713** Fax: (06) 328 7787
Mob: 027 4100931
johnhiamoe@clear.net.nz.
www.bnb.co.nz/hiamoe.html

Double $80 Single $50 (Full Breakfast)
Child $20 Preschool free Dinner $15 Child at home
Pet on property Children welcome Pets welcome
1 Queen 1 Double 1 Single (2 bdrm) 1 Ensuite

Toos, John, Edmund (9yrs), Julius (8yrs) and Guido (8yrs) look forward to giving you a warm welcome to "Hiamoe" and during your stay, it is our aim that you experience a home away from home.Third generation, farming our deer, cattle,sheep and forestry property and live in a restored 100-year-old colonial home. We have many interests ,enjoy visitors and as Holland is Toos original homeland ,we are accustomed to travel. Central heating ,open fires ,fenced pool.

Feilding   *Homestay*   *Feilding Central*

Avoca Homestay
Margaret Hickmott
12 Freyberg Street,
Feilding
Tel: **(06) 323 4699** Fax: (06) 323 4061
www.bnb.co.nz/avocahomestay.html

Double $80 Single $50 (Full Breakfast)
Dinner $25 by arrangement
1 Queen 2 Single (2 bdrm)
1 Ensuite 1 Family share

Enjoy a break in friendly Feilding, eleven times winner of New Zealand's Most Beautiful Town Award. You are assured of a warm welcome and an enjoyable stay in a comfortable smoke free home set in an attractive garden with mature trees and a spectacular shrubbery. Off street parking is provided for your vehicle. The main bedroom has a queensize bed, ensuite and an outside entrance for your convenience. We are within easy walking distance of the town centre and well situated for the Manfield Park complex.

Feilding - Palmerston North   *Country*   *13km NE of Feilding*

Puketawa B&B/Country Stay
Nelson & Phyllis Whitelock
987 Colyton Road, RD5, Feilding
Tel: **(06) 328 7819** Fax: (06) 328 7919
Mob: 025 298 0722   shane_maree@hotmail.com
www.homestaysnz.co.nz/puketawa.htm

Double $90 Single $50 (Full Breakfast)
Child half price Dinner $20 - $25 Pet on property
1 Queen 1 Twin 1 Single (3 bdrm)
1 Ensuite 1 Private

Discover Puketawa for yourself. Experience friendly Kiwi hospitality in our comfortable national award-winning home situated beside 10 acres of native bush, and surrounded by extensive gardens. Delicious meals are Phyl's speciality prepared from homegrown produce. We enjoy the great outdoors, gardening, travel, music, reading, etc, as well as meeting new friends from NZ and around the world. Four wheel drive tour of the farm is available. Situated handy to both Palmerston North and Feilding, 2 hours from Wellington and Napier.

All our B&Bs are non-smoking
unless stated otherwise in the text.

Palmerston North - Hokowhitu   *Homestay   Palmerston North Central*

Glenfyne
Jillian & Alex McRobert
413 Albert Street, Hokowhitu, Palmerston North
Tel: (06) 358 1626 Fax: (06) 358 1626
glenfyne@inspire.net.nz
www.bnb.co.nz/glenfyne.html

Double $80 Single $50 (Full Breakfast)
Credit cards accepted
1 Double 2 Single (2 bdrm)
1 Guests share

A warm welcome awaits you in our comfortable home. We are a retired, non-smoking couple with varied interests: meeting people, travel, cooking and golf. Our home is close to Massey University and the Manawatu Golf Club. There are some interesting walkways nearby, and two minutes will take you to the Hokowhitu Village (Post Office, Pharmacy, Restaurants etc). Jillian is a Kiwi Host, assuring you of great hospitality. Laundry facilities and covered off-street parking are available. We are happy to meet public transport.

Palmerston North   *Self-contained B&B   Palmerston North Central*

The Gables
Monica & Paul Stichbury
179 Fitzherbert Avenue, Palmerston North
Tel: (06) 358 3209 Fax: (06) 358 3209
Thegables.pn.nz@xtra.co.nz
www.friars.co.nz/hosts/gables.html

Double $80-$110 Single $50-$80
(Continental Breakfast) Dinner $20 by arrangement
Credit cards accepted
3 Queen 1 Single (4 bdrm)
1 Private 2 Guests share

Our fully restored 1930's home in a mature garden with historic trees is only 10 minutes walk from the CBD and numerous restaurants and a few minutes by car or bus from Massey University. Our self contained cottage in the style of a New England Barn is very popular, and, like the house, furnished with antiques and decorated in the country style. We host children only by arrangement. Our delightful pomeranian Bobby "the fluffy doorbell" will announce your arrival.

MANAWATU. HOROWHENUA

Palmerston North *Homestay B&B*

Karaka House
Lynn & David Whitburn
473 College Street, Hokowhitu, Palmerston North

Tel: (06) 358 8684 Fax: (06) 358 8685
Mob: 025 245 2765
dave_lynn@xtra.co.nz
www.bnb.co.nz/karakahouse.html

Double $90 Single $65
(Continental & Full Breakfast) Dinner by arrangement
Credit cards accepted Pet on property
2 Queen 2 Single (3 bdrm) 1 Guests share

Lynn and David offer you a warm welcome to Karaka House. We are a friendly couple who enjoy meeting people in the relaxed atmosphere of our home which is within an easy walk of the city centre, restaurants and theatres. The College of Education, Polytech and Massey are within easy reach. The tiled front entrance opens to a wide hall with a rimu staircase leading to the large sunny bedrooms which have been designed with your comfort in mind. We look forward to meeting you.

Palmerston North - Rongotea *Farmstay 20km W of Palmerston North*

Andellen
Kay and Warren Nitschke
RD 3, Palmerston North

Tel: (06) 324 8359 Fax: (06) 324 8359
Mob: 021 448 549 nitschkek@agriquality.co.nz
www.bnb.co.nz/andellen.html

Double $80 Single $45 (Continental Breakfast)
Child 1/2 price Dinner $25pp Credit cards accepted
Child at home Pet on property Pets welcome
1 Queen 2 Single (2 bdrm) 1 Ensuite 1 Family share

Kay, Warren and Libby (7yo) welcome you to "Andellen", a lovely large 90 year old farm villa set on 42 acres with extensive lawn, garden and orchard. We offer guests the opportunity to relax in a lovely tranquil country setting. Seasonal farm activities available. Children very welcome. Beach 10 minutes away. We have a pet cat and dog. Directions: Situated 11 kms South of Sanson or 11 kms North of Himitangi intersection. Off State Highway 1, into Kaimatarau Road and travel across first intersection. Next gate on LEFT - Farm no. 221. Our name is on the gate.

Palmerston North *B&B 3.5km E of Palmerston North*

Clairemont
Joy & Dick Archer
10 James Line,
RD 10, Palmerston North

Tel: (06) 357 5508 Fax: (06) 357 5501
clairemont@inspire.net.nz
www.bnb.co.nz/clairemont.html

Double $70 Single $45 (Full Breakfast)
1 Double 1 Twin (2 bdrm)
1 Guests share

Welcome to Clairemont. We are a rural spot within the city boundary, plenty of trees and a quite extensive garden. On our 1 1/4 acres we keep a few sheep, silky bantams, and our little dog Toby. We are handy to river walks, golf course, and shops are a few minutes away. We have a cosy, spacious family home we would like to share with you. Our interests are walking, gardening, model engineering and barbershop singing. Good off street parking provided, no smoking in house.

Palmerston North *B&B* *4km E of Palmerston North*

Panorama B&B
Claire & Bill Sawers
30 Moonshine Valley Road, RD1,
Aokautere, Palmerston North
Tel: (06) 354 8816 Fax: (06) 356 2757
panorama.bb@paradise.net.nz
www.homepages.paradise.net.nz/sawers/
Double $80 Single $50 (Full Breakfast) Child $20
Credit cards accepted Pet on property
1 Double 1 Twin (2 bdrm) 1 Guests share

A warm welcome awaits you at our home in Moonshine Valley. We offer a private and peaceful stay in a rural-residential area. Situated only eight minutes drive to the Square, four minutes to Massey University and closer to the International Pacific College. Guests share a lounge/dining room with refreshments always available. The bathroom includes a bath and shower. Interesting walkways and gardens are nearby, or just relax on the terrace and enjoy the panoramic city, rural and mountain views with our cat Sophie.

Palmerston North *Homestay B&B* *13km E of Palmerston North*

Country Lane Homestay
Fay and Allan Hutchinson
52 Orrs Road, RD1 Aokautere, Palmerston North
Tel: (06) 326 8529 Fax: (06) 326 9216
Mob: 025 485 833 ashhurst.timber@xtra.co.nz
www.bnb.co.nz/user82.html
Double $90-$120 Single $50
(Continental & Full Breakfast) Dinner $25-$30
1 King/Twin 1 Queen 1 Double 1 Single (3 bdrm)
2 Private 1 Family share

Country living, a short distance from Palmerston North near the Manawatu Gorge and below the wind farm. 10km from the Pacific College and 2km from Equestrain Centre. Our large home is newly decorated, with some antiques in a country traditional style and is surrounded by our pleasant garden. We have our sawmill on the property as well as coloured sheep, horses, and raise a few calves. Hill country farm visits may be arranged as well as trout fishing. The Manawatu river borders our property. It is our pleasure to provide home cooked meals for you with some of our local produce.

Palmerston North *Self-contained B&B* *5.5km SW of Central Palmerston North*

Udy's B&B
Tim & Glenda Udy
52 Anders Road, Palmerston North,
Tel: (06) 354 1722 Fax: (06) 354 1711
Mob: 025 409 299
kiwitim@clear.net.nz
www.bnb.co.nz/udysbb.html
Double $90 Single $60 (Full Breakfast)
Dinner neg. Credit cards accepted
1 Queen (1 bdrm) 1 Ensuite

Our beautiful home is located on a 4.5 acre lawn. Quiet country location, but very close to town (6-7 minutes to CBD). Our tennis court is available (with racquets) for our guests to use. Our accommodation is a fully self-contained flat in our home. We are ex-farmers. We have travelled extensively and enjoy meeting and talking to people. Our 3 cats keep to themselves. Less than 15 mins to Massey , UCOL, Manfield and International Pacific College. House - smoke-free. Dinner possible by prior arrangement.

Oroua Downs *Farmstay   14km N of Foxton*

Oroua Downs Farmstay
Bev & Ian Wilson
Omanuka Road, RD 11, Foxton
Tel: (06) 329 9859 Fax: (06) 329 9859
Mob: 025 986 023
getwilsons@xtra.co.nz
www.bnb.co.nz/orouadownsfarmstay.html
Double $70 Single $40 (Full Breakfast)
Child $20 Dinner $20pp
1 Double 3 Single (3 bdrm)
1 Guests share

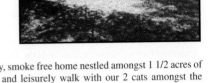

Bev and Ian invite you to share their spacious 2 storey, smoke free home nestled amongst 1 1/2 acres of tree-lined gardens. Enjoy the opportunity to relax and leisurely walk with our 2 cats amongst the garden listening to the bird song. We also operate a Building and Wooden Toy manufacturing business. Directions: turn off at Bed & Breakfast sign on State Highway 1, 14km north of Foxton and 16km south of Sanson. Travel 2 km down Omanuka Road.

Foxton *Farmstay   1km E of Foxton*

Karnak Stud
Margaret Barbour
Ridge Road, Foxton
Tel: (06) 363 7764 Fax: (06) 363 8941
www.bnb.co.nz/karnakstud.html
Double $80 Single $55 (Full Breakfast)
Child under 6 free Dinner By arrangement
Credit cards accepted Pet on property Pets welcome
1 Double 1 Twin 1 Single (2 bdrm)
1 Ensuite 1 Private

Karnak Stud, mini farm, is an ideal quiet stopover 1 1/2 hours from Wellington. Perfect for children to meet friendly farm dog Meg, cat Mousie, thoroughbred horses. Relaxing country living , excellent meals and organic farmstay food. Enjoy table tennis, darts, pool, children's toys, guests' library. Stroll through our sixteen acres of pasture and woodland. Follow Farmstay arrow on State Highway One for 1 km up Purcell Street to white fence, next wide gateway on your left. One night just isn't long enough! See animal friends on website.

Our B&Bs range from homely to luxurious,
but you can always be assured of superior hospitality.

Waitarere Beach *Homestay   14km W of Levin*

The Pines
Grant and Robyn Powell
Ngati Huia Place, Waitarere Beach,
Tel: (06) 368 7957 Mob: 025 285 3643
thepines@xtra.co.nz
www.bnb.co.nz/thepines.html

Double $100 Single $75 (Continental Breakfast)
Dinner $30 Credit cards accepted
2 Queen (2 bdrm)
2 Ensuite

Grant & Robyn (formerly of Miranui Homestay, Palmerston North) welcome you to our new absolute beachfront retreat - under construction - completion January 2003. Enjoy beach walks and magnificent view of Kapiti and Mounts Taranaki and Ruapehu. We offer two queensiZe bedrooms, ensuites, own living areas with TV, microwave, tea/coffee making facilities and continental breakfast provided. Situated 14km north west of Levin, approx. 1.5 hours from Wellington and 35 minutes from Palmerston North. Laundry facilities, off-street parking and non-smoking. Dinner by arrangement.

Levin *Self-contained B&B   5min Levin*

Fantails
Heather Watson
40 MacArthur Street, Levin
Tel: (06) 368 9011 Fax: (06) 368 9279
fantails@xtra.co.nz   www.fantails.co.nz

Double $90-$120 Single $60-$80 (Full Breakfast)
Child neg Dinner $35 S/C Cottages $100 - $140
Credit cards accepted
1 King 1 Queen 1 Twin 4 Single (4 bdrm)
3 Ensuite 1 Private

"Every picture tells a story" - Two acres of native bush, English trees and lots of birdlife and butterflies. Tranquillity and security. Our bedrooms all have a lovely outlook onto the garden, a good night's sleep on very comfortable beds, with all those extras. Home cooked eats on arrival and many more surprises when you stay at the Fantails (organic food a speciality). We also offer Retreat cottages (they sleep 2-4 people). Wheelchair friendly and smoke free. Laundry facilities available. Directions, please phone. Courtesy coach available.

Levin *Farmstay   3.4km E of Levin*

Lynn Beau Ley
Beverley & Peter Lynn
Queen Street East, RD 1, Levin
Tel: (06) 368 0310 Fax: (06) 368 0310
Mob: 025 274 4564   lynnbeauley@paradise.net.nz
www.bnb.co.nz/lynnbeauley.html

Double $85 Single $60 (Full Breakfast)
Dinner $20 by arrangement
Credit cards accepted Pet on property
1 Double 2 Single (2 bdrm) 1 Ensuite 1 Private

A 10 acre pastoral retreat 4 minutes from town centre. Comfortable distance for ferry/air travel. We farm sheep and cattle, and enjoy entertaining. Our home is spacious, ranch-style with warm aspect, situated in one acre of lawns and gardens. Tastefully appointed guest rooms, delicious breakfasts and many extras. Beverley has many years experience in hospitality business. Peter a background in management and financial services. Turn east off SH1 at Post Office into Queen Street East. We are 3.4km on left. Sign at gate.

Levin   *Farmstay   9km SE of Levin*

Buttercup Acres
Ivan & Pat Keating
55 Florida Road, RD 20, Levin
Tel: (06) 368 0557 Fax: (06) 368 0557
buttercupacres@xtra.co.nz
www.bnb.co.nz/buttercupacres.html
Double $90 Single $45 (Full Breakfast)
Dinner $20 Credit cards accepted
1 Double 2 Single (2 bdrm)
1 Ensuite 1 Private

Buttercup Acres is a small tranquil rural property at the foothills of the Tararua Ranges. We specialise in breeding Miniature Horses and Alpaca's. Our home is surrounded by 3 acres of gardens and a large pond. In the evenings you can relax in the lounge. Learn to spin or weave in our weaving studio or view the stars through our telescope. Our model railway will fascinate visitors. Free laundry facilities available. Directions: At Ohau turn into Muhunoa East Road. 5km to Florida Road.

Levin   *Self-contained Farmstay   2.5km S of Levin*

Range View Farmstay
Errol and Ann Quinn
112 Buller Rd, RD 1, Levin
Tel: (06) 368 5530 Fax: (06) 368 5810
Mob: 025 494 533
www.bnb.co.nz/rangeview.html
Double $90-$110 Single $90 (Full Breakfast)
Child under 10: $15.00 $20 pp extra person
Credit cards accepted Children welcome
2 Queen 1 Double 2 Single (2 bdrm)   2 Private

Errol and Ann welcome you to their private, quiet, fully self contained two bedroom cottage and separate bedsitter offering you all the comforts. Set on 8 acres of land with quiet animals one hour drive to Wellington, 35 minute drive to Palmerston North. The cottage has modern kitchen facilities, sleeps 6, has separate toilet, laundry, bathroom with shower and bath. Large verandah with view of Tararua Ranges. Walking distance to tranquil Lake Papatonga and Bush Walks. Directions: Turn off State Highway One 2.5km south of Levin (Farmstay sign) then 1km along Buller Rd.

All our B&Bs are non-smoking
unless stated otherwise in the text.

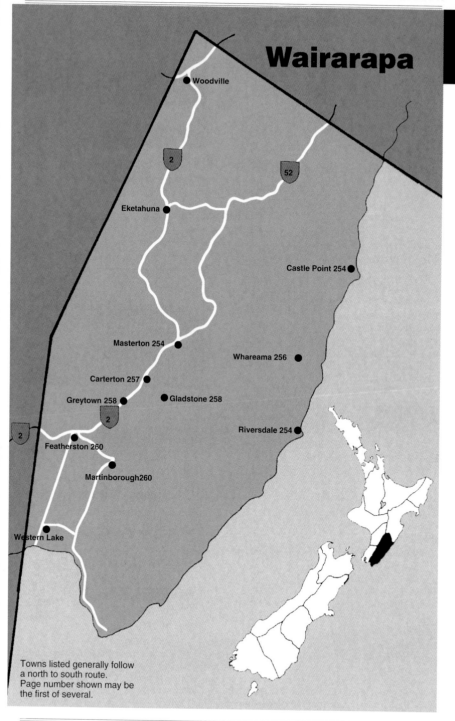

Wairarapa

Woodville

2

52

Eketahuna

Castle Point 254

Masterton 254

Whareama 256

Carterton 257

Greytown 258 ● Gladstone 258

2

Riversdale 254

2

Featherston 260

Martinborough260

Western Lake

Towns listed generally follow
a north to south route.
Page number shown may be
the first of several.

Masterton   *Self-contained Farmstay B&B*   *3km W of Masterton*

Harefield
Marion Ahearn
147 Upper Plain Road, Masterton
Tel: (06) 377 4070 Fax: (06) 377 4070
www.bnb.co.nz/harefield.html
Double $80 Single $45 (Full Breakfast)
Child 1/2 price Dinner $20 by arrangement
S/C Flat for 2 $55 Children welcome
1 Double 1 Single (1 bdrm)
1 Private

A warm welcome awaits you at Harefield, a small farmlet on the edge of town. A quiet country garden surrounds the cedar house and s/c flat. The flat has one bedroom with double and single beds. Two divan beds in living area. Self-cater or have breakfast in our warm dining room. Convenient for restaurants, showgrounds, vineyards, schools, tramping. 1 1/2 hour drive to Picton Ferry. We enjoy meeting people, travel, reading, art, farming and tramping. Baby facilities available. One outside cat. Smoke free.

Masterton   *Farmstay Homestay B&B Rural Homestay*   *10km W of Masterton*

Tidsfordriv
Glenys Hansen
4 Cootes Road, RD 8, Matahiwi, Masterton
Tel: (06) 378 9967 Fax: (06) 378 9957
ghansen@contact.net.nz
www.bnb.co.nz/tidsfordriv.html
Double $75 Single $40 (Full Breakfast)
Child 1/2 price Dinner $20 by arrangement
Credit cards accepted Pet on property
1 Queen 2 Single (2 bdrm)   1 Private

A warm welcome awaits you at 'Tidsfordriv' - a 64 acre farmlet - 7 kms off the main bypass route. A comfortable modern home set in park like surroundings with large gardens, ponds and many species of wetland birds. Enjoy bird watching with ease. Glenys has home-hosted for 14 years and invites you to join her for dinner. Conservation, gardening and travel are her interests. A Labrador dog is the family pet. Local Wairarapa attractions - National Wildlife Centre, gardens, vineyards, Tararua Forest Park.

Riversdale - Castlepoint   *Self-contained Farmstay B&B*   *40km E of Masterton*

Alderford Farmstays
Carol & Les Ross
RD 12, Masterton
Tel: (06) 372 3705 www.bnb.co.nz/alderford.html
Double $75 Single $45
(Continental & Full Breakfast)
Dinner $25pp. 3 course dinner
Cooked breakfast $7.50pp Credit cards accepted
1 Double (1 bdrm)
1 Ensuite

Les, Carol, Barney the Labrador, offer you a warm friendly welcome to "Alderford". Tastefully decorated warm cottage room away from main homestead. Cosy double iron bedstead, TV, fridge, tea, coffee, home-made biscuits. Delicious country meals with home-made jams, bottled fruits, fresh veges, free range eggs. "Alderford" is a 200 acre sheep, cattle, deer farm. 10 minutes to Riversdale beach with lovely 9 hole golf course, 10 minutes to Tinui pub, 25 minutes to the picturesque Castlepoint beach, canoe trips in area. "Alderford" 30 minutes drive from Masterton.

Masterton   *B&B Guesthouse   Central Masterton*

Victoria House
Marion and Sara Monks and Mike Parker
15 Victoria Street, Masterton
Tel: (06) 377 0186 Fax: (06) 377 0186
parker.monks@xtra.co.nz
www.bnb.co.nz/victoriahouse.html

Double $80 Single $50 (Continental Breakfast)
Twin $80 Credit cards accepted
3 Double 1 Twin 2 Single (6 bdrm)
2 Guests share

Victoria House is a two storey house built pre 1886, renovated to retain the character of the period. The peaceful nature of the furnishings and outdoor area create a quiet, relaxing atmosphere, great for a "get away from it" weekend. We are also only a three minute walk from the town centre and Masterton's excellant restaurants. Being "wine friendly" hosts we enjoy discussing wines and freely offer advice on the Wairararapa's growing wine industry.

Masterton   *Homestay   1km E of Masterton*

Mas des Saules
Mary & Steve Blakemore
9A Pokohiwi Road, Homebush, Masterton
Tel: (06) 377 2577 Fax: (06) 377 2578
Mob: 025 620 8728
mas-des-saules@wise.net.nz
www.bnb.co.nz/masdessaules.html

Double $110 Single $65 (Full Breakfast)
Child $40 Dinner $25 Credit cards accepted
2 Queen (2 bdrm) 1 Guests share

Down a country lane, amongst apple orchards, discover our tranquil French Provencal farmhouse with its stream, water fowl, and petanque court. Our children have departed, leaving us with a cat, two small dogs and cattle on our small farm. Guest lounge and bathroom with bath and shower. Open fire and central heating. Enjoy farmhouse cooking with fresh vegetables from our large country garden. We can also provide barbecues and picnic lunches. We are a well travelled couple who enjoy helping guests discover the unspoilt Wairarapa.

Masterton   *Farmstay   2km E of Masterton*

Apple Source Orchard Stay
Niel & Raewyn Groombridge
Te Ore Ore, RD 6, Masterton
Tel: (06) 377 0820 Fax: (06) 370 9401
Mob: 021 667 092   raeg@wise.net.nz
www.bnb.co.nz/applesource.html

Double $100 Single $75 (Continental Breakfast)
Child 1/2 price Dinner $30 Pet on property
2 Queen 1 Single (2 bdrm)
2 Ensuite

Try an experience that's a little different! Our colonial style homestead is set in an operating apple orchard and has a separate guest wing with lounge and two bedrooms with ensuites. You are welcome to share dinner or a country breakfast with us and enjoy the ambience of stanley range based cooking along with relaxing by the open fire or on the deck. There are orchard walks and a garden haven. Watch the daily orchard activities and pick some fruit in season. Ask us about the Model A tourer courtesy car.

Masterton   *B&B*   *7km N of Masterton*

Taravista
Pam & Ray Ward
49 Loop Line, RD 1, Masterton
Tel: (06) 377 2987 Fax: (06) 377 2987
Mob: 025 285 8709   pam.ray.ward@xtra.co.nz
www.bnb.co.nz/taravista.html
Double $80-$130 Single $50-$80 (Full Breakfast)
Child $15 Dinner $25 Children welcome
1 Double 1 Twin (2 bdrm)
1 Private

Looking for a warm Wairarapa welcome and superb mountain views? Relax in our spacious home with private guest lounge, log fire and tea making facilities. Enjoy a hearty dinner with your hosts, or privately, in smokefree comfort. Loop Line is the Wairarapa's "nouveau vin" and olive grove area, and Taravista is ideally situated for excursions to the seaside, Mount Bruce, Museums, Golf Courses and fishing/hunting adventures. Walk to a winery, river or playground or, drive five minutes to Masterton's shops, restaurants etc.

Masterton   *Self-contained B&B*   *Masterton Central*

Natusch Town House
Anne Bohm
55 Lincoln Road, Masterton,
Tel: 06 378 9252 Fax: 06 378 9330
Mob: 027 436 3732   anne@natusch.co.nz
www.natusch.co.nz
Double $150 (Continental Breakfast)
Credit cards accepted
4 Queen (4 bdrm)
1 Ensuite 1 Private

Self contained, hosts live off-site. Booking is for the whole house. You choose who, if any, are to share with you. A marvellous old two storied self-contained home built in 1893. Right in the centre of town within easy reach of great dining, bars, parks etc. Four double bedrooms each with a queen sized bed, two bathrooms, parlour, dining room and well appointed modern kitchen, off-street parking for up to four cars. Old style with luxury appointments. This is a Historic Places Trust listed home - a delight to stay in. A delicious breakfast is included on a self help basis.

Masterton - Whareama   *Self-contained Homestay B&B*   *32 km E of Masterton*

Blairlogie Homestead
Barbara & Graham Ingram-Monk
Langdale Rd, Masterton,
Tel: 06 372 3777 Fax: 06 372 3778
Mob: 021 185 5309   blairlogie@wise.net.nz
www.wairarapa.co.nz/blairlogie
Double $100-$130 Single $65 (Special Breakfast)
Child $25 Dinner $30 S/C cottage $100-$140
Pet on property Children welcome
1 Queen 2 Double 2 Twin 1 Single (4 bdrm)
1 Ensuite 1 Private 2 Guests share

Chill out in our historic homestead. Enjoy a luxury breakfast on the sunny verandah, take a picnic to Castlepoint beach, return to dinner in front of a log fire. Relax in our elegant sitting room, choose a video or book, or watch Sky TV. Swim in our solar-heated pool, walk the discovery trail set in 25 acres of woodland and gardens with many native birds, play pool or petanque. Children welcome. Come join us in our peaceful, country lifestyle!

Masterton *Homestay   1km S of Masterton*

Carrbridge House
Ross & Cushla Hollings
31 Andrew Street, Masterton,
Tel: (06) 370 2999 Fax: (06) 370 2950
hols@xtra.co.nz
www.carrbridge-house.co.nz
Double $100-$120 Single $90-$100
(Special Breakfast) Credit cards accepted
2 Queen (2 bdrm)
2 Ensuite

At Carrbridge House we offer you a relaxing stay in our comfortable home set in four parklike acres in rural Masterton. Unwind with afternoon tea before unpacking in one of our well-appointed rooms with flowers, complimentary port, bath robes, and hairdryers. Both have ensuites and one has its own private lounge and TV. Start the day with our special breakfast which can be enjoyed in the dining room or on our large verandah. For your added enjoyment we offer petanque, croquet and bicycles. Come visit us in the beautiful Wairarapa

Carterton *B&B   3km S of Carterton*

Portland House
Judy Betts
Portland Road, State Highway 2, Carterton
Tel: (06) 379 8809 Mob: 025 602 8358
portlandhouse@paradise.net.nz
www.bnb.co.nz/portlandhouse.html
Double $80 Single $50 (Full Breakfast)
Dinner by prior arrangement
Credit cards accepted Pet on property
1 Double 1 Twin (2 bdrm)   1 Private 1 Family share

A warm and friendly welcome awaits you at Portland House, a 125 year old refurbished villa and home to Birmans Missy and George. You can rest, relax and enjoy the country air of the Wairarapa in our peaceful surroundings and comfortable home. We are just off the main highway (SH2) and within 5 to 10 minutes drive to Masterton, the cafes in Greytown, the vineyards in Martinborough, the scenic Waiohine Gorge, the Tararua Forest Park and many wonderful Wairarapa Gardens. Smoking outside only please.

Carterton *Separate/Suite B&B   1km N of Carterton*

Homecroft
Christine & Neil Stewart
Somerset Road,
RD 2, Carterton
Tel: (06) 379 5959 homecroft@xtra.co.nz
www.bnb.co.nz/homecroft.html
Double $85 Single $50 (Full Breakfast)
Dinner $25 Pet on property
1 Queen 1 Double 1 Twin (3 bdrm)
1 Ensuite 1 Guests share

Homecroft is surrounded by our country garden and farmland yet handy to the vineyards, crafts, antiques, and golf courses of the Wairarapa. Wellington and the inter-island ferry 90 minutes away. Accommodation, with own entrance, in a separate wing of the house with small lounge, the sunny bedrooms open onto a deck. The double room with ensuite is separate from the house. All bedrooms overlook the garden. A leisurely breakfast at Homecroft is an enjoyable expereince. We look forward to making your stay with us happy and relaxing.

Gladstone *Homestay B&B   22km E of Carterton*

Hinana Cottage
Louise (and George & Jessa, the Schnauzers) Walker
Fire No 15, Admiral Road, RD 3, Masterton
Tel: (06) 372 7667 Mob: 027 499 8928
hinanacottage@xtra.co.nz
www.bnb.co.nz/hinanacottage.html

Double $110-$135 (Special Breakfast)
Dinner By arrangement Credit cards accepted
Pet on property
1 Queen 1 Double (2 bdrm) 1 Ensuite 1 Family share

Experience the peace and tranquility of Hinana Cottage, a delightfully restored 1930's bungalow nestling in the Gladstone hills, with spectacular views of the Tararuas and Wairarapa Valley. Handy to Masterton, Carterton and Greytown and an easy 35 minutes from Martinborough. Ideally situated for the exploration of Wairarapa's vineyards, walkways, caves and rivers. Relax in the outdoor spa pool, play petanque, or laze by the open fire and enjoy Hinana's native timber floors, ornate plaster ceilings, fine china and beautiful linen - all reminders of a bygone era.

Gladstone *Self-contained Farmstay B&B   15km SE of Masterton*

Cavelands Homestay
Belinda & Rod Cranswick
Fire No 10, Cavelands Road, RD 4, Masterton
Tel: (06) 372 7733 Fax: (06) 372 7773
Mob: 027 436 5738
cranswick@wise.net.nz
www.bnb.co.nz/cavelands.html

Double $125 Single $90 (Full Breakfast)
Dinner $40pp by arr. S.C $75 Credit cards accepted
1 Queen 1 Double (2 bdrm) 1 Private

Country hospitality awaits in our homestead (1870s circa) on our 200 acre sheep and cattle stud. Queen bedroom opens on a sunny verandah, elegant private sitting room with open fire. Delicious hearty breakfasts and homemade panforte with coffee. Foxy Ollie and two cats share our home. Experience Caveland's beauty and explore glowworm caves, walks, sheep mustering demos, mountain biking and grass tennis. Central to Gladstone's attractions, gardens, vineyards, ostrich and cheese farms. Close to homestead, peaceful hideaway for two in simple, self contained "whare". Open fire.

Greytown *Homestay B&B*

Westwood
Jill Kemp
PO Box 34, 82 West Street, Greytown
Tel: (06) 304 8510 Fax: (06) 304 8610
Mob: 027 471 6466   westwood.kemp@xtra.co.nz
www.westwood.greytown.co.nz

Double $150-$175 Single $100-$150 (Full Breakfast)
Credit cards accepted
3 King/Twin 1 Single (4 bdrm)
2 Ensuite 1 Private

A top category award winner in 'New Zealand House of the Year', Westwood has been designed to blend with its picturesque surroundings - nine acres of magnificent trees, with mountain views, a tranquil stream and formal Herb Garden. Just a short stroll to historic Greytown's cafes and specialty shops. Enjoy stylish comfort with an old fashioned ambience in your spacious ensuite room with private entrance, verandah, tea/coffee making facilities and SKY television. Breakfast poolside in summer or fireside in winter. Experience country hospitality at its best! King Beds are Super Kings.

Greytown   *Homestay B&B   80km N of Wellington*

The Ambers
Marilla & Steve Davis, 78 Kuratawhiti Street, Greytown
Tel: (06) 304 8588 Fax: (06) 304 8590 Mob: 025 994 394
ambershomestay@xtra.co.nz
www.ambershomestay.co.nz

Double $100-$110 Single $70 (Continental Breakfast) Child $25 self-contained cottage
Credit cards accepted
1 King 1 Queen 1 Double (3 bdrm)
1 Ensuite 1 Private 1 Guests share

Built in the 1800's The Ambers exudes the ambience of its era. The house is nestled in two acres of gardens with many beautiful old trees.

Our guest wing is separate enough to provide privacy or the intimate atmosphere you desire without feeling isolated from us. We offer guests secluded verandahs, a spa pool for those starry summer nights, lounge with open fire for winter.

The Cherub Room has a queen bed and private bathroom. The Vintage Room has a king bed with ensuite bathroom. If two couples wish to share a bathroom we also have our Oak Aged Room with double bed.

Breakfast includes homemade muffins and fresh fruit in season.

We are within walking distance of Greytown's Main Street with unique wooden Victorian architecture, cafes, and ten minutes drive to Martinborough's vineyards.

If you desire the ultimate privacy or a 'romantic getaway' we offer a "Blissful" cottage set in its own private garden featuring lovely old trees. Country Bliss Cottage has two double bedrooms, with own amenities including fire and bath. For tariff please contact Marilla Davis at above numbers.

Greytown   *Homestay B&B*   *Greytown central*

Kuratawhiti
Mary & Geoff Major
40 Kuratawhiti Street, Greytown,
Tel: (06) 304 9942 Fax: (06) 304 8942
Mob: 021 484 018   info@kuratawhiti.co.nz
www.kuratawhiti.co.nz

Double $120-$150 Single $90-$120 (Full Breakfast)
Child $30 Dinner $40 Credit cards accepted
Child at home Children welcome
1 King/Twin 2 Queen (3 bdrm)
1 Ensuite 1 Private 1 Guests share

Kuratawhiti, built in 1892, is one of South Wairarapa's finest historic properties, set in an acre of mature trees and gardens. A short walk to Greytown village, it is the ideal place for a relaxing retreat or as a base to explore the Wairarapa region. We are a young family with children; families are welcome and we offer babysitting. We have travelled extensively, love reading, music and meeting new people. Enjoy our outdoor spa, designer bed linen, fine wine, gourmet breakfasts and dinners.

Featherston   *B&B*

Woodland Holt Bed & Breakfast   Judi Adams
47 Watt Street, Featherston
Tel: (06) 308 9927 Mob: 025 291 2774
woodland-holt@xtra.co.nz
www.bnb.co.nz/woodlandholtbedbreakfast.html

Double $100-$125 Single $60-$65
(Continental Breakfast) Dinner $35
Credit cards accepted Pet on property
1 Queen 1 Double 1 Twin 1 Single (4 bdrm)
1 Ensuite 1 Guests share

Providing friendly hospitality. Interests include travelling, gardening, books, music, cross-stitch and collecting. Secluded gardens contain native, exotic and rare plants. Warm, luxury accommodation with off street parking. Breakfast includes home made treats and preserves. Explore beautiful Wairarapa or relax in comfort. View Meakin-at-Woodland, an extensive private collection of china by Alfred Meakin, and J&G Meakin. Dine at a local restaurant or arrange to join me for an evening meal. Picnic hampers are available (additional charge). We look forward to your company and making your stay enjoyable.

Martinborough   *Homestay B&B*   *0.5km NW of Martinborough*

Oak House
Polly & Chris Buring
45 Kitchener Street, Martinborough
Tel: (06) 306 9198 Fax: (06) 306 8198
chrispolly.oakhouse@xtra.co.nz
www.bnb.co.nz/oakhouse.html

Double $100-$120 Single $55
(Special Breakfast) Child by arrangement
Dinner by arrangement Pet on property
2 Queen 2 Single (3 bdrm)   1 Ensuite 1 Guests share

Our characterful eighty year old Californian bungalow offers gracious accommodation. Our spacious lounge provides a relaxed setting for sampling winemaker Chris' wonderful products. Our guest wing has its own entrance, bathroom (large bath and shower) and separate wc. Our new bedroom has ensuite facilities. Bedrooms enjoy afternoon sun and garden views. Breakfast features fresh croissants, home preserved local fruits and conserves. Creative cook Polly matches delicious dishes (often local game) with Chris' great wines. Tour our onsite winery with Chris. Meet our multi-talented cats.

Martinborough
Homestay gardens   *1km SW of Martinborough*

Ross Glyn
Kenneth & Odette Trigg
1 Grey Street, Martinborough
Tel: (06) 306 9967 Fax: (06) 306 8267
rossglyn1@hotmail.com
www.bnb.co.nz/rossglyn.html

Double $90 Single $55 (Continental & Full Breakfast)
Dinner $25+ Credit cards accepted
Pet on property Children welcome
1 Double 2 Single (2 bdrm) 1 Private 1 Guests share

Our home nestles in over three acres of landscaped gardens which includes a Camellia Walk, Woodlands, Sunken Rose Garden, Orchard and Pond area, and we are surrounded by Vineyards. Both our guestrooms have french doors opening onto a sunny deck with private access. Guests are welcome to relax with us and our small spoilt dog and cat in our large cosy (woodburner heated) lounge. Breakfast includes fresh croissants, homemade jams, jellies and preserved fruit. Cooked breakfast on request and dinner by arrangement.

Martinborough
B&B Country B&B   *4km E of Martinborough*

Alder Hey
Sheryll & John Lett
Hinakura Road, RD 4, Martinborough
Tel: (06) 306 9599 Fax: (06) 306 9598
Mob: 025 247 5012
bnb@alderhey.co.nz
www.alderhey.co.nz

Double $110-$120 Single $80 (Full Breakfast)
 Credit cards accepted Pet on property
2 Queen 1 Twin (2 bdrm) 1 Ensuite 1 Private

Nestled in a pretty valley five minutes drive east of Martinborough, we are close to the golf course and vineyards. The spacious and comfortable guest wing has its own entrance, with a lounge/library overlooking our olive grove which leads down to the trout stream on our boundary. Great country breakfasts with farm fresh eggs in our farmhouse kitchen or on the deck on a lovely Wairarapa morning. Walk in the country, visit a vineyard. John speaks conversational German and French. We warmly welcome you!

Martinborough
Self-contained   *Martinborough Central*

Martinborough Retreat
John & Jenny Simpson
79 Dublin Street, Martinborough
Tel: (04) 474 4494 Fax: (04) 473 7717
Mob: 025 760 115   jns@sievwrights.co.nz
www.bnb.co.nz/martinboroughretreat.html

Double $140 (Continental Breakfast)
Child $30 Additional adults $40
1 Queen 1 Double 1 Twin 1 Single (3 bdrm)
1 Ensuite 1 Private

The "Martinborough Retreat" is only five minutes walk from the Square, close to vineyards cafes/restaurants, golf course, tennis courts etc. Contemporary, spacious, fully furnished, character, two storey home (open plan), el fresco dining on large deck with outdoor furniture and gas barbecue. All facilities, TV/Video, radio/CD, microwave, dishwasher, washing machine, gas heater, and wood burner. Large flat grassed area with fruit trees. Ideal for self-catering family or group. Futons in lounge and mezzanine (plus 2 foldaway beds) - sleep 6 - 13.

Martinborough - Wairarapa *Self-contained B&B   Martinborough Central*

Beatson's of Martinborough

John Cooper & Karin Beatson
9A Cologne Street,
Martinborough, Wairarapa

Tel: (06) 306 8242 Fax: (06) 306 8243 Mob: 0274 499 827
beatsons@wise.net.nz
www.bnb.co.nz/beatson.html

Double $120-$150 Single $100 (Full Breakfast)
Dinner by arrangement Credit cards accepted Pet on property
3 King/Twin 4 Queen 1 Double (8 bdrm)
8 Ensuite

Hosts Karin Beatson and John Cooper offer you a friendly and relaxed stay in their 1905 houses "Harrington" and "Cologne", lovingly restored as boutique accommodation, to ensure your year-round comfort.

Furnishing includes some antiques and an interesting collection of New Zealand paintings and crafts. Polished matai floors, high ceilings and individually decorated, spacious bedrooms with ensuites feature. In the living areas, french doors open onto verandahs, with tables overlooking the garden with its cottage plantings, natives, fruits trees and herbs. Woodburners provide winter warmth. Great home cooking includes speciality country breakfasts using local products, homemade breads and preserves. (Dinners and functions by arrangement).

"Heriot Cottage" is a one-bedroomed self-contained comfortable colonial garden cottage featuring an original clawfoot bath, and a verandah to sip wine on.

Beatson's of Martinborough are just five minutes walk from Martinborough Square with its cafes, restaurants and speciality shops. Close to vineyards.

Martinborough   *Homestay   1km Martinborough*

The Old Manse
Sandra & John Hargrave
Cnr Grey & Roberts Streets, Martinborough,
Tel: (06) 306 8599 Fax: (06) 306 8540
Mob: 025 399 229   Tollfree: 0800 399 229
info@oldmanse.co.nz
www.oldmanse.co.nz
Double $130-$150 (Full Breakfast)
Credit cards accepted
5 Queen 1 Twin (6 bdrm) 6 Ensuite

In the heart of the wine district, a beautifully restored Presbyterian Manse, built in 1876, has been transformed into a boutique homestay. Spacious relaxed accommodation in quiet, peaceful setting. One twin plus five Queensize bedrooms all with their own ensuites. All day sun. Off street parking and open fireplace. Amenities include spa pool, petanque and billiards. Enjoy breakfast or wine overlooking vineyard. Walking distance to Martinborough Square with a selection of excellent restaurants. Close to vineyards, antique and craft shops, adventure quad bikes and golf courses.

Western Lake   *Homestay Rural   35km S of Featherston*

Tarawai
Maria Wallace & Ron Allan
Western Lake Road, Palliser Bay
Tel: (06) 307 7660 Fax: (06) 307 7661
Mob: 025 218 5889
tarawai@xtra.co.nz
www.bnb.co.nz/tarawai.html
Double $150-$190 (Continental Breakfast)
Credit cards accepted
2 King/Twin 1 Queen (3 bdrm)   3 Ensuite

We enjoy welcoming guests to our award winning contemporary home which overlooks the dramatically scenic Palliser Bay. The house is designed for space, comfort and warmth and to take advantage of the spectacular views. We also have a sauna. We offer delicious meals of fresh healthy food. We have walking tracks through our 20 hectares of native bush and there is good tramping, mountain biking, fishing, beach and bush walking close to Tarawai. Smoking outdoors only please. 24 hour Internet access available, laundry service available.

Ensuite and private bathrooms
are for your use exclusively.
Guest share bathroom means you
will be sharing with other guests.
Family share means you
will be sharing with the family.

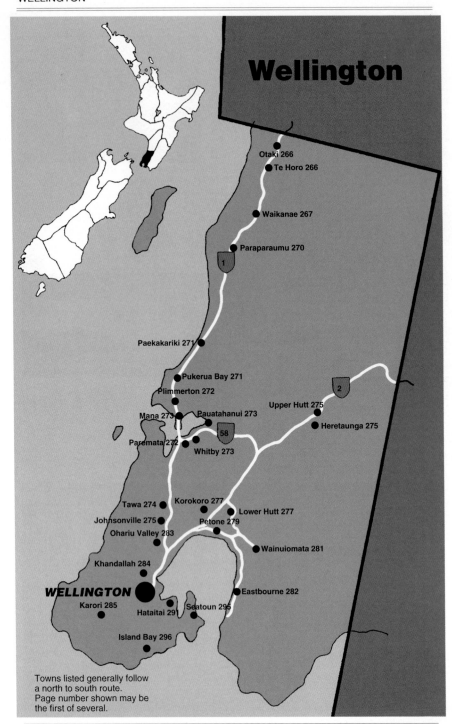

Wellington

Otaki 266
Te Horo 266

Waikanae 267

Paraparaumu 270
1

Paekakariki 271

Pukerua Bay 271
Plimmerton 272

2

Mana 273
Pauatahanui 273

Upper Hutt 275

Heretaunga 275

Paremata 272
58
Whitby 273

Tawa 274
Korokoro 277

Lower Hutt 277

Johnsonville 275
Petone 279

Ohariu Valley 283

Wainuiomata 281

Khandallah 284

WELLINGTON

Eastbourne 282

Karori 285
Hataitai 291
Seatoun 295

Island Bay 296

Towns listed generally follow
a north to south route.
Page number shown may be
the first of several.

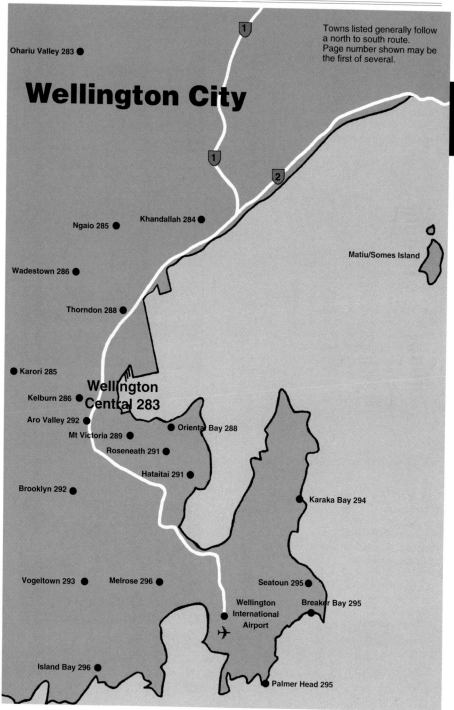

Wellington City

Ohariu Valley 283 ●

Towns listed generally follow
a north to south route.
Page number shown may be
the first of several.

WELLINGTON

Matiu/Somes Island

Ngaio 285 ●

Khandallah 284 ●

Wadestown 286 ●

Thorndon 288 ●

● Karori 285

Wellington Central 283

Kelburn 286 ●

Aro Valley 292 ●

● Oriental Bay 288

Mt Victoria 289 ●

Roseneath 291 ●

Hataitai 291 ●

Brooklyn 292 ●

● Karaka Bay 294

Vogeltown 293 ●

Melrose 296 ●

Seatoun 295 ●

Breaker Bay 295 ●

Wellington
International
Airport

Island Bay 296 ●

● Palmer Head 295

Otaki   *Homestay B&B & Art Studio*   *72km N of Wellington City*

Waitohu Lodge
Mary & Keith Oldham
294 Main Highway, Otaki, Wellington

Tel: (06) 364 5389 Fax: (06) 364 5350
Tollfree: 0800 364 239   waitohulodge@xtra.co.nz
www.bnb.co.nz/waitohulodge.html

Double $75-$95 Single $60 (Full Breakfast)
Child $30 Credit cards accepted Pet on property
1 Queen 4 Single (3 bdrm)
1 Private 1 Guests share

Waitohu Lodge, your "QUALITY AWARD" winning homestay is ideally located, easy to find and only 50 mins drive to Wellington City and the Picton ferry. Set back from the highway in trees and gardens we offer you quality, spacious, smokefree accommodation and friendly country hospitality. Enjoy comfortable beds, garden views, spabath and showers, guest lounge with television, books and complimentary tea/coffee, delicious breakfasts. Keith taught Geography, Mary paints, we enjoy people, travel, wines, our own homegrown produce and Burmese cat Raj. WELCOME.

Te Horo   *Homestay Country*   *65km N of Wellington*

Te Horo Lodge
Craig Garner
109 Arcus Road, Te Horo, Kapiti Coast

Tel: (06) 364 3393 Fax: (06) 364 3323
Mob: 025 306 009   Tollfree: 0800 483 467
reservations@tehorolodge.co.nz
www.bnb.co.nz/tehorolodge.html

Double $185-$230 Single $135-$165 (Full Breakfast)
Dinner $45 by arrangement Credit cards accepted
4 King/Twin 1 Single (4 bdrm)   4 Ensuite

Our purpose-built Lodge offers a relaxing tranquil environment set next to five acres of gardens and orchards and surrounded by another five acres of native bush. The downstairs guest rooms open on to a veranda and expansive lawns. The upstairs master suite features a large cathedral window looking into the tree tops and the serenity of the bush. A feature stone fireplace anchors the lounge. The grounds include a swimming pool, spa, gazebo and petanque court. Home cooked evening meals are available by prior arrangement.The Lodge is not suitable for children.

Te Horo   *Homestay B&B*   *3km S of Otaki*

Cottle Bush
Jon Allan & Roz White
990a State Highway 1, Te Horo 5560,

Tel: (06) 364 3566 Mob: 021 254 3501
jonandroz@msn.com
www.bnb.co.nz/cottlebush.html

Double $90-$120 Single $65-$80 Dinner $30
Pet on property
2 Queen 1 Twin (3 bdrm)
1 Ensuite 1 Guests share

Roz and Jon invite you to share their spacious two storey, smoke free home, nestled among the mature native totara, matai and titoki trees of Cottle Bush. Join us and our friendly dogs for a relaxing stay in a secluded rural atmosphere, not far from local attractions and ammenities and only an hour from Wellington. When you wake,enjoy your choice of cooked or continental breakfast. In the evening dine at a local restaurant or join us for dinner. Please make contact prior to arrival by letter, phone or e-mail.

Waikanae Beach   *Homestay B&B*   *5km W of Waikanae*

Waikanae Beach Homestay
Pauline & Allan Jones
115 Tutere Street, Waikanae
Tel: (04) 293 6532 Fax: (04) 293 6543
Mob: 025 300 785
albeach@paradise.net.nz
www.bnb.co.nz/joneswaikanaebeach.html
Double $90 Single $50 (Full Breakfast)
Child $20, under 8 $10 Credit cards accepted
2 Queen 1 Single (2 bdrm)   1 Ensuite 1 Private

Pauline and Allan invite you to enjoy the relaxing comfort of their sunny open plan home, with panoramic views of Kapiti Island and the Tararua Ranges. We have direct access to a sandy beach. An ideal place to break your journey. Guest laundry, tea and coffee making facilities are available at all times. Local attractions include Lindale Tourist Centre, Southwards Car Museum, Nga Manu Nature Reserve, a golf course and Kapiti Island Reserve - visits need to be booked. Our interests include music and crafts. Directions: Please phone.

Waikanae Beach   *Self-contained*   *5km W of Waikanae*

Konini Cottage
Maggie & Bob Smith
26 Konini Crescent, Waikanae Beach
Tel: (04) 904 6610 Fax: (04) 904 6610
konini@paradise.net.nz
www.bnb.co.nz/koninicottage.html
Double $80 (Full Breakfast)
Child $10 Optional full breakfast
$15pp $20 extra person Credit cards accepted
1 Double 2 Single (2 bdrm)   1 Private

The Lockwood cottage, set in one acre of grounds, bordering the golf links, is 300 metres from the beach. Fully equipped kitchen for self-catering, open plan living area, laundry facilities and tastefully furnished. If you choose to have breakfast you may either join us in our home or have it served in the privacy of the cottage. Directions: turn off SH1 at traffic lights to beach. 4kms to old petrol station, take right fork, then 1st right, 1km to Konini Crescent.

Waikanae   *Self-contained*   *1km E of Waikanae*

Country Patch
Sue & Brian Wilson
18 Kea Street, Waikanae
Tel: (04) 293 5165 Fax: (04) 293 5164
Mob: 027 457 8421 booking@countrypatch.co.nz
www.bnb.co.nz/countrypatch.html
Double $95-$160 Single $70-$120
(Continental Breakfast) Child $25
Dinner By arrangement Credit cards accepted
Pet on property Children welcome
2 King/Twin 1 Queen 2 Single (3 bdrm)   3 Ensuite

Two delightful self contained accommodation sites with. Country patch studio with its own entrance and deck has a queen bed with ensuite and twin beds on the mezzanine floor of the kitchen lounge. Country patch villa has an open fire and a large verandah with magic views. It is wheelchair accessible and the two bedrooms (each with ensuite) have king beds that unzip to twin. We warmly invite you to share our patch of the country with Kate (16), Simon (14) and Holly our labrador.

Waikanae *Homestay* *58km N of Wellington*

Millrest
Colleen & Gordon Butchers
57 Park Avenue, Waikanae, Kapiti Coast
Tel: (04) 904 2424 Fax: (04) 904 2424
topdog@paradise.net.nz
www.bnb.co.nz/millrest.html
Double $90 Single $65 (Full Breakfast)
Dinner by arrangement Credit cards accepted
Less 10% if prebooked by night before
1 Queen 1 Twin (2 bdrm) 1 Private

We invite you to share the informal lifestyle in our warm spacious home set in park like surroundings on your next holiday. We are an active retired couple who enjoy welcoming new friends and helping them to take advantage of the attractions of the Kapiti Coast and New Zealand. Alternatively if you feel like peace and tranquillity this will suit you too as we host only one party at a time. Buffy, our beagle cross dog shares our smoke free home. Not suitable for children under 10 years. Directions: Please phone, write or fax.

Waikanae *Self-contained & Homestay*

Sudbury Homestay and Garden
Glenys and Brian Daw
39 Manu Grove, Waikanae 6010
Tel: (04) 902 8530 Fax: (04) 902 8531
Mob: 021 129 6970 stay@sudbury.co.nz
www.sudbury.co.nz
Double $120-$150 Single $100-$120
(Continental Breakfast) (Special Breakfast)
Dinner by arrangement Credit cards accepted
2 Queen (2 bdrm) 1 Ensuite 1 Guests share

'Our place is yours' while you're here! Set in a beautiful 2.5 acre garden with its natural bush and native birds, rhododendrons, camellias, roses, and water-lilies in the large pond, Sudbury provides a very tranquil environment in which to relax. Your hosts enjoy entertaining, wine, having people to stay and while you are here your comfort is their priority. Sudbury's modern buildings offer you the choice of traditional homestay or charming self-contained cottage. Ample off-street parking available. Handy to SH1, rail and local award-winning restaurants.

Waikanae *Self-contained Rural Homestay* *6km E of Waikanae*

RiverStone
Paul & Eppie Murton
111 Ngatiawa Road, Waikanae
Tel: (04) 293 1936 Fax: (04) 293 1936
riverstone@paradise.net.nz
www.bnb.co.nz/riverstone.html
Double $100 Single $70 (Full Breakfast)
Child $45 Credit cards accepted
1 Queen 1 Twin (2 bdrm)
1 Private

Birdsong, the sound of the river and complete privacy. Peace and quiet with a scrumptious breakfast and comfortable accommodation. Riverstone has five hectares of paddocks and garden with river walks and local pottery and cafe. Waikanae, Raumati and Paraparaumu have a variety of cafes, shops, boutiques, Lindale farm park, the Southward Car museum, Nga Manu bird sanctuary, golf courses and beautiful beaches. Pick up from train or bus. Laundry facilities. Smoke free. No pets.

Discover Tranquillity ... and ... Luxurious Relaxation

Waikanae   *B&B Boutique Lodge*   *52km N of Wellington*

HURUNUI HOMESTEAD

Erica & Geoff Lineham, 15 Hurunui Street, Waikanae

Tel: (04) 902 8571 Fax: (04) 902 8572

hurunui@lineham.co.nz   www.hurunui.lineham.co.nz

Double $130-$160 Single $100-$120 (Special Breakfast)
Credit cards accepted
2 Queen 1 Double (3 bdrm)
1 Ensuite 1 Private 1 Guests share

Just 50 minutes from Wellington city centre is the pretty seaside village of Waikanae, and the romantic retreat of **Hurunui Homestead**. This gracious boutique lodge is for the discerning guest wanting to enjoy warm hospitality with superb accommodation and facilities in a unique garden and native bush setting.

Hollybrook Room has antique furniture and ensuite bathroom. **Country Garden Room** has french country style furnishings and separate private bathroom. If friends/family travelling together wish to share a bathroom we have the **South Pacific Room** with four poster iron double bed.

Downstairs living rooms open onto large sunny courtyard. The 2 acre park-like secluded gardens contain heated pool (summer), private spa (jacuzzi), tennis and petanque courts, gazebo, native bush walk, and ample off-street parking. Erica is an art quilter with onsite studio/gallery. Restaurants, shopping, top class golf courses and long sandy beaches nearby. **Indulge and Enjoy!**

Directions: Take SH1 to Waikanae. Turn at BP petrol station into Ngaio Rd. Take first right into Parata St, left into Sylvan Ave, right into David St, left into Hurunui St. Hurunui Homestead is signposted at the end of the cul-de-sac.   Member Tourism Industry Assn. NZ. & Kapiti Home Hosts Assn.

Waikanae *Self-contained B&B*   *3km E of Waikanae*

Burnard Gardens
Mary & Robert Burnard
236 Reikorangi Road, Waikanae,
Tel: (04) 293 3371 Fax: (04) 293 3378
mary@burnardgardens.co.nz
www.burnardgardens.co.nz
Double $100-$120 Single $80-$100 (Full Breakfast)
Child $10 Pet on property
1 Queen 1 Single (1 bdrm)
1 Private

We have a 20-acre property of which half is an English-style garden, featured in 'Great Gardens of New Zealand' (pub. HarperCollins) by Derek Fell. The B&B studio unit, situated directly behind the house, is very spacious and occupies the top floor above a 3-car garage. It has cosy dormer alcoves and barndoors overlooking part of the garden. The room has two beds, a kitchenette, lounge and dining areas as well as toilet facilities. A private bathroom is downstairs. Guests are welcome to stroll through the garden, play tennis or swim in the Waikanae River, which bounds the property.

Paraparaumu *Homestay*   *60km N of Wellington*

Jude & Vic Young
72 Bluegum Road,
Paraparaumu
Tel: (04) 902 0199 Fax: (04) 902 0199
www.bnb.co.nz/youngparaparaumu.html
Double $75 Single $45 (Full Breakfast)
Child 1/2 price Dinner $20
1 Double 1 Single (2 bdrm)
1 Private 1 Family share

Our 1950's beach house has hill and island views and is situated two blocks back from Marine Parade. Shops, golf course, airport, cafes and excellent restaurants are 1-2km walk away. Off-street parking is provided and we will meet bus or train. Jude is, with prior notice, pleased to provide meals for those on special diets. We love walking, food, music, and Citroens. Non smokers preferred. We have a cat. Directions: watch for yellow letterbox on seaward corner of Bluegum and Rua Roads.

Paraparaumu *Self-contained*   *55km N of Wellington*

M & S Homestay
Sytske & Marius Kruiniger
60A Ratanui Road, Paraparaumu
Tel: (04) 299 8098 Fax: (04) 297 3447
After hours no: (04) 297 3447
www.bnb.co.nz/mshomestay.html
Double $65 Single $50
Child $5 under 5yrs extra persons $10
Continental breakfast (optional), $5 pp.
Credit cards accepted Children welcome
1 Queen 2 Single (2 bdrm) 1 Private

Our self-contained accommodation is peaceful and sunny. A view across small lake, full with wildlife. Beach, shopping centre and excellent restaurants close by. Sunny lounge with t.v., books and games; well equipped kitchen, bathroom and laundry facilities. Information about indoor and outdoor attractions available. No dogs please and guests are asked not to smoke indoors. Please phone or fax for bookings and directions. We look forward meeting you.

Paraparaumu Beach *Homestay   5.5km NW of Paraparaumu*

Beachstay
Ernie & Rhoda Stevenson
17 Takahe Drive, Kotuku Park, Paraparaumu Beach
Tel: (04) 902 6466 Fax: (04) 902 6466
Mob: 025 232 5106
www.bnb.co.nz/beachstayparaparaumu.html

Double $75 Single $50 (Continental Breakfast)
Child $20 Dinner $25 by arrangement
Credit cards accepted
1 Double 2 Single (2 bdrm) 1 Private

Enjoy warm friendly hospitality in the relaxing atmosphere of our modern new home. Peaceful surroundings next to river estuary and beach. Wonderful views of sea, lake and hills. Lovely coastal and river walks. Tourist attractions include trips to Kapiti Island Bird Sanctuary. Paraparaumu Beach world ranking Golf Course six minutes drive. South Island Ferry Terminal 45 minutes away. We are newly retired non smokers who enjoy meeting people. We love our NZ scenery and bush walking. Ernie paints landscapes. Enquiries welcome. NZAFFH members.

Paekakariki *Homestay   10km S of Paraparaumu*

Killara Homestay
Carole & Don Boddie
70 Ames Street, Paekakariki
Tel: (04) 905 5544 Fax: (04) 905 5533
Mob: 025 944 551
killara@paradise.net.nz
www.killarahomestay.co.nz

Double $110-$130 Single $100-$110
(Continental Breakfast) Credit cards accepted
1 Queen 1 Twin (2 bdrm) 1 Private

Relax, enjoy the sound of the sea, fabulous views and direct beach access from our absolute beachfront home. Spacious accommodation upstairs includes a guest lounge,with outstanding views from Kapiti Island to the South Island. Internet and laundry facilities available. We host one party at a time. Have a relaxing spa bath; enjoy beach activities (surf-casting gear available); walk to local cafes/restaurants; or explore the Kapiti Coast. 15 minutes to 5 golf courses, 30 minutes to Wellington. Close to shops/transport.

Pukerua Bay *Homestay   32km N of Wellington*

Sheena's Homestay
Sheena Taylor
2 Gray Street, Pukerua Bay 6010, Kapiti Coast
Tel: (04) 239 9947 Fax: (04) 239 9942
Mob: 025 602 1503 homestay@sheenas.co.nz
www.bnb.co.nz/sheenashomestay.html

Double $70 Single $45 (Full Breakfast) Child $20
Dinner by arrangement Credit cards accepted
Pet on property Children welcome
1 Double 1 Twin 1 Single (2 bdrm) 1 Family share

Come share our warm, sunny refurbished smokefree home. Relax in the conservatory - enjoy the views. We have two friendly cats -Tabitha & Sienna. Pukerua Bay, home of creative people, has an interesting beach about 15 mins walk. Railway station closeby. Sheena is a keen spinner - spinning wheel/fibre available to use. Restaurants & cafes 5-15 mins drive. Most special diets catered for, lunches arranged. Smokers seat. Undercover off-street parking; laundry facilities; garaging for bikes; powerpoint small campervans; cot & highchair. Personal care for people with disabilities.

Plimmerton   *B&B*   *20mins N of Wellington*

Beachside
Brian & Mary Wesley-Smith
9 Beach Road, Plimmerton,

Tel: (04) 233 9469 Fax: (04) 233 9427
Mob: 021 620 782   wesley-smith@xtra.co.nz
www.bnb.co.nz/user11.html

Double $120 Single $110 (Continental Breakfast)
Child $50 Credit cards accepted Pet on property
1 Queen (1 bdrm) 1 Ensuite

We would love to share our 90 year old beachside house with you. Our guest accommodation is in a private wing with its own entrance from a charming courtyard. It features a spacious bed-sitting room with ensuite, as well as TV, coffee-making facilities, and fridge. We are situated right on the beach - so you can dive into the waves right from our front steps (providing the tide is in!) or simply laze on the sand! We have a kayak and mountain bikes which you are welcome to use. At our back door is Plimmerton village with a wide selection of restaurants, and the railway station is a two minute walk away. We have a cat and a friendly back Labrador. Children are welcome.

Plimmerton   *Self-contained Farmstay Separate/Suite*   *20min N of Wellington*

Southridge Farm
Katrina and Andrew Smith
Southridge, 96 The Track, Plimmerton, Wellington

Tel: (04) 233 1104 Fax: (04) 233 1112
aksmith@paradise.net.nz
www.bnb.co.nz/southrigefarm.html

Double $90 Single $70 (Continental Breakfast)
Child negotiable Child at home Pet on property
Children welcome Pets welcome
1 Queen 1 Single (1 bdrm) 1 Ensuite

We have it all at 'Southridge Farm'. Rural but very central. State Highway 1, beach, trains and restaurants all only 1km away. Major shopping centre 7km away. We have a lovely modern self-contained cottage with kitchen including washing machine if self-catering is preferred. Couch has a sofabed. Cot and foldaway bed also available. All outside animals including horses can be accommodated with notice. Andrew & Katrina, child Lachlan and farm dog Penny warmly invite you to share in our relaxing rural experience.

Paremata   *Homestay*   *26km N of Wellington*

Penryn Cove
Eleanor & John Clark
32 Penryn Drive, Paremata, Wellington

Tel: (04) 233 8265 Fax: (04) 233 8265
Mob: 025 815 525   JWClark@xtra.co.nz
www.bnb.co.nz/penryncove.html

Double $120 Single $95 (Full Breakfast)
Child Neg. Dinner by arrangement
Credit cards accepted Pet on property
2 Queen (2 bdrm) 1 Private 1 Guests share

We extend a warm welcome to our guests. Enjoy the tranquil, peaceful setting of 'Penryn Cove' surrounded by native bush reserve, set on the edge of a peninsula overlooking the Pauatahanui inlet and bird sanctuary. Easy access onto inlet walkway will provide you with some relaxing recreation. We have travelled extensively, enjoy meeting and sharing with fellow travellers. Easy walking distance to cafes, restaurants, shops, rail. Private spacious guest area with magical views, private deck. Directions: 2 minutes from State Highway 1. Please phone for directions.

Mana *B&B* *13km N of Wellington*

Le Solaire
Irene Denford
16A Mana View Road, Mana, Wellington
Tel: (04) 233 8407 Fax: (04) 233 8450
Mob: 025 439 822   irene.denford@xtra.co.nz
www.bnb.co.nz/lesolaire.html

Double $110-$135 Single $80 (Special Breakfast)
Child free Credit cards accepted
1 King 1 Queen (2 bdrm) 2 Ensuite

Dream away the evenings on one of the many decks whilst listening to good music and watching the sun set over the South Island. Modern, sunny three level home, with off street parking. Situated just 2 minutes walk from restaurants, train station, beaches and beautiful Pauatahanui Inlet. Wellington CBD 20 minutes by car or train, and Porirua city 4 kilometres. Home has spectacular sea views and spacious lounges. Guest rooms have lounge chairs, television, tea/coffee facilities and internet lines. Both have ensuit bathrooms, one with spa bath. Host is well travelled and has many interests, including art, theatre, music and trout fishing.

Whitby *Homestay* *10km NE of Porirua*

Oldfields
Elaine & John Oldfield
22 Musket Lane,
Whitby, Wellington
Tel: (04) 234 1002 Mob: 021 254 0869
oldfields@paradise.net.nz
www.bnb.co.nz/oldfield.html

Double $85 Single $55 (Full Breakfast)
Dinner $25 Credit cards accepted Pet on property
2 Queen (2 bdrm)
1 Guests share

Our home is situated in a quiet cul-de-sac street, with large decks overlooking garden and bush. As we are on our own with our two pet cats, we would really enjoy the company of New Zealand and overseas visitors. Having travelled and lived overseas we are always interested in other peoples experiences. We are ten minutes by car to Paremata train station and main highway, 25 minutes to Wellington city. We assure you of a warm welcome and memorable stay. House smoke free.

Pauatahanui *Homestay Self-contained Suites* *25km N of Wellington*

Braebyre Rural Homestay
Jenny & Randall Shaw
Flightys Rd, Pauatahanui, RD 1, Porirua
Tel: (04) 235 9311 Fax: (04) 235 9345
Tollfree: 0800 36 93 11   braebyre@paradise.net.nz
www.braebyrehomestay.co.nz

Double $100-$160 Single $90-$150 (Full Breakfast)
Child neg Dinner $40 Credit cards accepted
1 King/Twin 1 King 1 Queen 1 Double 1 Twin (5 bdrm)
3 Ensuite 1 Guests share

Looking for something special away from city noise? Stay near but not in the City. "Braebyre", one of Wellington's fine countryhomes, is easily found on state Highway 58 - the Northern Gateway. Two luxury studio suites nestle in the large landscaped gardens surrounding "Braebyre", on a mohair goat farm. The guest wing (with separate entrance) includes a lounge with table tennis, log fire and indoor spa pool. Evening dinner with your hosts, featuring homegrown produce, is available on request. Laundry $5.

Tawa   *Homestay   15km N of Wellington*

Tawa Homestay
Jeannette & Alf Levick
17 Mascot Street, Tawa, Wellington
Tel: (04) 232 5989 Fax: (04) 232 5987
milsom.family@xtra.co.nz
www.bnb.co.nz/tawahomestay.html
Double $85 Single $50 (Special Breakfast)
Dinner $20pp Credit cards accepted
1 Queen 1 Single (2 bdrm)
1 Family share

Our comfortable family home is in a quiet street in Tawa. We have a separate toilet, shower and spa bath. Freshly ground coffee a speciality, with breakfast of your choice. Jeannette's interests are: Ikebana, Japanese, German languages, porcelain painting, knitting, dressmaking, playing tennis, learning to play golf and the piano and gardening. Alf's interests are: Amateur radio, woodwork, Toastmasters international - and being allowed to help in the garden. We are both members of LIONS INTERNATIONAL.

Tawa   *Homestay   15km N of Wellington*

Joy & Bill Chaplin
3 Kiwi Place, Tawa, Wellington
Tel: (04) 232 5547 Fax: (04) 232 5547
Mob: 025 349 078
chapta@xtra.co.nz
www.bnb.co.nz/chaplin.html
Double $90 Single $45 (Full Breakfast)
Dinner by arrangement
1 Double 1 Single (2 bdrm)
1 Guests share

No. 3 is situated in a quiet street 7 minutes by car and rail to Porirua City and 15 minutes from Wellington and the InterIsland Ferry Terminal. Our house is wheelchair friendly and we have an extra bedroom downstairs with single bed or cot if required at reduced rate of $25. Spa, laundry facilities also available. Safe off-street parking. Tawa is close to beaches, ten-pin bowling, swimming pool and fine walks. Our house is 'smokefree'. Dinner by arrangement. Please phone for directions.

Tawa   *Homestay B&B   15km NW of Wellington*

Jocelyn & David Perry
5 Fyvie Avenue, Linden, Tawa
Tel: (04) 232 7664 djperry@actrix.co.nz
www.bnb.co.nz/perry.html
Double $75 Single $40 (Continental Breakfast)
Child $20 Dinner $20pp by Arrangement
Credit cards accepted
1 Double 1 Twin 1 Single (3 bdrm)
1 Guests share 1 Family share

We are a retired couple. Together we welcome you to stay with us. We are 15kms from Wellington city. A five minute walk to the suburban rail station with half hourly service into the city (15 minutes) and north to the Kapiti Coast. Alternatively you can drive north to the Coast, enjoying sea and rural views before sampling tourist attractions in this area. We are happy to provide transport to and from the Interisland ferry. We are a smoke free household. Laundry facilities available.

Johnsonville *B&B   Homestay   1km N of Johnsonville*

Cherswud
Marilyn and David McDonald
121 Helston Rd, Johnsonville, Wellington
Tel: (04) 478 5017 Fax: (04) 478 5516
Mob: 025 84 12 15
marilyn@macmaz.co.nz
www.bnb.co.nz/cherswud.html

Double $90 Single $65 (Full Breakfast)
Child $40 Dinner $30 Credit cards accepted
2 Queen 1 Single (3 bdrm) 2 guests share

We are delighted to welcome you to join us at Cherswud, our fully restored 1919 home with two cats, two lounges, conservatory, sunny deck, spacious bedrooms and luxurious guest-share bathroom with spa bath and massage shower. Bedrooms with comfortable beds, electric blankets, feather duvets, well-stocked bookcases, tea and coffee. We offer smokefree accommodation and warm hospitality with delicious meals. Dinner, with wine, by prior arrangement, although eight restaurants are within 12 minutes' walk. Two minutes off SH1 and 10 minutes from the ferry.

Upper Hutt - Te Marua *Homestay   7.4km N of Upper Hutt*

Te Marua Homestay
Sheryl & Lloyd Homer
108A Plateau Road, Te Marua, Upper Hutt
Tel: (04) 526 7851 Fax: (04) 526 7866
Mob: 025 501 679 Tollfree: 0800 110 851
sheryl.lloyd@clear.net.nz
www.bnb.co.nz/homer.html

Double $80 Single $50 (Continental Breakfast)
Dinner $25pp b/a Credit cards accepted
1 Queen 1 Double (2 bdrm)
1 Private

Our home is situated in a secluded bush setting. Guests may relax on one of our private decks or read books from our extensive library. For the more energetic there are bush walks, bike trails, trout fishing, swimming and a golf course within walking distance. The guest wing has a kitchenette and television. Lloyd is a landscape photographer with over 30 years experience photographing New Zealand. Sheryl is a teacher. Travel, tramping, skiing, photography, music and meeting people are interests we enjoy.

Heretaunga *Self-contained Homestay B&B   7Km S of Upper Hutt*

Woodhenge Studio and Garden
Johanna and Andrew King
60 Barton Rd, Upper Hutt,
Tel: (04) 528 2680 Fax: (04) 528 2682
Mob: 025 241 8449 johanna@kingconsultants.co.nz
www.kingconsultants.co.nz

Double $130 Single $130
(Continental & Full Breakfast) Child $25
Credit cards accepted Pet on property
1 Queen 1 Single (1 bdrm) 1 Ensuite

We are a landscape architect and an earthquake research engineer. "Woodhenge" our large old colonial home and office is located in the Conservation Zone 20 minutes from Wellington, overlooking Wellington's premier golf course, (games arranged) adjacent to Trentham Memorial Park, Hutt River and Racecourse. Our garden is beautiful with historic trees, home to endangered native bird life. The studio is private, fully self-contained with ensuite, antique furniture, quality linen, queenbed, single sofabed, flowers, fruit, continental breakfasts. PS. We have excellent restaurants nearby.

Upper Hutt *Homestay B&B   30mins Wellington*

Tranquility Homestay
Elaine & Alan
136 Akatarawa Road,
Birchville, Upper Hutt

Tel: (04) 526 6948 Fax: (04) 526 6968 Mob: 025 405 962
Tollfree: 0800 270 787
tranquility@xtra.co.nz
www.bnb.co.nz/tranquility1.html

Double $98 Single $50-$98 (Continental Breakfast) Child neg. Dinner $20 by prior arrangement
Credit cards accepted Children welcome Pets welcome
1 Queen 2 Single (3 bdrm)
1 Ensuite 2 Family share

Executive Timeout/Homestay. Escape from the stress of City
Life just approx 30 minutes from Wellington off SH2. Close to
Upper Hutt - Restaurants, Cinema, Golf, Racecourse, leisure Centre (swimming), Bush Walks etc. We are near the confluence of
the Hutt and Akatarawa Rivers which is noted for its fishing.
13km to Staglands. Country setting, relax and listen to the New
Zealand Tuis and watch the fantails or Wood Pigeons, or just
simply relax and read. Comfortable and warm and friendly hospitality, Good New Zealand style food.

Upper Hutt   *Self-contained B&B*   *40km N of Wellington*

Eirane Rural Retreat
David and Mary Beachen
1029 Akatarawa Road, Birchville, Upper Hutt
Tel: (04) 526 3638 Fax: (04) 526 3628
beachen@paradise.net.nz
www.bnb.co.nz/eiraneruralretreat.html
Double $150 Single $130 (Full Breakfast) Child $40
Dinner $30 Credit cards accepted Child at home
1 King/Twin 2 Single (2 bdrm)
1 Private

Our luxurious home nestles on the banks of the Akatarawa River with a native bush backdrop. You can enjoy a walk down to the best private swimming hole on the river, tennis on the grass court, feed the sheep and shetland pony or soak in the spa pool. We are 35 minutes from Wellington CBD. We are close to golf courses, good restaurants and a large shopping centre. Our interests include travel, gardening,property investment and sport. We have three young children.

Lower Hutt - Korokoro   *Homestay*   *12km N of Wellington*

Western Rise
Virginia & Maurice Gibbens
10 Stanhope Grove, Korokoro, Lower Hutt
Tel: (04) 589 1872 Fax: (04) 589 1873
Mob: 025 438 316
www.bnb.co.nz/westernrise.html
Double $85-$100 Single $55-$85 (Full Breakfast)
Dinner $15 Credit cards accepted
1 Queen 2 Single (2 bdrm)
1 Guests share

Just off State Highway 2, very quiet area, a warm, welcome awaits. Our Terrier/Cross dog Ben loves guests. View Wellington's magnificent harbour relaxing over a meal in or out doors. Maurice is a fingerprint expert with the New Zealand Police and Virginia enjoys the time spent with guests. Laundry free if staying 2 consecutive nights. 10-13 minutes to Picton Ferry, handy to many restaurants. Of street parking. Telephone for directions.

Lower Hutt   *Homestay*

Judy & Bob's Place
Judy & Bob Vine
11 Ngaio Crescent, Lower Hutt
Tel: (04) 971 1192 Fax: (04) 971 6192
Mob: 021 510 682   bob.vine@paradise.net.nz
www.bnb.co.nz/judybobsplace.html
Single $50 (Full Breakfast) Dinner $25
Credit cards accepted
1 Queen 2 Single (2 bdrm)   1 Guests share

Our home is situated plumb in the centre of Woburn, a picturesque and quiet central city suburb of Lower Hutt, known for its generous sized houses and beautiful gardens. Within walking distance of the Lower Hutt downtown, 15 minutes drive from central Wellington and its Railway Station and Ferry terminals; Airport 25 minutes; 3 minutes walk to Woburn Rail Station. Separate lounge and TV. Love to entertain and share hearty Kiwi style cooking with good New Zealand wine. Laundry facilities. Directions: Please phone, fax, email or write. Transfer transport available. High speed and dial up Internet connections available.

Hutt City   *Self-contained*

Casa Bianca
Jo & Dave Comparini
10 Damian Grove,
Hutt City

Tel: (04) 569 7859 Fax: (04) 569 7859
dcompo@xtra.co.nz
www.bnb.co.nz/casabianca.html

Double $90 Single $65 (Continental Breakfast)
1 King 1 Single (1 bdrm)
1 Private

Our comfortable house is situated in the peaceful eastern hills of Lower Hutt. We are within easy reach of the city centre, the Open Polytech, Waterloo railway station. Wellington is 20 minutes by train or car. We have a self contained apartment with bedroom (double), bathroom, large lounge, fully equipped kitchen, extra single bed in lounge. Breakfast provisions provided in apartment. We aim to provide guests with time to relax at their leisure, and enjoy our special hospitality. Off street parking. No smoking please.

Lower Hutt   *Homestay   2km SE of Lower Hutt*

Dungarvin
Beryl & Trevor Cudby
25 Hinau Street, Woburn, Lower Hutt

Tel: (04) 569 2125 Fax: (04) 569 2126
t.b.cudby@clear.net.nz
www.bnb.co.nz/dungarvin.html

Double $90 Single $70 (Full Breakfast)
Dinner $30 by arrangement Credit cards accepted
2 Single (1 bdrm)
1 Private

Our 70-year-old cottage has been fully refurbished while retaining its original charm. It is 15 minutes from the Ferry terminal and the Stadium, and 20 minutes from the Museum of NZ, "Te Papa". Our home is centrally heated and the sunny guest bedroom looks over our secluded garden. The beds have electric blankets and down duvets. Vegetarians are catered for, laundry facilities are available and we have ample offstreet parking. Our main interests are travel, music, gardening, shows and NZ wines.

Lower Hutt   *Homestay B&B   0.5km SE of Lower Hutt Central*

Rose Cottage
Maureen & Gordon Gellen
70A Hautana Street, Lower Hutt, Wellington

Tel: (04) 566 7755 Fax: (04) 566 0777
Mob: 021 481 732   gellen@xtra.co.nz
www.bnb.co.nz/rosecottagelowerhutt.html

Double $95-$105 Single $60-$75 (Full Breakfast)
Dinner $30 by arrangement Credit cards accepted
Pet on property
1 Queen 1 Single (2 bdrm) 1 Ensuite 1 Family share

Relax in the comfort of our cosy home which is just a five minute walk to the Hutt City Centre. Originally built in 1910 the house has been fully renovated. We have travelled extensively Overseas and in NZ. Interests include Travel, Gardening, Sports and live Theatre. As well as TV in Guest room there's Coffee and Tea-making facilities. Breakfast will be served in our Dining room at your convenience. Unsuitable for children. We look forward to welcoming you into our smoke-free home which we share with Scuffin our cat.

Lower Hutt - Korokoro *12km N of Wellington*

B&B Vineyard Accommodation

Devenport Estate Alasdair, Christopher, Marlene
1 Korokoro Road, Korokoro, Lower Hutt
Tel: (04) 586 6868 Fax: (04) 586 6869
Mob: 025 274 0394   devenport_estate@hotmail.com
homepages.paradise.net.nz/devenpor

Double $100-$120 Single $80 (Continental Breakfast)
for private bathroom $150 Credit cards accepted
Pet on property Children welcome
1 Queen 1 Double 1 Single (2 bdrm)   1 Guests share

Stay at the closest vineyard to the capital. Close to Ferry/City & Stadium. An Edwardian-styled homestead overlooking Wellington Harbour, built at the turn of the century [2000!] based upon the MacDonald family home in Scotland. Built for views and comfort: guest living-room with woodburner; chairs, TV, writing-desk, hand-basin in guest bedrooms. Free Internet access, laundry service, Petone Station pickup – see Devenport's website for more details. Alasdair, Christopher, Marlene and two cocker spaniels, welcome you to a comfortable stay in Wellington on our vineyard estate.

Petone - Korokoro *2km W of Petone*

Matairangi
Kate & Barry Malcolm
29 Singers Road,
Korokoro, Petone
Tel: (04) 566 6010
barrym@actrix.co.nz
www.bnb.co.nz/malcolm.html
Double $80 Single $55 Child $30
1 Twin (1 bdrm)
1 Private

Welcome to our hectare of peaceful natural bush and native birds, a hilltop perch with amazing views over Wellington Harbour and surrounding hills. Here you can enjoy your own private ground floor space including sitting room with tea/coffee facilities. Upstairs, Kate and Barry look forward to your company. Our interests are forest restoration, beekeeping, gardening and local history. New laid eggs and freshly baked bread are on the breakfast menu. The ferry terminal is a 15 minute drive away. Also email, laundry, parking.

Lower Hutt - Stokes Valley *Homestay B&B*   *8km NE of Lower Hutt*

Kowhai B&B
Glenys & Peter Lockett
88a Manuka Street, Stokes Valley, Lower Hutt
Tel: (04) 563 6671 Mob: 025 433 341
p_g.lockett@xtra.co.nz
www.bnb.co.nz/kowhaibb.html
Double $85-$95 Single $70 (Full Breakfast)
Credit cards accepted Pet on property
1 Queen 1 Double (2 bdrm)
1 Private

We are surrounded by bush and gardens in a quiet street. Your rooms and large guest lounge are upstairs with private deck, Sky TV, stereo, tea/coffee facilities. We want you to feel relaxed, so take only one booking at a time. Lucy the cat shares our home. Nearby: golf, boutique cinema, racecourse, swimming pool, bush walks. Wellington CBD/Picton ferry 25 minutes. Lower/Upper Hutt, 15 minutes. We have travelled extensively and enjoy meeting people.

Petone   *Homestay*   *3km S of Lower Hutt*

Anne & Reg Cotter
1 Bolton Street,
Petone, Wellington
Tel: (04) 568 6960 Fax: (04) 568 6956
www.bnb.co.nz/cotter.html

Double $60 Single $30 (Full Breakfast)
Child 1/2 price over 10yrs Dinner $15
Credit cards accepted
1 Double 2 Single (2 bdrm)
1 Family share

We have a 100 year old home by the beach. We are two minutes from a Museum on beach, shop and bus route to the city. A restaurant is nearby. We are ten minutes from Picton Ferries. Off street parking available. Children are very welcome. Reg is a keen amateur ornithologist and goes to the Chatham Islands with an expedition trying to find the nestling place of the Taiko - a rare sea bird, on endangered list. Other interests are Genealogy and conservation. Laundry facilities are available.

Petone - Korokoro   *Homestay*   *2km W of Petone*

Korokoro Homestay
Bridget & Jim Austin
100 Korokoro Road, Korokoro, Petone
Tel: (04) 589 1678 Fax: (04) 589 2678
Mob: 025 260 4948   Tollfree: 0800 116 575
jaustin@clear.net.nz
www.bnb.co.nz/korokorohomestay.html

Double $90 Single $50 (Continental Breakfast)
Child by arrangement Dinner by arrangement
Credit cards accepted
1 Queen 1 Twin (2 bdrm)   1 Guests share

We have a large garden and Bush reserve, in a very quiet locality yet only 12 minutes to Wellington and Ferries. Easy to find. We came from England to New Zealand in 1957 and enjoy travel. Jim is a desultory woodworker with a background in machinery. Bridget teaches and is a weaver/feltmaker, working and selling from home. We enjoy visual arts, theatre, cinema, music, books and the outdoors. Your food will be home-cooked and mainly organic as we prefer an environmentally friendly lifestyle.

Petone - Korokoro   *B&B*   *10km N of Wellington*

Sea Breeze
Craig & Bronnie Lyne
4 Green Park Lane, Petone, Lower Hutt
Tel: (04) 586 0025 Fax: (04) 586 0026
Mob: 025 453 742   info@seabreezehomestay.co.nz
seabreeze.co.nz

Double $245 Single $175 (Special Breakfast)
Child $175 Dinner $45 Credit cards accepted
Pet on property Children welcome
1 King/Twin (0 bdrm) 1 Ensuite 1 Private

Welcome to our home. Bronnie and Craig enjoy having people to stay and we would make your stay a memorable one. Our home has all the elements of a secluded executive, romantic or business retreat, with all day sun and panoramic views of the ocean and Wellington city. The spacious guestroom comprises of private lounge, bathroom, Sky TV, kingsize bed, central heating, tea and coffee-making facilities. We have all the benefits of the city, cafes, shopping and entertainment - or for the outdoor type - golf, beaches and bushwalks. We love it here, so will you.

Wainuiomata   *Self-contained Homestay B&B   6km E of Lower Hutt*

Kaponga House
Hilary Wharemate
22 Kaponga Street,
Wainuiomata

Tel: (04) 564 3495 after 5pm Fax: (04) 564 3495
hilwha@xtra.co.nz
www.bnb.co.nz/kaponga.html

Double $80 Single $50
(1 bdrm)
1 Private

Hilary and Neville offer you top quality accommodation in a quiet bush setting just 20 minutes drive from Wellington City. Our ground floor apartment includes one double bedroom, private bathroom with heated towel rail, laundry, spacious lounge/living room with gas heating, TV, tea/coffee making facilities and fridge. Nearby attractions include the Rimutaka Forest Park, seal colony, and 18 hole golf course. We enjoy gardening, golf, tennis and travel, and meeting new people. We look forward to welcoming you to our home. Genuine 'kiwi' hospitality guaranteed.

Just as we have a variety of B&Bs
you will also be offered a variety of breakfasts,
and they will always be generous.

Eastbourne   *Homestay   3km N of Eastbourne*

Bush House
Belinda Cattermole
12 Waitohu Rd, York Bay,
Eastbourne, Wellington
Tel: (04) 568 5250 Fax: (04) 568 5250
Mob: 025 654 5433
www.bnb.co.nz/bushhouse.html

Double $90 Single $60 (Full Breakfast)
Dinner by arrangemet Pet on property
1 Double 1 Single (2 bdrm)
1 Private 1 Family share

Come and enjoy the peace and tranquillity of the Eastern Bays. You will be hosted in a beautifully restored 1920's settler cottage nestled amongst native bush and looking towards the Kaikoura mountains of the South Island. My love of cordon-bleu cooking and the pleasure of the table are satisfied through the use of my country kitchen and dining room. Other attractions: Outdoor spa and a Devon Rex cat. Eastbourne is a small seaside village across the harbour from Wellington city with a range of attractions.

Eastbourne   *Self-contained B&B   12km E of Wellington*

Treetops
Robyn & Roger Cooper
7 Huia Road, Days Bay, Eastbourne
Tel: (04) 562 7692 Fax: (04) 562 7690
Mob: 025 616 9826   bnb@treetops.net.nz
www.treetops.net.nz

Double $110-$130 Single $95-$110
(Continental Breakfast) sofabeds in lounge $20 pp
Credit cards accepted
1 Queen + 2 single divans in lounge (1 bdrm) 1 Private

Secluded, romantic retreat in stunning location above Wellington harbour. Ride our private cablecar through native bush to the front door, or walk up through ferns and beech trees. Seaviews from stylish, spacious guest apartment comprising bedroom, lounge, kitchenette, bath/shower/toilet. Wake to songs of the bellbird; breakfast on your private garden patio; relax indoors with books, games, TV, radio. Phone/jackpoint. Portacot, highchair available. Laundry $6. Picturesque beach, cafes, galleries 200 metres. Central Wellington 20 minutes by local ferry or car. Seasonal weekly rates.

Eastbourne   *Homestay B&B   17km E of Wellington*

Lowry Bay Homestay
Pam & Forde Clarke
35 Cheviot Road, Lowry Bay, Eastbourne, Wellington
Tel: (04) 568 4407 Fax: (04) 568 2474
Tollfree: 0508 266 546   forde.clarke@xtra.co.nz
www.bnb.co.nz/lowrybayhomestay.html

Double $100-$130 Single $80-$110 (Full Breakfast)
Child Negotiable Child at home Pet on property
1 King 1 Queen 1 Single (2 bdrm)
1 Private

Enjoy our hospitality. Welcome to our special home. Warm, restful, peaceful, yet close to Wellington and Hutt Cities, transport, restaurants and art galleries. Play tennis on our court, stroll to the beach, walk in the bush, sail on our 28 foot yacht, or relax under a sun umbrella on the deck. Native birds abound. Our sunny, elegant bedrooms have garden views, TV, tea/coffee and central heating. We have two daughters, Isabella 19 and Kirsty 13, a cat and many interests. Laundry. Non-smoking indoors. From SH2 follow Petone signs then Eastbourne.

Eastbourne   *Homestay B&B*   *17km NE of Wellington*

Jennifer & Ken's Homestay
Jennifer & Ken
Marine Drive, Sorrento Bay, Eastbourne
Postal address - P.O.Box 3717 Wellington
Tel: +64 4 568 4817 Fax: +64 4 568 4817
Mob: +64 25 500 670   Tollfree: 0800 390 385
kjackson@pop.ihug.co.nz
www.bnb.co.nz/jenniferkenshomestay.html
Double $75-$95 Single $60-$75 (Full Breakfast)
Child by arrangement Dinner by arrangement
Credit cards accepted Pet on property
1 Double 1 Single (2 bdrm) 1 Private

Jennifer, Ken and our friendly cat Tuppence look forward to giving you a warm welcome to our home. It is nestled amongst native bush by the beach. Share with us the magical views of Wellington harbour and the city. You may wish to join us on a deck in summer, or in front of a cosy fire in winter. As non-smokers we appreciate no smoking inside. At any time we would be pleased to assist you with your stay.

Eastbourne   *Homestay B&B*   *17km E of Wellington*

2 Lady Bell
Mary and Neil Prichard
2 Lady Bell Grove, Lowry Bay, Eastbourne
Tel: (04) 576 9016 Mob: 025 484 671
prichards@xtra.co.nz
www.bnb.co.nz/user201.html
Double $120 Single $80 (Full Breakfast)
Dinner by arrangement Credit cards accepted
2 Double 1 Twin (3 bdrm)
2 Private 1 Guests share

Enjoy hospitality in beautiful native bush. Relax in the sauna and spa, explore the surrounding walks, go sailing, kayaking, golfing or stroll to the beach and soak up the beauty of the glorious Wellington harbour. Wellington and all it's sporting and cultural activities,restaurants and cafes are within easy reach by car, ferry or bus. Courtesy passenger transfer available. From State highway 1 or 2 follow signs to Petone and Seaview Marina. Lowry Bay is the third bay past the Marina.

Ohariu Valley - Wellington   *Farmstay B&B*   *12km NW of Johnsonville*

Papanui Station Farm Stay
Bev & Cliff Inglis
Boom Rock Rd, Ohariu Valley,
RD, Johnsonville, Wellington
Tel: (04) 478 8926
www.bnb.co.nz/papanuistationfarmstay.html
Double $76 Single $38 (Full Breakfast) Dinner $25
1 Double 1 Twin (2 bdrm)
1 Guests share

As the name suggests Mill Cottage is the cosy and intimate home of Bev and Cliff. We would like to invite you to experience a stay on a sheep and cattle station, 3200 acres within the Wellington city boundary. Papanui Station has Colonial Knob 1500ft at the north, Boom Rock to the south sea level, offers some most rugged coastline of New Zealand, along with great views of Cook Strait and South Island Mountains. We offer you an extreme location unique home hospitality and surroundings.

Khandallah - Wellington   *Homestay   6km N of Wellington*

Genevieve and Peter Young
10A Izard Road,
Khandallah, Wellington
Tel: (04) 479 5036 Fax: (04) 479 5037
www.bnb.co.nz/youngkhandallah.html
Double $80 Single $50
(Continental & Full Breakfast)
Pet on property
Children welcome
5 Single (3 bdrm)

We enjoy relaxing and meeting people. Our interests are travel, sport, food, wine, and the Arts. We have an elderly tabby cat. Khandallah is a hillside suburb handy to all the attractions of the capital, with a village atmosphere and a ten minute bus or train ride to town. Very close to the ferry terminal. We look forward to making your stay an enjoyable one. Local Pub/Cafe within easy walking distance. Please phone and we will arrange to pick you up.

Khandallah - Wellington   *Homestay   7km N of Wellington*

Sue & Ted Clothier
22 Lohia Street, Khandallah, Wellington
Tel: (04) 479 1180 Fax: (04) 479 2717
www.bnb.co.nz/clothier.html
Double $100 Single $70 (Full Breakfast)
Credit cards accepted Pet on property
1 Twin (1 bdrm)
1 Ensuite

This is a lovely, sunny and warm open plan home with glorious harbour and city views. A quiet easily accessible street just ten minutes from the city and five minutes from the ferry. Close to Khandallah village where you can make use of the excellent local restaurant, cafe or English country pub. We are a non-smoking household. Another family member is an aristocratic white cat called Dali. We enjoy sharing our home with our guests.

Khandallah - Wellington   *B&B   7km N of Wellington Central*

Khandallah Bed & Breakfast
Tim & Margaret Fairhall
50 Clark Street,
Khandallah, Wellington
Tel: (04) 479 5578 fairhall@paradise.net.nz
www.bnb.co.nz/fairhall.html
Double $150 Single $120 (Full Breakfast)
Credit cards accepted Pet on property
1 Queen 1 Twin (2 bdrm)
1 Ensuite 1 Private

A large home filled with antiques and New Zealand art. Lovely garden with heated pool and tennis court, guests welcome to use. We enjoy golf and can arrange a game. Lovely bush walks nearby. Walk to local pub or restaurant for dinner. The bedroom includes TV, tea/coffee, home baking, electric blankets, heating. Laundry facilities available. Breakfasts continental or full, with homemade jams, muffins and preserved fruit. Children at university, Buffy the cat at home. We love sports, Wellington and meeting pepole. Phone or e-mail for directions.

Khandallah - Wellington *B&B* *6km NW of Wellington*

Imran on Khandallah
Sonja & Terry FitzGerald
28 Imran Tce, Khandallah,
Tel: 064 4 4790570 Fax: 064 4 4790571
Mob: 025 2412101 terryf@xtra.co.nz
www.bnb.co.nz/imran.html
Double $150 Single $150 (Full Breakfast)
Dinner n/a Credit cards accepted Children welcome
1 Queen 1 Twin (2 bdrm)
1 Private

An extensive modern villa completed mid 2000 with panoramic views located in the exclusive suburb of Khandallah, minutes from city centre and travel terminals. We cater for the discerning corporate and leisure traveller. Elegantly decorated the guest bedroom includes a queensize bed, with an additional twin bedroom available if required (single party bookings only). Private courtyard, native garden, and library with business facilities. Full breakfast includes freshly squeezed juice, and delicous cooked options. Sonja and Terry will respect your privacy but you are most welcome to share their company.

Ngaio - Wellington *Self-contained or Homestay B&B* *7km NW of Wellington*

Ngaio Homestay
Jennifer & Christopher Timmings
56 Fox St, Ngaio, Wellington
Tel: (04) 479 5325 Fax: (04) 479 4325
jennifer.timmings@clear.net.nz
www.bnb.co.nz/ngaiohomestay.html
Double $100-$120 Single $80-$100
(Continental Breakfast) Child neg Dinner $25pp
S/C extra person $40 Credit cards accepted
1 Queen 2 Double 2 Twin 2 Single (5 bdrm)
3 Ensuite 1 Private 1 Family share

Our multi-level family home is in Ngaio, 5 mins to ferry terminal, 10 mins to CBD. We offer: views, sun, off street parking, quiet surroundings, 2 mins bush walk to local train station, dinner by arrangement, homely atmosphere. Children welcome. Our 2 self contained units are adjacent to our property, 1 double, 1 twin, each unit can sleep up to 4 persons. Equipped kitchen, laundry facilities, phone, Cable TV, perfect for relocating or immigrating. Weekly rates offered. All accommodation is smoke free.

Karori - Wellington *Homestay* *5km W of Wellington*

Campbell Homestay
Murray & Elaine Campbell
83 Campbell Street, Karori, Wellington
Tel: (04) 476 6110 Fax: (04) 476 6593
Mob: 025 535 080 ctool@ihug.co.nz
www.bnb.co.nz/campbellhomestay.html
Double $85 Single $50 (Continental Breakfast)
Child 1/2 price Dinner $25 Credit cards accepted
Pet on property Children welcome Pets welcome
1 Queen 1 Twin 3 Single (3 bdrm)
1 Guests share

Welcome to our home in the suburbs, easy to find from motorway or ferry terminal. Telephone and we will meet you at ferry, train, bus or air terminals. Join us for pre-dinner drinks, dine with us, or eat out at the local pub/cafe or licenced restaurant. We are close to the city on three bus routes. Make use of our laundry, large garden, spacious home, email/internet facilities. Meet Charlie our border collie dog and Honey the cat.

Karori - Wellington *B&B* *4 km we of Wellington CBD*

Bristow Place
Helen & Tony Thomson
8 Bristow Place, Karori, Wellington
Tel: +64 4 476 6291 Fax: +64 4 476 6293
Mob: +64 21 656 825
h.t.thomson@xtra.co.nz
www.bnb.co.nz/bristowplace.html
Double $150 Single $110 (Full Breakfast)
Dinner by arrangement Credit cards accepted
1 Queen (1 bdrm) 1 Private

Quiet, sunny location 5 minutes drive from city centre. Easy to find with parking available. We are happy to meet you at ferry, airport, etc. Close to transport or walk to local shops, restaurants. Guest bedroom provides Sky TV, tea / coffee facilities, electric blankets. Private bathroom with full bath, separate shower. Enjoy sole use of a lounge or join us for coffee and conversation. Our interests include sport, music, bridge, travel. German spoken. Gourmet dinner by arrangement. Internet, fax, laundry service at small charges.

Wadestown - Wellington *Homestay* *5km W of Wellingtom*

Ti Whanake
Julie Foley
72 Wilton Road, Wadestown, Wellington
Tel: (04) 499 6602 Fax: (04) 473 7332
Mob: 025 203 2228
www.bnb.co.nz/foley.html
Single $60 (Continental Breakfast) Dinner By neg.
Credit cards accepted Pet on property
1 Twin 1 Single (2 bdrm)
1 Private

A short walk to Otari Native Botanic Gardens and bus from door to central city 10 minutes. Own bathroom, separate lounge if preferred, electric blankets and heaters. Share the fireside in the evening with the host and Persian cat or attend some of the varied activities in the 'Cultural Capital'. Gardening, embroidery, playing the cello and mahjong are some of the interests the host enjoys. Visitors can be collected from the ferry etc. Parking on the street. Phone for directions.

Kelburn - Wellington *1km W of Wellington Central*

Self-contained Boutique B&B
Ruby House
Elizabeth Barbalich, 14B Kelburn Parade, Wellington
Tel: (04) 934 7930 Fax: (04) 934 7935
Mob: 021 483 980 elizabeth@rubyhouse.co.nz
www.rubyhouse.co.nz
Double $150-$185 (Special Breakfast)
Child $45 by arrangement Credit cards accepted
Long term, weekly & house rates avaliable.
1 King/Twin 1 King 1 Queen (3 bdrm) 3 Ensuite

Nestled on a private section amongst native trees, Ruby House offers guests a perfect balance of luxury, privacy and location. This villa style guesthouse boasts three spacious, beautifully appointed rooms that provide the essential ingredients for a memorable stay in the capital city - firm comfortable beds, antique furniture, ensuite bathrooms, private telephone/modem line. Ruby House is just around the corner from Victoria University and only two minutes walk to the Cable Car, which takes you directly into the main street of Wellington's CBD. Non-smoking/covered carparks.

Kelburn - Wellington *Boutique B&B 1km W of Wellington central*

'Rawhiti'
Annabel Leask
40 Rawhiti Terrace, Kelburn, Wellington
Tel: (04) 934 4859 Fax: (04) 972 4859
Mob: 025 276 8240   rawhiti@paradise.net.nz
www.rawhiti.co.nz

Double $140-$185 Single $130-$150
(Special Breakfast) Credit cards accepted
1 King/Twin 1 King (2 bdrm)
1 Ensuite 1 Family share

"Rawhiti" is located in the prime suburb of Kelburn and within walking distance of the city centre. Magnificent views of harbour and city are seen from all rooms including the small private garden at the rear. A charming 1905 two-storeyed home furnished to create an elegant and tranquil ambience. Its historical features, wonderful outlook and quality chattels combine to offer guests a special stay in Wellington. Annabel has travelled widely with interests in the Arts and golf. A two minute walk to the Cable Car, Botanic Gardens and Victoria University.

Kelburn - Wellington *B&B 2km W of Wellington*

Rangiora B&B
Lesley and Malcolm Shaw
177 Glenmore Street, Kelburn, Wellington 6005
Tel: (04) 475 9888 rangiora.bnb@xtra.co.nz
www.bnb.co.nz/rangiora.html

Double $100 Single $90 (Continental Breakfast)
Credit cards accepted Pet on property
1 Queen 1 Double (2 bdrm)
1 Guests share

LOCATION LOCATION LOCATION!!! We are very easy to find. Our modern hillside home is just 5 minutes drive from central Wellington, the Hawkestone Street motorway exit, and ferry terminals. Easy walking distance from several excellent restaurants. Cable Car, Botanic Gardens, Victoria University and Wildlife Sanctuary are also a short walk. Katherine Mansfield Birthplace is a short drive away. Tea/coffee making,TV,in rooms. Free E-mail access. Ample on-street parking. Courtesy car from/to ferry, bus, train. On city bus route. We have a small dog named Patsy.

Kelburn - Wellington *B&B 1km W of Wellington*

Glenlodge
Brenda Leighs
5 Glen Road, Kelburn, Wellington
Tel: (04) 973 7881 Fax: (04) 802 5268
Mob: 025 416811   glenlodge@paradise.net.nz
www.bnb.co.nz/glenlodge.html

Double $130 (Full Breakfast)
weekly rate available on request Credit cards accepted
1 Queen (1 bdrm)
1 Ensuite

There is no better location for your stay in Wellington than at Glenlodge. The Botanical Gardens and Cable Car, which will have you in downtown Wellington within minuntes, are literally at our front door. There are excellent cafes,galleries and shops within walking distance. With your beautifully appointed bedroom, ensuite and private guest lounge a memorable visit is guaranteed. Start your day with a full breakfast before heading off for a days sightseeing. Dinner by arrangement. Meet and greet and laundry facilities available. Unsuitable for children. Smokefree. We have a miniature Schnauzer.

Thorndon - Wellington   *Self-contained Separate/Suite B&B*

1km W of Wellington Central

Thorndon Views
Pieter & Jeanette de Villiers
37 Newman Terrace, Thorndon, Wellington

Tel: (04) 938-0783 Mob: 025 898 875
pieterdevil@hotmail.com
www.bnb.co.nz/thorndonviews.html

Double $115 Single $95 (Continental Breakfast)
Child $15
1 Queen 1 Double (1 bdrm) 1 Private

A stylish private, studio with great views of Wellington Harbour. The setting is a magnificent restored Victorian home surrounded by bush. Thorndon Views is a ten-minute walk to the CBD, close to the Inter-island Ferry and Westpac Stadium. Bush walks on your doorstep lead to breathtaking vistas of the harbour. Facilities include ensuite bathroom with warm towels and hairdryer, cooking facilities, SKY TV and spa. Healthy continental breakfast with a selection of breads, croissants, freshly brewed coffee, fresh fruit and yoghurt.

Oriental Bay - Wellington   *B&B   0.75km N of Wellington*

No 11
Virginia Barton-Chapple
11 Hay Street,
Oriental Bay, Wellington

Tel: (04) 801 9290 Fax: (04) 801 9295
www.bnb.co.nz/noorientalbay.html

Double $120 Single $95 (Full Breakfast)
Credit cards accepted Pet on property
1 King/Twin (1 bdrm)
1 Guests share

Oriental Bay is perhaps the finest location in Wellington. No 11 has an intimate view of the city and is an easy stroll to Te Papa: the Museum of New Zealand, the City Art Gallery, all the major theatres and cinemas, great restaurants and cafes. Virginia has extensive knowledge of what's going on, and where to go. The accommodation is in a comfortable room for two, with bathroom adjacent, electric blankets and tea & coffee facilities. Breakfast will be an occasion. Cat in residence.

The difference between a B&B and a hotel
is that you don't hug the hotel staff when you leave.

Mt Victoria - Wellington *Homestay B&B   Wellington Central*

Dream Catcher - Arts & Accommodation
Taly & John Hoekman
56 Pirie Street, Mt Victoria, Wellington
Tel: (04) 801 9363 Mob: 021 210 6762
www.bnb.co.nz/dreamcatcher.html
Double $110-$130 Single $90-$110
(Special Breakfast) Child $40 2nd child free
Credit cards accepted Pet on property
1 Queen 2 Double 2 Single (3 bdrm)
1 Ensuite 2 Private 1 Guests share

Dream Catcher is a renovated spacious Victorian house in central, picturesque Mount Victoria, only 5 minutes stroll from Wellington's vibrant attractions. Quality accommodations available: 1) "VIP Suite" - private livingroom, double bedroom and ensuite. 2) "Upstairs" - a self contained 2nd storey includes two bedrooms, guests shared bathroom, deck, verandah, living/kitchen, sun, and city views. Taly, John, their teenage daughter and two cats, keen travellers themselves, welcome the city visitor to enjoy the relaxed comfort of home, and the fresh generous breakfasts in the main kitchen or the back garden.

Mt Victoria - Wellington *Self-contained B&B Wellington Central*

Austin Street B&B
Andrew & Kate Chapman
103 Austin Street, Mt Victoria, Wellington
Tel: (04) 385 8384 Fax: (04) 385 8374
Mob: 021 385 833 austinstbb@hotmail.com
www.bnb.co.nz/austinstreetbb.html
Double $125 Single $125
(Continental Breakfast) $25.00 extra person
Credit cards accepted Child at home
1 Queen 1 Double 1 Sofa bed (1 bdrm) 1 Ensuite

Our self-contained studio is relaxing and private. We are a few minutes by foot to Courtenay Place (Wellington's restaurant, cafe and theatre district) and Te Papa. Our studio has an ensuite, TV and external access so you can come and go at your own leisure. Breakfast, you can make in your own time at the kitchenette while browsing through the provided paper. Laundry facilites available. Andrew works in the banking industry and Kate looks after our young children. A generous continental breakfast is provided.

Mt Victoria - Wellington *Homestay B&B   Wellington Central*

Scarborough House
Sue Hiles & Miles Davidson
36 Scarborough Tce, Mt Victoria, Wellington
Tel: + 64 4 801 8534 Fax: + 64 4 801 8536
Mob: 025 501 346
info@scarborough-house.co.nz
www.scarborough-house.co.nz
Double $130-$150 Single $120 (Full Breakfast)
Child $50 Credit cards accepted
1 King/Twin 1 Queen (2 bdrm) 1 Private

Welcome to Scarborough House, our modern centrally-heated home in a quiet, sunny Mt Vic street with views over the city, close to Courtenay Place - the restaurant, cafe and theatre district, Te Papa Museum, Westpac Stadium and the waterfront. King, queen or twin accommodation. Private guest bathroom. Breakfast of your choice. Tea/coffee facilities, hairdryer, bathrobes, Sky Digital TV, laundry and garaging available. Our interests include travel, skiing, golf and many of the activities our magnificent city offers. Children over 12 welcome; we are smokefree.

Mt Victoria - Wellington

Homestay B&B   0.5km E of Central Wellington

Villa Vittorio
Annette & Logan Russell
6 Hawker Street, Mt Victoria, Wellington

Tel: (04) 801 5761 Fax: (04) 801 5762
Mob: 025 321 267
l&a@villavittorio.co.nz
www.villavittorio.co.nz

Double $130-$160 Single $110-$125 (Full Breakfast)
Dinner from $40p.p. Credit cards accepted
1 Double (1 bdrm)
1 Private

WELCOME TO VILLA VITTORIO. Centrally located
close by Courtenay Place. Short walk to restaurants,
theatres, shopping, conference centres, Te Papa Museum,
Parliament and Stadium.

Guest bedroom with TV, tea and coffee facilities.
Adjoining sitting room with balcony overlooking city.
Bathroom with shower and bath.

Breakfast served in Italian styled dining room or outside
in courtyard.

We enjoy having guests, having travelled extensively
ourselves.

Transport and gourmet dinner by arrangement.

Garaging and laundry at small charge.

No children or pets.

Direction: Phone, fax, email or write.

Mt Victoria - Wellington *Self-contained B&B   Wellington City*

Austinvilla
Averil & Ian Wotton
11 Austin Street, Mt Victoria, Wellington
Tel: (04) 385 8334 Fax: (04) 385 8336
Mob: 027 273 7760   info@austinvilla.co.nz
www.austinvilla.co.nz

Double $140-$160 (Continental Breakfast)
Credit cards accepted Children welcome
2 Queen (2 bdrm)
2 Ensuite

A warm welcome to one of Mt Victoria's most elegant turn-of-the-century villas. Set amongst beautiful gardens, and only a five minute walk to theatres, restaurants, Oriental Bay, and Te Papa museum. Close to public transport, and a 10 minute drive to airport, ferries, and Westpac Stadium. Spacious, elegant apartments offer privacy and include kitchen, queen bed, ensuite with bath, lounge, Sky TV, phone, CD player. One apartment with French doors to private courtyard. Laundry facilities and garaging available. Continental breakfast provided. Smokefree. We welcome children over 10 years old.

Roseneath - Wellington *Homestay B&B   3km E of Wellington*

Harbourview Homestay and B&B
Hilda & Geoff Stedman
125 Te Anau Road, Roseneath, Wellington
Tel: (04) 386 1043 Tollfree: 0800 0800 78
hildastedman@clear.net.nz
www.bnb.co.nz/harbourviewhomestayandbb.html

Double $115-$130 Single $80-$100
(Continental & Full Breakfast) Dinner $35
Credit cards accepted
1 Double 2 Single (2 bdrm)   2 Private

This boutique guesthouse is 5 minutes drive from Wellington city, 10 minutes drive from the airport and on the No. 14 bus route. The house offers comfortable hospitality and elegance. Each bedroom opens on to a wide deck, offering expansive views of Wellington harbour. Pleasantly decorated rooms feature quality beds and linen. There is a choice of a double bedroom and/or share twin room, separate guest's bathroom with shower and spa bath. Harbourview is situated in a peaceful setting close to the city, catering for Businesspeople, Tourists and Honeymooners.

Hataitai - Wellington *3km E of Wellington CBD*
Self-contained Homestay B&B

Top O' T'ill
Cathryn & Dennis Riley
2 Waitoa Rd, Hataitai, Wellington 6003
Tel: (04) 386 2718 Fax: (04) 386 2719
Mob: 025 716 482   top.o.hill@xtra.co.nz
www.bnb.co.nz/topotill.html

Double $90-$120 Single $60-$110 (Full Breakfast)
Credit cards accepted
2 Queen 1 Twin 1 Single (4 bdrm)
2 Ensuite 1 Private 1 Guests share

Hataitai - 'breath of the ocean', is a popular suburb midway between the Airport and central Wellington. City attractions are 5-10 minutes by bus or car. Our comfortable family home of 60 years is a welcome retreat for guests. The quality studio is fully equipped, including cable television and phone. Long term rates available. We share a range of cultural interests, have travelled widely, and will be glad to help you make the most of your visit to Wellington. Not suitable for young children.

Hataitai - Wellington   *B&B Boutique*   *3km E of Wellington City Centre*

Matai House
Raema & Rex Collins
41 Matai Road, Hataitai, Wellington 6003
Tel: (04) 934 6985 Fax: (04) 934 6987
matai@paradise.net.nz
www.bnb.co.nz/mataihouse.html
Double $190-$250 (Special Breakfast)
Visa MasterCard Amex JCB Diners accepted
2 King (2 bdrm)   2 Ensuite

Panoramic sea views. 1913 villa, purpose-built private guest floor downstairs with guest rooms and adjoining lounge with private entrance. Suites have cable TV, modem points, bi-fold doors opening on to decking. King beds, thick pillow-top mattresses, goosedown covers, plump pillows. Bathrooms feature hairdryers, toiletries, robes and heated towel rails. Fresh flowers, tea/coffee-making facilities, fridge, laundry and ironing. Telephone/fax/email access. Off-street parking. Flexitime gourmet breakfast, freshly squeezed oranges, espresso coffee, muesli, fruit and cooked options. Four minutes to city and eight minutes to ferry. Qualmark™ applied for.

Aro Valley - Wellington   *Self-contained B&B*   *1km S of Wellington*

206 Aro Self-Contained Cottage
Russell and Shirley Martin
206 Aro St, Aro Valley
Tel: (04) 973 7008 Mob: 021 177 1957
info-206aro@paradise.net.nz
www.206aro.co.nz
Double $140 Single $140 (Continental Breakfast)
Child $10 Credit cards accepted Pets welcome
1 Queen 1 Double (1 bdrm)
1 Private

206Aro is a self-contained cottage, with complete privacy in Aro Valley. Fully fitted with quality accommodation touches - 100% cotton sheets, new futon sofa, etc. Native bush behind cottage and over the road; Plus a deck for sunny weather. Wellington downtown city is a 5-10 minutes drive (Free parking), or a nice 20 minute walk. Complimentary breakfast materials, drinks and daytime snacks, and free cable TV, range of videos, and use of stereo. Kids/pets welcome. Discounts for stays more than 2 nights. Run by Russell and Shirley.

Brooklyn (city end) - Wellington   *3km SW of Wellington City Centre*

Homestay

Karepa
Ann and Tom Hodgson
56 Karepa Street, Brooklyn, Wellington
Tel: (04) 384 4193 Fax: (04) 384 4180
Mob: 025 KAREPA golf@xtra.co.nz
www.holidayletting.co.nz/karepa
Double $130-$165 Single $95-$125 (Full Breakfast)
Child by arrangement Dinner $30 by arrangement
extra person $35 Credit cards accepted
2 King 1 Double 1 Single (3 bdrm) 1 Ensuite 1 Guests share

Stay at 'Karepa' our sunny, spacious home overlooking city, harbour and mountains. The secluded rear garden adjoins native bush. Private guest rooms have TV, and tea/coffee facilities. City 5 minutes, ferry 10 and airport 15. Residents of 18 years, ex UK, we have travelled widely, play golf and tennis, and enjoy Wellington's many attractions. Ann gardens and Tom watches from his deckchair. On-site parking. Bus at door. Laundry facilities. Sorry, no smokers or pets. Please phone/fax for directions.

Brooklyn City Side - Wellington *Homestay B&B 2km S of Wellington*

Quintessential Wellington
Georgie Jones
2A Coolidge Street, Brooklyn, Wellington
Tel: +64 4 380 1982 Fax: +64 4 380 1985
Mob: 025 243 5674 georgie.jones@xtra.co.nz
www.bnb.co.nz/quintessentialwellington.html

Double $100-$120 Single $80-$100
(Continental & Full Breakfast) Child negotiable
Credit cards accepted
1 Queen 2 Single (2 bdrm) 1 Private 1 Guests share

Choose personal hospitality, city centre 5 minutes - travellers and business visitors welcome. Home features striking architecture and stunning harbour, city, sky and bush vistas. Relax or work in warm peaceful surroundings. City and bush walks, local and national transport handy. Front door parking; private guestroom; luxury bathroom (shower and double bath); own secluded deck. Guidance available on local and regional attractions and activities. Interests include travel, visual and performing arts, architecture, contemporary design, current affairs. Free laundry. Email, TV, fridge, tea/coffee facilities.

Vogeltown - Wellington *Homestay 3km S of Wellington Central*

Vogeltown Homestay
Valerie Tait
14 Krull Street, Vogeltown, Wellington
Tel: (04) 934 2004 Fax: (04) 934 2004
valerie.tait@paradise.net.nz
www.bnb.co.nz/vogeltownhomestay.html

Double $80 Single $50 (Continental Breakfast)
Credit cards accepted
1 Queen 2 Single (2 bdrm)
1 Guests share

Vogeltown is a quiet suburb 10-15 minutes from airport and ferry. The city's many attractions are easily reached by bus or car. Two comfortable rooms share a guest bathroom and look out onto a private, sunny deck. Originally from northern England, I've lived in Wellington for many years and enjoy sharing my home and knowledge of the city with visitors. I've travelled extensively around NZ and tramped most of the major tracks. The house is smoke-free. Well-behaved children and pets welcome. Laundry facilities.

A homestay is a B&B where you
share the family's living area.

Karaka Bay - Wellington *Homestay   5km S of Wellington*

Edge Water Boutique Homestay
Stella & Colin Lovering
459 Karaka Bay Road, Seatoun, Wellington

Tel: (04) 388 4446 Fax: (04) 388 4446 Mob: (021) 613 357
edgewaterwellington@xtra.co.nz
www.edgewaterwellington.co.nz

Double $160-$250 Single $140-$220 (Full Breakfast) Dinner $70 wines extra Off Peak rates apply
Credit cards accepted Pet on property Children welcome
1 King/Twin 2 Superking 1 Queen (4 bdrm)
4 Ensuite

Edgewater is situated on the seafront at Karaka Bay, Seatoun. Only 10 minutes from Wellington City and Airport.

Featuring expansive ocean views, this mediterranean-style home offers 4 airy guest bedrooms with peaked cedar ceilings beneath seperate roofs.

Stella serves fresh fruits, homemade breads, pancakes and egg dishes for breakfast in the dining room or alfresco on the guest balcony in the morning sun.

Dinner is also offered, specialising in premium quality meats, seafood and game.

As ex-owner/chef of an award winning Wellington Restaurant, Stella's motto is "fresh is best".

We have a tabby cat and a small scruffy dog.

Please phone, fax or email for directions.

Breaker Bay - Wellington   *Homestay B&B*   *10km SE of Wellington*

Breaker Bay Homestay
Sheridan & Graham Evans
115 Breaker Bay Road, Seatoun,

Tel: (04) 972 3043 Fax: (04) 972 3046
Mob: 027 4455 624
breakerbay@paradise.net.nz
breakerbay.co.nz

Double $100-$140 Single $80-$120 (Full Breakfast)
Credit cards accepted Pet on property
1 King/Twin 1 Queen (2 bdrm)
1 Guests share

Just 12 minutes from the city and 5 minutes from the airport, Breaker Bay Homestay offers you a coastal retreat in a friendly community. The view is stunning, looking over the entrance to Wellington Harbour and watching the ships. Just relax, walk along our bay or explore Wellington's many attractions - restaurants, Te Papa, art gallerys, shopping, sporting facilities. We offer you breakfast of your choice and can provide dinner if required. Smokefree. Internet.

Seatoun - Wellington   *Homestay B&B*   *9km S of Wellington*

Francesca's
Frances Drewell
10 Monro Street, Seatoun, Wellington

Tel: (04) 388 6719 Fax: (04) 388 6719
francesdrewell@paradise.net.nz
www.bnb.co.nz/francescas.html

Double $90 Single $55 (Full Breakfast) Child $25
Dinner $25 by arrangement Credit cards accepted
1 Double 2 Single (2 bdrm)
1 Guests share

Although handy to Wellington Airport (3 kms away) our modern home is located in a quiet seaside village. A warm welcome awaits you in a home away from home. Choice of restaurants nearby. Flat off-street parking. Laundry facilities available. Directions: entering Wellington from the north follow the signs to the Airport then the signs to Seatoun. Monro Street is the second street on the left after the shops. From the Airport first turn right then as above. Bus stop one minute, frequent service.

Palmer Head - Wellington   *Self-contained B&B*   *6km S of Wellington*

Birkhall House
Mary & Brent & Joss
14 Birkhall Grove, Palmer Head, Wellington 6003

Tel: (04) 388 2881 Fax: (04) 388 2833
Mob: 027 6400 296
madammary@xtra.co.nz
www.bnb.co.nz/birkhallhouse.html

Double $90-$120 Single $70-$100
(Continental Breakfast)
self-contained unit $120 - $160 Pet on property
1 King 2 Single (3 bdrm) 1 Guests share

Relax in my lovely sunny home and enjoy the magic views of Wellington - South Island to Inner Harbour. We're only 6 mins from the airport and 11 mins to the city, and for the energetic a golf course, aquatic centre, and walking tracks are nearby. Enjoy at your leisure a continental breakfast (cooked on request) on the deck. We would be delighted to have you as our guest and welcome house trained kids. Smoke free inside, centrally heated. Laundry facilities available. Self/con unit available.

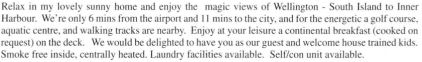

Island Bay - Wellington   *Self-contained B&B*

The Lighthouse
Bruce Stokell
326 The Esplanade, Island Bay, Wellington
Tel: (04) 472 4177 Fax: (04) 472 4177
Mob: 025 425 555
bruce@sportwork.co.nz
www.bnb.co.nz/thelighthouse.html

Double $150-$180 (Full Breakfast)
Credit cards accepted
1 Double (2 bdrm)
1 Private

Island Bay - 10 minutes city centre, 10 minutes airport, 20 minutes ferry terminal. The Lighthouse is on the South coast and has views of the island, fishing boats in the bay, the beach and rocks, the far coastline, the open sea, the shipping and, on a clear day, the South Island. There are local shops and restaurants. The Lighthouse has a kitchen and bathroom on the first floor, the bedroom/sitting room on the middle floor and the lookout/bedroom on the top. Romantic.

Island Bay/Melrose - Wellington   *8 km S of Wellington Central*

Self-contained Homestay B&B
Buckley Homestay
Kerry and Willy Muller
51 Buckley Road, Melrose, Island Bay, Wellington
Tel: (04) 934 7151   kandwmuller@paradise.net.nz
Mob: 025 607 1853   www.bnb.co.nz/buckley.html

Double $95-$130 (Continental & Full Breakfast)
Dinner by arrangement Credit cards accepted
Children welcome Smoking area inside
1 Double 2 Single (1 bdrm) 1 Private

Large sunny home with spectacular scenery and beautiful views over Wellington, Cook Strait and Mountains. New tastefully decorated, private entrance, 1 Bedroom, self contained, double flat with private balcony, T.V, tiled Conservatory, fridge and microwave. Surf or swim at our safe local beach. Close to hospitals. We are interested in food, wine, travel, relaxing and meeting people. Willy is a nurse, enjoys cooking, gardening and speaks Dutch. Kerry has travelled and has a background with animals, is retired and enjoys bowling.

Just as we have a variety of B&Bs
you will also be offered a variety of breakfasts,
and they will always be generous.

Chatham Islands   *Farmstay*

Te Matarae
Pat & Wendy Smith
PO Box 63, Te Matarae, Chatham Islands
Tel: (03) 305 0144
Fax: (03) 305 0144
www.bnb.co.nz/smithchathamislands.html

Double $95 Single $80 (Continental Breakfast)
Dinner $25 Pet on property Children welcome
2 Queen 2 Single (3 bdrm)
2 Ensuite 1 Family share

Relax in our natural wood home which is situated in eighty acres of bush on lagoon edge with mown walkways throughout. The lagoon is ideal for swimming and fishing and has nice sandy beaches. Farm activities and kayaks available. Farm is eleven hundred acres and includes four other bush reserves. Guests may meal with family or in separate dining room. Bedrooms are separated from main house by covered swimming pool. We are a non smoking household; so request guests to refrain from doing so in our home. Most meal ingredients are home produced.

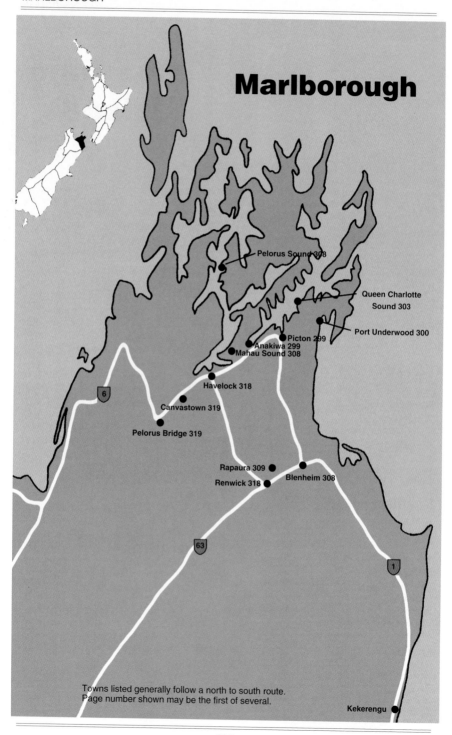

Marlborough

Pelorus Sound 308

Queen Charlotte
Sound 303

Port Underwood 300

Picton 299
Anakiwa 299
Mahau Sound 308

Havelock 318

Canvastown 319

Pelorus Bridge 319

6

Rapaura 309
Renwick 318
Blenheim 308

63

1

Towns listed generally follow a north to south route.
Page number shown may be the first of several.

Kekerengu

Picton - Waikawa Bay   *B&B*   *4km NE of Picton*

Bayside
Pam & John
33 Beach Road,
Waikawa Bay, Picton

Tel: (03) 573 7783 Fax: (03) 573 7783
Mob: 021 104 4011
pamjohn@xtra.co.nz
www.bnb.co.nz/seaviewpicton.html

Double $80 Single $45 (Full Breakfast)
1 Queen 2 Single (2 bdrm)
1 Ensuite 1 Private

Only a minute from the South Island's largest marina where one can enjoy a stroll around the berths and admire some of the beautiful craft, a pleasant way to start or finish the day. We are 4km from the ferry terminal and offer a full breakfast. A cafe/bar is within easy walking distance for an evening meal. With Picton being the gateway to the South Island and the Marlborough Sounds, we are able to advise on all activities in the area. Laundry available.

Picton - Anakiwa   *Self-contained Homestay*   *22km W of Picton*

Crafters Homestay & Gallery
Leslie & Ross Close
Anakiwa Road, RD 1, Picton

Tel: (03) 574 2547 Fax: (03) 574 2947
Mob: 025 231 2245
crafters@actrix.gen.nz
www.bnb.co.nz/craftershomestaygallery.html

Double $85 Single $50 (Continental Breakfast)
Dinner $25 by arrangement
Credit cards accepted Pet on property
2 Single (1 bdrm)   1 Private

Our home at the head of Queen Charlotte Sound has a magnificent view, this tranquil and peaceful area is noted for bush walks, bird life, boating and kayaking. Our warm and comfortable self-contained guest area has twin bedroom, sunny lounge, private bathroom and fully equipped kitchen. Ross is a wood turner and Leslie a potter, both are happy to demonstrate their skills and their Gallery is open every day. Jack Russell terrier, Lofty, enjoys fishing trips in the motor launch as much as his owners do.

Picton   *Homestay B&B Historic Homestay*   *Picton Central*

House of Glenora
Birgite Armstrong
22 Broadway, Picton

Tel: (03) 573 6966 Fax: (03) 573 7735
Mob: 025 229 0594   glenora.house@clear.net.nz
www.glenora.co.nz

Double $95-$130 Single $60-$85
(Continental Breakfast) Credit cards accepted
3 Queen 3 Double 3 Single (6 bdrm)
2 Ensuite 1 Private 1 Guests share

Welcome to the House of Glenora, one of Marlborough Sounds historical homes. Built in 1860 and surrounded by a sprawling garden that is situated in the heart of Picton, yet very secluded and peaceful. Scandinavian creativity and NZ hospitality is blended into a colourful and vibrant home with a difference. As Birgite is a Masterweaver, House of Glenora incorporates the International Weaving School, studio and gallery. The large bedrooms offer extensive living areas, wide sunny verandas and patios are decorated with a stunning mixture of antiques and contemporary pieces.

Picton   *Homestay B&B   1km E of Picton Central*

Retreat Inn
Alison & Geoff
20 Lincoln Street, Picton
Tel: (03) 573 8160 Fax: (03) 573 7799
elliott.orchard@xtra.co.nz
www.retreat-inn.co.nz

Double $95 Single $65 (Special Breakfast)
Dinner $30 pp by arrangement
enquire re. private facilities $115
Credit cards accepted Pet on property
1 Queen 2 Single (2 bdrm) 2 Guests share

'RETREAT INN' is an ideal spot to relax and ponder! Nestled on a hillside, surrounded by natural vegetation (& native birds), it is quiet & restful ... & only 1km from the quaint waterside village of Picton. Cosy guest bedrooms are upstairs, facing the sun ... very comfortable beds all have electric blankets. Breakfast at 'Retreat Inn' is special. Transport provided locally. Laundry facilities. Flat off-street parking. Sorry, no smoking indoors. We are a 2 person/2 cat household!

Picton   *Self-contained B&B   Picton Central*

Grandvue
Rosalie & Russell Mathews
19 Otago Street, Picton
Tel: (03) 573 8553 Fax: (03) 573 8556
grandvue-mathews@clear.net.nz
www.nzhomestays.co.nz/mathews.htm

Double $90 Single $60 (Full Breakfast)
Child $15 Credit cards accepted
1 Queen (1 bdrm)
1 Ensuite

Situated on the hills overlooking Picton, Grandvue offers panoramic views of Queen Charlotte Sound. At the end of a cul-de-sac Grandvue is a quiet haven in a secluded garden, five minutes walk to town and its assortment of restaurants. Accommodation is a comfortable, warm self-contained apartment with TV, video, and access to a barbecue. Feast on scenic views from our upstairs conservatory, while enjoying a delicious and satisfying breakfast. A portable cot and highchair are available. Courtesy transport & laundry facilities available.

Port Underwood Sound   *Self-contained   35km SE of Picton*

Ocean Ridge
Sara & Ken Roush
Ocean Bay, Private Bag, Blenheim
Tel: (03) 579 9474 Fax: (03) 579 9474
roush@nmb.quik.co.nz
www.nmb.quik.co.nz/roush

Double $150-$300
Light breakfast available $10 pp by arrangement
Credit cards accepted
2 Queen 1 Double 1 Single (3 bdrm) 3 Ensuite

Self-contained apartment with majestic views of Port Underwood Sound's rocky shoreline and sandy beaches, the open Pacific Ocean, and distant snow capped mountains. Magnificent sunrises, sunsets. Possibly see Orcas, dolphins or seals nearby. Experience nature on the several walking tracks. Apartment contains 3 bedrooms (each with linen provided and private ensuite), kitchen, lounge, dining area, private entrance, spa pool. You will want to obtain your food provisions in Picton or Blenheim BEFORE arriving at Ocean Ridge, as it is a 45 minute drive on a partly gravel road.

Picton   *Homestay B&B   200mtr S of Picton*

Rivenhall
Nan & Malcolm Laurenson
118 Wellington Street, Picton,
Tel: (03) 573 7692 Fax: (03) 573 7692
rivenhall.picton@xtra.co.nz
www.bnb.co.nz/rivenhall.html

Double $80 Single $55 (Full Breakfast)
Child $15 Dinner $25pp by arrangement
Credit cards accepted
1 Queen (1 bdrm) 1 Private

We offer you a warm friendly atmosphere at Rivenhall, one of Picton's older more gracious homes, situated at the top of Wellington Street, overlooking the town, a four minute walk from Picton centre and easy walking to the ferry. Nan will provide the breakfast of your choice (evening meal upon request). Laundry facilities available. Marlborough Sounds tours leave from the bottom of Wellington Street. And of course just ring for directions or to have us pick you up from the ferry, bus, train or aircraft.

Picton   *Homestay B&B   800m N of Picton*

Echo Lodge
Lyn & Eddie Thoroughgood
5 Rutland Street,
Picton

Tel: (03) 573 6367 Fax: (03) 573 6387
www.bnb.co.nz/echolodge.html

Double $65-$75 Single $55
(Special Breakfast) Pet on property
1 Double 1 Twin 1 Single (3 bdrm)
2 Ensuite 1 Private

Lyn and Eddie and our little dog Osca welcome you to a relaxed atmosphere at Echo Lodge. Breakfast is our speciality. Come and experience our home-made bread, jams, omelettes and treats. Comfortable bedrooms with ensuites. Also tea and coffee-making facilitie ensure a good nights sleep. We are five minutes walk to shops, restaurants, ferries, busses and bush walks. Make yourself comfortable in our large lounge with a cosy wood fire for those chilly nights. A courtesy car is available, as is off-street parking.

Picton - Kenepuru Sounds   *Farmstay B&B   80km NE of Havelock*

The Nikaus
Alison & Robin Bowron
Waitaria Bay, RD 2, Picton
Tel: (03) 573 4432 Fax: (03) 573 4432
Mob: 025 544 712
www.bnb.co.nz/thenikaus.html

Double $80 Single $45 (Full Breakfast)
Dinner $25 Credit cards accepted Pet on property
1 Double 2 Single (2 bdrm) 1 Guests share

The Nikaus is a Sounds sheep & cattle farm situated in Waitaria Bay, Kenepuru Sound, 2 hours drive from Blenheim or Picton. We offer friendly personal service in our comfortable spacious home. The large gardens (in AA Garden Book) contain many rhododendrons, roses, Camellia, lilies and perennials with big sloping lawns and views out to sea. A swimming pool is available for guests use. We have three adult children. A non-smoking household with interests in farming, boating, fishing and gardening. We have a dog, Minny (Jack Russel x). Other animals include the farm dogs, donkeys, pet wild pigs. "Miss Piggy", turkeys, hens and peacocks.

Picton   *Homestay*   *Picton Central*

The White House
Gwen Stevenson
114 High Street, Picton

Tel: (03) 573 6767
Fax: (03) 573 8871
thewhitehousepicton@xtra.co.nz
www.bnb.co.nz/thewhitehousepicton.html

Double $60 Single $40 (Continental Breakfast) Twin $60
2 Double 3 Single (4 bdrm)
2 Guests share

The White House in Pictons main street offers affordable luxury - just ask any previous guest - in a friendly, quiet, warm home environment. It nestles on a sunny 1/4 acre, surrounded by mature trees and gardens, and is just a minutes walk to Picton's fabulous cafes and restaurants for your evening meal.

Located conveniently in the middle of town, this delightful 70 year old home is filled with Gwen's porcelain doll collection and numerous 'old worlde' touches. It has been immaculately maintained throughout with all refurbishments reflecting the era in which it was built.

Guest bedrooms are upstairs, all of which have quality beds to ensure a good nights sleep. Also on the same floor is the guest lounge which affords panoramic views over Picton to the harbour and hills beyond. However, if they prefer, guests are most welcome to share the downstairs lounge with their host.

Gwen's long association with the hospitality industry has made her aware that some of the things people miss when travelling is being able to pop into the kitchen and make a pot of tea or a cup of coffee when they like. White House guests are invited to do just that.

The laundry facilities are also available for guests. We look forward to making our guests' Picton visit an enjoyable and memorable one.

And while The White House is a non-smoking residence, guests are most welcome to smoke on the front verandah or the back deck areas. We regret our home is unsuitable for children.

Picton   *Homestay B&B*   *Picton central*

Palm Haven
Dae & Peter Robertson
15A Otago Street,
Picton

Tel: (03) 573 5644 Fax: (03) 573 5645
palmhaven@xtra.co.nz
www.bnb.co.nz/palmhaven.html

Double $70-$85 Single $50 (Continental Breakfast)
Child $25 Dinner $25 Pet on property Pets welcome
2 Queen 2 Twin 2 Single (4 bdrm)
1 Ensuite 1 Guests share

Couples, families and singles are welcome in our new, spacious home, designed for your comfort and convenience. It's just a few minutes walk from the centre of town and all leisure activities. Our guest rooms - one queen ensuite, one twin, one queen with single and one king single - can be adapted to your needs. We provide cot, highchair, a laundry service and courtesy pick-up. We're keen lawn bowlers, and we share our home with Toby, a very handsome red tabby.

Picton - Queen Charlotte Sounds   *Self-contained Homestay*   *11km Picton*

Ngakuta Bay Homestay
Eve & Scott Dawson
Manuka Drive, RD 1, Ngakuta Bay

Tel: (03) 573 8853 Fax: (03) 573 8353
Mob: 025 237 3300   ngakutabayhouse@xtra,co.nz
www.picton.co.nz/ngakuta

Double $100-$120 Single $80 (Continental Breakfast)
Self-contained unit $100 - $150
Weekly rates from $500
1 King 1 Double 2 Twin (4 bdrm) 2 Ensuite 2 Private

Ngakuta Bay Homestay is on the scenic Queen Charlotte Drive set in an acre of bush, the Homestay is built of NZ beach with large verandahs giving magnificent views over Ngakuta Bay. Each room has French doors onto the verandah with fridge, complimentary tea & coffee. Large lounge area with Sky TV. Also available from the Homestay are sailing dinghys, windsurfers and kayaks. The Bay has landscaped recreational area with safe swimming and barbecue facilities making it an ideal holiday resort for water sports, walking and fishing.

Picton - Queen Charlotte Sounds   *16km W of Picton*
Self-contained Homestay B&B

Tanglewood
Stephen and Linda Hearn
Queen Charlotte Drive, The Grove, RD 1, Picton

Tel: (03) 574 2080 Fax: (03) 574 2044
Mob: 027 481 4388   tanglewood.hearn@xtra.co.nz
www.bnb.co.nz/tanglewoodpicton.html

Double $95-$105 Single $70 (Full Breakfast)
Dinner $35 S/C Unit $150 Credit cards accepted
2 King/Twin (2 bdrm)   2 Ensuite

Nestled amongst the native ferns overlooking Queen Charlotte Sounds. Relax in our luxurious spacious rooms with ensuite. Our private guest wing includes lounge, kitchenette and barbeque area. Guests may choose to self-cater or home cooked meals are available by arrangement. Listen to the birds sing. Walk with us to view the glow-worms or enjoy our beautiful native garden. Swim at the beach only 100 metres away or enjoy a spot of fishing. Drop off and pick up by arrangement. Only 10 minutes away Queen Charlotte Track. We look forward to making you welcome

Picton - Ngakuta Bay *Self-contained Homestay B&B   11km W of Picton*

Bayswater
Paul & Judy Mann
25 Manuka Drive, Ngakuta Bay,
Queen Charlotte Drive, RD 1, Picton
Tel: (03) 573 5966 Fax: (03) 573 5966
www.bnb.co.nz/bayswater.html

Double $80 Single $50
(Continental Breakfast)
1 Queen 1 Twin (2 bdrm)
1 Ensuite 1 Private

A warm welcome awaits you at Bayswater B&B in Ngakuta Bay, situated 11km from Picton and 24km from Havelock on Queen Charlotte Drive in the beautiful Marlborough Sounds. Our modern home has a self-contained apartment with 2 double bedrooms, ensuite and private bathroom, kitchen, lounge, dining and laundry. Spectacular views over surrounding bush and Ngakuta Bay from your own private balcony. We offer continental breakfast or self catering. Complimentary transport available. Suitable for longer stays. Come relax with us in our little piece of paradise.

Port Underwood Sound *Homestay B&B   20km E of Picton*

Oyster Bay Lodge
Jim & Lynnette Mark
Oyster Bay, PO Box 146, Picton
Tel: (03) 579 9644 Fax: (03) 579 9645
Mob: 025 316 630
www.bnb.co.nz/oysterbaylodge.html

Double $85 Single $55 (Full Breakfast)
Dinner $30 Pet on property
2 Double 1 Single (2 bdrm)
1 Guests share

Our home/lodge is set in beautiful Oyster Bay where the first white man born in the South Island lived for many years. Oyster Bay Lodge has an uninterrupted view over the Bay in a charming historical part of Marlbourgh Sounds. We share this delightful spot with our lovely Bichon Frise Tammy. Lynnette is an avid patchwork and quilter, while Jim is a semi-retired bulider. We both enjoy music and look foward to your company.

Picton - Anakiwa *Self-contained Homestay   22km W of Picton*

Tirimoana House
Stephanie & Peter Bonser
257 Anakiwa Road, RD 1, Picton
Tel: (03) 574 2627 Fax: (03) 574 2627
tirimoana.bonser@xtra.co.nz
www.truenz.co.nz/tirimoana

Double $85-$140 Single $70 (Full Breakfast)
Dinner $35 S/C Flat $85 - 95, $15 each extra
Credit cards accepted Pet on property
1 King/Twin 2 Queen 2 Double 2 Single (4 bdrm)
3 Ensuite 1 Private

Every room in our long established homestay commands spectacular views along Queen Charlotte Sound. Our great reputation has been built on creating a warm and friendly environment for guests. Local cuisine is our speciality. All bedrooms and our stunning 'Sunrise Suite' have own bathrooms and our s/c flat has its own private deck. After activities such as kayaking walking, boating, mountain biking or the wineries, relax in our swimming and hot spa pools. 'Arrive as guests and leave as friends' is our maxim. We'd love to meet you.

Picton   *Self-contained B&B   Picton Central*

Lincoln Cottage
Laurel & Bruce Sisson
19 Lincoln Street, Picton

Tel: (03) 573 5285 Fax: (03) 573 5285
Mob: 021 658 140   lincolncottage@xtra.co.nz
www.bnb.co.nz/lincolncottage.html

Double $80-$100 Single $65 (Full Breakfast)
Credit cards accepted
2 Queen 2 Twin (4 bdrm)
2 Ensuite 1 Guests share

A warm welcome awaits you at our completely refurbished self contained cottage, set in a peaceful location within walking distance of town. We are surrounded by beautiful bush and delightful walkways. Enjoy a delicious breakfast - panoramic views from the dining room, the ambience (including a cosy fire in the winter), or just relax on the sundeck. A fully equipped kitchen, off-street parking, laundry facilities and courtesy transport are available for your convenience. We look forward to meeting you.

Picton - Karaka Point   *Homestay   8km E of Picton*

Karaka Point Lodge
Juliet & Brian Kirke
Karaka Heights, 312 Port Underwood Road, Picton

Tel: (03) 573 7700 Fax: (03) 573 5444
Mob: 021 103 1689   jb@karakapointlodge.co.nz
www.karakapointlodge.co.nz

Double $150-$195 Single $135-$180
(Full Breakfast) Dinner $55pp by arrangement
Credit cards accepted Pet on property
2 King 1 Queen 1 Single (3 bdrm) 2 Ensuite 1 Private

8km from Ferries, we welcome you and offer tasteful boutique/luxury accommodation. All rooms open onto spacious decks with the most extensive and best sea views. Secure rooms, best beds, air-conditioning, guest computer. Spa under the stars in secluded area! Relax on the decks. Walk to the beach. Explore the gorgeous area - one of New Zealand's best kept secrets - on our mountain bikes. Numerous activities nearby. Stay two nights or more to receive a bottle of delicious Marlborough Sauvignon Blanc. Enjoy a wine with us before dining.

Picton - Whatamango Bay   *Self-contained B&B   8km E of Picton*

'A Sea View'
Ann Holt
424 Port Underwood Road,
Whatamango Bay, Picton

Tel: (03) 573 8815 Mob: 021 189 1844
aseaview@paradise.net.nz
www.bnb.co.nz/aseaview.html

Double $185 Single $115
(Special Breakfast)
Dinner $55 Credit cards accepted
2 Queen 1 Double (3 bdrm)
3 Ensuite

For a truly magical adventure, we invite you to stay at 'A Sea View'. 9km from ferries, but worlds away! Experience a blend of English hospitality, romantic rooms, antiques, breathtaking sea views. Verdi on the veranda, or tea in the terraced gardens? Gourmet dinners upon request - diploma in Italian cuisine. Secluded romantic hideaway for the sophisticated traveller seeking a unique experience.

Picton - Whatamango Bay *Self-contained Homestay B&B   10km E of Picton*

Whatamango Lodge
Ralph and Wendy Cass
17 McCormicks Road, Whatamango Bay, Picton

Tel: (03) 573 5110 Fax: (03) 573 5110
whatamango.lodge@paradise.net.nz
www.picton.co.nz/whatamango

Double $90-$120 Single $75 (Full Breakfast) Dinner $30
2 Queen (2 bdrm)
2 Ensuite

Welcome to Whatamango Lodge, situated at the head of Whatamango Bay, looking out towards Queen Charlotte Sound. We invite you to share our modern, waterfront home and enjoy total peace and tranquillity. Relax on your own private balcony and watch the magnificent birdlife. Take a stroll around the beach or swim in the crystal clear water. There are also numerous bush walks. You may like to use our dinghy or fish off the rocks.

Kayaks are available to paddle round the bay. We are situated 10 mins on a sealed road from Picton. Follow the Port Underwood Road from Waikawa to Whatamango Bay, turn left into McCormicks Rd, waterfront location, no 17. A courtesy car is also available for transport to or from the ferry.

Guest accommodation comprises

1. A self contained unit (sleeps 4), Queen sized bedroom, lounge (sofa bed), full kitchen facilities, large deck.

2. Queen sized bedroom with ensuite. Use of spacious lounge and balcony. Laundry facilities available.

Dinner is available by arrangement and features traditional New Zealand cuisine, served with complimentary wine. For breakfast choose either a full country style cooked breakfast, or a light continental breakfast, or if you prefer a delectable combination of both. We are a non-smoking household. Not suitable for children.

Picton - Queen Charlotte Sound   *Homestay B&B   12 E of Picton*

Nestled in our private bay between palm trees and pohutukawas, and just a 20 minute boat ride from Picton through the stunning Marlborough Sounds, lies the **Lazy Fish**.

Our home sits eight metres from the sea. Breathtaking vistas can be enjoyed from hammocks and day beds on the verandas, from cushions sprawled along the decks, and from Adirondack chairs scattered along the beach. French doors lead into cosy sitting rooms stylishly decorated with paintings, sculptures and antique furniture.

Accommodation ranges from bedrooms in the homestead that open out on to the veranda (each with an ensuite), to secluded bungalows tucked in the gardens and along the beach. These provide a more private setting for you to enjoy your stay. They each have a spacious sleeping/living room with a four-poster bed and ensuite. Parquet floors lead out to a private terrace, veranda and garden where you can enjoy a candle-lit soak under the stars in your own outdoor bathtub.

There are many nooks and crannies to wile away the days. A terrace inlaid with intricate glass mosaics is the ideal spot for lounging in the sun or enjoying a long lunch. Moss covered walls encircle another courtyard; wisteria vines and recessed candle sconces create a magical place for evening dining.

For the more energetic there are: canoes, rowboat, wind surfer, fishing and snorkelling gear and a spa (right on the beach), walks, board games and puzzles. Let us organise a day walk on the Queen Charlotte track, dolphin watching or eco tours.

Come join us, pull up a chair and relax, enjoy the conversation or take time out to reflect, either way you're welcome at The Lazy Fish.

Regular water transport runs from Picton several times a day, which we will organise for you. Car storage available if necessary.

The Lazy Fish	**Tel: (03) 579 9049**	**Cost:**	Double $90-$200
Homestay	**Fax:** (03) 579 9089		Single $80-$175 (Full Breakfast)
Boat access from Picton	**E:** enquiries@lazyfish.co.nz		$50 for lunch and dinner
Chris Warren	**W:** www.lazyfish.co.nz		Credit cards accepted
Private Bag 429		**Beds:**	5 Double 1 Twin (6 bdrm)
Picton		**Baths**:	6 Ensuite

Pelorus - Mahau Sound *Homestay*   *33km W of Picton*

Ramona
Ken & Phyl Illes
460 Moetapu Bay Road,
Mahau Sound, Marlborough

Tel: (03) 574 2215 Fax: (03) 574 2915
Mob: 025 247 6668
www.bnb.co.nz/ramona.html

Double $95 Single $75
Lunch & dinner by arrangement
Credit cards accepted
2 Double 2 Twin (2 bdrm) 1 Guests share

Our new beachfront home on the beautiful Mahau Sound has been designed for you to share. Our guest floor has its own conservatory, here you can view the passing water traffic. Awake to the call of Bellbirds and Tuis, and after breakfast stroll around our rhododendron garden, or fossick on the beach. In the evening, see our glowworms. Phyl, a quilter and keen gardener, and Ken, a retired builder, will arrange visits to local art and craft studios, at your request.

Blenheim *Farmstay*   *1.5km S of Blenheim*

Rhododendron Lodge
Audrey & Charlie Chambers
St Andrews, RD 4,
State Highway 1, Blenheim

Tel: (03) 578 1145 Fax: (03) 578 1145
www.bnb.co.nz/rhododendronlodge.html

Double $80 Single $60 (Full Breakfast)
Suite $100 10% discount 3 days or more
2 Queen 2 Single (3 bdrm)
1 Ensuite 1 Private

Welcome to our small farm in Blenheim for quality accommodation in our spacious home with excellent beds. Bacon, eggs and tomatoes from our farm make a delicious breakfast. Our executive suite has a "Bechstein" piano. Tree ferns and gardens surround a large swimming pool. Spacious lawns with rhododendrons, roses and trees. We are close to Gourmet restaurants and have a selection of their menus. Marlborough has beautiful parks, wine trails, and scenic Marlborough sounds. Laundry available and courtesy phone call for next homestay. Happy Holidays.

Blenheim *Homestay*   *3km S of Blenheim*

Hillsview
Adrienne & Rex Handley

Tel: (03) 578 9562 Fax: (03) 578 9562
Mob: 025 627 6727 aidrex@xtra.co.nz
www.bnb.co.nz/hillsview.html

Double $75-$80 Single $50
(Full Breakfast) Dinner by arrangement
Cost less 10% if pre-booked by the night before.
1 King/Twin 1 Double 2 Twin 1 Single (4 bdrm)
2 Private

Welcome to our warm, spacious, non-smoking home in a quiet suburb with outdoor pool, off-street parking, and no pets. All beds have quality mattresses, electric blankets and wool underlays. Interests: Rex's (retired airline pilot) - are aviation oriented - models, microlights, homebuilts and gliding. Builds miniature steam locomotives, has 1930 Model A soft top tourer vintage car and enjoys barbershop singing. Adrienne's - cooking, spinning, woolcraft. Let us share these hobbies, plus our caring personal attention, complimentary beverages and all the comforts of home with you.

Blenheim   *Homestay B&B   2km W of Blenheim*

Mirfield
Pam & Charles Hamilton
24 Severne St, Blenheim

Tel: (03) 578 8220 Fax: (03) 578 8220
Tollfree: 0800 395 720   lifes4living@xtra.co.nz
www.bnb.co.nz/mirfield.html

Double $80 Single $50 (Full Breakfast)
Child $15 under 12yrs Dinner $17.50 by arrangement
Credit cards accepted
2 Queen 2 Single (3 bdrm)   2 Private 1 Family share

As keen travellers ourselves, we'd like to be sensitive to your needs, and warmly welcome you to our clean, comfortable accommodation,spacious living,guest lounge and proximity to Marlborough's diverse attractions.Although within the town boundary,we still offer a peaceful,rural aspect where we grow export flowers, fresh vegetables and can treat you to homemade jams/preserves at our table.Best of both worlds.Directions: Highway 6 from Blenheim. First left after Shell Service Station,right hand side, opposite last street light.

Blenheim   *Farmstay   8km S of Blenheim*

Maxwell Pass Farmstay
Jean & John Leslie
66 Maxwell Pass Road,
PO Box 269, Blenheim

Tel: (03) 578 1941 Fax: (03) 578 1941
www.bnb.co.nz/maxwellpassfarmstay.html

Double $80 Single $45 (Full Breakfast)
Child 1/2 price Dinner by arrangement
1 Double 3 Single (3 bdrm)
1 Private 1 Family share

We're 8kms from Blenheim on a Hill Country property running Beef Cattle. Our home is in a quiet valley with spacious grounds (350 roses) and native birds. Marlborough is a major grape growing area plus horticulture, agriculture and livestock farming. Marlborough Sounds nearby. Good trout fishing rivers, skifield 1 1/2 hours drive. Blenheim has golf courses, croquet greens and tennis courts set in beautiful gardens. We enjoy taking guests for a look around farm. Horse trekking 5 minutes drive. No pets. Laundry available. Directions: Please phone.

Blenheim - Rapaura   *Self-contained Vineyard Homestay   12km NW of Blenheim*

Thainstone
Vivienne & Jim Murray
120 Giffords Rd, RD 3, Rapaura

Tel: (03) 572 8823 Fax: (03) 572 8623
Mob: 021 283 1484   thainstone@xtra.co.nz
www.marlborough.co.nz/thainstone

Double $120 Single $70 (Full Breakfast)
Dinner $30 S/C House $120 - $180, 2-4 people
Credit cards accepted
1 King 2 Queen 1 Double 1 Twin 1 Single (5 bdrm)
1 Ensuite 1 Private 1 Guests share

Our large home is surrounded by vineyards and within walking distance of the Wairau River and several wineries. In our home there are three upstairs bedrooms and a guest lounge which opens onto a swimming pool courtyard. The self-catering house has two bedrooms and is fully equipped for longer stays. We are widely travelled and some interests are bird watching, trout fishing, woodworking and cards. Evening meals, by prior arrangement, are served with Marlborough wines. Unsuitable for children.

Blenheim   *Country Retreat*   *15km W of Blenheim*

The Sentinel
Lyn & Neil Berry
Wrekin Road, off Brancott Road, Fairhall, Blenheim
Tel: (03) 572 9143 Fax: (03) 572 9143
TheSentinel@xtra.Co.NZ
www.bnb.co.nz/thesentinel.html

Double $120 Single $100 (Full Breakfast)
Dinner $35 incl. wine Credit cards accepted
2 Queen 2 Single (2 bdrm)
2 Ensuite

Your hosts Neil and Lyn and their Labrador "Rusty" welcome you to their 14 ha property 15 km west of Blenheim, in the Brancott Valley beside Marlborough's famous wine trail. We overlook vineyards, olives and deer. A full breakfast is provided. Dinner is additional by arrangement. Our interests are pottery, almond growing and organic gardening. Directions: See Marlborough wine trail maps.

Blenheim   *Self-contained Homestay*   *500m W of Blenheim Central*

Beaver B&B
Jen & Russell Hopkins
60 Beaver Road, Blenheim
Tel: (03) 578 8401 Fax: (03) 578 8401
Mob: 021 626 151
rdhopkins@xtra.co.nz
www.bnb.co.nz/beaverbb.html

Double $80 Single $50 (Continental Breakfast)
Credit cards accepted Pet on property
1 Queen (1 bdrm)
1 Ensuite

Our self-contained unit can accommodate one couple or a single. Features include your own entrance, queensize bed, mini kitchen, bathroom - large bath, shower and separate toilet. Use of our laundry can be made upon request. Two cats and a bird live with us. We have off-street parking and are within ten minutes walk from central Blenheim. Please phone before 8 am or after 4.30 pm during the working week. If no response, Jennie can be contacted via her cell-phone. Fax us anytime.

Blenheim   *Homestay B&B*   *2km N of Blenheim*

Philmar
Wynnis & Lex Phillips
63 Colemans Road, Blenheim
Tel: (03) 577 7788 Fax: (03) 577 7788
www.bnb.co.nz/philmar.html

Double $70-$80 Single $50
(Continental Breakfast) Dinner $20pp
2 Queen 1 Twin (3 bdrm)
1 Ensuite 1 Guests share

Welcome to our home 2kms from the town centre. Guests can join us in our spacious sunny living areas. We both enjoy all TV sports and our other interests include wood turning, handcrafts and the Lions organisation. Blenheim is an ideal place to visit Picton, Nelson, whale watch and the many wineries, parks and craft shops in the area . We have two cats Snookie and Cuddles. Smoking is not encouraged. Just phone to be picked up at airport, train or bus. Dinner on request.

Blenheim   *Homestay Vineyard Homestay*   *9km SW of Blenheim*

Stonehaven
Jocelyn & David Wilson
414 Rapaura Road, RD 3, Blenheim
Tel: (03) 572 9730 Fax: (03) 572 9730
Mob: 021 442 433   stay@stonehavenhomestay.co.nz
www.stonehavenhomestay.co.nz
Double $160-$180 Single $90-$110
(Special Breakfast) Dinner by arrangement
Credit cards accepted Pet on property
1 King 1 Queen 1 Single (3 bdrm)
2 Ensuite 1 Private

Our new stone and cedar home is surrounded by gardens and 18 acres of Sauvignon Blanc vines. Close by are some of NZ's most outstanding wineries. We have the space, comfort and privacy to make your stay memorable. Share an interesting fresh breakfast with us in the "Pavilion" overlooking the swimming pool. We enjoy travel, skiing, books, music, gardening and good food. There are many fine restaurants locally. We have a friendly Burmese cat and are non smokers.

Blenheim   *Farmstay Homestay B&B*   *6km N of Blenheim*

Charmwood Rural Retreat
Linda & Peter Gibson
158 Murrays Road, RD 3, Blenheim
Tel: (03) 570 5409 Fax: (03) 570 5110
Mob: 025 847 403   charmwood@xtra.co.nz
www.bnb.co.nz/charmwood.co.nz.html
Double $100-$150 Single $90 (Full Breakfast)
Credit cards accepted Pet on property
2 Queen 2 Single (3 bdrm)
2 Ensuite 1 Private

Charmwood is located in beautiful wine & olive growing countryside within easy reach of the town, airport, seaport and recreational Marlborough. Charmwood facilities include tranquil gardens, asphalt tennis court and swimming pool. In the colder months enjoy bubbling away in the spa or relaxing beside our cosy fire. We share our home with Murdoch and Smudge the cats who also enjoys the rural tranquility that Charmwood provides. Start the day with our Country Fare breakfast where we would be happy to help you plan your itinerary.

Blenheim   *Homestay B&B Vineyard Homestay*   *12km W of Blenheim*

Black Birch Lodge
Margaret & David Barnsley
Jeffries Road, RD 3, Blenheim
Tel: (03) 572 8876 Fax: (03) 572 8806
barnsley@ihug.co.nz
www.bnb.co.nz/blackbirchlodge.html
Double $130-$140 Single $85-$100 (Full Breakfast)
Child 1/2 price Dinner $35 by arrangement
Credit cards accepted Pet on property
2 Queen 3 Single (3 bdrm)   2 Ensuite

Black Birch Lodge is ideally situated for exploring Marlborough's wine trail. Your hosts have been involved in the wine industry since 1981 both as growers and David as editor of Winepress. Most Marlborough wineries are only a matter of minutes away, the closest being the prestigious Herzog Winery and Restaurant situated at the bottom of Black Birch's vineyard. Other features include tennis court, pool, bikes, library, laundry, wine trail advice, vineyard walks and trout fishing in nearby Wairau River. We have a small friendly dog, "Perro".

Blenheim   *Homestay*

Baxter Homestay
Kathy & Brian Baxter
28 Elisha Drive, Blenheim
Tel: (03) 578 3753 Fax: (03) 578 3796
baxterart@clear.net.nz
www.bnb.co.nz/.html

Double $90-$130 (Continental Breakfast)
Credit cards accepted
2 King/Twin 1 Double (3 bdrm)
2 Private 1 Guests share

Brian, a renowned NZ artist, and Kathy, a keen gardener, welcome you to their spacious, sunny, modern home & art gallery. T.V. in all bedrooms (smokefree). Guests can enjoy magnificent panoramic views over Blenheim and nearby vineyards, or explore terraced gardens of roses, rhododendrons, camellias, perennials, deciduous trees etc. We can arrange tours to wineries, gardens, ski-field, golf courses etc. Laundry facilities. Our interests include gardening, music, travel, fishing, skiing, art, video production, and meeting people from all over the world.

Awatere Valley - Blenheim   *Farmstay*   *63km S of Blenheim*

Duntroon
Trish & Robert Oswald
Awatere Valley, Private Bag, Blenheim
Tel: (03) 575 7374 Fax: (03) 575 7374
Mob: 025 865 223   oswald@xtra.co.nz
www.bnb.co.nz/duntroon.html

Double $110 Single $70 (Full Breakfast) Child $70
Dinner $45 Backpacker accommodation $20
1 Double 4 Single (3 bdrm)
1 Guests share 1 Family share

Come and enjoy the peaceful surroundings of our 3500 acre high country Merino property in the beautiful Awatere Valley. The large homestead set in established grounds with tennis court and swimming pool offers warm spacious bedrooms with comfortable beds. Lunch and dinner served with local wines by arrangement. Farm tours on request. Our interests include clay-target shooting, travel, flying, tennis, boating and handcrafts. Over the summer the Awatere Valley Road is open through Molesworth Station to Hamner Springs.

Blenheim   *Farmstay*   *5km S of Blenheim*

Windmill Farm
Millie Amos
3516 Main Road, Riverlands, Blenheim
Tel: (03) 577 7853 Fax: (03) 577 7853
www.bnb.co.nz/windmillfarm.html

Double $80 Single $50 (Continental Breakfast)
Pet on property
1 Double 2 Twin (2 bdrm)
1 Ensuite 1 Private

Only 5km south of Blenheim on SH1, you will find Windmill Farm, a spacious and modern home in close proximity to the golf driving range and to Montana Winery. Comfortably appointed spacious twin bedroom with private ensuite and one double bedroom with private bathroom and spa. We have travelled to many countries overseas and aim to make our guests feel welcome and relaxed. We are non smokers who enjoy gardens, travel and meeting people. We welcome you to our home. Please phone first.

Blenheim   *Homestay B&B Family*   *Blenheim Central*

Grove Bank
Pauline & Peter Pickering
2652 State Highway 1, Grovetown, Blenheim
Tel: (03) 578 8407 Fax: (03) 578 8407 Tollfree: 0800 422 632
grovebank@xtra.co.nz   www.grovebank.co.nz

Double $70-$85 Single $50-$55 (Full Breakfast) Dinner $20 - $35
Groups $75 - $150 Credit cards accepted
2 King/Twin 3 Queen 2 Single (8 bdrm)   6 Ensuite 1 Private 1 Spa bath

Pauline and Peter invite you to stay at our 8 acre olive grove and vineyard, which is located conveniently on SH1 on the northern boundary of Blenheim.

We offer 8 double bedrooms with ensuites plus bedroom and bathroom appliances. Our home is designed especially with homestay guests in mind. Spacious guest lounges (with televisions) opening onto large balconies, offer panoramic views of the plains ranges and river.

After a day of sightseeing and enjoying the delights of the "Gourmet Province", cool off in the swimming pool, relax in the spa, take a stroll in Pauline's gardens the olive grove/vineyard. Some courtesy transport is available for evening dining.

We offer continental and cooked breakfast and meals as requested. A former restaurateur and butcher, peter's breakfasts are legendary. Evening meals may consist of meats and fresh grown vegetables or fish caught by Peter from the Marlborough Sounds, rivers and lakes. If you feel like dining out, Marlborough's finest Italian Restaurant (Best pasta in the world - "Cuisine"), the Whitehaven winery and cafe and local bar and bistro are within 5 minutes walking distance.

We are happy to share our extensive local knowledge and contacts which will enable you to personalise and optimise your stay in the "Gourmet Province"/ Free laundry facilities. Directions: On Blenheim's north boundary definitely 100 metres north of narrow concrete bridge, on state highway 1, turn into multi signed entrance shared by the Research Centre. Then immediately turn left into gravel drive and follow to house.

Blenheim   *Homestay   Blenheim Central*

Maxwell House
John and Barbara Ryan
82 Maxwell Road, Blenheim

Tel: (03) 577 7545 Fax: (03) 577 7545
Mob: 025 234 9977
www.bnb.co.nz/maxwellhouse.html

Double $125 Single $100 (Full Breakfast)
Credit cards accepted
1 Queen 1 Twin (2 bdrm)
2 Ensuite

Welcome to Marlborough. We invite you to stay at Maxwell House, a grand old Victorian residence.
Built in 1880 our home has been elegantly restored and is classified with the Historic Places Trust. Our
large guest rooms are individually appointed with ensuite, lounge area, television and tea and coffee
making facilities. Breakfast will be a memorable experience, served around the original 1880's Kauri
table. Set on a large established property Maxwell House is an easy ten minute walk to the town centre.
Non Smoking.

Rapaura - Blenheim   *Self-contained Vinestay   8km N of Blenheim*

Twiga
Andy & Kris Bibby
35 Selmes Road, Rapaura, RD 3, Blenheim

Tel: (03) 570 5706 Fax: (03) 570 5726
Mob: 021 267 4011   Tollfree: 0800 284 670
twiga@agrimech.co.nz
www.twiga.co.nz

Double $175 Single $100
(Continental & Full Breakfast)
Twin $150 Credit cards accepted
1 Queen 1 Twin (2 bdrm)   2 Ensuite

Our self-contained, double storey accommodation has views across the garden and vineyard to the
Richmond Ranges. The living area includes a kitchenette, TV and wood-burner and a sun-deck outside
to sit and enjoy sundowners. Our double room ensuite has a relaxing spa bath. We are at the heart of the
Marlborough wine region and close to the Marlborough Sounds, renowned for its mussel industry. We
look forward to welcoming you to this special corner of New Zealand.

If you would like dinner
most hosts require 24 hours' notice.

Blenheim - Rapaura   *15km SW of BlenheimB&B*

Self-contained Vineyard Cottage

Tamar Vineyard
Clive & Yvonne Dasler
67 Rapaura Road, RD 3, Blenheim
Tel: (03) 572 8408 Fax: (03) 572 8405
Tollfree: 0800 429 922   tamar.vineyard@xtra.co.nz
www.tamarvineyard.co.nz

Double $140-$160 Single $120 (Special Breakfast)
Child negotiable Credit cards accepted
1 Queen 1 Single (1 bdrm) 1 Private

Situated in the heart of the wine region, Tamar is one of Marlborough's oldest vineyards. Our newly built cottage is a romantic retreat with breathtaking views through the vines to the Richmond Ranges. Luxuriate in an ornately carved four poster bed under a feather down duvet, then enjoy a gourmet breakfast before taking a leisurely stroll to nearby wineries and restaurants. Or let us help organise your wine trail, skifield, or Marlborough Sounds experience. Our secluded, smoke free cottage is self-contained and a warm welcome and memorable stay is assured.

Blenheim   *Homestay   2km N of Blenheim*

Orchard View
Lynley & John McGinn
20 Nolans Road, Grovetown, Blenheim, New Zealand
Tel: (03) 578 5444 Fax: (03) 578 5444
Mob: 021 295 7031   www.bnb.co.nz/orchardview.html
Tollfree: 0800 006 903   orchardview@xtra.co.nz

Double $90-$110 Single $70
(Continental & Full Breakfast) Ensuite $110
Credit cards accepted Pet on property
2 Queen 1 Double 2 Single (3 bdrm)
1 Ensuite 1 Family share

Set in 3/4 acre of parklike gardens, 3 mins drive to Blenheim and 10 mins to Picton. Our home is very popular with guests for its spaciousness and homely atmosphere. Orchard View is an ideal base for exploring the many wineries, craft shops and walkways. It is also close to our beautiful Marlborough Sounds and handy to some good restaurants. We are very relaxed and encourage our guests to be also. Full breakfast supplied. Own guests lounge with refreshments, TV, stereo.

Blenheim   *Self-contained Homestay B&B   2 s/c villas6min N of Blenheim*

Chardonnay Lodge
George and Ellenor Mayo
1048 Rapaura Road, Spring Creek, Blenheim
Tel: (03) 570 5194 Fax: (03) 570 5196
chardonnaylodge@xtra.co.nz
www.chardonnaylodge.co.nz

Double $105-$130 Single $85-$100 (Special Breakfast)
Child $20 (5 yrs & over) Dinner $35 pp by arr.
extra persons in villa $20 pp Credit cards accepted
3 Queen 3 Single (3 bdrm) 3 Ensuite

We offer excellent accommodation and facilities, including secluded solar heated swimming pool, private spa, sun lounges, barbecue and a full sized tennis court. Central to the superb vineyards and restaurants, with Blenheim just 6 minutes away we provide homestay with own ensuite or high standard self-contained villas. You will find everything you and your family need for a comfortable and relaxing stay. Our fluffy persian cats will welcome you to the lawns and garden. We are 2.2km from the Spring Creek turn off on SH1. Courtesy vehicle for all transport terminal transfers.

Blenheim *B&B* *2km W of Blenheim*

Karere House David & Maggie Cleveland
6 Karere Place, Springlands, Blenheim
Tel: (03) 579 1159 Fax: (03) 579 1160
Mob: 021 502 995 david@karerehouse.co.nz
www.karerehouse.co.nz
Double $150-$200 Single $130-$150 (Full Breakfast)
Unsuitable for children under 12
Dinner $60 Credit cards accepted
1 King/Twin 1 King 1 Queen (3 bdrm)
1 Ensuite 1 Private

Karere House enjoys a rural aspect, offering modern elegant accommodation in the heart of the Marlborough wine district. Three luxuriously appointed guest bedrooms, with terraces and outstanding views. Walk or cruise the Marlborough Sounds, wine tasting, arts and crafts, whale watching at Kaikoura, just a few of the local amenities. On your return enjoy a glass of wine followed by one of Maggie's (Cordon Bleu qualified) dinners. Heated swimming pool and petanque available. Welcome to Karere House, we look forward to meeting you.

Blenheim *Homestay* *3km Blenheim Centre*

Richmond View
Allan & Jan Graham
25 Elmwood Avenue, Blenheim,
Tel: (03) 578 8001 Fax: (03) 578 8001
Mob: 025 458 074 a.w.graham@xtra.co.nz
www.bnb.co.nz/richmondview.html
Double $90 Single $70 (Continental Breakfast)
Dinner by arrangement Pet on property
1 Queen 1 Twin (2 bdrm)
1 Guests share

We welcome you to our new home built on the slopes of Wither Hills situated to the South side of Blenheim, having panoramic views of town, Richmond ranges and Cook Strait in the distance. Offering Queen and Twin rooms with electric blankets and heating. Complimetary spa available. Bathroom and toilet are separate and private. Our interests comprise boating, vintage cars, flying and enjoying Marlborough's fantastic waterways and wineries which you can share by arrangement. Local pickup available on request. Dinner by arrangement.

Blenheim *B&B* *100m W of Blenheim*

Henry Maxwell's Central B&B
Rae Woodman
28 Henry Street, Blenheim
Tel: (03) 578 8086 Fax: (03) 578 8086
Mob: 025 200 9862 stay@henrymaxwells.co.nz
Tollfree: 0800 436 796 www.bnb.co.nz/maxwells.html
Double $90-$120 Single $65
(Full Breakfast) Pet on property
3 Queen 4 Twin 3 Single (4 bdrm)
2 Ensuite 1 Private 1 Guests share

Welcome to 'Henrys', a gracious 75 year old home. Guests have spacious quiet rooms, 2 with ensuites, 2 share bathroom. TV, tea, coffee, cookies and complimentary port. Queen size beds and large comfortable arm chairs. All overlook gardens. Breakfast in the unique dining room (maps and charts) is something to remember. Three minutes stroll to town, many excellent restaurants, shops, theatre, movies, etc. Find 'Henrys', corner of Henry and Munro Streets between High Street and Maxwell Road. Offstreet parking. Relax and enjoy the garden and sun.

Blenheim   *Homestay B&B Country Homestay*
1.5km S of Blenheim

Green Gables
Benjamin & Jeannine Van Straaten
RD4, Gate 3011, Blenheim
Tel: (03) 577 9205 Fax: (03) 577 9206
Mob: 025 547 520   Tollfree: 0800 273 050
green_gables_blenheim@xtra.co.nz
www.bnb.co.nz/greengables.html

Double $85-$100 Single $40-$60 (Continental Breakfast) Dinner $25 cooked breakfast $5 extra Credit cards accepted Pet on property Children welcome
2 Queen 2 Double (3 bdrm) 3 Ensuite

Enjoy your stay at our luxurious and exceptionally spacious two storey home located in rural Blenheim. Only 2km from the town centre, Green Gables is set in a tranquil, one acre landscaped garden and offers quiet, luxurious surroundings, although close to State Highway 1 and to town.

Guest accommodation comprises of three large bedrooms, all with en suite bathrooms. Two of our rooms have queen - sized beds and the third has a double bed. All rooms are fully equipped with electric blankets, radio clocks, hair dryers and room heating and two rooms have glass doors that open onto private balconies affording panoramic views of Blenheim. An adjoining guest lounge has a small library and television set and there are additional TV sets in the queen rooms. Coffee and tea making facilities are available and you are invited to use the laundry, fax and email facilities if required.

For breakfast choose either a full, country-style cooked breakfast or a light continental breakfast or if you prefer a delectable combination of both, served with delicious home-made jams and preserves. Dinner is available by arrangement and features traditional New Zealand cuisine served with a complimentary drink.

We are horticulturists and grow cut flowers. Bruce our friendly cocker spaniel would love to play ball with you and our ginger cat Sharky is visitor friendly and lives outside. Green Gables backs onto the picturesque Opawa river. In season this gentle river offers trout fishing, eeling and whitebaiting. A small rowing boat is available for your use at no extra charge. As an additional courtesy we would be pleased to help you with the on -booking of your B&B accommodation. Let us phone ahead for you and you'll make valuable savings on your phone card.

Directions: On SH1, 1/2 km south of Blenheim town, gate number 3011. 20 minutes form Picton ferry. Green Gables sign at drive entrance.

Renwick   *Self-contained Homestay Vineyard Lodge*   *15km W of Blenheim*

LeGrys Vineyard
Jennifer & John Joslin
PO Box 65, Renwick, Marlborough
Tel: (03) 572 9490 Fax: (03) 572 9491
Mob: 021 313 208   stay@legrys.co.nz
www.legrys.co.nz

Double $140 (Full Breakfast)
S/C double max 4 $225 + $45 pp Credit cards accepted
2 Queen 2 Single (3 bdrm) 2 Private

Waterfall Lodge - self-contained, vineyard setting. 2 beds. Queen, 2 single. Kitchen facilities, dining, lounge area, gas bbq. Main house - queen room, private bathroom. Both offer unique mud-brick construction and offer rustic charm combined with stylish furnishings. Breakfast hamper with full provisions daily. Ideal base for winery visits, golf, Sounds cruising, walking, Trout fishing. Blenheim Town 10 mins drive. Solar heated indoor pool. LeGrys & Mudhouse wines available, complimentary tasting and tray of nibbles to welcome you. John and Jennifer cruised the world in their yacht. We have a Springer Spaniel, Pippin.

Renwick   *Homestay*   *10km W of Blenheim*

Clovelly (formerly Devonia)
Don & Sue Clifford
2a Nelson Place, Renwick,
Marlborough 7352
Tel: (03) 572 9593 Fax: (03) 572 7293
clifford@actrix.gen.nz
www.bnb.co.nz/clovelly.html

Double $95-$110 Single $70-$80 (Full Breakfast)
Credit cards accepted Pet on property
1 Queen 1 Twin (2 bdrm)
2 Private

Our colonial style home is set in 1/2 an acre of lovely private grounds in the heart of vineyard country. We overlook orchards and out to the Richmond Range. Relax under the trees with refreshments or by a glowing fire in winter. Visit our quaint local English pub - dine in the village or vineyard restaurants. We are within 'stroll and taste' distance of a number of prestigious vineyards. Rest and unwind with Don and Sue and our two little Scottish terriers Chloe and Phoebe, who will welcome you warmly.

Havelock   *40km E of Picton*

Carnlough
Reg & Margaret Williams
101 Main Road,
Havelock, Marlborough
Tel: (03) 574 1444
Paregma@clear.net.nz
www.bnb.co.nz/carnlough.html

Double $80-$90 Single $80
Child $20 Pet on property
1 Queen (1 bdrm)
1 Ensuite

Our home is a gracious 1930's Villa, designed for space and comfort, 40 minutes from the Interisland Ferry. We have travelled widely abroad and have family here and overseas. We are members of the Lions club and we have a friendly West Highland Terrier who loves to greet our guests. Havelock is only 20 minutes from the Marlborough wine trail and a hub for many outdoor activities both on and off the water. Several excellent restaurants are within easy walking distance of our home.

Canvastown   *Homestay*   *50km W of Picton*

Woodchester
Wayne & Marilyn Te Amo
84 Te Hora Pa Road, Canvastown
Tel: (03) 574 1123 Fax: (03) 574 1123
Mob: 027 224 4765   marilynt@xtra.co.nz
www.embark.to/woodchesterlodge

Double $90 Single $55 (Full Breakfast)
Child $20 Dinner from $20 Credit cards accepted
1 Queen 1 Double 2 Twin (3 bdrm)
1 Guests share

We are down to earth people, our home is lodge style with country atmosphere. You will be accommodated in the guest wing but share meals and conversation in our dining room and lounge. Consider more than one night's stay as fishing and hunting are only minutes away. Walking and tramping tracks are prolific or cruise the fabulous sounds in comfort. Fishing and hunting parties must book forward. We love traditional Kiwi tucker and wines and encourage you to share evening meals with us. Welcome to Woodchester.

Pelorus Bridge   *Self-contained Guest House*   *45mins from Blenheim & Nelson*

Lord Lionel
Lionel & Monika Neilands
SH6 Pelorus, RD 2,
Rai Valley, Marlborough
Tel: (03) 574 2770 Fax: (03) 574 2770
www.bnb.co.nz/lordlionel.html

Double $80-$90 Single $50
(Full Breakfast) Child $20 (12 & under)
1 King 3 Double 2 Single (6 bdrm)
1 Private 2 Guests share

We wish to invite you to our riverbank lodge. A fishing paradise in the heart of the Pelorus River Country with excellent fishing for Rainbow, brown trout and some salmon. We are situated 45 minutes from Nelson and Blenheim on State Highway 6 in the midst of 1 1/2 acre of native forest with prolific bird life. We are in the heart of great walking tracks. We are 1 1/2km from Pelorus Bridge Scenic Reserve, which is one of the finest reserves in New Zealand. As we have our own private dwelling, the guests have the run of the house with excellent cooking facilities. Entire house available.

Please let your hosts know if you have to cancel
they will have spent time preparing for you.

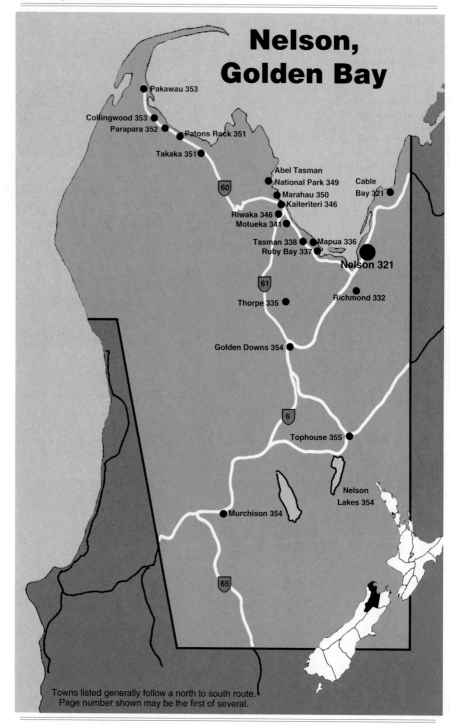

Nelson, Golden Bay

Pakawau 353
Collingwood 353
Parapara 352
Patons Rock 351
Takaka 351
Abel Tasman
National Park 349
Cable
Bay 321
Marahau 350
Kaiteriteri 346
Riwaka 346
Motueka 341
Tasman 338
Mapua 336
Ruby Bay 337
Nelson 321
60
61
Thorpe 335
Richmond 332
Golden Downs 354
6
Tophouse 355
Nelson
Lakes 354
Murchison 354
65

Towns listed generally follow a north to south route.
Page number shown may be the first of several.

Nelson - Cable Bay *B&B* *20km N of Nelson*

Quail Ridge
Ken and Gerrie Young
Cable Bay Rd, Hira, RD1, Nelson
Tel: (03) 545 1899 Fax: (03) 545 1890
quailridge@clear.net.nz
www.quailridge.co.nz

Double $120 Single $115 (Continental Breakfast)
Child $15 Dinner $30pp Credit cards accepted
2 Queen 2 Single (2 bdrm)
2 Ensuite

Quail Ridge offers a very special, memorable experience. The Cable Bay location is quiet and beautiful with wonderful water, island and farmland views. The two attractive separately located guest studios are designed for privacy and relaxation. Terraces provide socialising, barbecuing and outdoor dining areas. A quiet swimming beach, national walkway, and fishing are nearby with 4WD bikes, kayaking, and horse trekking locally. Restaurants and activities of Nelson city are 20 minutes away. Always a friendly welcome - our dog and cat enjoy sharing the moment.

Nelson *B&B Heritage Inn* *Nelson Central*

California House Inn
Tony & Glenis Aubrey
29 Collingwood St, Nelson
Tel: (03) 548 4173 Fax: (03) 548 4184
info@californiahouse.co.nz www.californiahouse.co.nz

Double $170-$220 Single $140-$170
(Full Breakfast) Credit cards accepted
4 Queen 1 Double 1 Twin 5 Single (5 bdrm)
5 Ensuite

Quiet, spacious, sunny; we invite you to enjoy the charm and character of our faithfully restored 1893 villa. Features include English oak panelling, stained glass windows, NZ native timbers and wide verandahs overlooking the garden. Your choice of five well appointed guestrooms with ensuite bathrooms, colonial furnishings, memorabilia & fresh flowers from the garden. Guest sitting room with library, open fire, refreshments, a congenial atmosphere and friendly hosts ensure relaxation and enjoyment. Delicious homebaked Californian breakfasts a highlight, all within five minutes walk of city centre!

Nelson *Homestay* *2km SW of Nelson*

Harbour View Homestay
Judy Black
11 Fifeshire Crescent, Nelson
Tel: (03) 548 8567 Fax: (03) 548 8667
Mob: 025 247 4445
www.bnb.co.nz/harbourviewhomestaynelson.html

Double $115-$135 Single $90-$125
(Continental Breakfast) Full breakfast $5pp extra
Credit cards accepted Pet on property
2 Queen 2 Single (3 bdrm) 2 Ensuite 1 Private

Harbour View Homestay

Our home is above the harbour entrance. Huge windows capture spectacular views of beautiful Tasman Bay, Haulashore Island, Tahunanui Beach, across the sea to Abel Tasman National Park and mountains. Observe from the bedrooms, dining room and decks, ships and pleasure craft cruising by as they enter and leave the harbour. If you can tear yourself away from our magnificent view, within walking distance along the waterfront there are excellent cafes and restaurants. Your hosts, Judy and David offer you a warm welcome and a memorable stay.

Nelson   *Homestay B&B*   *6km NE of Nelson*

Mike Cooper & Lennane Kent
4 Seaton Street, Nelson
Tel: (03) 545 1671 Fax: (03) 545 1671
cooperkent@actrix.gen.nz
www.bnb.co.nz/kent.html

Double $65-$70 Single $50 (Full Breakfast)
Child neg Dinner $30 with prior notice
Credit cards accepted Pet on property
1 Queen 1 Double 1 Single (2 bdrm)
2 Ensuite

Five minutes from Nelson City centre we give you a warm welcome to our comfortable home in a safe quiet neighbourhood with superb views over Tasman Bay and out to the Tasman mountains. Our guest accommodation is almost self-contained and is well equipped with a small lounge, fridge, TV, tea and coffee making facilities and a microwave. Laundry facilities are available for your use. Our interests include our large collection of books which you are welcome to use, sea fishing, education and our lively schnauzer dog.

Nelson   *B&B*   *Nelson Central*

Borogove
Judy & Bill Hiener
27 Grove Street, Nelson
Tel: (03) 548 9442 Fax: (03) 548 9443
Tollfree: 0800 379 308   hihiener@xtra.co.nz
www.bnb.co.nz/borogove.html

Double $100-$115 Single $85 (Full Breakfast)
2 Queen 1 Single (3 bdrm)
3 Ensuite

Behind a high laurel hedge you will discover BOROGOVE, our century-old heritage home set in a fragrant garden. Characteristic high ceilings, period furniture and antiques contribute to its unique charm. Bedrooms are elegantly decorated and have en-suite bathrooms. Relaxing arm-chairs, tea/coffee, heaters, electric blankets, reading-lights and TV ensure your comfort. Generous cooked breakfasts are served in our Victorian dining-room. It is a 3 minute walk to the Visitors' Centre, the shops and restaurants. Abel Tasman bus collection. Off-street parking.

Nelson   *Self-contained B&B Homestay Units*   *5km SW of Nelson*

Arapiki
Kay & Geoff Gudsell
21 Arapiki Road, Stoke, Nelson
Tel: (03) 547 3741 Fax: (03) 547 3742
bnb@nelsonparadise.co.nz
www.nelsonparadise.co.nz

Double $75-$110 Single $70-$90
(Continental breakfast optional, $7.50 pp)
Credit cards accepted Pet on property
1 Queen 1 Double 1 Single (2 bdrm)
2 Ensuite

Enjoy a relaxing holiday in the midst of your trip. The two quality smokefree units in our large home offer comfort, privacy and offstreet parking in a central location. The larger Unit 1 is in a private garden setting. A ranchslider opens on to a deck with outdoor furniture. It has an electric stove, microwave, TV, auto washing machine & phone. Unit 2 has a balcony with seating to enjoy sea and mountain views. It has a microwave, hotplate, TV & phone. We have two Tonkinese cats.

Nelson *Homestay B&B   6km S of Nelson*

Tarata Homestay
John & Mercia Hoskin
5 Tarata Street, Stoke, Nelson
Tel: (03) 547 3426 Fax: (03) 547 3640
Tollfree: 0800 107 308
hosts@taratahomestay.co.nz
www.taratahomestay.co.nz
Double $90-$95 Single $65-$70
(Continental Breakfast) Child $25
Credit cards accepted Pet on property
1 Queen 1 Twin (2 bdrm) 1 Private

In a quiet street surrounded by gardens and mature trees, we offer quality accommodation for only one party of guests at a time giving them exclusive use of all facilities. These include a comfortable lounge with a range of complimentary teas and coffee. We have a comprehensive selection of local information so that you can plan your stay, and we are always available to help you with ideas, expecially if time is limited. Our friendly Golden Labrador loves the opportunity to socialise with guests.

Nelson *Self-contained B&B   2.5km S of Nelson*

Sunset Waterfront B&B
Bernie Kirk & Louis Balshaw
455 Rock Road, Nelson

Tel: (03) 548 3431 Fax: (03) 548 3743
Mob: 025 363 300   waterfrontnelson@xtra.co.nz
www.bnb.co.nz/sunsetwaterfrontbb.html
Double $150 Single $120 (Full Breakfast)
Credit cards accepted
2 Queen 1 Twin 1 Single (2 bdrm) 2 Ensuite

Sunset Waterfront B&B provides wonderful panoramic sea and mountain views of Tasman Bay. Ideally situated to walk to quality seafood restaurants. Stroll along the promenade to enjoy the sunset or take an evening walk along the beach. We provide comfortable bedrooms with ensuites, TV, fridge, and sea views. One room for optional self catering. Freshly brewed coffee and local fresh produce provided. Home made fruitbread, scones and muffins. Also freshly picked raspberries and strawberries when in season. Off street parking. Regretfully no children under 12. Pet, Bono our Golden Retriever. Come enjoy our paradise!

Nelson *Self-contained B&B   7km N of Nelson*

Muritai Manor
Jan & Stan Holt
48 Wakapuaka Road, Wakapuaka, RD 1, Nelson

Tel: (03) 545 1189 Fax: (03) 545 0740
Mob: 025 370 622   Tollfree: 0800 260 662
muritai.manor@xtra.co.nz   www.muritaimanor.co.nz
Double $165-$195 Single $130-$160 (Full Breakfast)
Children & Dinner by arrangement Credit cards accepted
2 King/Twin 1 King 2 Queen 5 Single (5 bdrm)
5 Ensuite

Welcome to Muritai Manor, a unique Edwardian home in a semi-rural setting with superb views across Tasman Bay. Five luxury ensuite bedrooms furnished with antiques, TVs, refreshments, hairdryers, bathrobes, flowers, & toiletries; with electric blankets on all the beds. Enjoy gourmet breakfasts in the guest dining room. Open fires in both lounge & dining room in winter. Large solar heated swimming pool & spa in established garden with mature trees. Jess Gennie & Dande are the friendly canine family members. Your hosts - Jan & Stan.

Nelson   *Homestay*
2km W of Nelson Central

Jubilee House
Patsy & Sheridan Parris
107 Quebec Road, Nelson

Tel: (03) 548 8511
Fax: (03) 548 8511
Mob: 025 487 767
Tollfree: 0800 11 88 91
info@jubileehouse.co.nz
www.jubileehouse.co.nz

Double $90-$100   Single $60-$70
(Special Breakfast) Credit cards
accepted Pet on property
2 Double 2 Single (4 bdrm)
1 Guests share

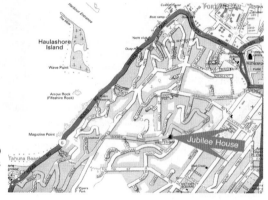

Visit our website : www.jubileehouse.co.nz

Many of our guests have told us we have some of the finest views of any Bed & Breakfast in New Zealand. High on a ridge overlooking the whole of Nelson City, beautiful Tasman Bay, mountains and harbour entrance. Drive downtown in three minutes, or try our new walkway from the top of Quebec Road to the valley below.

Breakfast is special, our own Muesli made with Beech honey and cinnamon, homemade yoghurt, breads, muffins and scones. Taste our local Pomeroy's fruit or spiced teas, or Sheridan's special blend of coffee beans. Waffles are our specialities, try a Vanilla and Cinnamon one, topped with seasonal fruit and real Canadian maple syrup. You might like to go savoury with salami, tasty bacon and Bratwurst sausage. We can serve something traditional or different, or cater for your special diet, with adequate notice.

As Nelson leads the rest of the country in sunshine hours stay a while in this beautiful region. You may even get to see one of our spectacular sunsets. We are happy to help or advise you on places of interest and things to do, or on the many great restaurants and cafes we have in our City.

We provide a smoke free environment, courtesy pick-up from the visitor centre or bus depot, and offer off street parking. KJ our Devon Rex cat may grace you with his presence; he is non-allegenic as his coat is wool.

Nelson   *Homestay B&B   2km E of Nelson*

Brooklands
Lorraine & Barry Signal
106 Brooklands Rd, Atawhai, Nelson
Tel: (03) 545 1423 bsignal@paradise.net.nz
www.bnb.co.nz/brooklands.html

Double $90-$110 Single $60 (Full Breakfast)
Child By arrangement Dinner $30
Credit cards accepted Children welcome
1 Queen 1 Double 2 Single (3 bdrm)
1 Ensuite 1 Guests share

Brooklands is a spacious, luxurious 4 level home with superb sea views. Guests have exclusive use of 2 levels. The large bathroom has a spa bath for two. One bedroom has a private balcony. There are spacious indoor/outdoor living areas. We enjoy sports, running, travel and outdoors. Lorraine makes dolls and bears and enjoys crafts, gardening and cooking. We are close to Nelson's attractions - beaches, crafts, wine trails, national parks, lakes and mountains. We enjoy making new friends. Smoke free. Courtesy transport available.

Nelson Central   *B&B   0.8km E of Nelson*

Sunflower Cottage
Marion & Chris Burton
70 Tasman Street, Nelson
Tel: (03) 548 1588 Fax: (03) 548 1588
marion@sunfloweraccommodation.co.nz
www.sunfloweraccommodation.co.nz

Double $95 Single $65 (Continental Breakfast)
2 King/Twin 2 Twin 2 Single (2 bdrm)
2 Ensuite

Welcome to our home on the banks of the Maitai River. Our large bedrooms, with ensuite bathrooms, are serviced daily with fresh flowers, complimentary basket of fruit and contain TV, microwave, fridge, tea/coffee making facilities, and toaster. Breakfast is self-service. We are very close to Queen's Gardens, Suter Art Gallery and the Botanical Hill, where after an easy walk to the centre of New Zealand, you experience wonderful views over Tasman Bay and Nelson township. Courtesy car to airport or bus depot.

Nelson   *B&B   Nelson Central*

The Baywick Inn
Tim Bayley & Janet Southwick
51 Domett Street, Nelson
Tel: (03) 545 6514 Fax: (03) 545 6517
Mob: 025 545 823   baywicks@iconz.co.nz
www.bnb.co.nz/thebaywickinn.html

Double $125-$155 Single $95-$120
(Special Breakfast) Dinner $40pp
Credit cards accepted Pet on property
3 Queen 1 Single (3 bdrm)   2 Ensuite 1 Private

Overlooking the Maitai River, Brook Stream and Centre of New Zealand this elegantly restored 1885 Victorian, offers spacious and luxuriously appointed rooms. Each has its own character and charm with antique furnishings, comfortable beds and modern amenities. Enjoy afternoon tea or cappuccino in the cozy guest lounge, sunroom or garden and chat with Tim about his classic MG's. Janet, a cook by profession, makes breakfast to order, healthy or indulgent, cooked or continental. This Canadian/New Zealand ambiance is enhanced by their lively fox terrier.

Nelson *B&B Historic Bed & Breakfast Hotel*   *500m E of Nelson Central*

The Sussex Bed & Breakfast Hotel
Carol & Stephen Rose
238 Bridge Street, Nelson
Tel: (03) 548 9972
Fax: (03) 548 9975
Mob: 025 784 846
Tollfree: 0800 868 687
reservations@sussex.co.nz
www.sussex.co.nz

Double $120-$150 Single $100-$130
(Continental Breakfast)
Credit cards accepted
Pet on property
5 Queen 3 Twin 3 Single (5 bdrm)
4 Ensuite 1 Private

Experience the peace and charm of yesteryear in our fully restored c1880's B&B, one of Nelson's original family homes. Situated beside the beautiful Maitai River, The Sussex has retained all the original character and romantic ambience of the era. It is only minutes walk from central Nelson's award winning restaurants and cafes, the Queens Gardens, Suter Art Gallery and Botanical Hill (The Centre Of NZ) and many good walks, river and bush.

The five sunny bedrooms all have TV's and are spacious and charmingly furnished. All rooms have access to the verandahs and complimentary tea & coffee facilities are provided. This is a musician's house and travelling musicians can enjoy the use of our instruments, including guitars, fiddles, mandolins, player piano, double bass and more.

Breakfast includes lots of fresh and preserved fruits, homemade muffins baked fresh every morning, hot croissants, homemade yoghurts, cheeses & salamis and a large variety of cereals, bagels, rolls, breads and crumpets. The Sussex provides a smoke free environment and all foods, to the best of our knowledge, are free from genetically modified ingredients.

We regret that we are not suited to children.

OTHER FACILITIES INCLUDE: Disabled facilities; Email/Internet station; fax; courtesy phone; laundry facilities; separate lounge for guest entertaining; complimentary port; tea & coffee facilities; very sociable cat (Riley); bread to feed the ducks.

Nelson - Tahunanui   *B&B*   *3km SW of Nelson*

Somerset House
Nicki & Richard Harden
33 Chamberlain Street, Tahunanui, Nelson
Tel: (03) 548 5998 Fax: (03) 548 5436
R.Harden@xtra.co.nz
www.bnb.co.nz/somersethouse.html

Double $110 Single $75
(Continental & Full Breakfast) Child Neg
Credit cards accepted Child at home Pet on property
1 Queen 1 Single (2 bdrm) 1 Ensuite

Our quiet hillside home, nestled in 1/2 acre of gardens, enjoys panoramic 180 degrees views - including Tasman Bay and Tahunanui Beach, with the distant mountain backdrop affording us glorious sunsets. The guest rooms,situated at the south western wing of house offer own access, tea/coffee facilities, elec blankets and outdoor spa. We invite you to enjoy a drink and chat on our large deck before going on to the fabulous waterfront restaurants just minutes away. A well travelled social family - including one son and two cats.

Nelson   *B&B*   *3km S of Nelson*

Beach Front B&B
Peter & Oriel Phillips
581 Rocks Road, Nelson
Tel: (03) 548 5299 Fax: (03) 548 5299
Mob: 025 216 5237 info@bnbnelson.co.nz
www.bnb.co.nz/beachfrontbb.html

Double $90-$95 Single $65
(Continental & Full Breakfast) Credit cards accepted
1 Queen 1 Double (2 bdrm)
1 Ensuite 1 Private

Our home is situated overlooking Tahunanui Beach, Haulashore Island and Nelson waterfront with amazing daytime mountain views and magnificent sunsets. Enjoy a wine out on the deck with your hosts. Excellent restaurants and cafes within walking distance, stroll to beach or a 5 minute drive to the city or World of Wearable Art. Golf course, tennis courts and airport nearby. Both rooms have ensuite/ private bathrooms, quality beds, electric blankets, fridge, TV, tea & coffee making facilities, heaters, iron, hairdryers. Laundry available.

Nelson   *B&B*   *Nelson Central*

Shelbourne Villa
Leon & Joyce Riebel
21 Shelbourne Street, Nelson
Tel: (03) 545 9059 Fax: (03) 546 7248
Mob: 025 423 0238 beds@shelbournevilla.co.nz
www.shelbournevilla.co.nz

Double $195-$250 (Full Breakfast)
Credit cards accepted
4 King (4 bdrm) 4 Ensuite

Experience tranquil garden setting with waterfall and private seating areas, only three blocks to city centre. All rooms have television, telephones, writing desks, hairdryers, curling irons, heated towel racks and cotton bed linens. Fax and email facilities available for business purposes. Large dining room, separate guest lounge with amenities. Extensively decorated with local arts and crafts. Walk to galleries, cinema, restaurants, shopping, churches, and exercise facility. Maitai River walks, Grampian Trails, trail to centre of New Zealand within five minutes walking distance from Villa. No pets, no children under 12.

Nelson Central   *B&B and Separate self-contained cottage*   *400m NE of Nelson Central*

Grove Villa
Lynne and Alf
36 Grove Street, Nelson

Tel: (03) 548 8895
Fax: (03) 548 8856
Tollfree: 0800 488900 (NZ)
lynne@grovevilla.co.nz
www.grovevilla.co.nz

Double $85-$140
Single $75-$115
(Continental Breakfast)
Credit cards accepted
Children welcome
1 King/Twin 2 Queen 1 Double
2 Twin 2 Single (6 bdrm)
3 Ensuite 1 Private 1 Guests share

Nearest town: Nelson City, 5 minutes walk.

Charming character historic home sympathetically restored. Many original features. Furnished with quirky memorabilia, antiques, original art. Set in attractive grounds including rare cycad 'cycas revoluta'. Easy access, off-street parking.

Close to cafes, shops, cinema, heated pool, Info. Centre, Post Office, churches, Maitai River walks, Centre of NZ, Suter Art Gallery, Queens Gardens, NMIT (polytechnic), Wearable Arts venue, bus station.

Each room (serviced daily) contains TV, comfortable quality beds, electric blankets, heaters, clock radios, iron/board, fresh flowers, bathrobes, sweet treats. Superior rooms have own access to large verandas (porches). Guests enjoy relaxing in guest lounge (anytime refreshments and guest fridge), garden courtyards, verandas, and browsing the guest library. Delicious breakfasts served in sunny dining room or courtyard. Guests rave about Alf's homemade bread! We serve an extensive breakfast may include sliced meats, NZ cheese, eggs, fresh fruit, homemade yoghurt, muesli, croissants, several toast/bread options.

A glance at our guest book will attest to the quality of our accommodation.

Many tell us that staying at Grove Villa has been a high spot of their NZ holiday! Meeting travellers including 'Kiwi' Bed and Breakfasts often turns breakfast into a 'mini party' with much swapping of notes and laughter.

We are seasoned travellers and sensitive to your requirements. You have anytime access to the house and your room with your own key. We are happy to discuss sights to see but also respect your privacy. Please ask if you would like help. Because there is so much to see in Nelson, we offer a discount for 3-plus night's stay.

We'd like you to relax and unwind so your days can be happily spent exploring and experiencing this wonderful regionl of NZ - Nelson, NZ's Sunshine Capital.

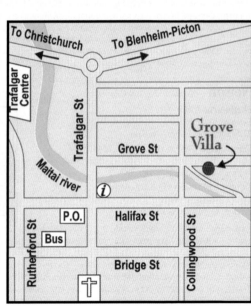

Nelson   *Nelson Central*

Peppertree B&B
Richard Savill & Carolyn Sygrove
31 Seymour Ave, Nelson
Tel: (03) 546 9881 Fax: (03) 546 9881
c.sygrove@clear.net.nz
www.bnb.co.nz/peppertreebb.html
Double $90 Child $15
Dinner $20 by arrangement each extra adult $25
1 Queen 1 Double 1 Single (1 bdrm)
1 Ensuite

Enjoy spaciousness and privacy in our Heritage Villa, only ten minutes riverside walk from Nelson's city centre. The master bedroom includes ensuite bathroom and walk in wardrobe. Your private adjoining rooms include a large lounge with additional double innersprung sofabed, log fire, Sky TV, fridge, kettle, toaster etc. and sunroom with cane setting and private entrance. Single bed available on request. Email/internet/fax facilities and off-street parking available. Children are welcome. We have two daughters aged eight and six and a cat called Chocolate.

Nelson - Tahunanui   *Self-contained B&B*   *8km W of Nelson*

Parkside Bed & Breakfast
Brent & Diane Williams
16 Centennial Road, Tahunanui, Nelson
Tel: (03) 548 6629 Fax: (03) 548 6621
Mob: 021 548 663   parkside.nelson@xtra.co.nz
www.bnb.co.nz/parkside.html
Double $95-$130 Single $75-$110
(Continental Breakfast) Credit cards accepted
Child at home Pet on property Children welcome
1 King 4 Queen 2 Single (4 bdrm)
2 Ensuite 1 Private

Welcome to our friendly atmosphere at Parkside. In our large modern bedrooms and separate guest lounge there are TV, fridge, tea/coffee facilities. Close to restaurants, golf course, sporting grounds, beach and airport. Shopping from Nelson City is only 8 mins drive. Have your breakfast in private or join us on our sunny deck. You can be sure of a warm friendly stay in our smoke free home with our two daughters aged 15 and 7 and friendly cat Mickey. There is off street parking for all guests.

Nelson - Stoke   *B&B*   *7KM SW of Nelson city centre*

Sakura Bed & Breakfast
Fumio & Sayuri Noguchi
604 Main Road, Stoke, Nelson
Tel: (03) 547 0229 Fax: (03) 547 0229
Mob: 021 547 022
fumio.noguchi@paradise.net.nz
homepages.paradise.net.nz/fumionog
Double $130 Single $65 (Full Breakfast)
Child at home Children welcome
1 King 4 Single (3 bdrm) 1 Ensuite 1 Family share

Modern, sunny and comfortable house with peacefull garden area. Situated in a quiet cul-de-sac off the Main Road. Ideally situated to visit Abel Tasman National Park and Nelson Lakes. Warm and friendly Japanese hosts. We serve either delicious Japanese breakfast or continental breakfast with home baked breads. Fresh vegetable salad and fruits are also included. Complimentary coffee and tea,home-made biscuits, fruits at all times. Why don't you try healthy, delicious Japanese breakfast? Children $15 for 3-12 years old.

Nelson *B&B* *Central*

Mikonui
Elizabeth Osborne
7 Grove Street, Nelson
Tel: (03) 548 3623 Tollfree: 0800 4 MIKONUI
bess.osborne@xtra.co.nz
www.bnb.co.nz/mikonui.html

Double $100 Single $70 (Full Breakfast)
Credit cards accepted
1 Queen 1 Double 1 Twin (3 bdrm)
3 Ensuite

100 metres from the Visitor Information Centre right in the heart of Nelson City is the Mikonui. This delightful old house built in the 1920's is constructed of New Zealand native timbers milled from the Mikonui Forest area in South Westland. The lovely Rimu staircase leads to 3 tastefully appointed bedrooms all with ensuites. Downstairs the old laundry has been transformed into a lovely dining room where guests can enjoy tea and coffee at any time, and where a tempting continental or cooked breakfast is served each morning.

Nelson *B&B* *5 min Nelson*

Brougham Gardens
Judith Nicholas
23 Brougham Street, Nelson
Tel: (03) 545 9049 Fax: (03) 545 9038
judith@broughamgardens.co.nz
www.bnb.co.nz/broughamgardens.html

Double $180-$240 Single $160-$180
(Continental Breakfast) (Full Breakfast)
Dinner $40 Credit cards accepted
3 King/Twin (3 bdrm) 2 Ensuite 1 Private

At Brougham Gardens B&B you are assured of a warm welcome and comfortable stay. Experience fine accommodation in quite secluded garden setting. Five minute walk to either city centre, restaurants, and cafes. Quality king/twin beds, down duvets, cotton linen, bathrobes, hairdryers, homemade chocolates and fresh flowers. Enjoy the swimming pool or spa. Breakfast in the garden room or on the verandah. A three course dinner including loca wine is available by prior arrangement. Barbeque, Internet, email and fax available for guest use. Laundry and off street parking.

Nelson Central *B&B* *Nelson*

Olverson House B&B
Darryl and Mandy Olverson
53 Brougham Street, Nelson
Tel: (03) 545 9936 Fax: (03) 545 9921
Mob: 027 415 6525 d.m.olverson@actrix.co.nz
www.olversonhouse.co.nz

Double $165-$185 Single $135-$155
(Continental & Full Breakfast)
Child $30 Credit cards accepted
3 Queen 1 Single (3 bdrm) 3 Ensuite

Share our elegant Edwardian villa with sea, mountain and town views. Lovingly restored, capturing the charm and ambience of yesteryear, with stained glass windows, rimu pannelled ceilings and doors. Guest bedrooms have ensuite facilities, two with balconies, are tastefully furnished with antiques, artwork and fresh flowers. You can enjoy continental and cooked breakfasts in the sunny dining room, on the verandah or in your bedroom. Join Darryl, Mandy, Adam, Joseph and the cat in our beautiful non-smoking home, only a short walk from town.

Nelson   *Self-contained   Nelson*

The Little Manor
Angela Higgins
12 Nile St West, Nelson
Tel: (03) 545 1411 Fax: (03) 545 1417
Mob: 025 247 1891   the.little.manor@xtra.co.nz
www.bnb.co.nz/thelittlemanor.html

Double $195   Single $185   (Full Breakfast)
Child $15   Credit cards accepted   Children welcome
1 King/Twin 1 Double (2 bdrm)
1 Private

Fully self-contained in historic inner city. This two storey uniquely designed cottage dates back to the 1860s. The ambience is quiet and tranquil with antiques throughout, open fire, claw foot bath with luxury comforts of today. Its quaintness unfolds with many rooms including upstairs spacious reading room, two bedrooms and deck. Front and back couryard. Moments away from art and pottery galleries, award winning restaurants, cafes, gardens and shopping district. Generous pantry of condiments and breakfast basket of bread, croissants, eggs, fresh fruit and much more.

Nelson   *Self-contained Homestay B&B   12km S of Nelson*

Monaco B&B by the sea
Bevin (Jack) and Paula Frost
105 Point Road, Monaco, Nelson
Tel: (03) 547 3110 Fax: (03) 547 3510
Mob: 025 284 7611   monacoseaside@xtra.co.nz
www.bnb.co.nz/monaco.html

Double $100-$135 Single $80-$120 Child $30
(Cont. Breakfast) Dinner b/a   Credit cards accepted
1 King/Twin 1 Queen 2 Single (3 bdrm)
1 Ensuite 1 Private 1 Guests share

Our spacious seaside home (including a self-contained unit with own entrance) is situated on tranquil Monaco Peninsula. Stroll to local artists, ie. Glass Gallery, pottery, woodturner, bonecarver, sculptor; swim, fish off nearby jetty, explore the estuary and nearby islands in our kayaks and sailboat, or relax and enjoy the birdlife and magical sunsets. Dine at popular local, olde English style "Honest Lawyer Country Pub". Courtesy pick-up from nearby airport. We love our "piece of paradise", and wish to share it with you! Winter rates apply. Cooked breakfast by arrangement.

Nelson Central   *B&B   500m Nelson Central*

About Time B&B
Martina Utz & Toby Pugno
13 Wainui Street, Nelson
Tel: (03) 546 7841 Fax: (03) 546 7841
aboutime@ihug.co.nz
www.bnb.co.nz/user64.html

Double $95-$115 Single $75 (Continental Breakfast)
Credit cards accepted
1 King/Twin 1 Queen 1 Single (3 bdrm)
2 Ensuite 1 Guests share

About Time B&B is a beautifully restored character villa. It's situated within walking distance to award-winning restaurants, cafes and many tourist attractions. We are a Swiss/Italian couple recently moved to New Zealand, much travelled and enjoy meeting people. Our home combines charm with modern facilities and offers a warm, friendly relaxed atmosphere. Relax in our cosy guest lounge or large,sunny verandah. Pleasantly decorated rooms feature quality beds and bedding. Free tea and coffee are available at all times. We have two Weimaraner dogs which are people-friendly. No children under 12.

Nelson   *Homestay B&B*   *4.5km S of Nelson*

Annesbrook House
Kath and Tony Charlton
201 Annesbrook Drive, Tahunanui, Nelson
Tel: (03) 548 5868
Fax: (03) 548 5802
tony.kath@paradise.net.nz
Double $75 - $90 Single $65
(Continental Breakfast)
2 Double
2 Ensuite

Drive up our private drive from Highway 6 to our peaceful home in a quiet sunny bush setting, with lovely views of the sea and mountains. Each bedsit has its own separate entrance, safe parking (some covered), ensuite, TV, fridge, electric blanket, hairdryer, heating, table and chairs, T+T facilities, microwave. Telephone available. We can book you in to many of the area's tourist attractions including boat trips and walks in the Abel Tasman National Park. We are centrally situated near Tahuna Beach, golf, airport, clubs, restaurants. Look for the lime green letterbox.

Richmond   *Homestay*   *0.5km E of Richmond*

Hunterville   Cecile & Alan Strang
30 Hunter Avenue, Richmond, Nelson
Tel: (03) 544 5852 Fax: (03) 544 5852
Tollfree: 0800 372 220   strangsa@clear.net.nz.
www.bnb.co.nz/hunterville.html
Double $80 Single $50 (Full Breakfast)
Child 1/2 price Dinner $20 by arrangement
Credit cards accepted Pet on property Pets welcome
1 King 1 Twin 1 Single (3 bdrm)
1 Private 1 Family share

A welcome with drinks poolside in summer, fireside in winter awaits you when you stay in our peaceful home where birdsongs greet you from surrounding bush. We are on the route to Golden Bay, Abel Tasman Park Region but just 15 minutes from Nelson. We travel frequently overseas so appreciate travellers' needs. With firm confortable beds, good laundry, dinner with local food, wine, and with travellers tales your stay with us will be memorable. Our other interests are music, reading, bridge and 'Coco', Dalmation, and 'Waldo' - both very friendly dogs.

Richmond   *Homestay*   *0.5km E of Richmond*

Anderson Homestay
Jean & Jack Anderson
46 Rochfort Drive, Richmond, Nelson
Tel: (03) 544 2175 Fax: (03) 544 2175
Mob: 025 440 530
www.bnb.co.nz/andersonhomestay.html
Double $60 Single $35 (Full Breakfast)
Child $15 Dinner $12.50
Credit cards accepted Pet on property
1 Double 2 Single (2 bdrm)
1 Guests share

We are a couple who like meeting people. Near by are lovely gardens, crafts, such as Pottery, Glass Blowing, Dried Flowers and Wood Turning. Beaches at Tahuna and Rabbit Island are only 10 minutes away by car. We are situated in an area very central for travellers going South, North or to Golden Bay and Tasman area. Buses and planes met. Enjoy Kiwi hospitality in Richmond. Directions: Above round-about in Queen Street turn into Wasbourn Drive, Farnham Drive and Rochfort Drive.

Richmond

Homestay B&B Country Homestay B&B   *2km S of Richmond*

Nicholls Country Homestay B&B
Alison & Murray Nicholls
87 Main Road, Hope, Nelson

Tel: (03) 544 8026 Fax: (03) 544 8026
Mob: 021 256 1359   m_a.nicholls@xtra.co.nz
www.bnb.co.nz/nicholls.html

Double $80 Single $40 (Full Breakfast)
Child $25 Dinner $12.50 Children welcome
1 Queen 1 Double 2 Single (3 bdrm)
1 Guests share 1 Family share

We are situated on a kiwifruit orchard on State Highway 6, 2km south of Richmond. A lengthy driveway ensures quiet surroundings in a lovely garden setting, with a pool. We are centrally situated, placing Nelson's many attractions within easy reach. We will happily provide information about these and make arrangements as required. Complimentary tea or coffee is offered to guests upon arrival and dinner may be provided by arrangement. A phonecall before arrival would be appreciated. Ours is a non smoking home.

Richmond

Self-contained Homestay B&B   *10km W of Nelson*

Chester Le House
Noelene & Michael Smith
39 Washbourn Drive, Richmond, Nelson

Tel: (03) 544 7279 Fax: (03) 544 7279
Mob: 025 213 5335   n.smith@xtra.co.nz
www.bnb.co.nz/chesterlehouse.html

Double $85 Single $50 (Full Breakfast)
Dinner $25 by arrangement Flat $90
Credit cards accepted
1 Double 4 Single (3 bdrm)
1 Ensuite 1 Guests share 1 Family share

We live in a fantastic part of New Zealand in a lovely modern home that we enjoy sharing with many people. Lovely views and all the comforts of home await you. Two twin rooms and queen suite with ensuite available. Lock your car in our garage and enjoy a barbecue or evening meal with us. Laundry and drier available. Pick up from terminals available. Only 10 minutes from Nelson city, Richmond is close to wineries and a scenic 40 minutes drive to Abel Tasman National Park.

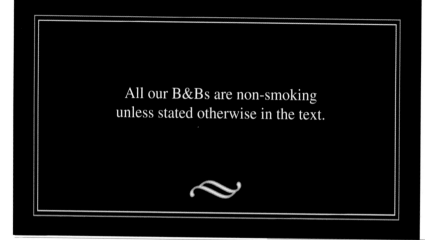

All our B&Bs are non-smoking
unless stated otherwise in the text.

Richmond   *B&B and Self-contained*   *10km S of Nelson*

Bay View
Janice & Ray O'Loughlin
37 Kihilla Road
Richmond
Tel: (03) 544 6541 Fax: (03) 544 6541 Mob: 025 623 0252
bayview@ts.co.nz
www.bnb.co.nz/bayviewrichmond.html
Double $80-$100 Single $65 (Full Breakfast)
Dinner by arrangement Credit cards accepted
Pet on property
2 Queen 1 Twin (3 bdrm)
1 Ensuite 1 Guests share

Bayview is a modern, spacious home built on the hills above Richmond township, with spectacular views of Tasman Bay and mountain ranges.

We offer rooms that are quiet, private and immaculately furnished with your complete comfort in mind. A large guest bathroom has shower and spa bath. The lounge opens onto a sheltered deck where you can relax, enjoy a drink or sit and chat. The self-contained suite with private entrance, off-street parking, kitchen, bathroom/laundry, lounge area and Queen bed offers privacy and all home comforts.

We have two miniature Schnauzer dogs, a variety of birds in a large aviary, tend our colourful garden and enjoy meeting people from new Zealand and overseas.

By car Bayview is 15 minutes from Nelson, 2 minutes from Richmond and award-winning restaurants, close to National parks, beaches, vineyards and crafts. Be assured of warm, friendly hospitality and a happy stay in our smokefree home.

Richmond *B&B Guesthouse 1km E of Richmond*

Antiquarian Guest House
Robert & Joanne Souch
12A Surrey Road, Richmond, Nelson
Tel: (03) 544 0253 Fax: (03) 544 0253
Mob: 025 417 504 souchjoanne@hotmail.com
www.bnb.co.nz/antiquarian.html
Double $95 Single $75 (Full Breakfast)
Credit cards accepted Pet on property
Children welcome Pets welcome
1 King 1 Queen 1 Twin (3 bdrm)
1 Ensuite 1 Guests share

Bob and Joanne Souch welcome you to their peaceful home only 2 minutes from Richmond (15 minutes drive south of Nelson) - excellent base for exploring National Parks, beaches, arts/crafts, skifields etc. Relax in the garden, beside the swimming pool or in our large TV/Guest lounge. Tea/coffee facilities, home baking and memorable breakfasts. Our family pet is Gemma (friendly border collie). As local antique shop owners we know the area well.

Richmond *Homestay B&B 12km SW of Nelson*

Idesia
Jenny & Barry McKee
14 Idesia Grove, Richmond, Nelson
Tel: (03) 544 0409 Fax: (03) 544 0402
Mob: 025 604 0869 Tollfree: 0800 361 845
idesian@xtra.co.nz
www.idesia.co.nz
Double $85-$95 (Full Breakfast)
Dinner $25 by arrangement Credit cards accepted
1 King/Twin 1 Queen 1 Twin (3 bdrm)
1 Ensuite 1 Private

A warm welcome to our home centrally located to explore the Nelson region. 2km from Highway 6, in a quiet grove neighbouring the country. Our modern house is elevated to catch the sun and views. For your comfort the bedrooms, recently furnished, have superior beds. Breakfast includes a continental selection and/or a cooked breakfast. Join us for dinner, by prior arrangement, and relax with us in the lounge over coffee. Our aim is to provide a home away from home and to offer tasty meals.

Thorpe *Homestay Rural Homestay 55km W of Nelson*

Rerenga Farm
Robert & Joan Panzer
Dovedale Road, Thorpe, Nelson
Tel: (03) 543 3825 Fax: (03) 543 3640
Mob: 025 243 1284
Robert@Customtours.co.nz
www.customtours.co.nz
Double $95 Single $75 (Special Breakfast)
Dinner $30 Credit cards accepted
Child at home Children welcome
1 Queen (1 bdrm) 1 Ensuite

You are offered a peaceful, rural retreat with international hosts (Dutch and North American). Our two children are real 'Kiwis'. The homestead is surrounded by rolling hills, forests and situated along the Dove River. We have a variety of trees, chickens, pigs, sheep, and an outdoor cat and dog. Note: our main business is 'Tailored Travel', personalized New Zealand Custom Tours (2-6 pax), tailored to your specific requirements and dates.

Mapua   *Country Accomodation*   *10km N of Richmond*

Atholwood Country Accommodation
Robyn & Grahame Williams
Bronte Road East
Off Coastal Highway 60, near Mapua
Tel: (03) 540 2925 Fax: (03) 540 3258
Mob: 025 310 309   atholwood@xtra.co.nz
www.atholwood.co.nz
Double $150-$170 Single $120-$150
(Special Breakfast) Child by arrangement
Dinner $40 by arrangement Credit cards accepted
2 Queen 1 Single (2 bdrm)   2 Ensuite

Our home is situated on the edge of the Waimea Inlet amid 2 acres of gardens and bush. The guest wing is upstairs and comprises 2 guest rooms with ensuites. Adjoining, is a guest lounge with fridge, tea/coffee etc. Special breakfasts, dinner by arrangement, award winning Cafes and Restaurants 10 minutes. Children welcome. Our beautiful cat Carlos completes the family. Our personal attention is assured in a relaxed and informal atmosphere.

Mapua - Nelson   *Coastal Village B&B Accommodation*   *30km W of Nelson*

Hartridge
Sue & Dennis Brillard
103 Aranui Road,
Mapua, Nelson
Tel: (03) 540 2079 Fax: (03) 540 2079
Mob: 025 247 4854   stay@hartridge.co.nz
www.hartridge.co.nz
Double $140-$180 Single $110-$140 Dinner $45
1 King/Twin 1 Queen 1 Double (3 bdrm)
2 Ensuite 1 Private

A friendly welcome over a cup of tea; dine in, or walk to cafes via the beach; wake to birdsong and the smell of fresh bread; enjoy gourmet breakfasts on the leafy verandah, or indoors with antiques and fine art: experience that rare luxury of special treatment - the very essence of your stay at Hartridge, the perfect antidote to city life. Romantic guestrooms have cotton bed linen, choice of pillows.Golf, swimming, kayaking, rainforest hiking, arts/crafts/winery trails nearby. Friendly terrier Jack, 1939 Morgan.

Mapua Village   *Homestay B&B*   *30km W of Nelson*

Mapua Seaview B&B
Murray & Diana Brown
40 Langford Drive, Mapua, Nelson
Tel: (03) 540 2006 Fax: 64 3 540 2006
Mob: 025 839 634   seaview@mapua.co.nz
www.mapua.co.nz
Double $89-$99 Single $80
(Continental & Full Breakfast) Dinner $30pp
Credit cards accepted
2 Queen (2 bdrm)   2 Ensuite

30 minutes from Nelson, 'Seaview' is nestled in the coastal village of Mapua (see photograph of our view.) Nearby choice of 'award'licensed restaurants. Enjoy vibrant sunsets , beach walk's, the busy birdlife of the estuary. Handy to Tasman & Golden Bays also Nelson's acclaimed National Parks (20 mins to Kaiteriteri). We are central to popular wineries, & craft studios. A homely friendly B&B with comfortable accommodation, queen beds, feather duvets, own bathrooms, TV etc. Cooked or continental breakfast . No stairs. Laundry & email facilities.

Mapua *B&B with self contained cottage*   *4km S of Mapua*

Kimeret Place Coastal B&B
Clare & Peter Jones
Bronte Road East (off SH60), RD 1,
Upper Moutere, Nelson

Tel: (03) 540 2727 Fax: (03) 540 2726
stay@kimeretplace.co.nz www.kimeretplace.co.nz

Double $110-$140 Single $90-$100 (Full Breakfast)
2 bdr cottage & luxury suites $180 - $265
Credit cards accepted Pet on property
3 King/Twin 2 Queen (5 bdrm) 4 Ensuite 1 Private

Soak up the stunning views from our heated swimming pool or spa. Set in 4 acres. Kimeret Place offers tranquility in relaxed but stylish surroundings. Our accommodation includes king/queen bedded rooms with en-suite or private facilities, a self-contained cottage, and Luxury suites with sitting areas, balconies and sumptuous bathrooms. An ideal base to explore the Abel Tasman National Park and the numerous local wineries and crafts. Dog-lovers may wish to meet our 2 black Labradors, who will give you a special welcome of their own.

Mapua Village *Homestay B&B*   *30km W of Nelson*

Mapua Estuary Bed & Breakfast
Elenore Searle
6A Moreland Place, Mapua Village,

Tel: (03) 5402458 Fax: (03) 5402458
Tollfree: 0800 114 099 estuarybnb@paradise.net.nz
homepages.paradise.net.nz/estuaryb

Double $90 Single $75 (Continental Breakfast)
Credit cards accepted
1 King/Twin 1 Queen (2 bdrm)
1 Ensuite 1 Private

Take a walk along the beach and explore the estuary. Enjoy the views, interesting bird life, estuary cruises, award winning aquarium, restaurants, cafes, craft shops. Make this your base for visits to Abel Tasman National Park or Nelson City (30 min. either way) Come back to a quality, comfortable, spotlessly clean timber home sited on the estuary itself. Sit outside in the garden and enjoy the tranquil view. Be assured of a warm welcome and a delicious breakfast.

Ruby Bay *B&B*   *20km W of Nelson*

Broadsea B&B
Rae & John Robinson
42 Broadsea Avenue, Ruby Bay, Nelson

Tel: (03) 540 3511 Fax: (03) 540 3511
42broadseabb@hotmail.com
www.bnb.co.nz/broadseabb.html

Double $110 Single $90
(Continental & Full Breakfast) Child not suitable
1 Queen (1 bdrm)
1 Ensuite 1 Private

Beach front accommodation, double room with own bathroom and toilet. Lovely walks on beach and reserve, cafes, Tavern, wineries, restaurants, in close vicinity. Fifteen minutes from Richmond & Motueka. Beaches, Rabbit Island, Kaiteriteri, Tahuna in close proximity. Near gateway to Abel Tasman National Park. Plenty of places to see, or 2 minutes to the beach with no maddening crowds. We want guests to feel at home and have their privacy. A continental and full cooked breakfast is served, and cups of coffee, tea and biscuits available. Birman cat and Labrador Sally will greet you outside.

NELSON
GOLDEN BAY

Ruby Bay *B&B   16km S of Motueka*

Tasman View
Gerald B & Jenny E Allsopp
106 Brabant Drive, Pine Hill Heights,
Ruby Bay, Mapua 7155
Tel: (03) 540 2966 Fax: (03) 540 2966
Mob: 027 439 0041   jg.allsopp@xtra.co.nz
www.tasmanview.co.nz

Double $175 Single $150 (Full Breakfast)
Credit cards accepted Pet on property
2 King/Twin 1 Single (3 bdrm) 2 Private

Extensive views of Tasman Bay from our new Mediterranean/Kiwi style home. Peaceful surroundings with native bush walks in adjoining reserve. Upstairs private wing. Take in the atmosphere while enjoying a meal or coffee at the excellent restaurants and patisserie/cafe at nearby Mapua village. 15 minutes to Motueka or Richmond, 30 minutes to Nelson or Marahau, gateway to Abel Tasman National Park. Transport by arrangement. Our spoilt Burmese cats have their own quarters but on request will be happy to socialise.

Ruby Bay *Rural Homestay   15km SE of Motueka*

Adobe Homestead
Tony & Jennie van der Koelen
151 Awa Awa Road, Ruby Bay, RD 1 Upper Moutere
Tel: (03) 540 2483 Fax: (03) 540 2483
Mob: 021 400 382   adobe.homestead@xtra.co.nz
www.bnb.co.nz/adobehomestead.html

Double $95-$115 Single $65-$75
(Continental Breakfast)
Child Half price by arrangement
Dinner $30 Credit cards accepted
1 Queen 2 Single (2 bdrm) 1 Guests share

Perched on a hilltop above Ruby Bay, the unusual and spacious Adobe Homestead enjoys 360 degrees views over farmland and vineyards. You can enjoy the peace of the house and gardens, reading from our extensive library or luxuriating in the hot spa pool on the deck. Ours is a small holding with usually a number of farm animals.. It is great for adults and children. We can help you plan your visit to vineyards, restaurants, craft workshops, beaches and parks close at hand.

Tasman *Boutique B&B   8km S of Motueka*

Aporo Pondsiders
Marian & Mike Day
Permin Road Tasman, RD 1, Upper Moutere, Nelson
Tel: (03) 526 6858 Fax: (03) 526 6258
Mob: 025 240 3757   marian@aporo.co.nz
www.aporo.co.nz

Double $200 Single $180 (Full Breakfast)
Credit cards accepted
4 King/Twin (4 bdrm)
2 Ensuite 1 Guests share

Secluded, peaceful, 3 stylish yet relaxed, spacious apartments, staggered for privacy and perched over a large ornamental pond with country and mountain views. Two having large sitting/dining room, kitchen galley, bedroom, ensuite (one with bath), balcony. One, as previous with 2 bedrooms, bathroom, full kictchen, balcony. Centrally situated off Highway 60, between Nelson/Motueka emabling travellers to explore the best of the province; Abel Tasman, Kahurangi National Parks; Golden Bay. Beautiful safe swimming beaches, walks, golf courses, trout rivers, arts, wineries are nearby.

Tasman   *B&B   12km S of Motueka*

Eagle Ridge B&B
Kathy & Phil Ward
Brooks View Heights, Permin Road,
Tasman, RD1, Upper Moutere

Tel: (03) 526 6063 Fax: (03) 526 6063
Mob: 025 283 2870   philkat@xtra.co.nz
www.eagleridge.co.nz

Double $120-$135 Single $80-$100
(Continental Breakfast) Child $25 - $50
Credit cards accepted Child at home Children welcome
2 King/Twin 1 Queen (2 bdrm)   2 Ensuite

Our mediterranean style home situated on a ridge overlooking the Tasman Golf Course and the sea beyond, with stunning mountain views, offers guests two rooms, twin/king or queen, both with comfort and privacy in a relaxing atmosphere. Our locality offers National Parks, Wineries, cafes, potteries, crafts, beaches, with a spectacular golf course at our doorstep. A quality continental breakfast will be served at a time to suit. Directions: on SH60 Tasman is located 12km south of Motueka, 8km from Mapua.

Tasman   *Self-contained B&B   8km S of Motueka*

Kina Cottage/D'Urville House
Irene & Len Edwards & Shirley Heine
Cliff Road, Kina, Tasman

Tel: (03) 526 6741 or (03) 526 6778
Fax: (03) 526 7737   l.i.edwards@xtra.co.nz
Mob: 025 223 3973   www.bnb.co.nz/kinacottage.html

Double $140 Single $100
1 Queen 1 Double 2 Single (3 bdrm)
2 Ensuite 1 Private

Thirty minutes from Nelson on Coastal Highway - gateway to Abel Tasman and Kahurangi National Parks. Relax in our tranquil garden setting overlooking Tasman Bay to D'Urville Island - beautiful sunrises across the bay. Private entrance to spacious ensuite room with comfortable chairs, TV, fresh fruit and flowers. Safe swimming and walking beach at doorstep. Picturesque golf club two mins drive, club/cart hire/cafe. Local award-winning wineries, pottery, and art galleries. Excellent waterfront restaurants in nearby Mapua. Full self-contained flat with all facilities, TV, double bed, continental breakfast, laundry available, plus extra double folding bed.

Motueka Valley   *Homestay   25km S of Motueka*

The Kahurangi Brown Trout
David Davies & Heather Lindsay
Westbank Road, Pokororo, RD 1, Motueka

Tel: (03) 526 8736 Tollfree: 0800 460 421
enquiries@kbtrout.co.nz
www.kbtrout.co.nz

Double $95-$125 Single $75-$105 (Full Breakfast)
Child $25 Dinner $18 - $35 Credit cards accepted
Pet on property Children welcome Pets welcome
2 King/Twin 1 Single (2 bdrm)
2 Ensuite

Comments from last season's visitors say it all. 'Wonderful in every way, including the trout (eventually) ... Good company, good food & the best bed in NZ ... The essence of tranquillity ... Will be back ... Your cooking is wonderful ... If only it could have been longer ... I dream of living somewhere like this ... Great house, fantastic garden ... thank you for your warm generous open hospitality ... We hope to be back one day ... A haven of peace and tranquillity ... Sorry we're not staying longer'.

Motueka Valley
Homestay B&B   28km S of Motueka

Doone Cottage Country Homestay
Glen & Stan Davenport
2455 Motueka Valley Highway
RD 1, Motueka

Tel: (03) 526 8740 Fax: (03) 526 8740 Mob: 021 258 7389
doone-cottage@xtra.co.nz www.doonecottage.co.nz

Double $130-$175 Single $110-$155 (Full Breakfast)
Dinner by arrangement Credit cards accepted
Pet on property 2 King/Twin 1 Queen (3 bdrm) 3 Ensuite

Overlooking Motueka River Valley and the Mt Arthur range, this charming 130 year old cottage has welcomed homestay guests for over 20 years.

Situated in 4 acres of secluded native trees, ferns and flower gardens on a natural river terrace neighbouring a 1000-acre deer farm, it offers homely hospitality, peace and tranquillity, friendly, helpful, experienced hosts, **very comfortable beds**, full ensuites, all home cooked meals, homemade breads, preserves, homegrown produce, free range eggs, etc. Comfortably furnished cottage style, guest rooms and private garden chalet have extensive garden/valley views. Native birds abound, sheep, chickens, ducks and donkeys. Your hostess spins wool from the raw fleece, her weaving studio offers sweaters, blankets, wall hangings, rugs, etc. which she has produced. A chuckling steam runs through the property, flowing into the Motueka, famous for its **brown trout**, with five more trout streams close by. Guiding & licences available.

Our central location offers **short distances** to excellent day trips/ activities in **Abel Tasman, Kahurangi** and **Nelson Lakes National Parks. Nelson** and **Golden Bay** - mountain and coastal bush walks, wilderness fishing, golf etc. (Bookings handled for cruising, water taxis, kayaking, horse trekking). Award winning wineries, arts and crafts. Or simply relax and soak up the country atmosphere of yesteryear in this special place.

2.5 hours to Picton; 3 hours to the West Coast; 5 hours to Christchurch.

Motueka Valley   *Self-contained Farmstay*   *34km S of Motueka*

River Island Lodge
Alistair Webber & Carol Mckeever
Baton Valley Road, Woodstock, RD 1, Motueka
Tel: (03) 543 3844 Fax: (03) 543 3802
relax@riverislandlodge.co.nz
www.riverislandlodge.co.nz

Double $180 Single $120 (Continental Breakfast)
Dinner $35 Credit cards accepted
4 Queen 4 Single (4 bdrm)
4 Ensuite

Experience the uniqueness of the Nelson Back Country. Surrounded by rivers and mountains, River Island Lodge offers stylish, self contained accommodation with a relaxed country feel. Fish for trout, swim in clear river pools, go horse trekking or kayaking or relax and enjoy the remote, rural atmosphere. Our farming family includes two school age children, farm dogs, horses, cattle and hens. Prepare your favourite meals in your own well equipped kitchen or by arrangement, have delicious meals prepared for you. Perfectly located to enjoy Nelson's wine and craft trails and national parks.

Motueka Valley   *Self-contained Farmstay*   *18km S of Motueka*

Mountain View Cottage/Dexter Farmstay
A & V Hall
Waiwhero Road,
RD 1, Motueka
Tel: (03) 526 8857 ajandvhall@xtra.co.nz
www.bnb.co.nz/mountainviewcottage.html

Double $85-$95 Single $50-$60 (Special Breakfast)
Dinner $20 Cottage $85-$95 Credit cards accepted
1 King/Twin 1 Double (2 bdrm)
1 Ensuite 1 Private

Your hosts Alan and Veronica offer B&B Farmstay and separate cottage accommodation on our 35 acre organic property complete with unique Dexter cows and Native Bush Covenanted area. Perfectly situated for anglers, close to 3 National Parks and art/craft/garden trails. Mountain View Cottage is completely self-contained while our homestead offers spacious bedroom with own ensuite, tea/coffee & TV facilities. Meals are cooked on our wood-fired range and breakfast comprises choice of homemade muesli, bread, yoghurt, pancakes and organic eggs. Mitzi the cat completes the picture.

Motueka   *B&B*   *2km SE of Motueka*

The Blue House
Gail & Doug Bayne
15 North Street, Motueka
Tel: (03) 528 6296 Mob: 021 263 0259
www.bnb.co.nz/thebluehouse.html

Double $70 Single $40 (Full Breakfast)
Child Age + $2, over 12 adult price
Dinner $15 by arrangement Credit cards accepted
1 Double 2 Single (2 bdrm)
1 Guests share 1 Family share

Our house, shared with one cat, is on a quiet road across from a beach with safe swimming, beautiful walks and an estuary for bird watching. Off-street parking. Guest annex comprises lounge, bathroom, two bedrooms and a private courtyard. Tea/coffee making. No smoking inside. We have travelled widely and we enjoy meeting guests from near or far away. DIRECTIONS: At the southern roundabout in High Street turn into Wharf Road, continue straight into Everett Street. At the end turn left into North Street.

Motueka   *An Artists Home*   *1km E of Motueka*

Copper Beech Gallery
John & Carol Gatenby
240 Thorp Street, Motueka

Tel: (03) 528 7456 Fax: (03) 528 7456
Mob: 021 256 0053   copper.beech.gallery@xtra.co.nz
www.CopperBeechGallery.co.nz

Double $180-$220 Single $150-$180
(Special Breakfast) Credit cards accepted
1 Queen 2 Single (2 bdrm)
2 Ensuite

Enjoy a unique and quality experience: attention to detail is our forte. Stay in the light and spacious home of John R Gatenby - one of New Zealand's leading landscape artists. Indulge in Carol's sumptuous breakfasts on the sun-drenched patio overlooking two acres of private garden and a bird sanctuary. At day's end return from Abel Tasman or Kahurangi National Parks to a warm welcome from Abbi, the outdoor Golden Labrador and enjoy a glass of locally produced wine with your kiwi hosts in the peace and tranquillity of their stylish home.

Motueka   *B&B*   *0.5km S of Motueka*

Rosewood
Barbara & Jerry Leary
48 Woodlands Avenue, Motueka

Tel: (03) 528 6750 Fax: (03) 528 6718
Mob: 021 251 0131
Barbara.Leary.Rosewood@xtra.co.nz
accommodation-new-zealand.co.nz/rosewood

Double $90 Single $55 (Full Breakfast)
Child 1/2 price Credit cards accepted Pet on property
1 Double 2 Single (2 bdrm) 1 Private 1 Family share

Hi, welcome to Rosewood your home from home where a warm and friendly atmosphere awaits you. A four minute walk to the centre of Motueka. Our rooms are clean and comfortable. The upstairs room has an adjacent lounge with TV and offers magnificent views of the bush-clad mountains. A delicious breakfast is provided. There is a spa available, notice is required. Our interests include travel, gardening, golf, and fishing. Love to see you as will Jasper our cat. "Rosewood", gateway to the beautiful Abel Tasman.

Motueka   *Self-contained B&B*   *1km S of Motueka*

Ashley Troubadour
Coral & John Horton
430 High Street, Motueka

Tel: (03) 528 7318 Fax: (03) 528 7318
Tollfree: 0800 222 046
www.bnb.co.nz/ashleytroubadour.html

Double $75 Single $52 (Continental Breakfast)
Child $10 S/C $85 - $110 Credit cards accepted
2 Queen 2 Double 2 Single (4 bdrm)
2 Ensuite 2 Guests share

Ashley Troubadour used to be a nunnery. Nowadays it is an Adventure Base for the Abel Tasman National Park and all other outdoor pursuits available in this area. You name it, we've got it, and John and Coral Horton, your friendly Ashley Troubadour hosts will gladly arrange all bookings etc. to make your stay a pleasure. Laundry facilities, security room, ample off-street parking all available for your peace of mind. Our ensuite rooms are near-new and fully self contained in quiet garden setting.

Motueka   *Self-contained B&B*   *Motueka Central*

Tri-angle Inn
Lesley & Daniel Jackson
142 Thorp Street, Motueka
Tel: (03) 528 7756 Mob: 025 484 778
daniel.hdt@xtra.co.nz
www.triangle-inn.co.nz
Double $120-$135 Single $90
(Continental Breakfast) (Full Breakfast) Child $35
Credit cards accepted Child at home Pet on property
2 King 4 Single (3 bdrm)   2 Ensuite

At the Tri-angle Inn you will find: a dazzling array of baked and locally grown delights for breakfast, large, comfortable beds, guest pantry with tea, coffee and juice, large colourful private suites with television, refrigerators, private ensuites and entrance. Set in one acre of garden with wonderful views of Mt Arthur and only 5 min walk from restaurants, cafes and golf course. Our family, which includes Liam our 12 year old son and 1 dog snow, actively participate in the multitude of recreational facilities available. Daniel is also a part-time local trout guide. Children over 10 most welcome.

Motueka   *Homestay B&B*   *1.4km E of Motueka*

Rebecca & Ian Williams
186 Thorp Street, Motueka
Tel: (03) 528 9385 Fax: (03) 528 9385
Mob: 025 480 466
www.bnb.co.nz/williams.html
Double $100 Single $50
(Continental & Full Breakfast) Child $20
Dinner by arrangement
Credit cards accepted Pet on property
2 Queen 2 Single (2 bdrm)
2 Ensuite

We only look expensive. We are 1.4 km to Motueka shopping centre and 1.2 km to 18 hole golf course. Each bedroom has own ensuite. The guest lounge has tea and coffee making facilities and fridge. Motueka is the stop-over place for visitors to explore Abel Tasman and Kahurangi National Parks. Golden Bay and Kaiteriteri golden sands beach is 10km away. We have a Jack Russell dog. Visa and M/C.

Motueka   *Self-contained B&B*   *5km N of Motueka*

Sea Haven
Barbara & Tim Robson
43 Green Tree Road, Riwaka, RD 3, Motueka
Tel: (03) 528 8892
seahaven@ihug.co.nz
www.bnb.co.nz/seahaven.html
Double $90-$100 Single $80 (Continental Breakfast)
Child $15 extra adult $25 Credit cards accepted
2 Double 1 Single (1 bdrm)
1 Private

Enjoy the serenity and rustic charm of the Riwaka estuary while using us as your base to explore Abel Tasman National Park, Kaiteriteri and Golden Bay. Our spacious modern apartment has a FULLY EQUIPPED KITCHEN and LAUNDRY, large living area, and a patio with barbecue. We offer delicious continental breakfasts or you may self -cater. Directions: Take Kaiteriteri Road from Motueka, across the Motueka River Bridge. Take 1st right into Lodders Lane, left into School Road, right into Green Tree Road. Discounts for longer stays, and for self-catering.

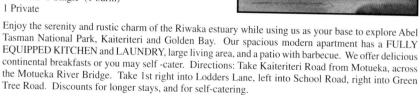

Motueka   *Homestay B&B   2km S of Motueka*

Grey Heron B&B - Airone Cinerino
Sandro Lionello & Laura Totis
110 Trewavas Street, Motueka 7161

Tel: (03) 528 0472 Fax: (03) 528 0472 Mob: 021 266 0345
sandro@greyheron.co.nz www.greyheron.co.nz

Double $75-$115 Single $50-$80 (Full Breakfast)   Dinner $30 Budget Twin $65
1 King 2 Queen 2 Single (4 bdrm)   1 Ensuite 1 Guests share

We are a couple recently moved form the North of Italy to the South of New Zealand, much travelled and keen on tramping and mountaineering.

Our beautiful garden faces the Moutere River Estuary: you will enjoy our breakfast (traditional English and Italian specialities including organic home-made bread and jams) overlooking a super tidal view of the estuary and of the Kahurangi National Park mountain range. You will appreciate our Mediterranean atmosphere in the heart of New Zealand nature, among native trees and lovely singing birds. Depending on the season, you will have the chance to see the spectacular White Herons and Royal Spoonbills feeding in the estuary.

PLAN a longer holiday in this Region and PROFIT by Sandro's experience in Geology, Mountaineering and Outdoor (Registered Instructor) and Italian Language Teaching: BOOK with us as extra geological and botanical guided walks along the tracks of the surrounding National Parks, Rock-climbing and Ice-climbing by special arrangements or Cultural weeks including Italian Cooking Classes, Entertaining with slides about Italy, and, on request, Italian Language lessons for beginners and advanced.

Our house is close to the beach: you can have a jog or a quiet walk along the Quay, safe wind-surfing and swimming just across the road. The 18 hole golf course is 15 min. walking. The Ensuite bedroom is small and cosy and includes a private driveway and ground-floor entrance.

On request we prepare delicious recipes of our Italian Cuisine, famous all around the world, using fresh herbs from our garden. You can enjoy dinner with us, overlooking wonderful sunsets beyond the mountains. Coffee, tea, laundry facilities. Secure off-street parking. Links with kayaking and trout fishing companies for booking tours. BENVENUTI TUTTI GLI AMICI ITALIANI.

Directions: From Nelson, at the Southern roundabout in High street, turn right towards Port Motueka, then turn left into Trewavas Street. From the West Coast, at the Clock Tower in High Street, go straight and then turn right into Trewavas Street. Look for our sign.

Motueka   *B&B   2km S of Motueka*

Estuary
Eric & Bonnie Stretton
543 High St South,
Motueka

Tel: (03) 528 6391 b.stretton@xtra.co.nz
www.bnb.co.nz/estuary.html

Double $95 Single $75 (Full Breakfast)
Credit cards accepted Pet on property
1 Queen (1 bdrm)
1 Ensuite

Guest's room with ensuite and private entrance has views through our olive trees to the estuary. Full breakfast, on deck or in family dining room. Swimming pool, craft gallery, Sky TV, internet and laundry facilities. 500 metres to The Sea Kayak Company and we also offer advice/make bookings on Abel Tasman National Park, tramping, sightseeing, wine trails, restaurants, beaches, crafts and activities. Our family includes two teenagers and friendly spaniel. Entrance into Motueka off coastal highway from Nelson, left at roundabout.

Motueka   *Homestay B&B   2km S of Motueka*

Time Out
Valerie Rae & Ian McLauchlan
41 King Edward Street, Motueka 7161

Tel: (03) 528 4696 Tollfree: 0800 005 097
rae.mclauchlan@xtra.co.nz
www.bnb.co.nz/timeout.html

Double $60-$85 Single $45-$80
(Continental Breakfast) Child upon application
Pet on property Children welcome
1 Queen 1 Double 2 Twin 2 Single (3 bdrm)
2 Guests share

100 year old villa. Park like garden, beautiful trees. The guest bedrooms and bathroom are upstairs and have lovely views of the garden and surrounding mountain ranges.The bedrooms are spacious and quiet with comfortable beds. We offer you a friendly home to use as a base whilst you enjoy the many attractions of this region. Our kitchen and laundry are available for your use and emails may be accessed. Early bookings are recommended during Dec/Jan/Feb. We have a small dog called Rocky.

Motueka   *B&B + Self Contained Apartment   500m E of Motueka*

Golf View Chalet
Kathleen & Neil Holder
20A Teece Drive, Motueka

Tel: (03) 528 8353 Mob: 025 234 8471
info@golfviewchalet.co.nz
www.GolfViewChalet.co.nz

Double $85-$95 Single $70 (Special Breakfast)
Child $15 S.C Apartment sleeps 7 $95(2persons)
$15extra adult Credit cards accepted
1 Queen 1 Double 2 Single (2 bdrm)
1 Ensuite 1 Private

Welcome to our sunny home "on 18 hole golf course", beside the sea. Listen to the native birds fantail and tui. View sunsets from the deck. Close to restaurants. National Parks and golden beaches nearby, your choice of the many activities the region has to offer. Then sleep well in our comfortable beds. Generous flexitime breakfast is served in hosts' dining room or alfresco. Breakfast option is available for self-cater apartment (extra). Complimentary laundry, tea, coffee making facilities. BBQ available.

Riwaka Valley   *Self-contained   15km NW of Motueka*

Kaiweka Farm
Reginald & Pauline Dysart
RD 3, Riwaka Valley, Motueka

Tel: (03) 528 9267 Fax: (03) 528 9267
Mob: 025 605 2753   rdysart@ihug.co.nz
www.bnb.co.nz/kaiwekafarm.html

Double $100 Single $85 (Continental Breakfast)
Child $10 Dinner by arrangement
Credit cards accepted
1 Double 1 Single (1 bdrm)
1 Private

Kaiweka Farm is situated in the north branch of the Riwaka Valley adjacent to the scenic reserve at the Riwaka River source. We are close to the Abel Tasman National Park, Kaiteriteri Beach and beautiful walks. We offer accommodation in a modern self contained flat, sleeps four with day bed, fully equipped with fridge, TV, microwave. Laundry, phone, fax, available. We have four children and enjoy the company of our dogs and two cats. Smoking outside please.

Kaiteriteri   *B&B   9km N of Motueka*

Seaview B&B
Jackie & Tig McNab
259 Riwaka-Kaiteriteri Road,
RD 2, Motueka

Tel: (03) 528 9341 Fax: (03) 528 9341
www.bnb.co.nz/seaviewbb.html

Double $90 Single $60 (Continental Breakfast)
Child $20 Credit cards accepted Children welcome
2 Queen 1 Single (2 bdrm)
1 Guests share

Jackie and Tig welcome you to our peaceful and ideally located coastal property just 5 minutes to Kaiteriteri beach and handy to Abel Tasman and Kahurangi National Parks. Nearby attractions include sea kayaking, water taxi trips, beach and bush walks, golden sands and safe swimming beaches. Set against a large area of private native bush with abundant birdlife we offer panoramic views of Tasman Bay with breathtaking sunrises and sunsets. Large continental breakfast with homemade jams. Guest lounge with tea/coffee making facilities. Bar and restaurant 4 minutes.

Kaiteriteri   *B&B Not Suitable for Children   10km N of Motueka*

Bracken Hill B&B
Grace & Tom Turner
265 Riwaka Kaiteriteri Road., R.D. 2., Motueka.

Tel: (03) 528 9629 Fax: (03) 528 9629
gracet@actrix.co.nz
www.bnb.co.nz/brackenhillbb.html

Double $105-$115 Single $90 (Continental Breakfast)
Credit cards accepted
2 Queen 1 Twin (3 bdrm)   3 Private

"AFFORDABLE COASTAL LUXURY" WELCOME, to our tasteful, spacious modern home. Cosy rooms, all have wonderful sea views over blue Tasman Bay. Surrounding mountains, native bush, magical sunrises & stars, provide spectacular romantic highlights! A large sundeck leads to a unique rock garden. GUESTS T/V Lounge, Tea/Coffee, Fridge, "Pool Table" & Brochures. (Laundry Facility) EXPERIENCE, (5-15min.) - Kaiteriteri Beach, Marahau, Kahurangi / Abel Tasman National Parks. Beautiful golden beaches, safe water activities, & scenic walks.   MEET Jake, our gentle Golden Labrador. (outdoor dog) ENJOY, a refreshing breakfast, helpful hospitality, & our "Peaceful Haven".

Kaiteriteri   *B&B*   *16km N of Motueka*

Bayview
Aileen & Tim Rich
Kaiteriteri Heights, RD 2, Motueka
Tel: (03) 527 8090 Fax: (03) 527 8090 Mob: 025 545 835
kaiteri.bayview@xtra.co.nz www.bayviewbandb.webnz.co.nz
Double $135-$150 (Full Breakfast) Dinner by arrangement Credit cards accepted
1 King/Twin 1 King 1 Twin (2 bdrm) 2 Ensuite

We welcome you to Paradise. Kaiteriteri Beach, the gateway to the Abel Tasman National Park with the most beautiful coastline in New Zealand and the sunniest weather.

Here we can offer you Bed and Breakfast at its very best. Your rooms are large and beautifully furnished with extensive views of the Bay. You have a comfortable sitting area, outside terrace, ensuite with heated towel rail and hair dryer, fridge, tea/coffee making facilities, radio and TV. Laundry, phone, fax and email are available. You are welcome to share our living area, terraces, extensive collection of books, or be as private as you wish.

A full breakfast is served at your convenience, on your terrace or in the dining room. Dinner, of fresh New Zealand fish, meat and produce is available by prior arrangement. There are 2 restaurants, seasonal, within walking distance and a variety of cafes and hotels within 5-10 minutes drive.

From Bayview you can enjoy coastal and bush walks, see plenty of birdlife, or relax and swim at one of three beautiful beaches. Stay an extra day and explore the Abel Tasman National Park. We can book your trip by launch, water-taxi or kayak. They all operate from Kaiteriteri Beach. There is excellent trout fishing in the Riwaka River, 5 minutes away. Visit craft people and wineries, take a day trip over the Takaka Hill to Golden Bay.

Our location is quiet and peaceful . Turn off 4kms along the Kaiteriteri Road at the Blue B&B sign on Cederman Drive corner. Our name is on the gate. Map on homepage.

What our guests say!

Everything has a Touch of Class
Wonderful stay in fabulous home, thanks for hospitality
Absolutely delightful. Wonderful views and hospitality
Wonderful place, excellent hospitality enjoyed our stay & time in Abel Tasman immensely.
Our best stay in every way. Many many thanks.

Kaiteriteri *B&B* *13km N of Motueka*

Everton
Martin & Diane Everton
Kotare Place, Little Kaiteriteri, RD 2, Motueka
Tel: (03) 527 8301 Fax: (03) 527 8301
Mob: 027 450 5944 everton@xtra.co.nz
www.bnb.co.nz/everton.html

Double $95 Single $80 (Full Breakfast)
Credit cards accepted
1 Queen 1 Twin (2 bdrm) 1 Guests share

We live 3 minutes walk from the golden sands of Kaiteriteri Beach with wonderful sea views. Full breakfast includes fresh home baked bread or muffins. Our interests include golf, music, travel, walking, conversation and reading. The Abel Tasman National Park is right here with all the associated activities of kayaking, walking and boat trips, plus restaurants, wineries and craft shopping. Trout and sea fishing can be arranged. We are licensed also to take you on a personalised trip in our boat if you choose. Email access is offered and even a piano to play! We have no pets and are non-smokers, but guests are welcome to smoke outside.

Kaiteriteri *Homestay B&B* *15km N of Motueka*

Bellbird Lodge
Anthea & Brian Harvey
Kaiteriteri - Sandy Bay Road, RD1, Motueka
Tel: (03) 527 8555 Fax: (03) 527 8556
Mob: 0256 788 441 bellbirdlodge@xtra.co.nz
www.bnb.co.nz/bellbirdlodge.html

Double $110-$140 Single $85-$115
(Special Breakfast) Credit cards accepted
1 King/Twin 1 Double 1 Twin (3 bdrm)
1 Ensuite 1 Private

Situated in a tranquil hillside setting with panoramic sea views, Bellbird Lodge is close to Kaiteriteri Beach and Abel Tasman National Park. The tastefully furnished guest rooms are on the ground floor and have tea/coffee making facilities. Enjoy a buffet breakfast with sumptuous hot course of the day served in the dining room or alfresco on the terrace with its stunning view, accompanied by songs of bellbirds and tuis. Welcome to our modern home where warm friendly hospitality and quality food and accommodation await you.

Kaiteriteri *Self-contained* *13km N of Motueka*

The Haven
Tom & Alison Rowling
Kaiteriteri, RD2, Motueka
Tel: (03) 527 8085 Fax: (03) 527 8065
thehaven@internet.co.nz
www.thehaven.co.nz

Double $150 extra couple $50
Credit cards accepted
1 King 2 Twin (2 bdrm)
1 Ensuite 1 Private

The Haven - the name says it all. Just the sound of the waves, bird song, and the occasional haunting cry of the big back back gulls as they soar overhead. A retreat from the stress of everyday life with a nautical theme reflecting Tom's lifetime association with ships and the sea. Self-contained, two bedrooms, the Captain's Cabin with king size bed and ensuite, the Crew's quarters with 2 large single beds and private bathroom. The galley kitchen has generous breakfast provisions and two decks provide outdoor living. Not suitable for small children. We are smokefree.

Abel Tasman National Park
B&B   17km NW of Motueka

Twin Views
Ellenor & Les King
Tokongawa Drive, Split Apple Rock, RD 2, Motueka
Tel: (03) 527 8475 Fax: (03) 527 8479
Mob: 025 318 937
twinviews@xtra.co.nz   www.twinviews.co.nz
Double $125-$135 Single $100 (Special Breakfast)
Credit cards accepted
1 King/Twin 1 Queen (2 bdrm)   2 Ensuite

Wake to the sound of waves breaking on the beach below in this new architect designed home with magnificent sea views overlooking Tasman Bay. Each room has panoramic sea views, ensuite, fridge, tea/coffee making facilities, TV, hair dryer, heated towel rails, comfortable seating. Breakfast can be served in either the guest lounge or on your own private terrace. We are only minutes away from two beaches, bush walks and five minutes drive to start of Abel Tasman Track. Photos of the view are taken from guest balcony. Directions: Go past Kaiteriteri Beach towards Marahau for 4km. Turn right onto Tokongawa Drive and go right to the top. Beachfront house near Collingwood also available.

Abel Tasman National Park - Marahau *18km NW of Motueka*

Homestay B&B Self-contained Motels

Abel Tasman Stables
George Bloomfield
Abel Tasman National Park, Marahau

Tel: (03) 527 8181 Fax: (03) 527 8181
abel.tasman.stables.accom@xtra.co.nz
www.abletasmanstables.co.nz

Double $95-$115 Single $60 (Special Breakfast)
Dinner $30 by arrangement Credit cards accepted
5 Queen 2 Double 3 Single (6 bdrm)
5 Ensuite 1 Private 1 Family share

Great views, hospitality, peaceful garden setting are yours at Abel Tasman Stables accommodation. Closest ensuite facility to Abel Tasman National park. Guests comments include 'I know now that hospitality is not just a word', TH, Germany. 'Wonderful place, friendly hospitality. The best things for really special holidays. We leave a piece of our hearts', P&M, Italy. 'The creme-de-la-creme of our holiday. What a view', MN & JW, England. Homestay bed & breakfast or self-contained options. Cafe close by.

Marahau - Abel Tasman National Park *B&B* *17km NW of Motueka*

Sandspit
Paul & Marieann Kennedy
Lady Barkly Grove off Tokongawa Drive,
Split Apple Rock, RD 2, Motueka

Tel: (03) 527 8388 Fax: (03) 527 8388
Mob: 025 240 4370 kennedy.keenan@xtra.co.nz
www.ozpal.com/sandspit

Double $130 Single $100 (Full Breakfast)
2 Queen (2 bdrm) 2 Ensuite

Sandspit is set in the Split Apple Rock sanctuary overlooking Marahau and the tranquil waters of Abel Tasman National Park. Sit on the deck and enjoy our freshly prepared delicious breakfast while looking out over the bay. Take a leisurely, stroll to Split Apple Beach or a dip in the pool. Kayak, walk and swim in the park or just sit on the deck and take in the magnificent view. Swimming pool, private entrance, TV, fridge, tea/coffee and home baking. Internet access. Directions: On the Marahau - Kaiteriteri Road, take the Tokongawa Drive turnoff. 0.6km up Tokongawa Drive turn left into Lady Barlky Grove. Sandspit is 100m on your left

Takaka Hill - Motueka *Self-contained Farmstay* *17km NW of Motueka*

Kairuru Farmstay
Wendy & David Henderson
Kairuru, State Highway 60, Takaka Hill, Motueka

Tel: (03) 528 8091 Fax: (03) 528 8091
Mob: 025 337 457 Tollfree: 0800 524 787
kairuru@xtra.co.nz www.kairurufamstay.co.nz

Double $150 Single $130 (Full Breakfast)
Dinner by arrangement Self catering $110
Credit cards accepted Children welcome
2 King/Twin 2 Queen 1 Twin (5 bdrm) 2 Private

Accommodation is offered in two modern well equipped cottages. The cottages are exclusively yours, with wonderful sea views and very private. A good selection for breakfast is supplied at the cottage but made by yourselves. Both the cottages are comfortable with sitting room, kitchen, laundry, bathroom, telephone, TV, electric blankets, microwave. Our 4000 acre sheep and cattle farm is set high on the unique marble mountain and offers guests a chance to stay on a working hill country cattle farm. Children are welcome and enjoy feeding and handling our pet sheep, goats, pig and chickens.

Patons Rock Beach - Takaka *10km W of Takaka*

Self-contained Farmstay 4 villas

Patondale
Vicki & David James
Patons Rock, RD 2, Takaka
Tel: (03) 525 8262 Fax: (03) 525 8262
Mob: 025 936 891 Tollfree: Res.0800306697
patondale@xtra.co.nz www.bnb.co.nz/patondale.html
Double $120 Single $70
(Continental & Full Breakfast) Child $20 $120 dbl.
Villas Credit cards accepted
4 King 1 Queen 10 Single (10 bdrm) 5 Private

Farmstay: A "Bay Beauty" awake to the sound of the sea below and enjoy with us a hearty breakfast.Our lovely home has "simply magic" views,pretty gardens and is very peaceful "above the rest" surrounded by our 200 acre dairy farm. Villas: four new, spacious, deluxe self-contained units, own attached carports. Two bedrooms. Peaceful rural setting a few minutes walk to the beach.Central location. "Simply the Best" Your kiwi hosts David & Vicki invite you to be our guests.

Takaka - Tata Beach *Homestay B&B 15km NE of Takaka*

The Devonshires
Brian & Susan Devonshire
Tata Heights Drive, RD 1, Takaka
Tel: (03) 525 7987 Fax: (03) 525 7987
Mob: 025 463 118 devs.1@xtra.co.nz
www.bnb.co.nz/thedevonshires.html
Double $90 Single $55 (Full Breakfast)
Child not suitable Dinner $25 - $30 by arrangement
Credit cards accepted
1 Queen (1 bdrm) 1 Ensuite

The Devonshires have moved to Tata Beach and invite you to enjoy their newly built home and stroll to the beautiful golden beach. A tranquil base for exploring the truly scenic Golden Bay, the Abel Tasman walkway, Kahurangi National Park, Farewell Spit, amazing coastal scenery, fishing the rivers or visiting interesting craftspeople. Brian, an educator, wine and American Football buff is a keen fisherman. Susan enjoys crafts, painting, gardening and practising her culinary skills. Mindy and Charlie Brown are the residents cats. Longer visits welcomed.

Takaka *Self-contained B&B 5km S of Takaka*

Rose Cottage
Margaret & Phil Baker
Hamama Road, RD 1, Takaka
Tel: (03) 525 9048 Fax: (03) 525 9048
www.bnb.co.nz/rosecottage.html
Double $75-$85 Single $55-$65
(Continental Breakfast)
Self contained units $85 - $125 Credit cards accepted
1 Queen 2 Single (2 bdrm)
1 Guests share

Rose cottage, much loved home of Phil and Margaret situated in the beautiful Takaka valley, in 2 1/2 acres of garden amongst 300 year old Totara trees, is ideally situated to explore Golden Bay's many attractions. Our 3 self contained units have full kitchens, private sun decks and quality furniture made by Phil in his craft workshop. The 12 metre indoor solar-heated swimming pool is available to our guests. Our interests are travel, photography, gardening, arts and crafts and helping to make our guests' stay a memorable one.

Takaka   *Homestay*   *Takaka Township*

Haven House
Pam Peacock
177 Commercial Street, Takaka, Golden Bay
Tel: (03) 525 9554 Fax: (03) 525 8720
www.bnb.co.nz/havenhouse.html
Double $85 Single $65 (Full Breakfast)
Child neg Triple $110
Credit cards accepted Pets welcome
1 Queen 1 Twin 2 Single (3 bdrm)
1 Guests share 1 Family share

A relaxed 'home away form home' atmosphere, happy echoes from the past in furnishings and character. Guest lounge. A large secluded, tranquil garden, to enjoy afternoon tea, picnic, barbecue. Your Haven. 'Home' goodies and orchard fruits compliment the traditional English breakfast, served in sunny conservatory or outside on terrace overlooking rose garden. Central to all tourist attractions, 10 minutes stroll to shops and cafes. Our aim is friendly personal service and hospitality endeavouring to make your stay a memorable one. Looking forward to meeting you.

Takaka   *Homestay*   *2km S of Takaka*

Croxfords Homestay
Pam & John Croxford
Dodson Road, RD 1, Takaka, Golden Bay
Tel: (03) 525 7177 Fax: (03) 525 7177
Tollfree: 0800 26 41 56
croxfords@xtra.co.nz
www.kahurangiwalks.co.nz
Double $100 Single $70 (Full Breakfast)
Child $10 Dinner $25 Credit cards accepted
1 Double 3 Single (2 bdrm)   2 Ensuite

You are welcome to our spacious home in a peaceful rural setting close to Takaka. Views of Kahurangi National Park are spectacular. Pam loves cooking evening meals, including special diets, using home grown produce. Breakfasts include home made bread, muesli, yoghurt and preserves. We enjoy assisting visitors make the most of their visit. We are near beaches and national parks. We have many New Zealand books. No children at home, or pets. Non smokers preferred. We offer guided walks in the ABEL TASMAN and KAHURANGI national parks.

Parapara   *B&B*   *20km NW of Takaka*

Hakea Hill House
Vic & Liza Eastman
PO Box 35, Collingwood 7171
Tel: (03) 524 8487 Fax: (03) 524 8487
vic.eastman@clear.net.nz
www.bnb.co.nz/hakeahillhouse.html
Double $120 Single $80 (Full Breakfast)
Child $40 Dinner by arrangement
Credit cards accepted Children welcome
2 Double 6 Single (3 bdrm)
1 Guests share

Hakea Hill House at Parapara has views from its hilltop of all Golden Bay. The two story house is modern and spacious. Two guest rooms have large balconies; the third for children has four bunk beds and a cot. American and New Zealand electric outlets are installed. Television, tea or coffee, and telephone lines are available in rooms. Vic is a practicing physician with an interest in astronomy. Liza is a quilter and cares for two outdoor dogs. Please contact us personally for reservations and directions.

Collingwood   *Self-contained B&B*   *25km N of Takaka*

Skara Brae Garden Motels & Bed and Breakfast
Joanne & Pax Northover
Elizabeth Street, Collingwood

Tel: (03) 524 8464 Fax: (03) 524 8474
Tollfree: 0800 752 722
skarabrae@xtra.co.nz
www.accommodationcollingwood.co.nz

Double $110 Single $80 (Continental Breakfast)
2 self-contained units $85 Credit cards accepted
2 Queen 1 Double 1 Twin 2 Single (4 bdrm)
1 Ensuite 3 Private

Skara Brae, the original police residence in Collingwood built in 1908, has been tastefully renovated over the years. Our historic home is in a quiet, peaceful garden setting. Join us in the house for bed and breakfast or our two self contained motel units. Either way you will experience a warm welcoming atmosphere and individual attention. We are a minute away from the excellent Courthouse Cafe and local tavern bistro bar and it is a short stroll to the beach. Farewell Spit trips depart close by.

Collingwood   *Homestay B&B*   *3km SE of Collingwood, 25km Takaka*

Win's B&B
Heather Margaret Win
State Highway 60, at start of Plain Road
Tel: (03) 524 8381
www.bnb.co.nz/wins.html

Double $60 Single $35 (Full Breakfast)
Dinner by arrangement Pet on property
Children welcome
1 Queen 1 Double 2 Twin (4 bdrm)
1 Guests share 1 Family share

A warm welcome to Win's Bed & Breakfast. 100km onto a sheep and cattle farm with mountain range in back ground, close to walking tracks and beach. 3km from Collingwood where there are 2 excellent cafes and a tavern bistro bar also bookings for Farewell Spit trips. I have 1 cat Bibbee.

Pakawau Beach - Collingwood   *Self-contained Homestay*   *12km N of Collingwood*

Pakawau Homestay
Val & Graham Williams
Pakawau Beach,
RD, Collingwood

Tel: (03) 524 8168 Fax: (03) 524 8168
www.bnb.co.nz/pakawauhomestay.html

Double $80 Single $70
(Full Breakfast) Dinner $25
S/C $70 Pet on property
1 Queen 2 Double 1 Single (2 bdrm)
1 Ensuite 1 Family share

We are the northern most homestay in the South Island, 9km from Farewell Spit. We offer self-contained accommodation from $70 per night. The Farewell Spit Tours will pick you up from our gate. You only have to walk a few metres through our garden to a safe swimming beach. Local seafoods available, eg. whitebait, scallops, or you can walk across the road to a licensed cafe. We are non smokers, have two cats and look forward to sharing our lifestyle with you.

Golden Downs   *Lodge   20km SW of Wakefield*

Golden Downs Lodge
William Cameron
Cnr Valley Road and Kerr Hill Road,
Kohatu, SH6, Wakefield
Tel: (03) 522 4175 Fax: (03) 522 4611
goldendowns@clear.net.nz
www.bnb.co.nz/goldendownslodge.html
Double $95 Single $50 (Full Breakfast) Child $20
Dinner $25 - $35 Pet on property Pets welcome
2 Double 6 Single (3 bdrm) 3 Private

Golden Downs lodge is a quirky, homely retreat at the heart of Golden Downs forest. Set on thirty acres of tree covered grounds, the lodge occupies the old Golden Downs village hall. We are proud of our fine food prepared from local produce, and an atmosphere of intelligent and entertaining hospitality.

Nelson Lakes   *Homestay   85km S of Nelson*

Nelson Lakes Homestay
Merv & Gay Patch
RD 2, State Highway 63, Nelson
Tel: (03) 521 1191 Fax: (03) 521 1191
Mob: 021 261 8529 Home@Tasman.net
www.bnb.co.nz/nelsonlakeshomestay.html
Double $95 Single $60 (Full Breakfast)
Dinner $30pp by arrangement
Credit cards accepted Pet on property
2 King/Twin 1 Queen (2 bdrm) 2 Ensuite

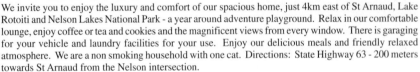

We invite you to enjoy the luxury and comfort of our spacious home, just 4km east of St Arnaud, Lake Rotoiti and Nelson Lakes National Park - a year around adventure playground. Relax in our comfortable lounge, enjoy coffee or tea and cookies and the magnificent views from every window. There is garaging for your vehicle and laundry facilities for your use. Enjoy our delicious meals and friendly relaxed atmosphere. We are a non smoking household with one cat. Directions: State Highway 63 - 200 meters towards St Arnaud from the Nelson intersection.

Murchison   *Self-contained Homestay B&B   0.5km N of Murchison*

Coch-Y-Bondhu Lodge
Mike & Noela Buchanan
15 Grey Street, Murchison. 7191. South Island. NZ,
Tel: (03) 523 9196 Fax: (03) 523 9196
Mob: 027 415 1019   cochybondhu@xtra.co.nz
www.homestays.net.nz/cochybondhu.htm
Double $100-$130 Single $85 (Full Breakfast)
Dinner By Arrangement S/C
Credit cards accepted Pet on property
2 Queen 1 Double 1 Twin 1 Single (4 bdrm)
2 Ensuite 1 Private 1 Family share

Kia-ora. Welcome!! Our large, uniquely crafted home is set on 3 acres, secluded, quiet, surrounded by mature trees and overlooking the Buller River. We pride ourselves on warm Kiwi hospitality, good food and comfortable beds. We are 10 minutes walk from the town centre but you get the feeling you are in the middle of the wilderness. We actively encourage native birds and see many varieties. We have two friendly dogs, several cows and hens. Mike is a professional fishing guide, a member of the NZPFGA.

Tophouse - Nelson Lakes   *Self-contained Farmstay   9km N of St Arnaud*

Tophouse
Gladys & Mac Hollick
Nelson Lakes, RD 2, Nelson

Tel: (03) 521 1848
Fax: (03) 521 1848
Tollfree: 0800 867 468
tophouse@clear.net.nz
www.tophouse.co.nz

Double $80 Single $40 (Continental Breakfast)
Child $20 Dinner $20 Credit cards accepted
Children welcome
1 Queen 5 Double 19 Single (13 bdrm)
4 Private 2 Guests share

We, Gladys and Mac Hollick together with our two cats, invite you to share our unique home with huge open fires, lovely setting and homely atmosphere. Tophouse, a cob (mud) building, dating from the 1880's when it was a hotel, and reopened in 1989 as a Farm Guest House, has that 'good old days' feel about it.

Situated on a 300 ha (730 acre) picturesque high country farm running cattle, with much native bush and an abundance of bird life also a unique 9 hole golf course. A popular holiday spot for its peace and beauty, bush walks, fishing and in the winter serves the two local ski fields. Tophouse is only 9km from St Arnaud, gateway to Nelson Lakes National Park.

A typical farmhouse dinner is taken with family and since the fire's going 'real' toast for breakfast. Cottages are 2 bedroom, fully self contained including kitchen, with great views of the surrounding mountains.

Directions: Just off State Highway 63 between Blenheim and Murchison and 9km from St Arnaud is Tophouse, that's us. The area took its name from the building. If travelling from Nelson, leave State Highway 6 at Belgrove and travel towards St Arnaud, we're signposted from the main road and looking forward to your visit. Come, see and feel the living history of this unique place.

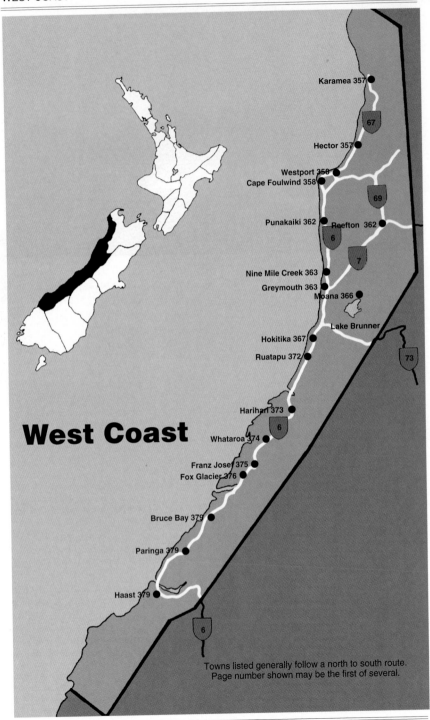

West Coast

Karamea 357

67

Hector 357

Westport 358
Cape Foulwind 358

69

Punakaiki 362   Reefton 362

6

7

Nine Mile Creek 363

Greymouth 363

Moana 366

Lake Brunner

73

Hokitika 367

Ruatapu 372

Harihari 373

6

Whataroa 374

Franz Josef 375
Fox Glacier 376

Bruce Bay 379

Paringa 379

Haast 379

6

Towns listed generally follow a north to south route.
Page number shown may be the first of several.

Karamea   *Farmstay B&B*   *84km N of Westport*

Beachfront Farmstay
Dianne & Russell Anderson
Karamea, SH 67, Karamea

Tel: (03) 782 6762 Fax: (03) 782 6762
Mob: 021 782676   farmstay@xtra.co.nz
www.WestCoastBeachAccommodation.co.nz

Double $110-$145 Single $80-$100 (Special Breakfast)
Child $35 Dinner $40 Credit cards accepted
1 King 1 Queen 1 Twin (3 bdrm)
2 Ensuite 1 Family share

Welcome to a spectacular area of the West Coast.Our home is 2 mins walk to a beautiful sandy beach with awesome views and amazing sunsets, great for walking or jogging. Relax in our spacious home and garden. We milk 330 friesian cows on our undulating pasture. Join us for delicious country cuisine, organic vegetables, homemade desserts, NZ wine also generous cooked breakfasts. Our area offers scenic walks, guided tours in limestone caves with extinct birds, unique limestone arches,9 hole golf course, horse riding, bird watching, fishing, guides available.

Karamea   *Self-contained Farmstay*   *0.5km Karamea*

Bridge Farm
Rosalie & Peter Sampson
Bridge Street, Karamea, RD 1, Westport

Tel: (03) 782 6955 Fax: (03) 782 6748
Tollfree: 0800 KARAMEA
Enquires@karameamotels.co.nz
www.bnb.co.nz/karameamotels.co.nz.html

Double $85-$100 (Continental Breakfast)
Child $10 Credit cards accepted
6 Queen 8 Single (10 bdrm) 8 Private

Since relinquishing their dairy farm to daughter Caroline and son-in-law Bevan, Rosalie and Peter has purpose built on the property accommodation that neatly bridges the gap between motel and farm stay. Both are happy to share their extensive knowledge of their district, its people and environment and introduce guests to the many short walks that Karamea offers. Each quality suite is self contained and has a private lounge that overlooks the farm to Kahurangi National Park beyond. A small mob of deer and alpaca graze nearby.

Hector   *Homestay B&B*   *35km N of Westport*

Beachfront Boutique
Dennis van der Giessen
33 Main Rd,
Hector, Westport

Tel: 03 782 8804 Fax: 03 782 8804
beachfront@thewebshed.co.nz
www.thewebshed.co.nz/beachfront

Double $60 Single $40
(Continental Breakfast) Child $15.00
2 Queen 1 Single (2 bdrm)

The Beachfront Boutique is a cozy Bed & Breakfast, located directly on the wonderfully unspoiled West Coast beach in Hector. We rent out two double rooms from $60 per night and provide a rich English or Country Style breakfast. Spend some time with us and explore the area from here. The area offers excellent walking and tramping, fishing, surfing, dolphin watching, carving, horse riding and tracking and much more. We are more than happy to help you plan your days.

Westport   *Boutique Country Lodge*   *7km SE of Westport*

River View Lodge
Noeline Biddulph
State Highway 6, Lower Buller Gorge,
PO Box 229, Westport

Tel: (03) 789 6037 Fax: (03) 789 6037
Mob: 025 249 1286   Tollfree: 0800 18 46 56
info@rurallodge.co.nz   www.rurallodge.co.nz

Double $145-$190 Single $145 (Full Breakfast)
Dinner $45 by arrangement Credit cards accepted
1 King/Twin 2 Queen 1 Twin (4 bdrm)   4 Ensuite

The Lodge is a peaceful retreat overlooking the Buller River. On the main road form Picton and Nelson to the West Coast. The suites are private, tastefully decorated with ensuites. Rooms open onto a large verandah and look out onto part of the garden and lawn. The garden is also featured in the NZ Gardens to Visit. Lunch and dinner by arrangement. Laundry facilities. Smoking outside only. Unsuitable for pets. We have one small very friendly dog. Reservations are recommended. Ample parking. Children by arrangement.

Westport - Cape Foulwind   *Homestay B&B*   *11km S of Westport*

Steeples Homestay
Pauline & Bruce Cargill
Lighthouse Road, Cape Foulwind, RD 2, Westport

Tel: (03) 789 7876 Mob: 021 663 687
Steepleshomestay@xtra.co.nz
www.bnb.co.nz/steepleshomestay.html

Double $80 Single $40 (Full Breakfast)
Child $15 Credit cards accepted
1 Queen 2 Single (2 bdrm)
1 Private

Enjoy our peaceful rural home, magnificent views of Tasman Sea, rugged coastline beaches, great swimming, surfing, fishing, walking. Within 5 minutes walk the very popular seal colony walkway, great dining at Bay House Restaurant and friendly local Star Tavern, or play a round of golf at Carters Beach Golf links. Other local attractions include Coaltown Museum, horse riding, underworld and white water rafting, bush walks, Punakaiki National Park. We are keen gardeners and enjoy all sports and have a Jack Russell dog and a cat. All laundry facilities available and off street parking.

Westport   *Self-contained Homestay*   *2km N of Westport*

Chrystal Lodge
Ann & Bill Blythe
PO Box 128, Westport
Tel: (03) 789 8617 Fax: (03) 789 8617
Tollfree: 0800 259 953   chrystal@clear.net.nz
www.bnb.co.nz/chrystallodge.html

Double $80 Single $50 (Continental Breakfast)
Child 1/2 price S/C Double $75 Credit cards accepted
Pet on property Children welcome
2 Queen 1 Double 3 Single (4 bdrm)
2 Ensuite 1 Guests share

Ann and Bill would like to welcome you to Chrystal Lodge. Our home, built on 20 acres is beside a beach ideal for walking, surfing, fishing or swimming. The self-contained units have a fully equipped kitchen/lounge with en-suite bathrooms off the bedrooms. Breakfast is optional in units. Our garden setting has ample off-street parking. Free guest laundry. Continental breakfast includes croissants and muffins. Pony available for children. We have two cats. Smoking outside please. Off season rates.

Westport   *Homestay*   *Westport Central*

Havenlee Homestay
Jan & Ian Stevenson
76 Queen Street, Westport
Tel: (03) 789 8543 Fax: (03) 789 8502
Mob: 025 627 2702   Tollfree: 0800 673 619
havenlee76@hotmail.com   www.havenlee.co.nz

Double $90 Single $60 (Continental Breakfast)
Child neg Credit cards accepted Children welcome
1 Queen 1 Double 1 Twin (3 bdrm)
1 Guests share suite

Peace in Paradise - this is Havenlee, offering tranquil, central location 300 metres from town centre. Born and bred West Coasters - hospitality is part of our heritage. Share our modern, spacious home set amongst native and exotic trees and shrubs. With breathtaking scenery, Westport is sited between the Kahurangi and Paparoa National Parks. Close by are Tauranga Bay Seal Colony and Punakaiki Pancake Rocks. Enjoy a generous continental-plus breakfast, warm, comfortable beds, full laundry facilities, local knowledge in a friendly, relaxed smokefree environment.

Westport - Cape Foulwind   *Homestay*   *11km W of Westport*

Clifftop Homestay
Paddy & Gail Alexander
Clifftop Lane, Cape Foulwind, RD 2, Westport
Tel: (03) 789 5472
www.bnb.co.nz/clifftophomestay.html

Double $90-$120 Single $80 (Continental Breakfast)
Child $15 Dinner $25 (whitebait) Twin Bed/Sit $120
2 Double 1 Single (2 bdrm)
1 Private 1 Family share

We and 'Murphy the Beagle' invite you to discover the magic of the Cape. Our boutique clifftop homestay offers two private, stylish rooms, one with spacious bed/lounge room with breathtaking sea views and Sky TV. The upmarket bathroom has spa bath, heated towel rails, hairdryer and separate toilet. Enjoy complimentary tea/coffee/biscuits or a locally brewed beer on our balcony or in our garden courtyard. Whether you stroll the beach, explore coastal walks, visit the seal colony, watch spectacular sunsets from the lighthouse - you will find 'the Cape' restorative to body and soul. Directions: first right past Star Tavern, right at beach carpark. Full breakfast by arrangement.

Westport *B&B* *Westport Central*

Derby Street Bed & Breakfast
Judy and Ross Ferguson
118 Derby Street, Westport,
South Island, New Zealand

Tel: (03) 789 7757 Mob: (025) 238 2661
derbyst@xtra.co.nz
www.bnb.co.nz/derbystreetbedbreakfast.html

Double $70 Single $55 (Full Breakfast) Dinner $15
1 King 1 Queen 1 Double 2 Single (3 bdrm)
2 Ensuite 1 Private 1 Guests share

We offer you quality accommodation in a 1907 villa with original pressed steel ceilings and decor. Two of our three bedrooms are ensuite, one with spa-bath and one with shower. Comfortable guest lounge available with open fire and TV. We hope you will take the opportunity to dine in our pleasant dining room (all tastes catered for) with Whitebait our specialty. We have two friendly Jack Russell dogs. Basic laundry free. Directions: Entering Westport on Palmerston Street turn right at Mill Street then left into Derby St. Look at map on - www.colourcards.com/derby/

Westport - Cape Foulwind *Farmstay Homestay B&B* *10km W of Westport*

Lighthouse Homestay
Derek Parsons & Helen Jenkins
32 Lighthouse Road, Cape Foulwind, Westport

Tel: (03) 789 7942 Fax: (03) 789 7942
Mob: 025 857 583 Tollfree: 0800 227 322
derek.parsons@xtra.co.nz

Double $90-$120 Single $70 (Continental Breakfast)
2 Queen 1 Double 2 Single (3 bdrm)
1 Ensuite 1 Guests share

Enjoy the soothing tranquillity of amazing sea views from your bedroom/patio. Walk the impressive Cape Foulwind Walkway with its seals and captivating coastline, ending at the magic Bay House Restaurant overlooking Tauranga Bay. Numerous outdoor activities and attractions nearby. Helen and Derek can take you out on the farm shifting cattle or walking through native rainforest. Let "Poppy" our fox terrier take you beachwalking below the cliffs. Kayaks, mountain bikes available. Short walk to friendly country pub. Smokefree inside.

www.westcoast.org.nz/tourism/accommodation/lighthouse/lighthouse.html

Westport *Self-contained Homestay B&B* *3km S of Westport*

Bellaville
Marlene & Ross Burrow
4 Martin Place, Carters Beach, Westport

Tel: (03) 789 8457 Mob: 025 6131 689
Tollfree: 0800 789 845 fairhalls@xtra.co.nz
www.bnb.co.nz/bellaville.html

Double $80 Single $50 (Continental & Full Breakfast)
Child $15 Children welcome
1 Queen 1 Single (1 bdrm)
1 Ensuite 1 Private

Welcome to paradise at Carters Beach. Wake to the sound of the waves pounding on our safe swimming/walking beach. Situated on the main road to Cape Foulwind and only minutes from the Seal Colony walkway, Golf course, Airport, Coal Town museum, restaurants and town centre. Easy access to the private entrance of your large sunny self contained room. Your private bathroom has a spa bath, shower and separate toilet. There are tea making facilities, MA's homemade biscuits, TV, hairdryer. Having travelled extensively, we look forward to chatting with you.

Westport   *B&B*

Archer House
Kerrie Fairhall
75 Queen Street, Westport,
Tel: (03) 789 8778 Fax: (03) 789 8763
Mob: 025 260 3677   accom@archerhouse.co.nz
www.archerhouse.co.nz
Double $120-$150 Single $110-$140
(Full Breakfast) Credit cards accepted
3 Queen 2 Single (3 bdrm) 2 Ensuite 1 Private

3 large bedrooms, 2 with ensuites, 1 with private facilities. All bedrooms have TVs and tea/coffee facilities. Bathrooms have a hair dryer, heated towel rail and toiletries. Sunny balconies and relax in a sheltered private conservatory or one of the two guest lounges. New Zealand Heritage Home, with outstanding historic significance to the West Coast created by leadlighting masterpieces, fireplaces and antique furniture. Short stroll to all town amenities including Victoria Square and heated swimming pool. Whole home is available for rental for those who prefer privacy. See website for more details, www.archerhouse.co.nz.

Westport - Carters Beach   *B&B*   *5km S of Westport*

Carters Beach B&B
Sue & John Bennett
MacIntyres Road, Off SH 67, Westport
Tel: (03) 789 8056
www.bnb.co.nz/cartersbeachbb.html
Double $80-$90 Single $60-$70
(Continental Breakfast)
1 Queen 1 Double 1 Twin (2 bdrm)
1 Ensuite 1 Private

Welcome to our lovely relaxed atmosphere at Carters Beach with a very sunny self-contained unit with own decking and entranceway. Also available is a double/twin room with own separate bath/shower and separate toilet. We are within a three minute walk to our very clean safe beach and fully licenced bar and café. Situated only 5km from the town of Westport. Our golf course, airport, and the famous seal colony all within a few minutes drive.

A homestay is a B&B where you share the family's living area.

Reefton   *B&B*

Quartz Lodge
Toni and Ian Walker
78 Sheil Street, Reefton, West Coast
Tel: (03) 732 8383 Fax: (03) 732 8083
Mob: 025 619 4520   quartz-lodge@xtra.co.nz
Tollfree: 0800 302 725   www.bnb.co.nz/quartzlodge.html

Double $80-$100 Single $45-$75 (Full Breakfast)
Child $20 Dinner $35 Credit cards accepted
1 King 1 Queen 1 Twin 1 Single (3 bdrm)
1 Ensuite 1 Private 1 Guests share

Toni and Ian invite you to experience "Quartz Lodge" nestled within Victoria Forest Park and in the heart of the West Coast quartz gold/coal mining country. Let this be your home away from home - but with all the extras. Huge picture windows in every room offer best views in town. Guests only entrance, lounge/dining area. Luxurious beds-rooms serviced daily. Country style breakfast, tea/coffee facilities, laundry service and phone/fax. Evening meals available - arriving late? not a problem. Your comfort is our priority.

Reefton   *B&B*   *Reefton Central*

Historic Reef Cottage B&B and Cafe
Susan & Ronnie Standfield
51-55 Broadway, Reefton
Tel: (03) 732 8440 Fax: (03) 732 8440
Mob: 025 262 3855   Tollfree: 0800 770 440
reefton@clear.net.nz
www.bnb.co.nz/historicreefcottage.html

Double $78-$130 Single $58-$105 (Full Breakfast)
Child 1/2 price Single party bookings $195 - $325
Dinner $10 - $35 Credit cards accepted
1 King/Twin 1 Queen 2 Double (4 bdrm) 2 Ensuite 2 Private

Built in 1887 from native timbers for a local barrister. This historical Edwardian home has been carefully renovated to add light and space without losing its olde world charm. Elegantly decorated the house features open fires, original furniture, brassware and NZ artwork. Nestled in Historic Gold/Coal mining country between native beech forests and the Inangahua River, Reef Cottage is unrivalled as the finest accommodation in Reefton.

Punakaiki   *Homestay B&B*   *45km N of Greymouth*

The Rocks Homestay
Peg & Kevin Piper
No. 33 Hartmount Place, PO Box 16, Punakaiki
Tel: (03) 731 1141 Fax: (03) 731 1142
Tollfree: 0800 272 164   therocks@minidata.co.nz
www.therockshomestay.com

WELCOME!

Double $110-$155 Single $80-$95 (Special Breakfast)
Child $40 - $60 Dinner $30 - $45 by arrangement
S/C House $120 - $160 Credit cards accepted
2 Queen 2 Twin (3 bdrm) 3 Ensuite

Huge windows and astounding views in all directions - coast, sea, cliffs, rainforest, National Park. The Rocks Homestay sits above the forest - comfortable, modern, warm, friendly - unique in its wilderness location. Healthy breakfasts with home baking. Home-cooked evening meals may be arranged. Visit the Pancake Rocks and Blowholes, walk Truman Track to the beach, photograph the limestone gorges. Stay a while and experience unspoiled New Zealand. Enjoy the reference library. Between Greymouth and Westport, turn off 100m north of Truman Track. Visit www.therockshomestay.com

Nine Mile Bay   *Self-contained*   *15km N of Greymouth*

Tasman Beach B&B
Jill Cotton
9 Mile Coast Road, RD 1,
Runanga, Highway 6, Westland
Tel: (03) 762 7117 Fax: (03) 762 7161
www.bnb.co.nz/tasmanbeachbb.html
Double $110 Single $90
(Continental Breakfast) Child $5
1 Queen 1 Twin (2 bdrm)
1 Private

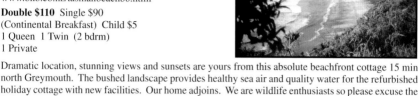

Dramatic location, stunning views and sunsets are yours from this absolute beachfront cottage 15 min north Greymouth. The bushed landscape provides healthy sea air and quality water for the refurbished holiday cottage with new facilities. Our home adjoins. We are wildlife enthusiasts so please excuse the little blue penguins who choose to visit us. Heaps of adventures await you at the Blow Holes Punakaiki 20 mins north. Breakfast always included. Full kitchen and laundry. Children enjoyed and welcome.

Nine Mile Creek   *Homestay B&B*   *14km N of Greymouth*

The Breakers
Frank & Barbara Ash
PO Box 188, Greymouth, Westland
Tel: (03) 762 7743 Fax: (03) 762 7733
Tollfree: 0800 350 590   stay@breakers.co.nz
www.breakers.co.nz
Double $145-$225 (Full Breakfast)
Dinner $55 Credit cards accepted
1 King 3 Queen 2 Twin (4 bdrm)
4 Ensuite

One of the West Coast's most spectacularly located B&B's, with stunning views over the ocean. Private beach access allows you to fossick for jade and beautiful stones. All rooms are 'en-suite' with TV and hot beverage making facilities. A gourmet dinner is available, with 24 hours notice, includes NZ wines and is constantly accompanied by the crashing waves! The Breakers is a wonderful base to visit the Pancake Rocks, the Paparoa National Park and the best stretch of coastline in NZ. Sorry, unsuitable for children

Greymouth   *Homestay*   *Greymouth Central*

Ardwyn House
Mary Owen
48 Chapel Street, Greymouth
Tel: (03) 768 6107 Fax: (03) 768 5177
Mob: 025 376 027
ardwynhouse@hotmail.com
www.bnb.co.nz/ardwynhouse.html
Double $75-$80 Single $50 (Full Breakfast)
Child 1/2 price Credit cards accepted
2 Queen 3 Single (3 bdrm)
1 Guests share

Ardwyn House is three minutes walk from the town centre in a quiet garden setting offering sea, river and town views. The house was built in the 1920's and is a fine example of an imposing residence with fine woodwork and leadlight windows, whilst being a comfortable and friendly home. Greymouths ideally situated for travellers touring the West Coast being central with good choice of restaurants. We offer a courtesy car service to and from local travel centres and also provide off street parking.

Greymouth   *Homestay*   *4km S of Greymouth*

Ib Pupich
5 Stanton Crescent,
Greymouth

Tel: (03) 768 4348 Fax: (03) 768 4348
pupich@xtra.co.nz
www.bnb.co.nz/pupich.html

Double $80 Single $50 (Full Breakfast)
1 King/Twin (1 bdrm)
1 Private

We offer warm hospitality in our lovely home overlooking the Tasman Sea and south to Mount Cook and Tasman. We have hosted for many years so you can be assured of a relaxed stay in this quiet street only five minutes walk from the beach. There is much to do and see, lakes and rivers, wonderful bush and coastline walks. Trout fishing and golf. Or just laze on the deck and watch the sun go down. Phone for direction please.

Greymouth   *Homestay B&B*   *3km N of Greymouth*

Oak Lodge
Zelda Anderson
Coal Creek, State Highway 6, Greymouth

Tel: (03) 768 6832 Fax: (03) 768 4362
Tollfree: 0800 351 000
NZH_OAK.LODGE@xtra.co.nz
www.oaklodge.co.nz

Double $100-$140 Single $90
(Continental & Full Breakfast) Credit cards accepted
1 Queen 1 Double 1 Twin 2 Single (3 bdrm)
3 Ensuite

Oak lodge is in a rural setting and was built in 1901, initially an old farmhouse and is surrounded with gardens. Many varities of Rhodddendrons and Azaleas. The interior is one of antiques and memorabilia, a unique atmosphere. Guests have their own lounge. The 20 acre hobby farm supports sheep and Scottish Belted Galloway cows. For our guest use a swimming pool and tennis court is available. We are half an hour from the Paparoa National Park and near to Lakes and excellent fishing rivers.

Greymouth   *Homestay*   *6km S of Greymouth*

Paroa Homestay (formerly Pam's Homestay)
Pam Sutherland, 345 Main South Road, Greymouth

Tel: (03) 762 6769 Fax: (03) 762 6765
Mob: 025 685 6280   Tollfree: 0800 116 922
paroahomestay@hotmail.com
www.bnb.co.nz/paroahomestay.html

Double $99-$115 Single $79-$99 (Special Breakfast)
Credit cards accepted Children over 5 welcome
1 King/Twin 1 King 1 Double (3 bdrm)
1 Ensuite 1 Private 1 Guests share

Relax on terraces overlooking sea, incredible sunsets. Three minutes walk to beach. Awake to chorus of native birds, nestling in towering powhutukawa tree. Luxurious guest lounge, bedrooms, in spacious classic home. Experience rainforest bushwalks, trout fishing tours. Superb breakfast, fresh fruit salad, hot bread, giant muffins, yoghurt, cereals, dried fruit/nuts. Pam enjoys hospitality, collects antiques, china, enjoys baking, organic gardening, bushwalking. Westcoast born, local knowledge is invaluable. most quoted comments "wonderful breakfast and hospitality". Courtesy pick-up from train/bus. Off-street parking.

Greymouth   *Lodge*   *15km N of Greymouth*

Kereru Lodge   Graeme Jenkinson
58 Herd Street, Dunollie, Greymouth
Tel: (03) 762 7077 Fax: (03) 762 7077
kereru.lodge@xtra.co.nz
www.bnb.co.nz/kererulodgegreymouth.html
Double $100-$120 Single $90-$120
(Continental Breakfast) Child by arrangement
Dinner $30 by arrangement Credit cards accepted
1 King/Twin 2 Queen 2 Twin (4 bdrm)
1 Ensuite 1 Private 1 Family share

Kereru Lodge: At the head of a sleepy, quiet valley surrounded by native forest. 5 minutes from the most fantastically, rugged beaches and shoreline in New Zealand. Great food, wine, coffee and music. Large comfortable beds. Warm fires. Cottage gardens and peaceful streams. This is the place to "take a holiday from your holiday". Your base for fantastic trout fishing, black-water rafting, Pancake Rocks, bush walks and treks. Kereru Lodge: A haven for discerning Travellers and Adventurers. Recommended by North and South magazine. Aug. 1999.

Greymouth   *Homestay*   *2.5km S of Greymouth*

Maryglen Homestay   Allison & Glen Palmer
20 Weenink Road, Karoro, Greymouth
Tel: (03) 768 0706 Fax: (03) 768 0599
Mob: 025 380 479   Tollfree: 0800 627 945
mary@bandb.co.nz
www.bnb.co.nz/maryglenhomestay.html
Double $85-$105 Single $65-$75 (Cont B'fast)
Dinner $20 Child neg Credit cards accepted
2 King/Twin 1 Queen 1 Single (3 bdrm)
2 Ensuite 1 Family share

What a view! What a quiet location? - Comments form guests about our home set in native bush overlooking the sea. From our downstairs rooms you step out to the large deck where you can enjoy the bush and beautiful sunsets. Spa pool available ($5pp). Our animals, dog "Lady", cat "Misty" enjoy visitors' company. Allison enjoys gardening, hospitality, playing bridge while Glen enjoys large jig-saws. Cable/Sky TV is available as are laundry facilities Transport to scenic spots (moderate charge).Level access and off street parking. Complimentary pick up from train/bus.

Greymouth   *B&B*   *1km S of Greymouth*

Rosewood
Rhonda & Stephan Palten
20 High St, Greymouth
Tel: (03) 768 4674 Fax: (03) 768 4694
Mob: 027 242 7080 Tollfree: 0800 185 748
rosewoodnz@xtra.co.nz
www.rosewoodnz.co.nz
Double $95-$130 Single $65-$90 (Full Breakfast)
Child $20 Credit cards accepted Child at home
1 King/Twin 4 Queen 1 Twin 2 Single (5 bdrm)
3 Ensuite 1 Private 1 Guests share

Rosewood is one of Greymouth's finest old restored homes, a few minutes walk from the town centre with its restaurants & Cafés. Rooms are well appointed & feature quality king and queen beds with modern ensuites or bathroom. Separate guest lounge/dining room with complimentary tea/coffee and homemade biscuits. Hosts Rhonda & her German husband Stephan allow you to recover from your journey or activities of the day and offer a superb breakfast making a perfect start to your day.

Greymouth *Homestay*   *6km S of Greymouth*

Sunsetview
Russell & Jill Fairhall
335 Main South Road, Greymouth 7801
Tel: (03) 762 6616 Fax: (03) 762 6616
sunsetview@xtra.co.nz
www.bnb.co.nz/sunsetview.html

Double $100-$140 Single $90 (Continental Breakfast)
Credit cards accepted
1 King/Twin 1 King 1 Queen (3 bdrm)
2 Ensuite 1 Private

Russell and Jill welcome you to our sunny modern home with amazing sea and mountain views. We offer well-appointed superior bedrooms. TV in rooms. Breakfast according to your needs. Tea, coffee and laundry facilities available. Outdoor areas with pool and barbecue. Short walk to beach. Trips arranged to visit modern and old gold mining sites. Fishing trips can be arranged. We offer a courtesy car service to and from local travel centres and provide off-street parking.

Greymouth - Runanga *Homestay*   *27km N of Greymouth*

Golden Sands Homestay
Sue & Tom Costelloe
4 Golden Sands Road, Barrytown, Runanga
Tel: (03) 731 1115 Fax: (03) 731 1116
goldensands@paradise.net.nz
www.bnb.co.nz/goldensandshomestay.html

Double $85-$95 Single $50 (Continental Breakfast)
Child by arrangement Dinner by arrangement
Credit cards accepted
2 Queen 1 Twin (3 bdrm)   3 Private

Nestled between the Paparoa Range and the Tasman Sea on the Greymouth to Westport Scenic Highway, Golden Sands Homestay offers a friendly atmosphere and comfortable rooms. It is handy to Punakaiki, the Pancake Rocks, and the Paparoa National Park to the north, with Greymouth a twenty-five minute drive to the south. As well as stunning views and wonderful sunsets, Golden Sands Homestay has Sky television, Internet facilities, a cosy fire in winter and a contented cat. Access and facilities for disabled people. Nearby restaurants.

Moana - Lake Brunner *Homestay B&B*   *35km E of Greymouth*

Lancewood
Simon and Jan Wilkins
2177 Arnold Valley Road, Moana, Lake Brunner
Tel: (03) 738 0844
lancewood.upon.moana@paradise.net.nz
www.bnb.co.nz/lancewood.html

Double $180 Single $120 (Continental Breakfast)
Dinner $30 pp by arrangement Credit cards accepted
1 Queen (0 bdrm)
1 Ensuite

We look forward to welcoming you to share our piece of paradise. Enjoy bush walks, gold panning, trout fishing, magnificent scenery, lake charters and float plane adventures. The fridge has complimentary wine and also available are tea and coffee facilities. Breakfast will be brought to your door. Join us in the evening for a BBQ tea on our balcony, enjoying captivating lake views and sunsets. Reservations essential. Phone for directions.

Lake Brunner - Moana   *Self-contained*   *Moana*

Lake View B&B
Brent & Madeline Beadle
18 Johns Road, Moana, Westland
Tel: (03) 738 0886 Fax: (03) 738 0887
Mob: 0274 318 022
browntrout@minidata.co.nz
www.fishnhunt.co.nz/guides/brunner/index.htm

Double $110 Single $90 (Continental Breakfast)
Child $30 Credit cards accepted
1 King 2 Single (2 bdrm)
1 Private

Lake View B&B offers guets fantastic views of Lake Brunner from the lounge, the decking or while lying in bed. Accommodation is a very private self-contained cottage adjacent to our house only five minutes walk to the village centre, cafe or hotel. The lake is famous for its trout fishing. Brent is a fishing guide. Lake tours, canoe hire, bush walks, pottery, and gold panning are all close. The Tranzalpine stops at Moana. Christchurch is three hours away by road.

Hokitika Central   *B&B*   *Hokitika*

Teichelmann's B&B Lodge
Frances & Brian Ward
20 Hamilton Street, Hokitika
Tel: (03) 755 8232 Fax: (03) 755 8239
Tollfree: 0800 743 742
teichel@xtra.co.nz
www.teichelmanns.co.nz

Double $125-$150 Single $115
(Continental & Full Breakfast) Credit cards accepted
2 King/Twin 2 King 1 Double 2 Twin 1 Single (6 bdrm)
5 Ensuite 1 Private

Frances and Brian welcome you to 'Catch your Breath and Breakfast' staying in our centrally situated, character home in the heritage area of Hokitika. Located opposite the information centre and museum, Teichelmann's is a short walk away from interesting craft galleries, shops, restaurants and cafes. Stroll on the beach in the evening and experience a West Coast sunset... the wild, romantic West Coast at its best. We look forward to your visit.

Hokitika   *Homestay B&B*   *0.5km N of Hokitika*

Terrace View Homestays
Dianne & Chris Ward
24 Whitcombe Terrace, Hokitika
Tel: (03) 755 7357 Fax: (03) 755 8760
Mob: 025 371 254   Tollfree: 0800 261 949
wardc@xtra.co.nz
www.bnb.co.nz/terraceviewhomestays.html

Double $95-$105 Single $85-$95 (Full Breakfast)
Dinner by arrangement Credit cards accepted
1 Queen 2 Single (2 bdrm) 1 Guests share

Welcome to our spacious native-rimu timber-featured home. Enjoy superb views of Hokitika, Tasman Sea, sunsets, and mountains including Cook and Tasman. Also enjoy our outside setting with beautiful landscaped private garden, or one of our lounges, to relax in. We will chauffeur you for a complimentary evening glowworm and town tour, to point out places of interest and history. Chris (Property Consultant, Rotarian) enjoys golf, fishing and property development. Dianne (Reading Teacher) enjoys handcrafts, ceramic dolls and cooking. Both enjoy family, travel and meeting people.

Hokitika   *Homestay Semi-rural B&B   4km E of Hokitika*

Prospect House
Danielle & Lindsay Smith
Blue Spur, RD 2, Hokitika
Tel: (03) 755 8043
Fax: (03) 755 6787
Mob: 025 221 2779
Tollfree: 0800 377 969
prospect@minidata.co.nz
www.prospecthouse.co.nz

Double $160-$180 (Full Breakfast) Dinner by arrangement
Credit cards accepted Pet on property
1 King 1 Queen 1 Double 1 Single (3 bdrm)
2 Ensuite 1 Private

Prospect House is situated on the outskirts of Hokitika on an ancient river terrace property of some 10 acres. This lovely colonial style family home commands sweeping views of the Southern Alps, has beautiful gardens and trees and is owned by a caring, friendly family.

Our guest books are full of accolades as to the space and luxurious comfort of our home and the friendliness of the host family.All say that they wish they had arranged their trip so that they could stay longer.

This spacious home features native rimu timbers, central heating, large deck and BBQ facilities, piped music throughout and full office facilities too. The main suite contains a King size double bed and full ensuite plus tea and coffee making facilities as well. Adjoining this is a separate bedroom with a double and single bed. The second suite has a Queen size bed and ensuite. Breakfast can be either continental or a full cooked breakfast.

Our interests vary from the garden to music, current affairs, sport flying and yes .... catering for guests. We can arrange scenic flights for you to the Glaciers or to the historic goldtown port of Okarito or to other interesting destinations. We can also assist to arrange other adventures for you. We have two dogs, a Westie and a Scotty. We also have two cats.

To find us, if travelling from North turn left into Hampden Street, continue on for 3km without turning again.

Hokitika   *Homestay   1km N of Hokitika*

Alpine Vista Homestay
Rayleine & Jon Olson
38 Bonar Drive, Hokitika
Tel: (03) 755 8732 Fax: (03) 755 8732
Mob: 025 202 2401   jolson@minidata.co.nz
www.bnb.co.nz/alpinevista.html
Double $100 Single $60 (Full Breakfast)
Credit cards accepted
2 Queen (2 bdrm)
1 Ensuite

Our comfortable home is on a terrace overlooking Hokitika with unsurpassed views of the Southern Alps, Tasman Sea and brilliant sunsets. The guest rooms have a private entrance and are connected by a small sitting room with TV. You are welcomed with home baking, tea/coffee making facilities available. We invite you to join us for a drink in the evening. Jon, a 4th generation Coaster, has abundant local knowledge. From main highway turn into Tudor Street signed Airport. Left into Bonar Drive, up into cul-de-sac.

Hokitika   *Homestay   1km N of Hokitika*

Montezuma
Russell & Alison Alldridge
261 Revell Street,
Hokitika,
Westland
Tel: (03) 755 7025
www.bnb.co.nz/montezuma.html
Double $80 Single $55
(Continental Breakfast)
1 Queen 1 Double (2 bdrm)
1 Ensuite 1 Guests share

Welcome to Montezuma by the sea. So named after a ship that was wrecked here in 1865. Alison a Queenslander, Russell a genuine West Coaster. Enjoy a leisurely walk along the beach, watch the breathtaking sunset, visit the nearby Glow Worm Dell and take time out to enjoy our West Coast hospitality. Directions: When travelling to Hokitika from North take first turn to your right (Richards Drive). Our house is the last on the street. When travelling from South turn left at the last street out of town.

Hokitika   *Rural Homestay   3km S of Hokitika*

Meadowbank
Tom & Alison Muir
Takutai, RD 3, Hokitika
Tel: (03) 755 6723 Fax: (03) 755 6723
www.bnb.co.nz/meadowbank.html
Double $80 Single $50 (Full Breakfast)
Child 1/2 price Dinner by arrangement
Pet on property
1 Double 2 Single (2 bdrm)
1 Guests share

Tom and Alison welcome you to their lifestyle property, situated just minutes south of Hokitika. Our large home, which we share with 2 cats, is modern, sunny and warm, and has a large garden. Nearby we have the beach, excellent golf-links, an old gold mine, river, and of course Hokitika, with all its attractions. Directions: Travel south 2kms from south end of Hokitika Bridge on SH6, turn right - 200 metres on right. North-bound traffic - look for sign 1km north of Golf-links.

Hokitika *B&B* *2km E of Hokitika*

Craidenlie Lodge
Bruce & Jenny Smith
Blue Spur, Hokitika
Tel: (03) 755 5063 Fax: (03) 755 8497 Tollfree: 0800 361 361
bruce@craidenlielodge.co.nz www.craidenlielodge.co.nz
Double $180-$220 Single $180-$220 (Full Breakfast) Credit cards accepted
4 Queen 2 Twin (6 bdrm) 4 Ensuite 1 Private 1 Guests share

Our visitors book has interesting entries:

Roger and Jane Somers from the UK, *'We have travelled to NZ five times. This is the best B&B we have every stayed at'.*

Roy and Mary Watts from the UK, *'Outstanding in all respects, great conducted tours'*

We converted our 6500 square foot family home into a lodge in 1999 located on a 40 acre section our home provides complete quiet and privacy. The native Kahikatea trees that surround the lodge are unique.

Bruce is a tennis nut, a born and bred fourth generation Coaster and entrepreneur, he will delight you with his local knowledge. Most of our guests allow us to chauffeur them to the local restaurant in the evening, pick them up take them to the glowworm dwell and other local sights.

Hokitika is the centre of the West Coast, most guests base themselves here for visits to the glaciers and the Punakaiki Pancake rocks, allow two nights.

Hokitika   *Homestay B&B   1km N of Hokitika*

Karnbach
Errol & Bill Amberger
41 Bonar Drive,
Hokitika
Tel: (03) 755 7102
www.bnb.co.nz/amberger.html
Double $95 Single $60
(Full Breakfast) Apartment $95
1 Double 1 Twin (1 bdrm)
1 Private 1 Family share

Fully furnished apartment - double bedroom, sunroom, lounge TV shower and laundry, own entrance plus internal access to house. Twin room in main house -share bathroom Relax in a friendly, homely atmosphere and enjoy panoramic views of the Southern Alps, Mount Cook and the Tasman Sea. We are retired farmers, have travelled extensively and enjoy meeting people from other countries. Bill is a keen gardener and sportsman, plays golf while his wife Errol is a spinner and weaver. From main highway turn into Tudor St, signed Airport. Left into Bonar Drive to end of cul-de-sac.

Hokitika   *Self-contained Homestay B&B   0.9 E of Hokitika*

Larry's Rest
Linda & Paul Hewson
188 Rolleston Street, Hokitika,
Tel: (03) 755 7636 Mob: 021 220 3295
info@larrysrest.co.nz   www.larrysrest.co.nz
Double $100 Single $80 (Continental Breakfast)
Credit cards accepted
2 Queen 2 Twin (4 bdrm)
1 Ensuite 1 Private 1 Family share

Self contained unit: Queen bedroom and twin room (also single bed settee in lounge. Portacot available). Spacious living/dining area, kitchen, laundry and wheelchair friendly bathroom. Private outdoor areas on secure, peaceful section. Ideal for families. Tariff: $110 double, breakfast extra. Homestay (next door), queen room with private ensuite, own entrance, tea/coffee facilities: $100 incl. breakfast. Twin room with host share bathroom: $90 twin, $80 single. Paul is a Regional Rep for the Correspondence School. Linda is an itinerant hairdresser. Interests include travel, tramping and kayaking. Friendly cat. (Signposted from main road).

Hokitika - Blue Spur   *B&B   4km E of Hokitika*

Villa Ruby Rock
Gerry & Corrie Commandeur
105 Brickfield Road, Blue Spur, Hokitika
Tel: (03) 755 7448 Fax: (03) 755 8622
Tollfree: 0800 38 87 03   rubyrock@nzrubyrock.com
www.nzrubyrock.com
Double $125-$200 (Continental Breakfast)
Dinner From $40 Credit cards accepted
1 King 2 Queen 1 Single (3 bdrm)
1 Ensuite 1 Guests share

At Villa Ruby Rock you can relax in luxury accommodation, enjoy the peaceful surroundings of the Southern Alps and look down at breathtaking sea views. Our first class bed and breakfast home offers you a chance to escape into a tranquil environment.Stay in the spacious Emerald suite, and enjoy your own personal spa ensuite, or take our Ruby or Sapphire room. A delicious continental breakfast is served, and home cooked meals are available. See Gerry and Corrie also at the Ruby Rock Gallery, Hokitika.

Hokitika - Lake Kaniere *15min E of Hokitika*
B&B studio apartment, fully self-contained

Serenity
Kay & Dave Clausen
6 Stuart Street, Lake Kaniere.
Postal: PO Box 133, Hokitika

Tel: (03) 755 5038 dmkeclausen@xtra.co.nz
Mob: 025 372 666 www.bnb.co.nz/serenity.html

Double $80 Single $60 (Continental Breakfast)
Child $20 under 15 years Extra adults (over dbl) $40
1 Queen 2 Single (1 bdrm) 1 Private

Lake Kaniere is set amongst beautiful New Zealand native bush. The scenery is breathtaking. There
are many bush-walks around the lake, and Dorothy Falls is just a short drive from 'Serenity'. Our
studio apartment is self-catering and has full kitchen and bathroom facilities. All linen is provided.
Restaurants and cafe-bars are just a shortdrive away, at Hokitika, or it's great to just relax and enjoy the
surroundings at Lake Kaniere - a very unspoilt place! 'Serenity' is two minutes walk from the Lake.
Separate access, studio apartment.

Ruatapu *B&B Country Stay* *12km S of Hokitika*

Berwick's Hill
Eileen & Roger Berwick
Ruatapu, Ruatapu-Ross Road,
State Highway 6, RD 3, Hokitika

Tel: (03) 755 7876 Fax: (03) 755 7876
Mob: 025 673 7387 berwicks@xtra.co.nz
www.bnb.co.nz/berwickshill.html

Double $90-$100 Single $60 (Full Breakfast)
Dinner $35 by arrangement Credit cards accepted
1 Queen 2 Single (2 bdrm)
1 Ensuite 1 Private

Welcome to Berwick's Hill. We offer you a warm and relaxed stay in our comfortable home. Magnificent views of the Tasman Sea and the Southern Alps are seen from the main living areas. We are close
to Lake Mahinapua, the beach and Golf Links with the opportunity to experience the Westland bush
sunsets and sunrises. We run sheep and cattle and grow pine trees on our hobby farm. We have one
farm dog and we share our home with our cat Sammy and our house dog Jed.

If you would like dinner
most hosts require 24 hours' notice.

Harihari *Farmstay Country Lodge* *0.5km S of Hari Hari*

Wapiti Park Homestead
Bev & Grant Muir
RD 1, Hari Hari 7953, South Westland
Tel: (03) 753 3074 Fax: (03) 753 3074 Tollfree: 0800 WAPITI
wapitipark@xtra.co.nz   www.countrylodge.co.nz

Double $145-$250 Single $125-$225 (Continental Breakfast) Dinner $45
Credit cards accepted
6 King 1 Twin 2 Single (7 bdrm) 6 Ensuite 1 Private

"A real tonic for weary travellers - food, facilities excellent. Hosting Incomparable" (RJ USA). "Absolutely Superb - Hosts, food, room - best stay in 5 weeks in NZ (GH UK) "This will be our 5th 4 night stay, it doesn't come any better than Wapiti Park" (I&B UK) Hosts Grant and Beverleigh invite you to discover the unique experience of staying at Wapiti Park Homestead, South Westlands premier hosted accommodation for the discerning traveller. Enjoy a special combination of elegance and warm hospitality. Relax in complete comfort and affordable luxury.

Set in tranquil surroundings, the modern colonial style lodge is set on the site of the original 1st Hari Hari accommodation house, coaching stop and post office and overlooks its own small farm which specialises in the breeding of Wapiti (Rocky mountain Elk).

The 6pm farm tour enables one to handfeed the Wapiti, meet the farm pet "Vicki" and learn about the elk velvet antler extract and its major health benefits. Enjoy spacious indoor/outdoor areas; large bedrooms with superior comfort beds and either ensuites or private facilities; 2 lounges and a trophy games room; a well stocked bar fridge; and our renowned "All you can eat" Country style dinners. Special diets can be catered for by prior arrangement.

Our location on state highway 6 makes us the ideal stopover between the Nelson/Christchurch - Wanaka/Queenstown areas. However to explore this scenic wonderland of rainforest glaciers, lakes and National Parks; to pursue the challenges of our renowned brown trout fishery, to hunt or to simply catch your breath and relax, you really need at least a 2 night stay. Guided hunting and fishing available and other activities arranged on request.

Unsuitable for children. No smoking indoors. Direct booking discounts available. Advance booking recommended. Spoil Yourself!

Whataroa   *Farmstay   35km N of Franz Josef*

Matai Lodge
Glenice & Jim Purcell
Whataroa, South Westland
Tel: (03) 753 4156 Fax: (03) 753 4156
Mob: 021 155 2506   Tollfree: 0800 787 235
jpurcell@xtra.co.nz   www.bnb.co.nz/matailodgewhataroa.html
Double $180 Single $100   (Full Breakfast) Dinner $40pp
1 King/Twin 1 King 2 Single (3 bdrm)   1 Ensuite 1 Private

Matai Lodge rests in the tranquil valley 20 minutes north of Franz Josef Glacier in the small farming community of Whataroa. You are welcome to share with us our modern spacious home on the 400 acre farm of sheep, cows, and farm dog. Upstairs is a suite of a king-size room and twin room with conservatory and private bathroom and downstairs a king-size ensuite you are welcome to join us for a home cooked dinner with NZ wine, over which we enjoy hearing tales from your home, and we will help you discover ours, with local advice and activity bookings available our motto is 'A STRANGER is a FRIEND we have yet to meet'.

You will need at least two days to see the Glaciers, walk in the World Heritage Park, kayak on the Okirito Lagoon, or visit the White Heron Bird Sanctuary by jet boat and see the spectacular scenery, or go horse trekking. Glenice and Jim play golf at the scenic golf course in Whataroa, green fees $10, clubs available.

Glenice has travelled to Japan teaching felting, weaving and spinning and enjoyed Japanese customs and language and being hosted by her many friends there. Jim and Glenice look forward to sharing their home and tranquil scenic paradise with you.

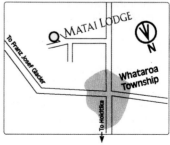

Driving Time from Matai Lodge to: Christchurch 5 hours, Picton 6 hours, Nelson 6 hours, Queenstown 6 hours, Wanaka 4 hours, Greymouth 2 hours, Whataroa 3km, and Franz Josef 20 minutes. Also available: Tel/Fax, Email, Sky TV, Laundry.

Whataroa - South Westland   *Farmstay B&B   13km N of Whataroa/10 mins*

Mt Adam Lodge
Elsa & Mac MacRae
State Highway 6, Whataroa, South Westland
Tel: (03) 753 4030 Fax: (03) 753 4264
Tollfree: 0800 675 137
mtadamlodge@paradise.net.nz
www.mountadamlodge.co.nz

Double $85-$110 Single $70-$80
(Continental Breakfast) Credit cards accepted
2 Queen 1 Double 4 Twin (7 bdrm)
5 Ensuite 2 Guests share

If you're wanting to escape the crowds in the busy tourist centres then we are an ideal place for you to stay. Just a short 35 minute drive north of Franz Josef Glacier. We are situated on our farm at the foot of Mt Adam surrounded by farmlands and beautiful native bush. Our lodge is just newly established and offers comfortable accommodation and a fully licensed restaurant. You can stroll along the river bank and the farm tracks meeting our variety of animals along the way.

Franz Josef Glacier   *Farmstay B&B   3km S of Franz Josef Glacier*

Knightswood B&B
Jackie & Russel Knight
PO Box 70, State Highway 6, Franz Josef
Tel: (03) 752 0059 Fax: (03) 752 0061
knightswood@xtra.co.nz
www.knightswood.co.nz

Double $125-$165 Single $100-$125 (Full Breakfast)
Child on request Credit cards accepted Child at home
2 King/Twin (2 bdrm)
2 Ensuite

Rusty built our house from local material in true pioneering spirit during 1998. Knightswood is surrounded by spectacular scenery, nestled in native bush which attracts prolific tuneful native birdlife. Both rooms offer breathtaking views of the Southern Alps. Jackie is a paediatric nurse from England, Rusty a local helicopter pilot and keen deer farmer. 200 deer run on the 250 acre farm. We, with our daughter Amy, look forward to helping you discover the magical qualities of the West Coast. Smoking outside only. Visit our website www.knightswood.co.nz

Franz Josef Glacier   *Homestay B&B   1.5km N of Franz Josef Glacier*

Holly Homestead
Gerard & Bernie Oudemans
State Highway 6, Franz Josef Glacier, South Westland
Tel: (03) 752 0299 Fax: (03) 752 0298
stay@hollyhomestead.co.nz
hollyhomestead.co.nz

Double $120-$180 Single $100-$130 (Full Breakfast)
Credit cards accepted
2 King/Twin 2 Queen (4 bdrm)
2 Ensuite 1 Private

Gerard and Bernie invite you to share their character home. Located on "The Glacier Highway", Holly Homestead (formerly Hollywood House) offers the peace and quiet of the country with the convenience of the township nearby. We happily provide local information and bookings for various activities for you to enjoy our magnificent region. There's plenty to do! Relax in our comfortable guest lounge after your adventures. Spectacular view from breakfast table, clouds permitting! Reservations recommended November to March (inclusive). Children aged 12+ welcome.

Fox Glacier   *Farmstay B&B*   *0.5km W of Fox Glacier*

The Homestead
Noeleen & Kevin Williams
PO Box 25, Cook Flat Road, Fox Glacier
Tel: (03) 751 0835 Fax: (03) 751 0805
foxhmstd@xtra.co.nz   www.bnb.co.nz/thehomestead.html
Double $110-$145 (Continental Breakfast) Cooked Breakfast $5pp
1 King/Twin 2 Queen (3 bdrm)   2 Ensuite 1 Private

Kevin, Noeleen and Chancey our friendly Corgi, welcome you to our 2,200 acre beef cattle and sheep farm. Beautiful native bush-clad mountains surround on three sides, and we enjoy a view of Mt Cook.

Our spacious 100 year old character home, built for Kevin's grandparents has fine stained glass windows. The breakfast room overlooks peaceful pastures to the hills, and you are served homemade yoghurt, jams, marmalade, scones etc, with a cooked breakfast if desired.

The guest lounge, with its beautiful wooden panelled ceiling, has an open plan fire for cool autumn nights.

A rural retreat within walking distance of village facilities, with Matheson (Mirror Lake) and glacier nearby. It is our pleasure to help you with helihikes, helicopter scenic flights and glacier walks. Unsuitable for small children. Bookings recommended. Smoke-free.

Directions: On Cook Flat Road, 5th house on right, 400m back off road before Church.

Fox Glacier   *Homestay   160km S of Hokitika*

Roaring Billy Lodge
Billy & Kathy
PO Box 16, 21 State Highway 6, Fox Glacier
Tel: (03) 751 0815 Fax: (03) 751 0085
Tollfree: 0800 352 121
kathynz@xtra.co.nz
www.bnb.co.nz/roaringbillylodge.html
Double $85-$95 Single $70-$75 (Special Breakfast)
Credit cards accepted Pet on property
1 Double 1 Twin (2 bdrm)
1 Guests share

Relax in the comfort and warmth of our renovated two-story home. Our upstairs living area is lined with local timbers and enjoys 360-degree views of the glacier valley, mountains, farms and the township. We're the closest homestay to the glacier and 2 minutes walk to all eating and tourist facilities. After a comfortable, quiet night's sleep, you can wear yourself out on the glacier and surrounding walks. We offer a special cooked breakfast. We have one cat and one dog.

Fox Glacier   *Homestay   Fox Glacier Central*

Reflection Lodge
Raelene Tuck
PO Box 46, Cook Flat Road, Fox Glacier
Tel: (03) 751 0707 Fax: (03) 751 0707
raelene@reflectionlodge.co.nz
www.reflectionlodge.co.nz
Double $110-$145 (Continental Breakfast)
Child $35 Twin $100 - $110 Children welcome
2 Queen 1 Single (3 bdrm)
1 Ensuite 1 Guest share

Welcome to the Glacier region. Reflection Lodge offers panoramic views of Mt Cook and Mt Tasman, New Zealand's two highest peaks reflecting in our own private lake. Myself and Colin (a local helicopter pilot), are fourth generation West Coasters and have lived in the Glacier region for 12 years. We invite you to share the comfort of our home and gardens. We are more than happy to assist you with any activities in our picturesque region. We enjoy meeting people and look forward to sharing our wonderful piece of paradise.

Fox Glacier   *Self-contained B&B Lodge   160km S of Hokitika*

Fox Glacier Lodge
F & L Buckton
Box 22, Fox Glacier, South Westland
Tel: (03) 751 0888 Fax: (03) 751 0888
Tollfree: 0800 36 98 00
www.bnb.co.nz/foxglacierlodge.html
Double $98-$180 (Continental Breakfast)
Child unsuitable for children Credit cards accepted
1 King 5 Queen (6 bdrm)
6 Ensuite

Fox Glacier lodge is in the heart of Fox Glacier Village. The recently completed solid timber lodge is warm, clean and modern. Bathrooms are ensuite, two have double spa-baths. Breakfast room is stocked for self-serve continental, available at any time. Short stroll to cafes, restaurants. Lodge is smoke free. Reservations recommended. Attractions: glow worm grotto (on site), Fox Glacier, Lake Matheson, Mt Cook views, scenic flights, heli-hikes, bush walks. Directions: Our home/office is opposite BP. The Lodge is beyond, nestled within a slice of Heaven. Welcome!

WEST COAST

Fox Glacier   *Homestay*

Fox Glacier Homestay
Eunice & Michael Sullivan
64 Cook Flat Road, Fox Gracier,
Tel: (03) 751 0817 Fax: (03) 751 0817
euni@xtra.co.nz
www.bnb.co.nz/foxglacier.html

Double $90-$110 Single $70-$90
(Continental Breakfast) Pet on property
Children welcome Pets welcome
1 Queen 1 Double 1 Single (3 bdrm)
1 Family share

Eunice and Michael are third generation farming and tourism family. We have three grown children, 1 dog (Ruff), 1 cat (Black Cat). Our grandparents were founders of the Fox Glacier Hotel. We are a couple who enjoy meeting people and would like to share the joys of living in our little paradise (rain and all). Our home is surrounded by a large garden and have views of the mountains and Mt Cook. A five minute walk from township.

Fox Glacier   *Self-contained B&B*   *2km W of Fox Glacier*

Mountain View
Julene & Phil Silcock
Williams Drive,
Fox Glacier
Tel: (03) 751 0770 Fax: (03) 751 0774
gingephil@actrix.co.nz
www.bnb.co.nz/user104.html

Double $110-$130 (Continental Breakfast)
1 King 1 Double 1 Twin (3 bdrm)
3 Ensuite

Our family welcomes you to Mountain View B&B. Set on 10 acres of farmland surrounded by bush clad hills with spectacular views of Mt Cook and Mt Tasman. Situated 2km from Fox Village our 4 year old country home has it all, peaceful surroundings and friendly hospitality. We have extensive knowledge of the area and can organise Glacier flights and walks. We are just 2 minutes drive to restaurants and cafes. We have 2 school age children Harry 8 and Katie 6, 1 cat, 1 toy poodle and 2 horses. Children welcome. Smoke free.

Fox Glacier   *Homestay B&B*   *0 km Fox Glacier*

Pekanga Homestay   Mike and Nicole Hall
Glacier Lane, Pekanga Drive, Fox Glacier
Tel: (03) 751 0016 Fax: (03) 751 0740
Tollfree: 0800 10 26 25   info@fox-glacier.co.nz
www.bnb.co.nz/pekangahomestay.html

Double $90-$130 Single $70-$110
(Continental Breakfast) Child $ by arrangement
Dinner $30 Credit cards accepted
1 King/Twin 1 Queen 1 Twin (3 bdrm)
1 Guests share

Nicole and Mike welcome you to their Bed and Breakfast built new in 2001. We are set agains the native bush with off street parking. Relax in the lounge with Warm Fire, huge selection of books and Sky TV. We are located in the centre of Fox Glacier, some 500 metres from Cafes, Restaraunts, Helicopter Flights and Guided Glacier walking companies. Mike is a local helicopter pilot and has a host of information on the area. Nicole has previously worked in tourist infomation and can help make your stay a well organised one.

Bruce Bay *Farmstay 50km S of Fox Glacier*

Mulvaney Farmstay
Peter & Malai Millar
PO Box 117, Bruce Bay, South Westland
Tel: (03) 751 0865 Fax: (03) 751 0865
Tollfree: 0800 393 297
mulvaney@xtra.co.nz
www.bnb.co.nz/millar.html

Double $80-$95 Single $65 (Continental Breakfast)
Child n/a Dinner $30
1 Queen 1 Double 1 Twin (3 bdrm)
1 Guests share 1 Family share

Welcome to Mulvaney Farmstays! We run a beef farm consisting mainly of Hereford and Limosin cattle. Our house was built in the 1920's by my Great Uncle Jack Mulvaney, for his bride to be but she never arrived. Jack Mulvaney was of Irish descent, just as the rest of his family was who settled in this valley 130 years ago. So he lived here by himself until 1971 raising Hereford cattle. We have now lived her for 20 years with our children (who are all grown up and studying away from home).

Paringa *Farmstay Homestay 70km S of Fox Glacier*

Condon Farmstays
Glynis & Tony Condon
NZ Post Ltd, Lake Paringa, South Westland
Tel: (03) 751 0895 Fax: (03) 751 0001
Mob: 025 647 4965 condonfarms@xtra.co.nz
www.bnb.co.nz/condonfarmstays.html

Double $85 Single $50 (Continental & Full Breakfast)
Child $20 Dinner $30 by arrangement Pet on property
1 Double 4 Single (3 bdrm) 1 Family share

We run a 4th generation working beef farm, with a few sheep. We enjoy meeting people and have travelled to America, England, Kenya, Australia and some parts of Europe. Our farm is nestled beneath the bush clad foothills of the Southern Alps, close to Lake Paringa and the Paringa River. We have three adult children and three grandchildren. Two children live in New Zealand and one overseas. Our interests include hunting, jet boating, fishing, spinning, knitting and reading. We have one house cat and a small dog. We are Kiwi Hosts and members of NZ Farm Home Hosts Association.

Haast *Self-contained Homestay B&B 16km S of Haast*

Okuru Beach
Marian & Derek Beynon
PO Box 59, Haast, South Westland
Tel: (03) 750 0719 Fax: (03) 750 0722
okurubeach@xtra.co.nz www.okurubeach.co.nz

Double $75-$80 Single $50 (Continental Breakfast)
Child $20 Dinner $20 by arrangement
Self-contained $85 Credit cards accepted Pet on property
3 Double 4 Single (5 bdrm)
1 Ensuite 1 Private 1 Guests share

Okuru Beach gives you the opportunity to stay in a unique part of our country, in a friendly relaxed environment. Enjoy coastal beaches with driftwood, shells and penguins in season. Walk in the rainforest and view the native birds. We and our friendly Labrador dog enjoy sharing our comfortable home and local knowledge. Dinner served with prior notice. Our interests are our handcraft shop, photography, fishing, shooting and tramping. Also available - Seaview Cottage, self-contained sleeps 4 persons. Directions - turn into Jacksons Bay Road, drive 14km turn into Okuru.

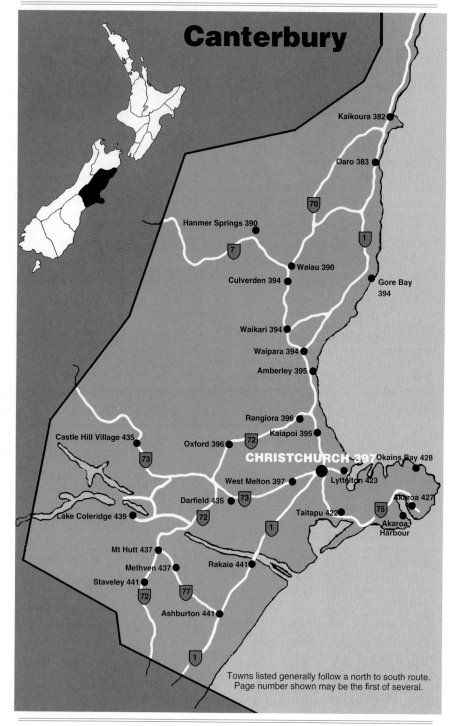

Canterbury

Kaikoura 382

Oaro 383

70

1

Hanmer Springs 390

7

Waiau 390

Culverden 394

Gore Bay
394

Waikari 394

Waipara 394

Amberley 395

Rangiora 396

Kaiapoi 395

Castle Hill Village 435

Oxford 396

72

CHRISTCHURCH 397 Okains Bay 428

73

West Melton 397

Lyttelton 423

Darfield 435

73

Akaroa 427

Lake Coleridge 439

72

Taitapu 422

75

Akaroa
Harbour

1

Mt Hutt 437

Methven 437

Rakaia 441

Staveley 441

72

77

Ashburton 441

1

Towns listed generally follow a north to south route.
Page number shown may be the first of several.

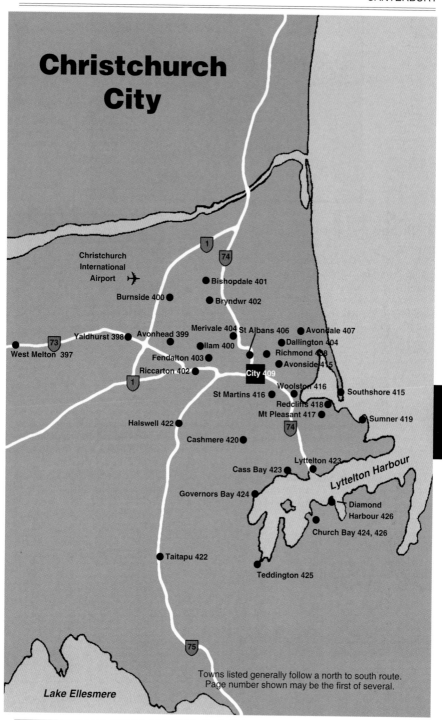

Christchurch City

Christchurch International Airport ✈

Bishopdale 401

Burnside 400 ●

● Bryndwr 402

Merivale 404 ● St Albans 406 ● Avondale 407

Yaldhurst 398 ● Avonhead 399 ●

● West Melton 397

● Ilam 400

Dallington 404

Fendalton 403 ●

Richmond 408

Avonside 415

Riccarton 402 ●

City 409

Woolston 416

St Martins 416 ●

Southshore 415

Redcliffs 418 ●

Mt Pleasant 417 ●

Halswell 422 ●

Sumner 419

Cashmere 420 ●

Lyttelton 423

Cass Bay 423 ●

Lyttelton Harbour

Governors Bay 424 ●

Diamond Harbour 426

Church Bay 424, 426

● Taitapu 422

Teddington 425

Lake Ellesmere

Towns listed generally follow a north to south route.
Page number shown may be the first of several.

CANTERBURY

Kaikoura *Homestay* *130km S of Blenheim*

Bay-View
Margaret Woodill, 296 Scarborough Street, Kaikoura
Tel: (03) 319 5480 Fax: (03) 319 7480
MSBSDH@xtra.co.nz
www.bnb.co.nz/bayviewkaikoura.html
Double/twin $75 Single $45 (Full Breakfast)
Child $15 under 14 Dinner $25 Queen ensuite $85
Pet on property Children welcome Pets welcome
1 Queen 1 Double 1 Twin 1 Single (4 bdrm)
2 Ensuite 1 Guests share 1 Family share

Our spacious family home on Kaikoura Peninsula has splendid mountain and sea views and is exceptionally quiet. Only five minutes from the Kaikoura township, off the main highway south. The house nestles in an acre of colourful garden and there is plenty of off-street parking. A guest lounge is available or you are more than welcome to socialise with the host. Laundry facilities and tea/coffee with homemade baking available. Traditional breakfast with home baked bread, muesli, home preserves, available early as required for whale/dolphin watching guests. Enjoy breakfast in the dining area or out on the sunny deck whilst taking in the magnificent mountain view.   We book local activities and happily meet bus or train.

Margaret, your friendly host, has lived in the area for most of her life. She has a grown family of four and seven grandchildren.   Margaret enjoys gardening, golf, bowls, sewing, choir and her amusing Burmese cat. She especially enjoys warmly welcoming guests into her home.

Guests comments:

"This B&B is an unforgettable memory for me in NZ five weeks travel" (Japan).

"Beautiful place, beautiful food, fabulous hospitality, Margaret. Thank you for opening up your home and welcoming us. Be back again" (Wellington).

"Thank you for meeting the train and showing us the area. You were highly recommended and we absolutely endorse this" (UK).

"Many thanks for your generous hospitality. You and your lovely home are a credit to B&B Homestays" (UK).

"The most amazing breakfast in all of New Zealand. The views are amazing too and so is Margaret's hospitality" (Australia).

"We felt like family! Thank you for such a lovely visit and wonderful, delicious meals. We thank you a million!" (USA).

"Let Our Home be Your Home".

Kaikoura - Oaro *Self-contained Homestay B&B* *22km S of Kaikoura*

Waitane Homestay
Kathleen & Peter King
Oaro, RD 2, Kaikoura
Tel: (03) 319 5494 Fax: (03) 319 5524
waitane@xtra.co.nz
www.bnb.co.nz/waitane.html

Double $70 Single $40 (Full Breakfast) Child $20
Dinner $20 Credit cards accepted Pet on property
1 Double 4 Single (3 bdrm)
2 Private

We are retired farmers, living on 48 acres close to the sea. Two cats share our home. We look north along the coast to Kaikoura Peninsula. Our home has one guest room with single beds, self contained unit has two bedrooms, sleeps four. Enjoy coastal walk to Haumuri Bluff with bird-watching, fossil hunting etc. Drive to Kaikoura alongside rocky coastline. This is a mild climate and we grow citrus and sub-tropical fruit - mainly feijoas. Join us for dinner - fresh vegies, our own preserves and homemade ice cream!!

Kaikoura *Homestay B&B* *Kaikoura Central*

Bevron
Bev & Ron Barr
196 Esplanade, Kaikoura
Tel: (03) 319 5432 Fax: (03) 319 5432
bevronhouse@hotmail.com
www.bnb.co.nz/bevron.html

Double $90 Single $80 (Full Breakfast)
Child 1/2 price
2 Double 2 Twin (2 bdrm)
2 Ensuite

We are a friendly active retired couple who enjoy meeting new people and sharing the delights of our home on the beachfront. The view from our balcony is breathtaking, giving an unobstructed panorama of sea and mountains. We have guest TV lounge and games room. There is a swimming beach opposite, with children's play area and BBQ. Kaikoura has many tourist attractions, we are happy to help with bookings. Our home is centrally located, being a short walk to restaurants, galleries and scenic attractions.

Kaikoura *Farmstay* *20km SW of Kaikoura*

The Kahutara Homestead Nikki & John Smith
P O Box 9, Kaikoura
Tel: (03) 319 5580 Fax: (03) 319 5580
Tollfree: 0800 27 33 51
kahutarahomestead@xtra.co.nz
www.bnb.co.nz/thekahutara.html

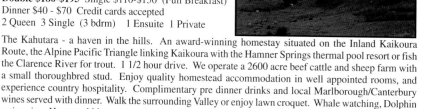

Double $180-$195 Single $110-$150 (Full Breakfast)
Dinner $40 - $70 Credit cards accepted
2 Queen 3 Single (3 bdrm) 1 Ensuite 1 Private

The Kahutara - a haven in the hills. An award-winning homestay situated on the Inland Kaikoura Route, the Alpine Pacific Triangle linking Kaikoura with the Hamner Springs thermal pool resort or fish the Clarence River for trout. 1 1/2 hour drive. We operate a 2600 acre beef cattle and sheep farm with a small thoroughbred stud. Enjoy quality homestead accommodation in well appointed rooms, and experience country hospitality. Complimentary pre dinner drinks and local Marlborough/Canterbury wines served with dinner. Walk the surrounding Valley or enjoy lawn croquet. Whale watching, Dolphin swimming, Horse trekking reservations made.

Kaikoura

Self-contained B&B   5km N of Kaikoura

Ardara Lodge
Alison & Ian Boyd
233 Schoolhouse Road, RD1, Kaikoura

Tel: (03) 319 5736 Fax: (03) 319 5732
Tollfree: 0800 226 164
aemboyd@xtra.co.nz   www.ardaralodge.com

Double $95-$100 Single $70-$80 (Continental Breakfast)
Cottage, 2-4 persons $120 - $200 Credit cards accepted
6 Queen 2 Twin 3 Single (6 bdrm)   5 Ensuite

You will enjoy a relaxed and peaceful stay in a beautiful rural setting near the magnificent Kaikoura mountains. Relax on our deck and enjoy Alison's colourful garden which completes the panoramic view.

Enjoy our outdoor hot tub (spa), view the Kaikoura mountains by day and the stars by night. Ian's Great, Great, Uncle Jim, left "Ardara", Ireland in 1876. He bought our land here in Kaikoura in 1883 and milked cows. He established an orchard and planted macrocarpa trees for shelter. One macrocarpa tree was milled and used to build the cottage which was designed and built by Ian in 1998.

The cottage has an upstairs bedroom with a queen and two single beds. Downstairs there is a bedroom with a queen bed, a bathroom with a shower, and a lounge, kitchen, dining room. The deck is private with a great view of the mountains. It has been very popular with groups, families and honeymoon couples.

The house has ensuite bathrooms with queen beds, TV, fridge, settee and coffee/tea facilities. You have your own private entrance and you can come and go as you please. We offer laundry facilities, off street parking, courtesy car from bus/train.

Bookings for local tourist attractions, restaurants and farm tours can be arranged. Ian's brother Murray, has Donegal House, an Irish Garden Bar and Restaurant, which is within walking distance. Ian is a retired teacher and Alison a librarian. Our hobbies are tennis, golf, designing and building houses, gardening, handcrafts, spinning and we like to travel. No smoking indoors please. We look forward to your company.

Directions: Driving north, 4km from Kaikoura on SH1, turn left, 1.5km along Schoolhouse Road.

Apartment Peterborough No 12

Our one bedroom upmarket apartment is in central Christchurch and within walking distance to all amenities such as the Arts Centre, Museum, Casino and Hagley Park. The third level apartment is in a quiet area and looks out onto a large grassed courtyard. View the clock tower from the terrace. Double queen bed, sofa bed, television, video, etc.

Tariff: $110 per night (min. 4 nights) or $595 per week. Serviced weekly.

For more information: http://ardaralodge.com/flat.htm

Kaikoura *B&B Inn* *3.6km N of Kaikoura*

Old Convent D & J Rooth
Mt Fyffe Road, Kaikoura
Tel: (03) 319 6603 Fax: (03) 319 6690
Mob: 025 353 954 Tollfree: 0800 365 603
o.convent@xtra.co.nz www.theoldconvent.co.nz

Double $135 Single $75 (Continental Breakfast)
Child $30 Dinner $50pp Family Suites $205
Credit cards accepted
3 King/Twin 3 Queen 6 Double
3 Twin 2 Single (17 bdrm) 14 Ensuite 2 Private

Experience the atmosphere in our preserved convent built in 1911. Your hosts offer personal service in a quiet and peaceful environment. For breakfast enjoy homemade yoghurt, muesli, breads, croissants and French Brioche. In the evenings the chef's passion for French cooking will ovewhelm you. Laundry facilities available. Fully licensed bar. Swimming pool. Bicycles and courtesy car complimentary. Spanish/French/Dutch spoken. Directions: The North edge of town, turn west off SH1 down Mill Road for 1.5kms.

Kaikoura *Self-contained B&B* *130km S of Blenheim*

Churchill Park Lodge
Moira & Stan Paul
34 Churchill Street, Kaikoura, Marlborough
Tel: (03) 319 5526 Fax: (03) 319 5526
Tollfree: 0800 363 690 cplodge@ihug.co.nz
www.bnb.co.nz/churchillparklodge.html

Double $90-$95 Single $75-$80
(Continental Breakfast) Child $20
Credit cards accepted Pet on property
1 Queen 1 Double 1 Single (2 bdrm) 2 Ensuite

We proudly offer two luxurious upstairs self contained units with private entrance and carparking facilities, designed and furnished to guarantee your holiday with us will be comfortable and enjoyable. The sea and mountain views from your balcony,are unbeatable in Kaikoura. Relax, soak up the sun, and eat your delicious Continental Breakfast within this very unique environment, only 5 minutes walk to the Beach, Town Centre, Shops and Restaurants. Our cat, like us, is friendly and welcoming. Experience genuine Kiwi hospitality. See you soon.

Kaikoura *Self-contained Homestay B&B* *130km S of Blenheim*

Austin Heights
Val & Ian Johnson
19 Austin Street, Kaikoura
Tel: (03) 319 5836 Fax: (03) 319 6836
www.bnb.co.nz/austinheights.html

Double $65 Single $40 (Continental Breakfast)
Child $20 (under 12) Dinner By arrangement
Queen Ensuite $85 - $100 Credit cards accepted
Pet on property Children welcome
1 Queen 1 Double 2 Single (3 bdrm)
1 Ensuite 1 Family share

We are a semi-retired couple who have moved from Southland and would like to welcome you to Austin Heights on the Kaikoura Peninsular. Our home is set in 1/2 acre of gardens and lawns offering lovely views of mountains and sea. The house is comfortable and modern and is situated on Austin Street which is the second turn left off Scarbrough Street off the main Highway South of town. We have two cats and are a non-smoking household. Courtesy transport available.

Kaikoura   *B&B Lodge*   *3km N of Kaikoura*

Carrickfin Lodge
Roger Boyd
Mill Road, Kaikoura

Tel: (03) 319 5165
Fax: (03) 319 5162
Tollfree: 0800 265 963
www.bnb.co.nz/carrickfinlodge.html

Double $100 Single $80 (Full Breakfast)
Not suitable for children
5 Queen 2 Single (6 bdrm)
6 Ensuite

Welcome to Kaikoura (Kai = food Koura = Crayfish). My name is Roger and I'm the fourth generation "Boyd" to live and farm "Carrickfin". It is an ancient Irish name from where my Great Gran father emigrated. Dongal is still the home of the "Boyds". He bought and settled this land in 1867 for 100 gold sovereigns which he got prospecting.

The Lodge is built on 100 acres adjoining the Kaikoura township. It is a large and spacious place with an open fire and a guests' bar. It was built well back from the road amidst two acres of lawns and shrubs to give complete privacy and security.

There are breathtaking views from all rooms looking directly at the "Seaward Kaikouras" a spectacular mountain range which rises to 8,500ft. These mountains are home to a unique and variety of wild life. Our sea and coastline is also unique for the Whales, Dolphins, Seals and many ocean going birds including the Wandering Albatros. It is one place in the world where Whales are found all the year round.

As well as fattening heifers I am a professional Wool Classer by trade and have worked in shearing sheds throughout the South Island high Country.

Another feature of "Carrickfin Lodge" is the big English Breakfast which is legendary. I am 3km from Whale Watch, Dolphin Encounter and some of the best restaurants.

Directions: At the north end of town turn west into Mill Road. I am up on the left (Easy to find - hard to leave).

Kaikoura *Farmstay B&B Licenced Rest & Accomodation*   *5km N of Kaikoura*

Donegal House
Murray Boyd & Mimi van Houten
Schoolhouse Road, Kaikoura

Tel: (03) 319 5083
Fax: (03) 319 5083
donegalhouse@xtra.co.nz
www.donegalhouse.co.nz

Double $120 Single $100 (Breakfast: everything!)
 Child $15 Dinner $24.50
Credit cards accepted
12 Queen 3 Single (13 bdrm)
13 Ensuite , 3 spa baths

"One Hundred Thousand Welcomes" - "Donegal House", the little Irish Pub in the country, brimming with warmth and hospitality, open fires and accordion music. Set on an historical dairy farm which has been farmed by the Boyd family since their arrival from Donegal, Ireland in 1865, "Donegal House" offers, accommodation, full bar facilities and a public licensed restaurant.

Caravan/motorhome facilities. The a-la-carte menu, specialising in Kaikoura's famous crayfish and seafood, plus locally farmed beef. NZ beers, Kilkenny and Guinness are on tap along with a good selection of Marlborough wines. Two spring fed lakes, home to Chinook salmon, Mute and Black Swans, Blue Teal, Paradise and Mallard ducks, are feature in the extensive lawns and gardens which surround "Donegal House". The towering Kaikoura Mountains make a perfect backdrop to this unique setting.

The Restaurant and Bar facilities at "Donegal House" have become a very popular place for visitors staying at the nearby Carrick-finn Lodge, Ardara Lodge, The Old Convent and Dylans Country Stay, to meet the Kaikoura locals and enjoy the rural hospitality in a unique Irish atmosphere.

We book whale watching, dolphin and seal swimming and hors trekking etc. "Even if you're not Irish-this is the place for you!" "A home away from home!"

Directions: Driving North 4kms from Kaikoura on SH1 turn left at Large transit signs, 1.6km along Schoolhouse Road.

Kaikoura *Self-contained Farmstay B&B motel* *20km N of Kaikoura*

Clematis Grove Retreat
Margaret & Ken Hamilton
Blue Duck Valley, RD 1, Kaikoura
Tel: (03) 319 5264 Fax: (03) 319 5278
clematisgrove@xtra.co.nz
www.virtual-kaikoura.com/clematis grove
Double $90-$130 Single $75 (Continental Breakfast)
Child 1/2 price Dinner $30 Credit cards accepted
Full breakfast by arrangement
1 King/Twin 1 Double 2 Single (2 bdrm)
1 Private 1 Family share

Coming to Kaikoura? Come and stay at Clematis Grove. Experience real NZ hospitality on a high country farm. Luxury accommodation at an affordable price, extremely private. Why stay in town? Come away from the crowds. At your door walk through our native forest, trees estimated up to 1100 years old. Listen to our native birds, watch our incredible native pigeons. You will be amazed at the stars at night, a morepork calls. Farm tours can be arranged. Incredible views of Kaikoura and the mountains.

Kaikoura *B&B Guesthouse* *130km S of Blenheim*

Nikau-the inn with the view
Judith Hughey
53 Deal Street,
Kaikoura
Tel: (03) 319 6973 Fax: (03) 319 6973
jhughey@xtra.co.nz
www.bnb.co.nz/nikau.html
Double $75-$90 Single $60-$70 (Special Breakfast)
Credit cards accepted
2 Queen 2 Double 3 Twin 6 Single (6 bdrm)
5 Ensuite 1 Private

It's big, it's blue and what a view. Sea and mountains fill the windows. Don't settle for less because it is Kaikoura's location that makes it unique. Nikau is just minutes walk to the main street where you can enjoy crayfish and seafood meals. At Nikau you can send your email from the desk overlooking the colourful garden, enjoy a special breakfast at the 4.2m table - once the council's - and chat to Judith who has travelled widely and grew up nearby. (Tea, coffee, laundry available.)

Kaikoura *Self-contained Homestay B&B*

Bendamere
Ellen & Peter Smith
37 Adelphi Tce, Kaikoura
Tel: (03) 319 5830 Fax: (03) 319 7337
www.bnb.co.nz/bendamere.html
Double $80-$100 Single $60-$70
(Continental & Full Breakfast)
Child $15 Smoking area inside
1 Queen 1 Double 1 Twin 4 Single (3 bdrm)
2 Ensuite 1 Private

We are retired dairy farmers and fourth generation Kaikourians with extensive knowledge of the area. Our 1930's restored home and large garden are just minutes from the township, beach, Whale Watch and other attractions. Incredible views of the Pacific Ocean and Seaward Kaikoura Mountains. Well appointed rooms offer electric blankets, heaters, hairdryers, television and tea-making facilities. Fax and laundry available. We enjoy helping visitors get the most of our their stay in our lovely seaside town. True country breakfast and other homemade treats.

Conway Flat - Kaikoura *Homestay B&B   45km S of Kaikoura*

Rafa Point Retreat
Geoff & Shirley Cant
509 Conway Flat Road, Conway Flat, RD Cheviot
Tel: (03) 319 2740 Fax: (03) 319 2749
Mob: 021 949 116   Tollfree: 0800 002 822
thecantz@paradise.net.nz
homepages.paradise.net.nz/thecantz

Double $75 Single $40 (Continental & Full Breakfast)
Child $15 Dinner $25 Children welcome
2 Queen 3 Single (3 bdrm)
1 Private 1 Family share

Our place is located on the coast with extensive sea views. Our home is a restored 1920 villa surrounded by 2 acres of extensive gardens with exotic plants and shrubs plus fruit trees. We are 40 minutes from Kaikoura for whale watching and central to Marlborough and North Canterbury wine areas. Hanmer Springs is 1 hour away for hot baths and winter skiing. We have no pets or children (welcome) and our home is a non-smoking zone.

Kaikoura *B&B   Central Kaikoura*

Lemon Tree Lodge
Andy & Tricia Pike
31 Adelphi Terrace, Kaikoura,

Tel: (03) 319 7464 Fax: (03) 319 7467
Mob: 025 648 0670 Tollfree: 0800 108 951
info@lemontree.co.nz   www.lemontree.co.nz

Double $100-$195 Single $90-$165
(Special Breakfast) Credit cards accepted
4 Queen 3 Single (3 bdrm)
4 Ensuite

Overlooking Kaikoura with spectacular views of the Pacific Ocean and mountain range. Four rooms newly designed and furnished in a classic and contemporary style all have en suite facilities. Two rooms are situated on the first floor of the main house with their own balconies with awesome sea views. The other two rooms are situated in a relaxing garden setting. All are non-smoking and equipped with colour TV, hairdryers, bathrobes, mini fridges, tea and fresh ground coffee. Couples and singles only. (Not suitable for children and pets.)

Kaikoura *B&B   130km S of Blenheim*

The Point
Peter & Gwenda Smith
Fyffe Quay, Kaikoura

Tel: (03) 319 5422 Fax: (03) 319 7422
pointsmith@xtra.co.nz
www.bnb.co.nz/thepoint.html

Double $85 Single $75 (Continental Breakfast)
Child at home Pet on property
1 Queen 1 Double (2 bdrm) 2 Ensuite

Welcome to our home. We are situated on the sea frontage, a picturesque location, only a short walk to the seal colony, which hosts shoreline and clifftop walks on and around the Peninsula. We live on a 90-acre Drysdale sheep farm, which is part of Kaikoura Peninsula. While enjoying breakfast you too can enjoy spectacular views of the land, sky and sea. We are within walking distance from one of Kaikoura's top restaurants and only five minutes drive from the town centre. The house is about 130 years old and over past years has seen numerous changes yet still contains some of the original character. Sheep shearing shows available daily.

Waiau   *Farmstay Homestay   21km N of Waiau*

Mason Hills   Averil & Robert Leckey
Inland Kaikoura Road, Waiau, RD, North Canterbury

Tel: (03) 315 6611 Fax: (03) 315 6611
Mob: 025 285 1333   Tollfree: 0800 101 961
mason_hills@xtra.co.nz
www.bnb.co.nz/masonhills.html

Double $120 Single $100 (Full Breakfast)
Dinner $30 by arrangement Credit cards accepted
Pet on property Children welcome
1 Queen 2 Single (2 bdrm)   1 Ensuite 1 Private

Conveniently situated midway between Kaikoura and Hanmer Springs on the "Alpine Pacific Triangle" (SH70), Mason Hills Station offers a real New Zealand rural experience: * Fourth generation New Zealanders. * Commercial Sheep and Beef Hill Country Station. * Large character Homestead in a genuine alpine setting. * 21 kms north of Waiau, 1km south of Mt Lyford ski field turn off. * 4WD Farm Tour encompassing spectacular Alpine to Pacific views available as an extra. Averil, Robert and Gracie the Labrador look forward to welcoming you.

Waiau   *Homestay   Waiau Central*

Waiau B&B
Sally & Vern McAllister
32 Lyndon Street, Waiau 8275, North Canterbury

Tel: (03) 315 6356 Fax: (03) 315 6356
Mob: 025 268 3024
vernandsally@xtra.co.nz
www.bnb.co.nz/waiaubb.html

Double $75 Single $45 (Full Breakfast) Child $25
Dinner $25 Pet on property Children welcome
1 Queen 1 Twin (2 bdrm)
1 Family share

Fresh air, clean green living, home baked food and home grown veggies. That is us. We enjoy people. Trout and salmon fishing, jet boating, golfing, skiing, 30 minutes to Hot Pools and horse trekking. One hour to wineries and whalewatch. Our home is on half an acre of gardens which we share with 2 cats. Waiau is one hour south of Kaikoura, 30 minutes from Hanmer Springs and ninety minutes north of Christchurch. Cyclists - we have a spa bath to rest those tired muscles.

Hanmer Springs   *Country Homestay   5km SW of Hanmer Springs*

Mira Monte
Anna & Theo van de Wiel
324 Woodbank Road, Hanmer Springs

Tel: (03) 315 7604 Fax: (03) 315 7604
Mob: 021 264 5809
vdwiel@xtra.co.nz
www.bnb.co.nz/miramonte.html

Double $110-$130 Single $85-$100
(Special Breakfast) Dinner $35. By arrangement
Credit cards accepted Pet on property
2 King 1 Single (2 bdrm)   2 Ensuite

Close to the thills of Hanmer Springs, at the foot of the mountains, lies our peaceful home. Our guest rooms have been tastefully decorated to make your stay special. Relax in your sittingroom or join us. We make a great espresso! Years in the hospitality trade have taught us how to pamper you. There is a piano and our large garden has a swimming pool. An elderly Labrador and young Jack Russell are part of the family. Come as a Stranger! Leave as a friend!

Albergo Hanmer

True Hospitality without compromise!

Hanmer Springs

WE ARE PASSIONATE ABOUT BREAKFASTS AND OUR EUROPEAN & PACIFIC RIM/NZ CUISINE! Renowned 3-course gourmet breakfasts, with the wafting smell of freshly baked swiss miniloaves and our superb Italian coffee. Dine by candle light: Prime NZ beef medallions, baby lamb, venison tenderloins, enveloped with Italian and Asian entrees and Swiss surprise desserts.

Guests comments: '... and the best coffee this side of Manhattan!' Sarah & Derek, London, UK. 'Renate and I have been captured by your magic once again - unparalleled! Renate & Richard Eckart, USA. 'Thank you for creating such an artistic, stimulating, get-comfortable environment' Bob Streeter, Fort Collins, USA.

Set in a magic mountain arena, Albergo Hanmer offers PEACE, PRIVACY and ALL DAY SUN, yet only 2 mins drive from the Thermal Pools and 18 hole golf.

ANOTHER TOUCH OF WELLNESS: relax in our newly created sunken feng shui courtyard with soothing waterfall.

Swiss brunch-style breakfast
Start your day with:
Fruit Juice, fresh fruit platter & home-made yoghurt, Swiss Birchermuesli or Bascha's low-fat muesli & other cereal selection.

Choose a hot main:
served with Béat's Swiss crunchy miniloaf.

Eggs Benedict on Salmon & fresh Hollandaise
Traditional French Omelettes
Spanish Fritatta with sage & apple
French Crêpes with lemon & maple syrup
Full English Breakfast
French Toast with Bacon & Banana
Freshly brewed italian coffee or teas

Special diets catered for!

The interior styling is modern European, creating a fresh, light and comfortable feel (u/floor heating). Unwind under a wonderful hot shower (high pressure), or in the double spa, then relax in the private guest lounge. Check out our new 2-room designer suite. Dedicated hosts, Bascha & Beat Blattner, are a young couple (NZ & Swiss origins) with 16 years experience in hospitality & tourism. Bascha's background is in Fashion, Teaching & Communications (NLP). Beat is a Tourism Expert & Desktop Publisher. We speak English, Swiss, German, French, Spanish and Italian. Come and view our seahorse memorabilia. WE CAN ARRANGE YOUR GOLFING, HUNTING AND FISHING TOURS.

DIRECTIONS: At junction before main village, 300m past Shell Garage, take ARGELINS ROAD (Centre branch), go past Hanmer Golf Club, take first road on left RIPPINGALE RD (no exit). Albergo Hanmer is 900m down at the end of this country lane.

Albergo Hanmer
B&B
130km N of Christchurch
Bascha & Beat Blattner
88 Rippingale Road
Hanmer Springs

Tel: (03) 315 7428
Fax: (03) 315 7428
Tollfree: 0800 342 313
E: albergohanmer@hotmail.com
W: www.albergohanmer.com
Check our website for specials!

Cost: Double $120-$220
Single $100
(Special Breakfast)
Dinner by prior arrangement
Credit cards accepted
Beds: 2 Super King/Twin
1 King (3 bdrm)
Bath: 3 Ensuite (spa)

Hanmer Springs *Self-contained B&B*

Cheltenham House
Maree & Len Earl
13 Cheltenham Street, Hanmer Springs
Tel: (03) 315 7545 Fax: (03) 315 7645
cheltenham@xtra.co.nz   www.cheltenham.co.nz

Double $140-$180 Single $115-$150
(Special Breakfast) Child by arrangement
Extra person $30 Credit cards accepted Pet on property
2 King/Twin 4 Queen 2 Single (6 bdrm)
5 Ensuite 1 Private

Cheltenham House offers luxury B&B accommodation, 200 metres from the Thermal Pools, restaurants and forest walks. This gracious 1930's home was renovated with the guests comfort paramount. The four spacious, sunny suites in the house and two cottage suites in the extensive garden, are all centrally heated. Enjoy breakfast of your choice, served in your suite, and local wine in the original rimu panelled billiard room in the evening. Together with our gentle labrador and sociable siamese, we look forward to meeting you.

Hanmer Springs *B&B*   *Hanmer Springs*

Hanmer View
Will & Helen Lawson
8 Oregon Heights, Hanmer Springs, 8273
Tel: (03) 315 7947 Fax: (03) 315 7958
Tollfree: 0800 92 0800
hanmerview@xtra.co.nz
www.hanmerview.co.nz

Double $110-$150 Single $80-$120 (Full Breakfast)
Dinner by arrangement Credit cards accepted
1 King/Twin 2 Queen (3 bdrm) 3 Ensuite

Hanmer View is surrounded by beautiful forest and adjoins Conical Hill track. Breathtaking alpine views. Purpose built to ensure guests enjoy a quiet, relaxing stay in warm, spacious luxury rooms. Each individually decorated room has ensuite, TV, wool duvets and hand made quilts. Tea, coffee and cake is always available and your hosts, Will and Helen delight in serving you a generous scrumptious breakfast. No-one goes away hungry. Short stroll to village, thermal pools and tourist attractions. See letterbox sign, on right, end Oregon Heights.

The best part about a homestay
is that you share the family's living area.

Hanmer Springs *Self-contained B&B lodge style* *1.5km W of Hanmer Springs*

Rippinvale Country Retreat
John & Helen Beattie, Rippingale Road, Hanmer Springs
Tel: (03) 315 7139 Fax: (03) 315 7139 Mob: 021 213 663 Tollfree: 0800 37 30 98
hjmbt@xtra.co.nz www.hamnersprings.net.nz
Double $195-$250 Single $155 (Full Breakfast) Credit cards accepted
2 Queen (2 bdrm) 2 Ensuite

Peace Privacy Comfort

Nestled in a secluded two and half acre wooded garden in a 50 acre lifestyle block adjacent to the Hanmer Springs golf course, RIPPINVALE COUNTRY RETREAT is an easy 10 min walk to the Hanmer Springs Thermal Reserve, village, restaurants and shops.

This large country home built in traditional NZ colonial style of mud brick boasts SPECTACULAR UNINTERRUPTED ALPINE VIEWS WITH ALL OF TODAYS MODERN COMFORTS.

A separate wing provides our guests with TOTAL PRIVACY AND COMFORT in their own cosy S/ C suite. Each centrally heated suite has a queen size bed, ensuite and sitting room, complimentary tea/coffee facilities DELICIOUS HOME BAKED TREATS, TV, fridge, hair dryers, woollen under-lays and electric blankets. French doors open onto your own private courtyard garden. (Guests are welcome to smoke in the garden.)

A FULL SPECIAL (MENU) BREAKFAST OF THE FRESHEST NZ PRODUCE, such as home made preserves, local Salmon, free range eggs and fruit from our orchard, can be served in your suite, the garden or join us in our farmhouse kitchen. By prior arrangement we will pack a picnic hamper or provide a supper tray if you are arriving late.

For total relaxation, Helen, a Massage Therapist, is able to provide THERAPEUTIC MASSAGE to ease tired and stressed muscles or for those wanting a more active stay John, an experienced hunting guide, can arrange free chase HUNTING/FISHING TRIPS, hiking, CAMERA HUNTS, or 4WD TREKS through our magnificent countryside. Other facilities include a tennis court and petanque terrain.

We both enjoy meeting new friends and sharing our love of this region with them.

Please phone for directions.

CANTERBURY

Culverden   *Farmstay   3km S of Culverden*

Ballindalloch
Diane & Dougal Norrie
Culverden, North Canterbury

Tel: (03) 315 8220 Fax: (03) 315 8220
Mob: 025 373 184
www.bnb.co.nz/ballindalloch.html

Double $110 Single $60 (Full Breakfast) Child $30
Dinner $30 Pet on property Children welcome
1 Queen 2 Single (2 bdrm) 1 Guests share

Welcome to 'Ballindalloch' a 2090 acre irrigated farm 3km south of Culverden. We milk 1100 cows through two floating rotary dairies at present but are in the process of building a 70 rotary dairy which will be in operation this year. We have 1000 Corriedale sheep stud. Our home is centrally heated in winter and has a log fire. We are just over 1 hour north of Christchurch and Hanmer Springs 1/2 hour to the north and Kaikoura whales 1.5 hours drive. We have travelled extensively overseas and appreciate relaxing in a homely atmosphere - we extend this to all guests. We have one cat Thomas, guests are welcome to smoke outdoors.

Gore Bay   *Homestay B&B   8km E of Cheviot*

Gore Bay B&B
Peter & Valerie McClatchy
6 Cathedral Road, Gore Bay,
Cheviot RD 3, North Canterbury 8271

Tel: (03) 319 8535 gorebay.bnb@xtra.co.nz
www.bnb.co.nz/gorebaybb.html

Double $80-$95 Single $60 (Continental Breakfast)
Children welcome
1 Double 2 Twin (2 bdrm)
1 Ensuite 1 Family share

We invite you to the natural beauty and peaceful tranquillity of Gore Bay. Enjoy panoramic sea-views from our beach-front home and our sun and sea paradise provides bush and beach walks, tennis, swimming, surfing, gardens and the spectacular Cathedral Cliffs. Golf and good restaurants nearby. Just 60 minutes drive from Hanmer Springs Thermal Resort and Kaikoura Whale Watch, 90 minutes north of Christchurch and 3 1/2 hours from Inter-island ferry. We are a retired couple enjoying sport, art and travel.

Waikari - Waipara   *Farmstay Homestay Historic Home   5km N of Waikari*

Waituna
Joanna & David Cameron
PO Box 7, Waikari, North Canterbury

Tel: (03) 314 4575 waituna.waikari@xtra.co.nz
Fax: (03) 314 4575 www.bnb.co.nz/waituna.html

Double $120-$130 Single $60
(Continental & Full Breakfast)
Dinner $40 by arrangement Credit cards accepted
1 King/Twin 1 Queen 4 Single (4 bdrm)
1 Ensuite 1 Private 1 Guests share

Waituna is a sheep farm halfway between Christchurch and Hanmer Springs and about 1 hour from Christchurch Airport. The large Homestead is listed with The Historic Places Trust, (the Limestone part built in 1879). Waituna is 15 mins from the Waipara wineries and close to golf courses, fishing rivers and horse treks. Hanmer has thermal pools, bungy jumping and jet boating. We lived in Ireland till 1972, (David is English) and enjoy sports, travelling and meeting people. We look forward to welcoming you to our gracious old home.

Waipara *Self-contained B&B   10km N of Amberley*

Winery Cottage
Julian Ball
RD 3, Amberley, North Canterbury
Tel: (03) 314 6909 Fax: (03) 314 6909
winery.cottage@xtra.co.nz   www.winerycottage.co.nz

Double $130 (Continental & Full Breakfast)
Dinner $40 Self Contained   Credit cards accepted
2 Queen (2 bdrm)   2 Ensuite

Situated on the northern edge of Waipara village, Winery Cottage offers you the ideal location to experience the many attractions that make our area unique. Base yourself in a cosy cottage with warm, spacious bedrooms and your very own modern ensuite bathroom. In the morning take a relaxed hearty breakfast with freshly baked breads, home-made muesli, fruit juice, hot porridge and filling cooked breakfast. Evening meal available upon request.Also now on offer is a modern self-contained house on it's own section with a fully equiped kitchen and laundry facilities. Within walking distance, the Weka Pass Railway will take you on a steam train excursion. Through the hills to Frog rock - a spectacular limestone outcrop. Smoke Free. Not suitable for children.

Amberley *Farmstay Homestay   1km S of Amberley*

Bredon Downs Homestay
Bob & Veronica Lucy
Bredon Downs, Amberley, RD 1, North Canterbury
Tel: (03) 314 9356 or (03) 314 8018
Fax: (03) 314 8994 Mob: 025 224 4061
lucy.lucy@xtra.co.nz
www.bnb.co.nz/bredondownshomestay.html

Double $100-$110 Single $60 (Full Breakfast)
Dinner $35 by arr. (incl. wine) Credit cards accepted
1 Queen 1 Twin 1 Single (3 bdrm) 1 Ensuite 1 Private

Our drive goes off SH1 and so we are conveniently en route to and from the inter-island ferry, just 48km north of Christchurch and 100km south of the Kaikoura whales, and easy to find. The house is surrounded by an English style garden with swimming pool, and close to the Waipara wineries, beach and attractive golf course. We breed ostriches which we are pleased to show visitors, have travelled extensively and lived abroad, and now share our lives with a Newfoundland and a Labrador, two geriatric donkeys and Rupert the cat!

Kaiapoi *B&B   15km N of Christchurch*

Morichele
Helen & Richard Moore
25 Hilton Street, Kaiapoi
Tel: (03) 327 5247 Fax: (03) 327 5247
morichele@xtra.co.nz
www.bnb.co.nz/morichele

Double $80 Single $50 (Full Breakfast) Child neg.
Dinner by arrangement Credit cards accepted
1 Double 1 Twin (2 bdrm)
1 Guests share

Kaiapoi is a riverside town close to the Waimakariri and Cam rivers, for fishing. It's within a 2 hour drive of skifields, Hanmer Springs, Akaroa and Kaikoura, each with their own attractions. We offer comfortable accommodation, with offstreet parking, and your own entrance, sitting/dining area with fridge, tea and coffee making facilities, TV and video. There are cafes and restaurants within walking distance, or you are welcome to bring back takeaways. Extra bed, fax, email and laundry available.

Rangiora   *B&B*   *30km N of Christchurch*

Willow Glen
Glenda & Malcolm Ross
419 High Street, Rangiora

Tel: (03) 313 9940 Fax: (03) 313 9946
Mob: 025 984 893
rosshighway@xtra.co.nz
www.willowglenrangiora.co.nz

Double $90 Single $60 (Full Breakfast)
1 Queen 1 Double (2 bdrm)
1 Guests share

Nestled on the northern side of Rangiora township on Highway 72, heading towards Oxford 30 minutes from Christchurch, roughly 1 hour to Mt Hutt. Walking distance to cafes and restaurants. Malcolm and I invite you to share our enchanting English style home for some Kiwi hospitality. Off street parking available. Warm comfortable beds, electric blankets, quality linen, and a hearty home style continental or cooked breakfast. Bedrooms overlook the garden with views of surrounding countryside. Meet Lucy our Foxy and Ralph our elderly cat. Email facilities available.

Rangiora   *B&B*   *7km W of Rangiora Town*

Springbank Vineyard Daphne Robinson
1035 Oxford Road, RD1, Rangiora

Tel: (03) 312 5653 Fax: (03) 312 5623
springbankvineyard@hotmail.com
www.bnb.co.nz/springbankvineyard.html

Double $100 Single $50 (Full Breakfast)
Credit cards accepted
2 Queen 2 Twin 1 Single (5 bdrm)
1 Ensuite 2 Family share

Historic Springbank Homestead, originally one of Canterbury's great estates, is encircled by spacious grounds and vineyards, with sheep, cattle, deer and horses grazing nearby. Exquisite lavender fields are also being established. Lovely large sunny bedrooms overlook the grounds, and many colonial antiques and paintings grace the 140 year old homestead. Situated just 30 minutes from Christchurch between Rangiora and Cust on AA's Scenic Highway 72, Springbank is close to golf courses and many famous tourist attractions. International skifield Mt Hutt is an hour's drive away. Relax, enjoy, unwind. It's a truly New Zealand experience.

Oxford   *Homestay*   *Oxford Central*

Glenariff
Beth & John Minns
136 High Street,
Oxford, Canterbury

Tel: (03) 312 4678
www.bnb.co.nz/glenariff.html

Double $70 Single $35 (Full Breakfast)
Child $15 Dinner $20 by arrangement
1 Double 2 Single (2 bdrm)
1 Guests share

'Glenariff' is a character home (circa 1886) operated as a Devonshire tea rooms set in a large country garden with mature trees. Oxford is a friendly country town with most leisure activities catered for. It will be our pleasure to welcome you to our home to relax and share our hospitality. A leisurely breakfast, candle light dinner or perhaps Devonshire tea served on the verandah. We have a pet cat and are smoke free. Directions: High Street is off Main Street - sign on gate.

Oxford *Farmstay B&B   3.7km W of Oxford*

Twin Bridge Farmstays
Anne & Don Manera
345 Woodside Road, Cooper Creek,
Oxford, North Canterbury
Tel: (03) 312 4964
www.bnb.co.nz/twinbridgefarmstays.html
Double $85 Single $50 (Continental Breakfast)
Child $40 Dinner $20 Pet on property
1 Double 1 Twin 1 Single (3 bdrm)
1 Family share

Welcome to our farm. A home away from home. Views of the Southern Alps, local mountains with walks through native bush and birds. Oxford offers most sports, horse riding, jet boating, golf, fishing. Come experience a working farm, cattle, sheep, three farm dogs or spend time enjoying the countryside. Our welcome includes tea, coffee and delicious home baking. Evening meals include local meat and produce. Situated 3.7 km west of Oxford. Look for sign on Main Road. 40 min from Christchurch. No smoking.

Oxford *Homestay B&B   40mins Christchurch Airport*

Hielan' House
Shirley & John Farrell
74 Bush Road, Oxford, North Canterbury
Tel: (03) 312 4382 Fax: (03) 312 4382
Mob: 025 359 435   www.bnb.co.nz/hielanhouse.html
Tollfree: 0800 279 382   meg29@ihug.co.nz
Double $95-$110 Single $70 (Full Breakfast)
Child price on application Dinner by arrangement
Credit cards accepted Pet on property Pets welcome
1 King/Twin 1 Queen (2 bdrm)   1 Ensuite 1 Private

Nestled in a peaceful, rural setting with the Oxford foothills as a backdrop, luxurious upstairs guest accommodation with separate entrance. Queen apartment has own lounge while both guest areas have TV, tea/coffee making facilities. Inground swimming pool, laundry, fax/internet facilities, cot available. On Inland Scenic Route 72 in the South Island. Christchurch 45 mins away. Delicious menu breakfasts, lunch and dinners organic meat and home grown vegetables available. Your warm welcome includes home baking and that inviting cup of coffee/tea. Pet farm animals.

West Melton - Christchurch *Rural Homestay   15km W of Christchurch*

Shettleston Farm
Cherry & Donald Moffat
Bells Road, West Melton, RD 1, Christchurch
Tel: (03) 347 8311 Fax: (03) 347 8391
Mob: 025 221 4707
shettlestonfarm@xtra.co.nz
www.bnb.co.nz/shettlestonfarm.html
Double $85 Single $65 (Continental Breakfast)
Dinner $25pp Credit cards accepted Pet on property
1 Double 1 Twin (2 bdrm)   1 Private

Enjoy the best of both worlds, 15 minutes from Christchurch Airport, 25 minutes from City Centre, yet a world away on our 10 acre country retreat. Our modern home is furnished with colonial furniture and our grounds display a collection of vintage farm machinery to complete the nostalgic atmosphere. We share our paradise with a flock of black and coloured sheep, "Poppyseed" our cow, goats, two donkeys, a collection of waterfowl on our pond, our faithful Golden Retriever and two spoilt cats. Smoke free home.

West Melton   *Farmstay B&B*   *25km W of Christchurch*

Hopesgate
Yvonne & Robert Overton
Hoskyns Road, RD 5, Christchurch
Tel: (03) 347 8330 Fax: (03) 347 8330
Mob: 025 311 234
robove@free.net.nz
www.bnb.co.nz/hopesgate.html

Double $90 Single $60 (Full Breakfast)
Dinner $20 Credit cards accepted
1 Queen 2 Single (2 bdrm)
1 Guests share

We have a 50 hectare property where we farm sheep and grow lavender. Close to all amenities, in a quiet rural setting with magnificent views of the mountains. Countless day trips can be taken from our home. We have enjoyed entertaining folk from different parts of the world and look forward to meeting and caring for many more. Relax with us and enjoy a farmhouse dinner. Begin or end a memorable holiday with us. 15 minutes from Christchurch Airport. Smoke free home. Friendly cat.

West Coast Road - Christchurch   *B&B*   *10km W of Christchurch*

GP's Place
Gwenda & Peter Bickley
164 Old West Coast Road, RD 6, Christchurch
Tel: (03) 342 9196 Fax: (03) 342 4196
Mob: 021 158 6208
gpsplace_@hotmail.com
www.bnb.co.nz/gpsplace.html

Double $90 Single $50
(Full Breakfast) Dinner $25
1 Queen 1 Twin (2 bdrm)
1 Private

Gwenda and Peter invite you to come and enjoy the ambience of our warm and spacious home set in a large garden with magnificent views of the Southern Alps. Our home is situated on 7.5 acres where we farm ostriches and various other farm animals. We are ideally located just 7 minutes from the airport and 10 minutes from the city. A full sized tennis court is available for guests use

Yaldhurst - Christchurch   *Homestay B&B*   *10km W of Christchurch*

Cherry Grove
Jan & Kirwan Berry
431 Old West Coast Road, RD 6, Christchurch
Tel: (03) 342 8629 Fax: (03) 342 4321
cherrygrove@netaccess.co.nz
users.netaccess.co.nz/cherrygrove/

Double $80-$90 Single $65 (Continental Breakfast)
Pet on property Children welcome
1 Queen 1 Twin (2 bdrm)
1 Ensuite 1 Private

Relax, enjoy the best of both worlds in a lovely rural setting just 20 minutes to the city centre. You are welcome to wander in our spacious gardens, feed the ducks and breathe our clear country air. We offer an Airport pickup only 10 minutes away, as is the Antarctic Centre. We are on the direct route to the West Coast and to many ski fields. Close by are several vineyards and golf courses. You are assured of a very warm welcome at Cherry Grove.

Yaldhurst - Christchurch
Homestay   5km W of Christchurch

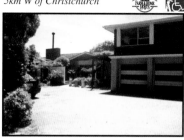

Gladsome Lodge   Stuart & Sue Barr
314 Yaldhurst Road, Christchurch 4
Tel: (03) 342 7414 Fax: (03) 342 3414
Mob: 025 299 1684 Tollfree: 0800 222 617
sue@gladsomelodge.com
www.bnb.co.nz/gladsomelodge.html

Double $80-$90 Single $60 (Continental Breakfast)
Child neg Dinner $25 Credit cards accepted
2 Queen 2 Double 2 Twin 3 Single (5 bdrm)
1 Ensuite 3 Guests share

Located close to Airport with easy access to key attractions. Be assured of professional, attentive hosting in a friendly environment. Enjoy our property which has a tennis court, swimming pool, spa and sauna available. We are able to accommodate couples travelling together as a group. Have knowledge of Maori history and culture. We are centrally heated. On bus route to City. On route to ski fields and West Coast Highway. Hosts Sue and Stuart, New Zealanders who have travelled and have a wide variety of interests.

Avonhead - Christchurch
Homestay   10km W of Christchurch

Fleur Lodge
Beverley & Harry Sweney
67 Toorak Ave,
Avonhead, Christchurch
Tel: (03) 342 5473 Fax: (03) 342 5475
www.bnb.co.nz/fleurlodge.html
Double $90 Single $70 (Full Breakfast)
Dinner $30 Pet on property
1 Double 1 Twin (2 bdrm)
1 Guests share 1 Family share

Come visit with us in our warm comfortable home which is situated close to Airport (4km), City Centre (9km) and well served by regular buses or with free pick up for sight seeing trips. Guest bedrooms are bright and have comfortable firm beds. Tea, coffee and homemade cookies are always available. We serve a delightful selection of breakfast dishes including homemade bread, muffins and jams. Our home is a smoke free zone and we share it with two Burmese cats.

Avonhead - Christchurch
B&B   10 kms W of City Centre

Russley 302
Sally & Brian Carpenter
302 Russley Road, Avonhead, Christchurch 8004
Tel: (03) 358 6543 Fax: (03) 358 6553
Mob: 025 224 3752   carpsrussley302@clear.net.nz
www.bnb.co.nz/russley.html
Double $100-$120 Single $60-$85 (Full Breakfast)
Credit cards accepted
1 Queen 1 Twin 1 Single (3 bdrm)
1 Ensuite 1 Private 1 Family share

Situated 2 minutes from Christchurch Airport "Russley 302" is an ideal first or last night stay. We are retired sheep farmers living in a rural setting farming, black/coloured sheep. Wool from these sheep form the basis of Sally's involvement in the handcraft industry. Brian's interests include Rotary & sport. Our modern home offers electric blankets, hairdryers, refrigerators, tea/coffee, laundry facilities with excellent off-street parking. We have enjoyed many years of farm hosting and invite you to share this experience with us.

Avonhead - Christchurch *10 min W of Christchurch central*

Self-contained modern townhouse accommodation

Ash Croft
Sky & Raewyn Williams
6 Fovant Street, Avonhead, Christchurch

Tel: (03) 342 3416 Fax: (03) 342 3415
Mob: 021 663 724   bookings@ashcroftgroup.com
www.ashcroftgroup.com

Double $85-$110 Child under 5 free
$10 each additional person   Credit cards accepted
2 Queen 1 Twin (3 bdrm)   1 Private

Ash Croft is a purpose built quality self-contained accommodation for the visitor to Christchurch. In a quiet residential area Ash Croft offers privacy and comfort with enclosed gardens and off-street parking. Fully equipped modern facilities, comfortable furnishings, spa bath, shower and separate toilet. Facilities include telephone, TV, VCR, video and book library, games for children. Laundry with washing machine and dryer. Portacot and highchair available. Wheelchair accessible. Easy access to airport, city centre, local shopping malls and restaurants.

Burnside - Christchurch *B&B*   *8km NW of Christchurch*

Burnside Bed & Breakfast
Elaine & Neil Roberts
31 O'Connor Place,
Burnside, Christchurch

Tel: (03) 358 7671 Fax: (03) 358 7761
elaine.neil.roberts@xtra.co.nz
www.bnb.co.nz/burnside.html

Double $90 Single $60 (Continental Breakfast)
1 Queen 1 Twin (2 bdrm)
1 Guests share

Welcome to our comfortable, modern home in quiet street, 5 minutes from the Airport and 15 minutes to city centre. Be greeted with fresh flowers and sweets in your bedroom. Relax in a garden setting with tea or coffee and freshly baked muffins. Enjoy a generous continental breakfast. A retired couple, we have travelled in New Zealand and overseas. Our interests include sport, walks, gardening, local history and our friendly cat. We enjoy sharing our home with guests and look forward to meeting you.

Ilam - Christchurch *Homestay*   *7.5km E of Christchurch*

Anne & Tony Fogarty Homestay
Anne & Tony Fogarty
7 Westmont Street,
Ilam, Christchurch 8004

Tel: (03) 358 2762 Fax: (03) 358 2767
tony.fogarty@xtra.co.nz
www.bnb.co.nz/annetonyfogartyhomestay.html

Double $80 Single $50 (Continental Breakfast)
Dinner $30 by arrangement Credit cards accepted
4 Single (2 bdrm)
1 Guests share

Our home is in the beautiful suburb of Ilam, ideally situated close to Christchurch Airport (7 mins by car), the Railway Station (10 mins), and the central City with its many attractions (10mins). We are adjacent to the city bus route. Guests are welcome to use our Laundry. We have a wide range of interests which include, our four adult children, Sport, Travel, Politics, and Gardening. We are able to provide conversational English classes for speakers of other languages (fee would apply).

Bishopdale - Christchurch   *Homestay B&B*

Fairleigh Garden, Allan & Valerie Carleton
411 Sawyers Arms Road, Harewood
Tel: (03) 359 3538 Fax: (03) 359 3548 Mob: 025 224 3746   Tollfree: 0800 611 411
fairleighgardenbb@xtra.co.nz   www.fairleighgarden.co.nz
Double $135-$185 Single $110-$145 (Special Breakfast) Honeymoon suite
Credit cards accepted Pet on property   Children welcome
1 King/Twin 2 Queen (3 bdrm)   3 Ensuite

Enjoy total relaxtion in the comfortable country styled Cedarwood Guesthouse and large tranquil garden on the outskirts of beautiful Christchurch. Experience warm and friendly hospitality with Valerie and Allan, who enjoy meeting and relaxing with their guests. They delight in sharing knowledge of the local area and of New Zealand. There is a very good map for you to use and they can recommend excellent restaurants, shops, walks, golf courses, Botanical gardens, Antartic Centre, Akaroa, Hamner Springs, TransAlpine train journey, musem, art gallery, Art Centre - the list could go on forever.

Delicious flexitime breakfasts are specially prepared for you, using the finest homegrown and local produce: fresh fruits in season, juices, cereals, homemade bread, muffins and jam. The farm bacon and fresh eggs are divine! Special diets are catered for by arrangement.

Great coffee, teas and homebaking are always available.

The three charming bedrooms - all with lovely garden views, modern ensuites, TV, telephone, heaters, hair dryers, firm comfortable beds, woollen underlays, cottin linen, bathrobes, fresh flowers and sheepskin rugs.

The honeymoon suite has a double spa bath ensuite and special honeymoon packages are available on request. Internet, laundry and ample parking are all available at any time. Valerie and Alan are gracious hosts and look forward to meeting you.

Fairleigh Garden Guest House is only four minutes from the airport and 10 minutes from the city - just 800 metres off Highway 1. Courtesy transfers are available.

Harewood - Christchurch
Homestay B&B

Highsted Homestead
Peter & Sherryn
132B Highsted Road, Christchurch
Tel: (03) 359 6486 Fax: (03) 359 6490
Mob: 025 676 4625 h.h@xtra.co.nz
www.bnb.co.nz/highstedhomestay.html
Double $110-$130 Single $80 (Full Breakfast)
Child $30 Credit cards accepted Child at home
2 Queen 1 Single (2 bdrm) 1 Private 1 Guests share

Ideally located five minutes from Christchurch airport, yet only 10 minutes drive to city. Our large colonial home is situated on a quiet private rear section amidst a 1/2 acre garden setting. Guest rooms include tea/coffee making facilities, TV, fridge, writing desk, electric blankets, heater, iron/ironing board and quality linen. Christchurch has many attractions and is well located for day trips including picturesque Akaroa. Enjoy NZ hospitality while you stay in our lovely garden city. Good local restaurants. Complimentary laundry. Rental car available. Courtesy airport pick-up

Riccarton - Christchurch
Homestay *4km W of city centre*

Riccarton Homestay
Caroline & Keith Curry
70A Puriri Street, Riccarton, Christchurch
Tel: (03) 348 4081 Fax: (03) 348 4081
curryc@xtra.co.nz
www.bnb.co.nz/riccartonhomestay.html
Double $90 Single $60 (Continental Breakfast)
Credit cards accepted
4 Single (2 bdrm)
1 Guests share

Our home is a comfortable, modern two storied townhouse in a quiet street near the University. Facilities for guests are two spacious upstairs twin bedrooms, a bathroom and separate toilet. The laundry is available for guest use. We are a pet and smoke free home. We offer a pick up service from the airport, railway station or city centre. Keith enjoys the outdoors and Caroline is a part time tourist guide interested in local history and embroidery and we both travel frequently locally and overseas.

Bryndwr - Christchurch
Homestay B&B *5km N of Christchurch City Centre*

Allisford
Peggy Crawford
1/61 Aorangi Road, Christchurch
Tel: (03) 351 7742 Fax: (03) 351 6451
Mob: 025 229 2486
saint@clear.net.nz
www.bnb.co.nz/allisford.html
Double $80 Single $50 (Full Breakfast)
2 Single (1 bdrm)
1 Family share

You are welcome to share my comfortable home and private garden, make tea or coffee and use laundry facilities. I have travelled in Europe, India, China etc and I enjoy meeting people. You are assured of comfortable beds and no waiting for the bathroom. I'm ten minutes from both Airport and City Centre, main highways are easily accessible. The Wairaiki Road-City bus is four minutes away. Various restaurants are closeby or you are welcome to bring home take-aways.

Bryndwr - Christchurch *5km NW of Christchurch Central*

Homestay B&B

Bryndwr Homestay
Patricia & Win Clancey
89A Aorangi Road, Bryndwr, Christchurch
Tel: (03) 351 6092 Fax: (03) 351 6092
wclancey@xtra.co.nz
www.bnb.co.nz/bryndwrbb.html
Double $100-$110 Single $80-$85
(Continental & Full Breakfast)
Child by arrangement Credit cards accepted
1 Queen 2 Single (2 bdrm) 1 Ensuite 1 Family share

We warmly welcome you to our spacious and comfortable home set in quiet attractive gardens. The ensuite room opens onto a balcony overlooking a secluded outdoor swimming pool. A sun room/TV room is ideal as a second (private) lounge. Tea/coffee, juice, home baking always available. Generous breakfasts. We have both travelled, have wide ranges of interest and enjoy talking to people. If needed, we are happy to help with travel plans. Courtesy pick-up, off street parking and laundry facilities are available.

Bryndwr - Christchurch *Homestay B&B   NW of Christchurch*

Bryndwr B&B
Brian & Kathy Moore
108 Aorangi Road, Christchurch,
Tel: (03) 351 6299
eroom.b@xtra.co.nz
www.bnb.co.nz/bryndwrbb2.html
Double $85 Single $65 (Full Breakfast)
1 Double 1 Single (2 bdrm)
1 Guests share

Welcome to share our comfortable family home with relaxing outdoor garden area. Located in the Northwest corner of Christchurch 5 km from the Airport off Wairakei Road or via Memorial Avenue, left onto Ilam Road, past Aqualand and on to Aorangi Road. Easy walking distances to local area shops and restaurants. Welcome to bring home takeaways. Complimentary tea or coffee any time. Laundry and ironing facilities available. Short 3 minutes walk to Bus route, only 10 minutes ride to the City Centre, passing Botanical Gardens, Museum and Art Centre. Inspection welcomed. Feel free to ring if you have any questions, we may be able to help.

Fendalton - Christchurch *Homestay B&B   1.5 km NW of Christchurch*

Fendalton House
Pam Rattray
50 Clifford Ave, Fendalton, Christchurch 1
Tel: (03) 355 4298 Fax: (03) 355 0959
Tollfree: 0800 374 298 fendaltonhouse@xtra.co.nz
www.fendaltonhouse.co.nz
Double $155-$195 Single $145-$185
(Special Breakfast) Credit cards accepted
1 Super King 1 King 1 Queen 1 Single (3 bdrm)
3 Ensuite

Recommended by Frommers Guide to NZ and the Rough Guide. Stay in a warm friendly family house in one of Christchurch's central and most prestigious garden suburbs within walking distance of town. You are welcome to share the sunny 'grapevine roofed' conservatory, and eat the grapes if they are ripe. After a large breakfast (which may include waffles, pancakes etc) we walk down to the bottom of garden to feed the wild ducks down there. Or you can borrow one of the canoes and paddle up our little stream. The friendly little cat stays downstairs.

Fendalton - Christchurch   *Homestay B&B Boutique   10 min City Centre*

Ambience on Avon
Lawson & Helen Little
9 Kotare Street, Fendalton, Christchurch
Tel: (03) 348 4537 Fax: (03) 348 4837
Mob: 025 333 627 lawsonh@amcom.co.nz
www.ambience-on-avon.co.nz

Double $120-$135 Single $90-$110
(Continental Breakfast) Credit cards accepted
1 Queen 1 Double (2 bdrm)
2 Private

Ambience on Avon in a private, picturesque garden on the Avon. We enjoy welcoming guests into our home with its elegant comfortable understated furnishings, guest lounge with a large open fire, TV. Enjoy complimentary coffee, tea, home baked cookies under the large elm tree or down at the river garden with friendly ducks, birds; or relax in our special leather therapeutic chairs in our family room opening into the garden. Art, comfortable beds, fine linen, electric blankets, room heaters and all modern conveniences for a relaxing friendly hosted stay.

Dallington - Christchurch   *Self-contained B&B   4km NE of Christchurch*

Killarney
Lynne & Russell Haigh
27 Dallington Terrace, Dallington, Christchurch
Tel: (03) 381 7449 Fax: (03) 381 7449
Mob: 025 235 2409   haigh.killarney@xtra.co.nz
www.bnb.co.nz/killarney.html

Double $90 Single $70 (Full Breakfast)
Child neg Pet on property
2 Double (2 bdrm)
1 Ensuite 1 Private 1 Family share

Peace, tranquillity and a cottage garden on the banks of the river Avon. Self-contained detached double accommodation is warm and cosy and includes fridge, microwave, extra single couch-bed, and a private garden. Double accommodation also available inside. Tea/coffee, home baking, and laundry service always available. Scenic river walks, or borrow our dinghy and row. Six minutes drive to city centre. Buses stop nearby. Courtesy pick-up sometimes available, or phone for directions. Both of us, and our two cats and bearded collie, look forward to meeting you.

Merivale - Christchurch   *B&B Inn   5mins to of Christchurch Central*

Villa Victoria
Kate McNeill
The Lane, 27 Holly Road, Christchurch 1
Tel: (03) 355 7977 Fax: (03) 355 7977
Mob: 025 397 376
villavictoria@xtra.co.nz
www.bnb.co.nz/villavictoria.html

Double $160-$175 Single $110-$125 (Full Breakfast)
Credit cards accepted
2 Double 1 Single (3 bdrm)   3 Ensuite

Built in 1901 "Villa Victoria" is situated in one of Christchurch's quiet historic suburbs just minutes from city activities. Authentically restored by owner Kate it reflects the elegance and charm of yesteryear. Furnishings are appropriate to Victoria/Edwardian era with lace curtains/bedspreads, brass/iron bed, antiques and collectables. This tranquil haven has been designed to be a home away from home, small and intimate with personalised hospitality. Delectable breakfasts a specialty using fresh local produce served at guests convenience. Off street parking. No pets or children.

Merivale - Christchurch *Homestay B&B   2km N of Christchurch*

Leinster Homestay B&B
Kay and Brian Smith
34B Leinster Road, Merivale, Christchurch
Tel: (03) 355 6176 Fax: (03) 355 6176
Mob: 025 330 771   brian.kay@xtra.co.nz
www.bnb.co.nz/leinsterhomestaybb.html

Double $115-$125 (Continental Breakfast)
Child neg Credit cards accepted Pet on property
1 Queen 1 Double 1 Single (2 bdrm)
1 Ensuite 1 Private

Kay and Brian invite you to their boutique bed and breakfast in Merivale, one of Christchurch's most beautiful suburbs and only a short stroll to many top cafes, wine bars, and shopping. Hagley Park, Arts Centre, Museum, Botanical Gardens, Museum, Casino, Conference and Antarctic Centre only 2/3 kilometres away. Quiet bedrooms with TV etc. Email/fax, laundry facilities. Off-street parking. Easy to find off main arterial route.

Merivale - Christchurch *B&B   3min Christchurch*

Melrose
Elaine & David Baxter
39 Holly Road, Merivale, Christchurch
Tel: (03) 355 1929 Fax: (03) 355 1927
Mob: 025 647 5564   BaxterMelrose@xtra.co.nz
www.melrose-bb.co.nz

Double $95 Single $65 (Continental & Full Breakfast)
Credit cards accepted Child at home Pet on property
3 Queen (3 bdrm)
1 Private 2 Guests share

A warm welcome awaits you at Melrose, a charming character home (1910) located in a small quiet street, just off Papanui Road only minutes away from the city and all the shops, restaurants and cafes of Merivale. Our house is spacious, we offer large rooms with tea and coffee making facilities and a private dining room/lounge. We have many interests and having travelled extensively, are keen to accommodate your needs. Our family comprises of two daughters and a boxer Milly. Off street parking. Children are welcome.

If you need any information ask your hosts,
they are your own personal travel agent and guide.

St Albans - Christchurch   *Homestay B&B*   *1mile N of Christchurch Central*

Barrich House
Barbara & Richard Harman
82 Caledonian Road, St Albans, Christchurch 8001

Tel: (03) 365 3985 Mob: 025 659 5787
r.harman@ext.canterbury.ac.nz
www.bnb.co.nz/barrichhouse.html

Double $80-$120 Single $50-$90 (Special Breakfast)
Child negotiable Dinner by arrangement
1 Queen 1 Twin (2 bdrm)
1 Ensuite 1 Private

Our welcoming home, startlingly alive and furnished with strong but tasteful interior colours, is in a quiet street within easy walking distance of the city and tourist amenities. Both rooms are well appointed and have very comfortable beds. The spacious queen room has arm chairs and overlooks a lovely courtyard. Excellent breakfast menu. Friendly hosts willing to help you plan your visit for best value. Complementary pick-up transport and use of laundry. Tea, coffee and biscuits are always available. Please contact us in advance.

St Albans - Christchurch   *B&B*   *1km N of Christchurch city centre*

Porticus Bed & Breakfast
Charlotte Barker
15 Dee Street, St Albans, Christchurch 8001

Tel: (03) 355 9828 Mob: 025 612 7920
c.barker@xtra.co.nz
www.bnb.co.nz/porticusbb.html

Double $125-$135 Single $95-$105 (Full Breakfast)
Child $65 Dinner $35 Credit cards accepted
2 Queen (2 bdrm)
1 Ensuite 1 Private

A warm welcome, relaxing atmosphere in 1920's villa, all combine to make a convenient comfortable "home from home" while exploring sightseeing highlights of Christchurch and Canterbury. Two queen rooms; one ensuite, one with private bathroom; guest sitting room, dining room, pleasant garden. Bedrooms have TV, heaters, electric blankets, tea/coffee facilities, fresh flowers. Phone and email available. Complimentary sherry. Evening meal on request - three course with glass of wine and coffee. I love visitors, my two dogs do too but they do respect your privacy.

All our B&Bs are non-smoking
unless stated otherwise in the text.

Avondale - Christchurch

B&B   8km NE of Christchurch Central

Hulverstone Lodge
Diane & Ian Ross
18 Hulverstone Drive, Avondale, Christchurch
Tel: (03) 388 6505 Fax: (03) 388 6025
Mob: 025 433 830   Tollfree: 0800 388 6505
hulverstone@caverock.net.nz
www.canterburypages.co.nz/hulverstone

Double $80-$120 Single $70-$100 (Full Breakfast)
Credit cards accepted Pet on property
3 King/Twin 1 Single (4 bdrm)
1 Ensuite 1 Private 1 Guests share

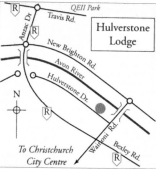

Gracing the bank of the Avon River in a quiet suburb, yet only 10 minutes from the city centre, stands picturesque Hulverstone Lodge. From our charming guest rooms watch the sun rise over the river, catch glimpses of the Southern Alps or enjoy views of the Port Hills.

Delightful riverside walks pass the door. A pleasant stroll along the riverbank leads to New Brighton with its sandy Pacific Ocean beach and pier. Numerous golf courses and the QEII leisure complex are close at hand.

Located just off Christchurch's Ring Road system, Hulverstone Lodge offers easy access to all major tourist attractions, while frequent buses provide convenient transport to the city.

Follow the Ring Road (marked with an Ⓡ on the big blue/green road signs) clockwise until it crosses the Avon River. Turn left then left again.

An ideal base for holidays year-round, Hulverstone Lodge is only a couple of hours from quaint Akaroa, Hanmer Hot Springs thermal attraction, Kaikoura's Whale Watch, and several ski-fields.

You are guaranteed warm hospitality and quality accommodation at Hulverstone Lodge. All our rooms are decorated with fresh flowers from our garden.

We offer: Complimentary pick-up; Fax and email facilities; King or twin beds;
Advice on onward travel planning; French and German languages spoken; A delicious breakfast.

Come and experience the ambience of Hulverstone Lodge.

Richmond - Christchurch   *Homestay B&B*   *1.5km E of Cathedral Square*

Willow Lodge
Grania McKenzie
71 River Road, Avonside, Christchurch 1
Tel: (03) 389 9395 Fax: (03) 381 5395
willow@inet.net.nz
www.bnb.co.nz/willowlodgerichmond.html
Double $100-$140 Single $70-$80 (Special Breakfast)
Child $25 Credit cards accepted Pet on property Children welcome
1 King/Twin 2 Queen 1 Single (3 bdrm)
1 Ensuite 2 Private

Beautiful river setting • Family suite • 1928 Art Deco style home • Stroll into town

Your perfect end to a wonderful journey - relax & unwind, read or chat, make yourself at home.

Enjoy a choice of 1 large suite of 2 large rooms.

We value our home's 1920/30's architecture & style, and mix it with plenty of contemporary art & books. Excellent large, firm beds. Breakfast is fresh & generous - organic bread, cereals, fresh fruit, eggs, good coffee & teas.

Christchurch bulges with good things - food & wine, bookshops, clothes, antiques and a lively arts scene.

We are happy to add our personal experience to enhance your stay. Sam is our elderly black Labrador.

Shuttle or taxi service to gate from air/rail/coach.

Also available: mountain bike, off street parking & laundry.

• Central city: walk/20 min

• Airport/rail: car/20 min

• Central city: car/5 min.

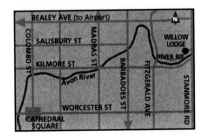

Christchurch City   *Self-contained B&B*   *Christchurch Central*

Riverview Lodge
Ernst and Sabine Wipperfuerth
361 Cambridge Terrace, Christchurch 1
Tel: (03) 365 2860 Fax: (03) 365 2845
riverview.lodge@xtra.co.nz
www.nz.com/travel/riverview

Double $150-$185 Single $95-$135
(Special Breakfast) S/C suites $200
Credit cards accepted
3 Queen 1 Double 1 Twin 1 Single (5 bdrm)
4 Ensuite 1 Private

Quality accommodation in a relaxed and quiet atmosphere, still just minutes walking away from the centre of an exciting city: this is the place to stay. Riverview Lodge is a restored residence that reflects the grace and style of the period. Balconies provide wonderful river views. The Edwardian townhouse next door has two very spacious (90m2) apartments for a private stay. As ex-tour operators we'll be happy to help you with planning and bookings. Kayaks, bicycles and golf clubs are for guests to use. We are multilingual.

Christchurch City   *B&B*   *Christchurch Central*

The Grange Guest House   Marie & Paul Simpson
56 Armagh Street, Christchurch
Tel: (03) 366 2850 Fax: (03) 374 2470
Mob: 021 366 608   Tollfree: 0800 93 2850
reservations@thegrange.co.nz
www.bnb.co.nz/thegrangeguesthouse.html

Double $120-$130 Single $95 (Full Breakfast)
Child $15 under 12yrs Credit cards accepted
2 King 3 Queen 1 Double 1 Twin (7 bdrm)
7 Ensuite 1 Guests share

At The Grange Guesthouse you will enjoy your visit in this tastefully "refurbished" Victorian mansion with wood panelling and a beautiful wooden feature staircase, you can relax in the guest lounge or in the garden. The Grange Guesthouse is situated within walking distance to most of Christchurch's favourite spots including; Cathedral Square, the Arts Centre, Art Gallery and Museum also the Botanic Gardens, Hagley Park and Mona Vale. During your stay at The Grange you will be treated to comfortable accommodation, complimentary tea and coffee, off-street parking, laundry service and sightseeing tours.

CANTERBURY

Just as we have a variety of B&Bs
you will also be offered a variety of breakfasts,
and they will always be generous.

Christchurch City *B&B Private Hotel*   *Christchurch Central*

Windsor B&B Hotel
Carol Healey & Don Evans
52 Armagh Street, Christchurch 1
Tel: (03) 366 1503 Fax: (03) 366 9796 Tollfree: 0800 366 1503
reservations@windsorhotel.co.nz
www.windsorhotel.co.nz

Double $108 Single $75 (Full Breakfast)
Child $15 under 12 yrs with Adult Quad/Family, $150 Triple, $132
Credit cards accepted Pet on property
(40 bdrm) 24 Guests share

Looking for Bed & Breakfast accommodation in Christchurch, then try "The Windsor". Built at the turn of the century this inner city residence is located on the Tourist Tram Route and is within 5-10 minutes walk of the City Centre, Restaurants, Banks, Town Hall, Convention Centre, Casino, Arts Centre, Museum and Botanical Gardens.

Guests are greeted on arrival by our pet dachshund "Miss Winnie" and shown around our charming colonial style home. Often described as "Traditional" this family operated Bed and Breakfast Hotel prides itself on the standard of accommodation that it offers. The nicely furnished bedrooms are all individually heated and decorated with a small posy of flowers and a watercolour by local artist Denise McCulloch.

The shared bathroom facilities have been conveniently appointed with bathrobes provided, giving warmth and comfort in the Bed and Breakfast tradition.

Such things as "Hotties" and "Brollies" add charm to the style of accommodation offered, as does our 1928 Studebaker sedan.

Our generous morning breakfast (included in the tariff) offers Fruit Juice, Fresh Fruits, Yogurt and Cereals followed by Bacon and Eggs, Sausages, Tomatoes, Toast and Marmalade, and is served in the dining room each morning between 6.30 and 9.00 am. The complimentary Tea and Coffee making facilities allow guests to help themselves at their own convenience and we serve "Supper" (Tea, Coffee and Biscuits) each evening in the lounge at 9.00 pm.

As part of our service the Hotel offers Laundry Facilities, off Street Parking for the motorist and bicycle and baggage storage.

QUOTE THIS BOOK FOR 10% DISCOUNT

Turret House

Christchurch City *B&B*

Turret House
Justine & Paddy Dougherty
435 Durham Street North, Christchurch

Tel: (03) 365 3900
Fax: (03) 365 5601
Tollfree: 0800 48 87 73
turretb.bchch@xtra.co.nz
www.turrethouse.co.nz

Double $95-$130 Single $65-$95
(Continental Breakfast)
Child $20 Credit cards accepted
2 King/Twin 4 Queen 1 Twin 1 Single (8 bdrm)
8 Ensuite

'Céad Míle Fáilte' (One hundred thousand welcomes)

Turret House is a gracious superior Bed & Breakfast accommodation located in downtown Christchurch. It is within easy walking distance of Cathedral Square, the Botanical Gardens, Museum, Art Gallery, the Arts Centre and Hagley Park 18 hole golf course. Also Casino, new Convention Centre, Town Hall.

Built around 1900 this historic residence is one of only three in the area protected by the New Zealand Historic Places Trust. It has been restored to capture the original character and charm. Situated within the grounds is one of Christchurch's best examples of our native kauri tree. Attractively decorated bedrooms with heaters and electric blankets combine comfort and old world elegance, with private bathrooms, some with bath and shower, all offering a totally relaxed and comfortable environment.

Tea, coffee and biscuits available 24 hrs. Cots and highchairs are also available. Family room sleeps 4.

If you're looking for a place to stay where the accommodation is superior and the atmosphere friendly - experience Turret House.

Just 15 minutes from Christchurch Airport. Situated on the corner of Bealey Ave and Durham Street. (Off-street parking).

Christchurch City   B&B B&B Hotel

Croydon House
Nita & Siegfried Herbst
63 Armagh Street, Christchurch
Tel: (03) 366 5111 Fax: (03) 377 6110
Tollfree: 0800 276 936   welcome@croydon.co.nz
www.croydon.co.nz

Double $120-$135 Single $85-$99 (Full Breakfast)
self-contained apartment $150 Credit cards accepted
1 King 4 Queen 2 Double 3 Twin 2 Single (12 bdrm)
10 Ensuite 2 Private

Croydon House is a charming, small Hotel offering fine Accommodation in the Heart of New Zealand's Garden City. All Bedrooms are tastefully refurbished with private or ensuite bathroom. Start your day with our scrumptious buffet and indulge yourself in a deliciously cooked breakfast prepared especially for you. Explore the city's major attractions, great restaurants, conference venues and the famous Botanical Gardens are within easy walking distance. We provide Internet access. For more information visit our Home Page on the Internet with on-line booking form.

Christchurch City   10min Christchurch Central

Home Lea B & B
Pauline & Gerald Oliver
195 Bealey Avenue, Christchurch
Tel: (03) 379 9977 Fax: (03) 379 4099
Tollfree: 0800 355 321
homelea@xtra.co.nz
www.bnb.co.nz/homelea.html

Double $85-$110 Single $60-$85
Child $15 Dinner B/A
1 King 2 Queen 5 Single (5 bdrm)
2 Ensuite 1 Private 1 Guests share

Home Lea offers the traveller a comfortable and enjoyable stay. Built in the early 1900's, Home Lea has the charm and character of a large New Zealand home of that era: Rimu panelling, leadlight windows, and a large lounge with a log fire. Tea, coffee, biscuits and fruit are available at all times. Off street parking, and email/fax facilities available for guests. Pauline and Gerald are happy to share there knowledge of local attractions and their special interests are travel, sailing and music.

Christchurch City   B&B   Christchurch Central

Orari B&B
Jenny Brown
42 Gloucester St, Christchurch 1
Tel: (03) 365 6569 Fax: (03) 365 2525
jenny@orari.net.nz
www.orari.net.nz

Double $150-$210 Single $130-$150
(Special Breakfast) Credit cards accepted
1 King/Twin 9 Queen 5 Single (10 bdrm)
8 Ensuite 2 Private

ORARI was built in 1893. Of Kauri construction with beautifully proportioned rooms, Orari is situated within easy walking distance of the Arts Centre, the Botanic Gardens, Museum, Hagley Park, Town Hall, Casino, Convention Centre, and Cathedral Square. Featuring 10 bedrooms with private bathrooms, off street parking and wheel chair access, it provides comfortable, friendly accommodation for travellers, business people and small group conferences. Enjoy the convenience of the inner city in an elegant heritage home. Children are welcome as guests but Orari is unsuitable for pets.

Christchurch City *B&B* *Christchurch Central*

Apartment 37 Lynne & David
PO Box 177, Christchurch
Apartment 37, Old Government Buildings,
Cathedral Square, Christchurch
Tel: (03) 377 7473 Fax: (03) 377 7863
Mob: 025 622 0849 apartment37@xtra.co.nz
www.bnb.co.nz/apartment.html
Double $145-$155 Single $130-$145
(Special Breakfast) Credit cards accepted
1 Queen 1 Twin (2 bdrm) 2 Ensuite

In the heart of Christchurch (Cathedral Square), Apartment 37 is unique offering warm friendly hospitality and elegant accommodation in a grand historic building with central city convenience. In addition enjoy many extras including Sky TV, tea/coffee making facilities, and access to in-building facilities (lap pool, gymnasium, spa, sauna, restaurant). Walk to Christchurch's vibrant attractions - Arts Centre, museum, botanic gardens, Hagley park, shops, cafes, conference centre, and entertainment or use transport right on door step. Perfect for holidays or business. Please phone for directions.

Christchurch City *B&B B&B Guesthouse*

Devon Bed & Breakfast Hotel
Sandra & Benjamin Humphrey
69 Armagh Street, Christchurch
Tel: (03) 366 0398 Fax: (03) 366 0398
Tollfree: 0800 283 386 bandbdevonhotel@xtra.co.nz
www.devonbandbhotel.co.nz
Double $95-$120 Single $70-$95 (Full Breakfast)
Child under 15, $1 per year of age
$20 Extra Adults Credit cards accepted
6 Queen 3 Twin 15 Single (11 bdrm)
6 Ensuite 1 Private 4 Guests share

The Devon is a personal guest house located in the heart of beautiful Christchurch city, which offers elegance and comfort in the style of an olde worlde English manor. Just 5 minute's walk to Christchurch Cathedral, Town Hall, and Convention Centre, casino, museum, hospital and botanical gardens in Hagley Park. TV lounge, tea & coffee making facilities. Off street parking.

Christchurch City *B&B*

Holly House
Erica & Allister Stewart
1/337 Cambridge Terrace,
Inner City, Christchurch
Tel: (03) 371 7337
a.e.stewart@xtra.co.nz
www.bnb.co.nz/hollyhouse.html
Double $110 Single $90
(Special Breakfast)
1 King/Twin (1 bdrm)
1 Private

We would be pleased to welcome you to our home which is within walking distance to anywhere in the inner city. We have one lovely bedroom which can be arranged as twin beds or one king size bed. The guests' bathroom is adjacent to the bedroom. The sitting room overlooks the beautiful tree-lined Avon River. A comment from our visitors' book: "Holly House is an absolute gem." Erica is an artist working with stained glass, and clay sculpture. Allister is a retired school teacher.

Christchurch City   *B&B*   *Christchurch Central*

The Manor
Alison & Ross Ruddenklau
82 Bealey Avenue, City Central
Christchurch

Tel: (03) 366 8584
Fax: (03) 366 4946
Tollfree: 0800 366 859
info@themanor.co.nz
www.themanor.co.nz

Room Rate $120-$197   (Full Breakfast)
Credit cards accepted
4 King/Twin 4 Queen 3 Twin 1 Single (10 bdrm)
8 Ensuite 2 Guests share

The Manor is a beautiful Victorian mansion, built in 1860. The original architecture includes a magnificent entrance foyer, coloured lead light windows and dining room are complimented with comfortable furnishings, antiques and collectables.

The bedrooms, all different, each with their own charm, are decorated in country cottage style.

The tariff includes breakfast with hot dish.

We are a short drive from the airport and conveniently situated 10-15 mins level walk to Art centre, Botanical gardens, Art galleries, City centre, golf course, museums, restaurants.

A day trip to Hanmer Springs, Akaroa, Kaikoura.

Stop a while and enjoy the hospitality at The Manor.

We welcome children but no pets please.

Southshore - Christchurch *Homestay B&B 10km E of Christchurch*

Southshore Homestay
Jan & Graham Pluck
71A Rockinghorse Road,
South Shore, Christchurch 7
Tel: (03) 388 4067 Fax: (03) 365 3775
grahamandjan@xtra.co.nz
www.bnb.co.nz/southshorehomestay.html

Double $90-$120 (Continental & Full Breakfast)
Dinner $25pp Credit cards accepted Pet on property
1 Queen (1 bdrm) 1 Ensuite 1 Family share

Twenty minutes from the city, Southshore lies between the ocean and the Avon Estuary. Sheltered by the dunes wilderness, our comfortable home is a quiet retreat set in an interesting seaside garden from where a private track over the dunes provides easy access to miles of safe, sandy beach. Nearby, the Estuary walkway offers expansive views and varied bird life. We are non-smokers, semi-retired with interests in gardening, vintage cars, embroidery and our cat. Please phone for reservations. Airport pickup available.

Avonside - Christchurch *4km E of Christchurch*
Homestay Separate/Suite B&B S.C Garden Studio

Avon Park Lodge Murray & Richeena Bullard
144A Kerrs Road, Avonside, Christchurch
Tel: (03) 389 1904 Mob: 025 641 9692
avonparklodge@clear.net.nz
www.bnb.co.nz/avonparklodge.html

Double $85 Single $60 (Full Breakfast)
Child by arrangement Dinner by arrangement
S.C. Garden Studio $110 Credit cards accepted
2 Queen 2 Twin (3 bdrm) 1 Ensuite 1 Guests share

Enjoy quiet, peaceful surroundings in our beautiful garden and two storey home close to parks and the Avon river. The two upstairs guest bedrooms are comfortably furnished and include tea and coffee making facilities, etc. Our self-contained garden studio with ensuite and kitchenette is complete with fridge and microwave. Close to frequent public transport (including bus to the railway station). Five min drive to the city. Your hosts and their lovable boxer dog Gus assure you of a warm, friendly welcome. Complimentary pick-up.

CANTERBURY

Please let us know how you enjoyed your B&B experience.
Ask your host for a comment form.

Woolston - Christchurch *Homestay B&B   4km E of Christchurch*

Treeview
Kathy & Laurence Carr
6 Lomond Place,
Woolston, Christchurch 6
Tel: (03) 384 2352
www.bnb.co.nz/treeview.html

Double $80 Single $45 (Continental Breakfast)
Child $20 Dinner $20
1 Double 2 Single (2 bdrm)
1 Guests share

Welcome. Kiwi hospitality. Smoke free sunny home in quiet cul-de-sac. Garden with seating. Guests carport. Comfortable beds, electric blankets, hair drier. Generous breakfast in dining room with cathedral ceilings. 10 mins by car to city and beaches. Bus handy. Courtesy transport from Railway Station. Airport shuttle service.   From Cathedral Square take Gloucester Street to roundabout at Linwood Avenue. turn right. Pass Eastgate Mall to traffic lights end of avenue of trees. Right into Hargood Street. First left into Clydesdale, first left Lomond Place.

St Martins - Christchurch *Self-contained B&B   4km S of Christchurch City Centre*

KLEYNBOS B&B
Gerda De Kleyne & Hans Van Den Bos
59 Ngaio Street, Christchurch
Tel: (03) 332 2896 Fax: (03) 332 2896
KLEYNBOS@xtra.co.nz
www.bnb.co.nz/kleynbosbb.html

Double $85 Single $75 (Continental Breakfast)
Credit cards accepted
1 Queen 1 Double 1 Single (2 bdrm)
2 Ensuite

ESPECIALLY FOR YOU, QUALITY ACCOMODATION WITH A PERSONAL TOUCH. Close, 4km, to the city centre, in an easy to find, friendly, tree-lined, residential street. THAT'S US! Your large room with ensuite bathroom is $85 and has its own microwave, fridge, waterboiler etc. We offer a 'no breakfast' rate by prior arragement. Our children are 10 and 13. Gerda works in Mental Health. Having guests is like family who have come to stay. Directions: SH74 Barbadoes Street, Waltham Road, Wilsons Road, Right into Gamblins Road, first left.

St Martins - Christchurch *Christchurch Central*

Self-contained two luxury self-catering apartments

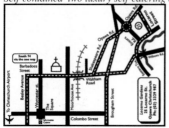

Locarno Gardens Aileen & David Davies, 25 Locarno Street, Christchurch 8002
Tel: (03) 332 9987 Fax: (03) 332 9687 Mob: 025 399 747, locarno@xtra.co.nz
www.cottagestays.co.nz/begonia/cottage.htm
Double $85-$110 Single $85-$110 (Continental Breakfast extra charge) extra person $25 ,
1 Super King 1 Queen 1 Twin (2 bdrm), 2 Ensuite

Mt Pleasant - Christchurch *Homestay 8km E of Christchurch*

Plains View
Robyn & Peter Fleury
2 Plains View, Mt Pleasant, Christchurch 8
Tel: (03) 384 5558 Fax: (03) 384 5558
Mob: 025 211 3606   Fleury@inet.net.nz
www.bnb.co.nz/fleury.html

Double $70-$85 Single $45 (Continental Breakfast)
1 Queen 1 Double 1 Single (3 bdrm)
1 Guests share

Enjoy our warm hospitality in the comfort of our modern home, spacious and sunny with wonderful views of the city and Southern Alps. Close by sumner beach, Ferrymead historical Park, Mt Cavendish Gondola and a variety of restaurants. Our interests include 4 wheel driving the outdoors, tapestry and gardening. our travels have taken us throughout New Zealand and overseas. We provide complimentary tea and coffee and are a non smoking household. Please phone for directions. Complimentary pickup available by arrangement (conditions apply).

Mt Pleasant - Christchurch *7km E of Christchurch Central*
Homestay B&B

The Cotterage
Jennifer Cotter
24B Soleares Avenue, Mt Pleasant, Christchurch 8008
Tel: (03) 384 2898 Fax: (03) 384 2898 jen@e3.net.nz
www.bnb.co.nz/thecotterage.html

Double $110 Single $60 (Continental Breakfast)
Child neg Dinner $20 Credit cards accepted
1 Queen 2 Single (2 bdrm)
1 Ensuite 1 Family share

Away from the city smog. Quiet secluded comfort in homely cottage down private lane. Charming tranquil garden. Sunny bedrooms opening on to covered terrace (for breakfast al fresco!) Tea and coffee always available. Many cafes, pubs, good restaurants 5 minutes drive. Estuary where bird life abounds 2 minutes walk. Nearby scenic attractions include Sumner beach, hills, walks, gondola, Lyttelton Harbour. City centre is 15 minutes. We enjoy company, have travelled extensively, enjoy creative pursuits, gardening, books. Two resident cats. Laundry facilities. Smoking outdoors. Please phone for directions.

Mt Pleasant - Christchurch *B&B 8km SE of Christchurch Centre*

Santa Maria
Anne & Ian Harris
57 Santa Maria Avenue, Mt Pleasant, Christchurch
Tel: (03) 384 1174 Fax: (03) 384 6474
Mob: 021 673 549
the-harris-family@xtra.co.nz
www.bnb.co.nz/santamaria.html

Double $120 Single $75
(Full Breakfast) Pet on property
1 Queen (1 bdrm)
1 Ensuite

Welcome to Santa Maria, our centrally heated home with panoramic views of the Pacific Ocean through to the Southern Alps. Our comfortable guestroom has ensuite bathroom, tea/coffee making facilities and access to a sunny courtyard. Enjoy our tennis court, pool or visit the nearby beach village of Sumner with its excellent selection of cafes, restaurants, bars and movie theatres. Windsurf, ride the Gondola or explore one of our many walkways. The choice is yours. Two adorable cats reside with us.

Mt Pleasant - Christchurch *7km E of Central Christchurch*

Self-contained B&B

The Nest on Mount Pleasant
Kathryn & Kai Tovgaard
24 Toledo Place, Christchurch 8
Tel: 0064 3 3 849 485 Fax: 0064 3 3 848 385
thenestonMP@xtra.co.nz
www.PlacesToStay.co.nz/places/5011.asp

Double $85-$105 Single $75-$90 (Full Breakfast)
Child discount Dinner b/a Credit cards accepted
2 Queen 2 Twin (3 bdrm) 1 Ensuite 1 Guests share

Unique self-contained home (including full kitchen and laundry facilities) yet with all the service of a homestay: This is the promise of THE NEST. Warm hospitality guaranteed with hosts next door. Situated in one of Christchurch's most exclusive Hill suburbs set in native bush. Views of Estuary, Sea and Mountains beyond. Tranquil and secure, with garage parking. TV, Stereo and BBQ. Very close to Chistchurch's best beaches with excellent cafes and restaurants, Ferrymead Historic Park, Lyttelton Harbour, and hillside walks with breathtaking views to the Southern Alps.

Balmoral Hill - Christchurch *B&B Luxury B&B* *8km E of Christchurch Centre*

Balmoral Oceanview
Dina & Russell Campbell
77 Glenstrae Road, Balmoral Hill, Christchurch 8008
Tel: (03) 384 4426 Fax: (03) 384 4491
Mob: 025 530978 Tollfree: 0800 671028
balmoraloceanview@xtra.co.nz
www.bnb.co.nz/balmoraloceanview.html

Double $170-$195 Single $155-$180
(Continental or Full Breakfast)
1 king/twin, 1 queen 1 ensuite and 1 private bathroom

Luxury, ambiance, relaxation and warm hospitality characterize our home with panoramic views of the Pacific Ocean. Stroll on Sumner's sandy beach and indulge in a latte or Kiwi cuisine at seaside cafes and restaurants. Wake to the smell of fresh bread and delight in a sumptuous cooked breakfast. Mount Cavendish Gondola 5 minutes away, City centre 15 mintues. Honeymoon package, luxurious double spa bathroom, pre diner drinks with guests, New Zealand artworks. Miniature Poodle nammed Beau.

Redcliffs - Christchurch *Homestay B&B* *8km E of Christchurch*

Redcliffs on Sea
Cynthia & Lyndsey Ebert
125 Main Road,
Redcliffs, Christchurch 8
Tel: (03) 384 9792 Fax: (03) 384 9703
redcliffs@nzhomestay.co.nz
www.nzhomestay.co.nz/ebert.htm

Double $100 Single $60 (Continental Breakfast)
Credit cards accepted
1 Queen 1 Double 2 Single (2 bdrm)
1 Ensuite 1 Family share

Relax and enjoy our comfortable home by the sea, situated approximately 15 minutes from the city, our home is "absolute water front ", on the Avon-Heathcote Estuary with magnificent views of the sea, birds and boating. We are non smoking and our guest facilities include a sunny queen and single bedroom with its own ensuite and TV, plus a twin bedroom with family share bathroom. Local restaurants offer a choice of cuisine, continental breakfast is included in the tariff, laundry facilities and off street parking.

Sumner - Christchurch   *Self-contained Homestay*   *10km E of Christchurch*

Villa Alexandra
Wendy & Bob Perry
1 Kinsey Terrace, Christchurch 8
Tel: (03) 326 6291 Fax: (03) 326 6096
villa_alexandra@xtra.co.nz   www.villaalexandra.co.nz
Double $85-$110 Single $70 (Full Breakfast)
Child $15, free under 12yrs.
Dinner $35 by arrangement.
1 Queen 1 Double 1 Twin 1 Single (4 bdrm)
2 Ensuite 2 Private

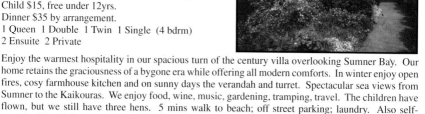

Enjoy the warmest hospitality in our spacious turn of the century villa overlooking Sumner Bay. Our home retains the graciousness of a bygone era while offering all modern comforts. In winter enjoy open fires, cosy farmhouse kitchen and on sunny days the verandah and turret. Spectacular sea views from Sumner to the Kaikouras. We enjoy food, wine, music, gardening, tramping, travel. The children have flown, but we still have three hens. 5 mins walk to beach; off street parking; laundry. Also self-contained beach front apartment, 2 double bedrooms, $135 per night, min. three nights.

Sumner Beach - Christchurch   *B&B Guesthouse*   *8km E of Christchurch*

Cave Rock Guest House
Gayle & Norm Eade
16 Esplanade, Sumner, Christchurch
Tel: (03) 326 6844 Fax: (03) 326 5600
Mob: 025 360 212   eade@chch.planet.org.nz
www.caverockguesthouse.co.nz
Double $95-$110 Single $80 (Continental Breakfast)
Child $15 Credit cards accepted Pet on property
3 Queen (3 bdrm)
3 Ensuite

The Cave Rock Guest House is Christchurch's only seafront accommodation directly opposite Sumner's famous "Cave Rock". Your hosts Gayle and Norm Eade have been in the hospitality industry for 15 years and enjoy meeting people from overseas and within NZ. Our large double rooms have seaviews and are self contained. All have colour TV, heating and ensuite bathrooms, and can sleep up to 4. Kitchen facilities available. Sumner Village is an ideal location, 15 minutes from Christchurch city, we have cafe/bars, shops, cinema, all walking distance. We have a very friendly Dalmatian dog.

Sumner - Christchurch   *B&B*   *8kms E of Christchurch*

Ocean View
Christian and Anna van Uden
65 Ocean View Terrace, Sumner, Christchurch
Tel: 0064 3 326 4888 Fax: 0064 3 326 4888
oceanview@clear.net.nz
www.bnb.co.nz/user5.html
Double $95-$130 Single $65-$90
(Continental Breakfast) Child neg
Credit cards accepted
1 Queen 1 Twin (2 bdrm) 2 Private

Chris, Anna and Dominic welcome you to Ocean View B&B. Fifteen minutes from Christchurch city and is set in the popular seaside suburb of Sumner. Sumner's relaxing village atmosphere has much to offer the traveller. Take advantage of the views up the coast and out to sea from the guest rooms that have direct access to expansive verandas and decking positioned to capture the sun. Guest lounge has television, tea and coffee facilities. Set on three acres of land providing a rural flavour.
DIRECTIONS : Please telephone, e-mail or visit our brochure.

Sumner - Christchurch *8km SE of Christchurch*

Self-contained B&B Apartment

c.u. at Sumner
Lisa Shannon
Tel: (03) 326 4044 Mob: 021 366 959
shayres@xtra.co.nz
www.bnb.co.nz/cuatsumner.html
Double $95-$140 (Continental Breakfast)
Credit cards accepted Children welcome
1 Queen 1 Double 2 Single (2 bdrm)
1 Private

Beachfront location, private courtyard. Situated in a unique coastal village near the heart of Christchurch. Step out the door of this stunning contemporary, modern apartment and treat yourself to delicious coffee, taste fine cuisine at Thai, Indian or cafe culture restaurants. View films at the cinema or wander along the surf beach at sunset. View local art on the walls, read from an extensive library or listen to an excellent choice of music. Sophisticated comfort with all the charm of seaside holiday living.

Sumner - Christchurch *Self-contained* *15km E of Central Christchurch*

Sumner on Sea Holiday Flat
Janet & Chris Abbott
104 Nayland Street,
Sumner, Christchurch
Tel: (03) 326 7034
janet.abbott@clear.net.nz
www.bnb.co.nz/user216.html
Double $100 Single $90 (Continental Breakfast)
Child $10 Credit cards accepted Children welcome
1 King 1 Double 1 Single (1 bdrm)
1 Private

Sumner on Sea

This self-contained garden flat is located on the ground floor of the historic villa built by the first mayor of Sumner around 1877. It has a large lounge with TV, video, divan & sofa bed; separate bedroom with king-sized bed, fully equipped kitchen and bathroom with shower. The quarter acre of rambling garden is patrolled by Levi the cat, and hens who provide fresh eggs. One block from beach, convenient for city bus, children welcome, café opposite, off street parking, surf toys weekly rental available.

Cashmere - Christchurch *Homestay B&B* *5km S of Christchurch*

Janet Milne
12A Hackthorne Road,
Cashmere,
Christchurch
Tel: (03) 337 1423
www.bnb.co.nz/milne.html
Double $100 Single $50
(Continental Breakfast)
1 Queen (1 bdrm)
1 Ensuite 1 Family share

Two storeyed home in quiet back section on Cashmere Hills. Lower storey is an independent suite comprising two hand basins, shower, lavatory, kingsize bed with electric blanket, two single bunks, television, telephone, heaters, and table and chairs. Tea/coffee making facilities. Non smokers only. I am a registered general nurse; obstetrics nurse; a university student studying for a degree in linguistics; and an English language teacher. The piano loves attention. Spanish and English are my favourite languages. 'Explorer' of foreign countries.

Cashmere - Christchurch *Homestay B&B* *5km S of Christchurch*

City Lights
Jan & Bob Thayer, 34 Harry Ell Drive, Cashmere, Christchurch
Tel: (03) 332 5566 Fax: (03) 337 0038 Mob: 021 105 8593
jancitylights@xtra.co.nz www.bnb.co.nz/citylightschristchurch.html

Double $120-$150 Single $100 (Full Breakfast) Dinner by arrangement Pet on property
1 King/Twin 1 Queen 1 Twin (3 bdrm) 1 Private

Stunning panoramic views and a warm welcome await you in our spacious modern Mediterranean style home nestled in the Cashmere Hills.

Enjoy the quiet and private gardens, beautiful heated saltwater swimming pool (Oct-April), piano, home gym, and the nearby Port Hills walkways. Relax in any of the sundrenched outdoor areas and enjoy the million dollar views from the mountains to the sea or curl up with a book in the spacious warm and well appointed living areas or private lounge.

Bedrooms have comfortable excellent quality beds and linen including cosy luxurious robes in which to relax.

Delicious full breakfasts with fresh locally grown produce, great coffee and freshly baked bread. Superb dinners available by arrangement and special diets catered for. Alternatively we can tell you about some great Christchurch restaurants in this area.

Our home is smokefree inside and we share it with our lovely old cat Che. Our interests include sports (arm chair), walking, gardening, kayaking, rotary, travel, good food and wine, and most importantly our two little grandchildren.

We prefer to host one couple or group of people at a time. This ensures your privacy and enables us to focus on your requirements.

Bob and Jan have travelled a lot and really appreciate our beautiful country. It would be our privilege to help you plan to get the very best our of your time here whether you are on holidays or business.

We look forward to welcoming you to our home with tea/coffee and fresh baking or a cool drink. Directions will be given at time of booking.

Cashmere   *Homestay B&B   5km S of Christchurch*

Burford Manor
Kathleen & David Burford
3 Lucknow Place, Cashmere 2, Christchurch
Tel: (03) 337 1905 Fax: (03) 337 1916
burfords@xtra.co.nz
www.webnz.co.nz/bbnz/burford.htm
Double $120-$130 Single $100 (Full Breakfast)
Credit cards accepted
2 Queen 2 Single (3 bdrm)
1 Ensuite 2 Private

Our home is 5 minutes drive from the city center with million dollar views of Rural Canterbury and the Southern Alps. Easy flat access and parking, quiet and peaceful, it incorporates the charm of yesteryear with the conveniences of a modern home, complemented by David's prizewinning garden and Kathleen's exhibition patchwork quilts. Interests include Rotary, Stamp collecting, Hiking, Gardening, Patchwork Quilting and Embroidery. Tim our friendly cat offers a special welcome. Flexible full home cooked breakfast. Directions: Please telephone or visit our web-page.

Halswell - Christchurch   *6km SE of Christchurch Central*
Self-contained B&B

Overton
Judi & Joe Brizzell
241 Kennedys Bush Road, Halswell, Christchurch 3
Tel: (03) 322 8326 Fax: (03) 322 8350
Mob: 025 623 0831   brizzell.accom@xtra.co.nz
www.canterburypages.co.nz/overton
Double $80-$95 Single $40-$85 (Full Breakfast)
Child $10-$15 Dinner from $20 Credit cards accepted
1 Queen 2 Single (2 bdrm) 1 Private 1 Family share

Tranquil, cosy and convenient. Only 20 minutes from the city and near the Akaroa highway, our 1/2 acre garden on the Port Hills overlooks the rural setting of the Canterbury Plains to the Southern Alps. For a warm, hosted experience our self-contained "Garden Lodge" canbe yours exclusively. The unit is fully equipped wit two bedrooms, (one with queen-sized bed, and one twin), toilet, shower, TV and cooking facilities, or, in our home, a room with twin beds. Our hobbies include gardening, fishing, walking, debating, and Cass, our Golden Retriever.

Tai Tapu - Christchurch   *Self-contained Farmstay   20km SE of Christchurch*

Ballymoney Farmstay & Garden
Merrilies & Peter Rebbeck
Wardstay Road, RD 2, Christchurch
Tel: (03) 329 6706 Fax: (03) 329 6709
Mob: 025 604 8353   rebbeckpandm@hotmail.com
www.bnb.co.nz/ballymoney.html
Double $100-$150 Single $90-$130
(Special Breakfast) Child neg Dinner $35
Full Farmstay $150 - $250 Credit cards accepted
1 King/Twin 1 Queen 1 Double 1 Single (3 bdrm)
2 Ensuite 1 Private

Country Retreat in two acre rambling garden. Character farmhouse with king/twin and double bedrooms. Self contained garden suite with queen and single bed, ensuite bathroom. Numerous extras. Seasonal cuisine featuring our own meat, eggs, fruits, nuts and vegetables. Local fish and wine. Irish/Kiwi hospitality. Masses of animals and birds, many rare breeds. Full farmstay includes all meals, farm tour on four-wheel motorbike, animal feeding and horseriding. Croquet, boules, bicycles on site. Golf and vineyards locally.

Tai Tapu - Christchurch   *Homestay B&B   15km S of Christchurch*

Pear Drop Inn   Erik & Paula Gray
Akaroa Highway 75, Tai Tapu, RD 2, Christchurch
Tel: (03) 329 6778 Fax: (03) 329 6661
Mob: 021 1266 873   peardropinn@clear.net.nz
www.bnb.co.nz/peardropinn.html
Double $90 Single $50 (Special Breakfast)
Child 1/2 price Dinner $25
Credit cards accepted Pet on property
1 King 1 Queen 4 Single (2 bdrm)
1 Ensuite 1 Guests share

Erik and Paula offer warm relaxed Kiwi hospitality. Welcome to our comfortable country home, nestled in 2 1/2 acres of trees, garden/orchard. Superbly located for City and Country activities, 15 mins to Christchurch. Paula's specialty, home cooking with organic fruit and vegetables from our garden. Meal times flexible. Fully appointed rooms provide ultimate comfort. Relax in the spa and informal landscaped garden with gazebo's and large pond. Local wineries, restaurants, walking tracks, golf, all within 5 minutes. Discounts available for longer stays.

Lyttelton   *Homestay B&B Self Contained Studio Apartment   0.5km E of Lyttelton*

Randolph House & The Crows Nest Gabby Corkery
Randolph House, 49 Sumner Road, Lyttelton
Tel: (03) 328 8877 Fax: (03) 328 8833
Mob: 021 279 3971gabby@exi.co.nz
www.exi.co.nz/bnb.htm
Double $100-$125 Single $85-$100
(Continental & Full Breakfast) Child neg
Dinner on request Credit cards accepted
Child at home Pet on property
1 King 1 Double 1 Twin 1 Single (3 bdrm)
1 Ensuite 1 Guests share

Historic Lyttelton, arrival point of the first European settlers. A bustling port town full of action and interest: restaurants, bars, historic buildings and walkways. Only 20 minutes to central Christchurch, but what a contrast! Welcome to Randolph House, built in 1870, lovingly restored and comfortably furnished. Enjoy the fantastic harbour views from our decks, a glass of wine at sunset, walk a short distance to dine in the lively atmosphere of the town. There's bed and then there's the breakfast. Superb!

Cass Bay - Lyttelton   *Homestay B&B semi-s/c   6km SE of Christchurch*

Harbour View Homestay   Susi & Hank Boots
Mariners Cove, Cass Bay, Lyttelton, Christchurch
Tel: (03) 328 7250 Fax: (03) 328 7251
Mob: 027 226 2633   harbourview.homestay@clear.net.nz
www.bnb.co.nz/harbourviewhomestaycassbay.html
Double $95-$110 Single $75 (Full Breakfast)
Dinner by arrangement Semi s/c from $130
Credit cards accepted Pet on property
1 King 1 Twin 1 Single (2 bdrm)
2 Ensuite 1 Family share

Cass Bay, nestled in the beautiful Lyttelton harbour basin with swimming beaches and walking tracks, offers easy access to all city amenities. It is also an ideal base for day-trips to many tourist attractions. Our new home incorporates warmth, luxury and comfort, has a relaxed atmosphere, a lovely garden-setting with a petanque area, sheltered patio, and breath-taking views. Our beds are very comfortable and extra long. Our semi-s/c accommodation offers microwave cooking possibility. Wir sprechen Deutsch, Schweizerdeutsch en spreken Nederlands. 10% discount from 3 days.

Lyttelton *B&B   9km E of Christchurch*

Shonagh O'Hagan's Guest House
Shonagh O'Hagan
Dalcroy House, 16 Godley Quay, Lyttelton
Tel: (03) 328 8577 Mob: (025) 346 351
shonagh.ohagan@xtra.co.nz
www.bnb.co.nz/shonaghohagans.html
Double $110 Single $82.5
(Continental & Full Breakfast) Child $25
Dinner $35 Credit cards accepted
1 King/Twin 2 Queen 1 Double (4 bdrm)
1 Guests share 2 Family share

Dalcory House built 1859, has been a Boarding School, private residents, rental property, and hostel for naval rating's in WW2. Shonagh your hostess is a Cook, Nurse, Educator, Health manager and mother. Have a comfortable nights sleep in pleasant surroundings with a clear view of Lyttelton Port and Harbour, 5 minutes walk from the centre of Lyttelton. Shonagh and her young son will ensure your stay is comfortable and memorable.

Church Bay - Lyttelton *Homestay   25km SE of Christchurch*

'The Priory'
Anne Prior
177 Marine Drive, Main Road, Church Bay, RD1, Lyttelton
Tel: (03) 329 4441 Mob: 025 644 9641
thepriory@xtra.co.nz
www.bnb.co.nz/thepriory.html
Double $70 Single $50 (Continental & Full Breakfast)
Child $8 Dinner $20 by arrangement Pet on property
1 Queen 1 Double 2 Single (1 bdrm)
1 Family share

"The Priory" at Church Bay is just 30 minutes from Christchurch city, located on the southern edge of Lyttelton Harbour. Upstairs studio sleeps six, with great elevated views overlooking Church Bay and the harbour. Pretty cottage garden. Shared bathroom, cooked & continental breakfast available, evening meals on request (complimentary "The Priory" homemade fruit wines). Be playing golf in just 5 minutes, with good swimming just a short walk away and other activities close by. Close boat ramp makes it ideal for sailing holidays. (Shy cat).

Governors Bay *B&B   13km SE of Christchurch*

Orchard House
Judy & Neil Wilkinson
Main Road, Governors Bay, RD 1,
Lyttelton, Christchurch
Tel: (03) 329 9622 n.j.wilkinson@xtra.co.nz
www.bnb.co.nz/orchardhouse.html
Double $100 Single $75 (Continental Breakfast)
Pet on property
1 Double (1 bdrm)
1 Ensuite

Governor's Bay is one of the many scenic bays surrounding Lyttelton Harbour. Our hillside home has beautiful views over the bay. The area is noted for its gardens and walking tracks, and is ideally situated for exploring Banks Peninsula. Our guest wing has a large sunny bedroom with ensuite. French doors open to a private balcony. The room has a TV and tea/coffee making facilities. A wide range of cuisine is offered by local restaurants. We have a cat called Suzy. Directions: Please phone.

Governors Bay *B&B 13 SE of Christchurch*

Governors Bay Bed & Breakfast
Karen & Kevin McGrath
14 Hays Rise, Governors Bay, Lyttelton RD1
Tel: (03) 329 9930 Mob: 021 622 657
karenkev@xtra.co.nz
www.bnb.co.nz/governorsbaybb.html

Double $100 Single $90 (Continental Breakfast)
Credit cards accepted Pet on property Pets welcome
1 Queen 1 Double (2 bdrm) 1 Private

Unique timber home designed to accommodate our B&B private guest wing. Separate entrance with sunny morning deck. Enjoy brekky in your room or on the deck. Queen room with picture window has panoramic views of Lyttelton Harbour. TV, fridge, and CD player. Rural walking tracks start at back of our 3 acre property. 20 min drive to Christchurch, 15 minutes to Lyttelton, only 2 mins to local hotel and cafe/wine bar. Karen operates Earth Healer Aromatherapy and offers complimentary aromatherapy baths. Full treatments by appointment. We and our lab X "Bella-Brae" look forward to welcoming you soon.

Governors Bay - Christchurch *Homestay B&B 13km S of Christchurch*

Heaven Can Wait
Glen and Katharin Walker
15 The Terrace, Governors Bay,
Tel: (03) 329 9411 Fax: (03) 329 9216
Mob: 025 201 7174
gee.walker@xtra.co.nz
www.bnb.co.nz/heavencanwait.html

Double $95-$120 Single $75 (Continental & Full Breakfast)
Credit cards accepted
3 Queen (3 bdrm) 1 Ensuite 1 Private 1 Guests share
Pets in residence

Heaven Can Wait. Warm welcoming atmosphere, rooms with a view. Breakfast in private tranquil garden. Blob out, take it all in, explore the area, Banks Peninsula, Akaroa on back doorstep. Play golf with or without passionate hosts, go hiking, shop till you drop with city only 15 minutes away, dine at the local cafe or pub. Bubbly and chocolates in the outdoor bath even. It's all there to be shared with Katharin, Glen and 2 friendly Jack Russell terriers, you won't be disappointed.

Teddington - Lyttelton Harbour *20km S of Christchurch*
Self-contained & Farmstay

Bergli Hill Farmstay Rowena & Max Dorfliger
265 Charteris Bay Road, Teddington,, R.D.1 Lyttelton
Tel: (03) 329 9118 Fax: (03) 329 9118
Mob: 025 829 410 bergli@ihug.co.nz
www.bnb.co.nz/berglihillfarmstay.html

Double $90 Single $65 (Full Breakfast)
Dinner $20 by arrangement S/C $50
Credit cards accepted Pet on property Children welcome
2 Queen 1 Double 3 Single (3 bdrm) 2 Ensuite 1 Family share

Lyttelton Harbour and the Port Hills create a dynamic panorama you can enjoy from our custom-built log chalet.Rowena speaks Japanese (but is a Kiwi)and Max speaks German. We are both self-employed (woodworker and shadow puppeteer) and enjoy sharing a sail on Max's yacht. Akaroa, Banks Peninsula and Christchurch are all close by. Our pet cat and sheep welcome guests enthusiastically. Whether relaxing on the veranda at Max's hand-crafted table or sipping wine in the spa bath, we are sure you will make good memories.

Church Bay - Diamond Harbour
Self-contained B&B *35km S of Christchurch*

Kai-o-ruru Bed & Breakfast
Robin & Philip Manger
32 James Drive, Church Bay,
RD 1, Lyttelton

Tel: (03) 329 4788 Fax: (03) 329 4788
manger@xtra.co.nz
www.bnb.co.nz/kaiorurubedbreakfast.html

Double $90 Single $50 (Full Breakfast)
Dinner $25 Pet on property
2 Single (1 bdrm)
1 Ensuite

Explore Banks Peninsula from Church Bay. Our cosy, ensuite unit overlooks Quail Island and our coastal garden. The room has a tea/coffee tray, home-made biscuits, books, TV. We are a non-smoking household with an unobtrusive cat. Philip and I are travelled, retired teachers who enjoy welcoming travellers to our wonderful area. Languages: German, Dutch (some Italian, Spanish).

If you would like dinner
most hosts require 24 hours' notice.

Akaroa - Barrys Bay *Farmstay Homestay B&B* *12km before Akaroa*

Rosslyn Estate
Ross, Lynette, Kirsty (10) & Matt (8) Curry
Christchurch-Akaroa Main Road (SH75), Rapid #5797, Barrys Bay, Akaroa Harbour
Tel: (03) 304 5804 Fax: (03) 304 5804
Rosslyn@xtra.co.nz   www.bnb.co.nz/rosslynestate.html

Double $110-$120 Single $90 (Full Breakfast) Child negotiable Dinner $25pp
Laundry no charge Credit cards accepted Children at home Pet on property
2 Queen (2 bdrm) 2 Ensuite

Experience the tranquility of farm life while conveniently situated on the main road between Christchurch and Akaroa, at the French Farm/Wainui intersection allowing you to explore this intriguing volcanic peninsula with ease. Our home is set amid rolling hills 400m along a meandering driveway, overlooking the Akaroa Harbour.

Rosslyn is a large historic homestead built in the 1860s. It has been our family home and life style for four generations. The homestead and farm buildings are rich in history including the original building that milled timber for the Christchurch Cathedral.

We take pride in offering quality home-grown and prepared produce from vegetables and fruit to preserves and baking. It is a pleasure for us to share our evening meal, served in the farm style kitchen at the family table. Breakfast ranges from fresh fruit to full cooked with smoke cured bacon and homemade bread toasted on the embers.

Two large ground floor rooms have been refurbished to accommodate you in comfort. Each room has ensuite bathroom, firm queen bed, central heating, screened windows and antiques of the period. A spa room, laundry, email and ph/fax are also available.

French doors leading to expansive verandahs and informal gardens make the most of serene harbour views.

Our 160 cow-working dairy farm also runs deer and much loved pets, most of whom live outside. The streams are lined with bush attracting an abundance of native birds.

We look forward to welcoming you with a fresh pot of tea, coffee or cool drink served with home baking, hearing of your adventures, and help plan new ones for the remainder of your holiday.

Directions: Main Christchurch-Akaroa road (SH75), 'Rosslyn Estate' sign behind red picket fence (left travelling to Akaroa) at French Farm/Wainui turn off.

Okains Bay - Banks Peninsula   *Farmstay   20km N of Akaroa*

Kawatea
Judy & Kerry Thacker
Okains Bay, Banks Peninsula
Tel: (03) 304 8621 Fax: (03) 304 8621
kawatea@xtra.co.nz   www.nzfarmstay.co.nz/thacker.htm

Double $90-$125 Single $65-$90 (Full Breakfast) Child B/A Dinner $25 - $30 Credit cards accepted
3 Queen 2 Single (3 bdrm)   1 Ensuite 1 Private 1 Guests share

Experience the grace and charm of yesteryear, while enjoying the fine food and wine of NZ today. Revel in the peace of country life, but still be close to sights and activities. Escape to 'Kawatea', an historic Edwardian homestead set in spacious gardens, and surrounded by land farmed by our Irish ancestors since the 1850s. Built in 1900 from native timbers, it features stained glass windows and handcrafted furniture, and has been carefully renovated to add light and space without losing its old world charm.

Linger over your choice of breakfast in the sunny conservatory. Join us for summer barbeques on the expansive verandahs, savouring seafood from the Bay, and creative country fare from our garden and farm. Gather around the dining table by the fire on cooler nights, sharing thoughts and experiences with our family and fellow travellers.

Participate in farm activities such as moving stock, feeding pet sheep, lambing, calving or shearing. Wander our 1400-acre hillside farm, climbing to enjoy a breath-taking panoramic view of Banks Peninsula. Relax or swim at Okains Bay, observe the birdlife on the estuary, or walk along the scenic coastline to secluded beaches and a seal colony with excellent photographic opportunities. Learn about Maori Culture and the life of early New Zealand settlers at the acclaimed Okains Bay Museum.

Explore Akaroa, with its strong French influence, visit art galleries and craft shops. Play golf, go horse riding, sample local wines and watch traditional cheeses being made. Take a harbour cruise or swim with the rare Hector's dolphin.

We have been providing farmstays since 1988, and pride ourselves on thoughtful personal service. Romantic weekends and special occasion dinners are also catered for. We hope you come as a visitor but leave as a friend.

Directions: Take Highway 75 from Christchurch through Duvauchelle. Turn left at signpost marked Okains Bay. Drive to the top of the Bay - we are 6km downhill on the right.

Akaroa *B&B 80km SE of Christchurch*

La Belle Villa

La Belle Villa
Deborah & Gordon Akaroa, 113 Rue Jolie, Akaroa

Tel: (03) 304 7084
Fax: (03) 304 7084   Mob: 025 227 2084
www.bnb.co.nz/labellevilla.html

Double $95-$110 Single $70 Winter rates apply
1 King 2 Queen 1 Twin (4 bdrm)
1 Ensuite 2 Private 1 Guests share

A warm welcome awaits you. Relax in the comfort of a bygone era, and appreciate the antiques in our picturesque historic villa. Built in the 1870's for a prominent businessman it became one of the 1st doctor's surgeries in Akaroa and is now established on approx. 1/2 acre of beautiful, mature grounds, surrounded by rolling hills and lush scenery.

Enjoy the indoor/outdoor living, large private swimming pool and gently trickling stream. We offer warm, spacious bedrooms, large guest lounge, fabulous fires in winter, breakfast 'Al Fresco' in the summer if you choose with the birds and trees. We offer to make your stay with us special.

It will be a pleasure to book you on to any cruises, fishing trips, swim with the dolphins, horse treks etc that you may require. Being centrally situated, restaurants, cafes, wine bars and the beach are all walking distance. So too, you will find, are the majority of galleries, shops and excursions available in New Zealand's most charming, quaint and quintessential French township.

Separate guest lounge

Outdoor swimming pool

Akaroa   *Farmstay   5km N of Akaroa*

Hanne & Paul LeLievre
Box 4, Akaroa, Banks Peninsula
Tel: (03) 304 7255 Fax: (03) 304 7255
Mob: 025 942 070
Double.L@Xtra.co.nz
www.bnb.co.nz/lelievre.html
Double $80 Single $45
(Full Breakfast) Dinner $20
1 Double 1 Single (1 bdrm)
1 Ensuite

Our home is situated 1.5km up the Takamatua valley and only 5km from Akaroa. We farm sheep, cattle and deer, and usually have a menagerie of dogs, cats and orphaned pets around. Hanne is Danish and speaks that language fluently. We have both worked in Australia for 10 years. We offer spacious accommodation in a sheltered position and invite you to enjoy some good old fashioned country hospitality. A trip to the "Akaroa Seal Colony Safari" should be considered a must.

Akaroa Harbour   *Farmstay   20km E of Akaroa*

Bossu
Rana & Garry Simes
Wainui, Akaroa, RD 2, Banks Peninsula
Tel: (03) 304 8421 Fax: (03) 304 8421
bossu@xtra.co.nz
www.bnb.co.nz/bossu.html
Double $130 Single $80 (Full Breakfast)
Dinner $25 Pet on property
1 Queen 3 Single (3 bdrm)
1 Private 1 Guests share

"Bossu" farm of 100 acres is on 2 kms of the harbour foreshore offering panoramic views of Akaroa and the surrounding countryside. Our farm tours are a specialty with sheep, cattle, forestry and a small vineyard. We also have a Jack Russell dog. We offer fishing, sightings of dolphin, penguin and nesting sea birds. A well used grass tennis court is a feature of our extensive garden. We enjoy golf, bridge, tennis and travel. Directions: first property on seaward side after Wainui.

Akaroa   *B&B Self-contained Cottage   Akaroa Central*

Blythcliffe
Rosealie & Jan Shuttleworth
37 Rue Balguerie, Akaroa 8161
Tel: (03) 304 7003 Fax: (03) 304 7003
Tollfree: 0800 393 877
blythcliffe@xtra.co.nz
www.blythcliffe.co.nz
Double $165 Single $140 S/C Cottage $180
3 Queen 1 Single (4 bdrm)
1 Ensuite 2 Private

Centrally located quiet, restful, historic home with category one listing. Also self-contained cottage at bottom of garden. Croquet lawn - petanque - full sized billiard table. 1 hectare garden and native bush, bordered by rocky stream. Email facilities. Laundry. Guest lounge with TV and tea/coffee making facilities. Continental/full breakfast, fresh fruit and home baking, crisp cotton damask linen. Fresh flowers. 1 family cat. Hair dryers, heated towel rails, toiletries. 5th generation local knowledge and history. B&B closed June/July. Cottage available, winter rates 1 April to 31 October @ $150 a night.

Akaroa - Paua Bay   *Farmstay*   *12km E of Akaroa*

Paua Bay Farmstay
Murray & Sue Johns
Postal - c/o 113 Beach Road,
Akaroa, Banks Peninsula
Tel: (03) 304 8511 Fax: (03) 304 8511
Mob: 021 133 8194   pauabay@inet.net.nz
www.pauabay.com

Double $90 Single $60 (Full Breakfast) Child neg
Dinner $25 Pet on property Children welcome
1 Queen 1 Twin (2 bdrm)
1 Guests share

Set in a private bay, our 900 acre sheep, deer and cattle farm is surrounded by coast-line, native bush and streams. You are spoilt for choice - Walk to the beach, enjoy seals and extensive bird life, join in seasonal farming activities or horse-riding. Swim in the pool, laze in the hammock and don't miss the secluded moonlit bath under the stars overlooking the pacific ... In the evening share a meal of fresh farm produce with relaxed conversation gathered around the large kitchen table.

Akaroa   *Self-contained*   *1km N of Akaroa*

Loch Hill Country Cottages Motel
Donna & David Kingan
PO Box 21, Main Highway, Akaroa
Tel: (03) 304 7195 Fax: (03) 304 7672
Tollfree: 0800 456 244   lochhill@xtra.co.nz
www.lochill.co.nz

Double $100-$150 Single $90 Child $12
(Continental Breakfast $10pp) Credit cards accepted
2 King/Twin 2 King 8 Queen 4 Single (11 bdrm)
5 Ensuite 3 Private

'Loch-Hill' with magnificent sea-views overlooking Akaroa, and cluster of fully self-contained luxurious cottages, nestled in surrounding bush, park and garden setting, offers privacy and tranquillity. Some large cottages have air-conditioning. Try our romantic honeymoon cottages with cozy log-fires and double spa-baths. Enjoy wonderful views form your balcony. Experience the hospitality of 'Loch-Hill' "Caid Mile Failte" (One hundred thousand welcomes). Explore or relax in these idyllic, secluded surroundings. Perfect for your holiday retreat, smaller business conference, or wedding group. Special rates available.

Akaroa Harbour   *Country B&B*   *7km N of Akaroa*

Cabbage Tree Corner
Prue Billings & Ben Kennard
RD 1, Akaroa
Tel: (03) 304 5155 Mob: 021 655 862
prueb@xtra.co.nz
www.breakfast.co.nz

Double $90-$100 Single $70 (Full Breakfast)
Dinner $25 Credit cards accepted
1 Queen 2 Single (2 bdrm)
2 Ensuite

Superbly sited in a commanding position above the north end of Akaroa harbour, this newly-restored 1920's farmhouse offers peace, comfort and views to die for. On the main highway it's close to all the Peninsula's attractions. Go walking, cycling or boating, see the dolphins, or enjoy the fine restaurants. Then relax in the peaceful atmosphere of our smoke free home. Expect a generous breakfast of fine fresh foods. Please phone for directions. The Akaroa/Christchurch bus stops at our gate.

Akaroa   *B&B   80km SE of Christchurch*

The Maples
Peter & Lesley Keppel
158 Rue Jolie, Akaroa
Tel: (03) 304 8767 Fax: (03) 304 8767
maplesakaroa@xtra.co.nz
www.themaplesakaroa.co.nz
Double $100-$110 Single $75-$85 (Full Breakfast)
Credit cards accepted
3 Queen 1 Single (3 bdrm)
3 Ensuite

The Maples is a charming historic two storey home built in 1877. It is situated in a delightful garden setting, three mins walk from the cafes and waterfront. We offer two queen bedrooms with ensuites upstairs and a separate garden room with a queen and single bed also ensuited. You can relax in the separate guests lounge were tea and coffee is available. Our delicious continental and cooked breakfasts usually include freshly baked brioche, croissants, and muffins.

Akaroa   *Homestay B&B   80km SE of Christchurch*

Lavaud House
Mary Farrell
83 Rue Lavaud, Akaroa
Tel: (03) 304 7121 Fax: (03) 304 7121
lavaudhouse@xtra.co.nz
www.nzhomestay.co.nz/lavaudhouse.html
Double $120-$155 Single $90-$125
(Continental Breakfast) Credit cards accepted
1 King 2 Queen 1 Twin (4 bdrm)
3 Ensuite 1 Private

'Lavaud House' is a gracious, historic home which overlooks the beach and harbour. Being centrally located, you are only five minutes walking distance from restaurants, galleries and shops. Relax in the comfort of elegant furnishings, listen to beautiful music (Bluthner grand piano), or wander in our peaceful garden with its magnificent harbour views and enchanting native birds. In the evening I invite you to enjoy a complimentary glass of wine with me and, in the morning, a delicious continental breakfast.

Akaroa   *Homestay B&B   80km SE of Christchurch*

Maison de la Mer
Laurice & Alan Bradford
1 Rue Benoit, Akaroa, Banks Peninsula
Tel: (03) 304 8907 Fax: (03) 304 8907
Mob: 025 376 982
maisondelamer@xtra.co.nz
www.maisondelamer.co.nz
Double $120-$170 Single $95 (Full Breakfast)
Credit cards accepted Pet on property
3 Queen 1 Single (3 bdrm)
3 Ensuite

Maisondelamer is a 1910 two-storey villa sited directly opposite the beach. Guests can easily walk to the shops, restaurants, and cafes. Two rooms have harbour views, and one has a double spa bath, and one has a private sitting room. All rooms are elegantly furnished and have television and tea/coffee facilities. Enjoy a complimentary glass of wine with us in our lounge or on the verandah in summer. It is our aim to provide a warm welcome, and we can assure you of an enjoyable stay.

Akaroa   *Farmstay B&B   5km S of Akaroa*

Onuku Heights - Historic Farmstay
Eckhard Keppler & Angelika Balsam, Onuku Heights, Akaroa
Tel: (03) 304 7112 Fax: (03) 304 7116   onuku.heights@paradise.net.nz   www.onuku-heights.co.nz
Double $120-$160 Single $100-$140   (Full Breakfast) Dinner $40 by arrangement Credit cards
accepted   3 King (3 bdrm) 3 Ensuite

Onuku Heights is a charming, carefully restored 1860's Homestead, overlooking the harbour, nestled
in orchard and tranquil gardens, with an abundance of bird life, surrounded by native bush reserves,
streams and waterfalls on a 309 ha working Sheep farm.

Enjoy spacious rooms furnished with antiques and comfortable, firm king size beds, and exquisite en
suite bathrooms. The two rooms in the Homestead have sea view, the sunny cottage room has garden
views. There is a separate guest lounge with an open fire and veranda.

Explore the beautiful scenery on well maintained walking tracks, going up to 700m altitude with breathtaking panoramic views of Akaroa Harbour, the Ocean and the Alps. Our property is part of the Banks
Peninsula Track. Join us in the farm activities, recline in a sunlounger, or just dream the day away
under an apple tree.

In the morning we prepare you a delicious breakfast with freshly baked bread, homemade jam, cereals,
fruits from the orchard; bacon and eggs if you like. In the evening you may choose one of Akaroa's fine
restaurants or we can spoil you with a three course Candlelit Dinner. Then relax on the veranda with a
glass of wine, enjoy the sunset and beautiful birdsong.

Akaroa   *Boutique B&B   80KM SE of Christchurch*

Wilderness House
Jim & Liz Coubrough
42 Rue Grehan, Akaroa,

Tel: (03) 304 7517 Fax: (03) 304 7518
Mob: 021 669 381   info@wildernesshouse.co.nz
www.wildernesshouse.co.nz

Double $150-$175 Single $120-$140 (Full Breakfast)
Dinner by arrangement Credit cards accepted
1 King/Twin 3 Queen (4 bdrm)
3 Ensuite 1 Private

Wilderness House is a beautiful historic home set in a large traditional garden containing protected trees, old roses and a private vineyard. Charming bedrooms, with their own character, feature fine linen, fresh flowers, tea/coffee and home baking. Elegant lounge opens to verandah and garden. Delicious continental and cooked breakfasts. We take particular care to make you feel comfortable, relaxed and welcome in our home. Join us for a glass of wine in the evening. Short stroll to harbour, restaurants and shops. Resident cats, Beethoven and Harry.

Akaroa   *B&B   85km E of Christchurch*

Aka-View Bed & Breakfast
Rosanne & Kelvin Downs
5 Langlois Lane, Akaroa,

Tel: (03) 304 8008 Fax: (03) 304 8008
Mob: 025 206 6591   aka-view@xtra.co.nz
www.aka-view.com

Double $150 Single $115 (Full Breakfast)
Credit cards accepted Pet on property
2 Queen 1 Twin (3 bdrm)
2 Private

Opened Nov.2001, after two years planning, Aka-View is a purpose built Country B&B.   The upper level features two queen and one twin rooms, private guest study, tea and coffee bar, all with unprecedented harbour views.   In addition guests have use of ground floor lounge, with cosy gas fire, stylish, but comfortable furnishings.   Gourmet breakfast is served either in the large kitchen, formal dining room, or alfresco, weather permitting. Fine teas, superb coffee, tasty treats are available in the guests study. Port and chocolates at bedtime. Not suitable for children, neither do we have facilities for pets.

Akaroa   *B&B   70km SE of Christchurch*

Bantry Lodge
Dolina & David Barker
French Farm, RD2, Akaroa

Tel: (03) 304 5161 Fax: (03) 304 5162
Mob: 025 284 8260
barkerd@ihug.co.nz
www.bnb.co.nz/bantrylodge.html

Double $110-$120 Single $80-$90 (Full Breakfast)
Dinner $40, by arrangement Credit cards accepted
1 Queen 1 Double (2 bdrm)
1 Guests share

Bantry Lodge occupies a prominent site in French Farm with views of the Akaroa hills and harbour. The 1995 guest wing, added to our 1880's home, has a spacious sitting room, two bedrooms, bathroom and servery. A full breakfast is served in the kitchen, dining room, or on the verandah overlooking the harbour. We have one shy cat, one dog. our home is non-smoking. Surrounded by developing gardens amongst established trees, our home is an idea place for guests to relax.

Castle Hill - Highcountry Canterbury
Homestay B&B   33km W of Springfield

The Burn Alpine B&B
Bob Edge & Phil Stephenson
11 Torlesse Place, Castle Hill Village, Christchurch
Tel: (03) 318 7559 Fax: (03) 318 7558
theburn@xtra.co.nz   www.theburn.co.nz

Double $120 Single $60 (Continental Breakfast)
Child 1/2 price Dinner $25 Dinner B&B $85
Credit cards accepted Children welcome
3 Double 2 Single (4 bdrm)
2 Guests share

One hour west of Christchurch. A carefree atmosphere prevails at "The Burn". Nestled in the heart of the Southern Alps, it's arguably New Zealand's highest B&B. We designed and built our alpine lodge to maximise mountain vistas. Centered in the mystic Castlehill basin, surrounded by native forest, this is a fantastic place to return after a days activity or just kick back and relax on the sunny deck. A host of outdoor sports include ski/snowboarding, hiking, mountain biking, and flyfishing. Professional flyfishing guiding available in house.

Glenroy - Darfield
Farmstay B&B   19km W of Darfield

Kerrilea
Robyn Prouse & Kerry Beveridge
Beckwith Rd, RD2 Coalgate, Canterbury
Tel: (03) 318 6569 Fax: (03) 318 6569
Mob: 021 153 727 info@kerrilea.com
www.kerrilea.com

Double $95 Single $65 (Full Breakfast) Child $40
Dinner $30 Pet on property Children welcome
2 Super King 1 Queen 2 Twin 4 Single (6 bdrm)
1 Ensuite 1 Family share

Our historical home is located in the Canterbury Foothills. 20 minutes North of Mt Hutt, 45 minutes to Christchurch Airport. Join in farm activities or enjoy golf, fishing or skiing. We farm the rare and distinctive Belted Galloway cattle, some dairy goats, sheep, and poultry. Horse wagon rides with Hank and Xena are optional and extra. Most foods are home grown, home cooked to ensure they are always fresh. Lots of tame animals to feed. Children and babies welcome. Email facilities available. Robyn was qualified Ambulance Officer.

Darfield *Farmstay   35km W of Christchurch*

Meychelle Manor
Brian & Michelle Walker
State Highway 73, Main West Coast Road, Kirwee/ Darfield
Tel: (03) 318 1144 Fax: (03) 318 1965 Tollfree: 0800 181 144
meychelle.m@inet.net.nz www.farmstaynewzealand.com
Double $170 Single $100 (Full Breakfast)
Child neg. Dinner neg. Credit cards accepted Child at home Children welcome
3 King/Twin (3 bdrm) 2 Ensuite 1 Private

Brian and Michelle warmly invite you to relax or have fun in their friendly, luxury family deer farm. Built in 1999, 25 minutes from Christchurch International Airport (on SH 73).

Shops/Restaurants • Ski-fields • Golf Courses • Horse riding: beginners and advanced
Beautiful Walkways • TransAlpine Scenic Train connection • Jetboat Rides • Wineries close by
We will be happy to assit you arranging these activities.

Meychelle Manor offers something special for guests from holidaymakers, honeymooners, business couples to children. We have a wide variety of farmyard and exotic animals. Lots of fun activities:

Farm Tour • Childrens Playarea • Putt on Golf Green • Petanque
Help Brian feed deer and farmyard animals • Walk to ostriches • Scatter wheat for chickens
Feed ducks and fish in lake • Swim in indoor heated pool

Guest lounge has a very comfortable leather lounge suite (very relaxing!), large screen TV, DVD home surround-sound theatre with large selection of movies and telescope. Also brochure and travel books to assist your travel plans. Three private, beautiful, warm rooms with comfortable super King/Twin beds, clock radios, blow dryers with 2 ensuites and private bathroom, private access, lake and mountain views from balconies with cafe style seating.

Complimentary bottle of wine • Tea of Coffee • Iced Lemon Water and Chocolates at night • Enjoy a delicious breakfast (at a time convenient with you) of • Brian's home-made bread 'yum' • Jams • Cereals • Yoghurt • Venison Sausages • Bacon
• Tomatoes • Eggs • Hash Browns • Fruit Juice • Variety of Teas • Ground Coffee • Evening meal: courtesy drive to and from lovely local restaurants • Modern Laundry facilities • Email • Internet access • Faxing.

We have 2 lovely, young girls, Chevonn and Chloe who adore meeting people but whom are also respectful of others. We ask guests not to smoke. Pets are not inside.

From our Visitors Book - "You made us feel part of your family", "Beautiful home".

Please phone for reservation/directions. Happy travelling. We look forward to meeting you.

Mt Hutt - Methven   *Farmstay*   *8km N of Methven*

Tyrone Deer Farm
Pam & Roger Callaghan
Mt Hutt Station Road, RD 12, Rakaia, Methven/Rakaia Gorge Alternative Route
Tel: (03) 302 8096 Fax: (03) 302 8099
tyronedeerfarm@xtra.co.nz   www.bnb.co.nz/tyronedeerfarm.html

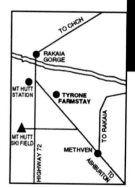

Double $120 Single $80 (Full Breakfast) Dinner $35pp by arrangement
self-contained $120 double   1 Queen 1 Double 1 Twin (3 bdrm) 2 Ensuite 1 Private

Welcome to TYRONE DEER FARM, centrally situated in the Mount Hutt, Rakaia Gorge, Methven area in the middle of the South Island, 5km from the Inland Tourist Route (Highway 72) and one hour from Christchurch International Airport, making TYRONE an ideal stopover heading south to Queenstown.

Our home is positioned with mountain views (Mt Hutt) and deer grazing a few metres away, and has ensuite bedrooms with electric blankets, wool underlays and duvets on the beds, also heater and hair dryers. The lounge has open fire, TV, tea & coffee making facilities and guest fridge.

Come meet Guz, our pet deer, her daughter $$s, 10.30 our cat. Laze in the garden, swim in the pool, relax. Evening meal served with New Zealand wine by arrangement.

We are able to arrange professional guides for fishing (salmon and trout) and for hunting; especially Tahr, Red Deer, and Chamois. Skiing at Mt Hutt, hot-air ballooning, jet-boating, golf on nearby 18 hole courses. Numerous walks - scenic, bush, garden alpine.

Directions: please refer to map.

In the Mt. Hutt village of Methven we have two fully equipped self contained units. Self catering $120 per night for two; extra person $40 per night or $20 extra child.

Mt Hutt - Methven *Farmstay B&B*   *4km NW of Methven Mt Hutt-Village*

Green Gables Deer Farm
Colleen & Roger Mehrtens
185 Waimarama Rd, Methven Mt Hutt-Village, Methven

Tel: (03) 302 8308 Fax: (03) 302 8309
Mob: 025 207 6925   Tollfree: 0800 466 093
greengables@xtra.co.nz
www.nzfarmstay.com

Double $130-$155 Single $80-$110 (Full Breakfast) Child $55 Dinner $40pp
Credit cards accepted Children welcome
2 King 2 Twin (3 bdrm)
2 Ensuite 1 Private

A warm welcome awaits you at Green Gables Farmstay just minutes from the picturesque village of Methven-Mt Hutt offering an impressive range of both summer and winter activities.

This area of freshness adventure and enjoyment situated 1 hour from the garden city of Christchurch and International Airport, Mt Cook 3hrs & Queenstown 5 hrs sth approx.   Relax in our peaceful farmhouse and tastefully appointed guest wing complete with ensuites, super-king beds, wool under-lays, electric blankets, heaters, hair dryers & clock radios.   French doors opening from each bedroom provides private access.

Green Gables presents magnificent views of Mt Hutt and surrounding mountains.

Hand feed pet deer Lucy and friends in a tranquil garden setting with white doves, Royal Danish White Deer and our Labrador.

Dine on delicious country cuisine and wine or at nearby restaurants. Our comfortable sitting room has an open fire and T.V.   A scrumptious home cooked Breakfast is served in our dining room.

We delight in sharing our knowledge of this fascinating area its history and all seasons activities.

Golf Terrace Downs High Country Resort •   Carts & Club Hire • Golf Methven - club hire 18 holes
Hot air Ballooning • Trout & Salmon Fishing - Lakes & Rivers • Skiing Mt Hutt - transport from gate
Scenic bush walks & Mt Somers sub alpine, walkway nearby • Horse riding/trekking
Riverland hovercraft scenic trips • Jet boating on the Rakaia River • Restaurants nearby
Members NZAFHH and HostLink N.Z.

Directions:- Green Gables is situated on S/H 77, 4kms NW of Methven- Mt Hutt Village. From Inland 72 Scenic-Route Turn onto S/H 77 - travel 5kms towards Methven-Mt Hutt Village.

Mt Hutt - Methven   *Farmstay   6km E of Methven*

Pagey's Farmstay
Shirley & Gene Pagey
Chertsey Road, Methven, Rakaia
Tel: (03) 302 1713 Fax: (03) 302 1714
www.bnb.co.nz/pageysfarmstay.html
Double $80 Single $50 (Full Breakfast)
Child 1/2 price under 12yrs Dinner $25pp
1 King 1 Queen 4 Single (3 bdrm)
1 Guests share

Come as guests but leave as friends who have enjoyed our beautiful 4500 sq ft home - set amidst aged trees, 1.5 acres of rose garden and lawns, wonderful homegrown cuisine, pre dinner drinks - mouth watering NZ wine, "hands on" tour of our 400 acre Romney Sheep stud farm, clean air-peace-tranqility-mountain views. Local activities include wonderful bush walks, ballooning, Methven's magnificent 18 hole golf course, skiing on Mt Hutt. We will arrange transport if required. YOU MAY NEVER WANT TO LEAVE. Directions: From Methven town centre, turn at the Medical Centre down Methven Chertsey Road, 6km on left.

Lake Coleridge - Canterbury High Country

120km W of Christchuch   Farmstay B&B Chalets

Ryton Station   Karen & Mike Meares
Harper Road, Lake Coleridge, Canterbury
Tel: (03) 318 5818 Fax: (03) 318 5819
Tollfree: 0800 92 868   ryton@xtra.co.nz
www.ryton.co.nz
Double $220 Single $120 (Full Breakfast)
Child by arrangement Child at home Pet on property
6 King/Twin 6 Queen 1 Double (13 bdrm)
7 Ensuite 1 Private 1 Guests share

Adventure and Hospitality in the South Island High Country. Ryton Station is a wonderful place for a personal experience of home hospitality on a working high country sheep station. The scenery is magnificent, the air and water crystal clear. 1 1/2 hours from Christchurch, accessible all year. Abundance of fishing, walks, tramping, station activities, jet boating, 4x4 trips, skiing, peace and quiet. Variety of accommodation for families, groups, individuals. Provide own transport, no pets. Ensuite chalets price includes dinner. Lodge: self catering or meals in homestead, price on application

Mt Hutt   *B&B   12km W of Methven*

The Homestead Mt Hutt Station
Brian & Karen Schultze
Junction of Inland Scenic Route 72 & Mt Hutt Station Road, No. 12 RD, Rakaia
Tel: (03) 302 8130 Fax: (03) 302 8102   Tollfree: 0800 754 684
your-hosts@the-homestead.co.nz
www.the-homestead.co.nz
Double $125 Single $90 (Full Breakfast)
Child $30 Dinner a la carte Credit cards accepted
6 Double 6 Twin (9 bdrm) 9 Private

The Homestead is beautifully situated on a privately owned 8,000 acre deer farm beneath Mt Hutt. Only one hours drive southwest of Christchurch or 12km west of Methven village.

We invite you to enjoy abundent natural beauty - and indulge yourself in the genuine, relaxed style of South Island hospitality. For those with the total holiday in mind ... From the subdued to the adventurous ... We can cater to your every need.

The Homestead offers quiet accommodation in serviced units with ensuite, fully licensed restaurant, spa pool, games room, grass tennis court, open fires throughout Homestead, panoramic views and lake view from restaurant and lounge.

Pets (4 sheep, 1 goat, 1 calf, 1 kunekune pig and 2 cats).

Closest accommodation to Mt Hutt ski field.

Staveley - Mt Hutt   *Farmstay B&B   20km SW of Methven*

Awaiti Farmstay
Jan & Graeme Crozier
Staveley, RD 1, Ashburton
Tel: (03) 303 0853 Fax: (03) 303 0851
graeme.a.c@xtra.co.nz
www.bnb.co.nz/awaitifarmstay.html
Double $130 Single $85 (Full Breakfast)
Child $40 Dinner $35pp Credit cards accepted
Pet on property Children welcome
1 King/Twin 1 King 1 Queen (3 bdrm)
2 Ensuite 1 Family share

Welcome to our cattle and sheep farm nestled in the Foothills of Mt Somers-15 Mins south of Mt Hutt Ski area. Relax in our warm comfortable homestead and large garden in the Staveley Village on Inland 72 Scenic Route - 75 minutes SW of Christchurch Airport, en route to Mt Cook and Queenstown. Enjoy a walk around our farm, hand feed pet sheep and meet "Bill" our large black cat. We delight in passing on our knowledge of the Geology, History and Attractions in our area.

Rakaia   *Homestay B&B Guesthouse   50km S of Christchurch*

St Ita's Guesthouse
Ken & Miriam Cutforth
11 Barrhill/Methven Road,
Rakaia Village, Canterbury
Tel: (03) 302 7546 Fax: (03) 302 7546
Mob: 0274 371 459 stitas@xtra.co.nz
www.stitas.co.nz
Double $100 Single $65 (Full Breakfast)
Child $30 Dinner $25pp Credit cards accepted
Pet on property Children welcome
2 Double 4 Single (3 bdrm) 3 Ensuite

A warm welcome is assured at St Ita's. Built in 1912 this spacious former convent is full of charm, set in an acre of grounds, and located on the western fringe of Rakaia. Nearby: Salmon fishing, horse trekking, golf, tennis, visiting local pubs and crafts. Within 30 minutes: Skiing, bushwalks, jetboating, bird watching, Tranzalpine Express. Evening 3 course meals include local produce and NZ wines, Full breakfasts Share the open fire with our cat and golden retriever.

Ashburton   *Homestay*

Pat & Dave Weir
1 Sudbury Street,
Ashburton Central
Tel: (03) 308 3534
d&pweir@xtra.co.nz
www.bnb.co.nz/weir.html
Double $70 Single $40 (Full Breakfast)
Dinner $20 Credit cards accepted
1 Double 2 Single (2 bdrm)
1 Family share

Our comfortable home is situated in a quiet street with the added pleasure of looking onto a rural scene. We are 10-15 mins walk from town or 3-5 mins to riding for the disabled grounds or river walkway. Guest rooms have comfortable beds with electric blankets. We welcome the opportunity to meet and greet visitors and wish to make your stay a happy one. Your hosts are semi-retired, hobbies general/ varied from meeting people to walking etc. Request visitors no smoking inside home. Laundry facilities available.

Ashburton   *Farmstay B&B*   *8km W of Ashburton*

Carradale Farm
Karen & Jim McIntyre, Ferriman's Rd (Rapid no. 200), RD 8, Ashburton
Tel: (03) 308 6577 Fax: (03) 308 6548 Mob: 025 338 044
carradale@ashburton.co.nz. www.ashburton.co.nz/carradale

Double $90-$100 Single $60 (Continental & Full Breakfast)
Child 1/2 price under 12yrs Dinner $25 by arrange-
ment Caravan powerpoint $25 Credit cards accepted
1 Double 2 Twin (3 bdrm)   1 Ensuite 2 Private

Our homestead which captures the sun in all rooms is
cosy and inviting. It is situated in a sheltered garden
where you can enjoy peace, tranquillity and fresh country air or indulge in a game of tennis. All guest rooms
have comfortable beds, electric blankets, reading lamps
and tea/coffee making facilities. Laundry and ironing
facilities available. Dinner is by arrangement and features traditional New Zealand cuisine. Including home
grown meat and vegetables. Breakfast is served with
delicious home made jams and preserves.

We have a 220 acre irrigated sheep and cattle farm.
You may like to join in farm activities or be taken for a
farm tour; sheep shearing demostration available (in
season).

As we have both travelled extensively in New Zealand,
Australia, United Kingdom, Europe, North America and
Zimbabwe. We would like to offer hospitality to fellow travellers. Our hobbies include meeting people,
travel, reading, photography, gardening, sewing, cake
decorating, rugby, cricket, Jim belongs to the Masonic
Lodge and Karen is involved in Community Affairs.

For the weary traveller a spa pool is available. For
young children we have a cot and high chair. There is
a power point for camper vans.

CARRADALE FARM "WHERE PEOPLE COME AS
STRANGERS AND LEAVE AS FRIENDS"

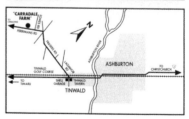

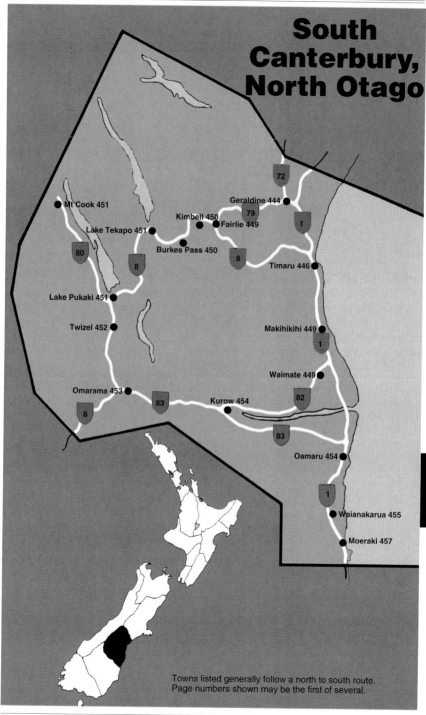

South Canterbury, North Otago

Mt Cook 451

Geraldine 444

Kimbell 450

Fairlie 449

Lake Tekapo 451

Burkes Pass 450

Timaru 446

Lake Pukaki 451

Twizel 452

Makihikihi 449

Waimate 449

Omarama 453

Kurow 454

Oamaru 454

Waianakarua 455

Moeraki 457

Towns listed generally follow a north to south route.
Page numbers shown may be the first of several.

STH CANT.
NTH OTAGO

Geraldine   *Guest Lodge*   *3km N of Geraldine*

The Crossing

Richard & Barbara Sahlie, 124 Woodbury Road, RD 21, Geraldine

Tel: (03) 693 9689 Fax: (03) 693 9789

srelax@xtra.co.nz   www.bnb.co.nz/thecrossing.html

Double $160-$190 Single $140-$170
(Full Breakfast) Dinner by arrangement
Extra Person $30 Visa/Mastercard accepted
3 Queen 1 Single (3 bdrm)   3 Ensuite

Experience New Zealand history on thirty seven tranquil acres near the base of the Four Peaks Range.

The Crossing is a beautifully restored and furnished English style manor house built in 1908. Our spacious lounges have open fires and comfortable seating. A shaded verandah overlooks the lovely gardens, where you can relax and read or enjoy a leisurely game of croquet or petanque.

Enjoy dinner and your choice of beverages in our fully licensed restaurant. Dinners by prior arrangement.

The Crossing is your perfect base for exploring the central South Island. Local attractions include fishing for salmon and trout, white water rafting, nature treks in Peel Forest, and ski fields are nearby. Golfers, spend a week and play fourteen uncrowded courses each within one hours drive. All have low green fees and welcome visitors.

We are located on the main route between Christchurch and Queenstown or Mount Cook. Directions: Signposted on SH 72/79 approx 3 km north of Geraldine, turn into Woodbury Road, then 1 km on right hand side. Children over 12 welcome. We are members of the Heritage and Character Inns Of NZ.

Geraldine *Farmstay   22km SW of Geraldine*

Camberdown
Susan & Colin Sinclair
2013 Geraldine/Fairlie Highway,
Beautiful Valley, RD 21, Geraldine
Tel: (03) 697 4849 Fax: (03) 697 4849
www.bnb.co.nz/camberdown.html
Double $110 Single $80 (Full Breakfast)
Dinner $25pp Credit cards accepted Pet on property
1 Queen 2 Single (2 bdrm)
2 Guests share

"Camberdown" is on Highway 79 between Geraldine and Fairlie, two hours from Christchurch. Our 1,000 acre sheep and cattle farm has mountain views with fishing and skiing nearby. Bird life abounds in areas of native bush. Relax on our sunny verandah or join in the daily activities of farm life. Susan enjoys patchwork and needlework. Colin is a member of Lions. Guests are welcome to share our home overnight or for longer stays to enjoy the surrounding attractions. Full board can be provided.

Geraldine *B&B   137km S of Christchurch*

Lilymay
Lois & Les Gillum
29 Cox Street, Geraldine,
Tel: (03) 693 8838 Mob: 025 228 2896
elgillum@chc.quik.co.nz
www.bnb.co.nz/lilymay.html
Double $75-$90 Single $55-$60 (Full Breakfast)
Child $15 - 20 Dinner n/a Credit cards accepted
2 Queen 1 Double 3 Twin 3 Single (3 bdrm)
2 Guests share

A charming character home set in a large garden where Sammy & Little Boy the cats play. A friendly, warm welcome is assurred with tea/coffee and Lois' homebaked cookies. Ample offstreet parking and separate guest entrance. Teas, coffee, etc available at all times in the guestlounge with cosy open fire. The Village,shops,cafes,restaurants, crafts a short stroll away. We are on the main highway to the Southern Lakes and mountains and the ideal stopover from Christchurch.

Geraldine *B&B   0.5km S of Geraldine*

Forest View
John & Joyce Leverno
128 Talbot Street, Geraldine, South Canterbury
Tel: (03) 693 9928 Fax: (03) 693 9928
Mob: 025 623 6384   Tollfree: 0800 572 740
forest.view@xtra.co.nz
www.bnb.co.nz/forestview.html
Double $80-$90 Single $65 (Full Breakfast)
Credit cards accepted Pet on property
1 King 1 Double 1 Twin (3 bdrm)
1 Ensuite 1 Private 1 Guests share

We have a charming two storey, character home set in a cottage garden where our cat "Fergus Roe" loves to hide. You will be warmly welcomed on arrival and a refreshing cup of tea or coffee is available in the guest lounge at all times. We are a short stroll to the cafes and restaurants in the charming village of Geraldine which is the ideal first stop from Christchurch (137km) as you travel towards the Southern Lakes and mountains.

Temuka   *Homestay B&B   20km N of Timaru*

Ashfield B&B
Ann & Martin Bosman
71 Cass Street, Temuka

Tel: (03) 615 6157 Fax: (03) 615 9062
ashfield@paradise.net.nz
www.bnb.co.nz/ashfieldbb.html

Double $90-$110 Single $55-$65 (Special Breakfast)
Child neg Credit cards accepted Pet on property
Children welcome
1 King 2 Queen 1 Double (4 bdrm)
1 Ensuite 1 Guests share

Ashfield is set on 4 acres of woodlands, 10 minutes walk from shops and restaurants. Built in in 1883 Ashfield features marble fireplaces and gilt mirrors, and a full size snooker table. Two of our upstairs bedrooms open up to a balcony with lovely views of the mountains. We enjoy spending the evening with guests by the open fire. In close proximity are skifields. salmon and trout fishing. So join us for a wonderful stay in a lovely setting. Two cats and one outside dog. Guests welcome to use laundry.

Timaru Central   *Homestay*

Margaret & Nevis Jones
16 Selwyn Street,
Timaru

Tel: (03) 688 1400
Fax: (03) 688 1400
www.bnb.co.nz/jonestimaru.html

Double $80-$90 Single $55 (Full Breakfast)
Child 1/2 price Dinner $25 Credit cards accepted
2 Double 2 Single (3 bdrm)
2 Ensuite 1 Guests share

Welcome to our spacious character brick home built in the 1920's and situated in a beautiful garden with a grass tennis court. A secluded property with off street parking and views of the surrounding sea and mountains. Centrally situated, only 5 minutes from the beach and town with an excellent choice of cafes and restaurants. On arrival tea is served on our sunny verandah. Hosts have lived and worked extensively overseas, namely South Africa, U.K and the Middle East, and enjoy music, theatre, tennis and golf. Dinner by arrangement.

Timaru - Seadown   *Homestay Country Homestay   4.8km N of Timaru*

Country Homestay
Margaret and Ross Paterson
491 Seadown Road, Seadown,RD 3, Timaru

Tel: (03) 688 2468 Fax: (03) 688 2468
www.bnb.co.nz/countryhomestay.html

Double $75 Single $50 (Full Breakfast)
Child 1/2 price Dinner $20 Credit cards accepted
1 Double 2 Single (3 bdrm)
1 Guests share

Our Homestay is approximately 10 minutes north of Timaru, situated 4.8 kms on Seadown Road off State Highway 1 at Washdyke - second house on left past Pharlap Statue. We have hosted on our farm for 11 years - now retired and have a country farmlet with some farm animals, with views of farmland and mountains. Day trips to Mt Cook, Hydro Lakes and ski fields, fishing, golf course few minutes away. Electric blankets on all beds - laundry facilities available. Interests are farming, gardening, spinning and overseas travel.

Timaru   *Homestay   Timaru Central*

Bidwill House
Dorothy & Ron White
15 Bidwill Street, Timaru
Tel: (03) 688 5856 Fax: (03) 688 5870
Mob: 025 238 8122
bookin@xtra.co.nz
www.bnb.co.nz/bidwillhouse.html
Double $100 Single $70 (Full Breakfast)
Child 1/2 price Dinner $15 - $25by arrangement
Credit cards accepted
1 King/Twin 2 Single (2 bdrm) 1 Ensuite

Bidwill House offers superior personalised homestay in a classic two storeyed home with a delightful garden in a quiet street in central Timaru - five minutes walk to the town centre, restaurants and Caroline Bay. The guest bedroom has a super-king/twin with a smaller bedroom with two single beds. The two rooms are only available to the one booking. Laundry facilities and a courtesy car are available. We look forward to welcoming guests to our home, and offer our hospitality to those who prefer a homestay.

Timaru   *Homestay B&B   5km N of Pleasant Point*

Ballyagan
Gail & Bill Clarke
State Highway 8 Levels, RD 4, Timaru
Tel: (03) 614 8221 Fax: (03) 614 8221
Mob: 025 653 7663   www.bnb.co.nz/ballyagan.html
Double $75 Single $50 (Full Breakfast)
Child 1/2 price Dinner $20 by arrangement
Credit cards accepted
1 Double 4 Single (3 bdrm)
1 Private 1 Guests share 1 Family share

Welcome to Ballyagan. Our home is among trees and gardens with native birds, small farm walk, pet sheep, cat and dog. Bedrooms have electric blankets and bedside lamps. Restaurants 5 mins to Pleasant Point vintage trains and golf course. We serve Devonshire afternoon tea, herbal-tea and fresh percolated coffee. Samlpe our local wine. Mount Cook ski fields and fishing within reasonable distance. Tea making, laundry facilities available. We enjoy meeting and hosting guests. Directions: SH8 7km from Washdyke. 5km from Pleasant Point. B&B Homestay sign at gate.

Timaru   *Homestay*

Okare Boutique Accommodation
Malcolm Smith
11 Wai-iti Road, Timaru
Tel: (03) 688 0316 Fax: (03) 688 0368
Mob: 025 229 7301   okare@xtra.co.nz
www.bnb.co.nz/okare.html
Double $95-$125 Single $80 (Full Breakfast)
Child $40 Credit cards accepted
1 King 1 Queen 1 Double 4 Single (5 bdrm)
1 Ensuite 1 Private 1 Guests share

STH CANT.
NTH OTAGO

Okare is a substantial Edwardian brick residence built in 1909 and offers discerning travellers and small families visiting the region comfortable accommodation with warm welcoming hospitality. Okare offers substantial sunny living spaces for our guests, upstairs there is a super King/twin and two twin rooms with share bathroom and a Double with twin spa-bath ensuite, downstairs a queen room with private facilities. We are situated only five minutes walk from a selection of restaurants, Boudicca's our own, offers a charge back facility. We have a baby and two huskies for your entertainment.

Timaru   *Farmstay Homestay   3.5km NW of Timaru*

Ranui
Margaret & Kevin Cosgrove
5 Kellands Hill, Timaru
Tel: (03) 686 1288 Fax: (03) 686 1285
Mob: 025 321 458
ranui@timaru.com
www.bnb.co.nz/ranui.html

Double $95-$120 Single $70 (Full Breakfast)
Child 1/2 price Dinner $25 Credit cards accepted
3 Queen 2 Single (4 bdrm)
1 Ensuite 1 Guests share

Our spacious home on 9 acres enjoys the best of both worlds - country living only 3 1/2 kms from the centre of Timaru. Set in 1 1/2 acres of established gardens with a magnificent view of Mt Cook we offer a relaxed atmosphere, heated swimming pool (summer), private spa pool, Sky TV in bedroom, dinner by arrangement. We run coloured sheep, the wool of which Margaret spins and knits. We enjoy golfing, boating and meeting people. Our family are all away. Children welcome. Phone for directions.

Timaru   *Farmstay   26km SW of Timaru*

Craigmore Farmhouse
Raewyn & Kerry Swann
Craigmore Hill Road, 2RD, Timaru
Tel: (03) 612 9822 Fax: (03) 612 9822
Mob: 025 337 718   farmstay@timaru.com
www.craigmore.com

Double $110-$120 Single $70 (Continental Breakfast)
Dinner $30 (BYO wine)   Credit cards accepted
1 King 1 Queen 1 Single (3 bdrm)
2 Private 1 Guests share

Craigmore Farmstay accommodation is within the Manager's Residence. Craigmore Farmhouse is designed to catch the sunshine and amazing views of the countryside. Sheep, deer and cattle are farmed on this limestone property. Farm tours optional. A popular nine hole golf course adjoins Craigmore. You can enjoy tramping to view ancient Rock Art or just relax while en route to summer lake sports or winter skiing. Please phone, fax or email to make a reservation. Raewyn and Kerry look forward to meeting you. Directions and map on website.

Timaru   *Homestay B&B   8km W of Timaru*

Rosebrook Lodge
Alastair & Janice Rowley
336 Gleniti Road, Hadlow, 4RD, Timaru
Tel: (03) 686 2771 Fax: (03) 686 2771
Mob: 025 264 9777   ajrowley@xtra.co.nz
www.bnb.co.nz/rosebrooklodge.html

Double $110 Single $70 (Continental & Full Breakfast)
Child $30 Dinner $25 Credit cards accepted
2 Double 1 Twin 1 Single (4 bdrm)
1 Private 1 Guests share

A warm welcome awaits you at Rosebrook Lodge. Our very comfortable home is nestled amongst 3 acres of mature trees, Rhododendrons, Azaleas and Roses - a mini park. Relax on one of the two patios and view the mountains with complimentary tea and coffee and homemade baking. Enjoy a walk in the surrounding countryside or mountain bikes available for further exploring. Guide available for the more energetic to Mt. Nimrod, a 3 hr walk - a 'mini Milford', just half an hour away. Golf course close by. Evening meals by arrangement.

Makikihi - Waimate   *Farmstay*   *37km S of Timaru*

Alford Farm
June & Ken McAuley
Lower Hook Road, RD 8, Waimate
Tel: (03) 689 5778 Fax: (03) 689 5779
Mob: 025 267 6008
alfordfarmstays@paradise.net.nz
www.bnb.co.nz/alfordfarm.html

Double $75 Single $50 (Continental Breakfast) Dinner $25 Credit cards accepted
1 Double 2 Single (2 bdrm)
1 Family share

Welcome to Alford Farm situated halfway between Dunedin and Christchurch. June and Ken offer Kiwi hospitality, comfortable beds, electric blankets, delicious meals and a relaxed atmosphere. If time permits, enjoy a complimentary farm tour. We raise cattle and deer. Visitors are welcome to view or participate in farm activities. We enjoy Square Dancing, hosting and gardening. Please feel free to call. 4kms south of Makikihi turn inland into Lower Hook Road. Alford Farm is 2nd on right (2kms). Rapid No 202.

Fairlie   *Farmstay Homestay*   *3km W of Fairlie*

Fontmell
Anne & Norman McConnell
Nixons Road 169, RD 17, Fairlie
Tel: (03) 685 8379 Fax: (03) 685 8379
www.bnb.co.nz/fontmell.html

Double $90-$110 Single $55 (Full Breakfast)
Child $25 Dinner $25
1 Queen 1 Double 2 Twin 1 Single (4 bdrm)
1 Private 1 Guests share

Our farm consists of 400 acres producing fat lambs, cattle and deer, with numerous other animals and bird life. The house is situated in a large English style garden with many mature trees in a tranquil setting. In the area are two skifields, golf courses, walkways and scenic drives. Informative farm tours available. Our interests include golf, gardening and music. Directions: Travel 1 km from town centre, along Tekapo highway, then turn left into Nixon's Road when two more kilometers will bring you to the "Fontmell" entrance.

Fairlie   *Farmstay Homestay Separate/Suite B&B*   *3km E of Fairlie*

Braelea Countrystay
Sandra & Les Riddle
State Highway 79, Fairlie, South Canterbury
Tel: (03) 685 8366 Fax: (03) 685 8943
Mob: 025 203 5151
braelea@chc.quik.co.nz
www.bnb.co.nz/braeleacountrystay.html

Double $90-$140 Single $60 (Full Breakfast)
Child neg Dinner $20pp Credit cards accepted P
et on property Children welcome
2 King/Twin 1 Twin (3 bdrm) 2 Private

Welcome to the MacKenzie Country. Our modern home is 2 hours south of Christchurch and 3 1/2 hours north of Queenstown on the main highway. We have a 50 acre sheep & beef farm with spectacular views of the mountains. Our 2 guest apartments have their own lounges with tea making facilities, but we hope you will join us for refreshments and a chat. We are interested in hunting and tramping. Our fare includes mainly home made and local produce. Relax with us and our resident puss Snoopy.

STH CANT.
NTH OTAGO

Kimbell   *Country Homestay*   *8km W of Fairlie*

Rivendell Lodge
Joan Gill
Stanton Road, Kimbell, RD 17, Fairlie
Tel: (03) 685 8833 Fax: (03) 685 8825
Mob: 027 481 9189   Rivendell.lodge@xtra.co.nz
www.fairlie.co.nz/rivendell

Double $95 Single $60 (Full Breakfast) Child neg
Dinner $35 Credit cards accepted Pet on property
2 Queen 3 Single (3 bdrm)
2 Private 1 Family share

Welcome to my one acre paradise; a haven of peace and tranquility offering quality country comfort and hospitality. I am a well travelled writer with a passion for mountains, literature and good conversation. I enjoy cooking and gardening and use home grown produce wherever possible. Take time out for fishing, skiing, walking, golf or water sports. Relax in the garden, complete with stream and cat, or come with us to some of our favourite places. Complimentary refreshments on arrival. Laundry facilities and internet access available.

Kimbell   *Farmstay Homestay*   *7km W of Fairlie*

Poplar Downs
Shirl & Robin Sinclair
Mt Cook Road, Kimbell, RD 17, Fairlie
Tel: (03) 685 8170 Fax: (03) 685 8210
Tollfree: 025 520 0878   poplardowns@xtra.co.nz
www.bnb.co.nz/poplardowns.html

Double $100 Single $70 (Full Breakfast) Child neg
Dinner $25 Credit cards accepted Pet on property
1 King/Twin 1 Double (2 bdrm)
1 Ensuite 1 Private

Our homestead is an elegant early 1900's villa tastefully restored with the comfort of modern amenities. Heated rooms open onto verandahs overlooking the garden where there are numerous quiet spots to sit and relax and view the surrounding mountains. We have the usual menagerie of farm animals including pet lambs, hens, pigs, house cows, horses, sheep dog and cocker spaniel as well as the household moggy. Locally there is skiing, golf, fishing and tramping. Our home is smoke free with children most welcome.

Burkes Pass   *Country Homestay*   *23km E of Lake Tekapo*

Dobson Lodge   Margaret & Keith Walter
Dobson Lodge, RD 17,
Burkes Pass, Mackenzie Country
Tel: (03) 685 8316 Fax: (03) 685 8316
Mob: 021 176 9138   dobson_lodge@xtra.co.nz
www.mtcook.org.nz/dobsonlodge/

Double $95, $120, $160 Single $70-$100
(Continental Breakfast) Child neg Dinner $25pp
S/c railway carriage $40 - $60 Credit cards accepted
2 Queen 1 Double 1 Single (3 bdrm)
2 Ensuite 1 Family share

Come and share with us our unique glacier stone homestead with exceptional character set in 17 acres. We are nestled in a picturesque valley, with views of Mount Dobson and close to Lake Tekapo. We are on the main tourist route approximately halfway between Christchurch and Queenstown. There is a small restaurant at Burkes Pass settlement. Our interests include photography, crafts and travel. We have one cat, a friendly collie and pet sheep. As well as the Lodge, self-contained railway carriage accommodation is available.

Lake Tekapo *Homestay B&B* *40km W of Fairlie*

Freda Du Faur House
Dawn & Barry Clark
1 Esther Hope Street, Lake Tekapo
Tel: (03) 680 6513
www.bnb.co.nz/fredadufaurhouse.html
Double $99-$105 Single $65
(Continental Breakfast) (Special Breakfast)
Child neg. Credit cards accepted Pet on property
1 Queen 1 Double 2 Single (3 bdrm) 1 Guests share

Experience tranquillity and a touch of mountain magic. A warm and friendly welcome. Comfortable home, mountain and lake views. Rimu panelling, heart timber furniture, attractive decor, blending with the McKenzie Country. Bedrooms in private wing overlooking garden, two opening onto balcony. Refreshments on patio surrounded by roses or view ever changing panorama from lounge. Walkways nearby. Mt Cook one hour away. Views of skifield. Our cat "Missy" welcomes you. Five minutes to shops and restaurants. From SH8 turn into Lakeview Heights and follow green B&B sign into Barbara Hay Street. Then right and see our Freda Du Faur sign.

Lake Tekapo *B&B* *43km W of Fairlie*

Creel House Grant & Rosemary Brown
36 Murray Place, Lake Tekapo
Tel: (03) 680 6516 Fax: (03) 680 6659
creelhouse.l.tek@xtra.co.nz
www.bnb.co.nz/creelhouse.html
Double $140 Single $70 (Special Breakfast)
$100 double/twin Off-season tariff
Credit cards accepted Pet on property
Children welcome
2 Queen 1 Twin (3 bdrm) 1 Ensuite 2 Private

Built by Grant, our three storied home with expansive balconies offers panoramic views of the Southern Alps, Mt John, Lake Tekapo and surrounding mountains. All rooms are spacious and comfortable, with guest lounge and separate guest entrance. A NZ native garden adds an attractive feature. Restaurants in township. Our two daughters are 12 & 14 years, we live on the ground floor with two cats thus separate from our guest accommodation. Grant is a professional flyfishing guide (NZPFGA) and offers guided tours.

Lake Pukaki - Mt Cook *Homestay* *12km N of Twizel*

Rhoborough Downs
Roberta Preston
Lake Pukaki, PB, Fairlie
Tel: (03) 435 0509 Fax: (03) 435 0509
Tollfree: 0800 420 007
ra.preston@xtra.co.nz
www.bnb.co.nz/rhoboroughdowns.html
Double $100 Single $50 (Continental Breakfast)
Child $30 Dinner $30 Pet on property
1 Double 3 Single (3 bdrm) 1 Guests share

A quiet place to stop, halfway between Christchurch and Queenstown or Christchurch and Dunedin via Waitaki Valley. 40 minutes to Mt Cook. The 18,000 acre property has been in the family 80 years. Merino sheep graze to 6,000 feet, Hereford cattle. Views of the Southern sky the homestead is set in tranquil gardens afternoon tea/drinks served on the veranda, have a cat and dog. Twizel has a bank, doctor, restaurants, shops. Dinner by arrangement. Please phone for bookings and directions. Cot available.

**STH CANT.
NTH OTAGO**

Lake Pukaki   *Farmstay*   *27km Lake Tekapo*

Tasman Downs Station
Linda, Bruce & Ian Hayman
Lake Tekapo

Tel: (03) 680 6841 Fax: (03) 680 6851
samjane@xtra.co.nz
www.bnb.co.nz/tasmandownsstation.html

Double $110-$120 Single $70 (Full Breakfast)
Dinner $35pp Pet on property
1 Queen 2 Single (2 bdrm)
1 Private 1 Family share

"A place of unsurpassed beauty" located on the shores of Lake Pukaki with magnificent views of Mount Cook and the Southern Alps. Our local stone home blends in with the natural peaceful surrounds. Bruce, an ex-RAF pilot, has rich pioneering and surprisingly wide experiences. This high country farm in the family since 1914, runs mainly cattle with crops grown for self-sufficiency. This is your great opportunity to experience true farm life with friendly hosts and a good natured corgi.

Twizel - Mt Cook   *B&B*

Artemis B&B
Jan and Bob Wilson
33 North West Arch, Twizel,

Tel: (03) 435 0388 Fax: (03) 435 0377
Mob: 025 265 4750   artemistwizel@paradise.net.nz
www.bnb.co.nz/user188.html

Double $115 Single $80 (Special Breakfast)
Credit cards accepted
2 Queen 1 Single (2 bdrm)
1 Ensuite 1 Private

Welcome to the magnicient Mackenzie basin. Our modern home has stunning mountain views along with peace and tranquillity. We are only 45 minutes from Mount Cook and 3 minutes drive to nearby restaurants. A guest sitting room with balcony - tea, coffee and complimentary snack and television. Our special continental breakfast includes a choice of juices, fruits, cereals, cheeses and homemade croissants, muffins and jams. A selection of teas and coffees. We look forward to sharing our home with you.

Twizel   *Homestay*

Aoraki Lodge
Oksana & Vlad Fomin
32 Mackenzie Drive, Twizel/Mt Cook 8773

Tel: (03) 435 0300 Fax: (03) 435 0305
Mob: 021 142 8229   aorakilodge@xtra.co.nz
www.bnb.co.nz/aorakilodge.html

Double $120-$140 Single $90 (Full Breakfast)
Child $15 Dinner $45pp Credit cards accepted
1 Queen 2 Double 4 Single (4 bdrm)
4 Ensuite 1 Family share

Haere Mai ki Aoraki (Welcome to Aoraki Lodge). If you prefer a casual informal atmosphere with friendly hosts then Aoraki Lodge is the place for you. Relax in our warm, sunny home and enjoy our private garden. Native birds can be seen and heard. Steve is a wellknown fishing guide and can offer helpful advice and information on all the attractions in the area. We look forward to meeting you.

Twizel *Homestay Self-contained Loft* *2km W of Twizel*

Heartland Lodge
Dave & Jenny Pullen
19 North West Arch, Twizel, South Canterbury
Tel: (03) 435 0008 Fax: (03) 435 0387
Mob: 0274 927 778   Tollfree: 0800 164 666
european@xtra.co.nz www.heartland-lodge.co.nz
Double $140 Single $90 (Full Breakfast) Child neg
Dinner $45 by arrangement 'Loft' from $70
Credit cards accepted
2 King/Twin (2 bdrm) 2 Ensuite

Welcome to our lovely, large Homestay Lodge, only 45 minutes from Mt Cook. Luxuriously appointed guest rooms feature ensuites with spa baths. Guests are invited to join us for a complimentary pre-dinner drink before sharing a delicious 3 course dinner complemented by New Zealand wine (by prior arrangement) or dining at one of several nearby restaurants. Our black Labrador, Megan and donkey, Monty, will extend a warm welcome. "The Loft" - a large self-service apartment above our garage sleeps up to 7. Directions: Please phone 0800 164 666.

Twizel - Lake Ruataniwha *Homestay* *4km SW of Twizel*

Lake Ruataniwha Homestay
Robin & Lester Baikie
Max Smith Drive, Twizel
Tel: (03) 435 0532 Fax: (03) 435 0522
Mob: 025 373 294   robinandlester@xtra.co.nz
www.bnb.co.nz/lakeruataniwhahomestay.html
Double $120-$140 Single $70-$90 Child neg.
Dinner $30 pp Children welcome
2 Queen 1 Twin (3 bdrm)
1 Ensuite 1 Guests share

Welcome to our new home, built on 4ha near Lake Ruataniwha. Panoramic views of the lake and mountains. We have travelled extensively overseas and enjoy meeting people. Bedrooms open on to a patio. Beds have woollen underlays, electric blankets and bedside lamps. Email, Internet and fax facilities available. Kitchen/living areas are unstairs opening on to large decks to relax on and enjoy the view. Our interests are farming, horse trekking, sport, CWI. Ideal stopover between Christchurch and Queenstown.

Omarama *Farmstay* *1km S of Omarama*

Omarama Station
Beth & Dick Wardell
Omarama, North Otago
Tel: (03) 438 9821 Fax: (03) 438 9822
wardell@paradise.net.nz
www.omaramastation.co.nz
Double $100 - $120 Single $60 (Full Breakfast)
Child $20 - $50 Dinner $35
2 Queen 2 Single (3 bdrm)
1 Ensuite 1 Private

Omarama Station is a merino sheep and cattle property adjacent to the Omarama township. The 100 year old homestead is nestled in a small valley in a tranquil parklike setting of willows, poplars and a fast flowing stream (good fly fishing), pleasant walking environs, and interesting historical perspective to the high country as this was the original station in the area. Swimming pool and a pleasant garden. An opportunity to experience day to day farming activities. Dinner by arrangement.

Kurow   *Self-contained Farmstay Campervans or tents*   *60km W of Oamaru*

Glenmac   Kaye & Keith Dennison
RD 7K, Oamaru
Tel: (03) 436 0200 Fax: (03) 436 0202
Mob: 025 222 1119   www.farmstaynewzealand.co.nz
glenmac@farmstaynewzealand.co.nz

Double $80-$100 Single $40-$50 (Full Breakfast)
Child 1/2 price Dinner $25 $15pp S/C POA
Credit cards accepted Smoking area inside
1 Queen 2 Double 1 Twin (4 bdrm)
1 Ensuite 1 Family share

The perfect place to get away from traffic noises, enjoy home cooked meals, have a comfortable bed, relax and be treated as one of the family. Explore our 4000 acre high country farm. See merino sheep and beef cattle. Either on farm or nearby enjoy horse riding, four wheel drive farm tour, walking/tramping, fishing (guide available), golf or explore the NEW Fossil Trail. ALSO AVAILABLE - SELF CONTAINED COTTAGE. DIRECTIONS: Situated at end of Gards Road which is 10km east of Kurow on right.

Kurow   *Self-contained B&B Homestyle*   *2.7km E of Kurow*

Western House
Bernadette & Michael Parish
Highway 83, Kurow, North Oago
Tel: (03) 436 0876 Fax: (03) 436 0872
mbparish@xtra.co.nz
www.westernhouse.co.nz

Double $100-$120 Single $90-$120 (Full Breakfast)
Dinner $35 Credit cards accepted Pet on property
2 Queen 1 Double 1 Twin (4 bdrm)
1 Ensuite 1 Private 1 Guests share

Western House, built in 1871, as an accomodation house is surrounded by extensive garden and orchard with mountain views. Enjoy wood fires, fresh flowers, hearty breakfasts and wholesome dinners. A warm welcome awaits guests for an enjoyable stay with us and our cat simba. Attractions: Trout and salmon fishing (guide available), golf (clubs on-site), tennis, squash, walks, mountain biking, 4WD, swimming pool, beehive tours, and historic water wheel built 1899.

Oamaru   *Homestay*

Wallfield
Pat & Bill Bews
126 Reservoir Road, Oamaru
Tel: (03) 437 0368
Mob: 025 284 7303
b&pbews@xtra.co.nz
www.bnb.co.nz/wallfield.html

Double $80 Single $45 (Continental Breakfast)
1 Double 2 Single (2 bdrm)
1 Guests share

Our modern home is situated high above the North end of Oamaru with superb views to the east and the mountains in the west. We have four children, all happily married, and an ever increasing number of grand children. We have been home hosting for the last eleven years and although recently retired from farming, still enjoy the buzz of meeting new friends. Our interests include gardening and tramping.

Oamaru   *Homestay   8km SW of Oamaru*

Tara
Marianne & Baxter Smith
Springhill Road, 3 ORD, Oamaru
Tel: (03) 434 8187 Fax: (03) 434 8187
smith.tara@xtra.co.nz
www.tarahomestay.com
Double $95 Single $55 (Full Breakfast)
Dinner $30 by arrangement
2 Single (1 bdrm)
1 Private

Want to be pampered? "Tara" is the place for you. Enjoy the comfort and luxuries of our character Oamaru stone home. "Tara" boasts all day sun and the privacy to soak up the country atmosphere. Nestled amongst eleven acres of roses, mature trees and rural farmland "Tara" is the perfect place to unwind. Our livestock include Alpacas, coloured sheep, donkeys and an aviary. We also have a Burmese cat and a Lassie Collie. My husband Baxter and I will ensure your visit is an enjoyable experience. Please phone for directions.

Oamaru   *Homestay   Oamaru Central*

Jenny & Gerald Lynch-Blosse
11 Stour Street, South Hill,
Oamaru, North Otago
Tel: (03) 434 9628
geraldlb@xtra.co.nz
www.bnb.co.nz/lynchblosse.html
Double $120 Single $75
(Continental Breakfast) Dinner $35
1 Double 2 Single (2 bdrm)
1 Private 1 Family share

We have a charming, character home surrounded by gardens, in a quiet street near the main highway. Our guest bedrooms are well appointed. Tea or coffee is available. Dinner by arrangement is preceded by drinks beside the fire. We have travelled, and enjoy meeting people, especially visitors to New Zealand. Oamaru has many fine, stone, Victorian buildings. Enjoy one of Oamaru's many lovely walks, the attractive public gardens, or visit our art gallery, museum or penguin colony. A warm welcome awaits you. Family cat.

Oamaru - Waianakarua   *Homestay   25km S of Oamaru*

Glen Foulis Margaret & John Munro
39 Middle Ridge Road,
Waianakarua, ORD 9, Oamaru
Tel: (03) 439 5559 Fax: (03) 439 5220
Mob: 021 940 777   hjm@wxc.net.nz
www.glenhomestays.co.nz
Double $90 Single $55 (Full Breakfast) Child $35
Dinner $12-$27 Campervans $25 Credit cards accepted
1 King/Twin 2 Single (2 bdrm)
1 Private 1 Family share

Up a country road surrounded by whispering pines, Glen Foulis overlooks the river valley and acres of green lawns. Comfy, warm bedrooms have alcove window seats overlooking woodland views. Enjoy a touch of our Scottish heritage by feeding our Highland cattle or sipping single malt from our mantelpiece collection. Curl up with books in our step down snug by the open fire. Golden retrievers, Adam & McDuff are well trained. Caolila is a young Abyssinian cat. Convenient stop between Christchurch and Southern Lakes.

Waianakarua - Oamaru   *Farmstay B&B*   *30km S of Oamaru*

Glen Dendron
Anne & John Mackay
284 Breakneck Road, Waianakarua, Oamaru
Tel: (03) 439 5288 Fax: (03) 439 5288 Mob: 021 615 287
anne.john.mackay@xtra.co.nz www.glenhomestays.co.nz

Double $90 Single $55 (Full Breakfast) Child $30 Dinner $30 with wine
Credit cards accepted Children welcome
1 King/Twin 1 Queen 2 Single (3 bdrm) 2 Guest share bathrooms

Enjoy tranquillity and beauty when you stay in our stylish modern home, spectacularly sited on a hilltop overlooking the picturesque Waianakarua river and surrounded by 5 acres of garden containing hundreds of different plants. After sumptuous farm cooked breakfast, feed sheep and alpacas. Then take a stroll through the forest, native bush complete with waterfalls and birds or beside the river. Play a round on the family golf course. Later, watch seals and penguins nearby. Then, complete a perfect day with our gourmet three course dinner with fine NZ wine before snuggling down for a peaceful sleep in the fresh country air.

After a lifetime spent in farming and forestry we relish the opportunity to share our home and semi-retired lifestyle with guests. Our adult family live overseas so we travel frequently and have a great interest in other countries and cultures. We are very keen gardeners, read widely and enjoy antiques. Anne is a floral artist and John involved with Lions.

With so much to see why not stay awhile!

We can plan customised itineraries of the area's many attractions.

• Oamaru's historic architecture.
• Garden and heritage trails.
• Beaches, fishing, seals, penguins.
• Famous Moeraki boulders.
Use us as a base for day visits to Oamaru, Dunedin, Waitaki Valley and Mt Cook. Christchurch International Airport - 3.5 hours.

We don't mind short notice!

Oamaru   *Homestay B&B   15min walk Oamaru Central*

Clyde House
Wenda & John Eason   32 Clyde St, Oamaru
Tel: (03) 437 2774 Fax: (03) 437 2774
Mob: 025 603 1363   Tollfree: 0800 259 334
eason.clydehouse@xtra.co.nz www.clydehouse.co.nz
Double $95-$120 Single $80 (Special Breakfast)
Child $25 Studio sleeps 3 $150 Credit cards accepted
Pet on property Children welcome
1 King 1 Queen 1 Double 1 Single (3 bdrm)
1 Ensuite 1 Private 1 Guests share 1 Family share

Unique private family home, built early 1900's, solid Oamaru limestone walls. Return verandah, set in spacious garden, in the centre of Oamaru. Close to town, restaurants, and the Blue Penguin Colony. Three rooms, ensuite, and private. Quiet area. Nature tours can be arranged. Electric blankets and feather duvets. Own TV or share our spacious living areas. Breakfast in our spacious conservatory 'Wintergarden'. Off street parking. We pride ourselves on our home baking and preserves. Sherry (our cat) and Wenda and John welcome you to our home.

Oamaru   *Self-contained Homestay full kitchen   3km S of Oamaru, just of SH1*

Springbank
Joan & Stan Taylor
60 Weston Road, Oamaru
Tel: (03) 434 6602 Fax: (03) 434 6602
Mob: 025 669 2902
www.bnb.co.nz/springbank.html
Double $75 Single $40 (Continental Breakfast)
Child $10 Credit cards accepted Pet on property
1 Double 1 Twin (1 bdrm)
1 Private

We look forward to sharing our retirement haven with visitors from overseas and New Zealand. Our modern home and separate guest flat are set in a peaceful and private large garden. Feed the gold fish and pamper Oscar our cat. Our guest flat is sunny, warm, spacious and comfortable. We enjoy helping visitors discover our district's best kept secrets! Penguins, gardens, Moeraki Boulders, beaches, pool, fishing and golf. Our interests - travel, gardening, grandchildren. Stan, Lions and follows sports. Joan all handcrafts, patchwork, floral design.

Moeraki - Oamaru   *Farmstay B&B   38km S of Oamaru*

Moeraki Boulder Downs Farmstay & B&B
Jan & Ken Wheeler
State Highway 1, Moeraki, RD 2, Palmerston
Tel: (03) 439 4855 Fax: (03) 439 4355
Mob: 025 614 6396 www.moerakiboulders.co.nz
farmstay@moerakiboulders.co.nz

Double $80-$100 Single $50-$60 (Full Breakfast)
Child $35 Dinner $30 (incl. wine) Credit cards accepted
1 Queen 2 Twin (2 bdrm) 1 Guests share

Indulge yourself and enjoy warm hospitality at our country retreat by the sea. We invite you to join us for a traditional New Zealand dinner - then relax by the fire in our charming 1920's homestead. Breakfast with the bellbirds - then stroll along the beautiful beach to Moeraki Boulders and quaint fishing village. Sheep farm tours a speciality. Stay two nights and expereince the Moeraki penguins, seals, historic Oamaru, golf courses and antique shops nearby. We are enroute to Christchurch, Dunedin, Queenstown and Mt Cook.

STH CANT.
NTH OTAGO

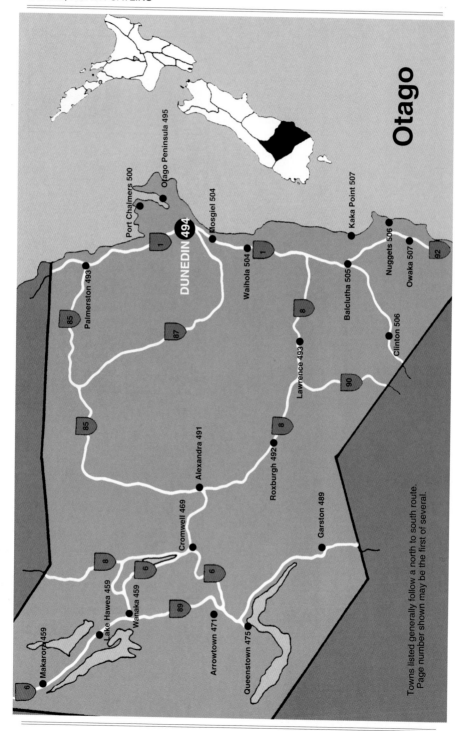

Otago

Port Chalmers 500
Otago Peninsula 495
Mosgiel 504
Kaka Point 507
Nuggets 506
Owaka 507

DUNEDIN 494

1

Palmerston 493

85

1
Waihola 504

Balclutha 505

Clinton 506

87

8

Lawrence 493

90

85

Alexandra 491

8

Roxburgh 492

Cromwell 469

6

6

Garston 489

8

Lake Hawea 459

89

Wanaka 459

Arrowtown 471

Makarora 459

Queenstown 475

6

92

Towns listed generally follow a north to south route.
Page number shown may be the first of several.

Makarora   *Homestay   Self-contained Cottage*   *65km N of Wanaka*

Larrivee Homestay
Andrea and Paul
Makarora, via Wanaka

Tel: (03) 443 9177 andipaul@xtra.co.nz
www.bnb.co.nz/larrivee.html

Double $110 Single $80
(Continental & Full Breakfast)
Child 1/2 price Dinner $35 BYO
Cottage: Double $100 $20 per extra
2 Double 2 Single (3 bdrm)
1 Ensuite 1 Private

Nestled in native bush bordering Mt Aspiring National Park, our unique home and cottage are secluded, quiet and comfortable. Originally from the USA, we have lived in Makarora for over 25 years and like sharing our mountain retreat and enjoying good food and conversation. Many activities are available locally, including fishing, bird watching, jet boating, scenic flights and bush walks - including the wonderful 'Siberia Experience', fly/walk/boat trip. We are happy to help make arrangements for activities.

Lake Hawea   *Homestay   15km N of Wanaka*

Sylvan Chalet
Lyall Campbell
4 Bodkin Street,
Lake Hawea, RD 2, Wanaka

Tel: (03) 443 1343 Mob: 025 224 9192
lyallc@xtra.co.nz
www.inow.co.nz/sylvanchalet

Double $80 Single $40 (Continental Breakfast)
Child $30 Pet on property Children welcome
1 Double 2 Single (2 bdrm)
1 Ensuite 1 Family share

I am a retired school teacher - now a craft dyer of silk, a spinner and cross-country skier. My three-storied A-frame is in a sheltered compound with many specimen trees. One guest room has an ensuite, the other opens to a balcony; both have mountain views. Access via a circular staircase. Washing machine available. Lake Hawea two minutes walk away. I have a cat and small dog. Directions: From Wanaka-Haast Rd turn off to Lake Hawea - past hotel to store - see A-frame through Archway.

Wanaka   *Homestay   Wanaka Central*

Lake Wanaka Homestay
Peter & Gailie Cooke
85 Warren Street, Wanaka

Tel: (03) 443 7995 Fax: (03) 443 7945
Tollfree: 0800 443 799 wanakahomestay@xtra.co.nz
www.bnb.co.nz/lakewanakahomestay.html

Double $90 Single $55 (Full Breakfast)
Child neg Credit cards accepted Pet on property
1 Double 2 Single (2 bdrm)
1 Guests share 1 Family share

Relax with us in our warm comfortable home ideally situated Centre Wanaka. Magnificent lake and mountain views, just 3 minutes walk to shops and restaurants. We both enjoy golf, skiing, boating, outdoor activities. Peter is a keen fly fisherman. Good comfortable beds, electric blankets, hairdryers, heaters. Tea, coffee, muffins, homemade biscuits any time. Cooked breakfast. We both enjoy helping people, and have shared our home with guests for 17 years and made many lovely friends. "Kim" our Labrador is everyone's friend. Directions: 4 blocks back Lake Front, opposite school.

OTAGO
NTH CATLINS

Wanaka *Self-contained Homestay B&B*

Temasek House
Doreen & Mike Allen
7 Huchan Lane, Wanaka
Tel: (03) 443 1655 Fax: (03) 443 1655
temasek.house@xtra.co.nz
www.wanakahomestay.co.nz/temasek.html
Double $105 Single $60 (Full Breakfast)
Child negotiable twin $90 Credit cards accepted
1 Queen 1 Twin 1 Single (3 bdrm)
1 Ensuite 1 Family share

Under New Management. We are a retired English couple, well travelled and actively involved in outdoor pursuits. Our main interests are flyfishing, tramping and skiing, but we happily share our knowledge of all this wonderful area's opportunities. Our comfortable home is ideally situated for local skifields and Mt Aspiring National Park. Lakeshore and restaurants a short stroll. Large lounge opens on to spacious sundeck overlooking established garden and offering mountain views with glimpses of lake through mature trees. A self-contained unit can be alternatively created. Families welcome.

Wanaka *Boutique Accommodation*   *2km Wanaka Central*

Oak Ridge Lake Wanaka
Rowland & Nora Hastings and John & Beth Haryett
cnr Cardrona Valley & Studholme Roads,
PO Box 220, Wanaka
Tel: (03) 443 7707 Fax: (03) 443 7750
Tollfree: 0800 869 262   info@oakridge.co.nz
www.oakridge.co.nz
Double $160-$240 Single $144-$216
(Special Breakfast) Child neg Credit cards accepted
Eftpos available Fully licensed restaurant/bar
12 Super King (12 bdrm) 12 Ensuite

Located only 2 minutes drive from the centre of Wanaka, the careful blending of the old and the new create at Oakridge a holiday experience unique in terms of comfort, design, location and ambience. Central to the development is a purpose-built hunting, fishing and skiing lodge. The existing lodge was extensively remodelled (July 2000) and new wings added to provide a range of accommodation designed to cater for the most judicious traveller. Fully licensed restaurant & bar offering sumptuous a la carte dining.

Wanaka *Homestay   Wanaka*

Aspiring Images
Betty & George Russell
26 Norman Terrace, Wanaka
Tel: (03) 443 8358 Fax: (03) 443 8327
grussell@xtra.co.nz
www.aspiringimages.co.nz
Double $110-$120 Single $75 (Full Breakfast)
Child $35 Dinner $35 B/A Credit cards accepted
1 King/Twin 1 Double (2 bdrm)
1 Ensuite 1 Private

The challenge - portray Wanaka and our homestay in 85 words! **Wanaka is:** magical; tranquil; dramatic; refreshing; exhilarating; captivatingly beautiful. **Wanaka has:** activities both challenging and restful, fascinating history, distinctive micro-climate, ecological diversity, mountain light ever changing. **Our homestay offers:** informative welcoming hosts, warmth and comfort, lake and mountain views, adjacent park with lake access, mountain bikes to ride. **We are:** ex-teachers with musical, sporting, photographic and Rotary interests; well travelled both nationally and internationally, qualified to help with NZ itineraries.

Lake Wanaka *Self-contained Homestay B&B* *Wanaka*

Beacon Point
Diana & Dan Pinckney
302 Beacon Point Road, PO Box 6, Lake Wanaka
Tel: (03) 443 1253 Fax: (03) 443 1254
Mob: Di 025 246 0222 / Dan 025 354 847
dan.pinckney@harcourts.co.nz
www.bnb.co.nz/beaconpoint.html

Double $90-$120 (Continental Breakfast)
Child $30 Dinner $30
1 Queen 1 Twin (2 bdrm)   2 Private

Our new home "Beacon Point" B & B is surrounded by 1 acre of lawn and garden for your enjoyment. It leads to a walking track to the village around the edge of the lake with snow capped mountains in winter. Private spacious studio with ensuite, Queen and single beds (2 rooms), kitchen, T.V, and sundeck. Studio equiped with every need for a perfect stay. We are very flexable and enjoy planning your days with you. Our intrests include farming, forestry, fly fishing, real estate, boating, gardening and our grandchildren. Turn right at lake - Lakeside Road - then to Beacon Point Road 302.

Wanaka *Homestay B&B*   *1km N of Wanaka*

Harpers
Jo & Ian Harper
95 McDougall Street, Wanaka
Tel: (03) 443 8894 Fax: (03) 443 8834
harpers@xtra.co.nz
www.bnb.co.nz/harpers.html

Double $110 Single $70 (Continental Breakfast)
Credit cards accepted
1 King/Twin 2 Twin (2 bdrm)
1 Ensuite 1 Guests share

We take pride in offering a friendly, comfortable home. Share breakfast and our awesome lake and mountain views with us. Also explore our extensive garden which provides a tranquil environment for relaxing. Recent guests' comments: '... surely one of the best B&Bs in NZ', '... nicest hosts we have encountered. I'll always remember the long breakfast talks', 'No Contest. The best 2 nights stay I've had in NZ. Long live the best pancake house', 'enjoyed the room ... the garden ... the view and most of all the warm hospitality.' We offer a drink and muffins on your arrival. Smokefree home.

Wanaka *Homestay Rural*   *4km S of Wanaka*

Stonehaven
Deirdre & Dennis
Halliday Lane, RD 2, Wanaka
Tel: (03) 443 9516 Fax: (03) 443 9513
moghul@xtra.co.nz www.stonehaven.co.nz

Double $95 Single $75 (Full Breakfast)
Child $20 neg portacots & high chairs avail.
Credit cards accepted Child at home Pet on property
1 Queen 1 Double 2 Single (2 bdrm)
1 Ensuite 1 Private

Our home is set in a developing two acres about five minutes drive from Wanaka. All beds have electric blankets, tea and coffee is freely available. We have extensive views of surrounding mountains. Children are welcome. Child care by arrangement. Our nearby tree collection has an accent on autumn colour. Local walks a speciality. Organic fruit both in season and preserved. We have twin thirteen year old girls, a small dog, and two cats. No smoking inside please. Please phone for directions.

Wanaka *Self-contained B&B* *10km N of Wanaka*

The Stone Cottage
Belinda Wilson
Wanaka, RD 2, Central Otago

Tel: (03) 443 1878 Fax: (03) 443 1276
stonecottage@xtra.co.nz www.stonecottage.co.nz

Double $215-$230 Single $200 (Full Breakfast)
Child 1/2 price under 12yrs Dinner $60 Credit cards accepted
1 King 2 Double 2 Single (2 bdrm) 1 Ensuite 1 Private

Fifty years ago, a spectacular garden was created at Dublin Bay on the tranquil shores of Lake Wanaka. Its beauty still blooms today against a backdrop of the majestic Southern Alps. Accommodation is private, comfortable and elegantly decorated.

The Stone Cottage offers two self-contained loft apartments with breathtaking views over lake Wanaka to snow clad alps beyond. Featuring your own bathroom, bedroom, kitchen, living room and balcony. Television, fax and email available. Private entrance.

Enjoy breakfast at leisure, made from fresh ingredients from your well stocked fully equipped kitchen, Pre dinner drinks, delicious 3 course dinner and NZ wines or a gourmet picnic hamper is available by arrangement.

Walk along the beach just 4 minutes from The Stone Cottage or wander in the enchanting garden. Guests can experience trout fishing, nature walks, golf, boating, horse riding, wine tasting and ski fields nearby.

Only 10 minutes from Wanaka, this is the perfect retreat for those who value privacy and the unique beauty of this area.

Relax in the magic atmosphere at The Stone Cottage and awake to the dawn bird chorus of native bellbirds and fantails.

Wanaka   *Homestay*   *2min N of Wanaka*

Hunt's Homestay
Bill & Ruth Hunt
56 Manuka Crescent, Wanaka 9192, Central Otago
Tel: (03) 443 1053 Fax: (03) 443 1355
Mob: 025 265 0114
relax@huntshomestay.co.nz
www.huntshomestay.co.nz

Double $100 Single $60 (Continental Breakfast)
Child by arrangement Credit cards accepted
1 Queen 2 Single (2 bdrm)
1 Guests share

Welcome to our modern home in Wanaka where we will greet you with tea or coffee in our smoke-free house and settle you in your spacious ground-floor accommodation. After farming near Wanaka, we built this house over looking the mountains and lake, and so have a good knowledge of the area. Through our membership of Lake Wanaka Tourism we are kept informed of all tourist activities in the area. Our interests are golf, gardening, travel and meeting people. We have no resident children or pets.

Wanaka   *Homestay Lodge*   *Wanaka Central*

Anubis Lodge
Michele or Bobbie Mercer
264 Beacon Point Road, Wanaka
Tel: (03) 443 7807 Fax: (03) 443 7803
Mob: 025 275 6124 or 025 407 816
m.b.mercer@xtra.co.nz
www.wanakahomestay.co.nz

Double $145 Single $120 (Special Breakfast)
Credit cards accepted Pet on property
2 King 1 Queen (3 bdrm)   3 Ensuite

Purpose built for bed & breakfast accommodation, rooms are large with own dressing rooms and ensuite bathrooms. Beds are luxuriously fitted with quality linen, feather duvets and electric blankets. Decor accented with native timber, fresh flowers, Italian art, Belgium rugs, Scottish leather and English linens. Wide open views of lake and mountains , a walk to lake edge for fishing, swimming or secluded relaxation. Central heating plus two fireplaces keep us cosy. Breakfast is varied and generous. We have two Pharaoh Hound dogs you may choose to meet. We certainly look forward to meeting you.....

Wanaka   *Homestay B&B*   *2km N of Wanaka Central*

Lake Wanaka Home Hosting
Joyce & Lex Turnbull
19 Bill's Way, Wanaka
Tel: (03) 443 9060 Fax: (03) 443 1626
Mob: 025 228 9160   lex.joy@xtra.co.nz
www.lakewanakahomehosting.co.nz

Double $100-$135 Single $65 (Full Breakfast)
Child $25 Dinner $30 Children welcome
1 King/Twin 1 Double 1 Twin (3 bdrm)
2 Private

We welcome visitors to Wanaka, enjoy sharing our natural surroundings with others. We have a large peaceful home where our guests can experience not only the austerity of the lake and mountains around them, but also experience the ambience of Wanaka itself. Guest room with super king bed has adjoining TV lounge with TV, tea coffee facilities, private bathroom. Good laundry facilities. We wish your stay in Wanaka will be a very happy one. Directions: please ring for directions. We enjoy your company.

Wanaka   *Homestay B&B*

Northridge
Richie & Sue Heathfield / Atkinson
11 Botting Place, PO Box 376, Wanaka

Tel: (03) 443 8835 Fax: (03) 443 1835
Mob: 025 950 436   stay@northridgewanaka.co.nz
www.northridgewanaka.co.nz

Double $120-$140 Single $100 (Full Breakfast)
Credit cards accepted
2 Queen 2 Single (3 bdrm)
1 Ensuite 1 Private 1 Guests share

Northridge is situated on a ridge with stunning views of the Lake and Mountains and within walking distance to restaurants, shops and the lakefront. Our quality 2 storey Native Timber and Schist stone home lends itself to indoor/outdoor living, where you can wander through the garden or sit on the patio with refreshments and take in the everchanging scenery. The rooms all with views are spacious and complete with quality linen, wool underlays and feather duvets. Northridge is centrally heated to keep us all cosy in winter.

Wanaka   *Boutique B&B Accommodation*   *Wanaka Central*

Crofthead B&B
Joan & Rodger Cross
19 Blacksmiths Lane,
PO Box 38, Wanaka

Tel: (03) 443 8883 Fax: (03) 443 6683
www.bnb.co.nz/croftheadbb.html

Double $100-$110 Single $60-$70
(Full Breakfast) Pet on property
1 King/Twin (1 bdrm)
1 Private

'Crofthead' - named after the family farm - is situated in peaceful Wanaka Station Park. The park has extensive plantings of mature English trees and rhododendrons and extends to the shores of beautiful Lake Wanaka - a few metres away. Stroll along the lakefront to shops and restaurants which are within easy walking distance. Enjoy the ambience of our new home. Relax in the walled outdoor room or admire the views from the sheltered courtyard areas. Washing and drying facilities available.

Wanaka   *Boutique B&B Lodge*   *Wanaka Central*

Wanaka Springs Boutique B&B Lodge
Lynne & Murray Dalziell
21 Warren Street, Wanaka 9192, Central Otago

Tel: (03) 443 8421 Fax: (03) 443 8429 Mob: 027 223 2512
relax@wanakasprings.com
www.wanakasprings.com

Double $230-$275 (Special Breakfast)
Honeymoon Room   Credit cards accepted
6 Queen 2 Twin (8 bdrm)
8 Ensuite

This 2001/2002 New Zealand Tourism Award Finalist for hosted accommodation offers a unique experience of 'informal sophistication' for the discerning traveller. In its intimate yet private setting, the Lodge's reputation as Wanaka's 'in-town retreat' is more than justified by its high standards of comfort, hospitality and facilities. Savour our special breakfast buffet and afternoon tea while you enjoy the stunning views and enjoy the services and facilities of a small hotel but retains the warmth, personality and charm of a boutique lodge just a three minute stroll from town centre.

Wanaka   *B&B   Boutique Hotel*   *Wanaka Central*

Te Wanaka Lodge
Graeme & Andy Oxley
23 Brownston Street, Wanaka

Tel: (03) 443 9224
Fax: (03) 443 9246
Tollfree: 0800 WANAKA (926252)
tewanakalodge@xtra.co.nz
www.tewanaka.co.nz

Double $145-$175 Single $135-$165
(Full Breakfast)
Self contained Cottage $185 - $195
Credit cards accepted
9 Queen 4 Twin (13 bdrm)   13 Ensuite

Nestled in the heart of Wanaka, Te Wanaka Lodge is a two minute walk to the lake, restaurants, shops and golf course. Tastefully decorated with fishing and skiing memorabilia, Te Wanaka Lodge has a distinctive Alpine ambience.

On a hot summer's day laze under our walnut tree with a cool drink from the House Bar, or in winter relax by the warmth of our log fire after enjoying a soak in our secluded garden hot tub.

- All bedrooms with ensuite and private balcony
- Full cooked breakfast included
- House Bar specialising in local beers and wines
- Sky TV, video, CD and book library
- Off street parking
- Ski drying room and laundry service
- Full business facilities
- In-house massage therapy.

OTAGO
NTH CATLINS

Wanaka   *B&B Luxury Lodge   60km E of Queenstown   6km from Wanaka*

Parklands Lodge
Margaret and Lawrence Mikkelsen
Ballantyne Road, RD2 Wanaka,
Tel: (03) 443 7305 Fax: (03) 443 7345
Mob: 025 955 160   parklandslodge@xtra.co.nz
www.parklandswanaka.co.nz

Double $210 Single $185 (Full Breakfast) Child $20
Dinner $35 (child $20) Credit cards accepted
3 King/Twin 2 Queen 2 Twin (6 bdrm)
4 Ensuite 1 Guests share

Parklands Lodge, nestled on 10 acres of rural land 6km from Wanaka, has spectacular mountain views, a refuge from the hustle and bustle of urban life. We have a guest dining room, 2 lounge rooms, cosy fires,laundry facilities,spa, swimming pool, BBQ area and a 5 hole pitch and putt golf course and a self-contained apartment. Plus a golden labrador dog. Guests are served a continental and cooked breakfast. Wanaka is a destination on its own with great activities and only 45 min by car from Queenstown, 6 min from Wanaka.

Wanaka   *B&B   16km S of Wanaka*

Smiths Settlement B&B
Chris & Mat Andrews
Cardrona Valley Road, R.D. 1, Wanaka
Tel: (03) 443 6680 Fax: (03) 443 6690
Mob: 025 836261
MAT-CHRIS.A@xtra.co.nz
www.bnb.co.nz/smithssettlementbb.html

Double $120 Single $90 (Continental Breakfast)
1 Queen 1 Double (2 bdrm)
1 Ensuite 1 Family share

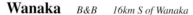

Smiths Settlement Bed and Breakfast OPENING JANUARY 2002. A secluded private location nestled beside the Cardrona River in a rural setting. Two double bedrooms, one with an ensuite. Just 5 minutes to the base of the Cardrona Resort Skifield ,The historic Cardrona Hotel and the Wairau Nordic Skifield. Only 10 minutes to Wanaka and 45 minutes to Queenstown. Come and enjoy a relaxing stay with us. We have two Golden Retriever dogs and three cats that will just love all your attention.

Wanaka   *Homestay B&B   2.5km E of Wanaka*

Riverside
Lesley & Norman West
11 Riverbank Road, RD 2, Wanaka
Tel: (03) 443 1522 Fax: (03) 443 1522
Mob: 025 601 4640
n.l.west@paradise.net.nz
www.bnb.co.nz/riverside.html

Double $100 Single $70 (Full Breakfast)
Credit cards accepted Pet on property
1 Queen 2 Twin (2 bdrm)   1 Guests share

We welcome guests to our lovely home on six developing acres with river boundary. Just 100 metres from SH84 and SH6 and 2.5km from Wanaka township. We offer you our friendly and peaceful environment with mountain and rural views. Cosy fires in winter, and shady terrace in summer, plsy two well-appointed guest rooms ensures your stay will be relaxing and enjoyable. Tea and coffee always available. Dinner by arrangement. Our boat is available for charter fishing or lake cruising. Our son is an experienced trout fishing guide.

Wanaka *Homestay B&B* *Wanaka central*

Ponderosa B&B
Janice & Mark Cochrane
10 Lismore Street, Wanaka,
Tel: (03) 443 4644 Fax: (03) 443 4645
Mob: 025 928 820
www.bnb.co.nz/ponderosabb.html
Double $120-$170 Single $120-$140 (Full Breakfast)
1 Queen 1 Twin (2 bdrm)
1 Ensuite 1 Guests share

Welcome to our new home in Wanaka that offers the most spectacular views. Breathtaking and uninterrupted lake, town and mountains. Relax in our guest lounge or on your own private balcony and soak up the wonderful sights. After experiencing some of Wanaka's many attractions enjoy a pre-dinner drink before venturing on a 2 minutes stroll to one of our many delightful restaurants. Guided hunting and fishing in the Clutha. Each room has electric blankets and TV. Driving time from Wanaka to Queenstown 1 hour, Christchurch 6 hours, Franz Josef 4 hours.

Wanaka *Homestay B&B* *6km N of Wanaka*

Riversong
Ann Horrax
5 Wicklow Terrace, Albert Town, RD 2, Wanaka
Tel: (03) 443 8567 info@happyhomestay.co.nz
www.happyhomestay.co.nz
Double $100-$120 Single $75 (Continental Breakfast)
Dinner $30 pp by arrangement
Pet on property Children welcome
1 King/Twin 1 Single (2 bdrm) 1 Private

"Riversong" ... named after the soft lament of nearby Clutha River, is situated at historic Albert Town, five minutes from Wanaka. Riversong is in the heart of Central Otago's natural and scenic beauty, trout fishing, three skifields, Mt Aspiring National Park, and much more. My background is healthcare and Ian's law. We invite you to share the comfort of our home and garden and Ian's knowledge of the region's fishing. We are committed to providing a friendly and relaxed atmosphere. We have two outside lab dogs. Directions: Albert Town is 6km north of Wanaka on State Highway 6 to Haast. Turn downriver at bridge over Clutha River and travel to end of Wicklow Terrace. Property signposted.

Wanaka *Self-contained B&B* *2 km NW of Wanaka*

Goldridge
Lyndon and Gill McKenzie
191 Anderson Road, Wanaka,
Tel: (03) 443 4160 Fax: (03) 443 4160
Mob: 025 377 302
lyndonandgill@xtra.co.nz
www.bnb.co.nz/goldridge.html
Double $90 Single $65 (Continental Breakfast)
$15 extra person $120 family Child at home
Pet on property Children welcome
1 Queen 3 Single (2 bdrm) 1 Private

Lyndon and Gill along with their children Cole,Tegan, and pet labrador Krammer welcome you to their home. Set within 6 acres of mature trees and gardens you can look out at some of Central Otago's magnificent views. Drive into the heart of Wanaka, where you'll find cafe's and wonderful shops ready to cater to you. The lake in summer is a very handy 5 minute drive. In winter ski fields a 25 minute drive to Cardrona or Treble Cone.

Wanaka   *Homestay B&B*   *3kms E of Wanaka*

The Cedars
Adrienne McPherson
7 Riverbank Road, Wanaka,
Tel: (03) 443 1544 Fax: (03) 443 1544
mcphersons@hyper.net.nz
www.bnb.co.nz/thecedars.html

Double $100-$140 Single $60-$90 (Full Breakfast)
Dinner By arrangement Credit cards accepted
2 Queen 2 Single (2 bdrm)
1 Ensuite 1 Family share

A warm country welcome awaits you at The Cedars, a spacious stacked stone home set on 11 acres. Panoramic views, expansive gardens, laneways between deer and sheep to wander or or relax in. We have sheltered verandah areas and a guest lounge with large open fire. Handy to golf course, three ski-fields and Mt Iron walking track. A full breakfst is served with fresh and homemade produce, percolated coffee and a selection of teas. By prior arrangement we offer an evening meal or BBQ. We look forward to meeting you.

Lake Wanaka   *Self-contained B&B*   *2.3km NW of Wanaka Central*

Peak-Sportchalet
Alex and Christine Schafer
36 Hunter Crescent, Lake Wanaka,
Tel: 0064 3 443 6990 Fax: 0064 3 443 4969
stay@peak-sportchalet.co.nz
www.Peak-Sportchalet.co.nz

Double $85-$95 Single $55-$65 (Full Breakfast)
Child at home Children welcome
1 King/Twin 1 King 1 Twin (3 bdrm)
1 Ensuite 1 Guests share

We invite you to stay in our full equipped, luxury chalet were you can relax and enjoy the view to Treble Cone and Black Peak. Or stay in our sunny B&B-Room with ensuite were you can enjoy a cooked Breakfast with homemade goods. We are equipped with a Ski- and Mountainbike workshop + guest-laundry. Enjoy a relaxation massage after your activities. We welcome you together with our daughter Josephine (3) in our smokefree home. Your holiday - an unforgettable adventure - that's our aim !!! Life the way it should be !!!

Wanaka   *Luxury Boutique Retreat*   *2km N of Wanaka*

Minaret Lodge
Gary Tate
34 Eely Point Road, Wanaka
Tel: (03) 443 1856 Fax: (03) 443 1846
Mob: 021 644 406
www.minaretlodge.co.nz

Double $250 Single $225 (Full Breakfast)
Credit cards accepted Pet in residence
5 King/Twin (5 bdrm)
5 Ensuite

Wanaka's luxury boutique retreat, bed & breakfast lodge, set in park-like setting, located within 10 minute walk to Wanaka town centre. The Lodge features a mud brick (adobe) construction with plastered finish, incoorporating local schist stone. All guest rooms have ensuites with heated tiled floor, fine furniture and linen, deck, sauna, spa, mountain bikes, ski storage and drying room included in facilities. Gourmet breakfast and aperitifs featuring local wine and cheese included in the tarrif.

Cromwell   *Homestay*

Stuart's Homestay
Elaine & Ian Stuart
5 Mansor Court, Cromwell
Tel: (03) 445 3636 Fax: (03) 445 3636
Mob: 025 203 3825   ian.elaine@xtra.co.nz
www.bnb.co.nz/stuart.html
Double $100-$120 Single $60 (Full Breakfast)
Dinner $15-$20 by arrangement Credit cards accepted
2 Queen 2 Single (3 bdrm)
1 Ensuite 1 Private

Welcome to our home which is situated within walking distance to most of Cromwell's amenities. We are semi-retired Southland farmers who have been home hosting for over ten years. Now enjoying living in the stone fruit and wine region of Central Otago. Cromwell is a quiet and relaxed tourist town which is known for historic gold diggings, vineyards, orchards, trout fishing, boating, walks and close to ski fields. Share dinner with us or just Bed and Breakfast. We enjoy sharing our home with visitors and a friendly stay is assured.

Cromwell   *Orchardstay*   *1km N of Cromwell*

Cottage Gardens
Jill & Colin McColl
3 Alpha Street, cnr State Highway 8B,
Cromwell, Central Otago
Tel: (03) 445 0628 Fax: (03) 445 0628
eco@xtra.co.nz   www.bnb.co.nz/cottagegardens.html
Double $80 Single $40-$55 (Continental Breakfast)
Child n/a Dinner $20 Credit cards accepted
1 Twin 4 Single (3 bdrm)
1 Ensuite 2 Family share

Apricots and Hospitality are our specialty. We offer good food and company and welcome you to join us anytime. Enjoy the privacy of our spacious guest room with ensuite, TV, fridge and teamaking facilities. Private entrance and verandahs overlooks gardens and Lake Dunstan. Experience Queenstown and Wanaka, 45min. Te Anau 2/5 hrs drive. Cromwell, surrounded by orchards and vineyards with everchanging scenery and excellent sports facilities. Golden labrador Jessica May will accompany you for lakeside walks. Fritter, our handsome ginger feline, enjoys fireside chats. Members Lions International.

Cromwell - Northburn   *Self-contained B&B*   *4km N of Cromwell*

Quartz Reef Creek Bed and Breakfast
June Boulton
Quartz Reef Creek, RD 3, Northburn,
State Highway 8, Cromwell
Tel: (03) 445 0404 quartz-reef@xtra.co.nz
Fax: (03) 445 0404 www.bnb.co.nz/boulton.html
Double $110 Single $70 (Continental Breakfast)
Twin Room $100 Credit cards accepted
1 Queen 1 Twin 2 Single (2 bdrm)
1 Ensuite 1 Private

OTAGO
NTH CATLINS

You are invited to stay at my peaceful and modern lakeside home located in Central Otago, a rapidly expanding wine growing region. Panoramic views from your sunny room include Lake Dunstan and surrounding mountains. Both rooms have total privacy with their own entrances. One has its own deck, tea making facilities, fridge, microwave and TV. Another room has twin beds, TV and sitting room. I enjoy making pottery in my studio and supply local galleries. I have two friendly pets, a dog Guinness and cat, Tom.

Cromwell   *Farmstay   10km NW of Cromwell*

Hiburn
Claire & Jack Davis
RD 2, Cromwell, Central Otago
Tel: (03) 445 1291 Fax: (03) 445 1291
Tollfree: 0800 205 104   hiburn@xtra.co.nz
www.bnb.co.nz/hiburn.html
Double $90 Single $60 (Full Breakfast)
Child $30 Dinner $20
1 Double 2 Single (2 bdrm)
1 Guests share

Welcome to Hiburn Farmstay, ideally situated between main tourist attractions yet off the beaten track at Cromwell, The Centre of beautiful Central Otago. Farming 400 hectares with Merino sheep and deer. Guests are welcome to join in and farm activities always included. Amazing working sheepdogs, great home cooking, children welcome. No pets. Peaceful and quiet, an ideal place to explore this region. Interests include sport, curling, gardening, handcrafts, sheepdog competitions. We treat our guests as friends and invite you to share our paradise.

Cromwell   *Homestay Lodge   6km N of Cromwell*

Lake Dunstan Lodge
Judy & Bill Thornbury
Northburn, RD 3, Cromwell
Tel: (03) 445 1107 Fax: (03) 445 3062
Mob: 025 311 415   william.t@xtra.co.nz
www.lakedunstanlodge.co.nz
Double $100-$120 Single $70 (Full Breakfast)
Child neg Dinner $25pp by arrangement
Credit cards accepted
2 Queen 3 Single (3 bdrm) 1 Ensuite 1 Guests share

Friendly hospitality awaits you at our home privately situated beside Lake Dunstan. We are ex-Southland farmers and have a cat "Ollie". Our interests include "Lions", fishing, boating, gardening and crafts. Bedrooms have attached balconies, fridge, tea and coffee facilities. Guests share our living areas, spa pool and laundry. Local attractions: orchards, vineyards, gold diggings, fishing, boating, walks, 4 ski fields nearby. Enjoy dinner with us or just relax in the peaceful surroundings. No smoking indoors please. Directions: 5km north of Cromwell Bridge on SH8.

Cromwell - Lowburn   *Homestay B&B   1.5km N of Cromwell*

Walnut Grove
Adrian & Olivia Somerville
State Highway 6, Lowburn, RD 2,
Cromwell, Rapid No 67
Tel: (03) 445 1112 Fax: (03) 445 1115
Mob: 027 477 4695   walnut.grove@xtra.co.nz
www.walnutgrove.co.nz
Double $125 Single $110 (Special Breakfast)
Credit cards accepted Pet on property
1 King/Twin 1 Queen (2 bdrm) 2 Ensuite

Let our home be your home for your visit to Central Otago - beautiful in all seasons! Our spacious home is on 4 acres, almost surrounded by a working orchard and with mountain views and glimpse of Lake Dunstan. Each comfortable guestroom has ensuite, TV, telephone and tea/coffee-making facilities. Breakfast is served when it suits you. We have two Siamese cats, a Labrador dog and our interests include meeting people, Rotary, travel, fishing and exploring Central Otago. Please ring ahead to make a reservation.

Cromwell - Bannockburn   *Self-contained Homestay B&B   6km Cromwell*

Aurum
Janette & Maurice Middleditch
RD 2, Bannockburn, Lawrence Street - Short Street
Tel: (03) 445 2024 Fax: (03) 445 2027
www.bnb.co.nz/aurum.html
Double $95-$110 Single $60-$75
(Continental Breakfast) Child neg.
Dinner by arrangement Credit cards accepted
1 Queen 1 Double (3 bdrm)
1 Private

Situated in Bannockburn and surrounded by local wineries and historic gold mining sites, Aurum provides private guest living. Maurice is a scenic artist who exhibits throughout the country and Janette speaks Dutch and loves meeting people. Two bedrooms and bedsitting room with big bathroom and bath, hairdryer, TV, tea and coffee, and laundry facilities available. A continental breakfast will be served at a time suitable to you. Reservations essential.

Arrowtown   *Self-contained Homestay   18km NE of Queenstown*

Bains Homestay
Ann & Barry Bain
R32 Butel Road, Arrowtown, Otago
Tel: (03) 442 1270 Fax: (03) 442 1271
Mob: 025 274 3360
bainshomestay@ihug.co.nz
www.dotco.co.nz/bainshomestay
Double $90-$105 (Full Breakfast) Child neg
Credit cards accepted Pet on property Pets welcome
1 Queen 4 Single (2 bdrm) 1 Ensuite 1 Private

We are a retired business couple who have travelled extensively. We welcome our guests to a peaceful, spacious, sunny self-contained upstairs suite complete with kitchen, and a balcony with panoramic views of surrounding mountains and the famous Millbrook golf resort. Meet our friendly Cocker Spaniel. Extra continental breakfast with freshly baked bread, jams etc is provided in your suite; or join us for a cooked starter. Complimentary laundry, road bikes, gold mining gear, BBQ etc. Our courtesy car is an Archbishop's 1924 Austin drophead coupe.

Arrowtown   *Homestay   19km E of Queenstown*

Rowan Cottage
Elizabeth & Michael Bushell
9 Thomson Street,
Arrowtown
Tel: (03) 442 0443
Mob: 025 622 8105
www.bnb.co.nz/rowancottage.html
Double $85 Single $50 (Continental Breakfast)
Dinner $25pp
1 Double 2 Single (2 bdrm)
1 Guests share

Rowan Cottage is situated in a quiet tree lined street with views to the mountains and hills. We are 10 minutes walk to the town and 20 minutes drive to Queenstown. We have a lovely cottage garden to relax and have coffee and homemade goodies. We are well travelled and can advise you on things to see and do in our beautiful part of the country. Guests comments: Wonderful Hospitality - Very Comfortable - Excellent Breakfasts.

OTAGO
NTH CATLINS

Arrowtown   *Homestay   Arrowtown*

Arrowtown Homestay
Anne & Arthur Gormack
18 Stafford Street,
Arrowtown
Tel: (03) 442 1747 Fax: (03) 442 1787
Tollfree: 0800 184 990   agormack@xtra.co.nz
www.bnb.co.nz/arrowtownhomestay.html
Double $100 (Continental Breakfast)
1 King 2 Single (2 bdrm)
2 Private

Our spacious home overlooking Millbrook Country Club and the Wakatipu Basin, offers spectacular views from every window. Although only 5 minutes walk from the town centre, our outlook is totally rural. We have a warm and comfortable home with plenty of space inside and out. During the Summer join us for a glass of wine beside our heated swimming pool, which is there for your use. Free use of laundry. Freephone: 0800 184 990

Arrowtown   *Self-contained B&B   20km N of Queenstown*

Polly-Anna Cottage
Daphne & Bill MacLaren
43 Bedford Street, Arrowtown
Tel: (03) 442 1347 Fax: (03) 442 1307
Mob: 025 220 3974
www.bnb.co.nz/pollyannacottage.html
Double $90-$95 Single $60 (Continental Breakfast)
Child $20 Dinner $25 Credit cards accepted
Pet on property Children welcome
1 Double 2 Single (2 bdrm)   1 Ensuite 1 Private

Daphne and Bill, retired business couple, have restored and renovated their quaint cute and cosy 100 year old cottage, nestled in an attractive garden, surrounded by spectacular mountains. Bill retired from Ford Dealer Industry; Have both travelled widely; Can inform on all local attractions and offer our warm hospitality, completely private ensuite facilities. 3 minutes from historic Arrowtown, 15 minutes to Queenstown. Try Daph's home preserves. Comments: "Highlight of our trip". "Thanks for Memory". Cat named Maggie. Come in, be surprised. Directions: Polly-Anna sign at front gate.

Arrowtown   *Homestay   20km N of Queenstown*

Wicky & Norman Smith
13 Stafford Street, Arrowtown
Tel: (03) 442 1092 Fax: (03) 442 1092
norman@queenstown.co.nz
www.bnb.co.nz/smitharrowtown.html
Double $85 Single $55 (Continental Breakfast)
Dinner $25 on request
1 Queen 2 Single (2 bdrm)
1 Guests share

A friendly welcome awaits you with tea or coffee on the patio of our home overlooking Arrowtown which is a popular holiday destination because of its charm and tranquillity. We are only 20 minutes drive from Queenstown where all the venturesome attractions are found. We have travelled widely and are keen trampers, and enjoy gardening, golf, computing and helping other people to enjoy the beauty of our area. Laundry is complimentary. Off street parking. We have a cat. Please phone, Fax or Email for bookings.

Arrowtown   *B&B B&B Lodge   Arrowtown Central*

Arrowtown Lodge & Hiking Co
John & Margaret Wilson
7 Anglesea Street, Arrowtown
Tel: (03) 442 1101 Fax: (03) 442 1108
Tollfree: 0800 258 802   hiking@queenstown.co.nz
www.arrowtownlodge.co.nz
Double $130-$160 Single $80-$110 (Full Breakfast)
Credit cards accepted
2 King/Twin 2 Queen (4 bdrm)
4 Ensuite

Located in the historic part of Arrowtown?< Arrowtown Lodge and Hiking Company is only 200 metres from the centre of the village where guests can enjoy a good selection of restaurants, cafes and pubs. Arrowtown Lodge is built in the old style using schist and mud brick. The four cottage style suites have king or queen size beds, TV, tea and coffee making facilities, hair driers, heated floors, guest phones, private guest entrance and off street car parking. Children welcome. Ancient Labrador resident. Guided walks available.

Arrowtown   *Self-contained   Arrowtown Central*

Pam Miller
23 Berkshire Street, Arrowtown
Tel: (03) 442 1126
www.bnb.co.nz/miller.html
Double $90 Single $70 (Full Breakfast)
Credit cards accepted Pet on property
1 Queen (1 bdrm)
1 Private

You will be made very welcome at my home which is centrally located on the main road, entering Arrowtown from Queenstown. I am three blocks from the Arrowtown village centre. My accommodation for guests has a private entrance, double bedroom, small sitting room with TV and tea/coffee making facilities. Also a private bathroom with laundry facilities. Delicious continental or full breakfast is served in the dining room upstairs. Elderly cat in residence. Off street parking. Only 20 minutes drive to Queenstown.

All our B&Bs are non-smoking
unless stated otherwise in the text.

Arrowtown   *Self-contained B&B   2min from Central Arrowtown*

Arrowtown Old Nick
Marie & Steve Waterhouse
70 Buckingham Street, Arrowtown,

Tel: (03) 442 0066 Fax: (03) 442 0066 Mob: 025 239 6091   Tollfree: 0800 653 642
host@oldnick.co.nz   www.oldnick.co.nz

Double $120-$150 Single $100-$130 (Full Breakfast) Child on application
Credit cards accepted Child at home Pet on property
4 King/Twin 1 King (5 bdrm) 3 Ensuite 1 Guests share

The Old Nick' was built in 1902 as the original residence & office of Arrowtown's police. By the late 1950s the residence was retired from active duty.

In 1995, transformation to lodgings of a more luxurious and inviting kind began, and today the original historic house set amidst Oak and Sycamore trees on a large lawn and gardens has become a place where people escape to (rather than from!)

Inside the main residence are two rooms (Super King/Twin and King)that share a bathroom complete with spa bath, fluffy towels, toiletries and hair dryers. Adjoining the main house on the site where the police horses were once housed is 'The Stables', with a choice of three Super King/Twin rooms, all with ensuites.

They say the heart of any home is the kitchen and The Old Nick has a huge, warm heart indeed. Its sumptuous breakfasts are reason alone to stay here.

You could forego all the activities this region offers and head straight for the lounge. Surrounded by local artwork, it's here that you can sink into a deep leather sofa in front of the open fire with a good book or good friend.

If the lure of the great outdoors is too much, you can throw yourself into activities that have made this part of the world famous or you can explore historic sites like the disused jail that stands on the adjoining property or spend time strolling through Arrowtown or Queenstown sampling various shopping & restaurants/cafes.

Share our hospitality with our 5 year old son Daniel and our outside dog - Halifax.

Arrowtown - Queenstown
Farmstay Separate/Suite B&B   4km S of Arrowtown

Golden Hills Homestead
Patricia Sew Hoy
Golden Hills Homestead, RD 1, Highway 6 rapid 1080, Queenstown
Tel: (03) 442 1427 Fax: (03) 4421 427 Mob: 025 238 8388
goldhill@xtra.co.nz   www.bnb.co.nz/goldenhills.html
Double $140-$195 Single $80-$100 (Special Breakfast)
Child 1/2 price Credit cards accepted   3 Queen 2 Single (3 bdrm) 2 Ensuite 1 Private

A superior, distinctive, sun-filled, quiet Homestead surrounded by a three acre award-winning garden on a 30acre farm.

Downstairs has a woodfire, large Lounge room leading to outside terraces with garden furniture as does the big Conservatory. Barbeque around a pond includes more outdoor living. Downstairs has two Ensuite Queen bedrooms with all the extras one would expect. Upstairs the Suite comprises one Queen and Single Bedroom; a heated floortiled bathroom with shower and spa bath. The Private Sitting room also has a large table for business people to work on. This Suite is private,sunny with spectacular mountain views from the Balconies. Fridge, complimentary wine/beer/port, nibbles, tea/coffee facilities, chocolates, T.V. Email, phone, fax, laundry and exchange book library included.

I have hosted for nine years in this beautiful area and look forward to showing you how to make the most of your holiday in special places. The House has just been redecorated to an even higher standard.

I look forward to your company.

WELCOME to Golden Hills Homestead!

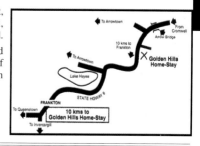

Arrowtown - Queenstown *B&B Self-contained Cottage   4km W of Arrowtown*

Willowbrook

Tamaki & Roy Llewellyn, Malaghan Road, RD 1, Queenstown

Tel: (03) 442 1773 Fax: (03) 442 1773 Mob: 025 516 739

info@willowbrook.net.nz   www.willowbrook.net.nz

Double $120-$140 Single $105-$125 (Continental Breakfast) Child POA Credit cards accepted
2 King 1 Queen 4 Single (5 bdrm)   4 Ensuite 1 Private

Willowbrook is a 1914 farmhouse at the foot of Coronet Peak in the beautiful Wakatipu Basin. The setting is rural, historical and distinctly peaceful, and with the attractions of Queenstown only 15 minutes away, Willowbrook can truly claim to offer the best of both worlds.

The old homestead has been beautifully renovated and while the character of the original house has been retained, it now boasts such modern comforts as central heating, Sky TV and a luxurious spa pool. Guest rooms all contain a bed (or beds) more comfortable than you would find in most hotels and are ensuite or have a private bathroom.

The 'Shearers Quarters' is a fully self-contained, two-bedroom cottage a short distance from the main house. With laundry facilities, open-plan kitchen/dining/lounge and spacious sundecks, it is ideally suited to families or two couples travelling together.

We have a tennis court in the garden and are within easy reach of 4 skifields and 3 golf courses. An Anglo/Japanese couple with a wealth of 'cross cultural experiences', we are only too happy to help with local bookings and itineraries in general.

Directions: We are on Malaghan Road (the 'back road' between Queenstown and Arrowtown). From Queenstown, take Gorge Road out through Arthurs Point, make no turns and after about 15 minutes, look for our sign on your right. From the north, turn right at Lake Hayes, go 5km and turn left into Malaghan Road. Millbrook Resort is on your left and we are 3 1/2 km further along the road, also on the left.

Arrowtown - Queenstown   *Homestay B&B   11km N of Queenstown*

Birchwood
Richard and Lynne Farrar
78 Lower Shotover Road, RD 1, Queenstown
Tel: (03) 442 3499 Fax: (03) 442 3498
Tollfree: 0800 36 45 50   bnb@birchwood.net.nz
www.birchwood.net.nz

Double $120-$150 Single $100 (Full Breakfast)
Child 1/2 price Credit cards accepted
1 King 1 Double 2 Single (3 bdrm)
1 Ensuite 1 Private

You are warmly invited to stay with us in our modern, classic style country home set in a sunny, sheltered two acre garden. Relax in a private, tranquil setting or enjoy a game of tennis on our court. The house is single storeyed with good access and easy parking. There is a spacious, elegant guest room (ensuite) with its own entrance, and a choice of twin or double bedroom. Located halfway between Arrowtown and Queenstown. Nearby attractions include cafes, restaurants, wineries, skifields and golf courses. Come and enjoy this unique area.

Queenstown - Arrowtown   *B&B   14km N of Queenstown*

Redbrick Bed & Breakfast
Paul & Leone Schoenbaechler
No. 319 Lower Shotover Road, R.D.1, Queenstown
Tel: 64-3-442-0855 Fax: 64-3-442-0884
Mob: 025-208-8097   redbrick@xtra.co.nz
www.red-brick.co.nz

Double $165 Single $145 (Continental Breakfast)
Credit cards accepted Child at home Pet on property
1 King/Twin (1 bdrm)
1 Ensuite

Redbrick is a quiet one room B&B with an old & worldly look, comfortable feel with a private balcony to watch the sunset. Surrounded by views of the mountains on a seven-acre lifestyle farm. The guest room has a seperate entrance, full ensuite, TV, radio, central heating, a super king bed. Breakfast includes a fresh baked loaf of bread. In house services: Make-up Artist and Therapeutic Massage. Leone, Paul and our kids Mandy (1988), Michelle (1991) and Joshua (2001)welcome you.

Queenstown   *right in the heart of Queenstown*

Mountvista Boutique Hotel
Ray & Eleanor Robins
4 Sydney St, Queenstown,
Tel: (03) 442 8832 Fax: (03) 442 4233
Mob: 021 62 77 62
stay@mountvista.com
www.mountvista.com

Double $345 Single $295
14 King/Twin (14 bdrm)
14 Ensuite

New and unique, this intimate small hotel offers the ambience and luxury of a remote exclusive lodge – while only 3 minutes' stroll to Queenstown's town centre & lakefront. Spacious Guest rooms are luxuriously furnished with SuperKing beds, plus a generous seating area with two supremely comfortable armchairs. The adjacent tiled ensuite bathroom has underfloor heating and a 2 person bath/shower. Rooms have fast internet, desk, phone, fridge, tea/coffee, & SKY TV with Sport-Movies-CNN. Sunny breakfast room, large guest lounge with wood fire, Ski drying & Sauna.

Queenstown   *Homestay   Health Retreat*   *1km N of Queenstown*

Bush Creek Health Retreat
Ileen Mutch
21 Bowen Street,
Queenstown
Tel: (03) 442 7260 Fax: (03) 442 7250
www.bnb.co.nz/bushcreek.html
Double $140 Single $70
(Special Breakfast) Child 1/2 price
1 Queen 4 Single (3 bdrm)
2 Guests share

The Retreat is one of the longest established in New Zealand, and Ileen is an internationally acclaimed specialist in Natural Healing. Recharge your energies in the renowned magical garden tucked away in 4 acres of total seclusion. Balcony bedrooms fully appointed with all the extras providing the ultimate in comfort. Lounge, sun decks, organically grown foods and deep tissue massage is available. Directions: Approaching Queenstown downhill, turn right at 2nd round-a-bout into Gorge Road + 1km to shops on left - 2 signposts up Bowen Street to the Retreat.

Queenstown   *Self-contained B&B*   *4km N of Queenstown*

Trelawn Place
Nery Howard & Michael Clark
PO Box 117, 412 Gorge Road, Queenstown
Tel: (03) 442 9160 Fax: (03) 442 9160
trelawn@ihug.co.nz   www.trelawnb-b.co.nz
Double $180-$250 Single $170 (Full Breakfast)
S/C $250 Credit cards accepted
Pet on property Children welcome
1 King/Twin 2 King 2 Queen 1 Twin (6 bdrm)
5 Ensuite 1 Private

Description: Sited dramatically above the Shotover River. Trelawn Place a superior country lodge is only 4kms from Queenstown. Five comfortably appointed ensuite rooms furnished with country chintz and antiques. Guest sitting room with open fire, shady vine covered verandas. Guest Laundry Facilities. Your well travelled hosts, Nery and Michael, Molly the cat, and the corgis welcome you. Our Honeymoon Cottage has two bedrooms. Directions: Take HW 6a into Queenstown, right at the second roundabout into Gorge Road, travel 4km toward Arthurs Point.

Queenstown   *Self-contained B&B*   *1.5km E of Queenstown Central*

Braemar House
Ann & Duncan Wilson
56 Panorama Terrace, Queenstown
Tel: (03) 442 7385 Fax: (03) 442 4385
Mob: 025 651 1035
www.bnb.co.nz/braemarhouse.html
Double $95 Single $60 (Continental Breakfast)
Child 1/2 price
1 Double 1 Single (1 bdrm)
1 Private

Our apartment is fully self-contained and occupies the middle floor of our home. A full breakfast is supplied if requested for $95 (double) or for the apartment only the tariff is $80. We have other beds available for groups of more than two people. There is a panoramic view of Lake Wakatipu and the surrounding mountains from the visitor's balcony and all rooms. Directions: Turn up Suburb Street off Frankton Road, then first right into Panorama Tce.

Queenstown   *Homestay*   *Queenstown Central*

The Stable
Isobel & Gordon McIntyre
17 Brisbane Street, Queenstown
Tel: (03) 442 9251 Fax: (03) 442 8293   gimac@queenstown.co.nz   www.thestablebb.com
Double $160-$180 Single $120 (Full Breakfast) Credit cards accepted
1 King/Twin 1 Double (2 bdrm)   1 Ensuite 1 Private

A 130 year old stone stable, converted for guest accommodation, and listed by the New Zealand Historic Places Trust, shares a private courtyard with our home. The "Garden Room" is in the house, providing convenience and comfort with lake and mountain views.

Our home is in a quiet cul-de-sac and set in a garden abundant with rhododendrons and native birds. It is less than 100 metres from the beach where a small boat and canoe are available for guests' use. The famous Kelvin Heights Golf Course is close and tennis courts, bowling greens and ice skating rink are in the adjacent park.   All tourist facilities, shops and restaurants are within easy walking distance, less than 5 minutes stroll on well lit footpaths.

Both rooms are well heated with views of garden, lake or mountains. Tea and coffee making facilities are available at all times. Guests share our spacious living areas and make free use of our library and laundry.   A courtesy car is available to and from the bus depots.

We can advise about and are booking agents for all sightseeing tours. Do allow an extra day or two for all the activities in the Queenstown region.

No smoking indoors.

Your hosts, with a farming background, have bred Welsh ponies and now enjoy weaving, cooking, gardening, sailing and the outdoors. We have an interest in a successful vineyard and enjoy drinking and talking about wine. We enjoy meeting people and have travelled extensively overseas.

Directions: Follow State Highway 6a (Frankton Road) to where it veers right at the Millenium Hotel. Continue straight ahead. Brisbane Street ("no exit") is 2nd on left. Phone if necessary.

Queenstown   *Self-contained B&B*   *Queenstown Central*

Birchall House
Joan & John Blomfield
118 Panorama Terrace,
Larchwood Heights, Queenstown
Tel: (03) 442 9985 Fax: (03) 442 9980
birchall.house@xtra.co.nz
www.bnb.co.nz/birchallhouse.html

Double $120-$130 Single $95 Child $30
(Continental & Full Breakfast) Credit cards accepted
1 Queen 2 Single (2 bdrm) 1 Private

Welcome to our new home in Queenstown, purpose built to accommodate guests in a beautiful setting. At Birchall House, you enjoy a magnificent 200 degree view of Lake Wakatipu and surrounding mountains, and are within walking distance of town centre. Our guest accommodation is spacious, private with separate entrance, centrally heated, smoke-free, electric blankets on all beds. A continental or cooked breakfast is available. Off-street parking, courtesy transport to/from the airport or bus terminal.From Frankton Road, turn up Suburb Street, then first right into Panorama Terrace. Access via Sunset Lane.

Queenstown   *Self-contained Homestay B&B*   *8km NE of Queenstown*

Collins Homestay
Pat & Ron Collins
Grant Road, RD 1, Queenstown
Tel: (03) 442 3801
rcollins@queenstown.co.nz
www.bnb.co.nz/collins.html

Double $90 Single $70 (Full Breakfast)
Garden Cottage $100 Credit cards accepted
2 Queen 2 Single (3 bdrm)
1 Ensuite 1 Private

We offer relaxed kiwi hospitality in rural environment with mountain views and lovely gardens. Accommodation: GARDEN COTTAGE with queen bed, ensuite, patio; GUEST WING, queen or twin, private bathroom. Laundry facilities. We are able to help with sightseeing arrangements. Our interests are golf, gardening, family, fishing and walking our dog Meg while BJ our cat prefers to lie in the sun. Directions: Grant Rd sign on Mailbox on S.H. 6 from North 2 km before Frankton. From South right at Frankton on S.H. 6 to Grant Rd 2 km on gravel Rd left turn.

Queenstown   *Guesthouse*   *0.8km*

Scallywags Guesthouse
Evan Jenkins
27 Lomond Cresent, Queenstown
Tel: (03) 442 7083 Fax: (03) 442 5885
www.bnb.co.nz/scallywagsguesthouse.html

Double $58 Single $50
Pet on property Children welcome
3 Queen 3 Twin (6 bdrm)
3 Guests share

A unique New Zealand home for you to share. We are a"B&B with no B". However bring your own food and use the excellent kitchen and great bbq area. Tea, coffee and milk is complimentary. Linen, towels, duvets and electric blankets are on all beds. Share excellent new bathroom facilities. Fantastic views - 180 degrees panorama - sunrise to sunset - lake, mountains, valleys. The ambience is casual and informal. Enjoy the company of other travellers. The house is situated adjacent to a bush reserve with native birdlife and song abundant. A peaceful haven just 10 minutes pleasant walk to village centre. "Luckie" the Lorikeet.

Queenstown

Bed & Breakfast
NUMBER 12

.... a quiet convenient location

Queenstown   *Self-contained Homestay B&B*   *Queenstown Central*

Number Twelve
Barbara & Murray Hercus
12 Brisbane Street, Queenstown

Tel: (03) 442 9511
Fax: (03) 442 9755
hercusbb@queenstown.co.nz
www.number12bb.co.nz

Double $120-$130 Single $90-$100
Mastercard and Visa accepted
2 King 2 Twin (2 bdrm)
1 Ensuite 1 Private

We would like you to come and share our conveniently situated house in a no exit street. You only have a 5 minute stroll to the town centre. Our home has mountain and lake views. Our home is warm and sunny, windows double glazed and we have central heating for the winter months. Our bedrooms have TVs, coffee/tea making facilities, hair dryers and instant heaters. Our studio apartment has full kitchen facilities. Email & laundry is available.

We have a solar heated swimming pool (Dec/March) the sun deck and BBQ are for your use. Our sun room is available for your comfort.

Guests have the choice of either a full or continental breakfast in our dining room with its panoramic views. Once settled in you will seldom need to use your car again. There are several easy walking routes into the town centre, restaurants, shops and tourist centres. We are very close to the lake and our botanical gardens. Whilst you are with us we will be happy to advise on tourist activities and sightseeing and make any arrangements you would wish. Barbara has a nursing/social work background and Murray is a retired chartered accountant. We have travelled extensively within our country and overseas. We have an interest in classical/choral music.

Directions: Highway 6a into Queenstown - the Millennium Hotel will be on your right, do NOT turn right at the sign Town Centre but continue straight ahead Brisbane St is second on the left and we are on the left.

OTAGO
NTH CATLINS

Queenstown   *B&B*   *1/2km N of Queenstown*

Adelaide Street Guest House
Dave, Mandy & family Wright
PO Box 998, 27 Adelaide Street, Queenstown
Tel: (03) 442 6207 Fax: (03) 442 6202
adelaidehouse@xtra.co.nz
www.bnb.co.nz/ahomeawayfromhome.html
Double $70-$95 Single $47-$59 (Continental Breakfast)
King with ensuite $120 Credit cards accepted
2 King 2 Double 2 Twin 4 Single (6 bdrm)
1 Ensuite 2 Guests share 1 Family share

Adelaide Street Guest House is perfectly situated just 35 metres from the shores of the beautiful Lake Wakatipu in the heart of Queenstown, just a short scenic walk to the centre of town. The sundecks, spacious lounge and most or our rooms enjoy breathtaking views of the lake and golf course enveloped by stunning mountain ranges. All rooms are heated and have electric blankets and duvets. Tea and coffee available anytime. Colourful sunsets in summer. Skiing in Winter. Book with us for tours and sightseeing. Off season rates.

Queenstown   *B&B*   *800m Queenstown*

Monaghans
Elsie & Pat Monaghan
4 Panorama Terrace,
Queenstown
Tel: (03) 442 8690 Fax: (03) 442 8620
patmonaghan@xtra.co.nz
www.bnb.co.nz/monaghans.html
Double $90 Single $80 (Continental Breakfast)
1 Queen (1 bdrm)
1 Ensuite

Welcome to our home in a quiet location, walking distance to town. Enjoy this panoramic view while you breakfast. One couple - personal attention. Spacious comfortable room with separate entrance and garden patio. Queen bed, own bathroom, TV, fridge and tea/coffee biscuits. Interests - music,gardening, sport, travel. We will enjoy your company but respect your privacy. Off street parking. Airport and bus transfers. Directions Turn right up Suburb Street off Frankton Road which is the main road into Queenstown then first right into Panorama Terrace.

Queenstown   *Self-contained*   *Queenstown Central*

Anna's Cottage & Rose Suite
Myrna & Ken Sangster
67 Thompson Street, Queenstown
Tel: (03) 442 8994 Fax: (03) 441 8994
Mob: 025 626 2165
www.bnb.co.nz/annascottage.html
Double $120-$160 Single $90
(Continental Breakfast $10 extra)
Credit cards accepted Smoking area inside
1 King/Twin 2 Queen (2 bdrm) 2 Private

A warm welcome to Anna's Cottage. Myrna a keen gardener and golfer, Ken with a love of fishing. Enjoy the peaceful garden setting and mountain views. Full kitchen facilities and living room combined. Washing machine. Tastefully decorated throughout, the bedroom is furnished with Sheridan linen. Only a few minutes from the centre of Queenstown. Private drive and parking at cottage. Attached to the end of our home The Rose Suite, self-contained, 1 Queen bed with ensuite, small kitchen, washing machine, furnished with Sheridan linen. Newly renovated suites.

Queenstown Central *Boutique Hotel*   *200m N of Queenstown*

Queenstown House
69 Hallenstein Street, Queenstown
Tel: (03) 442 9043 Fax: (03) 442 8755
Mob: 025 324 146
queenstown.house@xtra.co.nz
www.queenstownhouse.co.nz

Double $225-$495 Single $195 (Special Breakfast)
Credit cards accepted
10 King/Twin 4 Queen (14 bdrm)
14 Ensuite

"The best small B&B hotel in which we have stayed" comment our returning guests. Our elevated position has wonderful views over the town centre, lake and mountains. A delux breakfast menu served in our lakeview dining room is included, plus our very popular, complimentary cocktail hour each evening, hosted in either the fireside sitting room or rose filled courtyard. Guest laundry, bag storage, TV, hairdryer are supplied. Experience our unique style of hospitality, local knowledge and cheerful staff. Owner Louise Kiely, an ex restauranter & world traveller.

Queenstown *Self-contained & B&B*   *1.5km NE of Queenstown*

Ruth Campbell
10 Wakatipu Heights, Queenstown
Tel: (03) 442 9190 Fax: (03) 442 4404
Mob: 021 116 8801   roosterretreat@xtra.co.nz
www.bnb.co.nz/campbell.html

Double $100 Single $60 (Continental Breakfast)
SC unit $220 Credit cards accepted Child at home
Pet on property Children welcome
1 King/Twin 1 Queen 1 Double 1 Single (3 bdrm)
2 Private

Our 2 girls, 1 cat and 2 bantams welcome other children to share their playground. This tranquil home with off street parking has outstanding views over Lake Wakatipu and Queenstown. The fully self contained 2 bedroom cottage garden unit with full kitchen and laundry facilities has proved immensely popular with guests - especially those with children. Includes breakfast. A superking or twin room with private bathroom is in the house. Enjoy a generous continental breakfast including fresh baked bread and real coffee at your leisure. Complimentary tea, coffee and also laundry facilities.

Queenstown *Self-contained B&B*   *3km E of Queenstown*

Haus Helga
Helga & Ed Coolman
107 Wynyard Crescent, Fernhill, Queenstown
Tel: (03) 442 6077 Fax: (03) 442 4957
haushelga@xtra.co.nz
www.bnb.co.nz/haushelga.html

Double $195-$295 (Special Breakfast)
Child $25 Extra adult $50 Credit cards accepted
2 King/Twin 2 Queen 2 Single (4 bdrm)
4 Ensuite 4 Private

OTAGO
NTH CATLINS

Haus Helga overlooks Lake Wakatipu and the Remarkables Mountains and provides the "best view in all of New Zealand". Our luxurious home has extra large tastefully furnished guest rooms, each with a private deck or terrace. The self-contained suite includes a large kitchen/living/dining room. Our Voglauer guest room includes handpainted Austrian furniture and an ensuite with corner spa bath. We are now in our seventh year in operation and feel truly fortunate to have made so many great new friends, our wonderful guests.

Queenstown   *Boutique Accommodation*   *100m Queenstown*

The Dairy Guest House
Sarah & Brian Holding
10 Isle Street, Queenstown
Tel: (03) 442 5164 Fax: (03) 442 5164
Mob: 025 204 2585   Tollfree: 0800 33 33 93
info@thedairy.co.nz   www.bnb.co.nz/thedairy.html
Double $270-$325 (Full Breakfast)
Credit cards accepted
9 King/Twin 2 Queen (11 bdrm)   11 Ensuite

Discover a luxury Bed & Breakfast that offers the relaxed and comfortable hospitality of the Southern Alps of NZ, just 150 metres form the historic centre of Queenstown. The Dairy Guesthouse has 11 private rooms with en-suite, two lounge rooms, one with wood fire, separate TV lounge, ski storage, 6-seater hydrotherapy spa, and parking. Its focus is an original 1920's general store - from which the guesthouse takes its name. Begin each day with a sumptuous breakfast served in the Old Dairy from where you can view the beautiful surrounding mountains. NZ Tourism Awards Finalist 2001 and 2002. No Pets. No children under 12.

Queenstown   *Homestay B&B*   *Queenstown Central*

Larch Hill Home-stay B&B
Maria & Chris Lamens
16 Panners Way, Goldfields, Queenstown
Tel: (03) 442 4811 Fax: (03) 441 8882
chris@larchhill.com   www.larchhill.com
Double $105-$145 Single $95 (Special Breakfast)
Dinner $50 Apartment (twin share) $160
Credit cards accepted
2 King 1 Queen 2 Twin 2 Single (4 bdrm)
2 Ensuite 2 Private

A warm welcome awaits you at Larch Hill. Our comfortable and relaxing home-stay is just 3 min. drive from the centre of town. Public transport stops at the drive way. All rooms have lake and mountain views. In winter, there is a roaring log-fire awaiting your return from a days skiing or sightseeing. Maria provides three course dinners by prior arrangement. We have pleasure in organising any Queenstown experiences. We speak also Italian, German and Dutch. Directions: from HW6a turn into Goldfield Heights at Sherwood Manor. Second left is Panners Way.

Ensuite and private bathrooms
are for your use exclusively.
Guest share bathroom means you
will be sharing with other guests.
Family share means you
will be sharing with the family.

Queenstown   *Homestay & B&B   1/2km NW of central*

Coronet View Homestay and B&B
Karen & Neil Dempsey, Dawn & Warrick Goodman
28-30 Huff Street, Queenstown,

Tel: (03) 442 6766 Fax: (03) 442 6766 Mob: 025 320 895
dempsey@coronetview.com www.bnb.co.nz/coronetview.html

Double $100-$240 Single $100-$240
(Continental Breakfast) (Full Breakfast) (Special Breakfast)
Child POA Dinner $20 - $60 Hamper Lunches $20 - $60
Credit cards accepted
Child at home Children welcome
Pet on property
9 King/Twin 1 Queen 1 Twin (11 bdrm)
11 Ensuite

Neil & Karen or Dawn & Warwick
warmly Welcome you to the Elegant
Coronet View Homestay Located in the
Heart of Queenstown, New Zealands Adventure, Holiday and Shopping Playground.

Enjoy a award winning Local Wine in the
courtyard with Flower Garden , Jacuzzi,
Swimming pool and the Friendly persian
cats.

Wake-up in your Spacious ensuited rooms
with exquisitely home-made quilts to the
panorama views of the Lake, Mountains
and freshly Baked Crossiants, Danish Pastries, Bagels, Scones, Blueberry Muffins
and other Delights from our own Bakery.

Queenstown *B&B Boutique Hotel*   *300m NW of Central Queenstown*

Browns Boutique Hotel
Nigel & Bridget Brown
26 Isle Street, Queenstown
Tel: (03) 441 2050 Fax: (03) 441 2060
Mob: 025 222 0681   stay@brownshotel.co.nz
www.brownshotel.co.nz
Double $190-$220 Single $150-$180
(Continental Breakfast) Credit cards accepted
Child at home Pet on property
10 King/Twin (10 bdrm)   10 Ensuite

Browns Boutique Hotel was opened in August 2000. Located only two blocks walk from downtown Queenstown with views over Queenstown Bay to the Remarkables. Every guest room is well appointed, spacious and boasts a super king size bed along with French doors opening onto balconies over the courtyard. All rooms have their own generous sized ensuite including showers and baths (excluding two paraplegic rooms). The bathrooms are fully tiled and feature Italian and German fittings. The guest lounge and dining room feature leather couches, open fireplace and mahogany dining tables and chairs.

Queenstown *Homestay*

Delfshaven
Irene Mertz
11 Salmond Place (off Kent Street), Queenstown
Tel: (03) 441 1447 Fax: (03) 441 1383
Mob: 025 659 2609
www.bnb.co.nz/mertz.html
Double $150 Single $130 (Special Breakfast)
Credit cards accepted
1 Double (1 bdrm)
1 Private

Nestled at the base of Queenstown is my sunny warm modern home, offering magnificent unobstructed 180 degree views over town, lake and mountains. The comfortable guest room, with its own TV and tea-making facilities, opens out to the garden and those same views. It is only a five minute downhill walk to the town. I am a retired teacher, widely travelled, enjoy good food and wine, love art, music and enjoy meeting people. A piano is waiting to be played. Welcome to Salmond Place.

Queenstown *B&B Homestay Dinners*

Saxony Downs High Country Stay
Sandra & Ray Drayton
Moke Lake Road, PO Box 276, Queenstown
Tel: (03) 442 5389 Fax: (03) 442 5322
mail@saxonydowns.co.nz
www.saxonydowns.co.nz
Double from $110 Single from $70
(Full Breakfast) Dinner from $39pp
1 Double 1 Twin (2 bdrm)
1 Private

We offer a world of mountain walks amidst alpine flora, birdlife, native beech forest and stunning mountain views. Relaxed seclusion on 23 acres bordering two high country farm stations, only 10 minutes from town. Seven walking tracks, trout fishing on three alpine lakes nearby. Mountain bikes and fishing tackle available for guests' use. Guided walks available. Gourmet dinners with wine. Our valley contains one of 'Lord of the Rings' film sites. We assure guests of a quality relaxing experience.

Queenstown   *B&B   800m Queenstown central*

Balmoral Lodge
Les Walker
24 York Street, Queenstown
Tel: (03) 442 7209 Fax: (03) 442 6499
balmoral.lodge@xtra.co.nz
www.2qnbalmoral.co.nz
Double $250 Single $195-$225 (Full Breakfast)
two bedroom suite $295 Credit cards accepted
Pet on property Children welcome
10 King/Twin 2 King 2 Queen (4 bdrm)
4 Private

Balmoral Lodge provides luxury bed & breakfast. It is situated on Queenstown Hill just 800 metres from the town centre. Spectacular panoramic lake, mountain and township views from all rooms including exterior decks. Lavishly decorated. All rooms have ensuite bathrooms, baths with showers. Some have spa baths. Family suite shower only. Fridge and coffee-making. Full breakfast. Off-street parking. Laundry facilities. Honeymoon suite. Gracious hospitality.

Queenstown   *B&B   14km N of Queenstown*

Kahu Rise
Angela & Bill Dolan
455 Littles Road, RD1, Queenstown
Tel: (03) 441 2077 Fax: (03) 441 2078
Tollfree: 0800 436 111   info@kahurise.co.nz
www.kahurise.co.nz
Double $170 (Full Breakfast)
Credit cards accepted Pet on property
1 Queen 2 Twin (2 bdrm)
1 Private

In the country, yet close to Queenstown, Arrowtown and local attractions, Kahu Rise offers both tranquility and convenience. We cater only for single party bookings (1-4). Our guest wing has a private bathroom, underfloor heating, tea and coffee facilities, refrigerator, TV, hairdryer, etc. Both rooms have mountain views and open directly on to the lawn. We prepare you a delicious home-cooked breakfast each morning and will advise on and book activities. Bill, Angela and Tess, our friendly dog, warmly welcome you.

Queenstown   *B&B   3km W of Queenstown*

Wynard Lodge
Jane Shackel & Fraser Tyrrell
141 Wynyard Cres, Fernhill, Queenstown
Tel: (03) 441 3009 stay@wynyard-lodge.com
www.wynyard-lodge.com
Double $125-$150 Single $110-$135
(Special Breakfast) Family suite $225
Credit cards accepted Children welcome
2 Queen 2 Twin (3 bdrm)
1 Ensuite 1 Private

OTAGO
NTH CATLINS

Wynyard Lodge is a luxury B&B, high on Fernhill, just five minutes from central Queenstown, with spectacular uninterrupted views of the Remarkables and Lake Wakatipu. We offer comfortable beds, quality linens, individual heat pumps, TVs, tea/coffee facilities, electric blankets, and a full gourmet breakfast. Wynyard Lodge has a warm and inviting atmosphere with friendly, welcoming hosts. We also have a spa pool with the best view in Queenstown for our guests.   There is also plenty of storage room for skis and snowboards. Wynyard Lodge is a great place to unwind after a hard day of adventure or sightseeing.

Queenstown *B&B* *500m N of Queenstown*

Chalet Queenstown
Gillian & Kel Frame
1 Dublin Street, Queenstown,
Tel: (03) 442 7117
Fax: (03) 442 7508
Mob: 021 157 1425
Tollfree: 0800 222 457
chalet.queenstown@xtra.co.nz
www.chalet.co.nz

Double $125-$185 Single $90-$150 triple $150
- $210 Credit cards accepted
5 King/Twin 1 Queen 1 Single (6 bdrm)
6 Ensuite

You will love the location of Chalet Queenstown,
a sunny site 500m from the Central PO and Botanical Gardens. An easy stroll will bring you to
the lakeside walking track, and the Millenium
walk on Queenstown Hill is also on our doorstep.

Gillian and Kel have been involved in the tourism industry for many years and have a thorough
knowledge of Queenstown and surrounds. We enjoy meeting people, golf, scrabble, yoga and
books.

Our well appointed rooms all have views of lake
and/or mountains, ensuite facilities(shower), T.V,
refrigerator, tea and coffee, hair dryer, oil heating and super comfortable beds with electric blankets and lovely linen. Our guest lounge has facilities for preparing light meals.

We endeavour to provide guests with wholesome
organic and preservative-free food and beverages.
You will enjoy the hearty continental breakfast
consisting of organic yoghurt, fresh fruits, your
choice of milk, home made muesli, seeds, nuts
and dried fruits, 100% juices, home baked bread,
fresh baked croissants, cereals, toast, tea, coffee
and herbal tea.

Other features of our home
• Complimentary mountain bike use
• Second hand book library
• Off-street parking
• Laundry facilities (charge)
• Relaxed and friendly atmosphere
• Filtered water
• Airport and tour pick up and drop off

We are happy to assist with all your reservations
for activities and onward bookings through the
NZ B & B book. Seasonal rates apply.

Queenstown *B&B* *Queenstown Central*

Turner Lodge
Cara & Chris
Corner Gorge Road & Turner Street, Queenstown
Tel: (03) 442 9432 Fax: (03) 442 9409
Tollfree: 0800 488 763   turnerlodge@xtra.co.nz
www.turnerlodge.co.nz
Double $130-$165 Single $80-$100 (Full Breakfast)
self-contained country flat $150
1 King 3 Queen 1 Double 1 Twin 2 Single (6 bdrm)
3 Ensuite 1 Private 2 Guests share

Located in the heart of Queenstown. We offer warm hospitality in relaxed spacious surroundings. Plenty of off-street parking/guest lounge with open fire. The rooms are all non-smoking and recently refurbished. Full breakfast is available from 8am - 10am. All local activities can be booked through the friendly obliging staff. Hosts reside nearby; on-hand 8am-7pm daily. A self-contained country unit is also available. Close to major skifields, an easy 18km from Queenstown/.5km from Arrowtown.

Queenstown - Glenorchy *Homestay B&B* *40mins Queenstown*

Lake Haven
Ronda & John
Benmore Place, Glenorchy
Tel: (03) 442 9091 Fax: (03) 442 9801
lakehaven@xtra.co.nz
www.bnb.co.nz/lakehaven.html
Double $120 Single $80 (Full Breakfast)
Child by arrangement Dinner by arrangement
Credit cards accepted
2 King 1 Twin (3 bdrm)   3 Ensuite

Lake Haven offers quality accommodation and warm hospitality at our secluded Lakefront property with stunning lake and bush clad mountain views. Glenorchy is the base for several world famous walking tracks eg, Routeburn, renowned for its Trout fishing and a large range of activities. Ronda and John are longtime locals and are happy to assist you in exploring and enjoying our unique and beautiful area. Children welcome. Laundry facilities. Fishing guide available. Glenorchy - Gateway to paradise.

Garston *Self-contained Homestay B&B* *50km S of Queenstown*

Bev & Matt Menlove
17 Blackmore Road,
Private Bag, Garston 9660
Tel: (03) 248 8516
mattmenlove@xtra.co.nz
www.bnb.co.nz/menlove.html
Double $70 Single $40 (Continental Breakfast)
Dinner $20 by arrangement
1 Double 1 Single (1 bdrm)
1 Ensuite

We are organic gardeners and our other interests include lawn bowls, sailing, gliding and alternative energy. Garston is New Zealand's most inland village with the Mataura River (famous for its fly fishing) flowing through the valley, surrounded by the Hector Range and the Eyre Mountains. A fishing guide is available with advance notice. For day trips, Garston is central to Queenstown, Te Anau, Milford Sound or Invercargill. We look forward to meeting you.

Kingston - Garston   *High Country Station*   *20km SW of Kingston*

Mataura Valley Station
Robyn & David Parker, PO Box 2, Garston 9660, Southland
Tel: (03) 248 8552 Fax: (03) 248 8552 matauravalley@xtra.co.nz
www.bnb.co.nz/matauravalleystation.html

Double $130-$200 Single $100 (Special Breakfast) Child
$50 - $100 Dinner $50 Self-contained cottage $200 - $250
Credit cards accepted Pet on property
2 King 1 Double 2 Twin 1 Single (5 bdrm)
2 Ensuite 1 Private 1 Guests share 1 Family share

Welcome to our 19,000-acre High Country Sheep and Cattle
Station. Experience alpine tranquility, 45 minutes scenic
drive from Queenstown. Your farmstay experience includes
your host family's personal attention. Meet our two cats,
the working dogs, 400 hereford cattle and 8,000 merino
sheep.

Enjoy our sunny, self-contained cottage and comfortable
homestead, which have glorious views overlooking the
Mataura River, world famous for brown trout fishing.
Experienced, local, fishing guide available. Alpine walks on
farm trails, or in the neighbouring Eyre Mountains
Conservation Park.

Experience Farm activities, take a complimentary farm tour
or simply relax, enjoying the views and the skylarks. Paradise
ducks nest on the creek, hawks soar, and New Zealand falcons
may rest on the rooftop. Welcome to the farmhouse kitchen
for snacks and chats. All meals are available by arrangement.
Delicious, farm-style dinners with fresh garden vegetables,
home baking and local wines. Pamper yourself. Our
daughter, Kim, is an experienced massage therapist,
specialising in deep tissue and sports massage. Weddings
by arrangement – your hostess is a registered celebrant.

Vintage steam train, aerial or 4-wheel drive tours available.

Day trip distances to Queenstown, the Southern Scenic
Circuit, Milford and Doubtful Sounds. Tour bookings
available.

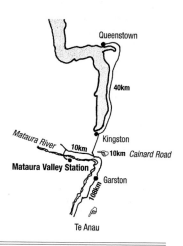

Alexandra - Earnscleugh   *Self-contained   Orchardstay   6km W of Alexandra*

Iversen
Robyn & Roger Marshall
47 Blackman Road, RD 1 Alexandra, Central Otago
Tel: (03) 449 2520 Fax: (03) 449 2519
Mob: 025 384 348   r.r.marshall@xtra.co.nz
www.bnb.co.nz/iversen.html

Double $110 Single $70 (Continental Breakfast)
Child by arrangement Dinner $25 by arrangement
Credit cards accepted
2 Queen (2 bdrm) 1 Guests share

Our self-contained guest accommodation offers you privacy and comfort. Combined with a warm welcome into our home, you can share with us, the peaceful and relaxing setting our our cherry orchard. While at Iversen , you can experience the grandeur and contrasts of the Central Otago landscape, walk the thyme covered hills, visit local wineries or just relax. Directions: From Alexandra or Clyde, travel on Earnscleugh Road, turn into Blackman Road and look for our sign on the left. Advanced bookings preferred.

Alexandra   *B&B Vineyard Homestay   6km N of Alexandra*

Hawkdun Rise Vineyard Stay
Judy & Roy Faris
Hawkdun Rise, Letts Gully Road,
Alexandra, Central Otago
Tel: (03) 448 7782 Fax: (03) 448 7752
Mob: 025 337 072   rfaris@clear.net.nz
www.vineyardstay.co.nz

Double $125 Single $90 (Full Breakfast)
Credit cards accepted
2 Queen 1 Double (3 bdrm)
2 Ensuite 1 Guests share

Welcome to our new home set in a small productive vineyard with commanding views of the surrounding hills. We are a professional couple with grown family and share our home with a Burmese cat, all non smokers. Complimentary wine and cheese served early evening and laundry and tea and coffee making facilities available. You can enjoy the privacy, views, spa and our wine cellar. If you are looking for privacy, tranquillity and executive accommodation you have found us.

Alexandra - Central Otago   *Homestay   3.5km N of Alexandra*

Duart   Mary & Keith McLean
Bruce's Hill, Highway 85, RD 3, Alexandra
Tel: (03) 448 9190 Fax: (03) 448 9190
duart.homestay@xtra.co.nz   www.duarthomestay.co.nz

Double $80 Single $50 (Continental Breakfast)
Child $30 Dinner $20 by arrangement
Credit cards accepted Pet on property
Children welcome Smoking area inside
1 Double 1 Twin 1 Single (3 bdrm)
1 Private 1 Family share

Your accredited Kiwi hosts, Mary and Keith, welcome you to our secluded home, 5 minutes from Alexandra. Your privacy is assured, but we enjoy company and conversation if that is your wish. Relish the spectacular views from our extensive stone terraced garden, or relax on the verandahs, sitting room or library area, while the laundry does itself and our cat sleeps peacefully. Or, you can walk in the hills or the Rail Trail, revel in the myriad activities and experiences Alexandra offers. Sky TV, complimentary tea, coffee, biscuits, fruit anytime.

Roxburgh - Millers Flat *Self-contained B&B*   *16km S of Roxburgh*

The Studio
Sheena & Wallace Boag
Millers Flat, RD 2, Roxburgh, Central Otago
Tel: (03) 446 6872 Fax: (03) 446 6872
www.bnb.co.nz/thestudio.html

Double $75 Single $45 (Continental Breakfast)
Child $20 Dinner $20 by arrangement
Double bed settee (upstairs) Credit cards accepted
2 Single (1 bdrm)   1 Ensuite

An easy 2-hour drive from Dunedin, Wanaka, Queenstown and Invercargill, Millers Flat is an attractive village in farming and fruitgrowing country, well-equipped with recreational facilities, easy access to fishing, walking tracks, gardens to visit, and the well-known community-owned store, "Faigan's". We live on 10 acres in a 110 year old house of rammed-earth construction. Our guest accommodation is a 2-storey building of more recent vintage, formerly Wallace's architectural studio, an interesting composition of space and light, comfortably-heated, with tea/coffee making facilities. Please phone ahead for directions.

Roxburgh - Ettrick *Self-contained Farmstay B&B*   *10km S of Roxburgh*

Clearburn Station
Margaret & Ian Lambeth
Dalmuir Road, RD 2, Roxburgh

Tel: (03) 446 6712 Fax: (03) 446 6774
JL.Lambeth@xtra.co.nz
www.bnb.co.nz/clearburnstation.html

Double $85 Single $50 (Continental Breakfast)
Child by arrangement Dinner $20 by arrangement
2 Single (1 bdrm)
1 Ensuite

Clearburn Station is a 5000 acre property with a Homestead Block and Hill Country Run stocked with sheep and cattle and operated as a family partnership with son John and his wife Linda and children. Guest accommodation is a detached self contained unit with electric blankets, heaters, fridge, TV and tea making facilities. Guests are very welcome to join in the farm activities during their stay. Restaurant, golf course and fishing are within 5 mins drive. Directions: Please phone. 1 3/4 hour drive from Dunedin.

Roxburgh *Country Inn*   *9km S of Roxburgh*

The Seed Farm
Elaine & John Buchan
4760 Roxburgh-Ettrick Road, RD 2, Roxburgh

Tel: (03) 446 6824 Fax: (03) 446 6024
elaine@theseedfarm.co.nz
www.bnb.co.nz/theseedfarm.html

Double $110 Single $85 (Continental Breakfast)
Dinner by arrangement Credit cards accepted
3 Queen 2 Single (4 bdrm)
4 Ensuite

Nestled in the Teviot Valley centre of NZ's cherry and apricot growing region, the Seed Farm comprises a two storeyed cottage and separate stables set amidst two acres of cottage garden. The buildings all carry Historic Places Trust 2 classification reflecting their historic significance to the district. The stables have been converted and offer four self-contained bedrooms with TV, tea making facilities etc. The cottage contains a restaurant offering an eclectic menu in an olde world ambience.

Lawrence   *B&B   45 min Balclutha*

The Ark
Frieda Betman
8 Harrington Place (Main Road),
Tel: (03) 485 9328 Fax: (03) 485 9222
lawrence.infocentre@xtra.co.nz
www.thearknz.homestead.com

Double $90 Single $45
(Full Breakfast) Child $15
2 Double 1 Twin 1 Single (4 bdrm)
1 Family share

My home is situated on the main road near the picnic ground with its avenue of poplars. My garden is special to me, the home is 100 years old, has character, charm and a lived in feeling. It's home to Ambrose Pumpkin my cats and Holly a miniature Foxie. Guestrooms are restful with fresh flowers, fruit and breakfast includes hot bread, croissants, home-made jams. Free-range eggs. There is a lovely peaceful atmosphere in our early gold mining town. Approx. 45 mins to Dunedin airport, just over an hour to Dunedin. Please refer to "The Ark" when you contact us.

Palmerston   *Homestay Boutique Lodge   8km S of Palmerston*

Centrewood Historic Homestead
Drs Jane & David Loten
Bobbys head Rd, RD1 Palmerston, Otago
Tel: (03) 465 1977 Fax: (03) 465 1977
david.loten@xtra.co.nz   www.ecostay.co.nz

Double $150 (Special Breakfast)
Dinner $40 by arrangement guest wing $200 - $250
Credit cards accepted
1 King 2 Queen 1 Single (3 bdrm)
2 Private

Set in 50 acres with rambling gardens and park-like grounds, Centrewood is a very large homestead offering complete peace and privacy. Guests enjoy elegant furnishings, spacious accommodation with private bathrooms (robes provided), and private living room. Adjacent is a cliff-top walk allowing easy viewing of seals and penguins and nearby sandy beaches. On site attractions include rose-gardens, tennis, native bird-watching. Wildlife tours by arrangement. Sited midway between Christchurch and Queenstown. Dinner by arrangement. Nearby attractions: Moeraki Boulders, Dunedin 40 minutes.

OTAGO
NTH CATLINS

Dunedin *B&B   2km W of Dunedin*

Magnolia House
Joan & George Sutherland
18 Grendon Street,
Maori Hill, Dunedin 9001

Tel: (03) 467 5999 Fax: (03) 467 5999
mrsuth@paradise.net.nz
www.bnb.co.nz/magnoliahouse.html

Double $95 Single $70 (Special Breakfast)
1 Queen 1 Double 2 Single (3 bdrm)
1 Private 1 Guests share

Our quiet turn-of-the-century villa sits in broad, flower-bordered lawns backed by native bush with beautiful, tuneful birds. All rooms have electric heating, comfortable beds with electric blanket, and antiques, while the Queen room has an adjoining balcony. Close by is Moana Pool, the glorious Edwardian house, "Olveston", and Otago Golf Course. Our special breakfast will set you up for the day. We have a courtesy car, a Burmese and a Siamese cat. It is NOT SUITABLE FOR CHILDREN OR SMOKERS.

Dunedin *Homestay B&B   7km NE of Dunedin*

Harbourside B&B
Shirley & Don Parsons
6 Kiwi Street, St Leonards, Dunedin

Tel: (03) 471 0690 Fax: (03) 471 0063
www.bnb.co.nz/harboursidebb.html

Double $75-$90 Single $55 (Full Breakfast)
Child $15 Dinner $25 Credit cards accepted
Pet on property Children welcome
1 Queen 1 Double 3 Single (2 bdrm)
1 Ensuite 1 Family share

We are situated in a quiet suburb overlooking Otago Harbour and surrounding hills. Within easy reach of all local attractions. Lovely garden or harbour views from all rooms. Children very welcome. Directions: Drive into city on one-way system watch for Highway 88 sign follow Anzac Avenue onto Ravensbourne Rd. Continue approx 5 kms to St Leonards turn left at Playcentre opposite Boatshed into Pukeko St then left into Kaka Rd, straight ahead to Kiwi St turn left into No. 6.

Dunedin *B&B   Dunedin Central*

Deacons Court
Keith Heggie & Gail Marmont
342 High Street, Dunedin

Tel: (03) 477 9053 Fax: (03) 477 9058
Tollfree: 0800 268 252 Deacons@es.co.nz
www.deaconscourt.bizland.com

Double $100-$130 Single $60-$80 (Full Breakfast)
Child $20 - $30 Credit cards accepted Pet on property
1 King 1 Queen 1 Double 3 Single (3 bdrm)
2 Ensuite 1 Private

Deacons Court is a charming superior spacious Victorian Villa 1km walking distance from the city centre and on a bus route. We offer you friendly but unobtrusive hospitality in a quiet secure haven. Guests can relax in our delightful sheltered back garden and conservatory. All our bedrooms are large, have ensuite or private bathrooms, heaters, TV & electric blankets. Complimentary 24hr tea or coffee, ample free parking and laundry service available. We cater for non-smokers and have an unobtrusive cat. Family groups welcome.

Dunedin   *800m W of Dunedin Central*

Castlewood
Donna & Peter   Mitchell
240 York Place, Dunedin

Tel: (03) 477 0526   Fax: (03) 477 0526
relax@castlewood.co.nz
www.bnb.co.nz/castlewood.html

Double $100 Single $70
Twin $90 $145 ensuite
2 Queen 1 Twin 1 Single (3 bdrm)
1 Ensuite 1 Private 1 Guests share

CASTLEWOOD

Relax at Castlewood and experience the character and charm of a bygone era. Castlewood offers superior homestay accommodation in a gracious restored 1912 Tudor style town house located a mere 10 minutes walk away from Dunedin's leading attractions and city centre. Delight in Castlewood's sunny fragrant walled garden. Your hosts Peter & Donna appreciate the needs of discerning travellers and offer a sumptuous continental breakfast plus a guest's sauna. Peter is a skilled artist, and author of 'Great Escapes'. For further information, references and maps, view www.castlewood.co.nz.

Dunedin   *Bed & Breakfast Inn*   *2km SW of Dunedin Central*

Glenfield House
Cal Johnstone & Wendy Gunn
3 Peel St,
Mornington, Dunedin

Tel: (03) 453 5923 Fax: (03) 453 5984
www.bnb.co.nz/glenfieldhouse.html

Double $135-$175 Single $110-$135
(Full Breakfast) Credit cards accepted
2 Queen 2 Double (4 bdrm)
2 Ensuite 1 Guests share

We welcome you to our restored Victorian residence on the edge of the green belt. We offer you warmth, elegance and informality. In all bedrooms we provide heating, cotton and feather bedding, TV, telephone and freshly ground coffee. Our blue suite incorporates an ensuite, a sun room and the opportunity for intimate dining overlooking the city and harbour. With notice, a sumptuous three course meal prepared from Otago produce will be served in the guest dining room. We thank you for not smoking.

Broad Bay - Otago Peninsula   *Self-contained B&B*   *16km E of Dunedin*

Chy-an-Dowr
Susan & Herman van Velthoven
687 Portobello Road, Broad Bay, Dunedin

Tel: (03) 478 0306 Fax: (03) 478 0306
Mob: 025 270 5533   hermanvv@xtra.co.nz
www.visit-dunedin.co.nz/chyandowr.html

Double $120-$150 (Full Breakfast)
Cottage $95 - $120 Credit cards accepted
Pet on property
1 King/Twin 1 Queen 1 Double (3 bdrm)   2 Ensuite

CHY~AN~DOWR" ("House by the Water"), our character home located on scenic Otago Peninsula offers quality accommodation with panoramic harbour views. The upstairs guest area is spacious and private with comfortable rooms, private facilities, sunroom and wonderful views. "SLEEPY HOLLOW", a peaceful, private SELF-CONTAINED COTTAGE secluded in its own private garden, situated in a quiet rural location. The cottage has one bedroom, queen bed, bedsettee in lounge. Breakfast optional. We emigrated from Holland in 1981 and we enjoy welcoming people into our home.

Dunedin - Otago Peninsula   *Homestay*   *8km Dunedin City*

Captains Cottage
Christine & Robert Brown
422 Portobello Road, RD 2, Dunedin
Tel: (03) 476 1431 Fax: (03) 476 1431
Mob: 0274 352 734
wildfilm@actrix.co.nz
www.bnb.co.nz/captainscottage.html
Double $135 Single $100 (Special Breakfast)
Dinner $25 Pet on property
1 King/Twin 1 Double (2 bdrm)
1 Ensuite 1 Private

Captains Cottage is on the waterfront set in bush with spectacular views. Enroute to Albatross, Penguin and Seal Colonies. Christine and Robert are wildlife film makers, Robert having filmed for BBC, National Geographic and Discovery has many a tale to tell. Our local and wildlife knowledge can help plan your stay. Come in our boat fishing or view the unique bird and marine life. If you enjoy great food, hospitality, BBQ's or relaxing by our fire come and share our interesting home with us.

Dunedin   *Homestay*   *3km NE of Dunedin*

Harbour Lookout
Ron & Maire Graham
3 Taupo Street,
Ravensbourne, Dunedin
Tel: (03) 471 0582 Mob: 025 263 7244
rongra@xtra.co.nz
www.bnb.co.nz/harbourlookout.html
Double $65 Single $40 (Continental Breakfast)
2 Single (1 bdrm)
1 Family share

We are a retired couple who issue a warm welcome to you our guests. Directions: follow Port Chalmers Highway 88 e.g. Anzac Ave and Ravensbourne Road to Adderley Tce turning uphill behind the Hotel. Entering the first bend be alert for signpost on right for Taupo Street and Lane. Turn downhill and right into our drive. Your bedroom with private toilet is on this level. Bathroom and living areas upstairs. We and Beethoven the Budgie look forward to meeting you. Come in and relax.

Dunedin   *Homestay B&B*   *2km W of Dunedin*

Kincaple
Delys Cox
215 Highgate, Roslyn, Dunedin
Tel: (03) 477 4384 Fax: (03) 477 4380
Mob: 025 2488 968   kincaple@xtra.co.nz
Tollfree: 0800 269 384 pin 4774
www.welcometodunedin.co.nz/kincaplehomestay/.html
Double $85-$120 Single $60 (Continental Breakfast)
Child half price, under 12 Credit cards accepted
1 King/Twin 1 Twin (2 bdrm)
1 Ensuite 1 Guests share

Beyond our cottage style entrance is a delightful and sizeable character family home built in 1903. There is a welcoming, warm atmosphere with relaxing decor. The family dog is a small dachshund. The beds have quality mattresses, duvets and electric blankets. Large guest lounge with tea and coffee making facilities. There is a north facing garden, off street parking and a bus stop at the door. It is a short distance to local shops, restaurants, Moana Pool and the centre of town.

Broad Bay - Otago Peninsula   *Self-contained*   *18km E of Dunedin*

The Cottage
Lesley Hirst & Janet Downs
Contact Only - 7 Frances Street, Broad Bay, Dunedin
Tel: (03) 478 0073 Fax: (03) 478 0272
Mob: 025 381 291   thecottage@xtra.co.nz
www.visit-dunedin.co.nz/thecottage.html
Double $100-$135 (Special Breakfast)
$100 without breakfast   Credit cards accepted
1 Double (1 bdrm)
1 Ensuite

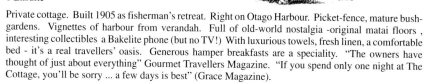

Private cottage. Built 1905 as fisherman's retreat. Right on Otago Harbour. Picket-fence, mature bush-gardens. Vignettes of harbour from verandah. Full of old-world nostalgia -original matai floors , interesting collectibles a Bakelite phone (but no TV!) With luxurious towels, fresh linen, a comfortable bed - it's a real travellers' oasis. Generous hamper breakfasts are a speciality. "The owners have thought of just about everything" Gourmet Travellers Magazine. "If you spend only one night at The Cottage, you'll be sorry ... a few days is best" (Grace Magazine).

Dunedin   *B&B*   *1km S of Dunedin*

Cill Chainnigh
Eileen & Wallie Waudby
33 Littlebourne Road, Roslyn, Dunedin
Tel: (03) 477 4963 Fax: (03) 477 4965
Mob: 025 228 7840
wallie.waudby@xtra.co.nz
www.bnb.co.nz/cillchainnigh.html
Double $90 Single $55 (Continental Breakfast)
1 Double 2 Single (2 bdrm)
1 Guests share

Eileen and Wallie would like to welcome visitors to Dunedin to their smoke-free home, situated in a quiet street just off Stuart Street and opposite Roberts Park. We have travelled extensively ourselves and understand how visitors feel when they arrive in a new town. Our home is in short walking distance to Dunedin's stately home "Olveston", the Moana swimming Complex and just over one kilometre to the town centre. The guest bedrooms, situated on the top floor for privacy and quietness, are warm and sunny .

Dunedin   *Homestay B&B*   *3.2km N of Dunedin Central*

Dalmore Lodge
Loraine & Mike Allpress
9 Falkirk Street, Dalmore, Dunedin
Tel: (03) 473 6513 Fax: (03) 473 6512
Mob: 025 287 1517   bookings@dalmorelodge.co.nz
www.dalmorelodge.co.nz
Double $95-$110 Single $75-$85 (Special Breakfast)
Child neg. Credit cards accepted Pet on property
1 King/Twin 1 Queen 1 Double 1 Single (4 bdrm)
1 Private 1 Guests share

OTAGO
NTH CATLINS

In its peaceful setting just two minutes off the Northern Motorway you'll find Dalmore Lodge. Our Larchwood home offers views of harbour, Pacific Ocean, city lights, Botanical Gardens, and hills. A three minute drive/20 minute walk takes you into the main business/shopping area. Public transport available end of driveway. We will meet you to/from airport, bus by prior arrangement (extra minimal cost) . Off street parking. We look forward to meeting you and sharing knowledge of Dunedin and local attractions.

Dunedin   *Homestay B&B   4.5km SE of Dunedin Central*

Alloway
Lorraine & Stewart Harvey
65 Every Street, Andersons Bay, Dunedin
Tel: (03) 454 5384 Fax: (03) 454 5364
Tollfree: 0800 387 245   alloway@xtra.co.nz
www.alloway.co.nz

Double $95-$140 Single $85-$115
(Continental Breakfast) Child neg.
Credit cards accepted
2 Queen 2 Single (2 bdrm) 1 Private 1 Guests share

We are situated on the gateway to the Otago Peninsula, which features wildlife, Walking Tracks, Taiaroa Head Albatross Colony, Disappearing Gun, Seal Colonies, Yellow Eyed Penguins, Glenfalloch Gardens, and much more. We are seven minutes to town centre. Our home is a modern interpretation of a traditional Scottish house, and set in 1 acre of gardens and lawns, with indoor/outdoor living. Awake to the sound of abundant bird life in a quiet and secure neighbourhood. We serve delicious healthy breakfasts. Two luxury bedrooms complete with one queen and one single bed.

Portobello - Otago Peninsula   *B&B   25min NE of Dunedin*

Peninsula Bed & Breakfast   Rachel & Mike Kerr
4 Allans Beach Road,
Portobello, Otago Peninsula, Dunedin
Tel: (03) 478 0909 Fax: (03) 478 0909
otago_peninsula@hotmail.com
www.bnb.co.nz/peninsulahomestaybb.html

Double $85-$145 Single $75-$125
(Continental Breakfast) Child $5 - $20
Credit cards accepted Children welcome
3 Queen 1 Twin (4 bdrm)   2 Ensuite 1 Guests share

We are a sixth generation Otago Peninsula family with two children, Jackson (4) and Rueben (2). Adjacent to our home is an historic villa set in a 1/2 acre of beautiful gardens with sea views & rural outlook. Luxury accommodation with ENSUITES, spacious guest lounge & dining area, return verandahs, off street parking. Situated overlooking Lathum Bay, opposite the 1908 Cafe & Restaurant. Albatross, penguins, seals, bird watching, Larnach Castle, scenic walks & drives name only a few of the attractions we are most central to on the pituresque Otago Peninsula.

Dunedin   *B&B   3.5km E of Dunedin*

Ardgowan
Ken & Margaret Turner
218 Musselburgh Rise,
Musselburgh,
Dunedin

Tel: (03) 456 0411
ardgowan@paradise.net.nz
www.bnb.co.nz/ardgowan.html

Double $100-$130 Single $70-$100
(Full Breakfast) Credit cards accepted
1 King/Twin 2 King 1 Queen (3 bdrm)
2 Ensuite 1 Private

Our spacious Edwardian villa, at the gateway to Otago Peninsula, is six minutes from central Dunedin. We offer a private lounge/dining area with Sky Television, upstairs bedrooms and sitting area with tea/ coffee facilities. Our knowledge of local attractions and restaurants is at our guests' disposal. We cater for older children. Laundry facilities and off-street parking is available. Our family has pet dogs.

Dunedin   *B&B*   *Dunedin Central*

Hulmes Court
Norman Wood, 52 Tennyson street, Dunedin
Tel: (03) 477 5319 Fax: (03) 477 5310   Mob: 025 351 075   Tollfree: 0800 448 563
normwood@earthlight.co.nz   www.hulmes.co.nz

Double $100-$160 Single $65-$150 (Continental Breakfast) Child please inquire
Credit cards accepted
3 King 10 Queen 4 Twin 1 Single (14 bdrm)
8 Ensuite 3 Guests share

Hulmes Court and Hulmes Too are two beautiful homes situated right in the heart of Dunedin, only a few minutes walk from the Visitor Centre, restaurants, shops and theatres. Tennyson Street is a quiet side Street and the property has private gardens, trees, decks and sitting areas, a tranquil retreat from the hustle and bustle so near by.

The Victorian Hulmes Court is one of the oldest and most historic homes in Dunedin. It was built in the 1860's by the first provincial surgeon Edward Hulme who helped found the Otago Medical School. Hulmes Too is a large Edwardian home built next to Hulmes Court on the grounds of the original estate. For the first time in over a century the properties are back together again.

Hulmes Court & Too have a variety of rooms which cater for all tastes from the economical cute single Rose room at $65 per night to our large and grand en suite rooms in Hulmes Too at $160 per night.

Your host Norman owns an advertising business, is interested in history, philosophy, geography and has stood for parliament twice. At the same time Norman at 36 and his staff are youthful and full of energy. We have journeyed widely and know what travellers need: peace, relaxation, comfortable beds, warmth, continental breakfasts, friendly service and good information. In addition, we provide complimentary laundry, internet & email, BBQ, mountain bikes and off-street parking. We have a cute black cat called Solstice and we enjoy children staying with us.

Port Chalmers - Dunedin   *Farmstay Homestay   20km NE of Dunedin*

Atanui
Bob & Betty Melville
Heywards Point Road, RD 1, Port Chalmers, Dunedin
Tel: (03) 482 1107 Fax: (03) 482 1107
atanui@actrix.gen.nz   www.bnb.co.nz/atanui.html
Double $100-$120 Single $80-$100 (Continental
Breakfast) Child 1/2 price Dinner $25
Credit cards accepted   1 King/twin 1 Queen
1 Twin (2 bdrm) 1 Ensuite 1 Guests share

Betty & Bob welcome you to our spacious stonehouse in a peaceful rural setting, 30 mins from Dunedin, with a spectacular view across the Otago harbour. Feed the Emu's, Aplaca's, peacocks etc. Good surfing beach and walking tracks. Relax in our spa pool. Three friendly cats. Three course farm-style meals available. Morning and afternoon teas complimentary. Children and campervans welcome. We look forward to meeting you. Directions: from north: left at Waitati; follow signs to Port Chalmers; at crossroads, turn left (no exit); next junction Heywards Point Road (metal) 4km on right. From south: Port Chalmers Highway 88 follow sign up hill to Longbeach, at Heyward Point Road (metal) 4km on right.

Portobello - Otago Peninsula   *Self-contained   15km E of Dunedin*   ♿

Fern Grove Garden
Bill & Christine Strang
741 Portobello Road, Portobello, Dunedin
Tel: (03) 478 0321 Mob: 025 298 3110
strang@southnet.co.nz
www.bnb.co.nz/ferngrovegarden.html
Double $95-$125 (Continental Breakfast)
Credit cards accepted Pet on property
1 Queen 1 Single (1 bdrm)
1 Private

Harbourside frontage with panoramic water and peninsular views from comfortable three roomed PRIVATE SELF/CONTAINED COTTAGE including bedroom, kitchen-dining room, bathroom, and sundeck. Offstreet parking. Laundry. Tui and bellbirds in fern garden. Albatross, penguins, seals, bird-watching, launch trips, Larnach castle and scenic walks all nearby. 15 minutes from Dunedin; 5 minutes from Portobello.

Dunedin - Harington Point   *30km NE of Dunedin*

B&B Motel Self-contained Cottage
Harington Point Accommodation
Bourke & Sharon Thomas
932 Harington Point Road, RD 2, Dunedin
Tel: (03) 478 0287 Fax: (03) 478 0089
Mob: 025 398 080   southlight@clear.net.nz
www.bnb.co.nz/haringtonpoint.html
Double $85-$110 (Continental Breakfast)
Dinner $30 by arrangement Credit cards accepted
S/C Cottage (2 bedroom 1 bathroom) $110
2 Queen 4 Twin (4 bdrm)   4 Ensuite

Enjoy very comfortable self-contained or B&B units overlooking Otago Harbour. Local wildlife includes albatross, penguins, seals, shags and sealions. The area has many historic features. Two minute walk to the beach for a leisurely stroll - spectacular sunsets. Golf course, restaurant and cafes close by. Bourke has 7 years experience with Penguin Conservation and Sharon works at the Albatross Centre. We have two daughters, a dog called Missy and 3 pet sheep. Let our local knowledge enhance your stay on the Peninsula.

Dunedin   *Homestay B&B*   *Central*

Arden Street Homestay & B&B
Joyce Lepperd
36 Arden Street, Opoho, Dunedin
Tel: (03) 473 8860 Fax: (03) 473 8861
joyce-l@clear.net.nz
www.bnb.co.nz/ardenstreethouseb&b.html
Double $65-$75 Single $45-$60
(Continental Breakfast) Child $10 Dinner $10 - $25
Credit cards accepted Child at home Children welcome
2 Double 2 Twin 3 Single (4 bdrm) 1 Private 1 Guests share

Central Dunedin homestay. Comfortable warm 1930s character home, built by a sea captain, the house reflects this with stained glass themes throughout. Quirky, sunny, great views, birdsong and garden. Your host Joyce Lepperd hosts lively social evening dinners - a great way to meet the 'locals' using organic produce from her garden. Close Botanical Gardens and Knox college, and university. Children welcome. We practice recycling! Look out for Harry the ships cat! From the north turn left towards North east Valley (North Rd), then first right (Glendining Ave goes up to Arden St.)

Dunedin   *Homestay B&B*   *Dunedin*

Highbrae Guesthouse
Stephen & Fienie Clark
376 High Street, City Rise, Dunedin
Tel: (03) 479 2070 Fax: (03) 479 2100
Mob: 025 328 470   highbrae@xtra.co.nz
www.bnb.co.nz/highbraeguesthouse.html
Double $85-$110 Single $65 (Continental Breakfast)
Child $10 Credit cards accepted
1 King 1 Queen 1 Twin (3 bdrm)
1 Guests share

Experience a taste of early Dunedin. This heritage home in the centre of the city was built on the High Street Cable Car route in 1908 to provide first class accommodation to its residents. Today it is still an impressive home with spectacular views of the city and harbour. The three upstairs guest rooms are carefully restored to preserve their character for visitors, who delight in the many features in the home. A courtesy van can meet you at the bus or train if required.

Portobello - Otago Peninsula   *Self-contained*   *20km E of Dunedin*

Silverlea Cottage
Shaun & Helen Murphy
7 Blackwell Street,
Portobello, Otago Peninsula
Tel: (03) 478 0140 shhemu@xtra.co.nz
www.silverleacottages.com
Double $100 Single $80 (Continental Breakfast)
$10pp breakfast optional Credit cards accepted
1 Double 2 Single (1 bdrm)
1 Private

Fully self-contained cottage on owner's section. Situated on a quiet no exit street, well away from tour buses and campervans, but still only a five minute walk from the local restaurant, cafe, takeaway and shop. Beautiful harbour views and close to the albatross colony, yellow-eyed penguins and Larnach Castle. Ground floor comprises kitchen/lounge/diner, shower/toilet and access to a large sun deck. The first floor bedroom has a small bell turret. TV, Internet, music books and games provided. Washing machine available. No pets.

Macandrew Bay - Otago Peninsula   *Self-contained   11km E of Dunedin*

Mac Bay Retreat
Jeff & Helen Hall
38 Bayne Terrace,
Macandrew Bay, Dunedin 9003

Tel: (03) 476 1475 Fax: (03) 476 1975
Mob: 021 897 243   jhall9@ihug.co.nz
www.bnb.co.nz/macbayretreat.html

Double $95 Single $65 (Continental Breakfast)
1 King 1 Double (2 bdrm) Credit cards accepted
1 Ensuite

MACBAY RETREAT - OTAGO PENINSULA. Welcome to your private self-contained smoke-free restreat, 15 min from Dunedin centre on the Otago Peninsula. Relax with the spectacular view overlooking the harbour from Dunedin city to Port Chalmers. Your cosy retreat is separate from the host's house and gives you a choice of either a super/king or double bed plus an ensuite, modern kitchen and TV. Suitable for one couple, possibly two couples, travelling together. Only minutes from Dunedin's most popular attractions, Larnach Castle, albatross and penguin colonies, etc.

Dunedin   *B&B*

Highview Lodge   Diane & Graeme Connolly
70 Heriot Row, Dunedin

Tel: (03) 477 0997 Fax: (03) 477 6036
Mob: 025 611 4382   Tollfree: 0800 244 664
highviewlodgedunedin@xtra.co.nz
www.bnb.co.nz/highviewlodge.html

Double $85-$135 Single $65-$95
(Continental Breakfast) Child $20 Dinner $30
Full breakfast by arrangement   Credit cards accepted
1 King 3 Queen 1 Single (4 bdrm)   2 Ensuite 1 Guests share

Highview Lodge offers superior accommodation in a restored 1910 Edwardian home with all the comforts of modern living combined with the elegance of a bygone era. Lovely city and harbour views, and a garden with native birds. The city shops, university, hospital and many restaurants and attractions are within a five minute walk. City bus stop nearby. Well heated private rooms, guest lounge, kitchenettes, off-street parking, laundry, phone/fax, Sky TV. Cooked breakfast, dinner, city tours,optional extras. Pick up and deliver within city. Please phone for directions.

Blueskin Bay - Dunedin   *B&B   16km N of Dunedin*

Arden House
Geoff and Faye Bate
712 Waitati Valley Road, Waitati Valley,
Blueskin Bay, Dunedin
Tel: (03) 482 2040 Mob: 025 953 507
ardenhouse@hotmail.com
www.bnb.co.nz/ardenhouse.html

Double $100-$125 Single $80-$95
(Continental & Full Breakfast) Dinner $25
2 King/Twin 1 Queen (3 bdrm)
1 Ensuite 1 Guests share

Arden House is nestled in a grove of trees, 16 km north of Dunedin and in close proximity to beautiful beaches (kayaking, fishing, walks). Our home has the ambience of yesteryear plus the comfort of today. Enjoy the sight and sound of native birds while savouring a generous breakfast (including home produce). We share our 3.5 acres with Shadrach, miniature daschund, Pumpkin and Max, cats, and two adorable angora goats. Geoff and Faye, your Kiwi hosts, offer you the warmest of welcomes.

Dunedin *B&B* *Dunedin Central*

Albatross Inn

Glynis Rees, 770 George Street, Dunedin

Tel: (03) 477 2727 Fax: (03) 477 2108 Tollfree: 0800 441 441
albatross.inn@xtra.co.nz   www.bnb.co.nz/albatrossinn1.html

Double $75-$125 Single $65-$85 (Continental Breakfast) Child $15 Credit cards accepted
1 King 4 Queen 3 Double 5 Single (8 bdrm)   8 Ensuite

Welcome to Dunedin & Albatross Inn!

Our beautiful late Victorian House is ideally located on the main street close to the University, gardens, museum, shops and restaurants.

Our attractive rooms have ensuite bathrooms, telephone, TV, radio, tea/coffee, warm duvets and electric blankets on modern beds. Extra firm beds upon request. Very quiet rooms at rear of house. Several rooms have kitchenette and fridge. Enjoy your breakfast in front of the open fire in our lounge. We serve freshly baked bread and muffins, fresh fruit salad, yoghurt, juices, cereals, teas, freshly brewed coffee.

We are happy to recommend and book tours for you. All wildlife tours pick up and drop off here. We can recommend many great places to eat, most just a short walk down George Street.

Nearby laundry, non-smoking, cot and highchair.

Our visitor book says! "The convenience of your location is wonderful, you can walk everywhere! Combined with a gorgeous house, such friendly hosts" Joe & Cathy Wallace, Georgia, USA. "This is everything a B&B ought to be... our only regret is leaving... Dianna & William McDowey, England.

Homepage: www.albatross.inn.co.nz.

Winter special $69 Double - special conditions apply. Complimentary e-mail and Internet.

OTAGO
NTH CATLINS

Mosgiel   *Homestay*   *14km S of Dunedin*

The Old Vicarage
Lois & Lance Woodfield
14 Mure Street, Mosgiel, Otago
Tel: (03) 489 8236 Fax: (03) 489 8236
l.l.woodfield@clear.net.nz
www.bnb.co.nz/theoldvicarage.html
Double $65-$85 Single $45 (Continental Breakfast)
Credit cards accepted Children welcome
1 Queen 2 Single (2 bdrm)
1 Private

Welcome to our English-style cottage home. Built in 1913 and used as the Vicarage for 46 years, before passing to private owners who made sympathetic restorations. The outstanding feature is the exquisitely balanced garden, laid out in 'rooms'. Two upstairs guest rooms and bathroom enjoy a commanding view of the garden. Warm Oregan panelling and leadlight windows enhance the atmosphere. Situated in Mosgiel, close to the Airport, just 15 minutes from Dunedin. We are a retired Christian couple who enjoy gardening, architecture, tramping and history.

Waihola   *Self-contained Homestay B&B*   *40km S of Dunedin*

Lillian & Trevor Robinson
Sandown Street, Rapid No 13,
Waihola, South Otago
Tel: (03) 417 8218 Fax: (03) 417 8287
Mob: 025 545 935
www.bnb.co.nz/robinson.html
Double $70 Single $45 (Full Breakfast)
Dinner $20 by arrangement Credit cards accepted
1 Queen 2 Single (2 bdrm)
1 Ensuite 1 Family share

We have a very comfortable home situated in a quiet street, only 15 minutes drive to Dunedin Airport. Our double room has Queen sized bed with ensuite, teamaking facilities, TV, fridge and heater. Lake Waihola is popular for boating, fishing and swimming. We have one friendly cat. We enjoy meeting people and ensure a very pleasant stay. Please phone.

Waihola   *Homestay B&B Lakeside Cottage*   *40km S of Dunedin*

Ivy Cottage - Lake Waihola
Bryan & Robin Leckie
Rapid No7, State Highway 1, Waihola, Otago
Tel: (03) 417 8946 Fax: (03) 417 8966
Tollfree: 0800 112 996
www.bnb.co.nz/ivycottagelakewaihola.html
Double $75 Single $55 (Full Breakfast)
Child $20 under 14yrs Dinner $25 2 nights $135
Credit cards accepted Pet on property
1 Double 3 Single (2 bdrm) 2 Ensuite

"Ivy Cottage" is on the northern end of the "Southern Scenic Route". Guests enjoy uninterrupted views of Lake Waihola, farmlands, forests. An excellent base for day trips. North, Dunedin's Albatross, Heritage, South, "The Catlins" scenic beauty; West, Central Otago's orchards, vineyards; East, Taieri Mouth & Pacific coastline. Waihola features Wetlands, Limestone fossils, aquatic recreation. We have varied & wide interests. "The Shed" our detached accommodation has ensuites, tea facilities, TV, heating and laundry. Dining options include our cuisine with wines or Waihola restaurants. "Bud" is our friendly golden retriever.

Balclutha *Farmstay   26km W of Balclutha*

Argyll Farmstay
Trish & Alan May
Clutha River Road, Clydevale,
RD 4, Balclutha

Tel: (03) 415 9268 Fax: (03) 415 9268
Mob: 025 318 241   argyllfm@ihug.co.nz
www.bnb.co.nz/argyllfarmstay.html

Double $100 Single $50 (Full Breakfast)
Child neg Dinner $25 Credit cards accepted
1 Queen 1 Twin 2 Single (2 bdrm)   1 Private

We welcome guests to our comfortable country home with large garden, swimming pool, and beautiful views of green pasture and river flats. We farm 530 acres running 800 deer, 150 cattle and 1000 sheep. We offer our guests an extra option of a jet boat ride or fishing trips with Alan, an experienced fisherman on the Clutha River, in our commercial boat Blue Mountain Jet. We are centrally located for people travelling to the Catlins, Queenstown or Te Anau. Directions: please telephone.

Balclutha *Farmstay B&B   5km S of Balclutha*

Breadalbane
Carolynne & Ken Stephens
293 Freezing Works Road, RD 3, Balclutha

Tel: (03) 418 2568 Fax: (03) 418 2591
Mob: 025 6514 215   breadalbane@xtra.co.nz
www.bnb.co.nz/breadalbane.html

Double $80 Single $45
(Continental & Full Breakfast) Child $20 Dinner $25
S/C House - at Kaka Point $60, $10 per extra person
1 Double 2 Twin (3 bdrm)   1 Guests share

Welcome to Breadalbane, 1300 acres of rolling farm land, with sheep, deer and farm forestry, located within two minutes of the Southern Scenic Route and Telford Polytechnic. Relax in peaceful surroundings in our large country garden, or stroll along the farm lane enjoying the panoramic views. Our home is well heated, all beds have electric blankets, each room has tea/coffee making facilities, with TV in the double room. Complimentary laundry available. We have a friendly corgi dog and cat. Farm Tour by arrangement. Phone for directions.

Balclutha *Homestay B&B   4km N of Balclutha*

Lesmahagow
Noel & Kate O'Malley
Main Road, Benhar, RD 2, Balclutha

Tel: (03) 418 2507 Mob: 025 578 465
Tollfree: 0800 301 224   lesmahagow@xtra.co.nz
www.lesmahagow.co.nz

Double $85-$100 Single $70-$85 (Special Breakfast)
Child $30 Dinner $25 Lunches on request
1 Queen 3 Double 2 Single (4 bdrm)
2 Guests share 1 Family share

Experience the peace and charm of yesteryear in historic Benhar. We offer quality and comfort in our character home and extensive gardens. Our guestrooms are spacious and comfortably furnished, complete with individual robes and hairdryers. A leisurely continental breakfast with homemade breads and muffins can be enjoyed in our lounge or garden. Situated at the gateway to the Catlins, 40 mins. from Dunedin airport, your comfort is our objective. Your hosts, Noel and Kate, welcome you to our home, Lesmahagow. Come as strangers, leave as friends.

Clinton *Farmstay Country B&B*   *33km S of Balclutha*

Wairuna Bush
Kathleen & Roy Carruthers
Clinton, RD,
South Otago
Tel: (03) 415 7222
www.bnb.co.nz/wairunabush.html
Double $80 Single $40 (Full Breakfast)
Dinner $25 by arrangement
1 Queen 1 Double 1 Twin (3 bdrm)
1 Guests share

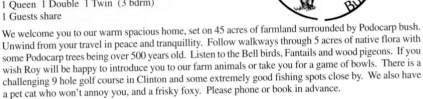

We welcome you to our warm spacious home, set on 45 acres of farmland surrounded by Podocarp bush. Unwind from your travel in peace and tranquillity. Follow walkways through 5 acres of native flora with some Podocarp trees being over 500 years old. Listen to the Bell birds, Fantails and wood pigeons. If you wish Roy will be happy to introduce you to our farm animals or take you for a game of bowls. There is a challenging 9 hole golf course in Clinton and some extremely good fishing spots close by. We also have a pet cat who won't annoy you, and a frisky foxy. Please phone or book in advance.

Clinton *Self-contained Farmstay B&B*   *8.2km W of Clinton*

Strathearn Cottage Farmstay
Ngaire & Warwick Taylor
Strathearn Road, Wairuna RD, Clinton
Tel: (03) 415 7444 Mob: 025 392 938
wf_na_taylor@xtra.co.nz
www.bnb.co.nz/strathearn.html
Double $85 Single $55 (Full Breakfast)
Child $10, under 5ys free Credit cards accepted
1 Double 1 Twin (1 bdrm)   1 Private

Introducing Strathearn's cosy self-contained cottage, "Grandma's House". Strathearn is an established 3000ac family operated sheep and beef farm. Join with us, our two kids, pets - kunekunes, alpacas, hens, ducks, cat & dog - and unwind whilst experiencing farm activities and hill vistas, or fishing the renowned Waipahi and Mataura Rivers. Breakfast at your leisure from our full breakfast hamper (sugar-free if required). Children welcome, cot available. "Grandma's House" overlooks SH1 between Clinton and Waipahi, making Strathearn halfway to everywhere Southern - Catlins, Fiordland, Invercargill, Dunedin and Central Otago.

Nuggets - The Catlins *Self-contained*   *24km Balclutha&Owaka*

Nugget Lodge
Kath & Noel Widdowson
Nugget Road 367, RD 1, Balclutha, South Otago
Tel: (03) 412 8783 Fax: (03) 412 8784
lighthouse@nuggetlodge.co.nz
www.nuggetlodge.co.nz
Double $95 (Full Breakfast) $15pp extra person
$15pp breakfast Credit cards accepted
1 Queen 1 Double 1 Single (2 bdrm)
2 Ensuite

A special place on a deserted beach above the incoming tide. Sleep to the roar of the waves and breathe the sea air from our modern, private, centrally-heated units. Nugget Lodge caters for the eco-enthusiasts who want seals, sealions, penguins, birds and walk tracks or for the guests who want only quiet time to rejuvenate the soul and take a break from the bustle of the city. Breakfast in hosts home. Restaurants nearby Host: wildlife Ranger/photographer.no pets, not suitable for children.

Kaka Point - The Catlins   *Self-contained B&B   21km S of Balclutha*

Rata Cottage
Jean Schreuder
31 Rata Street,
Kaka Point, South Otago
Tel: (03) 412 8779
www.bnb.co.nz/ratacottage.html
Double $65 Single $60
(Continental Breakfast) Child $7
1 Twin (1 bdrm)
1 Ensuite

A fully self contained sunny Bed & Breakfast unit in a tranquil bush garden setting, with sea view, bell birds and tuis. Bedroom with twin beds, plus double divan in lounge. Wheelchair facilities. Five minutes from a beautiful sandy beach for swimming or long walks. next door to scenic reserve and bush walks. You can have breakfast in the garden with the birds, or a visit from Baxter the cat if you wish. Non smoking. Laundry facilities available. Cooking facilities.

Owaka - The Catlins   *Self-contained Farmstay   15km S of Owaka*

Greenwood   Alan & Helen-May Burgess
739 Purakaunui Falls Road, Owaka, South Otago
Tel: (03) 415 8259 Fax: (03) 415 8259
Mob: 025 384 538   greenwoodfarm@xtra.co.nz
www.bnb.co.nz/greenwood.html
Double $80-$90 Single $55
(Continental & Full Breakfast) Child $25 Dinner $50
S/C house at Papatowai Beach $70 Double $10 extra
1 Queen 3 Single (3 bdrm)
1 Ensuite 1 Private 1 Family share

Welcome ... Situated within walking distance to the beautiful Purakaunui Falls, Alan enjoys taking people around our 1900 acre sheep, cattle and deer farm. Our home offers warm, comfortable accommodation. One guest bedroom has an ensuite, and day-room opening to a large garden. A private bathroom services other guest rooms. We enjoy dining with our guests. The Catlins area features the yellow-eyed penguin. Directions: Take Highway 92 to Owaka from Balclutha or Invercargill. From Owaka follow the signs to Purakaunui Falls. Our name is at gate entrance.

Owaka - The Catlins   *Farmstay   16 S of Owaka*

Tarara Downs
Ida & John Burgess
857 Puaho Road, RD 2, Owaka, South Otago
Tel: (03) 415 8293 Fax: (03) 415 8293
Mob: 025 215 1428   tarara@ihug.co.nz
www.bnb.co.nz/tararadowns.html
Double $55-$75 Single $45 (Full Breakfast)
Child 1/2 price Dinner $25 (2 course) Pet on property
1 King/Twin 1 Double (2 bdrm)
1 Ensuite 1 Family share

Our 2000-acre farm is situated in an area renowned for its bush and coastal scenery, within walking distance of the beautiful Purakaunui Falls. Our farm runs sheep, cattle, deer and horses. As well as seeing normal farm activities, horse riding, bush walks and fishing trips are available in the district. We live in a comfortable farmhouse, our family have all left home, and enjoy eating our own local produce. Children very welcome. Directions: Follow signs to Purakaunui Falls - we are the closest house to them.

OTAGO
NTH CATLINS

Owaka - The Catlins   *Homestay Separate/Suite B&B*   *6km E of Owaka*

Kepplestone-By-The-Sea   Gay & Arch Maley
9 Surat Bay Road, Newhaven, The Catlins, Owaka
Tel: (03) 415 8134 Fax: (03) 415 8137
Mob: 025 6767 253   Tollfree: 0800 105 134
kepplestone@xtra.co.nz
www.bnb.co.nz/kepplestonebythesea.html
Double $95-$110 Single $65 (Special Breakfast)
Dinner by arrangement
1 King/Twin 1 Queen 2 Twin (3 bdrm)
2 Ensuite 1 Family share

There are NO strangers here, only friends we haven't met. Situated metres from SuratBay, with Hooker sealions basking. Close to Catlins scenery, waterfalls, Royal Spoonbills, Golf. "Private Yelloweyed penguin viewing with Catlins Natural Wonders." Delicious homemade breakfasts. Fabulous meals served with Organically grown vegetables from garden. Alergy diets catered for, every care taken. Directions: Owaka, (Royal Terrace) Follow signs "towards" Pounawea, at golf course go "across" bridge,right to Newhaven, go 3km on metalroad,at Suratbay Road, right first house on left.

Owaka   *Self-contained Farmstay B&B*   *6km N of Owaka*

Hillview
Kate & Bruce McLachlan
Rapid 161 Hunt Road, Katea, RD 2, Owaka
Tel: (03) 415 8457 Fax: (03) 415 8650
Mob: 025 334 759   hillviewcatlins@xtra.co.nz
www.bnb.co.nz/hillview.html
Double $85 Single $40 (Continental Breakfast)
Child $20 Dinner from $20 Credit cards accepted
2 Queen 4 Single (4 bdrm)
2 Guests share

Our 450 acre cattle grazing unit is situated 15 min from Nugget Point, 10 mins from Cannibal Bay. Relax in our cosy private cottage set in a large developing garden, or enjoy the relaxed atmosphere of our home. Our 2 Burmese cats and miniature poodle live outside. Occassionally we host foreign students. Our interests are varied. Bruce is a shepherd and enjoys working with horses and training sheepdogs. Kate is a librarian who enjoys reading, gardening, spinning wool, and glass art. Breakfast with us or in private. Meals by arrangement. Bookings essential. Please phone after 4 pm.

Owaka - The Catlins   *Homestay B&B*   *1/2 km N of Owaka*

J T's Bed & Breakfast
John & Thelma Turnbull
Main Road, Owaka,
Tel: (03) 415 8127 Fax: (03) 415 8129
Mob: 025 649 7693   jtowaka@ihug.co.nz
www.bnb.co.nz/jts.html
Double $75-$85 Single $60 (Special Breakfast)
Child half price Dinner By arrangement
1 Queen 1 Twin (2 bdrm)
1 Guests share

Welcome to our warm and comfortable home, which is situated on a 25 acre farmlet, surrounded by colourful, peaceful gardens with splendid unspoilt views. Located in the heart of the Catlins, renowned for its wildlife and spectacular scenery, we are within walking distance of Owaka township with its restaurants, museum and other amenities. Our guests are encouraged to dine with us for the evening meal when we enjoy quality local food and wine. We look forward to meeting you. Travel safely.

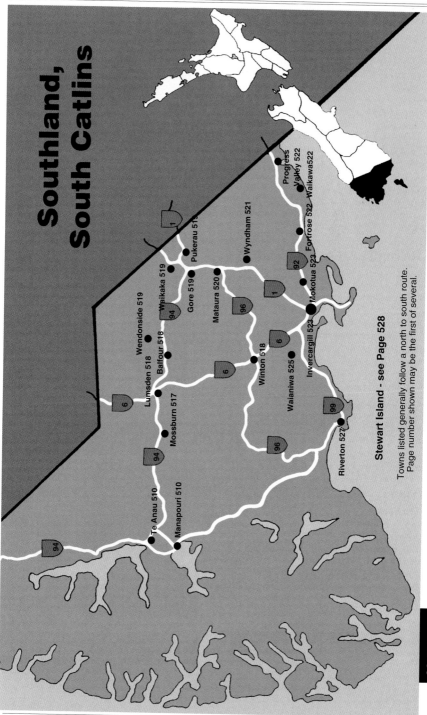

Southland, South Catlins

Progress
Valley 522
Waikawa 522
Fortrose 522
Mokotua 523
Wyndham 521
Pukerau 51
Waikaka 519
Gore 519
Mataura 520
Wendonside 519
Balfour 518
Winton 518
Waianiwa 525
Invercargill 523
Lumsden 518
Mossburn 517
Riverton 527
Te Anau 510
Manapouri 510

Stewart Island - see Page 528

Towns listed generally follow a north to south route.
Page number shown may be the first of several.

Te Anau   *Farmstay   20km E of Te Anau*

Tapua
Dorothy & Donald Cromb
RD 2, Te Anau
Tel: (03) 249 5805 Fax: (03) 249 5805
Mob: 025 201 9109   Tapua.Cromb@xtra.co.nz
www.bnb.co.nz/cromb.html

Double $110 Single $70 (Full Breakfast)
Dinner $30pp Credit cards accepted Pet on property
1 King/Twin 1 Twin (2 bdrm)
1 Guests share

You are surrounded by "Million Dollar" views while enjoying the comfort of our large modern family home. Electric blankets, heaters in rooms. Traditional farm style meals. Excellent base for day trips to Milford or Doubtful Sound. A two night stay is recommended. Farm tour prior to dinner of our 348ha farm which has 3700 sheep and approx 100 cattle. Excellent fishing rivers within a few minutes drive as are great walking tracks, golf course etc. We have a cat. Smoke free home. Directions: Please phone.

Te Anau   *Self-contained Homestay*

Rob & Nancy's Place
R & N Marshall
13 Fergus Square, Te Anau
Tel: (03) 249 8241 Fax: (03) 249 7397
Mob: 025 226 1820   rob.nancy@xtra.co.nz
www.bnb.co.nz/robnancysplace.html

Double $90-$110 Single $65 (Full Breakfast)
Credit cards accepted Pet on property
2 King 2 Single (3 bdrm)
1 Ensuite 1 Guests share

Rob, Nancy and Chardonnay our Burmese cat welcome you to our quiet and tranquil home facing a park, five minutes walk to the lake and town centre. We are a couple retired from farming and enjoy meeting people. Our modern home includes a courtyard barbecue and gardens. Te Anau is a special place to visit with the magnificent scenery of the Fiordland National Park including spectacular Milford and Doubtful Sounds. All tours are picked up and delivered to the door. Off street parking and storage available.

Manapouri   *Homestay B&B   20km S of Te Anau*

The Cottage
Don & Joy MacDuff
Waiau St, Te Anau - Manapouri
Tel: (03) 249 6838 Fax: (03) 249 6839
don.joymacduff@xtra.co.nz
www.bnb.co.nz/thecottagemanapouri.html

Double $85-$99 Single $65-$75 (Special Breakfast)
Credit cards accepted Pet on property
2 Queen 1 Single (2 bdrm)
2 Ensuite

GATEWAY TO THE MAJESTIC DOUBTFUL SOUND Our guests are welcome to leave their car here while they visit Doubtful Sound. Cozy Homestay B&B in tranquil bush setting, with lovely views. Warm ensuite rooms,cottage décor. French doors to cottage gardens. Tea & coffee facilities. Shared lounge with T.V. (Full breakfast and laundry.extra charge.) We,with Rosie our Skye Terrier extend a warm welcome to all who choose to stay with us. THERE ARE NO STRANGERS HERE, ONLY FRIENDS WE HAVE YET TO MEET.

Te Anau   *Homestay   Country Homestay*   *3km S of Te Anau*

The Farmyard
Helen & Ray Willett
Charles Nairn Road -24, Te Anau 9681
Tel: (03) 249 7833 Fax: (03) 249 7830
Mob: 025 289 0939
www.bnb.co.nz/thefarmyard.html
Double $90-$100 (Continental Breakfast)
Pet on property
1 Double 1 Single (1 bdrm)
1 Ensuite

Our country homestay, 3km from Te Anau, has detached, self contained cottage, privacy assured, peaceful rural setting and spectacular views of surrounding mountains. We are ideally situated for your Fiordland experience. Having for many years both worked on the Milford track and driven visitors to Milford Sound we are able to offer the very best advice for your Te Anau-Fiordland visit. Our pets - donkey, pony, sheep, pig, goats, terriers (2) are waiting to greet you!! Welcome to Te Anau-Fiordland. Please contact us for reservations.

Te Anau - Manapouri   *Self-contained Farmstay B&B*   *8km N of Manapouri*

Christies Cottage
Marie & Murray Christie
Hillside/Manapouri Road, Te Anau
Tel: (03) 249 6695 Fax: (03) 249 6695
mchristie@xtra.co.nz
www.christiescottage.co.nz
Double $90 (Continental Breakfast)
Child neg extra adult $15 Credit cards accepted
1 Double 2 Single (2 bdrm)
1 Private

Exclusively yours, in a tranquil setting, is a delightful sunlit self-contained cottage with courtyard garden, beautiful mountain backdrop overlooking the (famous trout fishing) Mararoa River. Murray and I with our two teenage children live on a sheep/cattle farm close to both Te Anau and Manapouri, Murray enjoys sharing his extensive knowledge of fishing and the region. I love gardening and helping with your travel plans if you wish. Bookings can be made for local tourist excursions. Looking forward to meeting you; travel safely, - Marie. www.christiescottage.co.nz

Te Anau   *Homestay*   *Te Anau Central*

House of Wood
Elaine & Trevor Lett
44 Moana Crescent, Te Anau
Tel: (03) 249 8404 Fax: (03) 249 7676
Mob: 025 220 4356
houseofwood@xtra.co.nz
www.bnb.co.nz/houseofwood.html
Double $95-$115 Single $80
(Continental Breakfast) Pet on property
1 Queen 1 Double 2 Single (3 bdrm)
1 Ensuite 1 Guests share

"House of Wood" with natural timber throughout interior is a uniquely designed two storey wooden house with outside balconies and beautiful views. We know the Otago/Southland area extremely well and can help you make the most of your time here. Now our three daughters have left home we have more time for woodturning, walking and spinning. Along with Kaidy our Westhighland Terrier, we welcome you to our smokefree home which is in a quiet residential area. Please phone for directions.

Te Anau   *B&B   1km S of Te Anau*

The Cats Whiskers
Irene & Terry Maher
2 Lakefront Drive, Te Anau
Tel: (03) 249 8112 Fax: (03) 249 8112
i.t.maher@paradise.net.nz
www.webnz.co.nz/bbnz/catwh.htm
Double $125-$135 Single $95 (Full Breakfast)
Child 1/2 price Credit cards accepted
1 King 2 Queen 4 Single (3 bdrm)
3 Ensuite

Situated opposite Department of Conservation headquarters, 10 min. walk to shops and restaurants. Comfortable pleasant rooms feature Queen or Twin. Family room - 1 King plus Twin. All ensuite, TV and tea making. Courtesy car to restaurants or meeting coaches. Off street parking and luggage storage for track walks or overnight kayaking. Agents for excursions to Milford and Doubtful Sounds. We have two Burmese cats. Directions: as you approach town, turn left where sign posted off Highway 94. First house on right. Off season rates. Guests laundry.

Te Anau   *Self-contained B&B Guesthouse   1km N of Te Anau Centre*

Shakespeare House Margaret & Jeff Henderson
10 Dusky Street, PO Box 32, Te Anau
Tel: (03) 249 7349 Fax: (03) 249 7629
Tollfree: 0800 249 349
marg.shakespeare.house@xtra.co.nz
www.bnb.co.nz/shakespearehouse.html
Double $80-$112 Single $60-$80 (Full Breakfast)
Child $5 - $15 S/C, 2 bedrooms, sleeps 5
Credit cards accepted Pet on property
4 King 3 Double 4 Single (8 bdrm) 8 Ensuite

Shakespeare House is a well established Bed & Breakfast where we keep a home atmosphere with personal service. We are situated in a quiet residential area yet are within walking distance of shops, lake and restaurants. Our rooms are ground floor and with the choice of King, Double or Twin beds. Each room has private facilities, TV, tea/coffee making. Tariff includes continental or delicious cooked breakfast. Guest laundry available. Winter rates May to September. Along with Brothersoul our pussy we welcome you to Te Anau.

Te Anau   *Self-contained Farmstay   26km E of Te Anau*

Country Cottage
Carolyn & John Klein
The Key, RD 2, Te Anau
Tel: (03) 249 5807 Fax: (03) 249 5807
kleinbnb@ihug.co.nz www.fishfiordland.com
Double $95 Single $75 (Continental Breakfast)
Child neg Credit cards accepted Pet on property
Children welcome Pets welcome
1 Queen 3 Single (2 bdrm)
1 Private

We live at 'The Key', a tiny village on the main Queenstown-Te Anau highway, nestled under the Takitimu mountains, just 15 minutes drive from Te Anau. Our modern self-contained cottage is exclusively yours, well-equipped, very warm and comfortable with a 'beautiful' country view. We all enjoy meeting people and sharing our extensive knowledge of the region with you. John offers guided fishing on many of our local rivers. If you're looking for a real country experience, come and see us, we'd love to see you!

Te Anau   *Farmstay Homestay B&B Rural Homestay*   *5km S of Te Anau*

Kepler Cottage
Jan & Jeff Ludemann
William Stephen Road, Te Anau
Tel: (03) 249 7185 Fax: (03) 249 7186
Mob: 027 431 4076   kepler@teanau.co.nz
www.fiordland.org.nz/html/kepcot.html
Double $110-$120 Single $90 (Full Breakfast)
Credit cards accepted Pet on property
1 Queen 3 Single (3 bdrm)
1 Ensuite 1 Private

Jeff, an aircraft engineer, and Jan, who works from home as a freelance journalist and marketing consultant, welcome you to their small farmlet on the edge of Fiordland, just five minutes drive from Te Anau. Relax outdoors in the garden and enjoy the peace and comfort of our rural location between visiting Milford or Doubtful Sounds, or walking one of the many nearby tracks. Our family includes a Cairn Terrier, and two cats. We can advise tours and sightseeing and make bookings where needed.

Te Anau   *Self-contained Farmstay*   *45km E of Te Anau*

Grassy Creek
Carol & Ray McConnell
RD 1, Te Anau
Tel: (03) 249 8553 Fax: (03) 249 8333
ray.mcconnell@xtra.co.nz
www.bnb.co.nz/grassycreek.html
Double $90 Single $20
(Continental Breakfast)
2 Double 6 Single (4 bdrm)
2 Private

This accommodation is a very comfortable, large self-contained farmhouse. All rooms are well equipped - Log burner, TV, good kitchen, auto washing machine, phone. It has a private country setting and is an excellent base for families or groups to explore Fiordland from. We are a keen farming family with cattle, sheep dogs and pets. Our farm is situated at the base of the Takitimu Mountains 15 mins from Manapouri, 25 mins from Te Anau. Good scenery, good fishing, good gardens. Please phone for directions.

Te Anau   *Farmstay Homestay B&B*   *8km S of Te Anau*

Lynwood Park
Trina & Daniella Baker
RD 2, Te Anau
Tel: (03) 249 7990 Fax: (03) 249 7990
Mob: 021 129 5626   lynwood.park@xtra.co.nz
www.bnb.co.nz/lynwoodpark.html
Double $70-$100 Single $50-$80 Child $30
(Continental & Full Breakfast) Winter rates, May - Oct
Credit cards accepted Child at home Pet on property
2 Queen 1 Double 3 Single (3 bdrm)
2 Ensuite 1 Private

Lynwood Park is a developing garden set amidst my families 450 acre sheep, cattle and deer farm. Each guest room has a private entrance, TV and tea/coffee making facilities. We offer free the use of our laundry facilities and childrens play area which Daniella my 4yr old, looks forward to sharing with you. We have three pet sheep, an old dog and a cat on the property. I am able to advise or arrange most activities to make your holiday a memorable experience.

SOUTHLAND, STH CATLINS

Te Anau   *B&B   Te Anau Central*

Cosy Kiwi
Virginia and Gerhard Hirner
186 Milford Road, Te Anau 9681
Tel: (03) 249 7475 Fax: 0064 3 249 8471
Tollfree: 0800 249 700   cosykiwi@xtra.co.nz
www.cosykiwi.com

Double $90-$115 Single $60-$85 (Special Breakfast)
Child neg Credit cards accepted Child at home
4 King/Twin 3 Queen 9 Single (7 bdrm)
7 Ensuite

Virginia an Gerhard and our two children welcome you to our new Bed & Breakfast (20 years experience in hospitality, we speak German). Privacy with comfort, quiet spacious, ensuited bedrooms, quality beds, individual heating and television. Gourmet breakfast buffet of home-made breads, jams, fresh fruits, home-bottled fruits, yoghurt, brewed coffee, special teas, mouthwatering pancakes with maple syrup and more. Centrally located, bookings arranged for all tours, pick-up at gate. Guest lounge with Internet access, laundry, off-street parking and luggage storage.

Te Anau   *Self-contained Farmstay   2km E of Te Anau*

Rose 'n' Reel
Lyn & Lex Lawrence
Benloch Lane, RD 2, Te Anau
Tel: (03) 249 7582 Fax: (03) 249 7582
Mob: 025 545 723   rosenreel@xtra.co.nz
www.fiordland.org.nz/html/rosenreel.html

Double $90 Single $60 (Full Breakfast)
Credit cards accepted
1 Queen 1 Double 1 Single (3 bdrm)
1 Private 1 Guests share

Genuine Kiwi hospitality in a magic setting 5 minutes from Te Anau. Hand feed tame fallow deer, meet two friendly cats. Sit on the veranda of our fully self contained cabin and enjoy watching deer with a lake and mountain view. The two room cabin has cooking facilities, fridge, microwave, TV, 1 Queen, 1 double plus bathroom. Our modern two storey smoke-free home is set in an extensive garden. Two downstairs guest bedrooms. Lex is a keen fly fisherman and average golfer, while I love to garden. Directions: Please phone.

Te Anau   *Self-contained B&B Rural Lifestyle   1.5km N of Te Anau*

The Croft
Jane & Ross McEwan
Te Anau Milford Sound Road,
RD 1, Te Anau
Tel: (03) 249 7393 Fax: (03) 249 7393
jane@thecroft.co.nz   www.thecroft.co.nz

Double $100-$120 (Continental Breakfast)
Credit cards accepted
2 Queen 1 Single (2 bdrm)
2 Ensuite

Warm hospitality and quality accommodation are guaranteed at 'The Croft', a small lifestyle farm only minutes from Te Anau. Our 2 new self contained cottages are set in private gardens and enjoy magnificent lake and mountain views. Timber ceilings, large ensuite bathrooms, window seats and elegant furnishings are some of the highlights. Microwaves, fridges, sinks & TV's. Enjoy breakfast with Jane & Ross or have it served in your cottage. Pets include Molly the sheep, Mac the Jack Russell, and 2 cats. Lake and river access from our farm.

Te Anau *Self-contained Farmstay* *26km E of Te Anau*

Davaar Country Lodge
James & Fiona Macdonald, RD 2, Te Anau, Southland
Tel: (03) 249 5838 Fax: (03) 249 5839 davaar@xtra.co.nz
www.bnb.co.nz/davaarcountrylodge.html
Double $95 Single $65 (Continental Breakfast) Child $15
1 Queen 3 Single (2 bdrm) 1 Private

A unique holiday experience awaits you at Davaar Country Lodge, nestled in the foothills of the Takitimu Mountains near Milford Sound in Fiordland. 'Davaar' is a 2800 acre sheep and cattle station, located in an idyllic rural setting on state highway 94, just 20 minutes east of Te Anau, at The Key.

The Lodge is exclusively yours and is fully self-contained with comprehensive kitchen and laundry facilities. A wood-burning log fire and electric blankets on all the beds make Davaar Country Lodge a cozy, warm retreat. We provide a continental style breakfast including fresh farm eggs, which is available in the lodge for you to breakfast at your leisure.

The lodge is perfect for tourists, families, mountain-bikers, trampers and hunters, it is also great for anyone just looking for a real Kiwi experience. Located on the Mararoa River, with the Oreti River and Mavora lakes nearby, it is a fisherman's paradise. A fishing or hunting guide can be arranged on request. 'Davaar' offers a wonderful combination of country hospitality with the freedom to suit your own special vacation needs.

Here you can get off the beaten track and explore some of New Zealand's most spectacular back country. Your hosts James and Fiona Macdonald look forward to welcoming you. We are really easy to find, situated on the main route between Queenstown and Milford Sound. Please phone for further directions.

Te Anau   *Self-contained*   *5km N of Te Anau*

Fiordland Lodge
Robynne & Ron Peacock
472 Te Anau - Milford Highway, RD 1, Te Anau
Tel: (03) 249 7832 Fax: (03) 249 7832
fiordlandguidesltd@xtra.co.nz
www.fiordlandguides.co.nz
Double $180 Single $160 (Full Breakfast)
Child $30 extra adult $40 Credit cards accepted
2 Queen 5 Single (4 bdrm)
2 Private

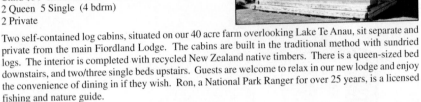

Two self-contained log cabins, situated on our 40 acre farm overlooking Lake Te Anau, sit separate and private from the main Fiordland Lodge. The cabins are built in the traditional method with sundried logs. The interior is completed with recycled New Zealand native timbers. There is a queen-sized bed downstairs, and two/three single beds upstairs. Guests are welcome to relax in our new lodge and enjoy the convenience of dining in if they wish. Ron, a National Park Ranger for over 25 years, is a licensed fishing and nature guide.

Te Anau   *Guesthouse*   *Te Anau Central*

Matai Lodge
Linda & Rod James
42 Mokonui Street, Te Anau
Tel: (03) 249 7360 Fax: (03) 249 7360
Tollfree: 0800 249 736   matailodge@hotmail.com
www.bnb.co.nz/matailodgeteanau.html
Double $76 Single $55 (Full Breakfast)
Credit cards accepted Pet on property
1 Queen 3 Double 3 Twin (7 bdrm)
2 Ensuite 2 Guests share

Matai Lodge is budget homestyle accommodation. Clean, comfy rooms with electric blankets, heaters and handbasins. Ideally situated clos to town centre and restaurants. Full cooked and continental breakfasts with homemade yoghurt. Lovely guestlounge dining area with exchange library and Internet. Complimentary tea, coffee, cookies, magazines and daily newspaper. BBQ in garden setting. Luggage and vehicle stored for free. Linda, Rod, and Lucky the cat offer you a warm welcome. All trips can be booked and paid for with your room. Genuine advice on all trips available.

Te Anau   *Self-contained B&B*

Edgewater XL B&B
Lynley Jones
52 Lakefront Drive, Te Anau,
Tel: (03) 249 7258 Fax: (03) 249 8099
Tollfree: 0800 433 439
edgewater.xl.motels@xtra.co.nz
www.bnb.co.nz/edgewaterxl.html
Double $185 Credit cards accepted Children welcome
1 Queen 2 Single (2 bdrm)
1 Ensuite 1 Private

Situated on the lakefront, Edgewater XL B&B provides unobstructed views of the lake and Fiordland National World Heritage Park. From your bedroom and private lounge, sliding doors open on to a balcony. Your unit has coffee and tea-making facilities and ensuite with spa bath. Teriff includes continental breakfast. We are a booking agent for all activities. Ian has good local knowledge of trout fishing areas. This magic setting is only three minutes from the town centre. Off-season rates apply.

Te Anau   *Self-contained B&B   5km E of Te Anau*

Stonewall Cottage
Nicky Harrison & Jim Huntington
36 Kakapo Road, RD2, Te Anau

Tel: (03) 249 8686 Fax: (03) 249 8686
Mob: 025 260 3414   hprojects@xtra.co.nz.
www.bnb.co.nz/stonewallcottage.html

Double $130 Single $100 (Continental Breakfast)
Child $20, neg. Credit cards accepted Child at home
Pet on property Children welcome
1 Queen (1 bdrm)   1 Ensuite

We welcome you to our new guest studio offering quality accommodation in a real rural retreat. Enjoy expansive mountain views from your own private courtyard. Our studio is self-contained with ensuite bathroom and full cooking facilities. A feature of our small deer farm is the dry stone walls which are ever increasing. You are invited to share in our daily farming and gardening activities or sit back and enjoy the tranquility after exploring the wonders of Fiordland.

Te Anau - Manapouri   *Farmstay   20 min Manapouri*

Crown Lea
Florence & John Pine
Gillespie Road, RD 1, Te Anau

Tel: (03) 249 8598 Fax: (03) 249 8598
Mob: 025 227 8366
crownlea@xtra.co.nz
www.crown-lea.com

Double $130-$150 Single $100 (Full Breakfast)
Dinner $30 Pet on property Smoking area inside
1 King/Twin 1 Queen 1 Twin (3 bdrm)
1 Ensuite 2 Private

Our 900 acre sheep, cattle and deer farm offers a farm tour after 6 pm, and views of Lake Manapouri, Fiordland mountains, and the Te Anau Basin. Day trips to Doubtful and Milford Sounds, visits to Te Anau, Glow-worm Caves, or hikes on the many walking tracks, in Fiordland are all within easy reach. Having travelled in the UK, Europe, Canada, Hong Kong and Singapore, we enjoy meeting guests from all over the world. We and Harriet the cat look forward to welcoming you to our home.

Mossburn   *Farmstay   25km S of Mossburn*

Joyce & Murray Turner
RD 1, Otautau, Southland

Tel: (03) 225 7602 Fax: (03) 225 7602
murray.joyce@xtra.co.nz
www.innz.co.nz/host/e/etalcreek.html

Double $80 Single $50 (Full Breakfast)
Child $20 Dinner $30 Pet on property
1 Queen 4 Single (3 bdrm)
1 Private

Our modern home on 301 hectares, 3000 sheep 200 beef cattle is situated half-way between Invercargill and Te Anau, which can be reached in 1 hour. We enjoy meeting people, will provide quality accommodation, farm fresh food in a welcoming friendly atmosphere. You can join in farm activities, farm tour or just relax. The Aparima River is adjacent to the property. Murray's a keen fly fisherman. Guiding available. Pet Bichon Frise. Evening meal on request. Directions please phone/fax. 24 hours notice to avoid disappointment.

SOUTHLAND, STH CATLINS

Lumsden *Farmstay self-contained room available* *9km S of Lumsden*

Josephville Gardens
Annette & Bob Menlove
Rapid sign 824, State Highway 6, RD 4, Lumsden
Tel: (03) 248 7114 Fax: (03) 248 7114
Mob: 025 204 9753 bobannette@menlove.net
www.bnb.co.nz/josephvillegardens.html
Double $100 Single $80 (Full Breakfast)
Dinner $25 Pet on property
1 King/Twin 2 Double 1 Twin (4 bdrm)
1 Ensuite 1 Private 1 Family share

We have a 480 hectare farm which runs sheep, cattle and deer. Surrounding our comfortable warm home, we have a large garden with a selection of specimen trees, rhododendrons, roses, peonys and perennials. The golf course is 3km away - golf clubs are available- a good fishing river nearby. We have hiked in our mountains a lot and can give advise on where and what to see. If you wish a four wheel drive trip is available.

Winton *Self-contained Farmstay* *10mins N of Winton*

Nethershiel Farm Cottage
Mrs Henderson & staff
710 Riverside No 3 Rd, Winton 9662
Tel: (03) 236 0791 Fax: (03) 236 0101
Mob: 025 340 598 nethershiel.farm@xtra.co.nz
www.nethershielfarm.co.nz
Double $95 Single $55
(Continental & Full Breakfast)
Child $20 under 12yrs Credit cards accepted
Children welcome Pets welcome
2 Queen 4 Single (3 bdrm) 1 Private

Enjoy your own comfortable fully equipped three bedroom house plus separate bunkhouse for energetic children. Set in historical garden on a sheep and flower farm, in the heart of Southland. Flowers bloom from October to May. Tennis court on property, trout river, excellent golf course nearby, only $15 per round. Plenty of trips, walks, tramps and adventure tours to do. Fishing guides available. Good central location for day trips everywhere in the south and Stewart Island. Weekly discounts.

Balfour *Farmstay* *3km N of Balfour*

Hillcrest
Liz & Ritchie Clark
206 Old Balfour Road, RD 1, Balfour
Tel: (03) 201 6165 Fax: (03) 201 6165
clarkrl@esi.co.nz
www.bnb.co.nz/hillcrestbalfour.html
Double $100 Single $70 (Full Breakfast)
Dinner $25pp Pet on property Children welcome
2 King/Twin (2 bdrm) 1 Private 1 Family share

Welcome to our 650 acre sheep and deer farm. Relax in our garden, enjoy a farm tour with mountain views or a game of tennis. Trout fish the Mataura, Oreti or Waikaia rivers. Fishing guide can be arranged on request. Enjoy a relaxing dinner with fine food, wine and conversation. Breakfast is served with fresh baked bread, home-made yoghurt, muesli, jams and preserves. Interests include handcrafts, tennis, photography and fishing. We have 3 school-age children and 2 cats. Directions: at Balfour crossroads, take the road to Waikaia, then first left Old Balfour Road and travel 2.5km, we are on right. Please phone.

Wendonside   *Farmstay   15km N of Riversdale*

Ardlamont Farm
Dale & Lindsay Wright
110 Wendonside Church Road North,
Wendonside, RD 7, Gore
Tel: (03) 202 7774 Fax: (03) 202 7774
ardlamont@xtra.co.nz
www.bnb.co.nz/ardlamontfarm.html
Double $90 Single $60 (Full Breakfast)
Child $20 Dinner $30
1 Double 2 Single (2 bdrm)   1 Private

Experience "Ardlamont", a 4th generation 1200 acre sheep and beef farm offering panoramic views of Northern Southland. Gourmet meals a specialty, served with fine New Zealand wines. Tour the farm, then return to the renovated comforts of our 90 year old homestead. Having travelled widely we enjoy welcoming visitors into our home. Our 3 teenage children attend university/boarding school in Dunedin. Two of New Zealand's best trout rivers only five minutes away. 15 minutes off SH94 (Queenstown - Gore - Dunedin route) Well worth the detour.

Waikaka   *Farmstay B&B   30km N of Gore*

Blackhills Farmstay
Dorothy & Tom Affleck
192 Robertson Road, RD 3, Gore, Southland
Tel: (03) 207 2865 Fax: (03) 207 2865
afflecks@ispnz.co.nz
www.bnb.co.nz/blackhillsfarmstay.html
Double $100 Single $50 (Full Breakfast) Child $25
Dinner $25 by arrangement Credit cards accepted
2 King/Twin 1 Queen (3 bdrm)
1 Private 1 Family share

Venture off HW1 for the refreshment of a quiet rural visit. Turn off HW90 on to the Waikaka Road. Drive approx. 10km, turn left at the T junction then first right on to Nicholson Road. Veer right to Robertson Road. Our 800 acre sheep and beef farm on a ridge above the Waikaka River offers superb views, a farm tour, sports facilities in nearby Waikaka and warm hospitality, midway between Dunedin and Fiordland. Both in our 50s, our interests include travel, golf, gardening, cooking and music. We appreciate guests of all ages.

Pukerau - Gore   *Country Homestay   12km E of Gore*

Connor Orchids
Dawn & David Connor
1158 State Highway 1, Pukerau, Southland
Tel: (03) 205 3896 Fax: (03) 205 3896
Mob: 025 669 1362   Tollfree: 0800 372 484
ddconnor@esi.co.nz
www.bnb.co.nz/connororchids.html
Double $80 Single $45 (Full Breakfast)
Dinner by arrangement Credit cards accepted
1 Queen 2 Single (2 bdrm)
1 Private 1 Guests share

Relax with us in our warm comfortable home set in a mature garden with a rural outlook. We are just minutes away from several rivers including the Mataura which is well known for Brown Trout fishing. Fishing guide available on request. Growing a variety of orchids is our main interest, we run a few pet sheep. We enjoy meeting people and have travelled extensively ourselves. Complimentary tea & coffee available. Smokefree accommodation.

Gore *Farmstay Homestay 6km W of Gore*

Irwin's Farmstay
Sandy & Trish Irwin
Croydon Bush, RD 7, Gore, Southland
Tel: (03) 208 6260
www.bnb.co.nz/irwinsfarmstay.html
Double $70 Single $45 (Full Breakfast)
Child neg Dinner $25pp by arrangement
1 Queen 4 Single (3 bdrm)
1 Guests share

Sandy and Tricia are semi-retired farmers living on 43 acres where we have sheep, farm dog and hens. We are 10 minutes from Gore on the road to Dolamore Park where there are several bush walking tracks. Golf course and fishing rivers a short drive away. We enjoy meeting people, sport, reading and gardening. Laundry facilities, cot and highchair available. A Bichon Frise dog and a cat share our home. No smoking indoors please. Please phone for directions.

Mataura - Gore *Farmstay 12km S of Gore*

Kowhai Place
JR & HM Williams
291 Glendhu Road, RD 4, Gore
Tel: (03) 203 8774 Fax: (03) 203 8774
kowhaiplace@hotmail.com
www.bnb.co.nz/kowhaiplace.html
Double $80 Single $45 (Full Breakfast)
Child 1/2 price Dinner $20 by arrangement
2 Queen 4 Single (4 bdrm)
1 Private 1 Guests share 1 Family share

John & Helen farm sheep and deer, on our 50 acre farmlet. We live 5 minutes, from one of the best brown trout fishing rivers in the world. Drive 1 hour south to the sea side and 1 1/2 hours northwest to lakes and ski fields. We both play golf, and enjoy gardening. Fishing guide, and garden tours can be arranged with prior notice. Over the past years, we have enjoyed sharing our spacious home and garden with lots of overseas guests. Enjoy the South.

Wyndham *Farmstay 3.65km E of Wyndham*

Smiths Farmstay
Beverly and Doug Smith
365 Wyndham - Mokoreta Road, RD 2, Wyndham, Southland
Tel: (03) 206 4840 Fax: (03) 206 4847 Mob: 025 286 6920
beverly@smithsfarmstay.co.nz   www.smithsfarmstay.co.nz

Double $90-$120 Single $65 (Continental Breakfast) (Full Breakfast)
Child Neg Dinner $30 Visa/mastercard accepted
2 King/Twin 1 Queen 1 Twin (4 bdrm) 1 Ensuite 1 Private 1 Guests share

Beverly and Doug assure you of a warm welcome to the Modern Farm house set in 265 hectare sheep farm. We are situated on the hills above Wyndham only 3.65 km, set in quiet and peaceful surroundings.

Farm tour included in tarif. Feeding the animals and sheep shearing when in season. Doug will demonstrate his sheep dogs working.

Beverly a registered nurse enjoys cooking, floral art, knitting, gardening and travel. We enjoy meeting people and both are of a friendly deposition, with a sense of humour.

"Each bedroom has a View and is tastefully furnished to meet your needs." "Genuine home cooking""Special Diets on request." "Packed Lunches if required" you are most welcome to join us for the evening meal, which is $30pp. We love sharing Christmas Day with guests, enquiries welcome.

Fishermans Retreat; The Mataura, Wyndham and Mimihau Rivers are renowned for its abundance of Brown trout. Each of these Rivers are only a short 5Km away. Doug, a keen experienced fisherman is only too happy to share his knowledge of these rivers with you. Enjoy the Mad Mataura evening Rise a site to experience.

Gateway to Catlins, Only two hours from Queenstown, Te Anau and Dunedin.

Laundry, Fax and email facilities available.

Directions: Come to Wyndham, follow signs to Mokoreta.

Progress Valley - South Catlins   *6km N of Waikawa*
Self-contained Farmstay B&B

Catlins Farmstay B&B
June & Murray Stratford
174 Progress Valley Road, South Catlins, Southland

Tel: (03) 246 8843 Fax: (03) 246 8844
catlinsfarmstay@xtra.co.nz   www.catlinsfarmstay.co.nz

Double $160-$220 Single $100 (Special Breakfast)
Child neg. Dinner $40 S/C Credit cards accepted
1 King 2 Queen 2 Single (3 bdrm)
3 Ensuite 1 Family share

Ours is a great location close to fossil forest at Curio Bay. Superior new guest rooms plus king s/c suite available with private entrances. I specialise in dinners using local fish, our homegrown venison, beef or lamb, and organic vegetables, followed by delicious desserts and breakfasts. We farm 1000 acres running, 2500 sheep, 500 deer, 150 cattle with 3 sheepdogs. Farm tours by arrangement. Directions: turn off at Niagara Falls into Manse Road, drive 2kms. Ask about our s/c cottage at Waikawa (www.cottagestays.co.nz/governors/cottage.htm)

Fortrose - The Catlins   *Farmstay B&B*   *50km SE of Invercargill*

Greenbush
Ann & Donald McKenzie
298 Fortrose - Otara Road, Fortrose,
RD 5, Invercargill

Tel: (03) 246 9506 Fax: (03) 246 9505
Mob: 025 239 5196   info@greenbush.co.nz
www.greenbush.co.nz

Double $120 Single $80
(Continental & Full Breakfast) Child neg
Dinner $30 by arrangement Credit cards accepted
1 King/Twin 1 Twin (2 bdrm)   1 Ensuite 1 Private

Greenbush Bed and Breakfast is ideally located off the Southern Scenic Route from Fortrose. Within 30 minutes drive from Greenbush you can enjoy Curio Bay, Waipapa Point and Slope Point the southern most point in the South Island. Greenbush is nestled in two acres of garden. You will wake to the song of birds and magnificent views of green rolling countryside. Enjoy our private beach access, lake and farm tour.

Waikawa Harbour - South Catlins   *80km SE of Invercargill*
Self-contained Farmstay B&B

Bay Farm
Alison & Bruce Yorke
595 Yorke Road, RD 1, Tokanui, Southland

Tel: (03) 246 8833 Fax: (03) 246 8833
BAYFARM@xtra.co.nz
www.bayfarm.co.nz

Double $120 Single $80 (Full Breakfast)
Dinner $30 Self Catering $100 Credit cards accepted
2 Queen 2 Single (3 bdrm)
1 Ensuite 1 Private 1 Family share

Bayfarm is a tranquil retreat situated in native forest overlooking Waikawa Harbour South Catlins. We farm sheep and cattle on 1200 acres. Dinner-fresh home grown produce. Non smokers preferred. Our interests include tramping, sailing, golf and meeting people. Fantail cottage is a modern self catering cottage for two adults, it has an extensive kitchen, queen bed, TV and ensuite. It is 150 metres from the homestead and completely private.

Lynfield - Catlins *Farmstay B&B   60 km SE of Invercargill*

Lynfield Farmstay
Shirley & Colin Jennings
Lynfield Otara, No 5 RD, Invercargill
Tel: 03 246 8463 Fax: 03 246 8463
www.bnb.co.nz/lynfieldfarmstay.html
Double $90 Single $45 (Continental & Full Breakfast)
Child neg. Dinner $25 by arrangement
1 Queen 1 Twin (2 bdrm)
1 Guests share

Lynfield Farmstay Catlins 998 Fortrose Otara Rd 60 km from Invercargill. The farm with a view includes Foveaux Straight, Waipapa Point and Lighthouse. Waipapa Beach with its Hooker Sea Lions, golf course 10 mins away at Fortrose, bush walks, southern most point of the South Island at Slope Point, Curio Bays Fossils and Hector Dolphins all within 25 min. drive. Traditional home cooking in comfortable surrounds. Let us drive you around the farm amongst sheep, lambs, cows and calves. Our friendly black cat usually wanders by.

Mokotua *Farmstay self-contained cottage   20km NE of Invercargill*

Fernlea
Anne & Brian Perkins
Mokotua, RD 1, Invercargill on Southern Scenic Route
Tel: (03) 239 5432 Fax: (03) 239-5432
Mob: 025 313 432   fernlea@southnet.co.nz
www.fernlea.co.nz
Double $100-$110 (Full Breakfast) Child $10
Dinner $30 by arrangement Credit cards accepted
2 Double (1 bdrm)
1 Private

Fernlea Bed and Breakfast was the SOUTHLAND SUPREME TOURISM AWARD WINNER 2000-2001. Anne's cottage is nestled in its own private olde world garden, is completely s/c and can sleep four people. Our dairy farm of 300 acres is home to 300 Holstein Friesian cows - farm tour included. Relax and enjoy a taste of real NZ farm life on your journey to discover the Catlins, or enroute to Stewart Island, Te Anau or Queenstown. Directions: From Invercargill on SH92, 20 mins from Invercargill turn left at Mokotua Garage.

Invercargill *Farmstay Country stay and Garden   15km N of Invercargill*

Tudor Park
Joyce & John Robins
21 Lawrence Road, RD 6, Invercargill
Tel: (03) 221 7150 Fax: (03) 221 7150
Mob: 025 310 031   tudorparksouth@hotmail.com
www.bnb.co.nz/tudorpark.html
Double $150 Single $80 (Continental Breakfast)
Child neg Dinner From $30
Twin $130 Credit cards accepted
1 King/Twin 1 Double 1 Twin (3 bdrm)
1 Ensuite 2 Private

When travelling in the Scenic South enjoy the peace and tranquillity of a comfortable country home set in a large 4 acre garden which was placed first in the "2000 SOUTHERN PRIDE BEAUTIFICATION AWARD" for large garden. Paeonies and Hellebores are also being grown. Fresh flowers, cotton sheets, private facilities and the 'best beds in NZ'. Close to Invercargill, Stewart Island, SH6 to Te Anau and Queenstown. We enjoy overseas travel. Please book ahead if possible.

Invercargill   *Homestay B&B*   *5km N of Invercargill city*

Glenroy Park Homestay
Margaret & Alan Thomson
23 Glenroy Park Drive, Invercargill
Tel: (03) 215 8464 Fax: (03) 215 8464
home_hosp@hotmail.com
www.bnb.co.nz/glenroypark.html
Double $95 Single $60 (Full Breakfast)
Child $12 Dinner $30 Pet on property
1 Queen 2 Single (2 bdrm)
1 Private 1 Guests share

Come and stay with us in our new warm and beautiful home. Interests: gardening, cooking, golfing and meeting people. Share an evening of relaxation and friendship - we look forward to having you visit us. Invercargill is the gateway to the Catlins, Stewart Island, Fiordland, and Queenstown, only 2-3 hours drive. Directions: travelling from Queenstown, left at first set of lights, Bainfield Rd, travel 500m, first left, third house on left. From Dunedin, travel 5kms from war memorial towards Queenstown, turn right at Bainfield Road, travel 500m, first left, third house on left.

Invercargill   *B&B*

The Oak Door
Lisa & Bill Stuart
22 Taiepa Road, Otatara,
RD 9, Invercargill 9521
Tel: 64 3 213 0633 Fax: 64 3 213 0633
blstuart@xtra.co.nz
www.bnb.co.nz/theoakdoor.html
Double $80 Single $70 (Full Breakfast) Child POA
1 Queen 1 Double 2 Twin 1 Single (3 bdrm)

Bill (Kiwi) & Lisa (Canadian) invite you to stay in a unique restful home built by them. Relax - enjoy the native bush setting and attractive gardens, just a five minute drive from Invercargill City Centre and two minutes from the airport. **DIRECTIONS:** Drive past the airport entrance. Take first left (Marama Ave South). Take first right Taiepa Road second drive on right (#22). Meet us at The Oak Door. Visit the area, enjoy sports (golf), scenery, gardens, shops, restaurants, walking, area events. (No smoking/no pets.)

Invercargill - Waikiwi   *B&B*

Aarden House
Dorothy & Raymond Shaw
193 North Road,
Invercargill
Tel: (03) 215 8825 Fax: (03) 215 8826
www.bnb.co.nz/aardenhouse.html
Double $70-$80 Single $45-$55
(Full Breakfast)
1 Queen 3 Single (2 bdrm)
1 Guests share

We enjoy meeting people and wish to make your stay as pleasant and comfortable as possible. Our home is five min's drive from the centre of Invercargill. On the main highway to/(from) Queenstown or Te Anau. Bus stops to Centre City. Visits to Stewart Island arranged. Catlands Information available. Guests have comfortable lounge, open fire, tea, coffee and TV facilities, conservatory, electric blankets on beds, off street parking. House is a non-smoking zone.

Invercargill   *Farmstay B&B   1km E of Invercargill*

The Grove Deer Farm
Alex & Eileen Henderson
154 Oteramika Road, RD 1, Invercargill
Tel: (03) 216 6492 Fax: (03) 216 6492
the_grove@xtra.co.nz
www.bnb.co.nz/thegrovedeerfarm.html
Double $90 Single $60 (Continental & Full Breakfast)
Child neg Credit cards accepted
1 Queen 4 Single (3 bdrm)
1 Guests share 1 Family share

Enjoy Bed & Breakfast on a deer farm. Situated in a unique rural setting only 1 kilometer from city boundary. See farmed deer and sheep. Guests welcome to tour of the farm. Ideal stopover on Southern Scenic/Catlins Route and Stewart Island National Park Easy access to Fiordland walking tracks. Alex is a vintage car & machinery enthusiast and can arrange good viewing. Famous trout fishing rivers. Directions: Find Tweed Street - travel East. Cross Rockdale Road. We are 1 kilometer on right. Look for "The Grove" sign.

Invercargill - Waianiwa   *Homestay   18km W of Invercargill*

Annfield Flowers
Margaret & Mike Cockeram
126 Argyle-Otahuti Road, Waianiwa,
RD 4, Invercargill
Tel: (03) 235 2690 Fax: (03) 235 2745
annfield@ihug.co.nz
www.bnb.co.nz/annfieldflowers.html
Double $90 (Full Breakfast)
Dinner $30, $20 - light meal Credit cards accepted
1 King/Twin (1 bdrm) 1 Ensuite

We are 1 km from the Southern Scenic Route (signposted Waianiwa/Drummound) and well placed for sightseeing, fishing and golf. Dating from 1866, Annfield has been renovated to retain character and include modern facilities. Our sunny guest room opens into the garden. Two cats and two dogs have limited access inside. We are semi-retired, grow flowers for export, keep coloured sheep and Dexter cattle. We enjoy meeting people and love to share dinner or a light meal, including our own produce. Complimentary laundry facilities.

Invercargill   *Self-contained Farmstay   10km E of Invercargill on Southern Scenic Rte*

Long Acres Farmstay
Helen & Graeme Spain
Waimatua, RD 11, Invercargill
Tel: (03) 216 4470 Fax: (03) 216 4470
Mob: 025 228 1308   longacres@xtra.co.nz
www.bnb.co.nz/longacres.html
Double $90 Single $60 (Full Breakfast) Child neg
Dinner $30 S/C $100 - $120 Children welcome
2 Double 4 Single (4 bdrm) 1 Private 1 Family share

Southland hospitality at its best awaits you at our warm and friendly home. Our farm is 850 acres carrying 3000 sheep and 80 cattle. We are a farming and shearing family. Shearing videos available to watch. Farm Tour available. Our farm is 30 minutes from Bluff. Transport to Stewart Island can be arranged. Our home and garden are relaxing and very peaceful. Being travellers ourselves we enjoy meeting visitors. Stay as long as you wish. A home cooked meal is always available. A welcome assured. Directions: From Invercargill east on Southern Scenic Route approx 15 mins. Look for Long Acres Farmstay Sign.

SOUTHLAND, STH CATLINS

Invercargill   *Homestay B&B   Invercargill Central*

Gala Lodge
Jeanette & Charlie Ireland
177 Gala Street, Invercargill
Tel: (03) 218 8884   charlie.ireland@xtra.co.nz
Fax: (03) 218 9148   www.bnb.co.nz/galalodge.html
Double $90 Single $50 (Continental & Full Breakfast)
Child neg. Dinner $25 b/a Budget room for backpackers
1 Queen 2 Twin 1 Single (3 bdrm)
2 Ensuite 1 Guests share 1 Family share

Gala Lodge, ideally situated for visitors to Invercargill, overlooks beautiful Queens Park, City centre, Museum and Information centre. The home has well appointed, upstairs bedrooms (electric blankets provided). Downstairs, kitchen and two guest lounges. Spacious gardens, ample car parking. Hosts background - Farming, Police work, Education & Training, Gardening. Interests - Reading, Genealogy, handcrafts, travel. Many years hosting students of many nationalities including Japan and China. We provide a relaxing, friendly base, support in welfare and travel arrangements. Courtesy car available. Most buses stop here. You are very welcome.

Invercargill   *Homestay B&B   4km N of Invercargill Central*

Stoneleigh Homestay
Joan & Neville Milne
15 Stoneleigh Lane, Invercargill
Tel: (03) 215 8921 Fax: (03) 215 8491
www.bnb.co.nz/stoneleighhomestay.html
Double $90 Single $65
(Continental & Full Breakfast)
Dinner $30 Credit cards accepted
1 Queen 3 Single (3 bdrm)
1 Guests share

Our home is warm and comfortable with underfloor heating and electric blankets. Neville owns a wholesale fruit and vegetable market so fresh produce is assured. Joan has been involved for years with catering and enjoys cooking, so we would love to share an evening meal with you. We are keen golfers and members of the Invercargill Golf Club rated in the top 10 courses in NZ. City and Airport pick-ups can be arranged. Five minutes drive from the City Centre on North Road. Bus stops, to city centre.

Invercargill   *Homestay B&B   6km NE of Invercargill*

The Manor
Pat & Frank Forde
9 Drysdale Road, Myross Bush, RD 2, Invercargill
Tel: (03) 230 4788 Fax: (03) 2304 788
Mob: 025 667 0904 gaz.di@xtra.co.nz
www.bnb.co.nz/themanor.html
Double $90 Single $65
(Continental & Full Breakfast) Child negotiable
Dinner $30 by arrangement Credit cards accepted
1 Queen 1 Double 2 Single (3 bdrm) 1 Guests share

Relax and enjoy our warm and comfortable home in a sheltered garden setting. Our 10 acre farmlet is situated on the outskirts of Invercargill. We are retired farmers, our interests include: keen golfers, gardening, horses, travel and meeting people. We have underfloor heating, electric blankets, pleasant outdoor areas and meals of fresh home grown produce, private guest area with television, fridge, tea and coffee making facilities. We are 5 minutes drive from Invercargill along State Highway One. Sign at Kennington corner.

Invercargill   *B&B*

Montecillo Lodge
Miss Bevron Sinclair
240 Spey Street, Invercargill
Tel: (03) 218 2503 Fax: (03) 218 2506
Tollfree: 0800 666 832   montecillo@hyper.net.nz
www.bnb.co.nz/montecillolodge.html

Double $100 Single $80 (Full Breakfast)
Child $15 Dinner $25 four motel units $70
Credit cards accepted
3 Queen 3 Double 8 Single (8 bdrm)
6 Ensuite 1 Guests share

Your friendly hosts Bevron & Ray extend you a warm welcome to our comfortable hotel. We are situated in a quiet street just 10-15 minutes walk from the city centre, museum, park, golf course and swimming centre. Each of our centrally heated rooms has it's own ensuite, telephone, TV, tea and coffee-making facilities. Cooked breakfast is available in our dining room. Dinner by arrangement. We can arrange trips to Stewart Island and your next night accommodation.

Riverton   *Self-contained B&B*   *35km S of Invercargill*

River Lodge Bed & Breakfast
Jocelyn and Russell Dore
93 Towack Street, Riverton
Tel: (03) 234 8732 Fax: (03) 234 8732
rbjmdore@actrix.co.nz
www.bnb.co.nz/dore.html

Double $80-$135 (Continental Breakfast)
Credit cards accepted Pet on property
3 Queen 1 Double (4 bdrm)
2 Ensuite 1 Guests share 1 Family share

Relax and enjoy our comfortable home by the sea, situated on the waterfront with our 3 double bedrooms opening onto a sunny veranda with peaceful water and garden views. We also have a private, spacious upstairs studio unit with spa bath and views from the mountains to the sea. Come and enjoy a relaxed homestyle stay. We are only 20 minutes from Invercargill on the Southern Scenic Route. Enjoy a meal at Riverton's great cafes. Laundry facilities available. We look forward to meeting you.

Riverton - Waimatuku   *Farmstay*   *15km E of Riverton*

Kildonan Farm
Jacqui and Bruce Fallow
83 Fraser Rd, Waimatuku,
Tel: (03) 224 6269 Fax: (03) 224 6284
Mob: 025 284 6882   fallow@southnet.co.nz
www.bnb.co.nz/user202.html

Double $90 Single $50 (Full Breakfast)
Dinner $30 Credit cards accepted
1 Double 1 Twin 1 Single (3 bdrm)
1 family share

Looking forward to meeting you and sharing this unique part of New Zealand. Our 200ha deer and cropping farm is situated 4km N of the Southern Scenic Route, 25mins NW of Invercargill and 15mins from Riverton (a historic fishing village). Our home has modern facilities, is warm and comforable, and set in a peaceful established garden. Conveniently located for excursions to Stewart Island, Hump Ridge track, Fiordland and Queenstown. Our interests include people, cooking, travel, gardening, fashion. Pets stay outside. Directions - please phone. Dinner by arrangement.

Stewart Island
Homestay B&B Self-contained   *3km N of Oban*

Thorfinn Charters & Accommodation

Barbara McKay & Bruce Story, PO Box 43,
Halfmoon Bay, Stewart Island

Tel: (03) 219 1210 Fax: (03) 219 1210
Mob: 025 201 1336

thorfinn@southnet.co.nz   www.thorfinn.co.nz

Double $140 Single $90 (Continental Breakfast)
(Full Breakfast) Dinner by arrangement
3 s/c units From $110 double Credit cards accepted
2 Queen 3 Single (2 bdrm)   1 Private 1 Family
share

Welcome to the tranquillity of our sunny open-plan
home 'On the Beach' with panoramic views of
Horseshoe Bay out to the offshore islands from all
rooms. Guest bedrooms on the second floor are
spacious with queen and single bed in each. You
may join us downstairs, or use the upstairs sitting area for reading, writing or quiet reflection in privacy.

With central heating, Sky TV, and transfers, you are assured a comfortable stay. Evening meals are by
arrangement and feature local seafood.

For groups and families we offer 3 self-contained houses just 10 minutes walk from the village. Two
quality houses, each 2-bedroom, sleep up to 7, while our 'Premium' house has 3 bedrooms, 2 ensuite,
dishwasher, etc. Sleeps up to 10. All feature Sky TV, central heating, superb sea views, conservatory,
bush surrounds and native birds.

Thorfinn, our luxury 12 metre launch provides 15
passengers with a comfortable ride, and great
visibility. Our specialities are pelagic (seabirds) and
terrestrial endemic birds and mammals with
commentary on island history, everywhere
magnificent scenery, and always the option to catch
a fish. The highest number of available birds in any
one place in NZ makes 30-40 species per day a
possibility. For 10 years we have operated nature
trips with a guided nature walk on Ulva Island to
explore unspoilt forest, rare and endangered birds. We
also do private charters including exclusive charters for up to six pax with deluxe seafood meal and fine
wine luncheon.

BJ, from the US East Coast and Hawaii, a medical doctor, brings botanical skill, while Bruce is a former
hill-country farmer with 40+ years' experience of the flora and fauna of Fiordland, the Catlins and
Stewart Island. Both are DoC Concessionaires, can access 'off the beaten track' areas, and are founda-
tion members of the NZ Birding Network. It will be our privilege to help you discover Stewart Island.

Stewart Island   *B&B*   *5min walk Oban*

Goomes B&B Homestay
Jeanette & Peter Goomes
PO Box 36,
Halfmoon Bay, Stewart Island
Tel: (03) 219 1057 Fax: (03) 219 1057
www.bnb.co.nz/goomesbb.html
Double $160 Single $130 (Special Breakfast)
Credit cards accepted
2 Queen 1 Single (2 bdrm)
2 Ensuite

Our quiet, private modern home is only five minutes walk from the township, on a bush clad point with panoramic views of Halfmoon Bay and islands beyond. Both rooms have sea views, ensuites, tea/ coffee facilities, and TV. Relax and watch the ever-changing moods of the sea, and see native birds feeding on our balcony. We are a fifth generation Stewart Island family and enjoy sharing our knowledge of this beautiful island with our guests. Courtesy transfers.

Stewart Island   *Self-contained B&B*   *5min 0 of Oban township*

Talisker Charters & Sails Ashore Accommodation
Iris and Peter Tait
11 View Street, Stewart Island
Tel: (03) 219 1151 Fax: (03) 219 1151
tait@taliskercharter.co.nz
www.taliskercharter.co.nz/sailsashore.htm
(Continental Breakfast) (Full Breakfast)
Credit cards accepted
1 Queen 2 Single (2 bdrm)
2 Ensuite

Enjoy with us our centrally located home with two new private apartments designed to maximise sun and scenery overlooking Halfmoon Bay. Stewart Island is New Zealands's newest National Park. Peaceful beaches, undisturbed forest and wonderful wildlife make the Island a haven. We have 33 years' of Island life as Ranger, District Nurse in charge, Commercial Fishers and now hosts of a charter yacht/ homestay. We and our Border Terriers will delight in sharing our Island and home with you.

A homestay is a B&B where you
share the family's living area.

Index

Y